Java Programming
Fourth Edition

Java Programming, Fourth Edition

Joyce Farrell

THOMSON

COURSE TECHNOLOGY

Java Programming, *Fourth Edition*

by Joyce Farrell

Vice President, Technology and Trades ABU:
Dave Garza

Director of Learning Solutions:
Sandy Clark

Acquisitions Editor:
Amy Jollymore

Managing Editor:
Tricia Coia

Development Editor:
Dan Seiter

Senior Content Project Manager:
Catherine G. DiMassa

Project Manager:
Mona Tiwary

Cover Designer:
Steve Deschene

Art Director:
Beth Paquin

Compositor:
International Typesetting and Composition

Manufacturing Coordinator:
Julio Esperas

Editorial Assistant:
Erin Kennedy

Copyeditor:
Gary Michael Spahl

Proofreader:
Vicki Zimmer

Indexer:
Liz Cunningham

ISBN-10 1-4239-0128-2
ISBN-13 978-1-4239-0128-0

BRIEF CONTENTS

TABLE OF CONTENTS

TABLE OF CONTENTS

CHAPTER 12   ADVANCED INHERITANCE CONCEPTS   481

PREFACE

Java Programming, Fourth Edition provides the beginning programmer with a guide to developing applications and applets using the Java programming language. Java is popular among professional programmers because it can be used to build visually interesting graphical user interface (GUI) and Web-based applications. Java also provides an excellent environment for the beginning programmer—a student quickly can build useful programs while learning the basics of structured and object-oriented programming techniques.

This textbook assumes that you have little or no programming experience. This book provides a solid background in good object-oriented programming techniques and introduces object-oriented terminology using clear, familiar language. The writing is nontechnical and emphasizes good programming practices. The examples are business examples; they do not assume a mathematical background beyond high-school business math. In addition, the examples illustrate only one or two major points; they do not contain so many features that you become lost following irrelevant and extraneous details. The explanations in this textbook are written clearly in straightforward sentences so that native and non-native English speakers alike can master the programming concepts. Complete, working code examples appear frequently in each chapter; these examples help the student make the transition from the theoretical to the practical. The code presented in each chapter is also provided on disk, so that students can easily run the programs and experiment with changes to them.

ORGANIZATION AND COVERAGE

Java Programming, Fourth Edition presents Java programming concepts, enforcing good style, logical thinking, and the object-oriented paradigm. Objects are covered right from the beginning, earlier than in many other textbooks. You create your first Java program in Chapter 1. Chapters 2, 3, and 4 increase your understanding of how data, classes, objects, and methods interact in an object-oriented environment.

Chapters 5 and 6 explore input and repetition structures, which are the backbone of programming logic and essential to creating useful programs in any language. You learn the special considerations of string and array manipulation in Chapters 7 and 8.

Beginning with Chapter 9, you will write applets—mini-programs meant to run in a browser. In Chapter 10, you learn to add graphics, images, and sound to your applets. Chapters 11 and 12 provide thorough coverage of inheritance, the object-oriented concept that allows you to develop new objects quickly by adapting the features of existing ones. In Chapters 13 and 14, you begin to use Swing components—Java's visually pleasing, user-friendly widgets. Exception handling, the object-oriented methods of error control, is covered in Chapter 15. Chapter 16 teaches you to save and retrieve data from files.

If instructors want to delay applet coverage, or postpone some advanced topics until a second-semester course, they can present Chapters 1 through 7 of *Java Programming, Fourth Edition*, and then teach the remaining chapters in a variety of sequences. For example, instructors who do not need to teach advanced array techniques can omit Chapter 8.

Instructors who want to delay applet coverage can work through Chapter 7 or 8; follow with Chapters 11, 12, and 13; and then return to Chapters 9 and 10.

In every chapter, *Java Programming, Fourth Edition* follows the text explanation with a "You Do It" section that contains step-by-step exercises to illustrate the concepts just learned, reinforcing the student's understanding and allowing concepts to be better retained. Creating the programs in the step-by-step examples also provides students with a successful experience in the language; finishing the examples provides them with models for their own creations.

The student using *Java Programming, Fourth Edition* builds applications and applets from the bottom up, rather than starting with existing objects. This facilitates a deeper understanding of the concepts used in object-oriented programming, and engenders appreciation for the existing objects students use as their knowledge of the language advances. When students complete this book, they will know how to modify and create simple Java programs and will have the tools to create more complex examples. They also will have a fundamental knowledge of object-oriented programming, which will serve them well in advanced Java courses or in studying other object-oriented languages such as C++, C#, and Visual Basic.

FEATURES

Java Programming, Fourth Edition is a superior textbook because it also includes the following features:

» **Objectives:** Each chapter begins with a list of objectives so you know the topics that will be presented in the chapter. In addition to providing a quick reference to topics covered, this feature provides a useful study aid.

» **Notes:** These highlighted tips provide additional information—for example, an alternative method of performing a procedure, another term for a concept, background information on a technique, or a common error to avoid.

» **Figures:** Each chapter contains many figures. Code figures are most frequently 25 lines long or less, illustrating one concept at a time. Frequently placed screen shots show exactly how program output appears.

NEW!

» **Color:** The code figures in each chapter contain all Java keywords in blue. This helps students identify keywords more easily, distinguishing them from programmer-selected names.

NEW!

» **Files:** The Student Disk holds more than 180 files that contain the code presented in the figures in each chapter. Students can run the code for themselves, view the output, and make changes to the code to observe the effects.

» **You Do It:** In each chapter, step-by-step exercises help the student create multiple working programs that emphasize the logic a programmer uses in choosing statements to include. This section provides a means for students to achieve success on their own— even those in online or distance learning classes.

» **Key Terms:** Each chapter includes a list of newly introduced vocabulary, shown in the order of appearance in the text. The list of key terms provides a mini-review of the major concepts in the chapter.

» **Summaries:** Following each chapter is a summary that recaps the programming concepts and techniques covered in the chapter. This feature provides a concise means for the student to recap and check understanding of the main points in each chapter.

» **Review Questions:** Each chapter includes 20 multiple-choice questions that serve as a review of chapter topics.

» **Exercises:** Each chapter concludes with meaningful programming exercises that provide additional practice of the skills and concepts learned in the chapter. These exercises vary in difficulty and are designed to allow exploration of logical programming concepts.

» **Case Project:** Each chapter contains a longer assignment that combines most of the concepts learned in the chapter.

» **Game Zone:** Each chapter provides one or more exercises in which the student creates interactive games using the programming techniques learned up to that point; 70 game programs are suggested in the book. The games are fun to create and play; writing them motivates students to master the necessary programming techniques. Students might exchange completed game programs with each other, suggesting improvements and discovering alternate ways to accomplish tasks.

NEW!

» **Up for Discussion:** Each chapter concludes with a few thought-provoking questions concerning programming in general or Java in particular. The questions can be used to start classroom or online discussions, or to develop and encourage research, writing, and language skills.

NEW!

» **Quality:** Every program example in the book, as well as every exercise, case project, and game solution, was tested by the author and then tested again by a Quality Assurance team using Java Standard Edition 6, the most recent version available. (The external version number used by Sun Microsystems is 6.0; the internal version number is 1.6.0. For more information on the features of the JDK, visit *http://java.sun.com*.)

» **CD-ROM included with book:** The CD that comes with this book includes the following items:

» Sun Microsystems Java Standard Edition 6, the Java language, compiler, and runtime environment

» Sun Microsystems Java Application Programming Interface (API) Specification, official documentation for the Java programming language

» The jGRASP integrated development environment for Java

» Code files for all Java program examples contained in the text

TEACHING TOOLS

The following supplemental materials are available when this book is used in a classroom setting. All of the teaching tools available with this book are provided to the instructor on a single CD.

Electronic Instructor's Manual. The Instructor's Manual that accompanies this textbook includes additional instructional material to assist in class preparation, including items such as Sample Syllabi, Chapter Outlines, Technical Notes, Lecture Notes, Quick Quizzes, Teaching Tips, Discussion Topics, and Key Terms.

ExamView®. This textbook is accompanied by ExamView, a powerful testing software package that allows instructors to create and administer printed, computer (LAN-based), and Internet-based exams. ExamView includes hundreds of questions that correspond to the topics covered in this text, enabling students to generate detailed study guides that include page references for further review. The computer-based and Internet testing components allow students to take exams at their computers, and they save the instructor time by grading each exam automatically.

PowerPoint Presentations. This book comes with Microsoft PowerPoint slides for each chapter. These are included as a teaching aid for classroom presentation, to make available to students on the network for chapter review, or to be printed for classroom distribution. Instructors can add their own slides for additional topics they introduce to the class.

Solution Files. Solutions to "You Do It" exercises and all end-of-chapter exercises are provided on the Teaching Tools CD, and can also be found on the Course Technology Web site at *www.course.com*. The solutions are password protected.

NEW!

Annotated solutions are provided for the multiple-choice Review Questions. For example, if students are likely to debate answer choices, or not understand the choice deemed to be the correct one, a rationale is provided.

Distance Learning. Course Technology is proud to present online test banks in WebCT and Blackboard to provide the most complete and dynamic learning experience possible. Instructors are encouraged to make the most of the course, both online and offline. For more information on how to access the online test bank, contact your local Course Technology sales representative.

ACKNOWLEDGEMENTS

I would like to thank all of the people who helped to make this book a reality, especially Dan Seiter, Development Editor. Dan's support, suggestions, and attention to detail made this a superior book.

Thanks also to Tricia Coia, Managing Editor; Mona Tiwary, Production Editor; and Catherine G. Dimassa, Senior Project Manager. Special thanks to Danielle Shaw and Serge Palladino, the Quality Assurance Testers, who provided thorough examination of the manuscript and consistently valuable suggestions. I am grateful to be able to work with so many fine people who are dedicated to producing quality instructional materials.

Thank you to Dick Grant of Seminole Community College, Sanford, Florida. He provided important technical and pedagogical suggestions based on his classroom use of this book. He possesses the rare combination of excellent teacher and programmer, and he made this book more accurate and more useful to students.

I am also grateful to the many other reviewers who provided comments and encouragement during this book's development, including Stefan Apperson, Yakima Valley Community College; James Chegwidden, Tarrant County College-Southeast; Kay Chen, Bucks County Community College; Efosa Idemudia, Middle Georgia College; and Soma Roy, Lehigh University.

Thanks, too, to my husband, Geoff, who makes my world a better place. This book is dedicated to him.

Joyce Farrell

READ THIS BEFORE YOU BEGIN

The following information will help you as you prepare to use this textbook.

TO THE USER OF THE DATA FILES

To complete the steps and projects in this book, you need data files that have been created specifically for this book. Your instructor will provide the data files to you. You also can obtain the files electronically from the Course Technology Web site by connecting to *www.course.com* and then searching for this book title. Note that you can use a computer in your school lab or your own computer to complete the exercises in this book.

USING YOUR OWN COMPUTER

To use your own computer to complete the steps and exercises, you need the following:

» **Software.** Java SE 6, available from *http://java.sun.com*. (Although almost all of the examples in this book will work with earlier versions of Java, the book was created using a preliminary "beta" version of Java 6. If you use a later version, you might notice minor cosmetic differences in the screen images.) The book clearly points out the few cases when an example does not work with earlier versions of Java. You also need a text editor, such as Notepad. A few exercises ask you to use a browser, such as Internet Explorer.

» **Hardware.** To install Java on your computer, the Java Web site suggests at least a Pentium III 500-MHz system with 512 MB of memory and at least 850 MB of disk space. A Pentium IV 1.4-GHz system with 1 GB of memory and 1 GB of disk space is recommended.

» **Data Files.** You cannot complete all the chapters and projects in this book using your own computer unless you have the data files. You can get the data files from your instructor, or you can obtain the data files electronically from the Course Technology Web site by connecting to *www.course.com* and then searching for this book title.

The following material is provided on the CD that comes with this book:

» Sun Microsystems Java Standard Edition 6, the Java language, compiler, and runtime environment

» Sun Microsystems Java Application Programming Interface (API) Specification, official documentation for the Java programming language

» The jGRASP integrated development environment for Java

» Code files for all Java program examples contained in the text

VISIT OUR WORLD WIDE WEB SITE

Additional materials designed especially for this book might be available for your course. Periodically search *www.course.com* for more details and updates.

CREATING YOUR FIRST JAVA CLASSES

In this chapter, you will:

Learn about programming
Be introduced to object-oriented programming
   concepts
Learn about Java
Analyze a Java application that uses console output
Add comments to a Java class
Save, compile, and run a Java application
Modify a Java class
Create a Java application using GUI output
Correct errors and find help

As you read your e-mail, your heart sinks. There's no denying the message: "Please see me in my office as soon as you are free—Lynn Greenbrier." Lynn is the head of programming for Event Handlers Incorporated, and you have worked for her as an intern for only two weeks. Event Handlers manages the details of private and corporate parties; every client has different needs, and the events are interesting and exciting.

"Did I do something wrong?" you ask as you enter her office. "Are you going to fire me?"

Lynn stands to greet you and says, "Please wipe that worried look off your face. I want to see if you are interested in a new challenge. Our Programming Department is going to create several new programs in the next few months. We've decided that Java is the way to go. It's object-oriented, platform independent, and perfect for applications on the World Wide Web, which is where we want to expand our marketing efforts."

"I'm not sure what 'object-oriented' and 'platform independent' mean," you say, "but I've always been interested in computers, and I'd love to learn more about programming."

"Based on your aptitude tests, you're perfect for programming," Lynn says. "Let's get started now. I'll describe the basics to you."

LEARNING ABOUT PROGRAMMING

A computer **program** is a set of instructions that you write to tell a computer what to do. Computers are constructed from circuitry that consists of small on/off switches, so you could create a computer program by writing something along the following lines:

```
first switch—on
second switch—off
third switch—off
fourth switch—on
```

Your program could go on and on, for several thousand switches. A program written in this style is written in **machine language**, which is the most basic circuitry-level language. The problems with this approach lie in keeping track of the many switches involved in programming any worthwhile task and in discovering the errant switch or switches if the program does not operate as expected. In addition, the number and location of switches vary from computer to computer, which means that you would need to customize a machine language program for every type of machine on which you want the program to run.

> **»NOTE**
> In every high-level programming language, the names of memory locations cannot include spaces.

Fortunately, programming has evolved into an easier task because of the development of high-level programming languages. A **high-level programming language** allows you to use a vocabulary of reasonable terms, such as "read," "write," or "add," instead of the sequences of on and off switches that perform these tasks. High-level languages also allow you to assign intuitive names to areas of computer memory, such as "hoursWorked" or "rateOfPay," rather than having to remember the memory locations (switch numbers) of those values.

Each high-level language has its own **syntax**, or rules of the language. For example, depending on the specific high-level language, you might use the verb "print" or "write" to produce output. All languages have a specific, limited vocabulary and a specific set of rules for using that vocabulary. When you are learning a computer programming language, such as Java, C++, or Visual Basic, you really are learning the vocabulary and syntax rules for that language.

Using a programming language, programmers write a series of **program statements**, similar to English sentences, to carry out the tasks they want the program to perform. After the program statements are written, high-level language programmers use a computer program called a **compiler** or **interpreter** to translate their language statements into machine code. A compiler translates an entire program before carrying out the statement, or **executing** it, whereas an interpreter translates one program statement at a time, executing a statement as soon as it is translated. Compilers and interpreters issue one or more error messages each time they encounter an invalid program statement—that is, a statement containing a **syntax error**, or misuse of the language. Subsequently, the programmer can correct the error and attempt another translation by compiling or interpreting the program again. Locating and repairing all syntax errors is part of the process of **debugging** a program—freeing the program of all errors. Whether you use a compiler or interpreter often depends on the programming language you use—for example, C++ is a compiled language and Visual Basic is an interpreted language. Each type of translator has its supporters—programs written in compiled languages execute more quickly, whereas programs written in interpreted languages are easier to develop and debug. Java uses the best of both technologies—a compiler to translate your programming statements and an interpreter to read the compiled code line by line at run time.

> **»NOTE**
> You will learn more about debugging Java programs later in this chapter.

In addition to learning the correct syntax for a particular language, a programmer must also understand computer programming logic. The **logic** behind any program involves executing the various statements and procedures in the correct order to produce the desired results. Although you begin to debug a program by correcting all the syntax errors, it is not fully debugged until you have also fixed all logical errors. For example, you would not write statements to tell the computer program to process data until the data had been properly read into the program. Similarly, you might be able to use a computer language's syntax correctly, but fail to end up with a logically constructed, workable program. Examples of logical errors include multiplying two values when you meant to divide them, or producing output prior to obtaining the appropriate input. Tools that will help you visualize and understand logic are presented in Chapter 5.

> **»NOTE** Programmers call some logical errors **semantic errors**. For example, if you misspell a programming language word, you commit a syntax error, but if you use a correct word in the wrong context, you commit a semantic error.

INTRODUCING OBJECT-ORIENTED PROGRAMMING CONCEPTS

Two popular approaches to writing computer programs are procedural programming and object-oriented programming.

PROCEDURAL PROGRAMMING

Procedural programming is a style of programming in which sets of operations are executed one after another in sequence. It involves using your knowledge of a programming language to create names for computer memory locations that can hold values—for example, numbers and text—in electronic form. The named computer memory locations are called **variables** because they hold values that might vary. For example, a payroll program written for a company might contain a variable named `rateOfPay`. The memory location referenced by the name `rateOfPay` might contain different values (a different value for every employee of the company) at different times. During the execution of the payroll program, each value stored under the name `rateOfPay` might have many operations performed on it—the value might be read from an input device, the value might be multiplied by another variable representing hours worked, and the value might be printed on paper. For convenience, the individual operations used in a computer program are often grouped into logical units called **procedures**. For example, a series of four or five comparisons and calculations that together determine a person's federal withholding tax value might be grouped as a procedure named `calculateFederalWithholding`. A procedural program defines the variable memory locations and then **calls** a series of procedures to input, manipulate, and output the values stored in those locations. A single procedural program often contains hundreds of variables and thousands of procedure calls.

> **>> NOTE** Procedures are also called modules, methods, functions, and subroutines. Users of different programming languages tend to use different terms. Java programmers most frequently use the term "method."

OBJECT-ORIENTED PROGRAMMING

Object-oriented programming is an extension of procedural programming in which you take a slightly different approach to writing computer programs. Writing **object-oriented programs** involves creating classes, creating objects from those classes, and creating **applications**, which are stand-alone executable programs that use those objects. After being created, classes can be reused over and over again to develop new programs. Thinking in an object-oriented manner involves envisioning program components as objects that belong to classes and are similar to concrete objects in the real world; then, you can manipulate the objects and have them interrelate with each other to achieve a desired result.

If you've ever used a computer that uses a command-line operating system (such as DOS), and if you've also used a graphical user interface (GUI), such as Windows, then you are familiar with one of the differences between procedural and object-oriented programs. If you want to move several files from a floppy disk to a hard disk, you can type a command at a prompt or command line, or you can use a mouse in a graphical environment to accomplish the task. The difference lies in whether you issue a series of commands, in sequence, to move the three files, or you drag icons representing the files from one screen location to another, much as you would physically move paper files from one file cabinet to another in your office. You can move the same three files using either operating system, but the GUI system allows you to manipulate the files like their real-world paper counterparts. In other words, the GUI system allows you to treat files as objects.

> **>> NOTE** Do not assume that all object-oriented programs are written to use GUI objects—they are not. However, the difference between command-line and GUI operating systems provides an analogy that helps you envision object-oriented concepts.

Understanding how object-oriented programming differs from traditional procedural programming requires understanding four basic concepts:

- » Objects
- » Classes
- » Inheritance
- » Polymorphism

UNDERSTANDING OBJECTS AND CLASSES

Objects, both in the real world and in object-oriented programming, are made up of attributes and methods. The attributes of an object are also referred to as its **states**. **Attributes** are the characteristics that define an object; attributes differentiate objects of the same class from one another. For example, some of your automobile's attributes are its make, model, year, and purchase price. Other attributes include whether the automobile is currently running, its gear, its speed, and whether it is dirty. All automobiles possess the same attributes, but not, of course, the same values for those attributes. Similarly, your dog has the attributes of its breed, name, age, and whether his shots are current.

>> NOTE
In object-oriented program grammar, a noun is equivalent to an object and an adjective is an attribute. Verbs are methods.

In object-oriented terminology, a **class** is a term that describes a group or collection of objects with common properties. An **instance** of a class is an existing object of a class. Therefore, your red Chevrolet `Automobile` with the dent can be considered an instance of the class that is made up of all automobiles, and your Golden Retriever `Dog` named Goldie is an instance of the class that is made up of all dogs. Thinking of items as instances of a class allows you to apply your general knowledge of the class to individual members of the class. A particular instance of an object takes its attributes from the general category. If your friend purchases an `Automobile`, you know it has a model name, and if your friend gets a `Dog`, you know the dog has a breed. You might not know the current state of your friend's `Automobile`, for example, its current speed, or the current status of her `Dog`'s shots, but you do know what attributes exist for the `Automobile` and `Dog` classes. Similarly, in a GUI operating environment, you expect each component to have specific, consistent attributes, such as a button being clickable or a window being closable, because each component gains these attributes as a member of the general class of GUI components.

> **>> NOTE** By convention, programmers using Java begin their class names with an uppercase letter. Thus, the class that defines the attributes and methods of an automobile would probably be named `Automobile`, and the class for dogs would probably be named `Dog`. However, following this convention is not required to produce a workable program.

> **>> NOTE** When you learn a programming language such as Java, you learn to work with two types of classes: those that have already been developed by the language's creators and your own new, customized classes.

Besides attributes, objects can use methods to accomplish tasks. A **method** is a self-contained block of program code, similar to a procedure. An `Automobile`, for example, can move forward and backward. It can also be filled with gasoline or be washed. Some methods can ascertain certain attributes, such as the current speed of an `Automobile` and the current status of its gas tank. Similarly, a `Dog` can walk or run, eat food, and get a bath, and there are methods to determine how hungry the `Dog` is or what its name is. GUI operating system components can be maximized, minimized, and dragged. Like procedural programs, object-oriented programs have variables (attributes) and procedures (methods), but the attributes and methods are encapsulated into objects that are then used much like real-world objects.

Encapsulation refers to the hiding of data and methods within an object. Encapsulation provides the security that keeps data and methods safe from inadvertent changes. Programmers sometimes refer to encapsulation as using a "black box," or a device that you can use without regard to the internal mechanisms. A programmer can access and use the methods and data contained in the black box but cannot change them.

If an object's methods are well written, the user is unaware of the low-level details of how the methods are executed, and the user must simply understand the interface or interaction

» NOTE
In this example, "your Automobile" is an instance of the Automobile class.

between the method and the object. For example, if you can fill your Automobile with gasoline, it is because you understand the interface between the gas pump nozzle and the vehicle's gas tank opening. You don't need to understand how the pump works mechanically or where the gas tank is located inside your vehicle. If you can read your speedometer, it does not matter how the displayed figure is calculated. As a matter of fact, if someone produces a superior, more accurate speed-determining device and inserts it in your Automobile, you don't have to know or care how it operates, as long as your interface remains the same. The same principles apply to well-constructed objects used in object-oriented programs.

UNDERSTANDING INHERITANCE AND POLYMORPHISM

An important feature of object-oriented programs is **inheritance**—the ability to create classes that share the attributes and methods of existing classes, but with more specific features. For example, Automobile is a class, and all Automobile objects share many traits and abilities. Convertible is a class that inherits from the Automobile class; a Convertible is a type of Automobile that has and can do everything a "plain" Automobile does—but with an added mechanism for and an added ability to lower its top. (In turn, Automobile inherits from the Vehicle class.) Convertible is not an object—it is a class. A specific Convertible is an object—for example, my1967BlueMustangConvertible.

Inheritance helps you understand real-world objects. For example, the first time you encounter a Convertible, you already understand how the ignition, brakes, door locks, and other Automobile systems work. You need to be concerned only with the attributes and methods that are "new" with a Convertible. The advantages in programming are the same—you can build new classes based on existing classes and concentrate on the specialized features you are adding.

A final important concept in object-oriented terminology is **polymorphism**. Literally, polymorphism means "many forms." It describes the feature of languages that allows the same word to be interpreted correctly in different situations based on the context. For example, in English the verb "run" means different things if you use it with "a footrace," a "business," or "a computer." You understand the word based on the other words used with it. Object-oriented programs are written so that the most useful verbs, such as "print" or "save," work differently based on their context. The advantages of polymorphism will become more apparent when you begin to create GUI applications containing features such as windows, buttons, and menu bars. In a GUI application, it is convenient to remember one method name, such as setColor or setHeight, and have it work correctly no matter what type of object you are modifying.

LEARNING ABOUT JAVA

» NOTE
When programmers call the JVM "hypothetical," they don't mean it doesn't exist. Instead, they mean it is not a physical entity created from hardware, but is composed only of software.

Java was developed by Sun Microsystems as an object-oriented language for general-purpose business applications and for interactive World Wide Web-based Internet applications. Some of the advantages that have made Java so popular in recent years are its security features and the fact that it is **architecturally neutral**, which means that you can use Java to write a program that will run on any platform (operating system).

Java can be run on a wide variety of computers because it does not execute instructions on a computer directly. Instead, Java runs on a hypothetical computer known as the **Java virtual machine (JVM)**.

Figure 1-1 shows the Java environment. Programming statements written in a high-level programming language are called **source code**. When you write a Java program, you first construct the source code using a text editor such as Notepad. The statements are saved in a file;
then, the Java compiler converts the source code into a binary program of **bytecode**. A program called the **Java interpreter** then checks the bytecode and communicates with the
operating system, executing the bytecode instructions line by line within the Java virtual
machine. Because the Java program is isolated from the operating system, the Java program
is also insulated from the particular hardware on which it is run. Because of this insulation,
the JVM provides security against intruders accessing your computer's hardware through the
operating system. Therefore, Java is more secure than other languages. Another advantage
provided by the JVM means less work for programmers—when using other programming
languages, software vendors usually have to produce multiple versions of the same product
(a Windows version, Macintosh version, UNIX version, Linux version, and so on) so all users
can run the program. With Java, one program version will run on all these platforms.

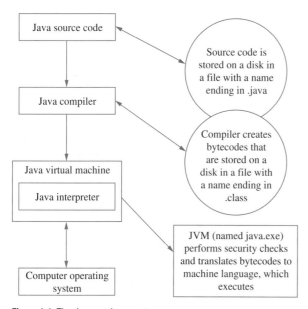

Figure 1-1 The Java environment

Java is also simpler to use than many other object-oriented languages. Java is modeled after
C++. Although neither language is easy to read or understand on first exposure, Java does
eliminate some of the most difficult-to-understand features in C++, such as pointers and multiple inheritance.

JAVA PROGRAM TYPES

You can write two kinds of programs using Java. Programs that are embedded in a Web page
are called Java **applets**. Stand-alone programs are called Java **applications**. Java applications can be further subdivided into **console applications**, which support character output
to a computer screen in a DOS window, for example, and **windowed applications**, which
create a GUI with elements such as menus, toolbars, and dialog boxes. Console applications
are the easiest applications to create (you start using them in the next section).

ANALYZING A JAVA APPLICATION THAT USES CONSOLE OUTPUT

At first glance, even the simplest Java application involves a fair amount of confusing syntax. Consider the application in Figure 1-2. This program is written on seven lines, and its only task is to print "First Java application" on the screen.

> **》NOTE** Some programmers prefer to reserve the term "print" for output that is produced on paper; they use "display" when referring to screen output. Because Java uses the `print()` and `println()` methods to display output on the screen, this book will use the term "print" to mean screen output.

```
public class First
{
    public static void main(String[] args)
    {
            System.out.println("First Java application");
    }
}
```

Figure 1-2 The `First` class

> **》NOTE** When you see program code in figures in this book, Java keywords will be blue and all other program elements will be black. A complete list of Java keywords is shown later in this chapter.

UNDERSTANDING THE STATEMENT THAT PRINTS THE OUTPUT

> **》NOTE**
> A statement does not necessarily end at the end of a line; a statement might run across several lines until it ends with a semicolon.

The statement `System.out.println("First Java application");` does the actual work in this program. Like all Java statements, this one ends with a semicolon.

The text "First Java application" is a **literal string** of characters; that is, it is a series of characters that will appear in output exactly as entered. Any literal string in Java is written between double quotation marks.

> **》NOTE** Most Java programming statements can be written on as many lines as you choose, as long as you place line breaks between words. However, a literal string cannot be broken and placed on multiple lines.

> **》NOTE**
> Data passed to a function can be called an argument or a **parameter**.

The string "First Java application" appears within parentheses because the string is an argument to a method, and arguments to methods always appear within parentheses. **Arguments** are pieces of information that are sent into, or **passed** to, a method, usually because the method requires the information to perform its task or carry out its purpose. As an example, consider placing a catalog order with a company that sells sporting goods. Processing a catalog order is a method that consists of a set of standard procedures—recording the order, checking the availability of the item, pulling the item from the warehouse, and so on. Each catalog order also requires a set of data items, such as which item number you are ordering and the quantity of the item desired; these data items can be considered the order's argument. If you order two of item 5432 from a catalog, you expect different results than if you order

8

1000 of item 9008. Likewise, if you pass the argument "Happy Holidays" to a Java method, you expect different results than if you pass the argument "First Java application".

> **NOTE** The `println()` method requires only one argument. Later in this chapter, you will learn about a method named `showMessageDialog()` that requires two arguments.

> **NOTE** You can use the `println()` method with no arguments when you want to print a blank line.

Within the statement `System.out.println("First Java application");`, the method to which you are passing `"First Java application"` is named `println()`. The `println()` method prints a line of output on the screen and positions the insertion point on the next line, so that any subsequent output appears on a new line.

> **NOTE** Method names are usually referenced followed by their parentheses, as in `println()`, so that you can distinguish method names from variable names.

Within the statement `System.out.println("First Java application");`, *out* is an object. The `out` object represents the screen. Several methods, including `println()`, are available with the `out` object. Of course, not all objects have a `println()` method (for instance, you can't print to a keyboard, to your `Automobile`, or to your `Dog`), but the creators of Java assume you frequently want to display output on a screen. Therefore, the `out` object was created and endowed with the method named `println()`. In the "You Do It" section later in this chapter, you will create your own objects and endow them with your own methods.

> **NOTE** The `print()` method is very similar to the `println()` method. With `println()`, after the message prints, the insertion point appears on the following line. With `print()`, the insertion point does not advance to a new line; it remains on the same line as the output.

Within the statement `System.out.println("First Java application");`, *System* is a class. Therefore, `System` defines the attributes of a collection of similar "System" objects, just as the `Dog` class defines the attributes of a collection of similar `Dog` objects. One of the `System` objects is *out*. (You can probably guess that another object is *in* and that it represents an input device.)

> **NOTE** Java is case sensitive; the class named `System` is a completely different class from one named `system`, `SYSTEM`, or even `sYsTeM`.

The dots (periods) in `System.out.println("First Java application");` are used to separate the names of the class, object, and method. You will use this same class-dot-object-dot-method format repeatedly in your Java programs.

The statement that prints the string "First Java application" cannot stand alone; it is embedded within a class, as shown in Figure 1-2.

UNDERSTANDING THE First CLASS

Everything that you use within a Java program must be part of a class. When you write `public class First`, you are defining a class named `First`. You can define a Java class using any name or **identifier** you need, as long as it meets the following requirements:

>> A class name must begin with a letter of the English alphabet, a non-English letter (such as α or π), an underscore, or a dollar sign. A class name cannot begin with a digit.

>> A class name can contain only letters, digits, underscores, or dollar signs.

>> A class name cannot be a Java reserved keyword, such as `public` or `class`. (See Table 1-1 for a list of reserved keywords.)

>> A class name cannot be one of the following values: `true`, `false`, or `null`. These three are not keywords (they are primitive values), but they are reserved and cannot be used.

>> NOTE Java is based on **Unicode**, which is an international system of character representation. The term "letter" indicates English-language letters as well as characters from Arabic, Greek, and other alphabets. You can learn more about Unicode in Appendix B.

abstract	double	int	super
assert	else	interface	switch
boolean	enum	long	synchronized
break	extends	native	this
byte	final	new	throw
case	finally	package	throws
catch	float	private	transient
char	for	protected	try
class	goto	public	void
const	if	return	volatile
continue	implements	short	while
default	import	static	
do	instanceof	strictfp	

Table 1-1 Java reserved keywords

It is a Java standard, although not a requirement, to begin class identifiers with an uppercase letter and employ other uppercase letters as needed to improve readability. Table 1-2 lists some valid and conventional class names that you can use when writing programs in Java. Table 1-3 provides some examples of class names that *could* be used in Java (if you use these class names, the class will compile) but that are unconventional and not recommended. Table 1-4 provides some class name examples that are illegal.

In Figure 1-2, the line `public class First` is the class header; it contains the keyword `class`, which identifies `First` as a class. The reserved word `public` is an access modifier. An **access modifier** defines the circumstances under which a class can be accessed and the

>> NOTE
Using an uppercase letter to begin an identifier and to start each new word in an identifier is known as **Pascal casing**.

Class Name	Description
Employee	Begins with an uppercase letter
UnderGradStudent	Begins with an uppercase letter, contains no spaces, and emphasizes each new word with an initial uppercase letter
InventoryItem	Begins with an uppercase letter, contains no spaces, and emphasizes the second word with an initial uppercase letter
Budget2009	Begins with an uppercase letter and contains no spaces

Table 1-2 Some valid class names in Java

>> NOTE You should follow established conventions for Java so your programs will be easy for other programmers to interpret and follow. This book uses established Java programming conventions.

Class Name	Description
Undergradstudent	New words are not indicated with initial uppercase letters; difficult to read
Inventory_Item	Underscore is not commonly used to indicate new words
BUDGET2009	Using all uppercase letters is not common

Table 1-3 Legal but unconventional and nonrecommended class names in Java

Class Name	Description
an employee	Space character is illegal
Inventory Item	Space character is illegal
class	class is a reserved word
2009Budget	Class names cannot begin with a digit
phone#	# symbol is illegal

Table 1-4 Some illegal class names in Java

other classes that have the right to use a class. Public access is the most liberal type of access; you will learn about public and other types of access in Chapter 3.

After the class header, you enclose the contents of a class within curly braces ({ and }). A class can contain any number of data items and methods. In Figure 1-2, the class First contains only one method within its curly braces. The name of the method is main(), and the main() method, like the println() method, contains its own set of parentheses. The main() method in the First class contains only one statement—the statement that uses the println() method.

> **NOTE** In general, whitespace is optional in Java. **Whitespace** is any combination of nonprinting characters—for example, spaces, tabs, and carriage returns (blank lines). However, you cannot use whitespace within any identifier or keyword. You can insert whitespace between words or lines in your program code by typing spaces, tabs, or blank lines because the compiler ignores these extra spaces. You use whitespace to organize your program code and make it easier to read.

For every opening curly brace ({) in a Java program, there must be a corresponding closing curly brace (}). The placement of the opening and closing curly braces is not important to the compiler. For example, the following method is executed exactly the same as the one shown in Figure 1-2. The only difference is that the layout of the method is different—the line breaks occur in different locations.

```
public static void main(String[ ] args){
    System.out.println("First Java application");
}
```

Many Java programmers prefer to write code using the style shown in this example, with the opening curly brace for the method at the end of the method header line. This format saves a line of type in the saved source code file. Others feel that code in which you vertically align each pair of opening and closing curly braces (as shown in Figure 1-2) is easier to read. Either style is acceptable, and both produce workable Java programs. When you write your own code, you should develop a consistent style.

UNDERSTANDING THE main() METHOD

The method header for the main() method is quite complex. The meaning and purpose of each of the terms used in the method header will become clearer as you complete this textbook; a brief explanation will suffice for now.

In the method header public static void main(String[ ] args), the word public is an access modifier, just as it is when you use it to define the First class. In Java, the reserved keyword **static** means that a method is accessible and usable even though no objects of the class exist. Of course, other classes eventually might have their own, different main() methods.

In English, the word "void" means empty. When the keyword **void** is used in the main() method header, it does not indicate that the main() method is empty, but rather that the main() method does not return any value when it is called. This doesn't mean that main() doesn't produce output—in fact, the method in Figure 1-2 does. It only means that the main() method does not send any value back to any other method that might use it. You will learn more about return values in Chapter 3.

Not all classes have a main() method; in fact, many do not. All Java *applications*, however, must include a class containing a public method named main(), and most Java applications have additional classes and methods. When you execute a Java application, the JVM always executes the main() method first.

In the method header public static void main(String[ ] args), you might recognize that the contents between the parentheses, (String[ ] args), must represent an argument passed to the main() method, just as the string "First Java application" is an argument passed to the println() method. String is a Java class that can be used to hold character strings. The identifier args is used to hold any String objects that might be sent to the main() method. The main() method could do something with those arguments, such as print them, but in Figure 1-2, the main() method does not actually use the args identifier. Nevertheless, you must place an identifier within the main() method's parentheses. The identifier does not need to be named args—it could be any legal Java identifier—but the name args is traditional.

》》 NOTE When you refer to the String class in the main() method header, the square brackets indicate an array of String objects. You will learn more about arrays and the String class in Chapter 6.

The simple application shown in Figure 1-2 has many pieces to remember. However, for now you can use the Java code shown in Figure 1-3 as a shell, in which you replace AnyClassName with a class name you choose and the line /******/ with any statements that you want to execute.

```
public class AnyClassName
{
    public static void main(String[] args)
    {
        /******/
    }
}
```

Figure 1-3 Shell code

ADDING COMMENTS TO A JAVA CLASS

As you can see, even the simplest Java class requires several lines of code and contains somewhat perplexing syntax. Large applications that perform many tasks include much more code, and as you write larger applications it becomes increasingly difficult to remember why you included steps or how you intended to use particular variables. Documenting your program code helps you remember why you wrote lines of code the way you did. **Program comments** are nonexecuting statements that you add to a program for the purpose of documentation. Programmers use comments to leave notes for themselves and for others who might read their programs in the future. At the very least, your Java class files should include comments indicating the author, the date, and the class's name or function. The best practice dictates that you also include a brief comment to describe the purpose of each method you create within a class.

> **NOTE** As you work through this book, add comments as the first three lines of every file. The comments should contain the class name and purpose, your name, and the date. Your instructor might ask you to include additional comments.

Comments can also be useful when you are developing an application. If a program is not performing as expected, you can comment out various statements and subsequently run the program to observe the effect. When you **comment out** a statement, you turn it into a comment so the compiler does not translate and the JVM does not execute its command. This can help you pinpoint the location of errant statements in malfunctioning programs.

There are three types of comments in Java:

» **Line comments** start with two forward slashes (//) and continue to the end of the current line. A line comment can appear on a line by itself or at the end (and to the right) of a line following executable code. Line comments do not require an ending symbol.

> **NOTE** The forward slash (/) and the backslash (\) characters are often confused, but they are two distinct characters. You cannot use them interchangeably.

» **Block comments** start with a forward slash and an asterisk (/*) and end with an asterisk and a forward slash (*/). A block comment can appear on a line by itself, on a line before executable code, or on a line after executable code. Block comments can also extend across as many lines as needed.

» **Javadoc** comments are a special case of block comments. They begin with a forward slash and two asterisks (/**) and end with an asterisk and a forward slash (*/). You can use javadoc comments to generate documentation with a program named javadoc.

> **NOTE** The Java Software Development Kit (SDK) includes the javadoc tool, which you can use when writing programs in Java. The tool produces HTML pages that describe classes and their contents.

Figure 1-4 shows how comments are used in code. In this example, the only statement that executes is the `System.out.println("Hello");` statement; everything else is a comment.

```
// Demonstrating comments
/* This shows
     that these comments
   don't matter */
System.out.println("Hello"); // This line executes
     // up to where the comment started
/* Everything but the println()
     is a comment */
```

Figure 1-4 A program segment containing several comments

SAVING, COMPILING, AND RUNNING A JAVA APPLICATION

SAVING A JAVA CLASS

» NOTE
Appendix A contains important information on saving, compiling, and running a Java application.

When you write a Java class, you must save it using some storage medium, most often a disk. In Java, if a class is `public` (that is, if you use the `public` access modifier before the class name), you must save the class in a file with exactly the same name and a .java extension. For example, the `First` class must be stored in a file named First.java. The class name and filename must match exactly, including the use of uppercase and lowercase characters. If the extension is not .java, the Java compiler does not recognize the file as containing a Java class.

COMPILING A JAVA CLASS

After you write and save an application, two steps must occur before you can view the application's output.

1. You must compile the class you wrote (called the source code) into bytecode.

2. You must use the Java interpreter to translate the bytecode into executable statements.

To compile your source code from the command line, your prompt should show the folder or directory where your program file is stored. Then, you type `javac` followed by the name of the file that contains the source code. For example, to compile a file named First.java, you type `javac First.java` and then press Enter. There will be one of three outcomes:

» You receive a message such as `'javac' is not recognized as an internal or external command, operable program or batch file.`

» You receive one or more program language error messages.

» You receive no messages, which means that the application compiled successfully.

» NOTE When compiling, if the source code file is not in the current path, you can type a full path with the filename. For example:

```
javac c:\java\myClasses\Chapter.01\First.java
```

» NOTE In a DOS environment, you can change directories using the `cd` command. For example, to change to a directory named `MyClasses`, you type `cd MyClasses` and press Enter.

If you receive an error message that the command is not recognized, it might mean one of the following:

» You misspelled the command `javac`.

» You misspelled the filename.

» You are not within the correct subfolder or subdirectory on your command line.

» Java was not installed properly. (See Appendix A for information on installation.)

» NOTE
Appendix A contains information on troubleshooting, including how to change filenames in a Windows environment.

If you receive a programming language error message, there are one or more syntax errors in the source code. Recall that a syntax error is a programming error that occurs when you introduce typing errors into your program or use the programming language incorrectly. For example, if your class name is `first` (with a lowercase f) in the source code but you saved the file as First.java (with an uppercase F), when you compile the application you'll receive an error message, such as `class first is public, should be declared in a file named first.java` because "first" and "First" are not the same in a case-sensitive language. If this error occurs, you must reopen the text file that contains the source code and make the necessary corrections.

If you receive no error messages after compiling the code in a file named First.java, the application compiled successfully, and a file named First.class is created and saved in the same folder as the application text file. After a successful compile, you can run the class file on any computer that has a Java language interpreter.

RUNNING A JAVA APPLICATION

To run the `First` application from the command line, you type `java First`. Figure 1-5 shows the application's output in the command window. In this example, you can see that the `First` class is stored in a folder named Java on the C drive.

>> **NOTE** If you want to confirm the storage location of your First.java class, the procedure varies depending on your operating system. In a Windows operating system, for example, you can open Windows Explorer, locate the icon representing the storage device you are using, find the folder in which you have saved the file, and expand the folder. You should see the First.java file.

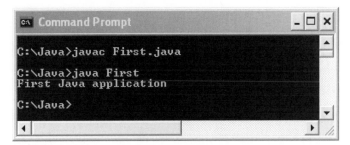

Figure 1-5 Output of the `First` application

MODIFYING A JAVA CLASS

After viewing the application output, you might decide to modify the class to get a different result. For example, you might decide to change the `First` application's output from `First Java application` to the following:

```
My new and improved
Java application
```

To produce the new output, first you must modify the text file that contains the existing class. You need to change the literal string that currently prints, and then add an additional text string. Figure 1-6 shows the class that changes the output.

```
public class First
{
    public static void main(String[] args)
    {
        System.out.println("My new and improved");
        System.out.println("Java application");
    }
}
```

Figure 1-6 `First` class containing modified output from original version

The changes to the `First` class include the addition of the statement `System.out.println` `("My new and improved");` and the removal of the word "First" from the string in the statement `System.out.println("Java application");`. However, if you make those changes to the file as shown in Figure 1-6, save the file, and type `java First` at the command line, you will not see the new output—you will see the old output without the added line. Even though you save a text file containing the modified source code for a class, it is the compiled class in the already-compiled class file that executes. After you save the file named First.java, the old compiled version of the class with the same name is still stored on your computer. Before the new source code will execute, you must do the following:

1. Save the file with the changes (using the same filename).

2. Compile the class with the `javac` command. (Actually, you are *re*compiling the class.)

3. Interpret the class bytecode and execute the class using the `java` command.

> **NOTE** When you complete these steps, the original version of the compiled file with the .class extension is replaced, and the new application executes. The original version no longer exists. When you modify a class, you must decide whether you want to retain the original version. If you do, you must give the new version a new class and filename.

CREATING A JAVA APPLICATION USING GUI OUTPUT

Besides allowing you to use the `System` class to produce command window output, Java provides built-in classes that produce GUI output. For example, Java contains a class named **JOptionPane** that allows you to produce dialog boxes. A **dialog box** is a GUI object resembling a window in which you can place messages you want to display. Figure 1-7 shows a class

```
import javax.swing.JOptionPane;
public class FirstDialog
{
    public static void main(String[] args)
    {
        JOptionPane.showMessageDialog(null,"First Java dialog");
        System.exit(0);
    }
}
```

Figure 1-7 The `FirstDialog` class

Figure 1-8 Output of the FirstDialog application

named FirstDialog; Figure 1-8 shows the output. The class in Figure 1-7 contains many elements that are familiar to you; only the three shaded lines are new.

In Figure 1-7, the first shaded line is an import statement. You use an **import statement** when you want to access a built-in Java class that is contained in a group of classes called a **package**. To use the JOptionPane class, you must import the package named javax.swing.JOptionPane.

The second shaded statement in the FirstDialog class in Figure 1-7 uses the showMessageDialog() method that is part of the JOptionPane class. Like the println() method that is used for console output, the showMessageDialog() method is followed by a set of parentheses. However, whereas the println() method requires only one argument between its parentheses to produce an output string, the showMessageDialog() method requires two arguments. When the first argument to showMessageDialog() is null, as it is in the class in Figure 1-7, it means the output message box should be placed in the center of the screen. The second argument, after the comma, is the string that should be output.

The last shaded statement in the main() method of the FirstDialog class shown in Figure 1-7 is System.exit(0);. You have already used the System class out object and its println() method; this application uses the System class exit() method. You must use this method with any application that uses a GUI; it returns control to the operating system. The zero contained within the parentheses of the exit() method is an argument that indicates the application ended successfully without error. Actually, you could use any integer as an argument to the exit() method, and the program would still end correctly. However, others who use this program expect a zero if the program ends normally, and so you should follow this convention in your programs.

When a user executes the FirstDialog class, the dialog box in Figure 1-8 is displayed. The user must click the OK button or the Close button to dismiss the dialog box.

CORRECTING ERRORS AND FINDING HELP

Frequently, you might make typing errors as you enter Java statements into your text editor. When you issue the command to compile the class containing errors, the Java compiler produces one or more error messages. The exact error message that appears varies depending on the compiler you are using. In the First class (shown in Figure 1-2), if you mistype the System.out.println() code using a lowercase 's' in System (as system.out.println ("First Java Application");), an error message similar to the one shown in Figure 1-9 is displayed. The first line of the error message displays the name of the file in which the error was found (FirstDialog.java), the line number in which it was found (7), and the nature of the error ("cannot find symbol"). The next two lines identify the symbol that cannot be found (system) and the name of the class (FirstDialog). This is a compile-time error, or syntax error; the compiler cannot find a symbol named system (with a lowercase initial letter) in this case-sensitive programming language. The compiler detects the violation of language rules and refuses to translate the class to machine code.

Figure 1-9 Error message generated when program contains "system" instead of "System"

When you compile a class, the compiler reports as many errors as it can find so that you can fix as many errors as possible. Sometimes, one error in syntax causes multiple error messages that normally would not be errors if the first syntax error did not exist. Consider the ErrorTest class shown in Figure 1-10. The class contains a single error—the

```
public class ErrorTest
/*   This class prints a test message
{
   public static void main(String[] args)
   {
      System.out.println("Test");
   }
}
```

Figure 1-10 The ErrorTest class with an unclosed comment

comment that starts in the second line is never closed. However, when you attempt to compile this class, you receive two error messages, as shown in Figure 1-11. The first error message correctly identifies the unclosed comment. The second error message is more confusing; it states that a closing curly brace is missing as the last line of the class. However, the class contains the correct number of curly braces. If you repair the first error by closing off the comment and then save and recompile the class, both error messages disappear. The second message is generated only as a side effect of the unfinished comment. When you compile a class and view a list of errors, correct the errors that make sense to you and then recompile; sometimes, when you correct an error or two, several others disappear.

Figure 1-11 Error messages generated by `ErrorTest` application in Figure 1-10

> **NOTE** In Figure 1-11, notice that the line number where the error was detected appears as part of the error message. For example, "ErrorTest.java:2: unclosed comment" means that the comment that is unclosed begins in line 2 of the file. Also, a caret appears below the location where Java detected the error—in this case, at the opening slash of the comment. When the compiler reports a line number in an error message, you can start to look at the indicated location. Frequently, however, the actual error you made is not precisely where Java first noticed it—only nearby.

Of course, no programmer intends to type a program containing syntax errors, but when you do, the compiler finds them all for you. A second kind of error occurs when the syntax of the program is correct and the program compiles but produces incorrect results when you execute it. This type of error is a **logic error**, which is usually more difficult to find and resolve. In the `First` class in Figure 1-2, typing the `System.out.println()` code as `System.out.println("Frst Java Application");` does not produce an error. The compiler does not find the spelling error of "Frst" instead of "First"; the code is compiled and the JVM can execute the statements. Other examples of logic errors include multiplying two values when you meant to add, printing one copy of a report when you meant to print five, or forgetting to produce a requested count of the number of times an event has occurred. Errors of this type must be detected by carefully examining the program output. It is the responsibility of the program author to test programs and find any logic errors. Good programming practice stresses programming structure and development that helps minimize errors. In addition, each chapter in this book contains four exercises in which you get the opportunity to locate and correct syntax and logic errors. Programmers call the process of correcting all these errors "debugging" a program.

> **NOTE**
> A logic error is a type of **run-time error**—an error not detected until the program asks the computer to do something wrong, or even illegal, while executing.

> **▶▶ NOTE** The process of fixing computer errors has been known as debugging since a large moth was found wedged into the circuitry of a mainframe computer at Harvard University in 1945. See these Web sites for interesting details and pictures: *www.jamesshuggins.com/h/tek1/first_computer_bug.htm* and *www.history.navy.mil/photos/images/h96000/h96566kc.htm.*

As you write Java programs, you can frequently consult this book as well as other Java documentation. A great wealth of helpful material exists at the Sun Microsystems Web site, *http://java.sun.com.* Of particular value is the Java application programming interface, more commonly referred to as the **Java API**. The Java API is also called the Java class library; it contains information about how to use every prewritten Java class, including lists of all the methods you can use with the classes.

> **▶▶ NOTE**
> The SDK previously was called the JDK, or Java Developer's Kit. You might see this term in other books.

Also of interest at the *java.sun.com* Web site are frequently asked questions (**FAQ**s) that provide brief answers to many common questions about Java software and products. You can also find several versions of the Java Software Development Kit (**SDK**) that you can download for free. Versions are available for Windows, Linux, and Solaris operating systems. You can search and browse documentation online or you can download the documentation file for the SDK and install it on your computer. After it is installed, you can search and browse documentation locally.

A downloadable Java tutorial titled "The Java Tutorial: A practical guide for programmers" with hundreds of complete working examples is available from *http://java.sun.com/docs/ books/tutorial/.* The tutorial is organized into trails—groups of lessons on a particular subject. You can start the tutorial at the beginning and navigate sequentially to the end, or jump from one trail to another. As you study each chapter in this book, you are encouraged to make good use of these support materials.

YOU DO IT

YOUR FIRST APPLICATION

Now that you understand the basics of an application written in Java, you are ready to enter your first Java application into a text editor. It is a tradition among programmers that the first program you write in any language produces "Hello, world!" as its output. You will create such a program now. You can use any text editor, such as Notepad, TextPad, or any other text-processing program.

> **▶▶ NOTE** It is best to use the simplest available text editor when writing Java programs. Multifeatured word-processing programs save documents as much larger files because of all the built-in features, such as font styles and margin settings, which you do not need in your Java programs.

To write your first Java application:

1. Start any text editor (such as Notepad or TextPad), and then open a new document, if necessary.

2. Type the class header **public class Hello**. In this example, the class name is `Hello`. You can use any valid name you want for the class. If you choose Hello, you must always refer to the class as Hello, and not as hello, because Java is case sensitive.

3. Press **Enter** once, type **{**, press **Enter** again, and then type **}**. You will add the `main()` method between these curly braces. Although it is not required, it is good practice to place

each curly brace on its own line and to align opening and closing curly brace pairs with each other. Using this format makes your code easier to read.

4. As shown in Figure 1-12, add the `main()` method header between the curly braces, and then type a set of curly braces for `main()`.

```
public class Hello
{
    public static void main(String[] args)
    {
    }
}
```

Figure 1-12 The `main()` method shell for the `Hello` class

5. Next add the statement within the `main()` method that will produce the output, "Hello, world!". Use Figure 1-13 as a guide for adding the shaded `println()` statement to the `main()` method.

```
public class Hello
{
    public static void main(String[] args)
    {
        System.out.println("Hello, world!");
    }
}
```

Figure 1-13 Complete `Hello` class

6. Save the application as **Hello.java** in the Chapter.01 folder on your Student Disk. Make certain that the file extension is .java. If it is not, the compiler for Java does not recognize the file as an application it can compile.

> **NOTE** Many text editors attach their own filename extension (such as .txt or .doc) to a saved file. Double-check your saved file to ensure that it does not have a double extension (such as Hello.java.txt). If the file has a double extension, rename the file. If you explicitly type quotation marks surrounding a filename (such as "Hello.java") in the Save As dialog box, most text editors save the file as you specify, without adding an additional extension. If you use a word-processing program to write your code, make certain that you save your .java files as text documents. The default for Notepad is to save all documents as text.

7. Go to the command-line prompt for the drive and folder or subdirectory in which you saved Hello.java.

8. At the command line, type **javac Hello.java**.

9. When the compile is successful, execute your application by typing **java Hello** at the command line, and then press **Enter**. The output should appear on the next line, as shown in Figure 1-14.

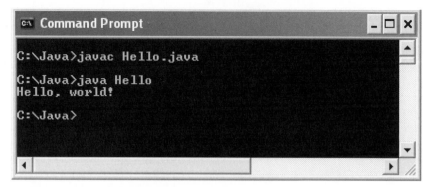

Figure 1-14 Output of `Hello` application

ADDING COMMENTS TO A CLASS

In this exercise, you add comments to your `Hello.java` application and save it as a new class named `Hello2`.

To add comments to your application and save it as a new class:

1. Position the insertion point at the top of the file that contains the `Hello` class, press **Enter** to insert a new line, press the **Up arrow** key to go to that line, and then type the following comments at the top of the file. Press **Enter** after typing each line. Insert your name and today's date where indicated.

   ```
   // Filename Hello2.java
   // Written by <your name>
   // Written on <today's date>
   ```

2. Scroll to the end of the line `public class Hello`, change the class name to **Hello2**, press **Enter**, and then type the following block comment:

   ```
   /*  This class demonstrates the use of the println()
   method to print the message Hello, world!  */
   ```

3. Save the file as **Hello2.java** in the Chapter.01 folder on your Student Disk. The file must be named Hello2.java because the class name is Hello2.

4. Go to the command-line prompt for the drive and folder or subdirectory in which you saved Hello2.java.

5. At the command line, type **javac Hello2.java**, and then press **Enter**.

> **»NOTE** If you receive an error message when you compile or run a program, look in the section "Saving, Compiling, and Running a Java Application" to find its cause and then make the necessary corrections. Save the file again and then repeat Steps 4 and 5 until your application compiles successfully.

6. When the compile is successful, execute your application by typing **java Hello2** at the command line, and then press **Enter**. The output should appear on the next line, as shown in Figure 1-15.

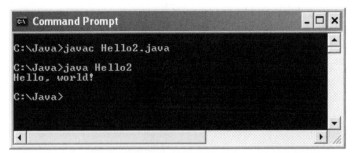

Figure 1-15 Successful compilation and execution of `Hello2` application

>> **NOTE** After the application compiles successfully, a file named Hello2.class is created and stored in the same folder as the Hello2.java file. If your application compiled without error but you receive an error message, such as "Exception in thread 'main' java.lang.NoClassDefFoundError," when you try to execute the application, you probably do not have your class path set correctly. See Appendix A for details.

>> **NOTE** When you run a Java application using the `java` command, do not add the .class extension to the filename. If you type `java First`, the interpreter looks for a file named First.class. If you type `java First.class`, the interpreter incorrectly looks for a file named First.class.class.

MODIFYING A CLASS

Next, you modify your Hello2 class, but to retain the Hello2 file, you save the modified file as the Hello3 class.

To change the Hello2 class to the Hello3 class and rerun the application:

1. Open the file **Hello2.java** in your text editor. Change both the comment name and the class name to **Hello3**.

2. Add the following statement below the statement that prints "Hello, world!":
   ```
   System.out.println("I'm ready for Java programming!");
   ```

   Be certain to type the semicolon at the end of the statement and use the correct case.

3. Save the file as **Hello3.java** in the Chapter.01 folder on your Student Disk.

4. At the command line, compile the file by typing the command **javac Hello3.java**.

5. Interpret and execute the class by typing the command **java Hello3**, and then press **Enter**. Your output should look like Figure 1-16.

>> **NOTE**
If you receive compile errors, return to the Hello3.java file in the text editor, fix the errors, and then repeat Steps 3 and 4 until the class compiles successfully.

Figure 1-16 Output of `Hello3` application

CREATING A DIALOG BOX

Next, you write a Java application that produces output in a dialog box.

To create an application that produces a dialog box as output:

1. Open a new file in your text editor. Type comments similar to the following, inserting your own name and today's date where indicated.

```
// Filename HelloDialog.java
// Written by <your name>
// Written on <today's date>
```

2. Enter the import statement that allows you to use the JOptionPane class:

```
import javax.swing.JOptionPane;
```

3. Enter the HelloDialog class:

```
public class HelloDialog
{
    public static void main(String[] args)
    {
        JOptionPane.showMessageDialog(null, "Hello, world!");
        System.exit(0);
    }
}
```

4. Save the file as **HelloDialog.java**. Compile the class using the command **javac HelloDialog.java**. Eliminate any syntax errors, resave the file, and recompile. Then execute the program using the command **java HelloDialog**. The output appears as shown in Figure 1-17.

5. Click **OK** to dismiss the dialog box.

Figure 1-17 Output of HelloDialog application

KEY TERMS

A computer **program** is a set of instructions that you write to tell a computer what to do.

A program written in circuitry-level language, as a series of on and off switches, is written in **machine language**.

A **high-level programming language** allows you to use a vocabulary of reasonable terms, such as "read," "write," or "add," instead of the sequences of on and off switches that perform these tasks.

Syntax is the rules of the language.

Program statements are similar to English sentences; they carry out the tasks that programs perform.

A **compiler**, or **interpreter**, is a program that translates language statements into machine code.

Executing a statement means to carry it out.

A **syntax error** is a programming error that occurs when you introduce typing errors into your program or use the programming language incorrectly. A program containing syntax errors will not compile.

The process of **debugging** a program frees it of all errors.

The **logic** behind any program involves executing the various statements and procedures in the correct order to produce the desired results.

Semantic errors occur when you use a correct word in the wrong context in program code.

Procedural programming is a style of programming in which sets of operations are executed one after another in sequence.

Variables are named computer memory locations that hold values that might vary.

Procedures are sets of operations performed by a computer program.

A procedural program **calls** a series of procedures to input, manipulate, and output values.

Writing **object-oriented programs** involves creating classes, creating objects from those classes, and creating applications that use those objects. Thinking in an object-oriented manner involves envisioning program components as objects that are similar to concrete objects in the real world; then, you can manipulate the objects to achieve a desired result.

An **application** is a stand-alone, executable program.

Objects are instances of a class; they are made up of attributes and methods.

The attributes of an object are also referred to as its **states**.

Attributes are the characteristics that define an object as part of a class.

In object-oriented terminology, a **class** is a term that describes a group or collection of objects with common properties.

An **instance** of a class is an existing object of a class.

A **method** is a self-contained block of program code, similar to a procedure.

Encapsulation refers to the hiding of data and methods within an object.

Inheritance is the ability to create classes that share the attributes and methods of existing classes, but with more specific features.

Polymorphism describes the feature of languages that allows the same word to be interpreted correctly in different situations based on the context.

Java was developed by Sun Microsystems as an object-oriented language used both for general-purpose business applications and for interactive World Wide Web-based Internet applications.

Java is **architecturally neutral**, which means that you can use it to write a program that runs on any platform (operating system).

Java runs on a hypothetical (software-based) computer known as the **Java virtual machine (JVM)**.

Source code consists of programming statements written in a high-level programming language.

Bytecode consists of programming statements that have been compiled into binary format.

A program called the **Java interpreter** checks the bytecode and communicates with the operating system, executing the bytecode instructions line by line within the Java virtual machine.

Java programs that are embedded in a Web page are called Java **applets**.

Stand-alone Java programs are called Java **applications**.

Console applications support character output to a computer screen in a DOS window.

Windowed applications create a graphical user interface (GUI) with elements such as menus, toolbars, and dialog boxes.

A **literal string** is a series of characters that appear exactly as entered. Any literal string in Java appears between double quotation marks.

Arguments are information passed to a method so it can perform its task.

Sending arguments to a method is called **passing** them.

Parameters are arguments passed to methods.

An **identifier** is a name of a class or object.

Unicode is an international system of character representation.

Using an uppercase letter to begin an identifier and to start each new word in an identifier is known as **Pascal casing**.

An **access modifier** defines the circumstances under which a class can be accessed and the other classes that have the right to use a class.

Whitespace is any combination of nonprinting characters—for example, spaces, tabs, and carriage returns (blank lines).

The reserved keyword **static** means that a method is accessible and usable even though no objects of the class exist. Of course, other classes eventually might have their own, different `main()` methods.

The keyword **void**, when used in a method header, indicates that the method does not return any value when it is called.

Program comments are nonexecuting statements that you add to a Java file for the purpose of documentation.

When you **comment out** a statement, you turn it into a comment so the compiler will not execute its command.

Line comments start with two forward slashes (//) and continue to the end of the current line. Line comments can appear on a line by themselves or at the end of a line following executable code.

Block comments start with a forward slash and an asterisk (/*) and end with an asterisk and a forward slash (*/). Block comments can appear on a line by themselves, on a line before executable code, or on a line after executable code. Block comments can also extend across as many lines as needed.

A special case of block comments are **javadoc** comments. They begin with a forward slash and two asterisks (/**) and end with an asterisk and a forward slash (*/). You can use javadoc comments to generate documentation with a program named javadoc.

The Java class named **JOptionPane** allows you to produce dialog boxes.

A **dialog box** is a GUI object resembling a window in which you can place messages you want to display.

You use an **import statement** when you want to access a built-in Java class that is contained in a package.

A **package** contains a group of built-in Java classes.

A **logic error** occurs when a program compiles successfully but produces an error during execution.

A **run-time error** occurs when a program compiles successfully but does not execute.

The **Java API** is the application programming interface, a collection of information about how to use every prewritten Java class.

FAQs are frequently asked questions.

The **SDK** is the Java Software Development Kit.

CHAPTER SUMMARY

» A computer program is a set of instructions that tells a computer what to do. You can write a program using a high-level programming language, which has its own syntax, or rules of the language. After you write a program, you use a compiler, or interpreter, to translate the language statements into machine code.

» Writing object-oriented programs involves creating classes, creating objects from those classes, and creating applications—stand-alone executable programs that use those objects, which are similar to concrete objects in the real world.

» A program written in Java is run on a standardized hypothetical computer called the Java virtual machine (JVM). When your class is compiled into bytecode, an interpreter within the JVM subsequently interprets the bytecode and communicates with your operating system to produce the program results.

» All Java programming statements end with a semicolon. Periods (called dots) are used to separate classes, objects, and methods in program code. The contents of all classes are contained within opening and closing curly braces. A series of characters that appears between double quotation marks is a literal string. Java programming methods might require arguments or messages to perform the appropriate task.

» Everything that you use within a Java program must be part of a class. A Java class might take any identifier that begins with either an uppercase or lowercase letter of the alphabet and contains only uppercase and lowercase letters, digits, and underscores. A class name cannot be a reserved keyword of Java.

» The reserved word `public` is an example of an access modifier—a word that defines the circumstances under which a class can be accessed. The keyword `static` in a method header indicates that you do not need to instantiate any objects to use the method. The keyword `void` in a method header indicates that the method does not return any value.

» All Java applications must have a method named `main()`. Most Java applications have additional methods.

» Program comments are nonexecuting statements that you add to a file for the purpose of documentation. Java provides you with three types of comments: line comments, block comments, and javadoc comments.

» To compile your source code from the command line, type `javac` followed by the name of the file that contains the source code. When you compile your source code, the compiler creates a file with a .class extension. You can run the .class file on any computer that has a Java language interpreter by entering the `java` command followed by the name of the class file.

» When you modify a class, you must do the following before the class will execute correctly: save the file with the changes using the same filename, compile the class with the `javac` command, and interpret the class bytecode with the `java` command.

» Java provides you with built-in classes that produce GUI output. For example, Java contains a class named `JOptionPane` that allows you to produce dialog boxes.

» To avoid and minimize syntax and logic errors, you must enter code carefully and closely examine your program's output.

REVIEW QUESTIONS

1. The most basic circuitry-level computer language, which consists of on and off switches, is _____ .

   a. a high-level language   c. Java

   b. machine language   d. C++

2. Languages that let you use a vocabulary of descriptive terms, such as "read," "write," or "add," are known as _____ languages.

   a. high-level   c. procedural

   b. machine   d. object-oriented

3. The rules of a programming language constitute its _____ .

   a. objects   c. format

   b. logic   d. syntax

4. A _____ translates high-level language statements into machine code.

a. programmer   c. compiler

b. syntax detector   d. decipherer

5. Computer memory locations are called _____ .

a. compilers   c. addresses

b. variables   d. appellations

6. The individual operations used in a computer program are often grouped into logical units called _____ .

a. procedures   c. constants

b. variables   d. logistics

7. Envisioning program components as objects that are similar to concrete objects in the real world is the hallmark of _____ .

a. command-line operating systems   c. object-oriented programming

b. procedural programming   d. machine languages

8. An object's attributes are also known as its _____ .

a. states   c. methods

b. orientations   d. procedures

9. An instance of a class is a(n) _____ .

a. object   c. method

b. procedure   d. class

10. Java is architecturally _____ .

a. specific   c. neutral

b. oriented   d. abstract

11. You must compile classes written in Java into _____ .

a. bytecode   c. javadoc statements

b. source code   d. object code

12. All Java programming statements must end with a _____ .

a. period   c. semicolon

b. comma   d. closing parenthesis

13. Arguments to methods always appear within _____ .

    a. parentheses

    b. double quotation marks

    c. single quotation marks

    d. curly braces

14. In a Java program, you must use _____ to separate classes, objects, and methods.

    a. commas   c. dots

    b. semicolons   d. forward slashes

15. All Java programs must have a method named _____ .

    a. `method()`   c. `java()`

    b. `main()`   d. `Hello()`

16. Nonexecuting program statements that provide documentation are called _____ .

    a. classes   c. comments

    b. notes   d. commands

17. Java supports three types of comments: _____ , _____ , and javadoc.

    a. line, block

    b. string, literal

    c. constant, variable

    d. single, multiple

18. After you write and save a Java application file, you _____ it.

    a. interpret and then compile

    b. interpret and then execute

    c. compile and then resave

    d. compile and then interpret

19. The command to execute a compiled Java application is _____ .

    a. `run`   c. `javac`

    b. `execute`   d. `java`

20. You save text files containing Java source code using the file extension _____ .

    a. .java   c. .txt

    b. .class   d. .src

EXERCISES

1. For each of the following Java identifiers, note whether it is legal or illegal:

    a. weeklySales   g. abcdefghijklmnop

    b. last character   h. 23jordan

    c. class   i. my_code

    d. MathClass   j. 90210

    e. myfirstinitial   k. year2008budget

    f. phone#   l. abffraternity

2. Name at least three attributes that might be appropriate for each of the following classes:

    a. TelevisionSet   c. PatientMedicalRecord

    b. EmployeePaycheck

3. Name at least three objects that are members of each of the following classes:

    a. Politician   c. Book

    b. SportingEvent

4. Name at least three classes to which each of these objects might belong:

    a. mickeyMouse   c. bostonMassachusetts

    b. myDogSpike

5. Write, compile, and test a class that prints your first name on the screen. Save the class as **Name.java** in the Chapter.01 folder on your Student Disk.

6. Write, compile, and test a class that prints your full name, street address, city, state, and zip code on three separate lines on the screen. Save the class as **Address.java** in the Chapter.01 folder on your Student Disk.

7. Write, compile, and test a class that displays the following pattern on the screen:

```
    X
   XXX
  XXXXX
 XXXXXXX
    X
```

Save the class as **Tree.java** in the Chapter.01 folder on your Student Disk.

8. Write, compile, and test a class that prints your initials on the screen. Compose each initial with five lines of initials, as in the following example:

```
      J     FFFFFF
      J     F
      J     FFFF
J     J     F
JJJJJJ      F
```

Save the class as **Initial.java** in the Chapter.01 folder on your Student Disk.

9. Write, compile, and test a class that prints all the objectives listed at the beginning of this chapter. Save the class as **Objectives.java** in the Chapter.01 folder on your Student Disk.

10. Write, compile, and test a class that displays the following pattern on the screen:

```
    *
  *   *
*   *   *
  *   *
    *
```

Save the class as **Diamond.java** in the Chapter.01 folder on your Student Disk.

11. Write, compile, and test a class that uses the command window to display the following statement about comments:

"Program comments are nonexecuting statements you add to a file for the purpose of documentation."

Also include the same statement in three different comments in the class; each comment should use one of the three different methods of including comments in a Java class. Save the class as **Comments.java** in the Chapter.01 folder on your Student Disk.

12. Modify the Comments.java program in Exercise 11 so that the statement about comments is displayed in a dialog box. Save the class as **CommentsDialog.java** in the Chapter.01 folder on your Student Disk.

13. From 1925 through 1963, Burma Shave advertising signs appeared next to highways all across the United States. There were always four or five signs in a row containing pieces of a rhyme, followed by a final sign that read "Burma Shave." One set of signs has been preserved by the Smithsonian Institution and reads as follows:

```
Shaving brushes
You'll soon see 'em
On a shelf
In some museum
Burma Shave
```

Find a classic Burma Shave rhyme on the Web. Write, compile, and test a class that produces a series of four dialog boxes so that each displays one line of a Burma Shave slogan in turn. Save the class as **BurmaShave.java** in the Chapter.01 folder on your Student Disk.

DEBUGGING EXERCISE

Each of the following files in the Chapter.01 folder on your Student Disk has syntax and/or logic errors. In each case, determine the problem and fix the errors. After you correct the errors, save each file using the same filename preceded with Fix. For example, DebugOne1.java will become FixDebugOne1.java.

a. DebugOne1.java

c. DebugOne3.java

b. DebugOne2.java

d. DebugOne4.java

»NOTE When you change a filename, remember to change every instance of the class name within the file so that it matches the new filename. In Java, the filename and class name must always match.

CASE PROJECT

GLAD TO MEET YOU

Glad To Meet You is a company that designs and prints personal business cards. The company has asked you to write a Java application to display the layout of the information in a typical business card order. Data items in a typical business card include the customer's name, address, city, state, zip code, home phone number, and work phone number.

Write, compile, and test a Java class that displays these data items in an attractive layout on the console screen, using your own name and other personal information. Be certain to include appropriate comments in your class. Save the class as **CardLayout.java** in the Chapter.01 folder on your Student Disk.

GAME ZONE

In 1952, A.S. Douglas wrote his University of Cambridge Ph.D. dissertation on human-computer interaction, and created the first graphical computer game—a version of Tic-Tac-Toe. The game was programmed on an EDSAC vacuum-tube mainframe computer. The first computer game is generally assumed to be "Spacewar!", developed in 1962 at MIT; the first commercially available video game was "Pong," introduced by Atari in 1973. In 1980, Atari's "Asteroids" and "Lunar Lander" became the first video games to be registered in the U. S. Copyright Office. Throughout the 1980s, players spent hours with games that now seem very simple and unglamorous; do you recall playing "Adventure," "Oregon Trail," "Where in the World is Carmen Sandiego?," or "Myst"?

Today, commercial computer games are much more complex; they require many programmers, graphic artists, and testers to develop them, and large management and marketing staffs are needed to promote them. A game might cost many millions of dollars to develop and market, but a successful game might earn hundreds of millions of dollars. Obviously, with the brief introduction to programming you have had in this chapter, you cannot create a very sophisticated game. However, you can get started.

For games to hold your interest, they almost always include some random, unpredictable behavior. For example, a game in which you shoot asteroids loses some of its fun if the asteroids follow the same, predictable path each time you play the game. Therefore, generating random values is a key component in creating most interesting computer games.

Appendix D contains information on generating random numbers. To fully understand the process, you must learn more about Java classes and methods. However, for now, you can copy the following statement to generate and use a dialog box that displays a random number between 1 and 10:

```
JOptionPane.showMessageDialog(null, "The number is "  +
    (1 + (int)(Math.random() * 10)));
```

Write a Java application that displays two dialog boxes in sequence. The first asks you to think of a number between 1 and 10. The second displays a randomly generated number; the user can see whether his or her guess was accurate. (In future chapters you will improve this game so that the user can enter a guess and the program can determine whether the user was correct. If you wish, you also can tell the user how far off the guess was, whether the guess was high or low, and provide a specific number of repeat attempts.) Save the file as **RandomGuess.java**.

UP FOR DISCUSSION

1. Have you written programs in any programming language before starting this book? If so, what do you think the advantages and disadvantages of using Java will be? If not, how difficult do you think writing programs will be compared to other new skills you have mastered?

2. What are the advantages to starting class names with an uppercase letter but method names with a lowercase one?

3. Most programming texts encourage students to use many comments in their programs. Many students feel that writing program comments are a waste of time. Do you agree? Why? Are there circumstances under which you would take the opposite stance?

4. Using the Web, try to discover which computer game is the most popular one ever sold. Have you played this game? What makes this game so appealing?

2

USING DATA WITHIN A PROGRAM

In this chapter, you will:

Use constants and variables
Learn about the `int` data type
Display variables
Write arithmetic statements
Use the Boolean data type
Learn about floating-point data types
Understand numeric type conversion
Work with the `char` data type
Use the `JOptionPane` class for GUI input

JAVA ON THE JOB, SCENE 2

"How are you doing with your first programs?" asks Lynn Greenbrier during a coffee break. "OK, I think," you reply with just a bit of doubt in your voice. "I sure wish I could do some calculations, though," you continue. "Writing code that only prints the output I coded using `println()` statements isn't exactly what I had in mind when I considered a job in programming."

"Well then," Lynn replies, "let's start learning how Java uses different data types to perform arithmetic and other kinds of calculations."

USING CONSTANTS AND VARIABLES

NOTE
Besides using literal constants, you can use symbolic constants, which you will learn about in Chapter 4.

You can categorize data items as constant or variable. A data item is **constant** when it cannot be changed while a program is running; a data item is variable when it might change. For example, if you include the statement `System.out.println(459);` in a Java class, the number 459 is a constant. Every time an application containing the constant 459 is executed, the value 459 prints. Programmers refer to the number 459 as a **literal constant** because its value is taken literally at each use.

> **NOTE** You might also hear programmers refer to a value such as 459 as a **numeric constant**. That means simply that 459 is a number, as opposed to an alphabetic character or string of characters.

On the other hand, you can set up a data item as a variable. A **variable** is a named memory location that you can use to store a value. A variable can hold only one value at a time, but the value it holds can change. For example, if you create a variable named `ovenTemperature`, it might hold 0 when the application starts, later be altered to hold 350, and still later be altered to hold 400.

Whether a data item is variable or constant, in Java it always has a data type. An item's **data type** describes the type of data that can be stored there, how much memory the item occupies, and what types of operations can be performed on the data. Java provides for eight primitive types of data. A **primitive type** is a simple data type. The eight types are described in Table 2-1.

Keyword	Description
byte	Byte-length integer
short	Short integer
int	Integer
long	Long integer
float	Single-precision floating point
double	Double-precision floating point
char	A single character
boolean	A Boolean value (`true` or `false`)

Table 2-1 Java primitive data types

The eight primitive data types are called "primitive" because they are simple and uncomplicated. Primitive types also serve as the building blocks for more complex data types, called **reference types**. The classes you will begin creating in Chapter 3 are examples of reference types.

» NOTE
The value of a reference type is actually a memory address.

DECLARING VARIABLES

You name variables using the same naming rules for legal class identifiers described in Chapter 1. Basically, variable names must start with a letter and cannot be any reserved keyword. You must declare all variables you want to use in a class. A **variable declaration** is a statement that reserves a named memory location and includes the following:

» A data type that identifies the type of data that the variable will store

» An identifier that is the variable's name

» An optional assignment operator and assigned value if you want a variable to contain an initial value

» An ending semicolon

Variable names usually begin with lowercase letters to distinguish them from class names. However, like class names, variable names can begin with either an uppercase or a lowercase letter.

> » NOTE Beginning an identifier with a lowercase letter and capitalizing subsequent words within the identifier is a style known as **camel casing**. An identifier such as `lastName` resembles a camel because of the uppercase "hump" in the middle.

For example, the variable declaration `int myAge = 25;` declares a variable of type `int` named `myAge` and assigns it an initial value of 25. This is a complete statement that ends in a semicolon. The equal sign (=) is the **assignment operator**. Any value to the right of the equal sign is assigned to the variable on the left of the equal sign. An assignment made when you declare a variable is an **initialization**; an assignment made later is simply an **assignment**. Thus, `int myAge = 25;` initializes `myAge` to 25, and a subsequent statement `myAge = 42;` might assign a new value to the variable.

Note that the expression `25 = myAge` is illegal; you cannot assign an identifying name to a literal. The assignment operator has right-to-left associativity. **Associativity** refers to the order in which operands are used with operators.

The variable declaration `int myAge;` also declares a variable of type `int` named `myAge`, but no value is assigned at the time of creation.

> » NOTE If you attempt to display an uninitialized variable, or use it as part of an arithmetic statement, you receive an error message stating that the variable might not have been initialized. Java protects you from inadvertently using the unknown value that is stored in an uninitialized variable. Programmers refer to an unknown value as a **garbage value**.

» NOTE
When you learn about creating classes, you will discover that variables declared in a class, but outside any method, are automatically initialized for you.

You can declare multiple variables of the same type in separate statements on different lines. For example, the following statements declare two variables: the first variable is named `myAge` and its value is 25; the second variable is named `yourAge` and its value is 19.

```
int myAge = 25;
int yourAge = 19;
```

You can also declare two (or more) variables of the same type in a single statement by separating the variable declarations with a comma and placing the declarations in the same line, as shown in the following statement:

```
int myAge = 25, yourAge = 19;
```

» NOTE
Even though this example covers three lines in your editor, it is a single Java statement, ending with a semicolon.

Another option is to declare two (or more) variables of the same type in a single statement, separating the variable declarations with a comma, but placing them on different lines, as shown in the following three-line statement:

```
int myAge = 25,
    yourAge = 19,
    grandpasAge = 87;
```

You can declare as many variables in a statement as you want, as long as the variables are the same data type. However, if you want to declare variables of different types, you must use a separate statement for each type. The following statements declare two variables of type int (myAge and yourAge) and two variables of type double (mySalary and yourSalary):

```
int myAge, yourAge;
double mySalary, yourSalary;
```

LEARNING ABOUT THE int DATA TYPE

» NOTE
The legal integer values are −2³¹ through 2³¹−1. These are the highest and lowest values that you can store in four bytes of memory, which is the size of an int variable.

In Java, you use variables of type **int** to store (or hold) **integers**, or whole numbers. A variable of type int can hold any whole number value from –2,147,483,648 to +2,147,483,647. When you assign a value to an int variable, you do not type any commas; you type only digits and an optional plus or minus sign to indicate a positive or negative integer.

The types **byte**, **short**, and **long** are all variations of the integer type. You use a byte or a short if you know a variable will need to hold only small values, so you can save space in memory. You use a long if you know you will be working with very large values. Table 2-2 shows the upper and lower value limits for each of these types. It is important to choose appropriate types for the variables you will use in an application. If you attempt to assign a value that is too large for the data type of the variable, the compiler issues an error message and the application does not execute. If you choose a data type that is larger than you need, you waste memory. For example, a personnel application might use a byte variable for number of dependents (because a limit of 127 is more than enough), a short for hours worked in a month (because 127 isn't enough), and an int for an annual salary (because even though a limit of 32,000 might be large enough for your salary, it isn't enough for the CEO's).

> **» NOTE** If your application uses a literal constant integer, such as 932, the integer is an int by default. If you need to use a constant higher than 2,147,483,647, you must follow the number with the letter L to indicate long. For example, long mosquitosInTheNorthWoods = 2444555888L; stores a number that is greater than the maximum limit for the int type. You can type either an uppercase or lowercase L to indicate the long type, but the uppercase L is preferred to avoid confusion with the number 1. You need no special notation to store a numeric constant in a byte or a short.

> **» NOTE** Because integer constants, such as 18, are type int by default, the examples in this book almost always declare a variable as type int when the variable's purpose is to hold a whole number. That is, even if the expected value is less than 127, such as hoursWorkedToday, this book will declare the variable to be an int. If you are writing an application in which saving memory is important, you might choose to declare the same variable as a byte.

Type	Minimum Value	Maximum Value	Size in Bytes
byte	−128	127	1
short	−32,768	32,767	2
int	−2,147,483,648	2,147,483,647	4
long	−9,223,372,036,854,775,808	9,223,372,036,854,775,807	8

Table 2-2 Limits on integer values by type

》NOTE In other programming languages, the format and size of primitive data types might depend on the platform on which a program is running. In contrast, Java consistently specifies the size and format of its primitive data types.

DISPLAYING VARIABLES

You can display a variable in a print() or println() statement alone or in combination with a string. For example, the NumbersPrintln class shown in Figure 2-1 declares an integer billingDate, which is initialized to 5. In the first shaded statement, the value of billingDate is sent alone to the print() method; in the second shaded statement, billingDate is combined with, or **concatenated** to, a String. In Java, when a numeric variable is concatenated to a String using the plus sign, the entire expression becomes a String. The println() method can accept either a number or a String, so both statements work. The output of the application shown in Figure 2-1 appears in Figure 2-2.

```
public class NumbersPrintln
{
    public static void main(String[] args)
    {
        int billingDate = 5;
        System.out.print("Bills are sent on the ");
        System.out.print(billingDate);
        System.out.println("th");
        System.out.println("Next bill: October " + billingDate);
    }
}
```

Figure 2-1 NumbersPrintln class

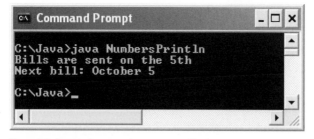

Figure 2-2 Output of NumbersPrintln application

》NOTE
Later in this chapter, you will learn that a plus sign (+) between two numeric variables indicates an addition operation. However, when you place a string on one or both sides of a plus sign, concatenation occurs.

Besides using the command line, you can also use a dialog box to display values. The JOptionPane.showMessageDialog() method, however, does not accept a single numeric variable as its display argument; it requires a String. Figure 2-3 shows a NumbersDialog class that uses the showMessageDialog() method twice to display an integer declared as creditDays and initialized to 30. In each shaded statement in the class, the numeric variable is concatenated to a String. In the first shaded statement, the String is empty; the empty String is created by typing a set of quotes with nothing between them. Even this empty String, or **null String**, is enough to make the entire expression a String, so the application produces the two dialog boxes shown in Figures 2-4 and 2-5. The first dialog box shows just the value 30; after it is dismissed by clicking OK, the second dialog box appears.

```java
import javax.swing.JOptionPane;
public class NumbersDialog
{
    public static void main(String[] args)
    {
        int creditDays = 30;
        JOptionPane.showMessageDialog(null,"" + creditDays);
        JOptionPane.showMessageDialog
            (null, "Every bill is due in " + creditDays + " days");
        System.exit(0);
    }
}
```

Figure 2-3 NumbersDialog class

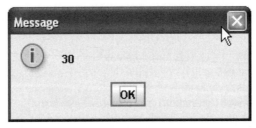

Figure 2-4 First dialog box created by NumbersDialog application

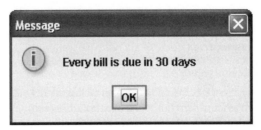

Figure 2-5 Second dialog box created by NumbersDialog application

WRITING ARITHMETIC STATEMENTS

Table 2-3 describes the five standard arithmetic operators for integers. You use **arithmetic operators** to perform calculations with values in your programs. A value used on either side of an operator is an **operand**. For example, in the expression 45 + 2, the numbers 45 and 2 are operands.

»NOTE
You will learn about the Java shortcut arithmetic operators in Chapter 6.

Operator	Description	Example
+	Addition	45 + 2, the result is 47
–	Subtraction	45 – 2, the result is 43
*	Multiplication	45 * 2, the result is 90
/	Division	45 / 2, the result is 22 (not 22.5)
%	Modulus (remainder)	45 % 2, the result is 1 (that is, 45 / 2 = 22 with a remainder of 1)

Table 2-3 Integer arithmetic operators

»NOTE When you perform paper-and-pencil division, you divide first to determine a remainder. In Java, you do not need to perform a division operation before you can perform a modulus operation. A modulus operation can stand alone.

»NOTE In arithmetic, you might be used to indicating multiplication with an X (as in 45 X 2), a dot (as in 45 • 2), or parentheses (as in 45(2)). None of these formats works in Java; you must use an asterisk to perform multiplication (as in 45 * 2).

The operators / and % deserve special consideration. When you perform **integer division**, whether the two operators used in the arithmetic expression are integer constants or integer variables, the result is an integer. In other words, any fractional part of the result is lost. For example, the result of 45 / 2 is 22, even though the result is 22.5 in a mathematical expression. When you use the modulus operator with two integers, the result is an integer with the value of the remainder after division takes place—the result of 45 % 2 is 1 because 2 "goes into" 45 twenty-two times with a remainder of 1.

»NOTE Later in this chapter, you will learn about values that contain decimal places. Unlike with integer division, you do not lose the fractional part of the result if at least one of the operands in a division operation is a floating-point data type.

When you combine mathematical operations in a single statement, you must understand **operator precedence**, or the rules for the order in which parts of a mathematical expression are evaluated. Multiplication, division, and modulus always take place prior to addition or subtraction in an expression. For example, the expression int result = 2 + 3 * 4; results in 14 because the multiplication (3 * 4) occurs before adding 2. You can override normal operator precedence by putting the operation to perform first in parentheses. The statement int result = (2 + 3) * 4; results in 20 because the addition within the parentheses takes place first, and then that result (5) is multiplied by 4.

»NOTE
You will learn more about operator precedence in Chapter 5.

> **NOTE** When multiple pairs of parentheses are added, the innermost expression surrounded by parentheses is evaluated first. For example, the value of the expression 2 * (3 + (4 * 5)) is 46. First, 4 * 5 evaluates to 20, and then 3 is added, giving 23. Finally, the value is multiplied by 2, giving 46.

> **NOTE** The associativity of the arithmetic operators is left-to-right. In a statement such as `answer = x + y + z;`, the x and y are added first, producing a temporary result, and then z is added to the temporary sum. After the sum is computed, the result is assigned to `answer`.

USING THE BOOLEAN DATA TYPE

Boolean logic is based on true-or-false comparisons. Whereas an `int` variable can hold millions of different values (at different times), a **Boolean variable** can hold only one of two values—`true` or `false`. The following statements declare and assign appropriate values to Boolean variables:

```
boolean isItPayday = false;
boolean areYouBroke = true;
```

You can also assign values based on the result of comparisons to Boolean variables. Java supports six comparison operators. A **comparison operator** compares two items; an expression containing a comparison operator has a Boolean value. Table 2-4 describes the comparison operators.

> **NOTE** When you use "Boolean" as an adjective, as in "Boolean operators," you usually begin with an uppercase B because the data type is named for Sir George Boole, the founder of symbolic logic, who lived from 1815 to 1864. The Java data type "`boolean`," however, begins with a lowercase "b."

> **NOTE**
> You will learn about other Boolean operators in Chapter 5.

Operator	Description	True example	False example
<	Less than	3 < 8	8 < 3
>	Greater than	4 > 2	2 > 4
==	Equal to	7 == 7	3 == 9
<=	Less than or equal to	5 <= 5	8 <= 6
>=	Greater than or equal to	7 >= 3	1 >= 2
!=	Not equal to	5 != 6	3 != 3

Table 2-4 Comparison operators

> **NOTE**
> Variable names are easily identified as Boolean if you use a form of "to be" (such as "is" or "are") as part of the variable name, as in `isSixBigger`.

When you use any of the operators that have two symbols (==, <=, >=, or !=), you cannot place any whitespace between the two symbols.

Legal declaration statements might include the following statements, which compare two values directly:

```
boolean isSixBigger = (6 > 5);
  // Value stored would be true
boolean isSevenSmallerOrEqual = (7 <= 4);
  // Value stored would be false
```

The Boolean expressions are more meaningful when variables (that have been assigned values) are used in the comparisons, as in the following examples. In the first statement, the `hours` variable is compared to a constant value of 40. If the `hours` variable is not greater than 40, the expression evaluates to `false`. In the second statement, the `income` variable must be greater than 100000 for the expression to evaluate to `true`.

```
boolean isOvertimePay = (hours > 40);
boolean isTaxBracketHigh = (income > 100000);
```

LEARNING ABOUT FLOATING-POINT DATA TYPES

A **floating-point** number contains decimal positions. Java supports two floating-point data types: `float` and `double`. A **float** data type can hold floating-point values of up to six or seven significant digits of accuracy. A **double** data type requires more memory than a float, and can hold 14 or 15 significant digits of accuracy. The term **significant digits** refers to the mathematical accuracy of a value. For example, a `float` given the value 0.324616777 displays as 0.324617 because the value is accurate only to the sixth decimal position. Table 2-5 shows the minimum and maximum values for each data type.

> **NOTE** A `float` given the value 324616777 displays as 3.24617e+008, which means approximately 3.24617 times 10 to the 8th power, or 324617000. The e stands for exponent; the format is called scientific notation. The large value contains only six significant digits.

> **NOTE** A value written as $3.4 * 10^{38}$ indicates that the value is 3.4 multiplied by 10 to the 38th power, or 10 with 38 trailing zeros—a very large number.

Type	Minimum	Maximum	Size in Bytes
float	$-3.4 * 10^{38}$	$3.4 * 10^{38}$	4
double	$-1.7 * 10^{308}$	$1.7 * 10^{308}$	8

Table 2-5 Limits on floating-point values

> **NOTE** A programmer might choose to store a variable as a `float` instead of a `double` to save memory. However, if high levels of accuracy are needed, such as in graphics-intensive software, the programmer might choose to use a `double`, opting for high accuracy over saved memory.

> **NOTE** A value stored in a `double` is a **double-precision floating-point number**; a value in a `float` is a **single-precision floating-point number**.

Just as an integer constant, such as 178, is a value of type `int` by default, a floating-point number constant such as 18.23 is a `double` by default. To store a value explicitly as a `float`, you can type the letter F after the number, as in `float pocketChange = 4.87F;`. You can type either a lowercase or an uppercase F. You can also type D (or d) after a floating-point value to indicate it is a `double`, but even without the D, the value will be stored as a `double` by default.

> **NOTE** The error message you receive when trying to use the modulus operator with floating-point values is "possible loss of precision." The class does not compile.

As with `int` values, you can perform the mathematical operations of addition, subtraction, multiplication, and division with floating-point numbers; however, you cannot perform modulus operations using floating-point values. (Floating-point division yields a floating-point result, so there is no remainder.)

UNDERSTANDING NUMERIC TYPE CONVERSION

When you are performing arithmetic with variables or constants of the same type, the result of the arithmetic retains the same type. For example, when you divide two `int`s, the result is an `int`, and when you subtract two `double`s, the result is a `double`. Often, however, you might want to perform mathematical operations on operands with unlike types.

When you perform arithmetic operations with operands of unlike types, Java chooses a unifying type for the result. The **unifying type** is the type to which all operands in an expression are converted so that they are compatible with each other; Java implicitly (or automatically) converts nonconforming operands to the unifying type. The following list shows the order for establishing unifying types between two variables:

1. `double`

2. `float`

3. `long`

4. `int`

» NOTE
Boolean values cannot be cast to another type. In some languages, such as C++, Boolean values are actually numbers. However, this is not the case in Java.

When two unlike types are used in an expression, the unifying type is the one with the lower number in the preceding list. In other words, the operand with the higher-numbered type is converted to the type of the operand that has a lower number.

For example, assume that an `int`, `hoursWorked`, and a `double`, `payRate`, are multiplied as follows:

```
int hoursWorked = 37;
double payRate = 6.73;
double grossPay = hoursWorked * payRate;
```

The result, `grossPay`, is a `double` because when a `double` and an `int` are multiplied, the `int` is promoted to the higher-ranking unifying type `double`—the type with the lower number in the preceding list. Similarly, the addition of a `short` and an `int` results in an `int`, and the subtraction of a `double` and a `long` results in a `double`. The following code will not compile because Java does not allow the loss of precision that occurs if you store the result in an `int`.

```
int hoursWorked = 37;
double payRate = 6.73;
int grossPay = hoursWorked * payRate;
```

> **» NOTE** The data types `char`, `short`, and `byte` all are promoted to `int` when used in statements with unlike types. If you perform a calculation with any combination of `char`, `short`, and `byte` variables, the result is an `int` by default. That is, the following code works:
>
> ```
> int a;
> byte b = 3, c = 4;
> a = b + c;
> ```
>
> However, the following code does not work because the `int` result of the addition cannot be stored in a `byte`.
>
> ```
> byte a, b = 3, c = 4;
> a = b + c;
> ```

You can explicitly (or purposely) override the unifying type imposed by Java by performing a type cast. **Type casting** forces a value of one data type to be used as a value of another type. To perform a type cast, you place the desired result type in parentheses, followed by the variable or constant to be cast. For example, a type cast is performed in the following code:

```
double bankBalance = 189.66;
float weeklyBudget = (float) bankBalance / 4;
   // weeklyBudget is 47.415, one-fourth of bankBalance
```

In this example, the `double` value `bankBalance / 4` is converted to a `float` before it is stored in `weeklyBudget`. Without the conversion, the statement that assigns the result to `weeklyBudget` would not compile. Similarly, a cast from a `float` to an `int` occurs in this code segment:

```
float myMoney = 47.82f;
int dollars = (int) myMoney;
   // dollars is 47, the integer part of myMoney
```

In this example, the `float` value `myMoney` is converted to an `int` before it is stored in the integer variable named `dollars`. When the `float` value is converted to an `int`, the decimal place values are lost.

> **》NOTE** It is easy to lose data when performing a cast. For example, the largest `byte` value is 127 and the largest `int` value is 2,147,483,647, so the following statements produce distorted results:
>
> ```
> int anOkayInt = 200;
> byte aBadByte = (byte)anOkayInt;
> ```
>
> A `byte` is constructed from eight 1s and 0s, or binary digits. The first binary digit, or bit, holds a 0 or 1 to represent positive or negative. The remaining seven bits store the actual value. When the integer value 200 is stored in the `byte` variable, its large value consumes the eighth bit, turning it to a 1, and forcing the `aBadByte` variable to appear to hold the value –72, which is inaccurate and misleading.

> **》NOTE** You do not need to perform a cast when assigning a value to a higher unifying type. When you write a statement such as as: `double payRate = 10;` Java automatically promotes the integer constant 10 to be a `double` so that it can be stored in the `payRate` variable. However, for clarity, you might prefer to write the following: `double payRate = 10.0;`

》NOTE
The word "cast" is used in a similar fashion when referring to molding metal, as in "cast iron." In a Java arithmetic cast, a value is "molded" into a different type.

WORKING WITH THE char DATA TYPE

You use the **char** data type to hold any single character. You place constant character values within single quotation marks because the computer stores characters and integers differently. For example, the following are typical character declarations.

```
char myMiddleInitial = 'M';
char myGradeInChemistry = 'A';
char aStar = '*';
```

A character can be any letter—uppercase or lowercase. It might also be a punctuation mark or digit. A character that is a digit is represented in computer memory differently than a numeric value represented by the same digit. For example, the following two statements are legal:

```
char aCharValue = '9';
int aNumValue = 9;
```

» NOTE
Appendix B contains more information on Unicode.

If you display each of these values using a `println()` statement, you see a 9. However, only the numeric value, `aNumValue`, can be used to represent the value 9 in arithmetic statements.

The following two statements might produce undesirable results:

```
char aCharValue = 9;
int aNumValue = '9';
```

» NOTE
A numeric constant can be stored as a character, but you cannot store an alphabetic letter in a numeric type variable.

If these variables are used in the following `println()` statement:

```
System.out.println("aCharValue is " + aCharValue +
    "aNumValue is " + aNumValue);
```

then the resulting output produces a blank and the number 57, which are Unicode values. Every computer stores every character it uses as a number; every character is assigned a unique numeric code using Unicode. Table 2-6 shows some Unicode decimal values and their character equivalents. For example, the character 'A' is stored using the value 65 and the character 'B' is stored using the value 66.

» NOTE
You will learn more about strings and the `String` class in Chapter 7.

A variable of type `char` can hold only one character. To store a string of characters, such as a person's name, you must use a data structure called a `String`. In Java, **String** is a built-in

Dec	Char	Dec	Char	Dec	Char	Dec	Char
0	nul	32		64	@	96	`
1	soh ^A	33	!	65	A	97	a
2	stx ^B	34	"	66	B	98	b
3	etx ^C	35	#	67	C	99	c
4	eot ^D	36	$	68	D	100	d
5	enq ^E	37	%	69	E	101	e
6	ack ^F	38	&	70	F	102	f
7	bel ^G	39	'	71	G	103	g
8	bs ^H	40	(	72	H	104	h
9	ht ^I	41	)	73	I	105	i
10	lf ^J	42	*	74	J	106	j
11	vt ^K	43	+	75	K	107	k
12	ff ^L	44	,	76	L	108	l
13	cr ^M	45	-	77	M	109	m
14	so ^N	46	.	78	N	110	n
15	si ^O	47	/	79	O	111	o
16	dle ^P	48	0	80	P	112	p
17	dc1 ^Q	49	1	81	Q	113	q
18	dc2 ^R	50	2	82	R	114	r
19	dc3 ^S	51	3	83	S	115	s
20	dc4 ^T	52	4	84	T	116	t
21	nak ^U	53	5	85	U	117	u
22	syn ^V	54	6	86	V	118	v
23	etb ^W	55	7	87	W	119	w
24	can ^X	56	8	88	X	120	x
25	em ^Y	57	9	89	Y	121	y
26	sub ^Z	58	:	90	Z	122	z
27	esc	59	;	91	[	123	{
28	fs	60	<	92	\	124		
29	gs	61	=	93	]	125	}
30	rs	62	>	94	^	126	~
31	us	63	?	95	_	127	del

Table 2-6 Unicode values 0 through 127 and their character equivalents

class that provides you with the means for storing and manipulating character strings. Unlike single characters, which use single quotation marks, string constants are written between double quotation marks. For example, the expression that stores the name Audrey as a string in a variable named `firstName` is:

```
String firstName = "Audrey";
```

You can store any character—including nonprinting characters such as a backspace or a tab—in a `char` variable. To store these characters, you can use an **escape sequence**, which always begins with a backslash followed by a character—the pair represents a single nonprinting character. For example, the following code stores a newline character and a tab character in the `char` variables `aNewLine` and `aTabChar`:

```
char aNewLine = '\n';
char aTabChar = '\t';
```

In the declarations of `aNewLine` and `aTabChar`, the backslash and character pair acts as a single character; the escape sequence serves to give a new meaning to the character. That is, the literal characters in the preceding code have different values from the "plain" characters 'n' or 't'. Table 2-7 describes some common escape sequences that you can use with command window output in Java.

Escape Sequence	Description
\b	Backspace; moves the cursor one space to the left
\t	Tab; moves the cursor to the next tab stop
\n	Newline or linefeed; moves the cursor to the beginning of the next line
\r	Carriage return; moves the cursor to the beginning of the current line
\"	Double quotation mark; prints a double quotation mark
\'	Single quotation mark; prints a single quotation mark
\\	Backslash; prints a backslash character

Table 2-7 Common escape sequences

>> **NOTE** When you display variables within `JOptionPane` dialog boxes rather than in a command window, the escape sequences '\n' (newline), '\"' (double quote), and '\\' (backslash) operate as expected within a `JOptionPane` object, but '\t', '\b', and '\r' do not work in the GUI environment.

When you want to produce console output on multiple lines in the command window, you have two options: You can use the newline escape sequence or you can use the `println()` method multiple times. For example, Figures 2-6 and 2-7 both show classes that produce the same output: "Hello" on one line and "there" on another. The version you choose to use is up to you. The example in Figure 2-6 is more efficient—both from a typist's point of view because the text `System.out.println` appears only once, and from the compiler's point of view because the `println()` method is called only once. The example in Figure 2-7, however, might be easier to read and understand. When programming in Java, you will find occasions when each of these approaches makes sense.

```
public class HelloThereNewLine
{
     public static void main(String[] args)
     {
          System.out.println("Hello\nthere");
     }
}
```

Figure 2-6 `HelloThereNewLine` class

> **NOTE** The `println()` method uses the local platform's line terminator character, which might or might not be the newline character '\n'.

```
public class HelloTherePrintlnTwice
{
     public static void main(String[] args)
     {
          System.out.println("Hello");
          System.out.println("there");
     }
}
```

Figure 2-7 `HelloTherePrintlnTwice` class

USING THE `JOptionPane` CLASS FOR GUI INPUT

In Chapter 1, you learned how to create GUI message boxes to display `String` objects. Earlier in this chapter, you learned to convert numeric variables to `String`s so their values could be displayed in a message box. You can also accept input using the `JOptionPane` class.

Two dialog boxes that can be used to accept user input are:

- `InputDialog`—Prompts the user for text input
- `ConfirmDialog`—Asks the user a question, providing buttons that the user can click for Yes, No, and Cancel responses

USING INPUT DIALOG BOXES

An **input dialog box** asks a question and provides a text field in which the user can enter a response. You can create an input dialog box using the **`showInputDialog()` method**. Six overloaded versions of this method are available, but the simplest version uses a single argument that is the **prompt**, or message requesting user input, which you want to display within the dialog box. The `showInputDialog()` method returns a `String` that represents a user's response; this means that you can assign the `showInputDialog()` method to a variable and the variable will hold the value that the user enters.

> **NOTE** In Chapter 3, you will learn how to write your own methods that return values. You will learn about overloaded methods in Chapter 4; they are methods that can be used with a variety of options.

For example, Figure 2-8 shows an application that creates an input dialog box containing a prompt for a first name. When the user executes the application, types "Audrey", then clicks the OK button or presses Enter on the keyboard, the response String will contain "Audrey". The response String can then be used like any other String object. For example, in the application in Figure 2-8, the response is concatenated with a welcoming message and displayed in a message dialog box. Figure 2-9 shows the dialog box containing a user's response, and Figure 2-10 shows the resulting output message box.

```java
import javax.swing.JOptionPane;
public class HelloNameDialog
{
    public static void main(String[] args)
    {
        String result;
        result = JOptionPane.showInputDialog("What is your name?");
        JOptionPane.showMessageDialog(null, "Hello, " + result + "!");
        System.exit(0);
    }
}
```

Figure 2-8 The HelloNameDialog class

»NOTE Recall from Chapter 1 that when you use dialog boxes, you must import the javax.swing.JOptionPane class into your program file and you must use the System.exit(0); command to terminate the application.

Figure 2-9 Input dialog box of the HelloNameDialog application

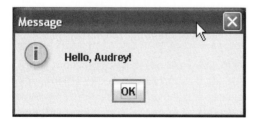

Figure 2-10 Output of the HelloNameDialog application

Within the JOptionPane class, an overloaded version of the showInputDialog() method allows the programmer flexibility in controlling the appearance of the input dialog box. The version of showInputDialog() that requires four arguments can be used to display a title in the dialog box title bar and a message that describes the type of dialog box. The four arguments to showInputDialog() include:

» The parent component, which is the screen component, such as a frame, in front of which the dialog box will appear. If this argument is null, the dialog box is centered on the screen.

» The message the user will see before entering a value. Usually this message is a String, but it actually can be any type of object.

» The title to be displayed in the title bar of the input dialog box.

» A class field describing the type of dialog box; it can be one of the following: ERROR_MESSAGE, INFORMATION_MESSAGE, PLAIN_MESSAGE, QUESTION_MESSAGE, or WARNING_MESSAGE.

For example, when the following statement executes, it displays the input dialog box shown in Figure 2-11.

```
JOptionPane.showInputDialog(null, "What is your area code?:",
     "Area code information", JOptionPane.QUESTION_MESSAGE);
```

Note that the title bar displays "Area code information," and the dialog box shows a question mark icon.

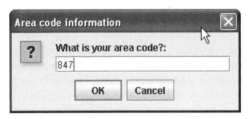

Figure 2-11 An input dialog box with a String in the title bar and a question mark icon

The showInputDialog() method returns a String object, which makes sense when you consider that you might want a user to type any combination of keystrokes into the dialog box. However, when the value that the user enters is intended to be used as a number, as in an arithmetic statement, the returned String must be converted to the correct numeric type. Earlier in this chapter, you learned how to cast a value from one data type to another. However, casting data only works with primitive data types—double, int, char, and so on— not with class objects (that are reference types) such as a String. To convert a String to an integer or double, you must use methods from the built-in Java classes Integer and Double. Each primitive type in Java has a corresponding class contained in the java.lang package; like most classes, the names of these classes begin with uppercase letters. These classes are called **type-wrapper classes**. They include methods that can process primitive type values.

> **NOTE**
> The term *parse* means to break into component parts. Grammarians talk about "parsing a sentence"— deconstructing it so as to describe its grammatical components. Parsing a String converts it to its numeric equivalent.

Figure 2-12 shows a SalaryDialog application that contains two String objects—wage String and dependentsString. Two showInputDialog() methods are called, and the answers are stored in the declared Strings. The shaded statements in Figure 2-12 show how the Strings are converted to numeric values using methods from the type-wrapper classes Integer and Double. The double value is converted using the Double.parseDouble() method, and the integer is converted using the Integer.parseInt() method. Figure 2-13 shows a typical execution of the application.

```
import javax.swing.JOptionPane;
public class SalaryDialog
{
    public static void main(String[] args)
    {
        String wageString, dependentsString;
        double wage, weeklyPay;
        int dependents;
        double hoursInWeek = 37.5;
        wageString = JOptionPane.showInputDialog(null,
            "Enter employee's hourly wage", "Salary dialog 1",
            JOptionPane.INFORMATION_MESSAGE);
        weeklyPay = Double.parseDouble(wageString) *
            hoursInWeek;
        dependentsString = JOptionPane.showInputDialog(null,
            "How many dependents?", "Salary dialog 2",
            JOptionPane.QUESTION_MESSAGE);
        dependents = Integer.parseInt(dependentsString);
        JOptionPane.showMessageDialog(null, "Weekly salary is $" +
            weeklyPay + "\nDeductions will be made for " +
            dependents + " dependents");
        System.exit(0);
    }
}
```

Figure 2-12 The `SalaryDialog` class

» NOTE
In the
`SalaryDialog`
application in
Figure 2-12,
the variable
`hoursInWeek`
holds 37.5. Instead
of creating a vari-
able to hold this
value, you might
prefer to create a
named constant. You
will learn how to do
this in Chapter 4.

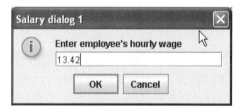

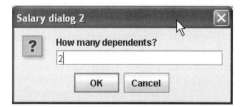

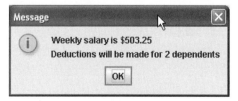

Figure 2-13 Sample execution of the `SalaryDialog` application

> **»NOTE** Chapter 1 explained that in Java, the reserved keyword `static` means that a method is accessible and usable even though no objects of the class exist. You can tell that the method `Double.parseDouble()` is a static method, because the method name is used with the class name `Double`—no object is needed. Similarly, `Integer.parseInt()` is also a static method.

USING CONFIRM DIALOG BOXES

Sometimes, the input you want from a user does not have to be typed from the keyboard. When you present simple options to a user, you can offer buttons that the user can click to confirm a choice. A **confirm dialog box** displays the options Yes, No, and Cancel; you can create one using the **showConfirmDialog() method** in the JOptionPane class. Four overloaded versions of the method are available; the simplest requires a parent component (which can be null) and the String prompt that is displayed in the box. The showConfirmDialog() method returns an integer containing one of three possible values: JOptionPane.YES_OPTION, JOptionPane.NO_OPTION, or JOptionPane.CANCEL_OPTION. Figure 2-14 shows an application that asks a user a question. The following statement displays the dialog box shown in Figure 2-15:

```
selection = JOptionPane.showConfirmDialog(null,
      "Do you want to upgrade to first class?");
```

The user's response is stored in the integer variable named selection. Then, a Boolean variable is set to the result of comparing selection and JOptionPane.YES_OPTION. If the

```
import javax.swing.JOptionPane;
public class AirlineDialog
{
    public static void main(String[] args)
    {
        int selection;
        boolean isYes;
        selection = JOptionPane.showConfirmDialog(null,
            "Do you want to upgrade to first class?");
        isYes = (selection == JOptionPane.YES_OPTION);
        JOptionPane.showMessageDialog(null,
            "You responded " + isYes);
        System.exit(0);
    }
}
```

Figure 2-14 The AirlineDialog class

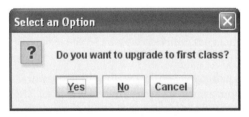

Figure 2-15 The confirm dialog box displayed by the AirlineDialog application

user has selected the Yes button in the dialog box, this variable is set to `true`; otherwise, the variable is set to `false`. Finally, the true or false result is displayed; Figure 2-16 shows the result when a user clicks the Yes button in the dialog box.

Figure 2-16 Output of `AirlineDialog` application when user clicks Yes

You can also create a confirm dialog box with five arguments, as follows:

» The parent component, which can be null

» The prompt message

» The title to be displayed in the title bar

» An integer that indicates which option button will be shown (It should be one of the class variables `YES_NO_CANCEL_OPTION` or `YES_NO_OPTION`.)

» An integer that describes the kind of dialog box (It should be one of the class variables `ERROR_MESSAGE`, `INFORMATION_MESSAGE`, `PLAIN_MESSAGE`, `QUESTION_MESSAGE`, or `WARNING_MESSAGE`.)

When the following statement is executed, it displays a confirm dialog box, as shown in Figure 2-17:

```
JOptionPane.showConfirmDialog(null,
        "A data input error has occurred. Continue?",
        "Data input error", JOptionPane.YES_NO_OPTION,
        JOptionPane.ERROR_MESSAGE);
```

Note that the title bar displays "Data input error," the Yes and No buttons appear, and the dialog box shows the error message, "A data input error has occurred. Continue?" It also displays the octagonal ERROR_MESSAGE icon.

Figure 2-17 Confirm dialog box with title, Yes and No buttons, and error icon

>> **NOTE** Confirm dialog boxes provide more practical uses when your applications can make decisions based on the users' responses. In Chapter 5, you will learn how to make decisions within programs.

YOU DO IT

WORKING WITH NUMERIC VALUES

In this section, you will write an application to declare and display numeric values.

To declare and display an integer value in an application:

1. Open a new document in your text editor.

2. Create a class header and an opening and closing curly brace for a new class named **DemoVariables** by typing the following:

```
public class DemoVariables
{
}
```

3. Position the insertion point after the opening curly brace, press **Enter**, press the **spacebar** several times to indent the line, and then type the following `main()` method and its curly braces:

```
public static void main(String[] args)
{
}
```

4. Position the insertion point after the opening curly brace in the `main()` method, press **Enter**, press the **spacebar** several times to indent the line, and then type the following to declare a variable of type `int` named `oneInt` with a value of 315.

```
int oneInt = 315;
```

> **NOTE** You can declare variables at any point within a method prior to their first use. However, it is common practice to declare variables first and place method calls second.

5. Press **Enter** at the end of the `oneInt` declaration statement, indent the line, and then type the following two output statements. The first statement uses the `print()` method to output "The int is " and leaves the insertion point on the same output line. The second statement uses the `println()` method to output the value of `oneInt` and advances the insertion point to a new line.

```
System.out.print("The int is ");
System.out.println(oneInt);
```

> **NOTE** When your output contains a literal string such as "The int is ", you can type a space before the closing quotation mark so there is a space between the end of the literal string and the value that prints.

6. Save the file as **DemoVariables.java** in the Chapter.02 folder on your Student Disk.

7. Compile the file from the command line by typing **javac DemoVariables.java** and pressing **Enter**. If necessary, correct any errors, save the file, and then compile again.

8. Execute the application from the command line by typing **java DemoVariables** and pressing **Enter**. The command window output is shown in Figure 2-18.

Figure 2-18 Output of the DemoVariables application

ADDING VARIABLES TO A CLASS

To declare two more variables in the application:

1. Return to the **DemoVariables.java** file in the text editor. Rename the class **DemoVariables2**.

2. Position the insertion point at the end of the line that contains the `oneInt` declaration, press **Enter**, and then type the following variable declarations on separate lines:

```
short oneShort = 23;
long oneLong = 1234567876543L;
```

3. Position the insertion point at the end of the line that contains the `println()` method that displays the `oneInt` value, press **Enter**, and then type the following statements to display the values of the two new variables:

```
System.out.print("The short is ");
System.out.println(oneShort);
System.out.print("The long is ");
System.out.println(oneLong);
```

4. Save the application using the filename **DemoVariables2.java**.

5. Compile the application by typing **javac DemoVariables2.java** and then pressing **Enter**. If necessary, correct any errors, save the file, and then compile again.

6. Execute the application by typing **java DemoVariables2** and then pressing **Enter**. The output is shown in Figure 2-19.

Figure 2-19 Output of the DemoVariables2 application

CONCATENATING STRINGS

In the previous application, you used two print methods to print a compound phrase with the following code:

```
System.out.print("The long is ");
System.out.println(oneLong);
```

To reduce the amount of typing, you can use one method and combine the arguments with a plus sign using the following statement:

```
System.out.println("The long is " + oneLong);
```

You are concatenating a variable to a `String`. It doesn't matter which format you use—the result is the same, as you will see next.

To change the two print methods into a single statement:

1. Open the **DemoVariables2.java** text file, and rename the class **DemoVariables3**.

2. Use the mouse to select the two statements that print "The int is " and the value of `oneInt`, and then press **Delete** to delete them. In place of the deleted statements, type the following `println()` statement:

   ```
   System.out.println("The int is " + oneInt);
   ```

3. Select the two statements that produce output for the short variable, press **Delete** to delete them, and then type the following statement:

   ```
   System.out.println("The short is " + oneShort);
   ```

4. Finally, select the two statements that produce output for the long variable, delete them, and replace them with the following statement:

   ```
   System.out.println("The long is " + oneLong);
   ```

5. Save the file as **DemoVariables3.java**, then compile and test the application. The output is shown in Figure 2-20.

Figure 2-20 Output of the `DemoVariables3` application

USING ARITHMETIC STATEMENTS

Next, you will add some arithmetic statements to the DemoVariables3.java application.

To use arithmetic statements in an application:

1. Open the **DemoVariables3.java** file in your text editor, and change the class to **DemoVariables4**.

2. Position the insertion point at the end of the last line of the current variable declarations, press **Enter**, and then type the following declarations:

```
int value1 = 43, value2 = 10, sum, difference,
    product, quotient, modulus;
```

3. Position the insertion point after the statement that prints the oneLong variable, press **Enter**, and then type the following statements on separate lines:

```
sum = value1 + value2;
difference = value1 - value2;
product = value1 * value2;
quotient = value1 / value2;
modulus = value1 % value2;
```

4. After the calculations you just added, type the following output statements:

```
System.out.println("Sum is " + sum);
System.out.println("Difference is " + difference);
System.out.println("Product is " + product);
System.out.println("Quotient is " + quotient);
System.out.println("Modulus is " + modulus);
```

5. Save the application as **DemoVariables4.java**.

6. Compile and run the application. Your output should look like Figure 2-21. Analyze the output and confirm that the arithmetic is correct.

Figure 2-21 Output of the DemoVariables4 application

USING BOOLEAN VARIABLES

Next, you will add two Boolean variables to the DemoVariables4.java file.

To add Boolean variables to an application:

1. Open the **DemoVariables4.java** file in your text editor and change the class to **DemoVariables5**.

2. Position the insertion point at the end of the line with the integer variable declarations, press **Enter**, and then type the following on one line to add two new Boolean variables to the application:

```
boolean isProgrammingFun = true, isProgrammingHard = false;
```

3. Next, add some print statements to display the values. Press **Enter** and then type the following statements:

```
System.out.println("The value of isProgrammingFun is "
  + isProgrammingFun);
System.out.println("The value of isProgrammingHard is "
  + isProgrammingHard);
```

4. Save the file as **DemoVariables5.java**, compile it, and then test the application. The output appears in Figure 2-22.

Figure 2-22 Output of the DemoVariables5 application

USING FLOATING-POINT VARIABLES

Next, you will add some floating-point variables to the DemoVariables5.java file and perform arithmetic with them.

To add floating-point variables to the application:

1. Open the **DemoVariables5.java** file in your text editor and change the class name to **DemoVariables6**.

2. Position the insertion point after the line that declares the Boolean variables, press **Enter**, and then type the following to add some new floating-point variables to the class:

```
double doubNum1 = 2.3, doubNum2 = 14.8, doubResult;
```

3. Press **Enter**, and then type the following statements to perform arithmetic and produce output:

```
doubResult = doubNum1 + doubNum2;
System.out.println("The sum of the doubles is "
    + doubResult);
doubResult = doubNum1 * doubNum2;
System.out.println("The product of the doubles is "
    + doubResult);
```

4. Save the file as **DemoVariables6.java**, compile it, and then run the program. The output is shown in Figure 2-23.

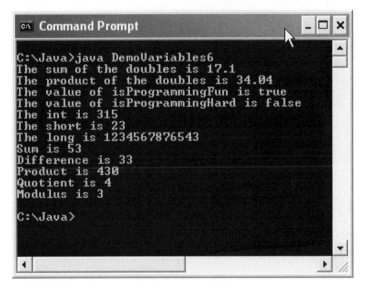

```
C:\Java>java DemoVariables6
The sum of the doubles is 17.1
The product of the doubles is 34.04
The value of isProgrammingFun is true
The value of isProgrammingHard is false
The int is 315
The short is 23
The long is 1234567876543
Sum is 53
Difference is 33
Product is 430
Quotient is 4
Modulus is 3

C:\Java>
```

Figure 2-23 Output of the DemoVariables6 application

USING CHARACTER VARIABLES

Next, you will add statements to your DemoVariables6.java file to demonstrate the use of some character variables.

To use a character variable in an application:

1. Open the **DemoVariables6.java** file in your text editor and change the class name to **DemoVariables7**.

2. Position the insertion point after the line that declares the `double` variables, press **Enter**, and then type the following statements. The first declares two character grades; the second displays them.

```java
char myGrade = 'A', myFriendsGrade = 'C';
System.out.println("Our grades are " + myGrade +
    " and " + myFriendsGrade);
```

3. Save the file as **DemoVariables7.java**, compile, and then test the application. Your output should look like Figure 2-24, which shows the characters in the first line of output.

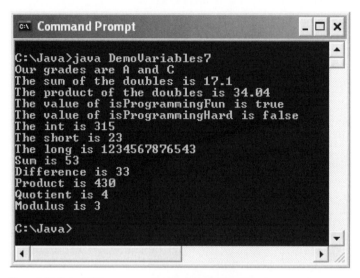

Figure 2-24 Output of the `DemoVariables7` application

USING ESCAPE SEQUENCES

Next, you will add statements to your DemoVariables7.java file to use the \n and \t escape sequences.

To use escape sequences in an application:

1. Open the **DemoVariables7.java** file in your text editor and change the class name to **DemoVariables8**.

2. Position the insertion point after the last method line in the class, just before the final closing curly brace of the `main()` method. Press **Enter** to start a new line, and then type the following:

```java
System.out.println("\nThis is on one line\nThis on another");
System.out.println("This shows\thow\ttabs\twork");
```

The complete class appears in Figure 2-25.

3. Save the file as **DemoVariables8.java**, compile, and then test the application. Your output should look like Figure 2-26. Notice how the '\n' character produces a new line of output where it is inserted, and how the '\t' character produces tab spacing.

```
public class DemoVariables8
{
    public static void main(String[] args)
    {
        int oneInt = 315;
        short oneShort = 23;
        long oneLong = 1234567876543L;
        int value1 = 43, value2 = 10, sum, difference,
            product, quotient, modulus;
        boolean isProgrammingFun = true,
            isProgrammingHard = false;
        double doubNum1 = 2.3, doubNum2 = 14.8, doubResult;
        char myGrade = 'A', myFriendsGrade = 'C';
        System.out.println("Our grades are " + myGrade +
            " and " + myFriendsGrade);
        doubResult = doubNum1 + doubNum2;
        System.out.println("The sum of the doubles is "
            + doubResult);
        doubResult = doubNum1 * doubNum2;
        System.out.println("The product of the doubles is "
            + doubResult);
        System.out.println("The value of isProgrammingFun is " +
            isProgrammingFun);
        System.out.println
            ("The value of isProgrammingHard is " +
            isProgrammingHard);
        System.out.println("The int is " + oneInt);
        System.out.println("The short is " + oneShort);
        System.out.println("The long is " + oneLong);
        sum = value1 + value2;
        difference = value1 - value2;
        product = value1 * value2;
        quotient = value1 / value2;
        modulus = value1 % value2;
        System.out.println("Sum is " + sum);
        System.out.println("Difference is " + difference);
        System.out.println("Product is " + product);
        System.out.println("Quotient is " + quotient);
        System.out.println("Modulus is " + modulus);
        System.out.println
            ("\nThis is on one line\nThis on another");
        System.out.println("This shows\thow\ttabs\twork");
    }
}
```

Figure 2-25 The DemoVariables8 class

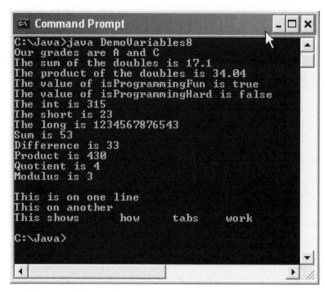

Figure 2-26 Output of the `DemoVariables8` application

USING VARIABLES IN DIALOG BOXES

Besides displaying variable values in the command window, you can use a GUI object, such as a dialog box, to display values. In this next example, assume you own several urban parking lots. Your lot named lot B is adjacent to Midtown Stadium, where football games are held. The Midtown City Council has awarded you a contract to provide parking for this Sunday's game. The stadium will pay you $7.25 per ticket sold to people parking in your lot. You have room for 210 cars and you assume the average car carries three passengers. Besides the per-ticket subsidy from the stadium, you decide you can charge drivers $1.25 per hour to park, and you assume the average game will require 3.5 hours of parking time. You want to write an application that calculates your potential earnings and displays the results in a dialog box.

To write a class that calculates your earnings and uses a dialog box to display the results:

1. Open a new file in your text editor, and type the first few lines you will need. You must import the `javax.swing.JOptionPane` class to support the style of output you want. The class name is `DemoVariables9`.

```
import javax.swing.JOptionPane;
public class DemoVariables9
{
    public static void main(String[] args)
    {
```

2. Declare variables that will hold the parking lot capacity, the average number of passengers per car, the parking fee per hour, the payment per ticket sold, the name of the parking lot, and the time anticipated for the game.

```
int lotCapacity = 210;
int avgPassengersPerCar = 3;
```

```
double feePerHourPerCar = 1.25;
double ticketPrice = 7.25;
char parkingLot = 'B';
double hoursForGame = 3.5;
```

3. Add variable declarations to hold your calculated answers—the total number of people who will park in your lot and the amounts of money you will earn from the parking, from the tickets, and in total.

```
int totalPeople;
double totalParking, totalTickets, grandTotal;
```

4. Enter the statements that perform the necessary calculations.

```
totalParking = lotCapacity * feePerHourPerCar
    * hoursForGame;
totalPeople = lotCapacity * avgPassengersPerCar;
totalTickets = totalPeople * ticketPrice;
grandTotal = totalParking + totalTickets;
```

5. Add the detailed call to the JOptionPane.showMessageDialog() method that will produce the output shown in Figure 2-27. The String argument to showMessage Dialog() is constructed from many pieces and includes several newline escape sequences.

```
JOptionPane.showMessageDialog(null, "Parking Lot " +
    parkingLot + " projected income:\n" + lotCapacity +
    " cars at $" + feePerHourPerCar + " for " +
    hoursForGame + " hours\n...................$" +
    totalParking + "\n" + totalPeople +
    " fans at $" + ticketPrice +
    " each\n...................$" + totalTickets +
    "\n\nTotal expected\nrevenue from lot " +
    parkingLot + " is.........$" + grandTotal);
```

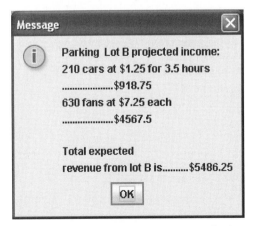

Figure 2-27 Output of the DemoVariables9 application

6. Add the statement that returns a 0 to the operating system. Recall from Chapter 1 that this statement is required when your application displays a dialog box. Then add closing curly braces for the `main()` method and for the class.

```
    System.exit(0);
  }
}
```

7. Save the file as **DemoVariables9.java** in the Chapter.02 folder on your Student Disk. Compile and execute the program. Your output should look like Figure 2-27. Make certain you understand how each line in the dialog box was produced.

8. Dismiss the dialog box by clicking **OK**.

USING A DIALOG BOX FOR INPUT

Next, you will modify the `DemoVariables9` application so that it becomes more useful. You will be able to alter the value of several variables interactively. This will allow you to experiment with the effect on profit that will result from changing both the average number of passengers in a car and the fee you charge per car.

To make the parking lot program interactive:

1. Open the `DemoVariables9` class in your text editor. Change the class name to **DemoVariables10** and immediately save the file as **DemoVariables10.java**.

   Remove the assigned values from the `avgPassengersPerCar` and `feePerHourPerCar` variables so their declarations become:

   ```
   int avgPassengersPerCar;
   double feePerHourPerCar;
   ```

2. After all the variable declarations, but before the value of `totalParking` is calculated, add this statement that prompts the user for the average number of passengers in a car, converts the `String` response to an integer, and stores the result in the appropriate variable.

   ```
   avgPassengersPerCar =
      Integer.parseInt(JOptionPane.showInputDialog (null,
      "What is the average number of passengers per car?"));
   ```

3. On the next line, prompt for and receive a value for the fee charged for each hour of parking.

   ```
   feePerHourPerCar =
      Double.parseDouble(JOptionPane.showInputDialog
      (null, "What is the fee per hour per car?"));
   ```

4. Save the file, compile, and execute. When the input dialog boxes appear, enter any numeric values you want and observe the results.

KEY TERMS

A data item is **constant** when it cannot be changed during the execution of an application.

A **literal constant** is a value that is taken literally at each use.

A **numeric constant** is a number whose value is taken literally at each use.

A **variable** is a named memory location that you can use to store a value.

An item's **data type** describes the type of data that can be stored there, how much memory the item occupies, and what types of operations can be performed on the data.

A **primitive type** is a simple data type. Java's primitive types are `byte`, `short`, `int`, `long`, `float`, `double`, `char`, and `boolean`.

Reference types are complex data types that are constructed from primitive types.

A **variable declaration** is a statement that reserves a named memory location.

Camel casing is a style in which an identifier begins with a lowercase letter and subsequent words within the identifier are capitalized.

The **assignment operator** is the equal sign (=); any value to the right of the equal sign is assigned to the variable on the left of the equal sign.

An **initialization** is an assignment made when you declare a variable.

An **assignment** is the act of providing a value for a variable.

Associativity refers to the order in which operands are used with operators.

A **garbage value** is the unknown value stored in an uninitialized variable.

The data type **int** is used to store integers.

Integers are whole numbers.

The **byte** data type holds very small integers, from –128 to 127.

The **short** data type holds small integers, from –32,768 to 32,767.

The **long** data type holds very large integers, from –9,223,372,036,854,775,808 to 9,223,372,036,854,775,807.

A value can be combined with, or **concatenated** to, another value.

An empty `String` created by typing a set of quotes with nothing between them is called a **null `String`**.

You use **arithmetic operators** to perform calculations with values in your applications.

An **operand** is a value used in an arithmetic statement.

Integer division is the operation in which one integer value is divided by another; the result contains no fractional part.

Operator precedence is the rules for the order in which parts of a mathematical expression are evaluated.

A **Boolean variable** can hold only one of two values—`true` or `false`.

A **comparison operator** compares two items; an expression containing a comparison operator has a Boolean value.

A **floating-point** number contains decimal positions.

A **float** data type can hold a floating-point value of up to six or seven significant digits of accuracy.

A **double** data type can hold a floating-point value of up to 14 or 15 significant digits of accuracy.

The term **significant digits** refers to the mathematical accuracy of a value.

A **double-precision floating-point number** is stored in a `double`.

A **single-precision floating-point number** is stored in a `float`.

A **unifying type** is a single data type to which all operands in an expression are converted.

Type casting forces a value of one data type to be used as a value of another type.

The **char** data type is used to hold any single character.

String is a built-in Java class that provides you with the means for storing and manipulating character strings.

An **escape sequence** begins with a backslash followed by a character; the pair represents a nonprinting character.

An **input dialog box** asks a question and provides a text field in which the user can enter a response.

You can create an input dialog box using the **showInputDialog() method**.

A **prompt** is a message requesting user input, which you want to display within the dialog box.

Type-wrapper classes, contained in the `java.lang` package, include methods that can process primitive type values.

A **confirm dialog box** displays the options Yes, No, and Cancel; you can create one using the **showConfirmDialog() method** in the `JOptionPane` class.

CHAPTER SUMMARY

» Data is constant when it cannot be changed after a class is compiled; data is variable when it might change.

» Variables are named memory locations that your programs can use to store values. You can name a variable using any legal identifier. A variable name must start with a letter and cannot be a reserved keyword. You must declare all variables you want to use in a program. A variable declaration requires a type and a name; it can also include an assigned value.

» Java provides for eight primitive types of data: `boolean`, `byte`, `char`, `double`, `float`, `int`, `long`, and `short`.

» You can declare multiple variables of the same type in separate statements or in a single statement, separated by commas.

» You can display variable values using `System.out.print()` and `println()` statements as well as by using dialog boxes.

» There are five standard arithmetic operators for integers: +, −, *, /, and %.

» Operator precedence is the order in which parts of a mathematical expression are evaluated. Multiplication, division, and modulus always take place prior to addition or subtraction in an expression. Right and left parentheses can be added within an expression when exceptions to this rule are required. When multiple pairs of parentheses are added, the innermost expression surrounded by parentheses is evaluated first.

» A Boolean type variable can hold a `true` or `false` value.

» There are six comparison operators: >, <, ==, >=, <=, and !=.

» A floating-point number contains decimal positions. Java supports two floating-point data types: `float` and `double`.

» When you perform mathematical operations on unlike types, Java implicitly converts the variables to a unifying type. You can explicitly override the unifying type imposed by Java by performing a type cast.

» You use the `char` data type to hold any single character. You type constant character values in single quotation marks. You type `String` constants that store more than one character between double quotation marks. You can store some characters using an escape sequence, which always begins with a backslash.

» You can accept input using the `JOptionPane` class. The `showInputDialog()` method returns a `String`, which must be converted to a number using a type-wrapper class before you can use it as a numeric value.

REVIEW QUESTIONS

1. When data cannot be changed after a class is compiled, the data is _____ .

   a. constant

   b. variable

   c. volatile

   d. mutable

2. Which of the following is not a primitive data type in Java?

   a. `boolean`

   b. `byte`

   c. `int`

   d. `sector`

3. Which of the following elements is not required in a variable declaration?

   a. a type

   b. an identifier

   c. an assigned value

   d. a semicolon

4. The assignment operator in Java is _____ .

   a. =

   b. ==

   c. :=

   d. ::

5. Assuming you have declared `shoeSize` to be a variable of type `int`, which of the following is a valid assignment statement in Java?

   a. `shoeSize = 9;`

   b. `shoeSize = 9.5;`

   c. `shoeSize = '9';`

   d. `shoeSize = "nine";`

6. Which of the following data types can store a value in the least amount of memory?

   a. `short`

   b. `long`

   c. `int`

   d. `byte`

7. The modulus operator _____ .

    a. is represented by a forward slash

    b. provides the remainder of integer division

    c. provides the quotient of integer division

    d. Answers b and c are correct.

8. According to the rules of operator precedence, when division occurs in the same arithmetic statement as _____ , the division operation always takes place first.

    a. multiplication

    b. modulus

    c. subtraction

    d. Answers a and b are correct.

9. A Boolean variable can hold _____ .

    a. any character

    b. any whole number

    c. any decimal number

    d. the values `true` or `false`

10. The "equal to" comparison operator is _____ .

    a. =

    b. ==

    c. !=

    d. !!

11. The value 137.68 can be held by a variable of type _____ .

    a. `int`

    b. `float`

    c. `double`

    d. Two of the preceding answers are correct.

12. When you perform arithmetic with values of diverse types, Java _____ .

    a. issues an error message

    b. implicitly converts the values to a unifying type

    c. requires you to explicitly convert the values to a unifying type

    d. requires you to perform a cast

13. If you attempt to add a `float`, an `int`, and a `byte`, the result will be a(n) _____ .

    a. `float`

    b. `int`

    c. `byte`

    d. error message

14. You use a _____ to explicitly override an implicit type.

    a. mistake

    b. type cast

    c. format

    d. type set

15. In Java, what is the value of 3 + 7 * 4 + 2?

    a. 21

    b. 33

    c. 42

    d. 48

16. Which assignment is correct in Java?

    a. `int value = (float) 4.5;`   c. `double value = 2.12;`

    b. `float value = 4 (double);`   d. `char value = 5c;`

17. Which assignment is correct in Java?

    a. `double money = 12;`   c. `double money = 12.0d;`

    b. `double money = 12.0;`   d. all of the above

18. Which assignment is correct in Java?

    a. `char aChar = 5;`   c. `char aChar = '*';`

    b. `char aChar = "W";`   d. Two of the preceding answers are correct.

19. An escape sequence always begins with a(n) _____ .

    a. e   c. backslash

    b. forward slash   d. equal sign

20. Which Java statement produces the following output?

```
w
xyz
```

    a. `System.out.println("wxyz");`

    b. `System.out.println("w" + "xyz");`

    c. `System.out.println("w\nxyz");`

    d. `System.out.println("w\nx\ny\nz");`

EXERCISES

1. What is the numeric value of each of the following expressions as evaluated by Java?

    a. 4 + 6 * 3   g. 16 % 2

    b. 6 / 3 * 7   h. 17 % 2

    c. 18 / 2 + 14 / 2   i. 28 % 5

    d. 16 / 2   j. 28 % 5 * 3 + 1

    e. 17 / 2   k. (2 + 3) * 4

    f. 28 / 5   l. 20 / (4 + 1)

2. What is the value of each of the following Boolean expressions?

    a. 4 > 1   f. 3 + 8 <= 10

    b. 5 <= 18   g. 3 != 9

    c. 43 >= 43   h. 13 != 13

    d. 2 == 3   i. −4 != 4

    e. 2 + 5 == 7   j. 2 + 5 * 3 == 21

3. Which of the following expressions are illegal? For the legal expressions, what is the numeric value of each as evaluated by Java?

   a. 2.3 * 1.2   d. 7.0 % 3.0

   b. 5.67 – 2   e. 8 % 2.0

   c. 25.0 / 5.0

4. Choose the best data type for each of the following so that no memory storage is wasted. Give an example of a typical value that would be held by the variable and explain why you chose the type you did.

   a. your age   c. your shoe size

   b. the U.S. national debt   d. your middle initial

5. Write a Java class that declares variables to represent the length and width of a room in feet. Use `Room` as the class name. Assign appropriate values to the variables—for example, `length` = 15 and `width` = 25. Compute and display the floor space of the room in square feet (area = length * width). Display more than just a value as output; also display explanatory text with the value—for example, `The floor space is 375 square feet`. Save the class as **Room.java** in the Chapter.02 folder on your Student Disk.

6. Write a Java class that declares variables to represent the length and width of a room in feet and the price of carpeting per square foot in dollars and cents. Assign appropriate values to the variables. Compute and display, with explanatory text, the cost of carpeting the room. Save the class as **Carpet.java** in the Chapter.02 folder on your Student Disk.

7. Write a class that declares variables to represent the length and width of a room in feet and the price of carpeting per square yard in dollars and cents. Use `Yards` as the class name. Assign the value 25 to the length variable and the value 42 to the width variable. Compute and display the cost of carpeting the room. (There are nine square feet in one square yard.) Save the class as **Yards.java** in the Chapter.02 folder on your Student Disk.

8. Write a class that declares a variable named `minutes`, which holds minutes worked on a job, and assign a value. Display the value in hours and minutes; for example, 197 minutes becomes 3 hours and 17 minutes. Save the class as **Time.java** in the Chapter.02 folder on your Student Disk.

9. Write a class that declares variables to hold your three initials. Display the three initials with a period following each one, as in J.M.F. Save the class as **Initials.java** in the Chapter.02 folder on your Student Disk.

10. Write a class that contains variables that hold your tuition fee and your book fee. Display the sum of the variables. Save the class as **Fees.java** in the Chapter.02 folder on your Student Disk.

11. Write a class that contains variables that hold your hourly rate of pay and the number of hours that you worked. Display your gross pay, your withholding tax (15% of gross pay),

and your net pay (gross pay – withholding). Save the class as **Payroll.java** in the Chapter.02 folder on your Student Disk.

12. a. Write a class that calculates and displays the conversion of $57 into currency denominations—20s, 10s, 5s, and 1s. Save the class as **Dollars.java** in the Chapter.02 folder on your Student Disk.

   b. In the Dollars.java class, alter the value of the variable that holds the amount of money. Run the application and confirm that the amount of each denomination calculates correctly.

13. Write a class that calculates and displays the amount of money you would have if you invested $1,000 at 5% interest for one year. Use the formula: Future Amount = Principal * Rate * Time. Save the class as **Interest.java** in the Chapter.02 folder on your Student Disk.

14. Write a class that displays the following heading on one line:

   "First Name   Last Name   Address   Phone Number"

   Display your first name, last name, address, and phone number on the second line, below the appropriate column headings. Save the class as **Escape.java** in the Chapter.02 folder on your Student Disk.

15. Write a class to convert Fahrenheit temperature to Celsius. Declare a variable to hold the normal human body temperature of 98.6 degrees Fahrenheit. A Celsius temperature can be calculated by subtracting 32 from the Fahrenheit value and multiplying the result by 5/9. Display the converted Celsius value. Save the class as **FahrenheitToCelsius.java** in the Chapter.02 folder on your Student Disk.

16. Write a class that declares variables that hold the following data fields about an inventory item: item number, item name, unit price (price each), and quantity on hand. Calculate the total value of the inventory items on hand (quantity times unit price) and display all the fields. Save the class as **Inventory.java** in the Chapter.02 folder on your Student Disk.

DEBUGGING EXERCISES

1. Each of the following files in the Chapter.02 folder on your Student Disk has syntax and/or logic errors. In each case, determine the problem and fix the application. After you correct the errors, save each file using the same filename preceded with Fix. For example, DebugTwo1.java will become FixDebugTwo1.java.

   a. DebugTwo1.java   c. DebugTwo3.java

   b. DebugTwo2.java   d. DebugTwo4.java

>> **NOTE** When you change a filename, remember to change every instance of the class name within the file so that it matches the new filename. In Java, the filename and class name must always match.

CASE PROJECT

TRAVEL TICKETS COMPANY

Travel Tickets Company sells tickets for airlines, tours, and other travel-related services. Because ticket agents frequently mistype long ticket numbers, Travel Tickets has asked you to write an application that will indicate if a ticket number entry is invalid.

The class displays an input dialog box that prompts a ticket agent to enter a six-digit ticket number. Ticket numbers are designed so that if you drop the last digit of the number, then divide the number by 7, the remainder of the division will be identical to the last dropped digit. This process is illustrated in the following example:

Step 1	Enter the ticket number; for example, 123454.
Step 2	Remove the last digit, leaving 12345.
Step 3	Determine the remainder when the ticket number is divided by 7. In this case, 12345 divided by 7 leaves a remainder of 4.
Step 4	Assign the Boolean value of the comparison between the remainder and the digit dropped from the ticket number.
Step 5	Display the result—`true` or `false`—in a message box.

Test the application with the following ticket numbers:

123454; the comparison should evaluate to `true`

147103; the comparison should evaluate to `true`

154123; the comparison should evaluate to `false`

Save the case as **TicketNumber.java** in the Chapter.02 folder on your Student Disk.

GAME ZONE

1. *Mad Libs*® is a children's game in which they provide a few words that are then incorporated into a silly story. The game helps children understand different parts of speech because they are asked to provide specific types of words. For example, you might ask a child for a noun, another noun, an adjective, and a past-tense verb. The child might reply with such answers as "table," "book," "silly," and "studied." The newly created Mad Lib might be:

   Mary had a little *table*

   Its *book* was *silly* as snow

   And everywhere that Mary *studied*

   The *table* was sure to go.

   Create a Mad Lib program that asks the user to provide at least four or five words, and then create and display a short story or nursery rhyme that uses them. Save the file as **MadLib.java**.

UP FOR DISCUSSION

1. What advantages are there to requiring variables to have a data type?

2. Some programmers use a system called Hungarian notation when naming their variables. What is Hungarian notation, and why do many object-oriented programmers feel it is not a valuable style to use?

3. Some languages do not require explicit type casting when you want to perform an unlike assignment, such as assigning a `double` to an `int`. Instead, the type casting is performed automatically, the fractional part of the `double` is lost, and the whole-number portion is simply stored in the `int` result. Are there any reasons this approach is superior or inferior to the way Java works?

4. Did you have a favorite computer game when you were growing up? Do you have one now? How are they similar and how are they different? Did you have a favorite board game? What does it have in common with your favorite computer game?

3

USING METHODS, CLASSES, AND OBJECTS

In this chapter, you will:

Create methods with no arguments, a single argument, and multiple arguments
Create methods that return values
Learn about class concepts
Create a class
Create instance methods in a class
Declare objects and use their methods
Organize classes
Begin to understand how to use constructors

JAVA ON THE JOB, SCENE 3

"How do you feel about programming so far?" asks your new mentor, Lynn Greenbrier, who is head of computer programming for Event Handlers Incorporated.

"It's fun," you reply. "It's great to see programs actually work, but I still don't understand what the other programmers are talking about when they mention 'object-oriented programming.' I *think* everything is an object, and objects have methods, but I'm not really clear on this whole thing at all."

"Well then," Lynn says, "let me explain methods, classes, and objects."

CREATING METHODS WITH ZERO, ONE, AND MULTIPLE ARGUMENTS

> **NOTE**
> The statements within a method execute only if and when the method is called.

A **method** is a program module that contains a series of statements that carry out a task. To execute a method, you **invoke** or **call** it from another method; the **calling method** makes a **method call**, which invokes the **called method**. Any class can contain an unlimited number of methods, and each method can be called an unlimited number of times. Within a class, the simplest methods you can invoke don't require any data items (called **arguments** or **parameters**) to be sent to them, nor do they send any data back to you (called **returning a value**). Consider the simple First class that you saw in Chapter 1, shown in Figure 3-1.

> **NOTE** Devices you own might contain features you never use. For example, you might use a VCR to play tapes, but never to record, or you might never use the "defrost" option on your microwave oven. Similarly, a class might contain any number of methods that are never called from a particular application.

```
public class First
{
    public static void main(String[] args)
    {
        System.out.println("First Java application");
    }
}
```

Figure 3-1 The First class

> **NOTE**
> Although there are differences, if you have used other programming languages, you can think of methods as being similar to procedures, functions, or subroutines.

Suppose you want to add three lines of output to this application to display your company's name and address. You can simply add three new println() statements, but instead you might choose to create a separate method to display the three new lines.

There are two major reasons to create a separate method to display the three lines. First, the main() method remains short and easy to follow because main() contains just one statement to call the method, rather than three separate println() statements to perform the work of the method. What is more important is that a method is easily reusable. After you create the name and address method, you can use it in any application that needs the company's name and address. In other words, you do the work once, and then you can use the method many times.

A method must include the following:

» A declaration (or header or definition)
» An opening curly brace
» A body
» A closing curly brace

» **NOTE** Using a method name to contain or encapsulate a series of statements is an example of the feature that programmers call **abstraction**. Consider abstract art, in which the artist tries to capture the essence of an object without focusing on the details. Similarly, when programmers employ abstraction, they use a general method name in a module rather than list all the detailed activities that will be carried out by the method.

The **method declaration** is the first line, or **header**, of a method. It contains the following:

» Optional access modifiers
» The return type for the method
» The method name
» An opening parenthesis
» An optional list of method arguments (you separate multiple arguments with commas)
» A closing parenthesis

You first learned about access modifiers in Chapter 1. The access modifier for a Java method can be any of the following modifiers: `public`, `private`, `protected`, or, if left unspecified, package. Most often, methods are given `public` access. Endowing a method with `public` access means any class can use it. In addition, like `main()`, any method that can be used without instantiating an object requires the keyword modifier `static`.

» **NOTE** You first learned the term "access modifier" in Chapter 1. Access modifiers are also called **access specifiers**.

» **NOTE** Besides the access modifiers `public`, `private`, and `protected`, Java uses additional modifiers that define how a method can be used. You will learn more about these terms, and about packages, in Chapter 12.

» **NOTE** Classes can contain instance methods and class methods. Instance methods operate on an object, and do not use the `static` keyword. Class methods do not need an object instance in order to be used. These methods use the `static` keyword. You will learn about these concepts when you create objects later in this chapter.

You can write the `nameAndAddress()` method shown in Figure 3-2. According to its declaration, the method is `public` and `static`, meaning any class can use it and no objects need to be created. Like the `main()` method you have been using in your Java applications, the `nameAndAddress()` method returns nothing, so its return type is `void`. The method receives nothing, so its parentheses are empty. Its body, consisting of three `println()` statements, appears within curly braces.

```
public static void nameAndAddress()
{
    System.out.println("Event Handlers Incorporated");
    System.out.println("8900 U.S. Hwy 14");
    System.out.println("Crystal Lake, IL 60014");
}
```

Figure 3-2 The `nameAndAddress()` method

>> **NOTE** Some methods you have used contain arguments within their parentheses. For example, when you write a `main()` method in a class, the parentheses in its header surround an argument (`String[] args`), and when you use the `println()` method, its parentheses usually contain text information you want to print. Unlike those two methods, the `nameAndAddress()` method header shown here does not contain any arguments within its parentheses. You will write methods that accept arguments later in this chapter.

You place the entire method within the class that will use it, but not within any other method. Figure 3-3 shows the two locations where you can place additional methods within the `First` class—within the curly braces of the class, but outside of (either before or after) any other methods.

>> **NOTE** Methods can never overlap. That is, no method can be placed within another method, and no method can start before another method has ended. Method *calls* lie within other methods, but the called method (header and body) is always placed outside the calling method. A called method is placed before the header or after the closing brace of the calling method, or in a totally different class.

>> **NOTE** The order in which you place methods' bodies in a class has no bearing on the order in which the methods are called. Any method in a file might call any of the other methods in any order and any number of times. The order in which you call methods does make a difference in how an application executes.

>> **NOTE**
The `main()` method executes first in an application, no matter where you physically place the `main()` method within its class.

```
public class First
{
    // You can place additional methods here, before main()
    public static void main(String[] args)
    {
        System.out.println("First Java application");
    }
    // You can place additional methods here, after main()
}
```

Figure 3-3 Placement of methods within a class

If you want the `main()` method to call the `nameAndAddress()` method, you simply use the `nameAndAddress()` method's name as a statement within the body of `main()`. Figure 3-4 shows the complete application. In this application, `main()` performs two actions. First, it calls the `nameAndAddress()` method, and then it prints "First Java application".

```
public class First
{
    public static void main(String[] args)
    {
        nameAndAddress();
        System.out.println("First Java application");
    }
    public static void nameAndAddress()
    {
        System.out.println("Event Handlers Incorporated");
        System.out.println("8900 U.S. Hwy 14");
        System.out.println("Crystal Lake, IL 60014");
    }
}
```

Figure 3-4 `First` class with `main()` calling `nameAndAddress()`

Figure 3-5 shows the output from the execution of the application shown in Figure 3-4. Because the main() method calls the nameAndAddress() method before it prints the phrase "First Java application", the name and address appear first in the output.

Figure 3-5 Output of the First application, including the nameAndAddress() method

The full name of the nameAndAddress() method is First.nameAndAddress(); the full name includes the class name, a dot, and the method name. When you use the nameAndAddress() method within its own class, you do not need to use the full name (although you can); the method name alone is enough. However, if you want to use the nameAndAddress() method in another class, the compiler does not recognize the method unless you use the full name, writing it as First.nameAndAddress();. This format notifies the new class that the method is located in the First class. You have used similar syntax (including a class name, dot, and method name) when calling the JOptionPane.showMessageDialog() method, in which JOptionPane is the class and showMessageDialog() is the method.

>> **NOTE** First.nameAndAddress() includes only a class name and a method name (separated by a dot) because nameAndAddress() is a static method—one that is used with the class name, without an object. Using System.out. println() includes a class name, an object name, and a method name (using a dot to separate each) because println() is not a static method, but is an instance method. You will learn more about instance methods later in this chapter.

>> **NOTE** Think of the class name as the family name. Within your own family, you might refer to an activity as "the family reunion," but outside the family people need to use a surname as well, as in "the Anderson family reunion." Similarly, within a class a method name alone is sufficient, but outside the class you need to use the fully qualified name.

>> **NOTE** Each of two different classes can have its own method named nameAndAddress(). Such a method in the second class would be entirely distinct from the identically named method in the first class. Two classes in an application cannot have the same name.

CREATING METHODS THAT REQUIRE A SINGLE ARGUMENT

Some methods require information to be sent in from the outside. If a method could not receive your communications, called arguments, you would have to write an infinite number of methods to cover every possible situation. As a real-life example, when you make a restaurant reservation, you do not need to employ a different method for every date of the year at every possible time of day. Rather, you can supply the date and time as information to the person who carries out the method. The method, recording the reservation, is then carried out in the same manner, no matter what date and time are involved. In a program, if you design a method to square numeric values, it makes sense to design a `square()` method that you can supply with an argument that represents the value to be squared, rather than having to develop a `square1()` method (that squares the value 1), a `square2()` method (that squares the value 2), and so on. To call a `square()` method, you might write a statement like `square(17);` or `square(86);`.

An important principle of object-oriented programming is the notion of **implementation hiding**, the encapsulation of method details within a class. That is, when you make a request to a method, you don't know the details of how the method is executed. For example, when you make a real-life restaurant reservation, you do not need to know how the reservation is actually recorded at the restaurant—perhaps it is written in a book, marked on a large chalkboard, or entered into a computerized database. The implementation details don't concern you as a client, and if the restaurant changes its methods from one year to the next, the change does not affect your use of the reservation method—you still call and provide your name, a date, and a time. With well-written object-oriented programming methods, using implementation hiding means that a method that calls another must know the name of the called method, what type of information to send, and what type of return data to expect, but the program does not need to know how the method works internally. In other words, the calling method needs to understand only the **interface** to the called method. The interface is the only part of a method that the method's client sees or with which it interacts. In addition, if you substitute a new or revised method implementation, as long as the interface to the method does not change, you won't need to make any changes in any methods that call the altered method.

> **»NOTE** At any call, the `println()` method can receive any one of an infinite number of arguments—"Hello", "Goodbye", or any other `String`. No matter what message is sent to `println()`, the message displays correctly. If the `println()` method could not accept arguments, it would not be practical to use it within applications.

> **»NOTE** Hidden implementation methods are often referred to as existing in a black box. Many everyday devices are black boxes—that is, you can use them without understanding how they work. For example, most of us use telephones, television sets, and automobiles without understanding much about their internal mechanisms.

> **»NOTE** As an example of how professional programmers use implementation hiding, you can visit the Java Web site at *http://java.sun.com* to see the interfaces for thousands of prewritten methods that reside in the Java prewritten classes. You are not allowed to see the code inside these methods; you see only their interfaces, which is all you need to be able to use them.

When you write the method declaration for a method that can receive an argument, you begin by defining the same elements as with methods that do not accept arguments—optional access modifiers, the return type for the method, and the method name. In addition, you must include the following items within the method declaration parentheses:

» The argument type

» A local name for the argument

For example, the declaration for a public method named `predictRaise()` that displays a person's salary plus a 10% raise could be `public void predictRaise(double moneyAmount)`. You can think of the parentheses in a method declaration as a funnel into the method—data arguments listed there are "dropped in" to the method. An argument passed into a method can be any data type, including the primitive types, such as `int`, `double`, `char`, and so on; it can also be a class type.

> **NOTE** In addition to accepting arguments that are primitive types, a method can accept a class type. If a class named `Customer` exists, a method might accept an instance of `Customer` as an argument, as in `public void approveCredit(Customer oneCustomer)`. In other words, a method can accept anything from a simple `int` to a complicated `Customer` that contains 20 data fields. You will learn more about class types later in this chapter.

The argument `double moneyAmount` within the parentheses indicates that the `predictRaise()` method will receive a value of type `double`, and that within the method, the passed value representing a salary will be known as `moneyAmount`. Figure 3-6 shows a complete method.

```
public static void predictRaise(double moneyAmount)
{
    double newAmount;
    newAmount = moneyAmount * 1.10;
    System.out.println("With raise, salary is " + newAmount);
}
```

Figure 3-6 The `predictRaise()` method

The `predictRaise()` method is a `void` method because it does not need to return any value to any other method that uses it—its only function is to receive the `moneyAmount` value, multiply it by 1.10 (resulting in a 10% salary increase), and then display the result.

> **NOTE**
> The phrases "void method" and "method of type void" mean the same thing. Both phrases refer to a method that has a return type of `void`.

Within a program, you can call the `predictRaise()` method by using either a constant value or a variable as an argument. Thus, both `predictRaise(472.25);` and `predictRaise(mySalary);` invoke the `predictRaise()` method correctly, assuming that `mySalary` is declared as a `double` variable and is assigned an appropriate value in the calling method. You can call the `predictRaise()` method any number of times, with a different constant or variable argument each time. Each of these arguments becomes known as `moneyAmount` within the method. The identifier `moneyAmount` represents a variable that holds any `double` value passed into the `predictRaise()` method; `moneyAmount` holds a copy of the value passed to it.

It is interesting to note that if the value used as an argument in the method call to `predictRaise()` is a variable, it might possess the same identifier as `moneyAmount` or a different one, such as `mySalary`. For example, the code in Figure 3-7 shows three calls to the `predictRaise()` method, and Figure 3-8 shows the output. One call uses a constant, 400.00. The other two use variables—one with the same name as `moneyAmount` and the other with a different name, `mySalary`. The identifier `moneyAmount` is simply a placeholder while it is being used within the `predictRaise()` method, no matter what name it "goes by" in the calling method. The variable `moneyAmount` is a **local variable** to the `predictRaise()` method; that is, it is known only within the boundaries of the method.

Within the `predictRaise()` method in Figure 3-7, if you later decide to change the way in which the 10% raise is calculated—for example, by coding `newAmount = moneyAmount + (moneyAmount * 0.10);`—no method that uses the `predictRaise()` method will ever know the difference. The calling method passes a value into `predictRaise()` and then a correct calculated result appears on the screen.

```
public class DemoRaise
{
    public static void main(String[] args)
    {
        double mySalary = 200.00;
        double moneyAmount = 800.00;
        System.out.println("Demonstrating some raises");
        predictRaise(400.00);
        predictRaise(mySalary);
        predictRaise(moneyAmount);
    }
    public static void predictRaise(double moneyAmount)
    {
        double newAmount;
        newAmount = moneyAmount * 1.10;
        System.out.println("With raise, salary is " + newAmount);
    }
}
```

Figure 3-7 The DemoRaise class with a main() method that uses the predictRaise() method three times

Figure 3-8 Output of the DemoRaise application

▶▶ **NOTE** Notice the output in Figure 3-8. Floating-point arithmetic is always imprecise. If you do not like the appearance of the numbers in this output, you can use the techniques described in Appendix C to format your output to a specific number of decimal places.

Each time the predictRaise() method in Figure 3-7 executes, a moneyAmount variable is redeclared—that is, a new memory location large enough to hold a double is set up and named moneyAmount. Within the predictRaise() method, moneyAmount holds a copy of whatever value is passed into the method by the main() method. When the predictRaise() method ends, at the closing curly brace, the local moneyAmount variable ceases to exist. After the raise is calculated in the method, if you placed a statement such as the following within predictRaise(), it would make no difference:

```
moneyAmount = 100000;
```

That is, if you change the value of moneyAmount after you have used it in the calculation within predictRaise(), it affects nothing else. The memory location that holds moneyAmount is released at the end of the method, and if you change its value within the

▶▶ **NOTE**
When a variable ceases to exist at the end of a method, programmers say the variable "goes out of scope."

method, it does not affect any value in the calling method. In particular, don't think there would be any change in the variable named `moneyAmount` in the `main()` method; that variable, even though it has the same name as the locally declared argument in the method, is a different variable with its own memory address, and is totally different from the one in the `predictRaise()` method.

CREATING METHODS THAT REQUIRE MULTIPLE ARGUMENTS

A method can require more than one argument. You can pass multiple arguments to a method by listing the arguments within the call to the method and separating them with commas. For example, rather than creating a `predictRaise()` method that adds a 10% raise to every person's salary, you might prefer creating a method to which you can pass two values—the salary to be raised as well as a percentage figure by which to raise it. Figure 3-9 shows a method that uses two such arguments.

» NOTE Note that a declaration for a method that receives two or more arguments must list the type for each argument separately, even if the arguments have the same type.

```
public static void predictRaiseUsingRate(double money, double rate)
{
   double newAmount;
   newAmount = money * (1 + rate);
   System.out.println("With raise, new salary is " + newAmount);
}
```

Figure 3-9 The `predictRaiseUsingRate()` method that accepts two arguments

In Figure 3-9, two arguments (`double money` and `double rate`) appear within the parentheses in the method header. A comma separates each argument, and each argument requires its own declared type (in this case, both are `double`) as well as its own identifier. When values are passed to the method in a statement such as `predictRaiseUsingRate (mySalary, promisedRate);`, the first value passed is referenced as `money` within the method, and the second value passed is referenced as `rate`. Therefore, arguments passed to the method must be passed in the correct order. The call `predictRaiseUsingRate (200.00,0.10);` results in output representing a 10% raise based on a $200.00 salary amount (or $220.00), but `predictRaiseUsingRate(0.10,200.00);` results in output representing a 200% raise based on a salary of 10 cents (or $20.10).

» NOTE If two method arguments are the same type—for example, two `doubles`—passing them to a method in the wrong order results in a logical error; that is, the program does compile and execute, but it probably produces incorrect results. If a method expects arguments of diverse types, passing arguments in the wrong order constitutes a syntax error, and the program does not compile.

You can write a method so that it takes any number of arguments in any order. However, when you call a method, the arguments you send to a method must match in order—both in number and in type—the arguments listed in the method declaration. Thus, a method to compute an automobile salesperson's commission amount might require arguments such as an integer dollar value of a car sold, a double percentage commission rate, and a character code for the vehicle type. The correct method executes only when three

»NOTE
The arguments in a method call are often referred to as **actual parameters**. The variables in the method declaration that accept the values from the actual parameters are the **formal parameters**.

arguments of the correct types are sent in the correct order. Figure 3-10 shows a class containing a three-argument method and a `main()` method that calls it twice, once using variable arguments and again using constant arguments. Figure 3-11 shows the output of the application.

```java
public class ComputeCommission
{
    public static void main(String[] args)
    {
        char vType = 'S';
        int value = 23000;
        double commRate = 0.08;
        computeCommission(value, commRate, vType);
        computeCommission(40000, 0.10, 'L');
    }
    public static void computeCommission(int value,
            double rate, char vehicle)
    {
        double commission;
        commission = value * rate;
        System.out.println("\nThe " + vehicle +
            " type vehicle is worth $" + value);
        System.out.println("With " + (rate * 100) +
            "% commission rate, the commission is $" +
            commission);
    }
}
```

Figure 3-10 The `ComputeCommission` class

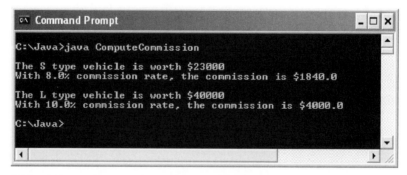

Figure 3-11 Output of the `ComputeCommission` application

»NOTE When you look at Java applications, you might see a method that appears to be callable in multiple ways. For example, you can use `System.out.println()` with no arguments to print a blank line, or with a `String` argument to print the `String`. You can use the method with different argument lists only because multiple versions of the method have been written, each taking a specific set of arguments. The ability to execute different method implementations by altering the argument used with the method name is known as method overloading, a concept you will learn about in the next chapter.

CREATING METHODS THAT RETURN VALUES

The return type for a method can be any type used in Java, which includes the primitive types int, double, char, and so on, as well as class types (including class types you create). Of course, a method can also return nothing, in which case the return type is void.

A method's return type is known more succinctly as a **method's type**. For example, the declaration for the nameAndAddress() method, shown earlier in Figure 3-4, is written public static void nameAndAddress(). This method is public and it returns no value, so it is type void. A method that returns true or false, depending on whether an employee worked overtime hours, might be public boolean workedOvertime(). This method is public and it returns a Boolean value, so it is type boolean.

> **» NOTE** In addition to returning the primitive types, a method can return a class type. If your application contains a class named BankLoan, a method might return an instance of a BankLoan, as in public BankLoan approval Process(). In other words, a method can return anything from a simple int to a complicated BankLoan that is composed of 20 data fields. You will learn more about class types later in this chapter.

The predictRaise() method shown earlier produces output, but does not return any value, so its return type is void. If you want to create a method to return the new, calculated salary value rather than display it, the header would be written as follows:

```
public static double predictRaise(double moneyAmount)
```

Figure 3-12 shows this method.

```
public static double predictRaise(double moneyAmount)
{
    double newAmount;
    newAmount = moneyAmount * 1.10;
    return newAmount;
}
```

Figure 3-12 The predictRaise() method returning a double

Notice the return type double that precedes the method name in the predictRaise() method header in Figure 3-12. Also notice the return statement that is the last statement within the method. A **return statement** causes a value to be sent from a called method back to the calling method. In this case, the value stored in newAmount is sent back to any method that calls the predictRaise() method. A method's declared return type must match the type of the value used in the return statement; if it does not, the class does not compile.

> **» NOTE**
> A method can return, at most, one value. The value can be a primitive data type, such as int, char, or double, or it can be a class type.

If a method returns a value, when you call the method you normally use the returned value, although you are not required to do so. For example, when you invoke the predictRaise() method, you might want to assign the returned value (also called the method's value) to a double variable named myNewSalary, as in the following statement:

```
myNewSalary = predictRaise(mySalary);
```

The predictRaise() method returns a double, so it is appropriate to assign the method's returned value to a double variable.

Alternatively, you can choose to use a method's returned value directly, without storing it in any variable. When you use a method's value, you use it in the same way you would use any variable of the same type. For example, you can print a return value in a statement such as the following:

```
System.out.println("New salary is " + calculateRaise(mySalary));
```

In the preceding statement, the call to the `calculateRaise()` method is made from within the `println()` method call. Because `calculateRaise()` returns a `double`, you can use the method call `calculateRaise()` in the same way that you would use any simple `double` value. As another example, you can perform arithmetic with a method's return value, as in the following statement:

```
spendingMoney = calculateRaise(mySalary) - expenses;
```

LEARNING ABOUT CLASS CONCEPTS

When you think in an object-oriented manner, everything is an object, and every object is a member of a class. You can think of any inanimate physical item as an object—your desk, your computer, and the building in which you live are all called objects in everyday conversation. You can also think of living things as objects—your houseplant, your pet fish, and your sister are objects. Events are also objects—the stock purchase you made, the mortgage closing you attended, and a graduation party that was held in your honor are all objects.

» NOTE
Programmers also use the phrase "is-a" when talking about inheritance relationships. You will learn more about inheritance in Chapter 11.

Everything is an object, and every object is a member of a more general class. Your desk is a member of the class that includes all desks, and your pet fish a member of the class that contains all fish. An object-oriented programmer would say that your desk is an instance of the `Desk` class and your fish is an instance of the `Fish` class. These statements represent **is-a relationships**—that is, relationships in which the object "is a" member of the class. Expressing an is-a relationship is correct only when you refer to the object and the class in the proper order. You can say, "My oak desk with the scratch on top *is a* Desk and my goldfish named Moby *is a* Fish." You don't define a Desk as, "A Desk *is an* oak desk with a scratch on top," or explain what a Fish is by saying, "A Fish *is a* goldfish named Moby," because both a Desk and a Fish are much more general. The difference between a class and an object parallels the difference between abstract and concrete. An object is an **instantiation** of a class, or one tangible example of a class. Your goldfish, my guppy, and the zoo's shark each constitute one instantiation of the `Fish` class.

» NOTE
Everything is an object—even a class.

The concept of a class is useful because of its reusability. Objects gain their attributes from their classes, and all objects have predictable attributes because they are members of certain classes. For example, if you are invited to a graduation party, you automatically know many things about the object (the party). You assume there will be a starting time, a certain number of guests, some quantity of food, and some kind of gifts. You understand what a party entails because of your previous knowledge of the `Party` class of which all parties are members. You don't know the number of guests, what food will be served, or what gifts will be received at this particular party, but you understand that because all parties have guests and refreshments, this one must too. Because you understand the general characteristics of a `Party`, you anticipate different behaviors than if you plan to attend a `TheaterPerformance` object or a `DentalAppointment` object.

» NOTE The data components of a class are often referred to as the instance variables of that class. Also, class object attributes are often called fields to help distinguish them from other variables you might use.

In addition to their attributes, class objects have methods associated with them, and every object that is an instance of a class is assumed to possess the same methods. For example, for all `Party` objects, at some point you must set the date and time. In a program, you might name these methods `setDate()` and `setTime()`. Party guests need to know the date and time and might use methods named `getDate()` and `getTime()` to find out the date and time of any `Party` object.

》 NOTE
Method names that begin with "get" and "set" are very typical. You will learn more about `get` and `set` methods in the next section.

Your graduation party, then, might have the identifier `myGraduationParty`. As a member of the `Party` class, `myGraduationParty` (like all `Party` objects) might have data methods `setDate()` and `setTime()`. When you use them, the `setDate()` and `setTime()` methods require arguments, or information passed to them. For example, statements such as `myGraduationParty.setDate("May 12")` and `myGraduationParty.setTime("6 P.M.")` invoke methods that are available for the `myGraduationParty` object. When you use an object and its methods, think of being able to send a message to the object to direct it to accomplish some task—you can tell the `Party` object named `myGraduationParty` to set the date and time you request. Even though `yourAnniversaryParty` is also a member of the `Party` class, and even though it also has access to `setDate()` and `setTime()` methods, the arguments you send to `yourAnniversaryParty` will be different from those you send to `myGraduationParty`. Within any object-oriented program, you are continuously making requests to objects' methods and often including arguments as part of those requests.

In addition, some methods used in an application must return a message or value. If one of your party guests uses the `getDate()` method, the guest hopes that the method will respond with the desired information. Similarly, within object-oriented programs, methods are often called upon to return a piece of information to the source of the request. For example, a method within a `Payroll` class that calculates federal withholding tax might return a tax figure in dollars and cents, and a method within an `Inventory` class might return `true` or `false`, depending on the method's determination of whether an item is at the reorder point.

With object-oriented programming, sometimes you create classes so that you can instantiate objects from them, and other times you create classes to run as applications; the application classes frequently instantiate objects that use the objects of other classes (and their data and their methods). The same programmer does not need to write every class he or she uses. Often, you will write programs that use classes created by others; similarly, you might create a class that others will use to instantiate objects within their own applications. You can call an application or class that instantiates objects of another prewritten class a **class client** or **class user**.

》 NOTE The `System` class that you have used to produce output in the Comm and Prompt window provides an example of using a class that was written by someone else. You did not have to create it or its object's `println()` method; both were created for you by Java's creators.

》 NOTE You can identify a class that is an application because it contains a `public static void main()` method. The `main()` method is the starting point for any application. You will write and use many classes that do not contain a `main()` method—these classes can be used by other classes that are applications or applets. (You will learn about applets in Chapters 9 and 10.)

》 NOTE A Java application can contain only one method with the header `public static void main(String[ ] args)`. If you write a class that imports another class, and both classes have a `main()` method, your application will not compile.

So far, you've learned that object-oriented programming involves objects that send messages to other objects requesting they perform tasks, and that every object belongs to a class. Understanding classes and how objects are instantiated from them is the heart of object-oriented thinking.

CREATING A CLASS

When you create a class, you must first assign a name to the class, and then you must determine what data and methods will be part of the class. Suppose you decide to create a class named `Employee`. One instance variable of `Employee` might be an employee number, and two necessary methods might be a method to set (or provide a value for) the employee number and another method to get (or retrieve) that employee number. To begin, you create a class header with three parts:

» An optional access modifier

» The keyword `class`

» Any legal identifier you choose for the name of your class

For example, a header for an `Employee` class is `public class Employee`. The keyword `public` is a class modifier. Public classes are accessible by all objects, which means that public classes can be **extended**, or used as a basis for any other class. The most liberal form of access is `public`. Public access means that if you develop a good `Employee` class, and someday you want to develop two classes that are more specific, `SalariedEmployee` and `HourlyEmployee`, then you do not have to start from scratch. Each new class can become an extension of the original `Employee` class, inheriting its data and methods.

> **» NOTE** You can use the following class modifiers when defining a class: `public`, `final`, `abstract`, or `strictfp`. You will use the `public` modifier for most of your classes. You use the other modifiers only under special circumstances.

After writing the class header `public class Employee`, you write the body of the `Employee` class, containing its data fields and methods, between a set of curly braces. Figure 3-13 shows the shell for the `Employee` class.

```
public class Employee
{
// Data fields (Instance variables) and methods go here
}
```

Figure 3-13 The `Employee` class shell

> **» NOTE**
> To help you determine whether a data field should be static or not, you can ask yourself how many times it occurs. If it occurs once per class, it is static, but if it occurs once per object, it is not static.

You place the data fields for the `Employee` class as statements within the curly braces. **Data fields**, also called simply **fields**, are variables you declare within a class, but outside of any method. Data fields are also called **instance variables** when they are not made static. When you eventually create, or instantiate, objects from a class, each will have its own copy of each nonstatic data field you declare. For example, to allow each `Employee` to have its own employee number, you can declare an employee number that will be stored as an integer simply by typing `int empNum;` within the curly braces of the `Employee` class (but not within any method). However, programmers frequently include an access modifier for each of the class fields, and so you would declare the `empNum` as follows:

```
private int empNum;
```

You have already learned that Java supports four distinct access levels for member variables and methods: private, protected, public, and, if left unspecified, package. Most class fields are private, which provides the highest level of security. Assigning **private access** to a field means that no other classes can access the field's values, and only methods of the same class are allowed to set, get, or otherwise use private variables. The principle used in creating private access is sometimes called **information hiding** and is an important component of object-oriented programs. A class's private data can be changed or manipulated only by a class's own methods and not by methods that belong to other classes. In contrast to fields, most class methods are public, not private. The resulting private data/public method arrangement provides a means for you to control outside access to your data—only a class's nonprivate methods can be used to access a class's private data. The situation is similar to hiring a public receptionist to sit in front of your private office and control which messages you receive (perhaps deflecting trivial or hostile ones) and which messages you send (perhaps checking your spelling, grammar, and any legal implications). The way in which the nonprivate methods are written controls how you use the private data.

>> **NOTE** The first release of Java (1.0) supported five access levels—the four listed previously plus private protected. The private protected access level is not supported in versions of Java higher than 1.0; you should not use it in your Java programs.

>> **NOTE** Data fields are most often private and not static. Only rarely is a class field made public. Class fields are made static only when you do not want each object to have its own copy of the field. You will learn more about how and why to create static and nonstatic class members in the next section.

>> **NOTE** The field modifiers are the same as the method modifiers, with one addition—the final modifier, which makes the value in a field unchangeable. You will learn to use the final modifier in Chapter 4.

>> **NOTE** Data fields are most frequently made public when they are both static and final—that is, when a class contains a nonchanging value that you want to use without being required to create an object. For example, the Java Math class contains a public field called PI that you can use without instantiating a Math object. You will learn about the Math class in Chapter 4.

The Employee class developed to this point appears in Figure 3-14. It defines a public class named Employee, with one field, which is a private integer named empNum.

```
public class Employee
{
    private int empNum;
}
```

Figure 3-14 The Employee class with one field

CREATING INSTANCE METHODS IN A CLASS

Besides data, classes contain methods. For example, one method you need for an Employee class that contains an empNum is the method to retrieve (or return) any Employee's empNum for use by another class. A reasonable name for this method is getEmpNum(), and its declaration is public int getEmpNum() because it will have public access, return an integer (the employee number), and possess the identifier getEmpNum(). Figure 3-15 shows the complete getEmpNum() method.

```
public int getEmpNum()
{
    return empNum;
}
```

Figure 3-15 The `getEmpNum()` method

The `getEmpNum()` method contains just one statement: the statement that accesses the value of the private `empNum` field.

Notice that, unlike the class methods you created earlier in this chapter, the `getEmpNum()` method does not employ the `static` modifier. The keyword `static` is used for classwide methods, but not for methods that "belong" to objects. If you are creating a program with a `main()` method that you will execute to perform some task, many of your methods will be static so you can call them from within `main()` without creating class objects. However, if you are creating a class from which objects will be instantiated, most methods will probably be nonstatic because you will associate the methods with individual objects. For example, the `getEmpNum()` method must be nonstatic because it returns a different `empNum` value for every `Employee` object you ever create. **Nonstatic methods**, those methods used with object instantiations, are called **instance methods**.

»NOTE You can call class (static) methods without creating an instance of the class. Instance methods require an instantiated object.

»NOTE You have used the method `System.out.println()`. This method is nonstatic—it is an instance method that is used with the `out` object. You have also used the method `JOptionPane.showMessageDialog()`. This method is static—you use it with the class `JOptionPane`, not with any specific object.

Understanding when to declare fields and methods as static and nonstatic is a challenge for new programmers. In summary:

- When you declare variables in a class, you most often declare nonstatic instance variables. (You do not need to use any special keywords to do this.) Every time you create an instance of a class, the system reserves enough computer memory to hold one copy of each class's instance variables for that object. For example, if you create an `Employee` class containing instance variables for ID number and pay rate, and then create four `Employee` objects, you create four ID numbers and four pay rates.
- Static class variables are not instance variables. The system allocates memory to hold class variables once per class, no matter how many instances of the class you instantiate. The system allocates memory for class variables the first time it encounters a class, and every instance of a class shares the same copy of any static class variables. For example, in your organization, you might include a maximum pay rate as a static member of an `Employee` class. Because every employee who works for your organization is subject to the limit imposed by the maximum pay rate, it would be a waste to store a copy of the same value once for every `Employee` instance. Instead, you might choose to make the variable static, store it once for the entire class, and allow every `Employee` object to have access to it.

When a class contains data fields, you want a means to assign values to them. For an `Employee` class with an `empNum` field, you need a method with which to set the `empNum`. Figure 3-16 shows a method named `setEmpNum()` that sets the value of an `Employee`'s `empNum`. The method is a `void` method because there is no need to return any value to a calling method. The method receives an integer, locally called `emp`, to be assigned to `empNum`.

```
public void setEmpNum(int emp)
{
   empNum = emp;
}
```

Figure 3-16 The `setEmpNum()` method

NOTE In Java, methods that set values within and get values from an object most frequently start with "get" and "set". Using these three-letter prefixes with your method names is not required, but it is conventional.

Figure 3-17 shows the complete `Employee` class containing one private data field and two public methods. This class becomes the model for a new data type named `Employee`; when `Employee` objects eventually are created, each will have its own `empNum` field, and each will have access to two methods—one that provides a value for its `empNum` field and another that retrieves the value stored there.

NOTE Methods that set values are called **mutator methods**; methods that retrieve values are called **accessor methods**.

```
public class Employee
{
   private int empNum;
   public int getEmpNum()
   {
      return empNum;
   }
   public void setEmpNum(int emp)
   {
      empNum = emp;
   }
}
```

Figure 3-17 The `Employee` class with one field and two methods

DECLARING OBJECTS AND USING THEIR METHODS

Declaring a class does not create any actual objects. A class is just an abstract description of what an object will be like if any objects are ever actually instantiated. Just as you might understand all the characteristics of an item you intend to manufacture long before the first item rolls off the assembly line, you can create a class with fields and methods long before you instantiate any objects that are members of that class.

A two-step process creates an object that is an instance of a class. First, you supply a type and an identifier—just as when you declare any variable—and then you allocate computer memory for that object. For example, you might define an integer as `int someValue;` and you might define an `Employee` as `Employee someEmployee;`, where `someEmployee` stands for any legal identifier you choose to represent an `Employee`.

When you declare an integer as `int someValue;`, you notify the compiler that an integer named `someValue` will exist, and you reserve computer memory for it at the same time.

When you declare the someEmployee instance of the Employee class, you are notifying the compiler that you will use the identifier someEmployee. However, you are not yet setting aside computer memory in which the Employee named someEmployee might be stored—that is done automatically only for primitive type variables. To allocate the needed memory for a class object, you must use the **new operator**. Two statements that actually set aside enough memory to hold an Employee are as follows:

```
Employee someEmployee;
someEmployee = new Employee();
```

You can also define and reserve memory for someEmployee in one statement, as in the following:

```
Employee someEmployee = new Employee();
```

» NOTE
Every object name is also a reference—that is, a computer memory location.

In this statement, Employee is the object's type (as well as its class), and someEmployee is the name of the object. The equal sign is the assignment operator, so a value is being assigned to someEmployee. The new operator is allocating a new, unused portion of computer memory for someEmployee. The value that the statement is assigning to someEmployee is a memory address at which someEmployee is to be located. You do not need to be concerned with what the actual memory address is—when you refer to someEmployee, the compiler locates it at the appropriate address for you.

» NOTE
You will write constructor methods later in this chapter.

The final portion of the statement after the new operator, Employee(), with its parentheses, looks suspiciously like a method name. In fact, it is the name of a method that constructs an Employee object. The Employee() method is a **constructor method**, a method that creates and initializes class objects. You can write your own constructor methods, but when you don't write a constructor method for a class object, Java writes one for you, and the name of the constructor method is always the same as the name of the class whose objects it constructs.

After an object has been instantiated, its methods can be accessed using the object's identifier, a dot, and a method call. For example, Figure 3-18 shows an application that instantiates two Employee objects. The two objects, clerk and driver, each use the setEmpNum() and getEmpNum() method one time. The DeclareTwoEmployees application can use these methods because they are public, and it must use them with an Employee object because the methods are not static. Figure 3-19 shows the output of the application.

```
public class DeclareTwoEmployees
{
    public static void main(String[] args)
    {
        Employee clerk = new Employee();
        Employee driver = new Employee();
        clerk.setEmpNum(345);
        driver.setEmpNum(567);
        System.out.println("The clerk's number is " +
            clerk.getEmpNum() + " and the driver's number is " +
            driver.getEmpNum());
    }
}
```

Figure 3-18 The DeclareTwoEmployees class

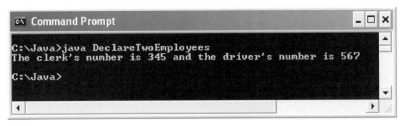

Figure 3-19 Output of the `DeclareTwoEmployees` application

UNDERSTANDING DATA HIDING

Within the `DeclareTwoEmployees` class, you must use the public methods `setEmpNum()` and `getEmpNum()` to be able to set and retrieve the value of the `empNum` field for each `Employee` because you cannot access the private `empNum` field directly. For example, the following statement would not be allowed:

```
clerk.empNum = 789;
```

This statement generates the error message "empNum has private access in Employee", meaning you cannot access `empNum` from the `DeclareTwoEmployees` class. If you made `empNum` public instead of private, a direct assignment statement would work, but you would violate an important principle of object-oriented programming—that of data hiding using encapsulation. Data fields should usually be private, and a client application should be able to access them only through the public interfaces—that is, through the class's public methods. However, you might reasonably ask, "When I write an application, if I *can't* set an object's data field directly, but I *can* set it using a public method, what's the difference? The field value is set either way!" Actually, the `setEmpNum()` method in the `Employee` class in Figure 3-17 *does* accept any integer value you send into it. However, you could rewrite the `setEmpNum()` method to prevent invalid data from being assigned to an object's data fields. For example, perhaps your organization has rules for valid employee ID numbers—they must be no fewer than five digits, or they must start with a 9, for instance—or perhaps you calculate a check-digit that is appended to every employee ID number. The statements that enforce these requirements would be part of the `setEmpNum()` method.

Similarly, a `get` method might control how a value is retrieved. Perhaps you do not want clients to have access to part of an employee's ID number, or perhaps you always want to add a company code to every ID before it is returned to the client. Even when a field has no data value requirements or restrictions, making data private and providing public `set` and `get` methods establishes a framework that makes such modifications easier in the future.

> **»NOTE**
> Checking a value for validity requires decision making. You will begin to learn about making decisions in Java in Chapter 5.

> **»NOTE** A check-digit is a number appended to a field, typically an ID number or account number. The check-digit ensures that the number is valid. For example, an organization might use five-digit employee ID numbers in which the fifth digit is calculated by dividing the first four by 7 and taking the remainder. As an example, if the first four digits of your ID number are 7235, then the fifth digit is 4, the remainder when you divide the first four digits by 7. So the five-digit ID becomes 72354. Later, if you make a mistake and enter your ID into a company application as 82354, the application would divide the first four digits, 8235, by 7. The remainder is not 4, and the ID would be found invalid.

> **»NOTE** You will not necessarily write `set` and `get` methods for every field in a class; there are some fields that clients will not be allowed to alter. Some fields will simply be assigned values, and some field values might be calculated from the values of others.

ORGANIZING CLASSES

Most classes you create have more than one data field and more than two methods. For example, in addition to requiring an employee number, an `Employee` needs a last name, a first name, and a salary, as well as methods to set and get those fields. Figure 3-20 shows how you could code the data fields for `Employee`.

```
public class Employee
{
    private int empNum;
    private String empLastName;
    private String empFirstName;
    private double empSalary;
    // Methods will go here
}
```

Figure 3-20 An `Employee` class with several data fields

Although there is no requirement to do so, most programmers place data fields in some logical order at the beginning of a class. For example, `empNum` is most likely used as a unique identifier for each employee (what database users often call a **primary key**), so it makes sense to list the employee number first in the class. An employee's last name and first name "go together," so it makes sense to store these two `Employee` components adjacently. Despite these common sense rules, you have a lot of flexibility in how you position your data fields within any class.

>> **NOTE** A unique identifier is one that should have no duplicates within an application. For example, an organization might have many employees with the last name Johnson or a weekly salary of $400.00, but there is only one employee with employee number 128.

Because there are two `String` components in the current `Employee` class, they might be declared within the same statement, such as:

```
private String empLastName, empFirstName;
```

However, it is usually easier to identify each `Employee` field at a glance if the fields are listed vertically.

You can place a class's data fields and methods in any order within a class. For example, you could place all the methods first, followed by all the data fields, or you could organize the class so that several data fields are followed by methods that use them, then several more data fields are followed by the methods that use them. This book will follow the convention of placing all data fields first so that you can see their names and data types before reading the methods that use them.

Even if the only methods created for the `Employee` class include one `set` method and one `get` method for each instance variable, eight methods are required. Consider an employee record for most organizations and you will realize that many more fields are often required (such as address, phone number, hire date, number of dependents, and so on), as well as many more methods. Finding your way through the list can become a formidable task. For ease in locating class methods, many programmers store them in alphabetical order. Other programmers arrange values in pairs of "get" and "set" methods, an order that also results in functional groupings. Figure 3-21 shows how the complete class definition for an `Employee` might appear.

```java
public class Employee
{
    private int empNum;
    private String empLastName;
    private String empFirstName;
    private double empSalary;
    public int getEmpNum()
    {
        return empNum;
    }
    public void setEmpNum(int emp)
    {
        empNum = emp;
    }
    public String getEmpLastName()
    {
        return empLastName;
    }
    public void setEmpLastName(String name)
    {
        empLastName = name;
    }
    public String getEmpFirstName()
    {
        return empFirstName;
    }
    public void setEmpFirstName(String name)
    {
        empFirstName = name;
    }
    public double getEmpSalary()
    {
        return empSalary;
    }
    public void setEmpSalary(double sal)
    {
        empSalary = sal;
    }
}
```

Figure 3-21 The `Employee` class with several data fields and corresponding methods

The `Employee` class is still not a particularly large class, and each of its methods is very short, but it is already becoming quite difficult to manage. It certainly can support some well-placed comments, as shown in Figure 3-22.

```
// Employee.java holds employee data
// Programmer: Lynn Greenbrier
// Date: September 24, 2009
public class Employee
{
   // private data members:
         private int empNum;
         private String empLastName;
         private String empFirstName;
         private double empSalary;

   // public mutator and accessor methods:
         public int getEmpNum()
         {
          return empNum;
         }
         public void setEmpNum(int emp)
         {
          empNum = emp;
         }
// ...and so on
```

Figure 3-22 Start of Employee class with data fields, methods, and comments

AN INTRODUCTION TO USING CONSTRUCTORS

When you create a class, such as Employee, and instantiate an object with a statement such as Employee chauffeur = new Employee();, you are actually calling a method named Employee() that is provided by default by the Java compiler. A constructor method, or more simply, a **constructor**, is a method that establishes an object. A **default constructor** is one that requires no arguments. A default constructor is created automatically by the Java compiler for any class you create whenever you do not write your own constructor.

When the prewritten, default constructor method for the Employee class is called, it establishes one Employee object with the identifier provided. A default constructor provides the following specific initial values to an object's data fields:

» Numeric fields are set to 0 (zero).
» Character fields are set to Unicode '\u0000'.
» Boolean fields are set to false.
» Fields that are nonprimitive objects themselves (for example, String fields) are set to null (or empty).

» NOTE
You never provide a return type for a constructor method—not even void.

If you do not want each field in an object to hold these default values, or if you want to perform additional tasks when you create an instance of a class, you can write your own constructor method. Any constructor method you write must have the same name as the class it constructs, and constructor methods cannot have a return type. Normally, you declare constructors to be public so that other classes can instantiate objects that belong to the class.

For example, if you want every `Employee` object to have a starting salary of $300.00 per week, you could write the constructor method for the `Employee` class that appears in Figure 3-23. Any `Employee` object instantiated will have a `salary` field value equal to 300.00, and the other `Employee` data fields will contain the default values.

```
public Employee()
{
    salary = 300.00;
}
```

Figure 3-23 The `Employee` class constructor

>> **NOTE** Even if you do not initialize an object's field, it always contains the default values listed previously, and even though you might want the field to hold the default value, you still might prefer to explicitly initialize the field for clarity. For example, if an `Employee` class contains an integer field named `yearsOnTheJob`, you might choose to place a statement in a constructor such as `yearsOnTheJob = 0;`. Although the `int` field would be initialized to 0 anyway, the explicit assignment allows anyone reading the constructor to clearly understand your intentions.

You can write any Java statement in a constructor. Although you usually have no reason to do so, you could print a message from within a constructor or perform any other task.

You can place the constructor anywhere inside the class, outside of any other method. Typically, a constructor method is placed with the other methods. Often, programmers list the constructor first because it is the first method used when an object is created.

YOU DO IT

CREATING A STATIC METHOD THAT REQUIRES NO ARGUMENTS AND RETURNS NO VALUES

Event Handlers Incorporated assists its clients in planning and hosting social events and business meetings. In this section, you will create a new class named `SetUpSite`, which you will eventually use to set up one `EventSite` object that represents the site where an event can be held. For now, the class will contain a `main()` method and a `statementOfPhilosophy()` method for Event Handlers Incorporated.

To create the `SetUpSite` class:

1. Open a new document in your text editor.

2. Type the following shell class to create a `SetUpSite` class and an empty `main()` method:

```
public class SetUpSite
{
    public static void main(String[] args)
    {
    }
}
```

>> **NOTE** The `Employee` class constructor in Figure 3-23 takes no arguments. You will learn about constructors that take arguments in the next chapter.

>> **NOTE** You are never required to write a constructor method for a class; Java provides you with a default version if the class contains no explicit constructor.

>> **NOTE** A class can contain multiple constructors. You will learn how to overload constructors in the next chapter.

>> **NOTE** When you write a constructor for a class, you no longer receive the automatically written version.

3. Place the insertion point to the right of the opening brace in the `main()` method, press **Enter** to start a new line, and then type the following between the curly braces of the `main()` method:

```
statementOfPhilosophy();
```

This statement calls a method named `statementOfPhilosophy()`.

4. Place the `statementOfPhilosophy()` method outside the `main()` method, just before the closing curly brace for the `SetUpSite` class code:

```
public static void statementOfPhilosophy()
{
    System.out.println("Event Handlers Incorporated is");
    System.out.println("dedicated to making your event");
    System.out.println("a most memorable one.");
}
```

5. Save the file as **SetUpSite.java** in the Chapter.03 folder on your Student Disk.

6. At the command line, compile the application by typing **javac SetUpSite.java** and pressing **Enter**.

If you receive any error messages, you must correct their cause. For example, Figure 3-24 shows the error message received when `println()` is spelled incorrectly within the SetUpSite.java file. Notice the message indicates that the file is SetUpSite.java, the line on which the error occurs is line 10, and the error is "cannot find symbol", followed by the name of the symbol that the compiler does not understand: "symbol: method prinln(java.lang.String)". To help you, Java tells you where the error might be: "location: class java.io.PrintStream"; Java assumes the error is in the `PrintStream` class because you are using the `System.out` object, which it knows is a `PrintStream` class object, and the compiler can't find a method with the name `prinln()` there. The compiler displays the offending line, and a caret appears just below the word that the compiler doesn't understand. When you view this error message, you should notice the misspelling of the `println()` method name. To correct the spelling error, return to the SetUpSite.java file, fix the mistake, save the file, and then compile it again.

Figure 3-24 Error message received when `println` is incorrectly spelled

> **NOTE** If you misspelled `println()`, but did not notice the typographical error when you read the message, or did not know how the method name should be spelled, your next course of action is to search the Java documentation for methods contained in the `PrintStream` class. You can find the Java documentation at *http://java.sun.com*.

7. Execute the application using the command **java SetUpSite**. Your output should look like Figure 3-25.

Figure 3-25 Output of the SetUpSite application

CALLING A STATIC METHOD FROM ANOTHER CLASS

Next, you will see how to call the statementOfPhilosophy() method from a method within another class.

To call a static method from a method within another class:

1. First, open a new document in your text editor, and then enter the class that appears in Figure 3-26.

```
public class TestStatement
{
    public static void main(String[] args)
    {
        System.out.println("Calling method from another class");
        SetUpSite.statementOfPhilosophy();
    }
}
```

Figure 3-26 The TestStatement class

2. Save the file as **TestStatement.java** in the Chapter.03 folder on your Student Disk.

> **NOTE** If you want one class to call a method of another class, both classes should reside in the same folder. If they are not saved in the same folder, when you compile the calling class, your compiler issues the error message "cannot find symbol" and the symbol it names is the missing class you tried to call.

3. Compile the application with the command **javac TestStatement.java**. If necessary, correct any errors, save the file, and then repeat this step to compile the file again.

4. Execute the application with the command **java TestStatement**. Your output should look like Figure 3-27.

CREATING A STATIC METHOD THAT ACCEPTS ARGUMENTS AND RETURNS VALUES

Next, you will add a method to the SetUpSite class; the new method both receives an argument and returns a value. The purpose of the method is to accept the current year and calculate how long Event Handlers has been in business.

Figure 3-27 Output of the `TestStatement` application

To add a method that receives an argument and returns a value:

1. Open the **SetUpSite.java** file in the text editor, and then change the class name to **SetUpSite2**. Immediately save the file as **SetUpSite2.java** in the Chapter.03 folder on your Student Disk.

2. Position the insertion point to the right of the opening curly brace of the `main()` method of the class, and then press **Enter** to start a new line.

3. Type **int currentYear = 2008;** to declare a variable to hold the current year, and then press **Enter**.

4. Type **int age;** to declare another variable to hold the age of Event Handlers Incorporated.

5. Position the insertion point at the end of the call to the `statementOfPhilosophy()` method in the `main()` method of the class, and then press **Enter** to start a new line. You will add a call to a method that will receive the current year as an argument and return the age of the organization. Type **age = calculateAge(currentYear);** as a call to a `calculateAge()` method.

6. Press **Enter** and then type the following to print the number of years the company has been in business:

```
System.out.println("Serving you for " + age + " years");
```

7. Now you will write the `calculateAge()` method. Position the insertion point after the closing brace of the `statementOfPhilosophy()` method, press **Enter** to start a new line before the closing brace of the program, and then enter the `calculateAge()` method as follows:

```
public static int calculateAge(int currDate)
{
    int originYear = 1977;
    int years;
    years = currDate - originYear;
    return years;
}
```

The `calculateAge()` method receives an integer value that locally is known as `currDate`. Note that the name `currDate` does not possess the same identifier as `currentYear`, which is the variable being passed in from the `main()` method, although it could. Notice also that the method declaration indicates an `int` value will be returned. The `calculateAge()` method subtracts the year Event Handlers was founded, 1977, from its argument and returns the age to the calling function.

100

>> **NOTE** The `calculateAge()` method is static because no `SetUpSite2` objects need to be created to use it; it is a class method.

8. Save the file (as SetUpSite2.java), compile it, and correct any errors. Execute the application and confirm that the results are correct. Figure 3-28 shows the complete application, along with some newly added comments, and Figure 3-29 shows the output.

```java
// SetUpSite2 class displays the statement
// of philosophy and calculates the age
// of the organization
public class SetUpSite2
{
    public static void main(String[] args)
    {
        int currentYear = 2008;
        int age;
        statementOfPhilosophy();
        age = calculateAge(currentYear);
        System.out.println("Serving you for " +
            age +  " years");
    }
// Event Handlers official philosophy statement
    public static void statementOfPhilosophy()
    {
    System.out.println("Event Handlers
            Incorporated is");
    System.out.println("dedicated to making
            your event");
    System.out.println("a most memorable one.");
    }
// calculateAge method, based on origin 1977
    public static int calculateAge(int currDate)
    {
      int originYear = 1977;
      int years;
      years = currDate - originYear;
      return years;
    }
}
```

Figure 3-28 The `SetUpSite2` application

Figure 3-29 Output of the `SetUpSite2` application

CREATING A CLASS CONTAINING INSTANCE FIELDS AND METHODS

Next, you will create a class to store information about event sites for Event Handlers Incorporated.

To create the class:

1. Open a new document in your text editor.

2. Type the following class header and the curly braces to surround the class body:

```
public class EventSite
{
}
```

3. Type **private int siteNumber;** between the curly braces to insert the private data field that will hold an integer site number for each event site used by the company.

4. Within the `EventSite` class's curly braces and after the declaration of the `siteNumber` field, enter the following `getSiteNumber()` method to return the site number to any calling class:

```
public int getSiteNumber()
{
   return siteNumber;
}
```

5. Add the following method to the file after the final curly brace for the `getSiteNumber()` method, but prior to the closing curly brace for the `EventSite` class:

```
public void setSiteNumber(int n)
{
   siteNumber = n;
}
```

The argument *n* represents any number sent to this method.

6. Save the file as **EventSite.java** in the Chapter.03 folder on your Student Disk, compile it, and then correct any syntax errors. (You cannot run this file as a program because it does not contain a `public static main()` method.) The complete class appears in Figure 3-30.

```
public class EventSite
{
    private int siteNumber;
    public int getSiteNumber()
    {
        return siteNumber;
    }
    public void setSiteNumber(int n)
    {
        siteNumber = n;
    }
}
```

Figure 3-30 The `EventSite` class

CREATING A CLASS THAT INSTANTIATES OBJECTS OF ANOTHER CLASS

Next, you will modify the `SetUpSite2` application so that it instantiates an `EventSite` object.

To instantiate an object:

1. Open the **SetUpSite2.java** file from the Chapter.03 folder in your text editor. Change the class name to **SetUpSite3**, then immediately save the file as **SetUpSite3.java** in the Chapter.03 folder on your Student Disk.

2. Place the insertion point at the end of `int age;` within the `main()` method, press **Enter** to start a new line, and then type **EventSite oneSite = new EventSite();** to allocate memory for a new `EventSite` object named `oneSite`. This declaration statement calls the default `EventSite` constructor.

3. Just below the newly entered declaration for `oneSite`, to provide the `SetUpSite3` application with a variable to hold any site number returned from the `getSiteNumber()` method, type **int number;** and then press **Enter**.

4. Next, call the method `setSiteNumber()` to set the site number for `oneSite`. Type **oneSite.setSiteNumber(101);**. The number in parentheses could be any integer number.

5. After the statement that prints the age of the company, enter the statement that calls the `getSiteNumber()` method and assign its return value to the number variable:

```
number = oneSite.getSiteNumber();
```

6. To add a call to the `println()` method to display the value stored in `number`, type the following:

```
System.out.println("The number of the event site is " +
    number);
```

7. Save the program file (as SetUpSite3.java) in the Chapter.03 folder on your Student Disk.

8. Compile the program by typing **javac SetUpSite3.java** and pressing **Enter**. Correct any errors and compile again, if necessary.

9. Execute the program by typing **java SetUpSite3** and pressing **Enter**. Your output should look like Figure 3-31.

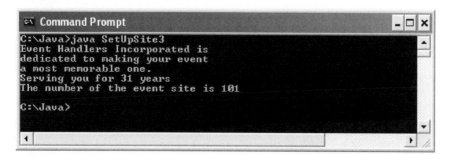

Figure 3-31 Output of the `SetUpSite3` application

MODIFYING A CLASS TO CONTAIN ADDITIONAL FIELDS AND METHODS

Currently, the `EventSite` class contains a single field and just two methods. To make the class more similar to a class a business might actually use, you will add private data fields and public methods that clients can use to access those fields.

To expand the `EventSite` class to contain data fields and methods:

1. In your text editor, open the **EventSite.java** file from the Chapter.03 folder. Add two new data fields to the `EventSite` class: a `double` to hold a usage fee for the site, and a `String` to hold the site manager's last name. Also add four new methods to set and get data from each of the two new fields. To ensure that the methods are easy to locate later, you place them in alphabetical order within the class. Figure 3-32 shows the new class with the newly added code shaded.

2. Save the file (as EventSite.java) and compile it. If necessary, correct any errors and compile it again.

```java
public class EventSite
{
    private int siteNumber;
    private double usageFee;
    private String managerName;
    public double getFee()
    {
        return usageFee;
    }
    public String getManager()
    {
        return managerName;
    }
    public int getSiteNumber()
    {
        return siteNumber;
    }
    public void setFee(double fee)
    {
        usageFee = fee;
    }
    public void setManager(String manager)
    {
        managerName = manager;
    }
    public void setSiteNumber(int n)
    {
        siteNumber = n;
    }
}
```

Figure 3-32 The `EventSite` class with three fields and six methods

WRITING AN APPLICATION TO DEMONSTRATE THE NEW CLASS

You have created an `EventSite` class that contains both data and methods. However, no actual event sites exist until you write an application that instantiates one or more `EventSite` objects to give actual values to the data fields for that object, and to manipulate the data in the fields using the class methods. Next, you will create a program to test the new, expanded `EventSite` class.

To create the test program:

1. Open a new document in the text editor, and then enter the class that tests the new expanded `EventSite` class. The class should look like Figure 3-33.

```
public class TestExpandedClass
{
    public static void main(String[] args)
    {
        EventSite oneSite = new EventSite();
        int number;
        double amount;
        String name;
        oneSite.setSiteNumber(101);
        oneSite.setFee(3125.75);
        oneSite.setManager("Nancy Kenneth");
        number = oneSite.getSiteNumber();
        amount = oneSite.getFee();
        name = oneSite.getManager();
        System.out.println("Site number " + number
            + " is managed by " + name);
        System.out.println("The usage fee is $" + amount);
    }
}
```

Figure 3-33 The `TestExpandedClass` application

> **NOTE** You should get into the habit of documenting your programs with your name, today's date, and a brief explanation of the program. Your instructor might also ask you to insert additional information as comment text.

2. Save the file as **TestExpandedClass.java** in the Chapter.03 folder on your Student Disk. Compile the program and correct any errors, if necessary.

3. Execute the class with the command-line statement **java TestExpandedClass**. Your output should look like Figure 3-34.

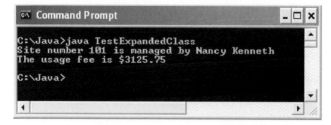

Figure 3-34 Output of the `TestExpandedClass` application

ADDING A CONSTRUCTOR TO A CLASS

Next, you will add a default constructor to the `EventSite` class and demonstrate that it is called automatically when you instantiate an `EventSite` object.

To add a constructor to the `EventSite` class:

1. Open the **EventSite.java** file in your text editor.

2. Place the insertion point at the end of the line containing the last field declaration (`managerName`), and then press **Enter** to start a new line.

3. Add the following constructor function that sets any `EventSite` `siteNumber` to 999 and any manager's name to "ZZZ" upon construction:

```
public EventSite()
{
    siteNumber = 999;
    managerName = "ZZZ";
}
```

4. Save the file (as EventSite.java), compile it, and correct any errors.

5. Open a new text file and create a test class named **TestConstructor** using the code shown in Figure 3-35.

> **NOTE** To save typing, you can create the class shown in Figure 3-35 by opening the TestExpandedClass.java file that you created earlier in this chapter, changing the class name to `TestConstructor`, deleting the three statements that set the object's values, and saving the modified file as TestConstructor.java.

```
public class TestConstructor
{
    public static void main(String[] args)
    {
        EventSite oneSite = new EventSite();
        int number;
        double amount;
        String name;
        number = oneSite.getSiteNumber();
        amount = oneSite.getFee();
        name = oneSite.getManager();
        System.out.println("Site number " + number
            + " is managed by " + name);
        System.out.println("The usage fee is $" + amount);
    }
}
```

Figure 3-35 The `TestConstructor` application

6. Save the file as **TestConstructor.java** in the Chapter.03 folder on your Student Disk, compile the file, and correct any syntax errors.

7. Execute the program and confirm that it declares a `oneSite` object of type `EventSite`, calls the constructor, and assigns the indicated initial values, as shown in Figure 3-36.

Figure 3-36 Output of the `TestConstructor` application

KEY TERMS

A **method** is a program module that contains a series of statements that carry out a task.

When you **invoke** or **call** a method, you execute it.

The **calling method** makes a **method call** that invokes the **called method**.

Arguments or **parameters** are the data items sent to methods.

Returning a value sends a data value from a called method back to the calling method.

Abstraction is the programming feature that allows you to use a method name to encapsulate a series of statements.

The **method declaration** is the first line, or **header**.

Access modifiers are also called **access specifiers**.

Implementation hiding is a principle of object-oriented programming that describes the encapsulation of method details within a class.

The **interface** to a method includes the method's return type, name, and arguments. It is the part that a client sees and uses.

A **local variable** is known only within the boundaries of a method.

The arguments in a method call are often referred to as **actual parameters**.

The variables in the method declaration that accept the values from the actual parameters are the **formal parameters**.

A method's return type is known more succinctly as a **method's type**.

A **return statement** sends a value from a called method back to the calling method.

An **is-a relationship** is the relationship between an object and the class of which it is a member.

An object is an **instantiation** of a class, or one tangible example of a class.

A **class client** or **class user** is an application or class that instantiates objects of another prewritten class.

Classes can be **extended**, or used as a basis for any other class.

Data fields, also called simply **fields**, are variables you declare within a class, but outside of any method.

Instance variables are nonstatic data fields; one copy exists for every object created.

Assigning **private access** to a field means that no other classes can access the field's values, and only methods of the same class are allowed to set, get, or otherwise use private variables.

Information hiding is the object-oriented programming principle used when creating private access for data fields; a class's private data can be changed or manipulated only by a class's own methods, and not by methods that belong to other classes.

Nonstatic methods, those methods used with object instantiations, are called **instance methods**.

Methods that set values are called **mutator methods**.

Methods that retrieve values are called **accessor methods**.

You use the **new operator** to allocate the needed memory for an object.

A **constructor method**, or more simply, a **constructor**, is a method that establishes an object.

A **primary key** is a unique identifier for data within a database.

A **default constructor** is one that is created automatically by the Java compiler.

CHAPTER SUMMARY

» A method is a series of statements that carry out a task. Methods must include a declaration (or header or definition), an opening curly brace, a body, and a closing curly brace. A method declaration contains optional access modifiers, the return type for the method, the method name, an opening parenthesis, an optional list of method arguments, and a closing parenthesis.

» When you write the method declaration for a method that can receive an argument, you need to include the argument type and a local name for the argument within the method declaration parentheses. You can call a method within a program using either a constant value or a variable as an argument.

» You can pass multiple arguments to methods by listing the arguments separated by commas within the call to the method. The arguments you send to the method must match (both in number and in type) the parameters listed in the method declaration.

» The return type for a method (the method's type) can be any Java type, including `void`. You use a return statement to send a value back to a class that contains a statement that calls a method.

» Class objects have attributes and methods associated with them. Class instance methods that will be used with objects are nonstatic. You can send messages to objects using their methods.

» A class header contains an optional access modifier, the keyword `class`, and any legal identifier you choose for the name of your class. The instance variables, or fields, of a class are placed as statements within the class's curly braces.

» Declaring a class does not create any actual objects; you must instantiate any objects that are members of a class. To create an object that is an instance of a class, you supply a type and an identifier, and then you allocate computer memory for that object using the `new` operator.

» A constructor method establishes an object and provides specific initial values for the object's data fields. A constructor method always has the same name as the class of which it is a member. By default, numeric fields are set to 0 (zero), character fields are set to Unicode '\u0000', Boolean fields are set to `false`, and object type fields are set to `null`.

» In object-oriented programming, everything is an object, and every object is a member of a more general class. An object is an instantiation of a class, or one tangible example of a class. The concept of a class is useful because of its reusability.

» With well-written object-oriented programming methods, using implementation hiding, or the encapsulation of method details within a class, means that the calling method needs to understand only the interface to the called method. In this case, the calling method only needs to know the name of the called method, what type of information to send it, and what type of return data to expect.

» Assigning private access to a field means that no other classes can access the field's values, and only methods of the same class are allowed to set, get, or otherwise use private variables. The principle used in creating private access is sometimes called information hiding, which means that a class's private data can be changed or manipulated only by a class's own methods, and not by methods that belong to other classes. Data fields should usually be private and a client application should be able to access them only through the public interfaces—that is, through the class's public methods.

REVIEW QUESTIONS

1. In Java, methods must include all of the following except _____ .

   a. a declaration   c. curly braces

   b. a call to another method   d. a body

2. All method declarations contain _____ .

   a. the keyword `static`

   b. one or more explicitly named access modifiers

   c. arguments

   d. parentheses

3. A public static method named `computeSum()` is located in `classA`. To call the method from within `classB`, use the statement _____ .

   a. `computeSum(classB);`

   b. `classB(computeSum());`

   c. `classA.computeSum();`

   d. You cannot call `computeSum()` from within `classB`.

4. Which of the following method declarations is correct for a static method named `displayFacts()` if the method receives an `int` argument?

   a. `public static int displayFacts()`

   b. `public void displayFacts(int data)`

   c. `public static void displayFacts(int data)`

   d. Two of these are correct.

5. The method with the declaration `public static int aMethod(double d)` has a method type of _____ .

   a. `static`   c. `double`

   b. `int`   d. You cannot determine the method type.

6. Which of the following is a correct call to a method declared as `public static double aMethod(char code)`?

   a. `double aMethod();`   c. `aMethod(char 'M');`

   b. `double aMethod('V');`   d. `aMethod('Q');`

7. A method is declared as `public static void showResults(double d, int i)`. Which of the following is a correct method call?

   a. `showResults(double d, int i);`

   b. `showResults(12.2, 67);`

   c. `showResults(4, 99.7);`

   d. Two of these are correct.

8. The method with the declaration `public static char procedure(double d)` has a method type of _____ .

   a. `public`   c. `char`

   b. `static`   d. `double`

9. The method `public static boolean testValue(int response)` returns _____ .

   a. a Boolean value   c. no value

   b. an integer value   d. You cannot determine what is returned.

10. Which of the following could be the last legally coded line of a method declared as `public static int getVal(double sum)`?

    a. `return;`   c. `return 2.3;`

    b. `return 77;`   d. Any of these could be the last coded line of the method.

11. The nonstatic data components of a class are often referred to as the _____ of that class.

    a. access types   c. methods

    b. instance variables   d. objects

12. Class objects can have both attributes and _____ .

    a. fields   c. methods

    b. data   d. instances

13. You send messages or information to an object through its _____ .

    a. fields   c. classes

    b. methods   d. type

14. A program or class that instantiates objects of another prewritten class is a (n) _____ .

    a. class client   c. object

    b. superclass   d. patron

15. The body of a class is always written _____ .

    a. in a single line, as the first statement in a class

    b. within parentheses

    c. between curly braces

    d. as a method call

16. Most class data fields are _____ .

    a. private   c. static

    b. public   d. final

17. The concept of allowing a class's private data to be changed only by a class's own methods is known as _____ .

    a. structured logic   c. information hiding

    b. object orientation   d. data masking

18. Suppose you declare a class object as `Book thisBook;`. Before you store data in `thisBook,` you _____ .

    a. also must explicitly allocate memory for it

    b. need not explicitly allocate memory for it

    c. must explicitly allocate memory for it only if it has a constructor

    d. can declare it to use no memory

19. If a class is named `Student`, the class constructor name is _____ .

    a. any legal Java identifier   c. `StudentConstructor`

    b. any legal Java identifier that begins with S   d. `Student`

20. If you use the default constructor when you create an object, _____ .

    a. numeric fields are set to 0 (zero)   c. Boolean fields are set to `true`

    b. character fields are set to blank   d. All of these are true.

EXERCISES

1. Create an application named `TestMethods` whose `main()` method holds two integer variables. Assign values to the variables. In turn, pass each value to methods named `displayIt()`, `displayItTimesTwo()`, and `displayItPlusOneHundred()`. Create each method to perform the task its name implies. Save the application as **TestMethods.java** in the Chapter.03 folder on your Student Disk.

2. a. Create an application named `Numbers` whose `main()` method holds two integer variables. Assign values to the variables. Pass both variables to methods named `sum()` and `difference()`. Create the methods `sum()` and `difference()`; they compute the sum of and difference between the values of two arguments, respectively. Each method should perform the appropriate computation and display the results. Save the application as **Numbers.java** in the Chapter.03 folder on your Student Disk.

    b. Add a method named `product()` to the `Numbers` class. The `product()` method should compute the multiplication product of two integers, but not display the answer. Instead, it should return the answer to the calling method, which displays the answer. Save the application as **Numbers2.java** in the Chapter.03 folder on your Student Disk.

3. Create a class named `Eggs`. Its `main()` method holds an integer variable named `numberOfEggs` to which you will assign a value. Create a method to which you pass `numberOfEggs`. The method displays the eggs in dozens; for example, 50 eggs is four full dozen (with two eggs remaining). Save the application as **Eggs.java** in the Chapter.03 folder on your Student Disk.

4. Create a class named `Monogram`. Its `main()` method has three character variables that hold your first, middle, and last initials, respectively. Create a method to which you pass the three initials and which displays the initials twice—once in the order first, middle, last and a second time in traditional monogram style (first, last, middle). Save the application as **Monogram.java** in the Chapter.03 folder on your Student Disk.

5. Create a class named `Exponent`. Its `main()` method holds an integer value and in turn passes the value to a method that squares the number and to a method that cubes the number. The `main()` method prints the results. Create the two methods that respectively square and cube an integer that is passed to them, returning the calculated value. Save the application as **Exponent.java** in the Chapter.03 folder on your Student Disk.

6. Create a class named `Cube` that displays the result of cubing a number. Pass a number to a method that cubes the number and returns the result. The result is displayed from within the `main()` method. Save the application as **Cube.java** in the Chapter.03 folder on your Student Disk.

7. Create an application that contains a method that computes the final price for a sales transaction. The `main()` method contains variables that hold the price of an item, the salesperson's commission expressed as a percentage, and the customer discount expressed as a percentage. Create a `calculation()` method that determines the final price and returns the value to the calling method. The `calculation()` method requires three arguments: product price, salesperson commission rate, and customer discount rate. A product's final price is the original price plus the commission amount minus the discount amount; the customer discount is taken as a percentage of the total price after the salesperson commission has been added to the original price. Save the application as **Calculator.java** in the Chapter.03 folder on your Student Disk.

8. Write an application that displays the result of dividing two numbers and displays any remainder. The `main()` method contains variables that hold the values. Perform the calculation and display the results in a separate method from the `main()` method. Save the application as **Divide.java** in the Chapter.03 folder on your Student Disk.

9. Write an application that calculates and displays the weekly salary for an employee who earns $25 an hour, works 40 regular hours and 13 overtime hours, and earns time and one-half (wage * 1.5) for overtime hours worked. Create a separate method to do the calculation and return the result to the `main()` method to be displayed. Save the program as **Salary.java** in the Chapter.03 folder on your Student Disk.

10. a. Write an application that contains a method that calculates and displays the conversion of any amount of money into the fewest bills; it displays the number of 20s, 10s, 5s, and 1s needed. Create a `main()` method that contains a variable that holds a number of dollars, initializes the value to 57, and passes the dollar figure to the conversion method. Save the program as **Dollars.java** in the Chapter.03 folder on your Student Disk.

    b. In the Dollars.java application, alter the value of the variable that holds the amount of money. For example, try rerunning the program with 12 and 99. Run the program and confirm that the amount of each dollar value is broken down into bills correctly.

11. Write an application that calculates and displays the amount of money you would have if you invested $1,000 at 5% interest for one year. Create a separate method to do the calculation and return the result to be displayed. Save the program as **Interest.java** in the Chapter.03 folder on your Student Disk.

12. a. Create a class named `Pizza`. Data fields include a `String` for toppings (such as pepperoni), an integer for diameter in inches (such as 12), and a `double` for price (such as 13.99). Include methods to get and set values for each of these fields. Save the class as **Pizza.java** in the Chapter.03 folder on your Student Disk.

    b. Create a class named `TestPizza` that instantiates one `Pizza` object and demonstrates the use of the `Pizza` set and get methods. Save this application as **TestPizza.java** in the Chapter.03 folder on your Student Disk.

13. a. Create a class named `Student`. A `Student` has fields for an ID number, number of credit hours earned, and number of points earned. (For example, many schools compute grade point averages based on a scale of 4, so a three-credit-hour class in which a student earns an A is worth 12 points.) Include methods to assign values to all fields. A `Student` also has a field for grade point average. Include a method to compute the grade point average field by dividing points by credit hours earned. Write methods to display the values in each `Student` field. Save this class as **Student.java** in the Chapter.03 folder on your Student Disk.

 b. Write a class named `ShowStudent` that instantiates a `Student` object from the class you created and assign values to its fields. Compute the `Student` grade point average, and then display all the values associated with the `Student`. Save the application as **ShowStudent.java** in the Chapter.03 folder on your Student Disk.

 c. Create a constructor method for the `Student` class you created. The constructor should initialize each `Student`'s ID number to 9999, his or her points earned to 12, and credit hours to 3 (resulting in a grade point average of 4.0). Write a program that demonstrates that the constructor works by instantiating an object and displaying the initial values. Save the application as **ShowStudent2.java**.

14. a. Create a class named `Circle` with fields named `radius`, `area`, and `diameter`. Include a constructor that sets the radius to 1. Also include methods named `setRadius()`; `getRadius()`; `computeDiameter()`, which computes a circle's diameter; and `computeArea()`, which computes a circle's area. (The diameter of a circle is twice its radius, and the area is 3.14 multiplied by the square of the radius.) Save the class as **Circle.java** in the Chapter.03 folder on your Student Disk.

 b. Create a class named `TestCircle` whose `main()` method declares three `Circle` objects. Using the `setRadius()` method, assign one `Circle` a small radius value and assign another a larger radius value. Do not assign a value to the radius of the third circle; instead, retain the value assigned at construction. Call `computeDiameter()` and `computeArea()` for each circle and display the results. Save the application as **TestCircle.java** in the Chapter.03 folder on your Student Disk.

>> **NOTE** If you were designing a `Circle` class, you might choose not to store the diameter or area because they can be recalculated from the radius value at any time. You might also choose to have the `setRadius()` method call the `computeDiameter()` and `computeArea()` methods because those calculations depend on the radius.

15. a. Create a class named `Checkup` with fields that hold a patient number, two blood pressure figures (systolic and diastolic), and two cholesterol figures (LDL and HDL). Include methods to get and set each of the fields. Include a method named `computeRatio()` that divides LDL cholesterol by HDL cholesterol and displays the result. Include an additional method named `ExplainRatio()` that explains that HDL is known as "good cholesterol" and that a ratio of 3.5 or lower is considered optimum. Save the class as **Checkup.java** in the Chapter.03 folder on your Student Disk.

 b. Create a class named `TestCheckup` whose `main()` method declares four `Checkup` objects. Provide values for each field for each patient, and then display the values. Blood pressure numbers are usually displayed with a slash between the systolic and diastolic values. (Typical numbers are values such as 110/78 or 130/90.) With the cholesterol figures, display the explanation of the cholesterol ratio calculation.

(Typical cholesterol numbers are values such as 100 and 40 or 180 and 70.) Save the application as **TestCheckup.java** in the Chapter.03 folder on your Student Disk.

16. a. Create a class named Invoice containing fields for an item number, name, quantity, price, and total cost. Create instance methods that set the item name, quantity, and price. Also include a displayLine() method that calculates the total cost for the item (as price times quantity), then displays the item number, name, quantity, price, and total cost. Save the class as **Invoice.java** in the Chapter.03 folder on your Student Disk.

   b. Create a class named TestInvoice whose main() method declares three Invoice items. Provide values for each, and display them. Save the application as **TestInvoice.java** in the Chapter.03 folder on your Student Disk.

17. Write an application that schedules several meetings for a meeting room. The application should contain the day of the week, starting time, and ending time for each meeting. Use two classes. The first class, named Meeting, is used to declare Meeting objects. The class contains fields that hold meeting data (day of the week, starting time, and ending time) and methods to get and set the values of the fields. The other class, named RoomSchedule, creates objects representing two Meetings, sets values, and displays the values. Save the classes as **Meeting.java** and **RoomSchedule.java**, respectively, in the Chapter.03 folder on your Student Disk.

DEBUGGING EXERCISES

Each of the following files saved in the Chapter.03 folder on your Student Disk has syntax and/or logic errors. In each case, determine and fix the problem. After you correct the errors, save each file using the same filename preceded with Fix. For example, DebugThree1.java will become FixDebugThree1.java.

   a. DebugThree1.java   c. DebugThree3.java

   b. DebugThree2.java   d. DebugThree4.java

> **>> NOTE** When you change a filename, remember to change every instance of the class name within the file so that it matches the new filename. In Java, the filename and class name must always match.

CASE PROJECT

HOWARD, FINE, AND HOWARD

The law firm of Howard, Fine, and Howard wants to develop two classes—a Client class that holds data about the firm's clients, and an Attorney class that holds data about each of the attorneys who work for the firm. Client data includes a client number, last name, first name, primary attorney's ID number, and balance owed to the firm. Attorney data includes an ID number, last name, first name, and annual salary. Each class includes public get and set instance methods for accessing the data. Create an application that instantiates five Clients and two Attorneys, assigns appropriate values to their data fields, and displays the values in an attractive format. Save the files as **Client.java**, **Attorney.java**, and **LawFirm.java** in the Chapter.03 folder on your Student Disk.

GAME ZONE

1. Playing cards are used in many computer games, including versions of such classics as Solitaire, Hearts, and Poker. Design a `Card` class that contains a character data field to hold a suit ('s' for spades, 'h' for hearts, 'd' for diamonds, or 'c' for clubs) and an integer data field for a value from 1 to 13. (When you learn more about string handling in Chapter 7, you can modify the class to hold words for the suits, such as "spades" or "hearts," as well as words for some of the values—for example, "ace" or "king".) Include `get` and `set` methods for each field. Save the class as **Card.java**.

   Write an application that randomly selects two playing cards and prints their values. Simply assign a suit to each of the cards, but generate a random number for each card's value. Appendix D contains information on generating random numbers. To fully understand the process, you must learn more about Java classes and methods. However, for now, you can copy the following statement to generate a random number between 1 and 13 and assign it to a variable:

   ```
   myValue = ((int)(Math.random() * 100) % 13 + 1);
   ```

   After you learn about decision making in Chapter 5, you will be able to have the game determine the higher card. For now, just observe how the card values change as you execute the program multiple times. Save the application as **PickTwoCards.java**.

   >> **NOTE** You use the `Math.random()` function to generate a random number. The function call uses only a class and method name—no object—so you know the `random()` method must be a static method.

2. Computer games often contain different characters or creatures. For example, you might design a game in which alien beings possess specific characteristics such as color, number of eyes, or number of lives. Design a character for a game, creating a class to hold at least three attributes for each character. Include methods to get and set each of the character's attributes. Save the file as **MyCharacter.java**. Then write an application in which you create at least two characters. In turn, pass each character to a display method that prints the character's attributes. Save the application as **TwoCharacters.java**.

UP FOR DISCUSSION

1. One of the advantages to writing a program that is subdivided into methods is that such a structure allows different programmers to write separate methods, thus dividing the work. Would you prefer to write a large program by yourself, or to work on a team in which each programmer produces one or more modules? Why?

2. In this chapter, you learned that hidden implementations are often said to exist in a black box. What are the advantages to this approach in both programming and real life? Are there any disadvantages?

3. In this chapter, you learned that instance data and methods belong to objects (which are class members), but that static data and methods belong to a class as a whole. Consider the real-life class named `StateInTheUnitedStates`. What are some real-life attributes of this class that are static attributes, and what are some that are instance attributes? Create another example of a real-life class and discuss what its static and instance members might be.

4. In this chapter, you learned that well-placed comments can be helpful. Can you think of any circumstances under which program comments would be a detriment?

4

MORE OBJECT CONCEPTS

In this chapter, you will:

Understand blocks and scope
Overload a method
Learn about ambiguity
Send arguments to constructors
Overload constructors
Learn about the `this` reference
Use static variables
Work with constants
Use automatically imported, prewritten constants and
    methods
Use the explicitly imported prewritten class
    `GregorianCalendar`

UNDERSTANDING BLOCKS AND SCOPE

Within any class or method, the code between a pair of curly braces is called a **block**. For example, the method shown in Figure 4-1 contains two blocks. The first block contains another, so it is an example of an **outside block** (also called an **outer block**). It begins immediately after the method declaration and ends at the end of the method. The second block (shaded in Figure 4-1) is called the **inside block** or **inner block**. It is contained within the second set of curly braces and contains two executable statements: the declaration of anotherNumber and a println() statement. The inside block is **nested**, or contained entirely within, the outside block. A block can exist entirely within another block or entirely outside and separate from another block, but blocks can never overlap. For example, if a method contains two opening curly braces, indicating the start of two blocks, the next closing curly brace always closes the inner (second) block—it cannot close the outer block because that would make the blocks overlap. Another way to state this concept is that whenever you encounter a closing brace that ends a block, it always closes the most recently started block.

```
public static void methodWithNestedBlocks()
{
   int aNumber = 10;   // aNumber comes into existence
   System.out.println("In outer block, aNumber is "  + aNumber);
   {
      int anotherNumber = 512;
         // anotherNumber comes into existence
      System.out.println("In inner block, aNumber is " +
         aNumber + " and another number is " + anotherNumber);
   }   // anotherNumber ceases to exist
   System.out.println("In outer block, aNumber is "  + aNumber);
} // aNumber ceases to exist
```

Figure 4-1 A method with nested blocks

If you declare a variable in one program that you write, you cannot refer to that variable in another program (although you can declare another variable with the same name in the new program). Similarly, when you declare a variable within a block, you cannot refer to that variable outside the block. The portion of a program within which you can refer to a variable is the variable's **scope**. A variable comes into existence, or **comes into scope**, when you declare it. A variable ceases to exist, or **goes out of scope**, at the end of the block in which it is declared.

In the methodWithNestedBlocks() method shown in Figure 4-1, the variable aNumber exists from the point of its declaration until the end of the method. This means aNumber exists both in the outer block and in the inner block and can be used anywhere in the method. The variable anotherNumber comes into existence within the inner block; anotherNumber ceases to exist when the inner block ends and cannot be used beyond its block. Figure 4-2 shows the output when the method in Figure 4-1 is called from another method.

> **NOTE**
> Although you can create as many variables and blocks as you need within any program, it is not wise to do so without a reason. The use of unnecessary variables and blocks increases the likelihood of improper use of variable names and scope.

```
Command Prompt                                      - □ ×
C:\Java>java TestMethodWithNestedBlocks
In outer block, aNumber is 10
In inner block, aNumber is 10 and another number is 512
In outer block, aNumber is 10

C:\Java>_
```

Figure 4-2 Output produced by application that uses methodWithNestedBlocks()

Figure 4-3 shows a method containing some invalid statements. The first assignment aNumber = 75; is invalid because aNumber has not been declared yet. Similarly, anotherNumber = 489; (Invalid statement 2) is invalid because anotherNumber has not been declared yet, and Invalid statement 3 is invalid because anotherNumber still has not been declared. After you declare anotherNumber, you can use it for the remainder of the block, but Invalid statement 4 is outside the block in which anotherNumber was declared,

```java
public static void methodWithInvalidStatements()
{
    aNumber = 75;  // Invalid statement 1
    int aNumber = 22;
    aNumber = 6;
    anotherNumber = 489;  // Invalid statement 2
    {
        anotherNumber = 165;  // Invalid statement 3
        int anotherNumber = 99;
        anotherNumber = 2;
    }
    aNumber = 50;
    anotherNumber = 34; // Invalid statement 4
}
aNumber = 29;  // Invalid statement 5
```

Figure 4-3 The methodWithInvalidStatements() method

> **NOTE**
> You are not required to vertically align the opening and closing braces for a block, but your programs are much easier to read if you do.

and by the time Invalid statement 4 executes, `anotherNumber` has gone out of scope. The last statement in Figure 4-3, `aNumber = 29;` does not work because it falls outside the block in which `aNumber` was declared; it actually falls outside the entire `methodWithInvalidStatements()` method.

Within a method, you can declare a variable with the same name multiple times, as long as each declaration is in its own nonoverlapping block. For example, the two declarations of variables named `someVar` in Figure 4-4 are valid because each variable is contained within its own block. The first instance of `someVar` has gone out of scope before the second instance comes into scope.

```
public static void twoDeclarations()
{
   { // Begin first block
     int someVar = 7;
     System.out.println(someVar);
   }  // End first block
   {  // Begin second block
     int someVar = 845;    // a new someVar
     System.out.println(someVar);
   }  // End second block
}
```

Figure 4-4 The `twoDeclarations()` method

You cannot declare the same variable name more than once within a block, even if a block contains other blocks. When you declare a variable more than once in a block, you are attempting to **redeclare the variable**—an illegal action. For example, in Figure 4-5, the second declaration of `aValue` causes an error because you cannot declare the same variable twice within the outer block of the method. By the same reasoning, the third declaration of `aValue` is also invalid, even though it appears within a new block. The block that contains the third declaration is entirely within the outside block, so the first declaration of `aValue` has not gone out of scope.

```
public static void invalidRedeclarationMethod()
{
   int aValue = 35;  // First declaration is okay
   int aValue = 44;  // Second declaration is invalid
   {
     int anotherValue = 0;  // Valid - different identifier
     int aValue = 10;  // Third declaration is also invalid
   }
}
```

Figure 4-5 The `invalidRedeclarationMethod()`

> **NOTE**
> Object-oriented programmers also use the term "override" when a child class contains a field or method that has the same name as one in the parent class. You will learn more about inheritance in Chapter 11.

Although you cannot declare a variable twice within the same method, you can declare a variable within one method of a class and use the same variable name within another method of the class. In this case, the variable declared inside each method resides in its own location in computer memory. When you use the variable's name within the method in which it is declared, it takes precedence over, or **overrides**, any other variable with the same name in another method.

In other words, a locally declared variable always masks or hides another variable with the same name elsewhere in the class. For example, consider the class in Figure 4-6. In the main() method of the OverridingVariable class, aNumber is declared and assigned the value 10. When the program calls firstMethod(), a new variable is declared with the same name but with a different memory address and a new value. The new variable exists only within firstMethod(), where it is displayed holding the value 77. After firstMethod() executes and the logic returns to the main() method, the original aNumber is displayed, containing 10. When aNumber is passed to secondMethod(), a copy is made within the method. This copy has the same identifier as the original aNumber, but a different memory address. So, within secondMethod(), when the value is changed to 862 and displayed, it has no effect on the original variable in main(). When the logic returns to main() after secondMethod(), the original value is displayed again. Examine the output in Figure 4-7 to understand the sequence of events.

```java
public class OverridingVariable
{
    public static void main(String[] args)
    {
        int aNumber = 10;
        System.out.println("In main(), aNumber is " + aNumber);
        firstMethod();
        System.out.println("Back in main(), aNumber is " + aNumber);
        secondMethod(aNumber);
        System.out.println("Back in main() again, aNumber is " + aNumber);
    }
    public static void firstMethod()
    {
        int aNumber = 77;
        System.out.println("In firstMethod(), aNumber is " + aNumber);
    }
    public static void secondMethod(int aNumber)
    {
        aNumber = 862;
        System.out.println("In secondMethod(), aNumber is " + aNumber);
    }
}
```

Figure 4-6 The OverridingVariable class

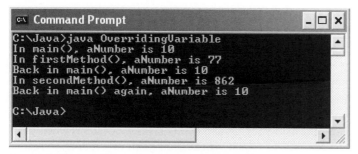

Figure 4-7 Output of the OverridingVariable application

> **»NOTE** You are familiar with local names overriding names defined elsewhere. If someone in your household is named "Eric," and someone in the house next door is named "Eric," members of your household who talk about "Eric" are referring to the local version. They would add a qualifier such as "Eric Johnson" or "Eric next door" to refer to the nonlocal version.

When they have the same name, variables within methods of a class also override class instance variables. Figure 4-8 shows an `Employee` class that contains two instance variables and three `void` methods. The `setValues()` method provides values for the two class instance fields. Whenever the method named `methodThatUsesInstanceAttributes()` is used with an `Employee` object, the instance values for `empNum` and `empPayRate` are used. However, when the other method, `methodThatUsesLocalVariables()`, is used with an `Employee` object, the local variable values within the method, 33333 and 555.55, override the class's instance variables. Figure 4-9 shows a short application that declares an `Employee` object and uses each method; Figure 4-10 shows the output.

```
public class Employee
{
    private int empNum;
    private double empPayRate;
    public void setValues()
    {
        empNum = 111;
        empPayRate = 22.22;
    }
    public void methodThatUsesInstanceAttributes()
    {
        System.out.println("Employee number is " + empNum);
        System.out.println("Pay rate is " + empPayRate);
    }
    public void methodThatUsesLocalVariables()
    {
        int empNum = 33333;
        double empPayRate = 555.55;
        System.out.println("Employee number is " + empNum);
        System.out.println("Pay rate is " + empPayRate);
    }
}
```

Figure 4-8 The `Employee` class

> **»NOTE**
> Programmers frequently use the same name for a class instance field and an argument to a method simply because it is the "best name" to use; in these cases, the programmer must use the `this` reference, which you will learn about later in this chapter.

When you write programs, you might choose to avoid confusing situations that arise when you give the same name to a class instance field and a local method variable. But, if you do use the same name, be aware that within the method, the method's local variable overrides the instance variable.

It is important to understand the impact that blocks and methods have on your variables. Variables and fields with the same names represent different memory locations when they are declared within different scopes. After you understand the scope of variables, you can more easily locate the source of many errors within your programs.

```
public class TestEmployeeMethods
{
    public static void main(String[] args)
    {
        Employee aWorker = new Employee();
        aWorker.setValues();
        aWorker.methodThatUsesInstanceAttributes();
        aWorker.methodThatUsesLocalVariables();
    }
}
```

Figure 4-9 The `TestEmployeeMethods` application

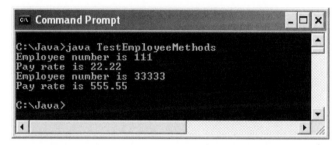

Figure 4-10 Output of the `TestEmployeeMethods` application

OVERLOADING A METHOD

Overloading involves using one term to indicate diverse meanings, or writing multiple methods with the same name but with different arguments. When you use the English language, you overload words all the time. When you say "open the door," "open your eyes," and "open a computer file," you are talking about three very different actions using very different methods and producing very different results. However, anyone who speaks English fluently has no trouble understanding your meaning because the verb *open* is understood in the context of the noun that follows it.

When you overload a Java method, you write multiple methods with a shared name. The compiler understands your meaning based on the arguments you use with the method. For example, suppose you create a class method to apply a simple interest rate to a bank balance. The method is named `calculateInterest()`; it receives two `double` arguments—the balance and the interest rate—and displays the multiplied result. Figure 4-11 shows the method.

```
public static void calculateInterest(double bal, double rate)
{
    double interest;
    interest = bal * rate;
    System.out.println("Simple interest on $" + bal +
        " at  " + rate + "% rate is " + interest);
}
```

Figure 4-11 The `calculateInterest()` method with two double arguments

NOTE The `calculateInterest()` method in Figure 4-11 can receive integer arguments, even though it is defined as needing `double` arguments, because integers are promoted or cast automatically to `doubles`, as you learned in Chapter 2.

When an application calls the `calculateInterest()` method and passes two `double` values, as in `calculateInterest(1000.00, 0.04)`, the interest is calculated correctly as 4% of $1000.00. Assume, however, that different users want to calculate interest using different argument types. Some users who want to indicate an interest rate of 4% might use 0.04; others might use 4 and assume that it means 4%. When the `calculateInterest()` method is called with the arguments $1000.00 and 0.04, the interest is calculated correctly as 40.00. When the method is called using $1000.00 and 4, the interest is calculated incorrectly as 4000.00.

A solution for the conflicting use of numbers to represent parameter values is to overload the `calculateInterest()` method. For example, in addition to the `calculateInterest()` method shown in Figure 4-11, you could add the method shown in Figure 4-12.

```
public static void calculateInterest(double bal, int rate)
                                             // Notice rate type
{
   double interest, rateAsPercent;
   rateAsPercent = rate / 100.0; // Converts whole number rate
      // to decimal equivalent
   interest = bal * rateAsPercent;
   System.out.println("Simple interest on $" + bal +
      " at  " + rate + "% rate is " + interest);
}
```

Figure 4-12 The `calculateInterest()` method with a `double` argument and an `int` argument

NOTE Note the `rateAsPercent` figure is calculated by dividing by 100.0 and not by 100. If two integers are divided, the result is a truncated integer; dividing by a `double` 100.0 causes the result to be a `double`. Alternatively, you could use an explicit cast such as `rateAsPercent = (double)rate / 100.0`.

If an application calls the method `calculateInterest()` using two `double` arguments—for example, `calculateInterest(1000.00, 0.04)`—the first version of the method, the one shown in Figure 4-11, executes. However, if an integer is used as the second parameter in a call to `calculateInterest()`—as in `calculateInterest(1000.00, 4)`—the second version of the method, the one shown in Figure 4-12, executes. In this second example, the whole number rate figure is correctly divided by 100.0 before it is used to determine the interest earned.

Of course, you could use methods with different names to solve the dilemma of producing an accurate interest figure—for example, `calculateInterestUsingDouble()` and `calculateInterestUsingInt()`. However, it is easier and more convenient for programmers who use your methods to remember just one method name that they can use in the form that is most appropriate for their programs. It is a convenience to be able to use one reasonable name for tasks that are functionally identical except for argument types.

LEARNING ABOUT AMBIGUITY

When an application contains just one version of a method, you can call the method using a parameter of the correct data type, or one that can be promoted to the correct data type. For example, consider the simple method shown in Figure 4-13.

```
public static void simpMeth(double d)
{
    System.out.println("Method receives double parameter");
}
```

Figure 4-13 The `simpMeth()` method with a `double` argument

If you write an application in which you declare `doubleValue` as a `double` variable and `intValue` as an `int` variable (as shown in Figure 4-14), either method call `simpMeth (doubleValue);` or `simpMeth(intValue);` results in the output "Method receives double parameter". When you call the method with the `double` argument, the method works as expected. When you call the method with the integer argument, the integer is cast as (or promoted to) a `double`, and the method also works. The output is shown in Figure 4-15.

```
public class CallSimpMeth
{
    public static void main(String[] args)
    {
        double doubleValue = 45.67;
        int intValue = 17;
        simpMeth(doubleValue);
        simpMeth(intValue);
    }
    public static void simpMeth(double d)
    {
        System.out.println("Method receives double parameter");
    }
}
```

Figure 4-14 The `CallSimpMeth` application that calls `simpMeth()` with a `double` and an integer

Figure 4-15 Output of the `CallSimpMeth` application

> **» NOTE** Note that if the method with the declaration `void simpMeth(double d)` did not exist, but the declaration `void simpMeth(int i)` did exist, then the method call `simpMeth(doubleValue);` would fail. Although an integer can be promoted to a `double`, a `double` cannot become an integer. This makes sense if you consider the potential loss of information when a `double` value is reduced to an integer.

When you properly overload a method, you can call it providing different argument lists, and the appropriate version of the method executes. Within the application in Figure 4-14, if you add a second overloaded `simpMeth()` method that takes an integer parameter (as shown in Figure 4-16, with the new method shaded), the output changes when you call `simpMeth(intValue);`. Instead of promoting an integer argument to a `double`, the compiler recognizes a more exact match for the method call that uses the integer argument, so it calls the version of the method that produces the output "Method receives integer parameter". Figure 4-17 shows the output.

```java
public class CallSimpMethAgain
{
    public static void main(String[] args)
    {
        double doubleValue = 45.67;
        int intValue = 17;
        simpMeth(doubleValue);
        simpMeth(intValue);
    }
    public static void simpMeth(double d)
    {
        System.out.println("Method receives double parameter");
    }
    public static void simpMeth(int d)
    {
        System.out.println("Method receives integer parameter");
    }
}
```

Figure 4-16 The `CallSimpMethAgain` application that calls `simpMeth()` with a `double` and an integer

Figure 4-17 Output of the `CallSimpMethAgain` application

When you overload methods, you risk creating an **ambiguous** situation—one in which the compiler cannot determine which method to use. Consider the following overloaded `calculateInterest()` method declarations:

```java
public static void calculateInterest(int bal, double rate)
public static void calculateInterest(double bal, int rate)
    // Notice rate type
```

A call to `calculateInterest()` with an `int` and a `double` argument (in that order) executes the first version of the method, and a call to `calculateInterest()` with a `double` and an integer argument executes the second version of the method. With each of these calls, the compiler can find an exact match for the arguments you send. However, if you call `calculateInterest()` using two integer arguments, as in `calculateInterest(300,6);`, an ambiguous situation arises because there is no exact match for the method call. Because two integers can be promoted to an integer and a `double` (thus matching the first version of the overloaded method), or to a `double` and an integer (thus matching the second version), the compiler does not know which version of the `calculateInterest()` method to use and the program does not execute.

It is important to note that you can overload methods correctly by providing different argument lists for methods with the same name. Methods with identical names that have identical argument lists but different return types are not overloaded—they are illegal. For example, `int aMethod(int x)` and `void aMethod(int x)` cannot coexist within a program. The compiler determines which of several versions of a method to call based on argument lists. If those two methods could exist within a class, when the method call `aMethod(17);` was made, the compiler would not know which method to execute because both methods take an integer argument.

SENDING ARGUMENTS TO CONSTRUCTORS

In Chapter 3, you learned that Java automatically provides a constructor method when you create a class. You also learned that you can write your own constructor method, and that you often do so when you want to ensure that fields within classes are initialized to some appropriate default value. In Chapter 3, you learned about automatically written default constructors that do not require arguments. However, when you write your own constructor methods, the constructors you write can receive arguments. Such arguments are often used for initialization purposes when the values that you want to assign to objects upon creation might vary.

For example, consider the `Employee` class with just one data field, shown in Figure 4-18. Its constructor method assigns 999 to the `empNum` of each potentially instantiated `Employee` object. Anytime an `Employee` object is created using a statement such as `Employee partTimeWorker = new Employee();`, even if no other data-assigning methods are ever used, you ensure that the `partTimeWorker Employee`, like all `Employee` objects, will have an initial `empNum` of 999.

```
public class Employee
{
    private int empNum;
    Employee()
    {
        empNum = 999;
    }
}
```

Figure 4-18 The `Employee` class with constructor that initializes `empNum` field

Alternatively, you might choose to create `Employee` objects with initial `empNum` values that differ for each `Employee`. To accomplish this when the object is instantiated, you can pass an employee number to the constructor. Figure 4-19 shows an `Employee` class containing a constructor that receives an argument. With this constructor, an argument is passed using a statement such as the following:

```
Employee partTimeWorker = new Employee(881);
```

When the constructor executes, the integer within the method call (881) is passed to `Employee()` as the argument `num`, which is assigned to the `empNum` within the constructor method.

```
public class Employee
{
    private int empNum;
    Employee(int num)
    {
        empNum = num;
    }
}
```

Figure 4-19 The `Employee` class with constructor that accepts a value

When you create an `Employee` class with a constructor such as the one shown in Figure 4-19, every `Employee` object you create must have an integer argument. In other words, with this new version of the class, the following statement no longer works:

```
Employee partTimeWorker = new Employee();
```

After you write a constructor for a class, you no longer receive the automatically written default constructor. If a class's only constructor requires an argument, you must provide an argument for every object of the class that you create.

> **NOTE** In Chapter 2, you learned that Java casts variables to a unifying type when you perform arithmetic with unlike types. In a similar way, Java can promote one data type to another when you pass a parameter to a method. For example, if a method has a `double` argument and you pass in an integer, it is promoted to a `double`. Recall that the order of promotion is `double`, `float`, `long`, `int`, and `char`. Any type in this list can be promoted to any type that precedes it.

OVERLOADING CONSTRUCTORS

If you create a class from which you instantiate objects, Java automatically provides you with a constructor. Unfortunately, if you create your own constructor, the automatically created constructor no longer exists. Therefore, after you create a constructor that takes an argument, you no longer have the option of using the automatic constructor that requires no arguments.

Fortunately, as with any other method, you can overload constructors. Overloading constructors provides you with a way to create objects with or without initial arguments, as needed. For example, in addition to using the provided constructor method shown in Figure 4-19, you can create a second constructor method for the `Employee` class.

Figure 4-20 shows an `Employee` class containing two constructors. When you use this class to create an `Employee` object, you have the option of creating the object either with or without an initial `empNum` value. When you create an `Employee` object with the statement `Employee aWorker = new Employee();`, the constructor with no arguments is called, and the `Employee` object receives an initial `empNum` value of 999. When you create an `Employee` object with `Employee anotherWorker = new Employee(7677);`, the constructor version that requires an integer is used, and the `anotherWorker Employee` receives an initial `empNum` of 7677.

```
public class Employee
{
    private int empNum;
    Employee(int num)
    {
        empNum = num;
    }
    Employee()
    {
        empNum = 999;
    }
}
```

Figure 4-20 The `Employee` class containing two constructors

>> **NOTE** You can use constructor arguments to initialize field values, but you can also use arguments for any other purpose. For example, you could use the presence or absence of an argument simply to determine which of two possible constructors to call, yet not make use of the argument within the constructor method. As long as the constructor argument lists differ, there is no ambiguity about which constructor method to call.

LEARNING ABOUT THE this REFERENCE

When you start creating classes, they can become large very quickly. Besides data fields, each class can have many methods, including several overloaded versions. On paper, a single class might require several pages of coded statements.

When you instantiate an object from a class, memory is reserved for each instance field in the class. For example, if a class contains 20 data fields, when you create one object from that class, enough memory is reserved to hold the 20 values for that object. When you create 200 objects of the same class, the computer reserves enough memory for 4,000 data fields—20 for each of the 200 objects. In many applications, the computer memory requirements can become substantial. Fortunately, it is not necessary to store a separate copy of each variable and method for each instantiation of a class.

Usually, you want each instantiation of a class to have its own data fields. If an `Employee` class contains fields for employee number, name, and salary, every individual `Employee` object needs a unique number, name, and salary value. (When you want each object to have a unique field value, you do not define the field as `static`.) However, when you create a method for a class, any object can use the same method. Whether the method performs a calculation, sets a field value, or constructs an object, the instructions are the same for each instantiated object. Not only would it take an enormous amount of memory to store a separate copy of each method for every class object, but memory would also be wasted because you would be storing identical copies of methods—that is, each copy of the method would have the same contents for each object. Luckily, in Java just one copy of each method in a class is stored, and all instantiated objects can use that copy.

When you use a nonstatic method, you use the object name, a dot, and the method name—for example, `aWorker.getEmpNum();`. When you execute the `aWorker.getEmpNum()` method, you are running the general, shared `Employee` class `getEmpNum()` method; `aWorker` has access to the method because `aWorker` is a member of the `Employee` class. However, within the `getEmpNum()` method, when you access the `empNum` *field*, you access `aWorker`'s private, individual copy of the `empNum` field. Many `Employee` objects might exist, but just one copy of the method exists no matter how many `Employee`s there are—so when you call `aWorker.getEmpNum();`, the compiler must determine *whose* copy of the `empNum` value should be returned by the single `getEmpNum()` method.

NOTE When you pass a reference, you pass a memory address.

The compiler accesses the correct object's field because you implicitly pass a reference to `aWorker` to the `getEmpNum()` method. A **reference** is an object's memory address. The reference is implicit because it is automatically understood without actually being written. The reference to an object that is passed to any object's nonstatic class method is called the **`this` reference**; `this` is a reserved word in Java. For example, the two `getEmpNum()` methods shown in Figure 4-21 perform identically. The first method simply uses the `this` reference without your being aware of it; the second method uses the `this` reference explicitly.

```
public int getEmpNum()
{
   return empNum;
}
public int getEmpNum()
{
   return this.empNum;
}
```

Figure 4-21 Two versions of the `getEmpNum()` method, with and without an explicit `this` reference

NOTE Recall that methods associated with individual objects are instance methods. Only instance methods implicitly receive a `this` reference.

Usually, you neither want nor need to refer to the `this` reference within the methods you write, but the `this` reference is always there, working behind the scenes, so that the data field for the correct object can be accessed.

On a few occasions, you must use the `this` reference to make your classes work correctly; one example is shown in the `Student` class in Figure 4-22. Within the constructor for this class, the parameter names `stuNum` and `gpa` are identical to the class field names. Within the constructor, `stuNum` and `gpa` refer to the locally declared names, not the class field names. The statement `stuNum = stuNum` accomplishes nothing—it assigns the local variable value to itself. The client application in Figure 4-23 attempts to create a `Student` object with an ID number of 111 and a grade point average of 3.5, but Figure 4-24 shows the output. The values are not assigned; instead, they are just zeroes.

```
public class Student
{
    private int stuNum;
    private double gpa;
    public Student(int stuNum, double gpa)
    {
      stuNum = stuNum;
      gpa = gpa;
    }
    public void showStudent()
    {
       System.out.println("Student #" + stuNum +
           " gpa is " + gpa);
    }
}
```

Figure 4-22 A `Student` class whose constructor does not work as expected

```
public class TestStudent
{
    public static void main(String[] args)
    {
        Student aPsychMajor = new Student(111, 3.5);
        aPsychMajor.showStudent();
    }
}
```

Figure 4-23 The `TestStudent` class that instantiates a `Student` object

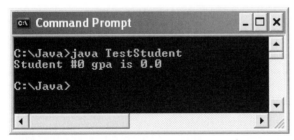

Figure 4-24 Output of the `TestStudent` application

Figure 4-25 shows a modified `Student` class. The only difference between this class and the one in Figure 4-22 is the explicit use of the `this` reference within the constructor. When the `this` reference is used with a field name in a class method, the reference is to the class field instead of to the local variable declared within the method. When the `TestStudent` application uses this new version of the `Student` class, the output appears as expected, as shown in Figure 4-26.

```
public class Student
{
    private int stuNum;
    private double gpa;
    public Student(int stuNum, double gpa)
    {
        this.stuNum = stuNum;
        this.gpa = gpa;
    }
    public void showStudent()
    {
        System.out.println("Student #" + stuNum +
            " gpa is " + gpa);
    }
}
```

Figure 4-25 The Student class using the explicit this reference within the constructor

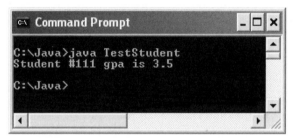

Figure 4-26 Output of the TestStudent application using the new version of the Student class

USING STATIC VARIABLES

In Chapter 3, you learned that most methods you create within a class are nonstatic—methods that you associate with individual objects. You also created static methods. For example, the main() method in a program and the methods that main() calls without an object reference are static. These methods do not have a this reference because they have no object associated with them; therefore, they are called **class methods**.

You can also create **class variables**, which are variables that are shared by every instantiation of a class. Whereas instance variables in a class exist separately for every object you create, there is only one copy of a static, class variable per class. For example, consider the BaseballPlayer class in Figure 4-27. The BaseballPlayer class contains a static field named count, and two nonstatic fields named number and battingAverage. The BaseballPlayer constructor sets values for number and battingAverage and increases the count by one. In other words, every time a BaseballPlayer object is constructed, it contains individual values for number and battingAverage, and the count field contains a count of the number of existing objects and is shared by all BaseballPlayer objects.

```
public class BaseballPlayer
{
   private static int count = 0;
   private int number;
   private double battingAverage;
   public BaseballPlayer(int id, double avg)
   {
   number = id;
   battingAverage = avg;
   count = count + 1;
   }
   public void showPlayer()
   {
   System.out.println("Player #" + number +
        " batting average is " + battingAverage +
        " There are " + count + " players");
   }
}
```

Figure 4-27 The `BaseballPlayer` class

The `TestPlayer` class in Figure 4-28 is an application that declares two `BaseballPlayer` objects, displays them, and then creates a third `BaseballPlayer` object and displays it. When you examine the output in Figure 4-29, you can see that by the time the first two objects are declared, the `count` value that they share is 2. Whether `count` is accessed using the `aCatcher` object or the `aShortstop` object, the `count` is the same. After the third object is declared, its `count` value is 3, as is the value of `count` associated with the previously declared `aCatcher` object. In other words, because the static `count` variable is incremented within the class constructor, each object has access to the total number of objects that currently exist. No matter how many `BaseballPlayer` objects are eventually instantiated, each refers to the single `count` field.

```
public class TestPlayer
{
   public static void main(String[] args)
   {
      BaseballPlayer aCatcher = new BaseballPlayer(12, .218);
      BaseballPlayer aShortstop = new BaseballPlayer(31, .385);
      aCatcher.showPlayer();
      aShortstop.showPlayer();
      BaseballPlayer anOutfielder = new BaseballPlayer(44, .505);
      anOutfielder.showPlayer();
      aCatcher.showPlayer();
   }
}
```

Figure 4-28 The `TestPlayer` class

135

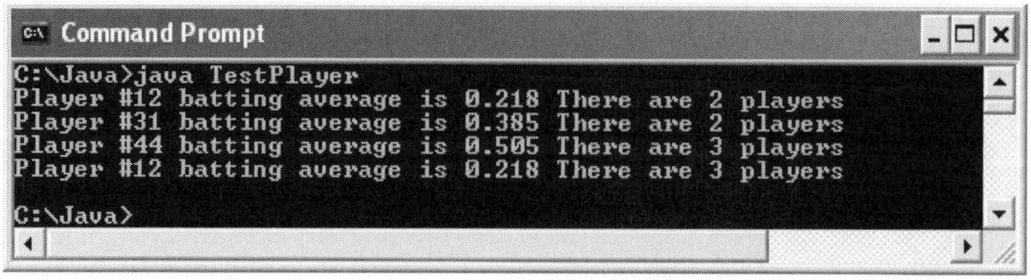

```
Command Prompt                                          _ □ ×
C:\Java>java TestPlayer
Player #12 batting average is 0.218 There are 2 players
Player #31 batting average is 0.385 There are 2 players
Player #44 batting average is 0.505 There are 3 players
Player #12 batting average is 0.218 There are 3 players

C:\Java>
```

Figure 4-29 Output of the `TestPlayer` application

WORKING WITH CONSTANTS

In Chapter 2, you learned to create literal constants within a program. A **literal constant** is a fixed value that does not change, such as the literal string "First Java program" or the integer 18. Variables, on the other hand, do change. When you declare int empNum;, you expect that the value stored in empNum will be different at different times or for different employees.

»NOTE
You can use the keyword final with methods or classes. When used in this manner, final indicates limitations placed on inheritance. You will learn more about inheritance as you become more proficient at object-oriented programming.

Sometimes, however, a variable or data field should be a **constant**; that is, it should not be changed during the execution of a program. For example, you might want to store a school ID value that is the same for every Student object you create, so you declare it to be static. In addition, if you want the value for the school ID to be fixed so that all Student objects use the same ID value—for example, when applying to scholarship-granting organizations or when registering for standardized tests—you might want to make the school ID unalterable. If you do not want any methods to alter the school ID value while a program is running, you can insert the keyword final in the school ID declaration. The keyword **final** indicates that a field value is permanent. A value such as "First Java program" or 18 is a literal constant; when you use final in a declaration, the name of the field becomes a **symbolic constant**. For example, the class in Figure 4-30 contains the symbolic constant SCHOOL_ID. When you compile any program that uses an object that contains the SCHOOL_ID, the field has a final, unalterable value. By convention, constant fields are written using all uppercase letters. The compiler does not require using uppercase identifiers for constants, but using uppercase identifiers helps you distinguish symbolic constants from variables. For readability, you can insert underscores between words in symbolic constants.

»NOTE
Fields that are final can also be initialized in a static initialization block. For more details about this technique, see *java.sun.com*.

»NOTE Mathematical constants are good candidates for receiving final status. For example, when PI is defined as static final double PI = 3.14159;, it appropriately becomes a constant that should never take on any other value. Later in this chapter, you will discover that the creators of Java have defined a PI constant for you. Constants you might declare within your own application include examples such as a fixed sales tax rate. When you declare a constant such as the following, the sales tax remains fixed for every use within an application:

```
static final double SALES_TAX = 0.075;
```

»NOTE When you declare SALES_TAX to be final, you are not implying that it can never change. You simply are saying that its value will not change when the application executes. When tax rates do actually change, you must alter and recompile the programs that use them.

You cannot change the value of a symbolic constant after declaring it; any attempt to do so results in a compiler error. You must initialize a constant with a value; this makes sense when you consider that a constant cannot be changed later. If a constant did not receive a value upon creation, it could never receive a value.

```
public class Student
{
    private static final int SCHOOL_ID = 12345;
    private int stuNum;
    private double gpa;
    public Student(int stuNum, double gpa)
    {
        this.stuNum = stuNum;
        this.gpa = gpa;
    }
    public void showStudent()
    {
        System.out.println("Student #" + stuNum +
            " gpa is " + gpa);
    }
}
```

Figure 4-30 The Student class containing a symbolic constant

>> **NOTE**
Programmers sometimes refer to named constants as "constant variables." Others think this is an oxymoron, or contradiction in terms.

A constant always has the same value within a program, so you might wonder why you cannot use the actual, literal value. For example, why not code 12345 when you need the school ID rather than going to the trouble of creating the SCHOOL_ID symbolic constant? There are at least four good reasons to use the symbolic constant rather than the literal one:

» The number 12345 is more easily recognized as the school ID if it is associated with an identifier such as SCHOOL_ID. Using symbolic constants makes your programs easier to read and understand.

» If the school ID changes, you would change the value of SCHOOL_ID at one location within your program—where the constant is defined—rather than searching for every use of 12345 to change it to a different number. Also, being able to make the change at one location saves you valuable programming time.

>> **NOTE**
Although many programmers use named constants to stand for most of the values in their programs, many make an exception when using 0 or 1.

» Even if you are willing to search for every instance of 12345 in a program to change it to the new school ID value, you might inadvertently change the value to one that is being used for something else, such as a student's personal ID number or tuition amount.

» Using named constants reduces typographical errors. If you must include 12345 at several places within a program, you might inadvertently type 13245 for one of the instances.

>> **NOTE** Some programmers refer to the use of a literal numeric constant, such as 12345, as using a **magic number**—a value that does not have immediate, intuitive meaning or a number that cannot be explained without additional knowledge. These programmers prefer that you use a named variable or constant in place of every numeric value. For example, you might write a program that uses the value 7 several times, or you might use constants such as DAYS_IN_WEEK and DEPARTMENTS_IN_COMPANY that both hold the value 7 but more clearly describe its purpose. Avoiding magic numbers helps provide internal documentation for your programs.

>> **NOTE** Static fields are not always final. If you want to create a field that all members of the class can access, but the field value changes, then it is static but not final. Similarly, final fields are not always static. If you want each object created from a class to contain its own final value, you would not declare the field to be static.

USING AUTOMATICALLY IMPORTED, PREWRITTEN CONSTANTS AND METHODS

» NOTE
You will begin to import optional classes explicitly later in this chapter.

There are many times when you need to create classes from which you will instantiate objects. You can create an `Employee` class with fields appropriate for describing employees in your organization and their functions, and an `Inventory` class with fields appropriate for whatever type of item you manufacture. However, many classes are commonly used by a wide variety of programmers. Rather than have each Java programmer "reinvent the wheel," the creators of Java created nearly 500 classes for you to use in your programs.

You have already used several of these prewritten classes; for example, you have used the `System` and `JOptionPane` classes to produce output. Each of these classes is stored in a **package**, or a **library of classes**, which is simply a folder that provides a convenient grouping for classes. Many Java packages containing classes are available only if you explicitly name them within your program; for example, when you use `JOptionPane`, you must import the `java.swing` package into your program. However, the group that contains classes such as `System` is used so frequently that it is available automatically to every program you write. The package that is implicitly imported into every Java program is named **java.lang**. The classes it contains are **fundamental classes**, or basic classes, as opposed to the **optional classes** that must be explicitly named.

> **» NOTE** Some references list a few other Java classes as also being "fundamental," but the `java.lang` package is the only automatically imported, named package. You will create your own packages in Chapter 12.

The class `java.lang.Math` contains constants and methods that you can use to perform common mathematical functions. All of the constants and methods in the `Math` class are `static`—they are class variables and class methods. A commonly used constant is `PI`. Within the `Math` class, the declaration for `PI` is as follows:

```
public final static double PI = 3.14159265358979323846;
```

» NOTE
In geometry, pi is an approximation of a circle's radius based on the ratio of the circumference of the circle to its diameter.

Notice that `PI` is:

- » `public`, so any program can access it directly
- » `final`, so it cannot be changed
- » `static`, so only one copy exists and you can access it without declaring a `Math` object
- » `double`, so it holds a floating-point value

> **» NOTE** For mathematicians, another useful constant is **E**, which represents the base of natural logarithms. Its definition is as follows:
> ```
> public final static double E = 2.7182818284590452354;
> ```

You can use the value of `PI` within any program you write by referencing the full package path in which `PI` is defined; for example, you can calculate the area of a circle using the following statement:

```
areaOfCircle = java.lang.Math.PI * radius * radius;
```

> **» NOTE** Because all constants and methods in the `Math` class are classwide (that is, static), there is no need to create an instance of the `Math` class. You cannot instantiate objects of type `Math` because the constructor for the `Math` class is private and your programs cannot access the constructor.

However, the `Math` class is imported automatically into your programs, so if you simply reference `Math.PI`, Java recognizes this code as a shortcut to the full package path. Therefore, the preferred (and simpler) statement is the following:

```
areaOfCircle = Math.PI * radius * radius;
```

In addition to constants, many useful methods are available within the `Math` class. For example, the `Math.max()` method returns the larger of two values, and the method `Math.abs()` returns the absolute value of a number. The statement `largerValue = Math.max(32, 75);` results in `largerValue` assuming the value 75, and the statement `posVal = Math.abs(-245);` results in `posVal` assuming the value 245. Table 4-1 lists some common `Math` class methods.

Method	Value That the Method Returns
`abs(x)`	Absolute value of *x*
`acos(x)`	Arc cosine of *x*
`asin(x)`	Arc sine of *x*
`atan(x)`	Arc tangent of *x*
`atan2(x, y)`	Theta component of the polar coordinate (r, theta) that corresponds to the Cartesian coordinate x, y
`ceil(x)`	Smallest integral value not less than *x* (ceiling)
`cos(x)`	Cosine of *x*
`exp(x)`	Exponent, where *x* is the base of the natural logarithms
`floor(x)`	Largest integral value not greater than *x*
`log(x)`	Natural logarithm of *x*
`max(x, y)`	Larger of *x* and *y*
`min(x, y)`	Smaller of *x* and *y*
`pow(x, y)`	*x* raised to the *y* power
`random()`	Random `double` number between 0.0 and 1.0
`rint(x)`	Closest integer to *x* (*x* is a `double`, and the return value is expressed as a `double`)
`round(x)`	Closest integer to *x* (where *x* is a `float` or `double`, and the return value is an `int` or `long`)
`sin(x)`	Sine of *x*
`sqrt(x)`	Square root of *x*
`tan(x)`	Tangent of *x*

Table 4-1 Common `Math` class methods

>> **NOTE** Unless you are a mathematician, you won't use many of these `Math` class methods, and it is unwise to do so unless you understand their purposes. For example, because the square root of a negative number is undefined, if you display the result after the method call `imaginaryNumber = Math.sqrt(-12);`, you see NaN. NaN stands for "Not a Number."

USING AN EXPLICITLY IMPORTED PREWRITTEN CLASS AND ITS METHODS

Java contains hundreds of classes, only a few of which—those in the `java.lang` package—are included automatically in the programs you write. To use any of the other prewritten classes, you must use one of three methods:

» Use the entire path with the class name.

» Import the class.

» Import the package that contains the class you are using.

For example, the `java.util` class package has useful classes containing methods that deal with dates and times. Within this package, one of the defined classes is named, `GregorianCalendar`.

> **» NOTE** The Gregorian calendar is the calendar you use to keep track of time. It was instituted on October 15, 1582, and is named for Pope Gregory XIII, who was instrumental in the calendar's adoption. For dates that fall before the Gregorian cutover date, the `GregorianCalendar` class uses the Julian calendar. The only difference between the two calendars is the leap-year rule. The Julian calendar specifies leap years every four years, whereas the Gregorian calendar omits century years that are not divisible by 400, such as 1900 and 2100.

> **» NOTE** Dates obtained using `GregorianCalendar` are historically accurate only from March 1, 4 A.D. onward, when modern Julian calendar rules were adopted. Before this date, leap-year rules were applied irregularly, and before 45 B.C. the Julian calendar did not exist. Obviously, these constraints are not a problem for most business applications.

You can instantiate an object of type `GregorianCalendar` from this class by using the full class path, as in the following:

```
java.util.GregorianCalendar myAnniversary =
     new java.util.GregorianCalendar();
```

Alternatively, when you include `import java.util.GregorianCalendar;` as the first line in your program, you can shorten the declaration of `myAnniversary` to this:

```
GregorianCalendar myAnniversary = new GregorianCalendar();
```

An `import` statement allows you to abbreviate lengthy class names by notifying the Java program that when you use `GregorianCalendar`, you mean the `java.util.GregorianCalendar` class. If you use `import` statements, you must place them before any executing statement in your Java file. That is, within a Java class file, you can have a blank line or a comment line—but nothing else—prior to an `import` statement.

> **» NOTE** `GregorianCalendar` is not a reserved word; it is a class you are importing. If you do not want to import the Java utility's `GregorianCalendar` class, you are free to write your own `GregorianCalendar` class.

An alternative to importing a class is to import an entire package of classes. You can use the asterisk (*) as a **wildcard symbol**, which indicates that it can be replaced by any set of characters. In a Java `import` statement, you use a wildcard symbol to represent all the classes in a package. Therefore, the `import` statement `import java.util.*;` imports the `Gregorian Calendar` class and any other `java.util` classes as well. There is no disadvantage to importing the extra classes, and you will most commonly see the wildcard method in professionally written Java programs. However, you have the alternative of importing each class you need individually. Importing each class by name, without wildcards, can be a form of documentation; this technique specifically shows which parts of the package are being used.

>> **NOTE** You cannot use the Java-language wildcard exactly like a DOS or UNIX wildcard because you cannot import all the Java classes with import java.* ;. The Java wildcard works only with specific packages such as import java.util.* ; or import java.lang.* ;. Also, note that the * in an import statement imports all of the classes in a package, but not other packages that are within the imported package.

>> **NOTE** Notice that the import statement ends with a semicolon. In particular, C++ programmers, who use *include* statements at the tops of their files, are likely to make the mistake of omitting this punctuation in Java.

>> **NOTE** The import statement does not move the entire imported class or package into your program, as its name implies. Rather, it simply notifies the program that you will be using the data and method names that are part of the imported class or package.

>> **NOTE**
Your own classes are included in applications because of your classpath settings. See Appendix A for more information on classpath.

Seven constructors are available for GregorianCalendar objects. These constructors are overloaded, requiring different argument lists, in exactly the same way that constructors for your own classes can be overloaded. The default constructor for the GregorianCalendar class creates a calendar object containing the current date and time in the default locale (time zone) that has been set for your computer. You can use other constructors to specify:

» Year, month, date
» Year, month, date, hour, minute
» Year, month, date, hour, minute, second
» Locale
» TimeZone
» TimeZone, Locale

>> **NOTE**
TimeZone and Locale are also Java classes. They respectively contain information about the time zone and the locale where the application is being used.

You can create a default GregorianCalendar object with a statement such as the following:

```
GregorianCalendar today = new GregorianCalendar();
```

Alternatively, you can create a GregorianCalendar object using one of the overloaded constructors—for example:

```
GregorianCalendar myGraduationDate = new GregorianCalendar(2010,5,24);
```

>> **NOTE** As you read this discussion of the GregorianCalendar class, go to *http://java.sun.com*, select API Specifications, select the version of Java with which you are working, and choose GregorianCalendar from the list of available classes. The online Java documentation provides valuable information about the data fields and methods that are available with every built-in class. This section discusses the GregorianCalendar class as an example of an interesting class, but you can apply what you learn here to any Java class; the techniques for importing and using any class are the same.

Specific data field values, such as the day, month, and year, can be retrieved from a GregorianCalendar object by using a class get() method and specifying what you want as an argument. You could retrieve the day of the year (for example, February 1 is the 32nd day of the year) with the following statement:

```
int dayOfYear = today.get(today.DAY_OF_YEAR);
```

The GregorianCalendar get() method always returns an integer. Some of the possible arguments to the get() method are shown in Table 4-2.

Arguments	Values Returned by `get()`
`DAY_OF_YEAR`	A value from 1 to 366
`DAY_OF_MONTH`	A value from 1 to 31
`DAY_OF_WEEK`	SUNDAY, MONDAY, . . . SATURDAY, corresponding to values from 1 to 7
`YEAR`	The current year; for example, 2008
`MONTH`	JANUARY, FEBRUARY, . . . DECEMBER, corresponding to values from 0 to 11
`HOUR`	A value from 1 to 12; the current hour in the A.M. or P.M.
`AM_PM`	A.M. or P.M., which correspond to values from 0 to 1
`HOUR_OF_DAY`	A value from 0 to 23 based on a 24-hour clock
`MINUTE`	The minute in the hour, a value from 0 to 59
`SECOND`	The second in the minute, a value from 0 to 59
`MILLISECOND`	The millisecond in the second, a value from 0 to 999

Table 4-2 Some possible returns from the `GregorianCalendar` `get()` method

▶▶NOTE Notice that the month values in the `GregorianCalendar` class are values from 0 through 11. Thus, January is month 0, February is month 1, and so on.

As an example of how to use a `GregorianCalendar` object, Figure 4-31 shows an `AgeCalculator` application. In this class, a default `GregorianCalendar` object named

▶▶NOTE
The `parseInt()` method is used in the application in Figure 4-31 to convert the user's input string to an integer. You learned about the `parseInt()` method in Chapter 2.

▶▶NOTE
For information about time, including how leap years and leap seconds are calculated, go to the U.S. Naval Observatory Web site at *http://tycho.usno.navy.mil.*

```java
import java.util.*;
import javax.swing.*;
public class AgeCalculator
{
    public static void main(String[] args)
    {
        GregorianCalendar now = new GregorianCalendar();
        int nowYear;
        int birthYear;
        int yearsOld;
        birthYear = Integer.parseInt
            (JOptionPane.showInputDialog(null,
            "In what year were you born?"));
        nowYear = now.get(Calendar.YEAR);
        yearsOld = nowYear - birthYear;
        JOptionPane.showMessageDialog(null,
            "This is the year you become " + yearsOld +
            " years old");
        System.exit(0);
    }
}
```

Figure 4-31 The `AgeCalculator` application

now is created. The user is prompted for a birth year, the current year is extracted from the now object using the get() method, and the user's age this year is calculated by subtracting the birth year from the current year. Figure 4-32 shows the output when a user born in 1982 runs the application in 2008.

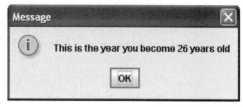

Figure 4-32 Execution of the AgeCalculator application

YOU DO IT

DEMONSTRATING SCOPE

In this section, you will create a method with several blocks to demonstrate block scope.

To demonstrate block scope:

1. Start your text editor, and then open a new document, if necessary.

2. Type the header for a class named DemoBlock as **public class DemoBlock**. On the next three lines, type the opening curly brace (**{**), the main() method header, **public static void main(String[ ] args)**, and the main() method's opening curly brace (**{**).

3. Add a statement that displays the purpose of the program:

```
System.out.println("Demonstrating block scope");
```

4. On a new line, declare an integer named x, assign the value 1111 to it, and display its value:

```
int x = 1111;
System.out.println("In first block x is " + x);
```

5. Begin a new block by typing an opening curly brace on the next line. Within the new block, declare another integer named y, and display x and y. The value of x will be 1111 and the value of y will be 2222:

```
{
    int y = 2222;
    System.out.println("In second block x is " + x);
    System.out.println("In second block y is " + y);
}
```

6. On the next line, begin another new block. Within this new block, declare a new integer with the same name as the integer declared in the previous block. Then display x and y. The value of y will be 3333. Call a method named demoMethod(), and display x and y again. Even though you will include statements within demoMethod() that assign values to x and y, the x and y displayed here will still be 1111 and 3333:

```
{
    int y = 3333;
    System.out.println("In third block x is " + x);
```

```
        System.out.println("In third block y is " + y);
        demoMethod();
        System.out.println("After method x is " + x);
        System.out.println("After method block y is " + y);
   }
```

7. On a new line after the end of the block, type **System.out.println("At the end x is " + x);**, and then type a closing curly brace. This last statement in the program displays the value of x, which is still 1111.

8. Finally, enter the following demoMethod() that creates its own x and y, assigns different values, and then displays them:

```
public static void demoMethod()
{
   int x = 8888, y = 9999;
   System.out.println("In demoMethod x is " + x);
   System.out.println("In demoMethod block y is " + y);
}
```

9. Type the final closing curly brace, and then save the file as **DemoBlock.java** in the Chapter.04 folder on your Student Disk. At the command prompt, compile the file by typing the command **javac DemoBlock.java**. If necessary, correct any errors and compile again.

10. Run the program by typing the command **java DemoBlock**. Your output should look like Figure 4-33. Make certain you understand how the values of x and y are determined in each line of output.

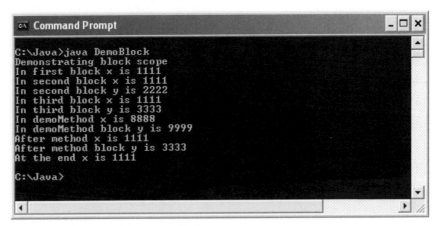

Figure 4-33 Output of the DemoBlock application

11. To gain a more complete understanding of blocks and scope, change the values of x and y in the program, and try to predict the exact output before resaving, recompiling, and rerunning the program.

OVERLOADING METHODS

Next, you will overload methods to display event dates for Event Handlers Incorporated. The methods take one, two, or three integer arguments. If there is one argument, it is the month, and the event is scheduled for the first day of the given month in the year 2008. If there are two arguments, they are the month and the day in the year 2008. Three arguments represent the month, day, and year.

> **▶▶ NOTE** In addition to creating your own class to store dates, you can use the built-in Java class GregorianCalendar to handle dates. This exercise provides you with an understanding of how some of the built-in class was constructed.

To create an application that calls an `overloadDate()` method that can take one, two, or three arguments:

1. Open a new file in your text editor.

2. Begin the following DemoOverload class, with three integer variables and three calls to an overloadDate() method:

```
public class DemoOverload
{
        public static void main(String[] args)
        {
              int month = 6, day = 24, year = 2008;
              overloadDate(month);
              overloadDate(month,day);
              overloadDate(month,day,year);
        }
```

3. Create the following overloadDate() method that requires one argument:

```
public static void overloadDate(int mm)
{
        System.out.println("Event date " + mm + "/1/2008");
}
```

4. Create the following overloadDate() method that requires two arguments:

```
public static void overloadDate(int mm, int dd)
{
        System.out.println("Event date " + mm + "/" +  dd + "/2008");
}
```

5. Create the following overloadDate() method that requires three arguments:

```
public static void overloadDate(int mm, int dd, int yy)
{
        System.out.println("Event date " + mm + "/" +  dd + "/" + yy);
}
```

6. Type the closing curly brace for the DemoOverload class.

7. Save the file as **DemoOverload.java** in the Chapter.04 folder on your Student Disk.

8. Compile the program, correct any errors, recompile if necessary, and then execute the program. Figure 4-34 shows the output. Notice that whether you call the `overloadDate()` method using one, two, or three arguments, the date prints correctly because you have successfully overloaded the `overloadDate()` method.

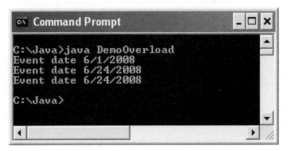

Figure 4-34 Output of the `DemoOverload` application

CREATING A CONSTRUCTOR THAT REQUIRES AN ARGUMENT

To demonstrate a constructor that requires an argument, you will use a new version of the `EventSite` class you created in Chapter 3.

To alter a constructor to require an argument:

1. Either open the **EventSite.java** file you created in Chapter 3, or open a new file in your text editor and type the `EventSite` class shown in Figure 4-35. Recall that the class contains three data fields (`siteNumber`, `usageFee`, and `managerName`) and a `get` and `set` method for each field. The class also contains a constructor that initializes the `siteNumber` field to 999 and the `managerName` to "ZZZ". Save the file as **EventSite.java** in the Chapter.04 folder on your Student Disk.

2. Modify the existing constructor by adding a required integer argument and assigning the argument value (instead of 999) to the `siteNumber` field:

```
public EventSite(int siteNum)
{
   siteNumber = siteNum;
   managerName = "ZZZ";
}
```

3. Save the file and then compile and correct any errors.

4. Open a new text file to create a short application that demonstrates the constructor at work by typing the following code:

```
public class DemoConstructor
{
   public static void main(String[] args)
   {
      EventSite aSite = new EventSite(678);
      System.out.println("Site number is "
         + aSite.getSiteNumber());
   }
}
```

```
public class EventSite
{
    private int siteNumber;
    private double usageFee;
    private String managerName;
    public EventSite()
    {
        siteNumber = 999;
        managerName = "ZZZ";
    }
    public double getFee()
    {
        return usageFee;
    }
    public String getManager()
    {
        return managerName;
    }
    public int getSiteNumber()
    {
        return siteNumber;
    }
    public void setFee(double fee)
    {
        usageFee = fee;
    }
    public void setManager(String manager)
    {
        managerName = manager;
    }
    public void setSiteNumber(int n)
    {
        siteNumber = n;
    }
}
```

Figure 4-35 The EventSite class

5. Save the file as **DemoConstructor.java** in the Chapter.04 folder, and then compile and test the program. The site number (678) should be assigned to the aSite object.

OVERLOADING A CONSTRUCTOR

Next, you will overload the EventSite constructor to take either no arguments, in which case the site number is 999, or to take an argument that is the site number.

To overload the EventSite constructor:

1. If necessary, open your text editor, and then open the **EventSite.java** text file from the Chapter.04 folder on your Student Disk.

2. Above the existing constructor that requires an argument, add the new overloaded constructor that requires no argument by typing the following:

```
public EventSite()
{
    siteNumber = 999;
    managerName = "ZZZ";
}
```

3. Save the file, compile, and correct any errors.

4. Next, modify the application that declares an EventSite so that it creates two EventSite objects—one using a constructor argument and the other without an argument. In your text editor, open the **DemoConstructor.java** file from the Chapter.04 folder on your Student Disk, and change the class name to **DemoConstructor2**.

5. After the declaration of the aSite object, create a new EventSite using no constructor argument by typing **EventSite anotherSite = new EventSite();**.

6. Position the insertion point after the println() statement that displays the site number of aSite, and then press **Enter** to start a new line. Then type the following statement to print the site number of anotherSite:

```
System.out.println("Another site number is "
    + anotherSite.getSiteNumber());
```

7. Save the file as **DemoConstructor2.java**, compile, and test the application. The two site numbers should print as 678 and 999.

USING THE this REFERENCE

You can create as many overloaded versions of a method as you want, as long as each version has a unique argument list. Next, you will create a third version of the EventSite constructor that uses the site manager's name as an argument. In addition, you will use the this reference.

To create a version of the EventSite constructor that uses the this reference to identify a class field:

1. Open the **EventSite.java** file in your text editor. After the two existing constructors, add a third constructor that accepts a manager's name as an argument. Because the identifier managerName is used as the constructor argument, as is the EventSite class field name, you must use the this reference with the field name to differentiate the two variables:

```
public EventSite(String managerName)
{
    this.managerName = managerName;
}
```

2. Save the EventSite class file, compile, and correct any errors.

3. Open the **DemoConstructor2.java** file in your text editor and change the class name to **DemoConstructor3**.

4. Below the instantiations of the two existing EventSite objects, add a third declaration that uses a manager name as an argument:

```
EventSite aThirdSite = new EventSite("Robin");
```

5. Remove the existing print statements from the file and replace them with three statements that will display the site numbers and manager names for all three objects:

```
System.out.println("Site number is "
    + aSite.getSiteNumber() + " Manager is " +
    aSite.getManager());
System.out.println("Another site number is "
    + anotherSite.getSiteNumber() + " Manager is " +
    anotherSite.getManager());
System.out.println("A third site number is "
    + aThirdSite.getSiteNumber() + " Manager is " +
    aThirdSite.getManager());
```

6. Save the file as **DemoConstructor3.java**. Compile and execute the application. The output appears in Figure 4-36. You can see that when an `EventSite` is created using an integer as the constructor argument, it becomes the site number and the manager name defaults to "ZZZ". When an `EventSite` is created using no constructor arguments, 999 is used for the site number and the manager's name is "ZZZ". Finally, when a `String` is used as the constructor argument, the `String` becomes the manager's name and the site number defaults to 0.

Figure 4-36 Output of the `DemoConstructor3` application

7. On your own, create a fourth overloaded constructor for the `EventSite` class. This constructor requires both a site number and manager name as arguments. Write an application to demonstrate that your constructor works as expected.

CREATING A static FIELD

Next, you will create a class variable to hold the location of the company headquarters for Event Handlers Incorporated. The location of the company headquarters is an ideal candidate for a class variable. Because the headquarters location is the same for every event no matter where the actual event is held, the value for the headquarters location should be stored just once, but every `EventSite` object should have access to the information.

To create a class variable for the EventSite class:

1. In your text editor, open the **EventSite.java** text file from the Chapter.04 folder on your Student Disk. Position the insertion point after the opening curly brace of the class, and then press **Enter** to start a new line. Type the class variable definition using an

identifier that consists of all uppercase letters; this identifies the field as a `final` field to those who read your class:

```
static final public String HEADQUARTERS = "Crystal Lake, IL";
```

> **》NOTE** A static variable can be either `public` or `private`. If the variable is `private`, you must write a method in your class to access it.

2. Save the file and compile.

3. Start a new file in your text editor, and create the demonstration application named **DemoStaticField** shown in Figure 4-37. This program shows the site number, manager name, and headquarters location for three `EventSite` objects.

```java
public class DemoStaticField
{
    public static void main(String[] args)
    {
        EventSite site1 = new EventSite();
        EventSite site2 = new EventSite(123);
        EventSite site3 = new EventSite("Carmen");
        System.out.println("site1 #" + site1.getSiteNumber() +
            " " + site1.getManager() + "      " +
            site1.HEADQUARTERS);
        System.out.println("site2 #" + site2.getSiteNumber() +
            " " + site2.getManager() + "      " +
            site2.HEADQUARTERS);
        System.out.println("site3 #" + site3.getSiteNumber() +
            " " + site3.getManager() + "      " +
            site3.HEADQUARTERS);
    }
}
```

Figure 4-37 The `DemoStaticField` application

4. Save the file as **DemoStaticField.java** in the Chapter.04 folder on your Student Disk. Compile and test the program. Figure 4-38 shows the application's output.

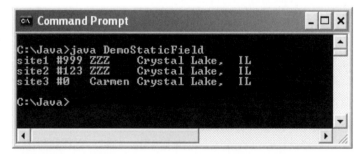

```
C:\Java>java DemoStaticField
site1 #999 ZZZ     Crystal Lake,  IL
site2 #123 ZZZ     Crystal Lake,  IL
site3 #0   Carmen Crystal Lake,  IL

C:\Java>
```

Figure 4-38 Output of the `DemoStaticField` application

USING AN AUTOMATICALLY IMPORTED PREWRITTEN CLASS

In this section, you will use the `Math` class to perform some basic calculations.

To write a program that uses some `Math` class methods:

1. Open a new file in your text editor. Type the beginning of a class named `DemoMath` as follows:

```
public class DemoMath
{
    public static void main(String[] args)
    {
        double val = 26.9;
        System.out.println("The value is " + val);
```

2. On separate lines, type the following statements to demonstrate the `Math` class methods:

```
System.out.print("Absolute value of val is ");
System.out.println(Math.abs(val));
System.out.print("Absolute value of -val is ");
System.out.println(Math.abs(-val));
System.out.print("The square root of val is ");
System.out.println(Math.sqrt(val));
System.out.print("Val rounded is ");
System.out.println(Math.round(val));
System.out.print("A random number is ");
System.out.println(Math.random());
System.out.print("8.0 raised to the 2 power is ");
System.out.println(Math.pow(8.0, 2));
```

> **» NOTE**
> The expression
> `-val` means "neg-
> ative val." In this
> code, the minus
> sign (-) used in the
> fourth output state-
> ment is a unary, or
> single-argument,
> operator. You will
> learn more about
> unary operators in
> Chapter 6.

3. Add closing curly braces for the `main()` method and for the class.

4. Save the program as **DemoMath.java** in the Chapter.04 folder on your Student Disk, compile the program, run it, and then compare your results to Figure 4-39.

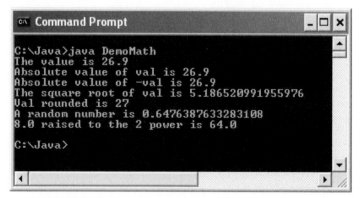

Figure 4-39 Output of the `DemoMath` application

5. Add more statements that demonstrate any of the other `Math` methods that you might use in your programs. Save, compile, and test the program again.

USING AN EXPLICITLY IMPORTED PREWRITTEN CLASS

Next, you will construct a program using the `GregorianCalendar` class and some of the arguments to the `GregorianCalendar` `get()` method.

To write a program that uses the `GregorianCalendar` **class:**

1. Open a new file in your text editor.

2. For the first line in the file, type **import java.util.*;**.

3. On the next lines, begin the class by typing the class header, the opening brace, the `main()` method header, and its opening brace, as follows:

```
public class CalendarDemo
{
    public static void main(String[] args)
    {
```

4. Declare a `GregorianCalendar` object named now that holds information about the current date and time. Then create a series of output statements that display a variety of `GregorianCalendar` fields containing information about the date:

```
GregorianCalendar now = new GregorianCalendar();
System.out.println("YEAR: " + now.get(Calendar.YEAR));
System.out.println("MONTH: " +
    now.get(Calendar.MONTH));
System.out.println("WEEK_OF_YEAR: " +
    now.get(Calendar.WEEK_OF_YEAR));
System.out.println("WEEK_OF_MONTH: " +
    now.get(Calendar.WEEK_OF_MONTH));
System.out.println("DATE: " + now.get(Calendar.DATE));
System.out.println("DAY_OF_MONTH: " +
    now.get(Calendar.DAY_OF_MONTH));
System.out.println("DAY_OF_YEAR: " +
    now.get(Calendar.DAY_OF_YEAR));
System.out.println("DAY_OF_WEEK: " +
    now.get(Calendar.DAY_OF_WEEK));
```

5. Add more statements that display information about the current time, as follows:

```
System.out.println("AM_PM: " +
    now.get(Calendar.AM_PM));
System.out.println("HOUR: " + now.get(Calendar.HOUR));
System.out.println("HOUR_OF_DAY: " +
    now.get(Calendar.HOUR_OF_DAY));
System.out.println("MINUTE: " +
    now.get(Calendar.MINUTE));
System.out.println("SECOND: " +
    now.get(Calendar.SECOND));
System.out.println("MILLISECOND: " +
    now.get(Calendar.MILLISECOND));
```

6. Add the closing curly brace for the `main()` method and the closing curly brace for the class.

7. Save the file as **CalendarDemo.java** in the Chapter.04 folder on your Student Disk. Compile and execute the program. Figure 4-40 shows the output from the program when it is executed a little after 1 p.m. on June 24, 2008. Notice that the month of June is represented by 5—the month values in the GregorianCalendar are 0 through 11. When you display month values in your own programs, you might choose to add 1 to any value before displaying it, so that users see month numbers to which they are accustomed.

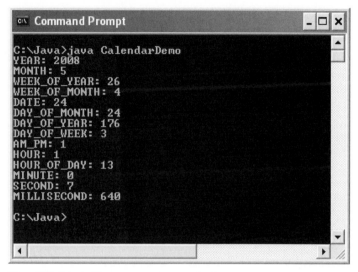

Figure 4-40 Output of the CalendarDemo application

CREATING AN INTERACTIVE APPLICATION WITH A TIMER

Next, you will use the GregorianCalendar class to create an application that outputs a user's response time to a question.

To create a timed interactive application:

1. Open a new file in your text editor and type the following two import statements. You need the JOptionPane class to use the showConfirmDialog() method, and you need the java.util package to use the GregorianCalendar class:

```
import javax.swing.JOptionPane;
import java.util.*;
```

2. Begin the DialogTimer application as follows. Use the milli1, milli2, sec1, and sec2 variables to compute time1 and time2 from calendar objects created at the beginning and end of the program; you then use time1 and time2 to compute a timeDifference:

```
public class DialogTimer
{
    public static void main(String[] args)
    {
        int time1, time2, milli1, milli2, sec1, sec2, timeDifference;
```

3. Instantiate a `GregorianCalendar` object and retrieve its `MILLISECOND` and `SECOND` values. Compute a `time1` value by multiplying the current `sec1` value by 1000 and adding it to the current `milli1` value:

```
GregorianCalendar before = new GregorianCalendar();
milli1 = before.get(GregorianCalendar.MILLISECOND);
sec1 =  before.get(GregorianCalendar.SECOND);
time1 = 1000 * sec1 + milli1;
```

4. Display a dialog box that asks the user to make a choice:

```
JOptionPane.showConfirmDialog(null, "Is stealing ever justified? ");
```

5. Next, create a new `GregorianCalendar` object. This statement does not execute until the user provides a response for the dialog box, so the time variables contain different values from the first `GregorianCalendar` object created:

```
GregorianCalendar after = new GregorianCalendar();
milli2 =  after.get(GregorianCalendar.MILLISECOND);
sec2 = after.get(GregorianCalendar.SECOND);
time2 = 1000 * sec2 + milli2;
```

6. Compute the difference between the times and display the result in a dialog box. Then add the `exit` statement that is required with GUI applications:

```
timeDifference = time2 - time1;
JOptionPane.showMessageDialog(null,"It took " +
    timeDifference + " milliseconds for you to answer");
System.exit(0);
```

7. Add two closing curly braces—one for the method and the other for the class—and then save the file as **DialogTimer.java** in the Chapter.04 folder on your Student Disk.

8. Compile and execute the program. When the question appears, choose a response. The second output looks like Figure 4-41; the actual time displayed varies depending on how long you wait before selecting an answer.

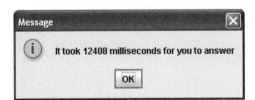

Figure 4-41 Output of the `DialogTimer` application

9. The output in the `DialogTimer` application is accurate only when the first and second `GregorianCalendar` objects are created during the same minute. For example, if the first object is created a few seconds before a new minute starts, and the second object is created a few seconds after the new minute starts, the second `SECOND` value appears to be much lower than the first one. On your own, modify the `DialogTimer` application to rectify this discrepancy.

KEY TERMS

A **block** is the code between a pair of curly braces.

An **outside block,** or **outer block,** contains another block.

An **inside block,** or **inner block,** is contained within another block.

An inside block is **nested** within an outside block.

A variable's **scope** is the portion of a program within which you can refer to the variable.

A variable comes into existence, or **comes into scope**, when you declare it.

A variable ceases to exist, or **goes out of scope**, at the end of the block in which it is declared.

To **redeclare a variable** is to attempt to declare it twice—an illegal action.

A variable **overrides** another with the same name when it takes precedence over the other variable.

Overloading involves using one term to indicate diverse meanings, or writing multiple methods with the same name but with different arguments.

An **ambiguous** situation is one in which the compiler cannot determine which method to use.

A method's **signature** is the combination of the method name and the number, types, and order of arguments.

A **reference** is an object's memory address.

The `this reference` is a reference to an object that is passed to any object's nonstatic class method.

Class methods are static methods that do not have a `this` reference (because they have no object associated with them).

Class variables are static variables that are shared by every instantiation of a class.

A **literal constant** is a specific value, such as "First Java program" or 18.

A **constant** is a memory location whose value cannot change.

The keyword `final` indicates that a field value is permanent.

A **symbolic constant** is a field that holds a fixed value.

A **magic number** is a value that does not have immediate, intuitive meaning. It cannot be explained without additional knowledge.

A **package** is a library of classes.

A **library of classes** is a folder that provides a convenient grouping for classes.

The package that is implicitly imported into every Java program is named `java.lang`.

The **fundamental classes** are basic classes contained in the `java.lang` package that are automatically imported into every program you write.

The **optional classes** reside in packages that must be explicitly imported into your programs.

A **wildcard symbol** is an asterisk—a symbol used to indicate that it can be replaced by any set of characters. In a Java `import` statement, you use a wildcard symbol to represent all the classes in a package.

CHAPTER SUMMARY

» A variable's scope is the portion of a program within which you can reference that variable. A block is the code between a pair of curly braces. Within a method, you can declare a variable with the same name multiple times, as long as each declaration is in its own nonoverlapping block. If you declare a variable within a class and use the same variable name within a method of the class, the variable used inside the method takes precedence over (or overrides, or masks) the first variable.

» Overloading involves writing multiple methods with the same name but different argument lists. Methods that have identical argument lists but different return types are not overloaded; they are illegal.

» When you overload methods, you risk creating an ambiguous situation—one in which the compiler cannot determine which method to use. Constructor methods can receive arguments and be overloaded. If you explicitly create a constructor for a class, the automatically created constructor no longer exists.

» You store separate copies of data fields for each object, but just one copy of each method. Within nonstatic methods, data fields for the correct object are accessed because you implicitly pass a `this` reference to class methods. Static methods do not have a `this` reference because they have no object associated with them; static methods are also called class methods.

» Static class variables are variables that are shared by every instantiation of a class.

» After a program is compiled, literal constants never change. Similarly, the values stored in symbolic constants never change. You create a symbolic constant by inserting the keyword `final` before a variable name. By convention, constant fields are written using all uppercase letters. A constant must be initialized with a value.

» Java contains nearly 500 prewritten classes that are stored in packages, which are folders that provide convenient groupings for classes. The package that is implicitly imported into every Java program is named `java.lang`. The classes it contains are the fundamental classes, as opposed to the optional classes, which must be explicitly named.

» The class `java.lang.Math` contains constants and methods that can be used to perform common mathematical functions. All of the constants and methods in the `Math` class are static—they are class variables and class methods.

» An `import` statement allows you to abbreviate lengthy class names by notifying the Java program that when you use class names, you are referring to those within the imported class. Any `import` statement you use must be placed before any executing statement in your file. An alternative to importing a class is to import an entire package of classes. To do so, you can use the asterisk (*) as a wildcard symbol to represent all the classes in a package.

» The `GregorianCalendar` class is the calendar generally used in the Western world. The `GregorianCalendar` class has seven constructors and a number of `get()` methods to define and manipulate dates and time.

REVIEW QUESTIONS

1. The code between a pair of curly braces in a method is a _____ .
   a. function
   b. block
   c. brick
   d. sector

2. When a block exists within another block, the blocks are _____ .
   a. structured
   b. nested
   c. sheltered
   d. illegal

3. The portion of a program within which you can reference a variable is the variable's
   _____ .
   a. range
   b. space
   c. domain
   d. scope

4. You can declare variables with the same name multiple times _____ .
   a. within a statement
   b. within a block
   c. within a method
   d. You can never declare multiple variables with the same name.

5. If you declare a variable as an instance variable within a class, and you declare and use the same variable name within a method of the class, then within the method, _____ .
   a. the variable used inside the method takes precedence
   b. the class instance variable takes precedence
   c. the two variables refer to a single memory address
   d. an error will occur

6. A method variable will _____ a class variable with the same name.
   a. acquiesce to
   b. destroy
   c. override
   d. alter

7. Nonambiguous, overloaded methods must have the same _____ .
   a. name
   b. number of arguments
   c. argument names
   d. type of argument

8. If a method is written to receive a `double` argument, and you pass an integer to the method, then the method will _____ .

 a. work correctly; the integer will be promoted to a `double`

 b. work correctly; the integer will remain an integer

 c. execute, but any output will be incorrect

 d. not work; an error message will be issued

9. A constructor _____ arguments.

 a. can receive

 b. cannot receive

 c. must receive

 d. can receive a maximum of 10

10. A constructor _____ overloaded.

 a. can be

 b. cannot be

 c. must be

 d. is always automatically

11. Usually, you want each instantiation of a class to have its own copy of _____ .

 a. the data fields

 b. the class methods

 c. both of the above

 d. none of the above

12. If you create a class that contains one method, and instantiate two objects, you usually store _____ for use with the objects.

 a. one copy of the method

 b. two copies of the method

 c. two different methods containing two different `this` references

 d. data only (the methods are not stored)

13. The `this` reference _____ .

 a. can be used implicitly

 b. must be used implicitly

 c. must not be used implicitly

 d. must not be used

14. Methods that you reference with individual objects are _____ .

 a. `private`

 b. `public`

 c. `static`

 d. `nonstatic`

15. Variables that are shared by every instantiation of a class are _____ .

 a. class variables

 b. `private` variables

 c. `public` variables

 d. illegal

16. The keyword `final` used with a variable declaration indicates _____ .

    a. the end of the program

    b. a static field

    c. a symbolic constant

    d. that no more variables will be declared in the program

17. Java classes are stored in a folder or _____ .

    a. packet   c. bundle

    b. package   d. gaggle

18. Which of the following statements determines the square root of a number and assigns it to the variable `s`?

    a. `s = sqrt(number);`

    b. `s = Math.sqrt(number);`

    c. `number = sqrt(s);`

    d. `number = Math.sqrt(s);`

19. A `GregorianCalendar` object can be created with one of seven constructors. This means that the constructors _____ .

    a. override each other   c. are overloaded

    b. are ambiguous   d. all of the above

20. The `GregorianCalendar` class `get()` method always returns a(n) _____ .

    a. day of the week

    b. date

    c. integer

    d. `GregorianCalendar` object

EXERCISES

1. a. Create a class named `Commission` that includes three variables: a `double` sales figure, a `double` commission rate, and an integer commission rate. Create two overloaded methods named `computeCommission()`. The first method takes two `double` arguments representing sales and rate, multiplies them, and then displays the results. The second method takes two arguments: a `double` sales figure and an integer commission rate. This method must divide the commission rate figure by 100.0 before multiplying by the sales figure and displaying the commission. Supply appropriate values for the variables, and write a `main()` method that tests each overloaded method. Save the file as **Commission.java** in the Chapter.04 folder on your Student Disk.

b. Add a third overloaded method to the `Commission` application you created in Exercise 1a. The third overloaded method takes a single argument representing sales. When this method is called, the commission rate is assumed to be 7.5% and the results are displayed. To test this method, add an appropriate call in the `Commission` program's `main()` method. Save the application as **Commission2.java** in the Chapter.04 folder on your Student Disk.

2. Create a class named `Pay` that includes five `double` variables that hold hours worked, rate of pay per hour, withholding rate, gross pay, and net pay. Create three overloaded `computeNetPay()` methods. When `computeNetPay()` receives values for hours, pay rate, and withholding rate, it computes the gross pay and reduces it by the appropriate withholding amount to produce the net pay. (Gross pay is computed as hours worked multiplied by pay per hour.) When `computeNetPay()` receives two arguments, they represent the hours and pay rate, and the withholding rate is assumed to be 15%. When `computeNetPay()` receives one argument, it represents the number of hours worked, the withholding rate is assumed to be 15%, and the hourly rate is assumed to be 5.65. Write a `main()` method that tests all three overloaded methods. Save the application as **Pay.java** in the Chapter.04 folder on your Student Disk.

3. a. Create a class named `Household` that includes data fields for the number of occupants and the annual income, as well as methods named `setOccupants()`, `setIncome()`, `getOccupants()`, and `getIncome()` that set and return those values, respectively. In addition, create a constructor that requires no arguments and automatically sets the occupants field to 1 and the income field to 0. Save this file as **Household.java** in the Chapter.04 folder on your Student Disk. Create an application named `TestHousehold` that demonstrates each method works correctly. Save the file as **TestHousehold.java** in the Chapter.04 folder on your Student Disk.

b. Create an additional overloaded constructor for the `Household` class you created in Exercise 3a. This constructor receives an integer argument and assigns the value to the occupants field. Add any needed statements to `TestHousehold` to ensure that the overloaded constructor works correctly, save it, and then test it.

c. Create a third overloaded constructor for the `Household` class you created in Exercises 3a and 3b. This constructor receives two arguments, the values of which are assigned to the occupants and income fields, respectively. Alter the `TestHousehold` application to demonstrate that each version of the constructor works properly. Save the application, and then compile and test it.

4. Create a class named `Box` that includes integer data fields for length, width, and height. Create three constructors that require one, two, and three arguments, respectively. When one argument is used, assign it to length, assign zeros to height and width, and print "Line created". When two arguments are used, assign them to length and width, assign zero to height, and print "Rectangle created". When three arguments are used, assign them to the three variables and print "Box created". Save this file as **Box.java** in the Chapter.04 folder on your Student Disk. Create an application named `TestBox` that demonstrates each method works correctly. Save the application as **TestBox.java** in the Chapter.04 folder on your Student Disk.

5. Create a class named `Shirt` with data fields for collar size and sleeve length. Include a constructor method that takes arguments for each field. Also include a static `String` variable named `material` and initialize it to "cotton". Write an application named `TestShirt` to instantiate three `Shirt` objects with different collar sizes and sleeve lengths, and then display all the data, including material, for each shirt. Save both the **Shirt.java** and **TestShirt.java** files in the Chapter.04 folder on your Student Disk.

6. Create a class named `CheckingAccount` with data fields for an account number and a balance. Include a constructor method that takes arguments for each field. Include a `double static` variable that holds a value for the minimum balance required before a monthly fee is applied to the account. Set the minimum balance to 200.00. Write an application named `TestAccount` in which you instantiate two `CheckingAccount` objects and display the account number, balance, and minimum balance without fee for both accounts. Save both the **CheckingAccount.java** and **TestAccount.java** files in the Chapter.04 folder on your Student Disk.

7. Write a Java application that uses the `Math` class to determine the answers for each of the following:

   a. The square root of 30

   b. The sine and cosine of 100

   c. The value of the floor, ceiling, and round of 44.7

   d. The larger and the smaller of the character K and the integer 70

   e. A random number between 0 and 10 (*Hint:* The `random()` method returns a value between 0 and 1; you want a number that is 10 times larger.)

   Save the application as **MathTest.java** in the Chapter.04 folder on your Student Disk.

8. Write an application to calculate how many days it is from today until the first day of next summer (assume that this date is June 21). Save the file as **Summer.java** in the Chapter.04 folder on your Student Disk.

9. Write an application to calculate how many days it is from today until the end of the current year. Save the file as **YearEnd.java** in the Chapter.04 folder on your Student Disk.

10. a. Create a `CollegeStudent` class for a college. The class contains data fields that hold a student's first name, last name, enrollment date, and projected graduation date, using `GregorianCalendar` class objects for each date. Provide `get()` and `set()` methods for each field. Also provide a constructor that requires first and last names and enrollment date, and sets the projected graduation date to exactly four years after enrollment. Save the class as **CollegeStudent.java** in the Chapter.04 folder on your Student Disk.

   b. Create an interactive GUI application that prompts the user for data for two `Student` objects. Prompt the user for first name, last name, enrollment month, enrollment day, and enrollment year for each `Student`, and then instantiate the objects. Display all the values, including projected graduation dates. Save the application as **TestCollegeStudent.java**.

DEBUGGING EXERCISES

» NOTE
When you change a filename, remember to change every instance of the class name within the file so that it matches the new filename. In Java, the filename and class name must always match.

Each of the following files in the Chapter.04 folder on your Student Disk has syntax and/or logic errors. In each case, determine the problem and fix the program. After you correct the errors, save each file using the same filename preceded with Fix. For example, save DebugFour1.java as FixDebugFour1.java.

a. DebugFour1.java

b. DebugFour2.java

c. DebugFour3.java and DebugBox.java

d. DebugFour4.java

CASE PROJECT

IN DEEP WATER ASSOCIATES

In Deep Water Associates operates a business that offers a variety of services to customers who own swimming pools. Each year, In Deep Water cleans local pools and fills the pools when needed. Because swimming pools require a different amount of time to service, your job is to write a program that calculates the price of a service call; the price includes a set $75 fee for cleaning plus an additional fee based on the amount of time it will take to fill a customer's pool with water. Table 4-3 provides the necessary parameters for estimating the price for a pool based on the fill-up time. Write an application that prompts the user for the length, width, and depth of a pool, and calculates the service and fill-up price. Save the application as **Swimming.java** in the Chapter.04 folder on your Student Disk.

Parameter	Explanation
Fee for cleaning	$75
Pool volume in cubic feet	length * width * average depth, all in feet
Gallons per cubic foot	7.5
Pool capacity in gallons	volume * gallons per cubic foot
Rate of flow	50 gallons per minute
Minutes per hour	60
Fee per hour for filling	$8

Table 4-3 Parameters for estimating pool fill-up price

GAME ZONE

1. Dice are used in many games. One die can be thrown to randomly show a value from 1 through 6. Design a Die class that can hold an integer data field for a value (from 1 to 6). Include a constructor that randomly assigns a value to a die object. Appendix D contains information on generating random numbers. To fully understand the process, you must learn more about Java classes and methods. However, for now, you can copy the following statement to generate a random number between 1 and 6 and assign it to a variable. Using this statement assumes you have assigned appropriate values to the static constants.

```
myValue = ((int)(Math.random() * 100) % HIGHEST_DIE_VALUE +
    LOWEST_DIE_VALUE);
```

Also include a method in the class to return a die's value. Save the class as **Die.java**.

Write an application that randomly "throws" two dice and displays their values. After you learn about decision making in Chapter 5, you will be able to have the game determine the higher die. For now, just observe how the values change as you execute the program multiple times. Save the application as **TwoDice.java**.

2. Using the Die class, write an application that randomly "throws" five dice for the computer and five dice for the player. Display the values and then, by observing the results, decide who wins based on the following hierarchy of Die values. (The computer will not decide the winner; the player will determine the winner based on observation.) Any higher combination beats a lower one; for example, five of a kind beats four of a kind.

» five of a kind
» four of a kind
» three of a kind
» a pair

After you learn about arrays in Chapter 8, you will be able to have the game efficiently determine whether you or the computer had the better roll. For now, just observe how the values change as you execute the program multiple times. Save the application as **FiveDice.java**.

UP FOR DISCUSSION

1. What are the advantages of declaring named constants in your programs? Can you think of any disadvantages?

2. In this chapter, you learned about prewritten classes such as Math and GregorianCalendar. Explore the Java documentation at *http://java.sun.com* and find at least three other built-in classes you think would be useful. Describe these classes and discuss the types of applications in which you would employ them.

3. So far, you have created extremely simple games that rely on random-number generation. However, most computer games are far more complex. If you are not familiar with them, find descriptions of the games Grand Theft Auto and Stubbs the Zombie. Why are some people opposed to these games? Do you approve of playing them? Would you impose any age restrictions on players?

5

MAKING DECISIONS

In this chapter, you will:

Understand decision making
Make decisions with the `if` and `if...else` structures
Use multiple statements in an `if` or `if...else` structure
Nest `if` and `if...else` statements
Use AND and OR operators
Learn to avoid common errors when making decisions
Use the `switch` statement
Use the conditional and NOT operators
Understand precedence

JAVA ON THE JOB, SCENE 5

Lynn Greenbrier asks, "Why are you frowning?"

"It's fun writing programs," you tell her, "but I don't think my programs can do much yet. When I use programs written by other people, I can respond to questions and make choices. And other people's programs keep running for a while—the programs I write finish as soon as they start."

"You're disappointed because the programs you've written so far simply carry out a sequence of steps," Lynn says. "You need to learn about decision-making structures."

UNDERSTANDING DECISION MAKING

▶▶ NOTE
You learned the difference between a program's logic and its syntax in Chapter 1.

When computer programmers write programs, they rarely just sit down at a keyboard and begin typing. Programmers must plan the complex portions of programs using paper and pencil. Programmers often use **pseudocode**, a tool that helps them plan a program's logic by writing plain English statements. Using pseudocode requires that you write down the steps needed to accomplish a given task. You write pseudocode in everyday language, not the syntax used in a programming language. In fact, a task you write in pseudocode does not have to be computer-related. If you have ever written a list of directions to your house—for example, (1) go west on Algonquin Road, (2) turn left on Roselle Road, (3) enter expressway heading east, and so on—you have written pseudocode. A **flowchart** is similar to pseudocode, but you write the steps in diagram form, as a series of shapes connected by arrows (see Figure 5-1).

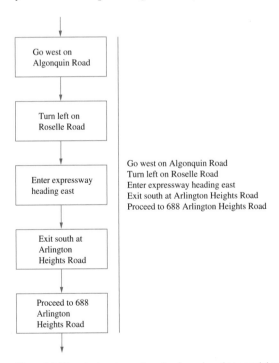

Go west on Algonquin Road
Turn left on Roselle Road
Enter expressway heading east
Exit south at Arlington Heights Road
Proceed to 688 Arlington Heights Road

Figure 5-1 Flowchart and pseudocode of a series of sequential steps

Some programmers use a variety of shapes to represent different tasks in their flowcharts, but you can draw simple flowcharts that express very complex situations using just rectangles and diamonds. You use a rectangle to represent any unconditional step and a diamond to represent any decision. For example, Figure 5-1 shows a flowchart and pseudocode describing driving directions to a friend's house. Notice how the actions illustrated in the flowchart and the pseudocode statements correspond. The logic in Figure 5-1 is an example of a logical structure called a **sequence structure**—one step follows another unconditionally. A sequence structure might contain any number of steps, but when one task follows another with no chance to branch away or skip a step, you are using a sequence.

Sometimes, logical steps do not follow in an unconditional sequence—some tasks might or might not occur based on decisions you make. Using diamond shapes, flowchart creators draw paths to alternative courses of action starting from the sides of the diamonds. Figure 5-2 shows a flowchart describing directions in which the execution of some steps depends on decisions.

Figure 5-2 shows a **decision structure**—one that involves choosing between alternative courses of action based on some value within a program. For example, the program that

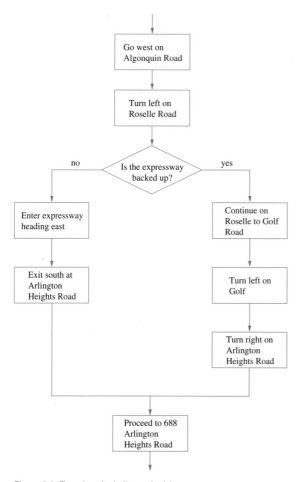

Figure 5-2 Flowchart including a decision

produces your paycheck can make decisions about the proper amount to withhold for taxes, the program that guides a missile can alter its course, and a program that monitors your blood pressure during surgery can determine when to sound an alarm. Making decisions is what makes computer programs seem "smart."

When reduced to their most basic form, all computer decisions are yes-or-no decisions. That is, the answer to every computer question is "yes" or "no" (or "true" or "false," or "on" or "off"). This is because computer circuitry consists of millions of tiny switches that are either "on" or "off," and the result of every decision sets one of these switches in memory.

The values `true` and `false` are **Boolean values**; every computer decision results in a Boolean value. Thus, internally, a program you write never asks, for example, "What number did the user enter?" Instead, the decisions might be "Did the user enter a 1?" "If not, did the user enter a 2?" "If not, did the user enter a 3?"

>> **NOTE** Sir George Boole lived from 1815 to 1864. He developed a type of linguistic algebra, based on 0s and 1s, the three most basic operations of which were (and still are) AND, OR, and NOT. All computer logic is based on his discoveries.

MAKING DECISIONS WITH THE if AND if...else STRUCTURES

In Java, the simplest statement you can use to make a decision is the **if statement**. For example, suppose you have declared an integer variable named `someVariable`, and you want to print a message when the value of `someVariable` is 10. The following is the `if` statement that makes the decision to print. Note that the double equal sign (==) is used to determine equality. Figure 5-3 shows a diagram of the logic expressed in this statement.

```
if(someVariable == 10)
    System.out.println ("The value of someVariable is 10");
```

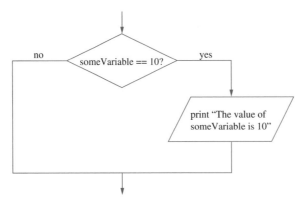

Figure 5-3 Decision structure illustrating an `if` statement

>> **NOTE** Traditionally, flowcharts use diamond shapes to hold decisions and rectangles to represent actions. Even though input and output statements represent actions, many flowchart creators prefer to show them in parallelograms; this book follows that convention.

In this example, if someVariable holds the value 10, the Boolean value of the expression someVariable == 10 is true, and the subsequent println() statement executes. If the value of the expression someVariable == 10 is false, the println() statement does not execute. Either way, the program continues with the statement that follows the if statement.

In a Java if statement, the Boolean expression, such as (someVariable == 10), must appear within parentheses. You can leave a space between the keyword if and the opening parentheses, but it is not required. Notice that there is no semicolon at the end of the first line of the if statement if(someVariable == 10) because the statement does not end there. The statement ends after the println() call, so that is where you type the semicolon. You could type the entire if statement on one line and it would execute correctly; however, the two-line format for the if statement is more conventional and easier to read, so you usually type if and the Boolean expression on one line, press Enter, and then indent a few spaces before coding the action that will occur if the Boolean expression evaluates as true. Be careful—if you use the two-line format and type a semicolon at the end of the first line, as in the following example, the logic executes as shown in Figure 5-4.

```
if(someVariable == 10);
// Notice the incorrect semicolon here
    System.out.println ("The value of someVariable is 10");
    // The indentation in the println() statement above makes no
    // difference
```

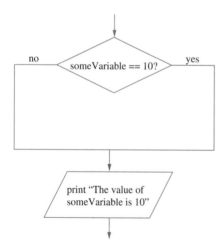

Figure 5-4 Flowchart of logic with extra semicolon at the end of the first line of the if statement

When this if expression is evaluated, the statement ends if it evaluates as true. Whether the expression evaluates as true or false, execution continues with the next independent statement that prints someVariable. In this case, because of the incorrect semicolon, the if statement accomplishes nothing.

Another common programming error occurs when a programmer uses a single equal sign rather than the double equal sign when attempting to determine equivalency. The expression someVariable = 10 does not compare someVariable to 10; instead, it attempts to assign the value 10 to the someVariable variable. When the expression containing the single equal sign is part of an `if` statement, the assignment is illegal. The confusion arises in part because the single equal sign is used within Boolean expressions in `if` statements in many other programming languages, such as COBOL, Pascal, and BASIC. Adding to the confusion, Java programmers use the word *equals* when speaking of equivalencies. For example, you might say, "If `someVariable` *equals* 10 . . .".

An alternative to using a Boolean expression, such as `someVariable == 10`, is to store the Boolean expression's value in a Boolean variable. For example, if `isValueTen` is a Boolean variable, then the following statement compares `someVariable` to 10 and stores `true` or `false` in `isValueTen`:

```
isValueTen = (someVariable == 10);
```

Then, you can write the `if` as:

```
if(isValueTen)...
```

This adds an extra step to the program, but makes the `if` statement more similar to an English-language statement.

> **NOTE** When comparing a variable to a constant, some programmers prefer to place the constant to the left of the comparison operator, as in `10 == someVariable`. This practice is a holdover from other programming languages, such as C++, in which an accidental assignment might be made when the programmer types the assignment operator (a single equal sign) instead of the comparison operator (the double equal sign). In Java, the compiler does not allow you to make a mistaken assignment in a Boolean expression.

THE `if...else` STRUCTURE

Consider the following statement:

```
if(someVariable == 10)
    System.out.println("The value of someVariable is 10");
```

Such a statement is sometimes called a **single-alternative `if`** because you only perform an action, or not, based on one alternative; in this example, you print a statement when `someVariable` is 10. Often, you require two options for the course of action following a decision. A **dual-alternative `if`** is the decision structure you use when you need to take one or the other of two possible courses of action. For example, you would use a dual-alternative `if` structure if you wanted to display one message when the value of `someVariable` is 10 and a different message when it is not. In Java, the **`if...else` statement** provides the mechanism to perform one action when a Boolean expression evaluates as `true`, and to perform a different action when a Boolean expression evaluates as `false`. For example, the following code displays one of two messages:

> **NOTE**
> In an `if...else` statement, the statement that executes when the `if` is true ends with a semicolon, as does the statement that executes when the `if` is false.

```
if(someVariable == 10)
    System.out.println("The value of someVariable is 10");
else
    System.out.println("No, it's not");
```

> **NOTE** The indentation shown in the preceding `if...else` example code is not required, but is standard usage. You vertically align the keyword `if` with the keyword `else`, and then indent the action statements that depend on the evaluation.

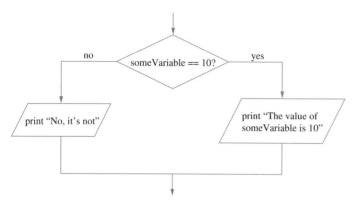

Figure 5-5 An `if...else` structure

Figure 5-5 shows a flowchart of the logic for this `if...else` structure. In this example, when the value of `someVariable` is 10, the message "The value of `someVariable` is 10" is printed. When `someVariable` is any other value, the program prints the message "No, it's not".

When you execute an `if...else` statement, only one of the resulting actions takes place depending on the evaluation of the Boolean expression following the `if`. Each statement, the one following the `if` and the one following the `else`, is a complete statement, so each ends with a semicolon.

>> **NOTE**
You can code an `if` without an `else`, but it is illegal to code an `else` without an `if`.

USING MULTIPLE STATEMENTS IN AN `if` OR `if...else` STRUCTURE

Often, you want to take more than one action following the evaluation of a Boolean expression within an `if` statement. For example, you might want to print several separate lines of output or perform several mathematical calculations. To execute more than one statement that depends on the evaluation of a Boolean expression, you use a pair of curly braces to place the dependent statements within a block. For example, the program segment shown in Figure 5-6 and diagrammed in Figure 5-7 determines whether an employee has worked more than 40 hours in a single week; if so, the program computes regular and overtime salary and then prints the results.

```
if(hoursWorked > 40)
{
    regularPay = 40 * rate;
    overtimePay = (hoursWorked - 40) * 1.5 * rate;
    System.out.println("Regular pay is " + regularPay);
    System.out.println("Overtime pay is " + overtimePay);
} // The if structure ends here
```

Figure 5-6 An `if` structure that determines pay

>> **NOTE** In Figure 5-6, no action is taken if `hoursWorked` is less than 40. An actual payroll calculation would include more comprehensive instructions, but they are not necessary for the sake of the example.

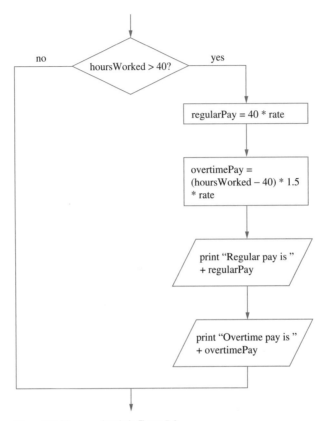

Figure 5-7 Diagram of code in Figure 5-6

NOTE When you create a block, you do not have to place multiple statements within it. It is perfectly legal to block a single statement.

When you place a block within an `if` statement, it is crucial to place the curly braces correctly. For example, in Figure 5-8, the curly braces have been omitted. Figure 5-9 illustrates the effect of this omission. Within the code segment in Figure 5-8, when `hoursWorked > 40` is `true`, `regularPay` is calculated and the `if` expression ends. The next three statements that compute `overtimePay` and print the results always execute every time the program runs, no matter what value is stored in `hoursWorked`. These last three statements are not dependent on the `if` statement; they are independent, stand-alone statements. The indentation might be deceiving; it looks as though four statements depend on the `if` statement, but indentation does not cause statements following an `if` statement to be dependent. Rather, curly braces are required if the four statements must be treated as a block.

```
regularPay = 0;
if(hoursWorked > 40)
   regularPay = 40 * rate; // The if structure ends here
   overtimePay = (hoursWorked - 40) * 1.5 * rate;
   System.out.println("Regular pay is " + regularPay);
   System.out.println("Overtime pay is " + overtimePay);
```

Figure 5-8 Erroneous overtime pay calculation with missing curly braces

>> **NOTE** The code shown in Figure 5-8 might not compile if `regularPay` is not assigned a starting value before the `if` statement—the compiler recognizes that `hoursWorked` might not be greater than 40, so the calculation that assigns a value to `regularPay` might not occur. In other words, you might be attempting to print the value of `regularPay` in the second-to-last line of code without having calculated the value.

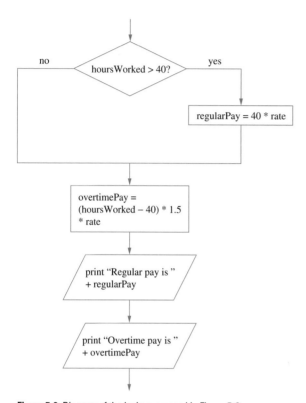

Figure 5-9 Diagram of the logic expressed in Figure 5-8

Because the curly braces are missing, regardless of whether `hoursWorked` is more than 40, each of the last three statements in Figure 5-8 is a new stand-alone statement that is not part of the `if`, and so each executes.

In Figure 5-8, if the `hoursWorked` value is 40 or less—30, for example—then the `regularPay` calculation does not execute (it executes only if `hoursWorked` is greater than 40), but the next three independent statements do execute. The variable `regularPay` holds 0 and the program calculates the value of `overtimePay` as a negative number (because 30 minus 40 results in −10). Therefore, the output is incorrect. Correct blocking is crucial to achieving valid output.

Just as you can block statements to depend on an `if`, you can also block statements to depend on an `else`. Figure 5-10 shows an application containing an `if` structure with two dependent statements and an `else` with two dependent statements. The program executes the final `showMessageDialog()` statement without regard to the `hoursWorked` variable's value; the `showMessageDialog()` statement is not part of the `if` structure. Figure 5-11 shows the output from two executions of the program. The dialog box on the left displays when the user enters 39 for the `hoursWorked` value; the dialog box on the right displays when the user enters 42.

```
import javax.swing.JOptionPane;
public class Payroll
{
   public static void main(String[] args)
   {
      String hoursString;
      double rate = 20.00;
      double hoursWorked;
      double regularPay;
      double overtimePay;
      hoursString = JOptionPane.showInputDialog(null,
         "How many hours did you work this week?");
      hoursWorked = Double.parseDouble(hoursString);
      if(hoursWorked > 40)
      {
         regularPay = 40 * rate;
         overtimePay = (hoursWorked - 40) * 1.5 * rate;
      }
      else
      {
         regularPay = hoursWorked * rate;
         overtimePay = 0.0;
      }
      JOptionPane.showMessageDialog(null, "Regular pay is " +
         regularPay + "\nOvertime pay is " + overtimePay);
      System.exit(0);
   }
}
```

Figure 5-10 `Payroll` application containing an `if` and `else` with blocks

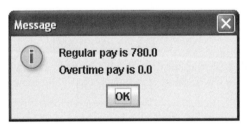
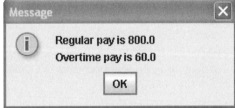

Figure 5-11 Output of the `Payroll` application

> **NOTE** When you block statements, you must remember that any variable you declare within a block is local to that block. For example, the following code segment contains a variable named `sum` that is local to the block following the `if`. The shaded statement causes an error because the `sum` variable is not recognized:
>
> ```
> if(a == b)
> {
>    int sum = a + b;
>    System.out.println("The two variables are equal");
> }
> System.out.println("The sum is " + sum);
> ```

NESTING `if` AND `if...else` STATEMENTS

Within an `if` or an `else` statement, you can code as many dependent statements as you need, including other `if` and `else` structures. Statements in which an `if` structure is contained inside another `if` structure commonly are called **nested `if` statements**. Nested `if` statements are particularly useful when two conditions must be met before some action is taken.

For example, suppose you want to pay a $50 bonus to a salesperson only if the salesperson sells more than three items that total more than $1000 in value during a specified time. Figure 5-12 shows the logic for this situation. Figure 5-13 shows the code to solve the problem.

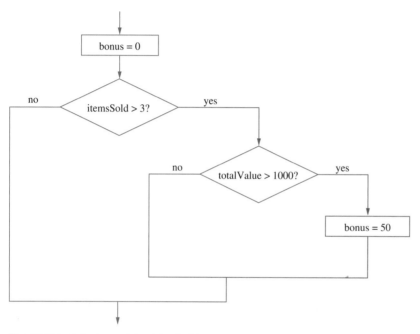

Figure 5-12 Logic for bonus-determining decision

```
bonus = 0;
if(itemsSold > 3)
    if(totalValue > 1000)
        bonus = 50;
```

Figure 5-13 Code for bonus-determining decision using nested `if` statements

Notice there are no semicolons in the `if` statement code shown in Figure 5-13 until after the `bonus = 50;` statement. The expression `itemsSold > 3` is evaluated. If this expression is `true`, the program evaluates the second Boolean expression `(totalValue > 1000)`. If that expression is also `true`, the bonus assignment executes and the `if` structure ends.

When you use nested `if` statements, you must pay careful attention to placement of any `else` clauses. For example, suppose you want to distribute bonuses on a revised schedule, as shown in Figure 5-14. If the salesperson does not sell more than three items, you want to give a $10 bonus; if the salesperson sells at least three items, the bonus is $25 if the value of the items is $1000 or less, or $50 if the value is more than $1000. Figure 5-15 shows the code that assigns the bonuses.

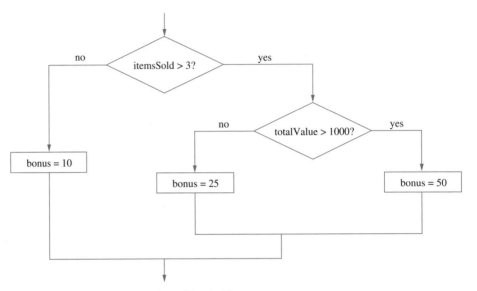

Figure 5-14 Logic for revised bonus-determining decision

As Figure 5-15 shows, when one `if` statement follows another, the first `else` clause encountered is paired with the most recent `if` encountered. The complete nested `if...else` structure fits entirely within the `if` portion of the outer `if...else` statement. No matter how many levels of `if...else` statements are needed to produce a solution, the `else` statements are always associated with their `if`s on a "first in-last out" basis.

> **NOTE** In Figure 5-15, the indentation of the lines helps to show which `else` is paired with which `if`. Remember, the compiler does not take indentation into account, but consistent indentation can help readers understand a program's logic.

```
if(itemsSold > 3)
   if(totalValue > 1000)
      bonus = 50;
   else   // This else goes with the second if
      bonus = 25;
else // This else goes with the first if
   bonus = 10;
```

Figure 5-15 Code for revised bonus-determining decision using nested `if` statements

USING LOGICAL AND and OR OPERATORS

For an alternative to some nested `if` statements, you can use the **logical AND operator** between two Boolean expressions to determine whether both are `true`. The AND operator is written as two ampersands (`&&`). For example, the code shown in Figure 5-16 works exactly

```
bonus = 0;
if(itemsSold > 3 && totalValue > 1000)
    bonus = 50;
```

Figure 5-16 Code for bonus-determining decision using the `&&` operator

the same as the code shown in Figure 5-13. The `itemsSold` variable is tested, and if it is greater than 3, the `totalValue` is tested. If `totalValue` is greater than $1000, the bonus is set to $50.

You are never required to use the AND operator because using nested `if` statements always achieves the same result, but using the AND operator often makes your code more concise, less error-prone, and easier to understand.

It is important to note that when you use the `&&` operator, you must include a complete Boolean expression on each side. If you want to set a bonus to $400 when a `saleAmount` is both over $1000 and under $5000, the correct statement is:

```
if(saleAmount > 1000 && saleAmount < 5000) bonus = 400;
```

Even though the `saleAmount` variable is intended to be used in both parts of the AND expression, the following statement is incorrect and does not compile because there is not a complete expression on both sides of the `&&`:

```
if(saleAmount > 1000 && < 5000)bonus = 400;
```

With the AND operator, both Boolean expressions that surround the operator must be `true` before the action in the statement can occur. You can use nested `if` statements, or you can use the **logical OR operator**, which is written as `||`, if you want some action to occur when at least one of two conditions is `true`. For example, if you want to give a bonus of $200 to any salesperson who satisfies at least one of two conditions—selling more than 100 items or selling any number of items that total more than $3000 in value—you can write the code using either of the ways shown in Figures 5-17 and 5-18. Figure 5-19 shows the program logic.

> **» NOTE**
> The two vertical lines used in the OR operator are sometimes called "pipes." The pipe appears on the same key as the backslash on your keyboard.

```
bonus = 0;
if(itemsSold > 100)
    bonus = 200;
else
    if(totalValue > 3000)
        bonus = 200;
```

Figure 5-17 Code segment for bonus-determining decision using nested `if`s

```
bonus = 0;
if(itemsSold > 100 || totalValue > 3000)
    bonus = 200;
```

Figure 5-18 Code segment for bonus-determining decision using the `||` operator

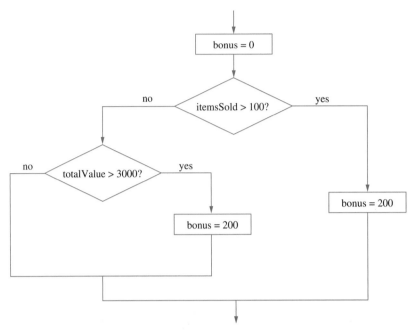

Figure 5-19 Logic for bonus-determining decisions in Figures 5-17 and 5-18

>> **NOTE** A common use of the OR operator is to decide to take action whether a character variable is uppercase or lowercase, as in if(selection == 'A' || selection == 'a') .... The subsequent action occurs whether the selection variable holds an uppercase or lowercase A.

AVOIDING COMMON ERRORS WHEN MAKING DECISIONS

New programmers frequently make errors when they first learn to make decisions. As you have seen, the most frequent errors include the following:

» Using the assignment operator instead of the comparison operator when testing for equality

» Inserting a semicolon after the Boolean expression in an if statement instead of after the entire statement is completed

» Failing to block a set of statements with curly braces when several statements depend on the if or the else statement

» Failing to include a complete Boolean expression on each side of an && or || operator in an if statement

In this section, you will learn to avoid two additional types of errors with if statements. Programmers often make errors at the following times:

» When performing a range check incorrectly or inefficiently

» When using the wrong operator with AND and OR

PERFORMING ACCURATE AND EFFICIENT RANGE CHECKS

When new programmers must make a range check, they often introduce incorrect or inefficient code into their programs. A **range check** is a series of if statements that determine
whether a value falls within a specified range. Consider a situation in which salespeople can
receive one of three possible commission rates based on their sales. For example, a sale total-
ing $1000 or more earns the salesperson an 8% commission, a sale totaling $500 through
$999 earns 6% of the sale amount, and any sale totaling $499 or less earns 5%. Using three
separate if statements to test single Boolean expressions might result in some incorrect commission assignments. For example, examine the code shown in Figure 5-20.

```
if(saleAmount >= 1000)
    commissionRate = 0.08;
if(saleAmount >= 500)
    commissionRate = 0.06;
if(saleAmount <= 499)
    commissionRate = 0.05;
```

Figure 5-20 Incorrect commission-determining code

>> **NOTE** As long as you are dealing with whole dollar amounts, the expression if(saleAmount >= 1000) can be
expressed just as well as if(saleAmount > 999). Use whichever has the clearest meaning for you.

Using the code shown in Figure 5-20, if a saleAmount is $5000, the first if statement exe-
cutes. The Boolean expression (saleAmount >= 1000) evaluates as true, and 0.08 is
correctly assigned to commissionRate. However, when a saleAmount is $5000, the next
if expression, (saleAmount >= 500), also evaluates as true, so the commissionRate,
which was 8%, is incorrectly reset to 6%.

A partial solution to this problem is to use an else statement following the if(saleAmount
>= 1000) expression, as shown in Figure 5-21.

```
if(saleAmount >= 1000)
    commissionRate = 0.08;
else if(saleAmount >= 500)
    commissionRate = 0.06;
else if(saleAmount <= 499)
    commissionRate = 0.05;
```

Figure 5-21 Improved, but inefficient, commission-determining code

>> **NOTE** You can place the if following an else on a new line and indent it, but a program with many nested
if...else combinations soon grows very long and "deep." With many indentations, later statements in the nest would
move farther and farther to the right on the page. For easier-to-read code, Java programmers commonly place each else
and its subsequent if on the same line, as shown in Figure 5-21.

With the new code in Figure 5-21, when the saleAmount is $5000, the expression
(saleAmount >= 1000) is true and the commissionRate becomes 8%; then the entire

if structure ends. When the saleAmount is not greater than or equal to $1000 (for example, $800), the first if expression is false and the else statement executes and correctly sets the commissionRate to 6%.

The code shown in Figure 5-21 works, but it is somewhat inefficient. When the saleAmount is any amount over $499, either the first if sets commissionRate to 8% for amounts over $999, or its else sets commissionRate to 6% for amounts over $499. In either of these two cases, the Boolean value tested in the next statement, if(saleAmount <= 499), is always false. After you know that the saleAmount is not at least $500, rather than asking if(saleAmount <= 499), it's easier and more efficient to use an else. If the saleAmount is not at least $1000 and is also not at least $500, it must by default be less than or equal to 499. Figure 5-22 shows this improved logic, and Figure 5-23 shows its code.

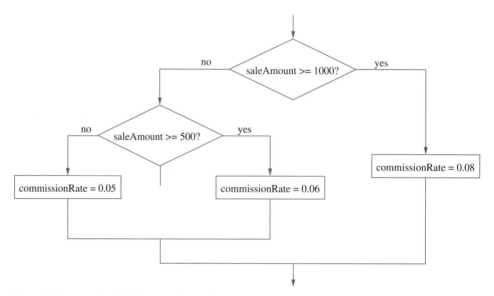

Figure 5-22 Improved and efficient commission-determining logic

```
if(saleAmount >= 1000)
    commissionRate = 0.08;
else if(saleAmount >= 500)
    commissionRate = 0.06;
else commissionRate = 0.05;
```

Figure 5-23 Code using logic in Figure 5-22

Within a nested if...else, like the one shown in Figure 5-23, it is most efficient to ask the most likely question first. In other words, if you know that most saleAmount values are over $1000, compare saleAmount to that value first. That way, you most frequently avoid asking multiple questions. If, however, you know that most saleAmounts are small, you should ask if(saleAmount < 500) first. The code shown in Figure 5-24 results in the same commission value for any given saleAmount, but is more efficient when most saleAmount values are small.

```
if(saleAmount < 500)
    commissionRate = 0.05;
else if(saleAmount < 1000)
    commissionRate = 0.06;
else commissionRate = 0.08;
```

Figure 5-24 Commission-determining code asking about smallest saleAmount first

USING AND and OR APPROPRIATELY

Beginning programmers often use the AND operator when they mean to use OR, and often use OR when they should use AND. Part of the problem lies in the way we use the English language. For example, your boss might request, "Print an error message when an employee's hourly pay rate is under $5.65 and when an employee's hourly pay rate is over $60." Because your boss used the word "and" in the request, you might be tempted to write a program statement like the following:

```
if(payRate < 5.65 && payRate > 60)
    System.out.println("Error in pay rate");
```

However, as a single variable, no payRate value can ever be both below 5.65 and over 60 at the same time, so the print statement can never execute, no matter what value the payRate has. In this case, you must write the following statement to print the error message under the correct circumstances:

```
if(payRate < 5.65 || payRate > 60)
    System.out.println("Error in pay rate");
```

Similarly, your boss might request, "Print the names of those employees in departments 1 and 2." Because the boss used the word "and" in the request, you might be tempted to write the following:

```
if(department == 1 && department == 2)
    System.out.println("Name is: " + name);
```

However, the variable department can never contain both a 1 and a 2 at the same time, so no employee name will ever be printed, no matter what department the employee is in.

> **NOTE** Another type of mistake occurs if you use a single ampersand or pipe when you try to indicate a logical AND or OR. Both & and | are valid Java operators, but they operate on bits rather than making comparisons in logical conditions as && and || do.

USING THE switch STATEMENT

By nesting a series of if and else statements, you can choose from any number of alternatives. For example, suppose you want to print a student's class year based on a stored number. Figure 5-25 shows one possible implementation of the program.

```
if(year == 1)
   System.out.println("Freshman");
else if(year == 2)
   System.out.println("Sophomore");
else if(year == 3)
   System.out.println("Junior");
else if(year == 4)
   System.out.println("Senior");
else System.out.println("Invalid year");
```

Figure 5-25 Determining class status using nested `if` statements

An alternative to using the series of nested `if` statements shown in Figure 5-25 is to use the `switch` statement. The **`switch` statement** is useful when you need to test a single variable against a series of exact integer or character values. The `switch` structure uses four keywords:

- `switch` starts the structure and is followed immediately by a test expression enclosed in parentheses.
- `case` is followed by one of the possible values for the test expression and a colon.
- `break` optionally terminates a `switch` structure at the end of each case.
- `default` optionally is used prior to any action that should occur if the test variable does not match any case.

Figure 5-26 shows the `case` structure used to print the four school years.

>> **NOTE** You are not required to list the `case` values in ascending order, as shown in Figure 5-26. It is most efficient to list the most common `case` first, instead of the `case` with the lowest value.

>> **NOTE** Besides `int` and `char`, you can use a `switch` statement to test values of type `byte` and `short`, which hold smaller integer values.

```
int year;
// Get year value from user input, or simply by assigning
switch(year)
{
   case 1:
      System.out.println("Freshman");
      break;
   case 2:
      System.out.println("Sophomore");
      break;
   case 3:
      System.out.println("Junior");
      break;
   case 4:
      System.out.println("Senior");
      break;
   default:
      System.out.println("Invalid year");
}
```

Figure 5-26 Determining class status using a `switch` statement

The `switch` structure shown in Figure 5-26 begins by evaluating the `year` variable shown in the `switch` statement. If the year is equal to the first `case` value, which is 1, the statement that prints "Freshman" executes. The `break` statement bypasses the rest of the `switch` structure, and execution continues with any statement after the closing curly brace of the `switch` structure.

If the year variable is not equivalent to the first case value of 1, the next case value is compared, and so on. If the year variable does not contain the same value as any of the case statements, the default statement or statements execute.

You can leave out the break statements in a switch structure. However, if you omit the break and the program finds a match for the test variable, all the statements within the switch statement execute from that point forward. For example, if you omit each break statement in the code shown in Figure 5-26, when the year is 3, the first two cases are bypassed, but "Junior", "Senior", and "Invalid year" all print. You should intentionally omit the break statements if you want all subsequent cases to execute after the test variable is matched.

You do not need to write code for each case in a case statement. For example, suppose that the supervisor for departments 1, 2, and 3 is "Jones", but other departments have different supervisors. In that case, you might use the code in Figure 5-27.

```java
int department;
String supervisor;
// Statements to get department
switch (department)
{
    case 1:
    case 2:
    case 3:
        supervisor = "Jones");
        break;
    case 4:
        supervisor = "Staples");
        break;
    case 5:
        supervisor = "Tejano");
        break:
    default:
        System.out.println("Invalid department code");
}
```

Figure 5-27 Using empty case statements so the same result occurs in multiple cases

>> NOTE When several char variables must be checked and you want to ignore whether they are uppercase or lowercase, one frequently used technique employs empty case statements, as in the following example:

```java
switch (departmentCode)
{
    case 'a':
    case 'A':
        departmentName = "Accounting");
        break;
    case 'm':
    case 'M':
        departmentName = "Marketing");
        break;
    // and so on
```

You are never required to use a `switch` structure; you can always achieve the same results with nested `if` statements. The `switch` structure is simply convenient to use when there are several alternative courses of action that depend on a single integer or character variable. In addition, it makes sense to use `switch` only when there are a reasonable number of specific matching values to be tested. For example, if every sale amount from $1 to $500 requires a 5% commission, it is not reasonable to test every possible dollar amount using the code in Figure 5-28. Because 500 different dollar values result in the same commission, one test—`if(saleAmount <= 500)`—is far more reasonable than listing 500 separate cases.

```
switch(saleAmount)
{
    case 1:
        commRate = .05;
        break;
    case 2:
        commRate = .05;
        break;
    case 3:
        commRate = .05;
        break;
    // ...and so on for several hundred more cases
}
```

Figure 5-28 Inefficient use of the `switch` statement

USING THE CONDITIONAL AND NOT OPERATORS

Besides using `if` statements and `case` structures, Java provides one more way to make decisions. The **conditional operator** requires three expressions separated with a question mark and a colon, and is used as an abbreviated version of the `if...else` structure. As with the `switch` structure, you are never required to use the conditional operator; it is simply a convenient shortcut. The syntax of the conditional operator is:

```
testExpression ? trueResult : falseResult;
```

The first expression, `testExpression`, is a Boolean expression that is evaluated as `true` or `false`. If it is `true`, the entire conditional expression takes on the value of the expression following the question mark (`trueResult`). If the value of the `testExpression` is `false`, the entire expression takes on the value of `falseResult`.

For example, suppose you want to assign the smallest price to a sale item. Let the variable *a* be the advertised price and the variable *b* be the discounted price on the sale tag. The expression for assigning the smallest cost is:

```
smallerNum = (a < b) ? a : b;
```

When evaluating the expression a < b, where *a* is less than *b*, the entire conditional expression takes the value of *a*, which then is assigned to smallerNum. If *a* is not less than *b*, the expression assumes the value of *b*, and *b* is assigned to smallerNum.

You could achieve the same results with the following if...else structure:

```
if(a < b)
    smallerNum = a;
else
    smallerNum = b;
```

The advantage of using the conditional operator is the conciseness of the statement.

USING THE NOT OPERATOR

You use the **NOT operator**, which is written as the exclamation point (!), to negate the result of any Boolean expression. Any expression that evaluates as true becomes false when preceded by the NOT operator, and accordingly, any false expression preceded by the NOT operator becomes true.

For example, suppose a monthly car insurance premium is $200 if the driver is age 25 or younger, and $125 if the driver is age 26 or older. Each of the following if...else statements correctly assigns the premium values:

```
if(age <= 25)
    premium = 200;
else
    premium = 125;

if(!(age <= 25))
    premium = 125;
else
    premium = 200;

if(age >= 26)
    premium = 125;
else
    premium = 200;

if(!(age >= 26))
    premium = 200;
else
    premium = 125;
```

The statements with the NOT operator are somewhat harder to read, particularly because they require the double set of parentheses, but the result of the decision-making process is the same in each case. Using the NOT operator is clearer when the value of a Boolean variable is tested. For example, a variable initialized as boolean oldEnough = (age >= 25); can become part of the relatively easy-to-read expression if(!oldEnough)....

UNDERSTANDING PRECEDENCE

You can combine as many AND or OR operators as you need to make a decision. For example, if you want to award 10 bonus points to any student who receives a perfect score on any of four quizzes, you might write a statement like the following:

```
if(score1 == 100 || score2 == 100 || score3 == 100 || score4 == 100)
    bonus = 10;
else
    bonus = 0;
```

In this case, if at least one of the score variables is 100, the student receives 10 bonus points. Although you can combine any number of AND or OR operators, special care must be taken when you combine them. You learned in Chapter 2 that operations have higher and lower precedences, and an operator's precedence makes a difference in how an expression is evaluated. For example, within an arithmetic expression, multiplication and division are always performed prior to addition or subtraction. Table 5-1 shows the precedence of the operators you have used so far.

Precedence	Operator(s)	Symbol(s)
Highest	Logical NOT	!
Intermediate	Multiplication, division, modulus	* / %
	Addition, subtraction	+ -
	Relational	> < >= <=
	Equality	== !=
	Logical AND	&&
	Logical OR	||
	Conditional	? :
Lowest	Assignment	=

Table 5-1 Operator precedence for operators used so far

In general, the order of precedence agrees with common algebraic usage. For example, in any mathematical expression, such as $x = a + b$, the arithmetic is done first and the assignment is done last, as you would expect. The relationship of && and || might not be as obvious. The AND operator is always evaluated before the OR operator. For example, consider the program segments shown in Figure 5-29. These code segments are intended to be part of an insurance company program that determines whether an additional premium should be charged to a driver who meets both of the following criteria:

» Has more than two traffic tickets or is under 25 years old

» Is male

Consider a 30-year-old female driver with three traffic tickets; according to the stated criteria, she should not be assigned the extra premium because she is not male. With the first `if` statement in Figure 5-29, the AND operator takes precedence over the OR operator, so `age < 25 && gender == 'M'` is evaluated first. The value is `false` because `age` is not less

```
// Assigns extra premiums incorrectly
if(trafficTickets > 2 || age < 25 && gender == 'M')
    extraPremium = 200;
// Assigns extra premiums correctly
if((trafficTickets > 2 || age < 25) && gender == 'M')
    extraPremium = 200;
```

Figure 5-29 Some comparisons using && and ||

than 25, so the expression is reduced to `trafficTickets > 2` or `false`. Because the value of the tickets variable is greater than 2, the entire expression is `true`, and $200 is assigned to `extraPremium`, even though it should not be.

In the second `if` statement shown in Figure 5-29, parentheses have been added so the OR operator is evaluated first. The expression `trafficTickets > 2 || age < 25` is `true` because the value of `trafficTickets` is 3. So the expression evolves to `true &&` `gender== 'M'`. Because gender is not 'M', the value of the entire expression is `false`, and the `extraPremium` value is not assigned 200, which is correct.

The following two conventions are important to keep in mind:

» The order in which you use operators makes a difference.

» You can always use parentheses to change precedence or make your intentions clearer.

YOU DO IT

USING AN if...else

In this section, you will start writing a program for Event Handlers Incorporated that determines which employee will be assigned to manage a client's scheduled event. To begin, you will prompt the user to answer a question about the event type, and then the program will display the name of the manager who handles such events. There are two event types: private events, handled by Dustin Britt, and corporate events, handled by Carmen Lindsey.

To write a program that chooses between two managers:

1. Open a new text file, and then enter the first lines of code to create a class named `ChooseManager`. You will import `JOptionPane` so that you can use GUI input and output objects. The class will contain a `main()` method that performs all the work of the class:

```
import javax.swing.JOptionPane;
public class ChooseManager
{
    public static void main(String[] args)
    {
```

2. On new lines, declare the variables and constants this application will use. You will ask the user to enter a `choiceString`, which you will convert to an integer `eventType`. The names of the managers for private and corporate events are stored as symbolic constants; the chosen manager will be assigned to the `chosenManager` string:

```
String choiceString, chosenManager;
int eventType;
final String PRIV_MANAGER = "Dustin Britt";
final String CORP_MANAGER = "Carmen Lindsey";
```

> **NOTE**
> In Chapter 4, you learned that the names of symbolic constants conventionally are declared using all uppercase letters.

3. Add the code that prompts the user to enter a 1 or 2 depending on the event type being scheduled, and accept the response into a string, which you then convert to an integer:

```
choiceString = JOptionPane.showInputDialog(null,
    "What type of event are you scheduling?" +
    "\nEnter 1 for Private, 2 for Corporate");
eventType = Integer.parseInt(choiceString);
```

> **»» NOTE** The prompt in the `showInputDialog()` method is split into two parts, joined with a +, so that it is easier to read. You could write the entire prompt as a single string.

4. Use an `if...else` statement to choose the name of the manager to be assigned to the `chosenManager` string, as follows:

```
if(eventType == 1)
    chosenManager = PRIV_MANAGER;
else
    chosenManager = CORP_MANAGER;
```

5. Display the chosen manager's name in a dialog box, and then exit the program:

```
JOptionPane.showMessageDialog(null,
    "Manager for this event will be " + chosenManager);
System.exit(0);
```

6. Type the two closing curly braces to end the `main()` method and the `ChooseManager` class.

7. Save the program as **ChooseManager.java** in the Chapter.05 folder on your Student Disk, and then compile and run the program. Confirm that the program selects the correct manager when you choose 1 for a private event or 2 for a corporate event. For example, Figure 5-30 shows the output when the user enters 1 for a private event.

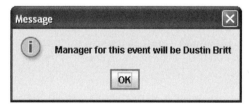

Figure 5-30 Output of the `ChooseManager` application after user enters 1

CREATING AN Event CLASS TO USE IN A DECISION-MAKING APPLICATION

Next, you will create an `Event` class. The class will be used by Event Handlers Incorporated to store data about a planned event. Each `Event` object includes three data fields: the type of event, the name of the manager for the event, and the hourly rate charged for handling the event. The `Event` class also contains a `get` and `set` method for each field.

To create the Event class:

1. Open a new text file and type the class header for the Event class, followed by declarations for the three data fields:

```
public class Event
{
    private int typeOfEvent;
    private double rate;
    private String manager;
```

2. Create three get methods; each returns one of the data fields in the Event class:

```
    public int getType()
    {
        return typeOfEvent;
    }
    public double getRate()
    {
        return rate;
    }
    public String getManager()
    {
        return manager;
    }
```

3. Also add three set methods; each sets a single data field:

```
    public void setType(int eventType)
    {
        typeOfEvent = eventType;
    }
    public void setRate(double eventRate)
    {
        rate = eventRate;
    }
    public void setManager(String managerName)
    {
        manager = managerName;
    }
```

4. Type the closing curly brace for the class.

5. Save the file as **Event.java** in the Chapter.05 folder on your Student Disk, then compile the file and correct any errors.

WRITING AN APPLICATION CONTAINING MULTIPLE STATEMENTS DEPENDING ON AN if...else

Now that you have created an Event class, you will create a ChooseEvent application. You will prompt the user for an event type, and then select both a manager and a rate for the Event based on the selected type. Private events are managed by Dustin Britt and cost $47.99 per hour. Corporate events are managed by Carmen Lindsey and cost $75.99 per hour. After the user selects an event type, you will instantiate an Event object containing appropriate event data.

To create an application containing an `if...else` with multiple consequences:

1. Open a new file in your text editor and type the following to begin the `ChooseEvent` class. The class contains `String` variables that hold user input data and the selected manager, an integer to hold the event type, constants for the managers' names, and a `double` to hold the charged rate. You also will declare a scheduled `Event` object:

```
import javax.swing.JOptionPane;
public class ChooseEvent
{
    public static void main(String[] args)
    {
        String choiceString, chosenManager;
        int eventType;
        final String PRIV_MANAGER = "Dustin Britt";
        final String CORP_MANAGER = "Carmen Lindsey";
        final double PRIV_RATE = 47.99;
        final double CORP_RATE = 75.99;
        double rate;
        Event scheduledEvent = new Event();
```

2. Prompt the user for an event type:

```
        choiceString = JOptionPane.showInputDialog(null,
            "What type of event are you scheduling?" +
            "\nEnter 1 for Private, 2 for Corporate");
        eventType = Integer.parseInt(choiceString);
```

3. Write a decision that selects the correct manager and rate based on the user's choice. Because two statements execute when the user selects 1, and two statements execute when the user does not select 1, the sets of statements following the `if` and the `else` must both be blocked using curly braces:

```
        if(eventType == 1)
        {
            chosenManager = PRIV_MANAGER;
            rate = PRIV_RATE;
        }
        else
        {
            chosenManager = CORP_MANAGER;
            rate = CORP_RATE;
        }
```

4. Set the three fields that are contained in the scheduled `Event` object as follows:

```
scheduledEvent.setType(eventType);
scheduledEvent.setManager(chosenManager);
scheduledEvent.setRate(rate);
```

5. To confirm that the `Event` was constructed properly, add a dialog box that displays the `Event` object's fields, then exit the application:

```
        JOptionPane.showMessageDialog(null,
            "Event type " + scheduledEvent.getType() +
            "\nManager for this event will be " +
```

```
            scheduledEvent.getManager() +
            "\nThe hourly fee will be $" +
            scheduledEvent.getRate());
        System.exit(0);
```

6. Add a closing curly brace for the `main()` method and another for the class.

7. Save the application as **ChooseEvent.java**. Compile and run the program several times with different input at the prompt. Confirm that the output shows that the event has the correct manager, type, and rate based on how you respond to the prompt (with 1 or not with 1). Figure 5-31 shows the output when the user enters 2 at the prompt.

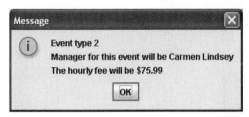

Figure 5-31 Output of the `ChooseEvent` application after user enters 2

NESTING `if` STATEMENTS

Currently, the `ChooseEvent` application identifies an event as private and assigns an appropriate manager and rate when the user enters 1 at the event-type prompt. When the user enters any other number, such as a 3 or 9, the event is considered to be corporate. Next, you will improve the `ChooseEvent` application so that if the user mistypes the entry (that is, does not enter either a 1 or 2), an `Event` object with an "invalid" type is instantiated.

To improve the `ChooseEvent` program:

1. If necessary, start your text editor and open the ChooseEvent.java file from the Chapter.05 folder on your Student Disk, and then change the class name to **ChooseEventImproved**. Immediately save the modified file as **ChooseEventImproved.java** in the Chapter.05 folder on your Student Disk.

2. Change the `if...else` structure that tests the `eventType` so that it becomes a nested `if...else` with three possibilities. When the user enters anything other than 1 or 2, display an error message and create an `Event` object with a code of 999 for the event type, "Unassigned" for the manager name, and 0.0 for the rate. The new `if...else` structure is:

```
if(eventType == 1)
{
    chosenManager = PRIV_MANAGER;
    rate = PRIV_RATE;
}
else if(eventType == 2)
{
    chosenManager = CORP_MANAGER;
    rate = CORP_RATE;
}
```

```
else
{
    eventType = 999;
    chosenManager = "Unassigned";
    rate = 0.0;
}
```

3. Save the application (as **ChooseEventImproved.java**), compile it, and then run the application several times to confirm that user responses of 1 or 2 result in valid `Event` objects, and that other responses result in an error message and an event of type 999. Figure 5-32 shows the output when a user enters 4 for the event type.

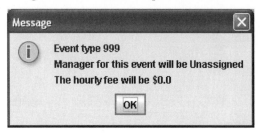

Figure 5-32 Output of the `ChooseEventImproved` application after user enters 4

USING THE switch STATEMENT

Next, you will modify the `ChooseEventImproved` application to account for a new type of event. Besides private and corporate, there will be special rates for nonprofit organizations. The entered code for nonprofit events is 3, and Robin Armanetti is the manager assigned to these events. The rate for nonprofit events is $40.99. Now that there are more options available within the application, you can avoid so many nested `if` statements by converting them to a `switch` structure.

To convert the `ChooseEventImproved` decision-making process to a `switch` structure:

1. If necessary, open the ChooseEventImproved.java file and change the class name to **ChooseFromMultipleEvents**. Immediately save the file as **ChooseFromMultipleEvents.java** in the Chapter.05 folder on your Student Disk.

2. Position the insertion point at the end of the statement that declares the constant for CORP_MANAGER, press **Enter** to start a new line, and then type a constant declaration for the nonprofit manager as follows:

```
final String NON_PROF_MANAGER = "Robin Armanetti";
```

3. Position the insertion point at the end of the statement that declares the constant for CORP_RATE, press **Enter** to start a new line, and then type the constant for NON_PROF_RATE as follows:

```
final double NON_PROF_RATE = 40.99;
```

4. To the list of current prompts, add a prompt to tell the user to enter 3 for nonprofit organization events. After the addition, the prompt becomes:

```
choiceString = JOptionPane.showInputDialog(null,
        "What type of event are you scheduling? " +
        "\nEnter 1 for Private, 2 for Corporate, 3 for Nonprofit");
```

5. Delete the `if...else` statements that currently determine whether the user entered 1 or 2, and then replace them with the following `switch` structure:

```
switch (eventType)
{
    case 1:
        chosenManager = PRIV_MANAGER;
        rate = PRIV_RATE;
        break;
    case 2:
        chosenManager = CORP_MANAGER;
        rate = CORP_RATE;
        break;
    case 3:
        chosenManager = NON_PROF_MANAGER;
        rate = NON_PROF_RATE;
        break;
    default:
        eventType = 999;
        chosenManager = "Unassigned";
        rate = 0.0;
}
```

6. Save the file (as **ChooseFromMultipleEvents.java**), compile, and test the application. Make certain the correct output appears when you enter 1, 2, 3, or any invalid number as keyboard input. Figure 5-33 shows the output when the user enters 3.

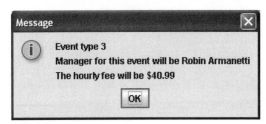

Figure 5-33 Output of the `ChooseFromMultipleEvents` application after user enters 3

KEY TERMS

Pseudocode is a tool that helps programmers plan a program's logic by writing plain English statements.

A **flowchart** is a tool that helps programmers plan a program's logic by writing the steps in diagram form, as a series of shapes connected by arrows.

A **sequence structure** is a logical structure in which one step follows another unconditionally.

A **decision structure** is a logical structure that involves choosing between alternative courses of action based on some value within a program.

`True` or `false` values are **Boolean values**; every computer decision results in a Boolean value.

In Java, the simplest statement you can use to make a decision is the **if statement**; you use it to write a single-alternative decision.

A **single-alternative if** is a decision structure that performs an action, or not, based on one alternative.

A **dual-alternative if** is a decision structure that takes one of two possible courses of action.

In Java, the **if...else statement** provides the mechanism to perform one action when a Boolean expression evaluates as true, and to perform a different action when a Boolean expression evaluates as false.

Statements in which an if structure is contained within another if structure commonly are called **nested if statements**.

You can use the **logical AND operator** between Boolean expressions to determine whether both are true. The AND operator is written as two ampersands (&&).

You can use the **logical OR operator** between Boolean expressions to determine whether either expression is true. The OR operator is written as two pipes (||).

A **range check** is a series of if statements that determines whether a value falls within a specified range.

The **switch statement** is useful when you need to test a single variable against a series of exact integer or character values. The switch structure uses four keywords: switch starts the structure and is followed immediately by a test expression enclosed in parentheses; case is followed by one of the possible values for the test expression and a colon; break optionally terminates a switch structure at the end of each case; and default optionally is used prior to any action that should occur if the test variable does not match any case.

The **conditional operator** requires three expressions separated with a question mark and a colon, and is used as an abbreviated version of the if...else structure.

You use the **NOT operator**, which is written as the exclamation point (!), to negate the result of any Boolean expression.

CHAPTER SUMMARY

» Making a decision involves choosing between two alternative courses of action based on some value within a program.

» You can use the if statement to make a decision based on a Boolean expression that evaluates as true or false. If the Boolean expression enclosed in parentheses within an if statement is true, the subsequent statement or block executes.

» A single-alternative if performs an action based on one alternative; a dual-alternative if, or if...else, provides the mechanism for performing one action when a Boolean expression evaluates as true. When a Boolean expression evaluates as false, a different action occurs.

» To execute more than one statement that depends on the evaluation of a Boolean expression, you use a pair of curly braces to place the dependent statements within a block. Within an if or an else statement, you can code as many dependent statements as you need, including other if and else statements.

» Nested if statements are particularly useful when two conditions must be met before some action occurs.

» You can use the AND operator (&&) within a Boolean expression to determine whether two expressions are both `true`. You use the OR operator (||) when you want to carry out some action even if only one of two conditions is `true`.

» New programmers frequently cause errors in their `if` statements when they do the following:

   » Use the assignment operator instead of the comparison operator when testing for equality.

   » Insert a semicolon after the Boolean expression in an `if` instead of after the entire statement is completed.

   » Fail to block a set of statements with curly braces when several statements depend on the `if` or the `else`.

   » Fail to include a complete Boolean expression on each side of an && or || operator in an `if`.

   » Perform a range check incorrectly or inefficiently.

   » Use the wrong operator when using AND and OR.

» You use the `switch` statement to test a single variable against a series of exact integer or character values.

» The conditional operator requires three expressions, a question mark, and a colon, and is used as an abbreviated version of the `if...else` statement.

» You use the NOT operator (!) to negate the result of any Boolean expression.

» Operator precedence makes a difference in how expressions are evaluated. You can always use parentheses to change precedence or make your intentions clearer.

REVIEW QUESTIONS

1. The logical structure in which one instruction occurs after another with no branching is a _____ .

   a. sequence   c. loop
   b. selection   d. case

2. Which of the following is typically used in a flowchart to indicate a decision?

   a. square   c. diamond
   b. rectangle   d. oval

3. Which of the following is not a type of `if` statement?

   a. single-alternative `if`   c. reverse `if`
   b. dual-alternative `if`   d. nested `if`

4. A decision is based on a(n) _____ value.

   a. Boolean   c. definitive
   b. absolute   d. convoluted

5. In Java, the value of `(4 > 7)` is _____ .

   a. 4   c. `true`

   b. 7   d. `false`

6. Assuming the variable `q` has been assigned the value 3, which of the following statements prints XXX?

   a. `if(q > 0) System.out.println("XXX");`

   b. `if(q > 7); System.out.println("XXX");`

   c. Both of the above statements print XXX.

   d. Neither of the above statements prints XXX.

7. What is the output of the following code segment?

```
t = 10;
if(t > 7)
{
    System.out.print("AAA");
    System.out.print("BBB");
}
```

   a. AAA   c. AAABBB

   b. BBB   d. nothing

8. What is the output of the following code segment?

```
t = 10;
if(t > 7)
    System.out.print("AAA");
    System.out.print("BBB");
```

   a. AAA   c. AAABBB

   b. BBB   d. nothing

9. What is the output of the following code segment?

```
t = 7;
if(t > 7)
    System.out.print("AAA");
    System.out.print("BBB");
```

   a. AAA   c. AAABBB

   b. BBB   d. nothing

10. When you code an `if` statement within another `if` statement, as in the following, then the `if` statements are _____ :

```
if(a > b)
    if(c > d)x = 0;
```

   a. notched   c. nested

   b. nestled   d. sheltered

11. The operator that combines two conditions into a single Boolean value that is `true` only when both of the conditions are `true`, but is `false` otherwise, is _____ .

    a. $$

    b. !!

    c. ||

    d. &&

12. The operator that combines two conditions into a single Boolean value that is `true` when at least one of the conditions is `true` is _____ .

    a. $$

    b. !!

    c. ||

    d. &&

13. Assuming a variable `f` has been initialized to 5, which of the following statements sets `g` to 0?

    a. `if (f > 6 || f == 5) g = 0;`

    b. `if (f < 3 || f > 4) g = 0;`

    c. `if (f >= 0 || f < 2) g = 0;`

    d. All of the above statements set `g` to 0.

14. Which of the following groups has the lowest operator precedence?

    a. relational

    b. equality

    c. addition

    d. logical OR

15. Which of the following statements correctly prints the names of voters who live in district 6 and all voters who live in district 7?

    a. `if (district == 6 || 7)`
       `System.out.println ("Name is " + name);`

    b. `if (district == 6 || district == 7)`
       `System.out.println ("Name is " + name);`

    c. `if (district = 6 && district == 7)`
       `System.out.println ("Name is " + name);`

    d. two of these

16. Which of the following prints "Error" when a student ID is less than 1000 or more than 9999?

    a. `if (stuId < 1000) if (stuId > 9999)`
       `System.out.println ("Error");`

    b. `if (stuId < 1000 && stuId > 9999)`
       `System.out.println ("Error");`

c. if(stuId < 1000)

    System.out.println("Error");

  else if(stuId > 9999)

    System.out.println("Error");

d. Two of these are correct.

17. You can use the _____ statement to terminate a `switch` structure.

    a. `switch`   c. `case`

    b. `end`   d. `break`

18. The `switch` argument within a `switch` structure requires a(n) _____ .

    a. integer value   c. `double` value

    b. character value   d. integer or character value

19. Assuming a variable `w` has been assigned the value 15, what does the following statement do?

    `w == 15 ? x = 2 : x = 0;`

    a. assigns 15 to `w`   c. assigns 0 to `x`

    b. assigns 2 to `x`   d. nothing

20. Assuming a variable `y` has been assigned the value 6, the value of `! (y < 7)` is _____ .

    a. 6   c. `true`

    b. 7   d. `false`

EXERCISES

1. a. Write an application that prompts the user for a checking account balance and a savings account balance. Display the message "Checking account balance is low" if the checking account balance is less than $10. Display the message "Savings account balance is low" if the savings account balance is less than $100. Save the file as **Balance.java** in the Chapter.05 folder on your Student Disk.

   b. Modify the application in Exercise 1a to display an additional message, "Both accounts are dangerously low", if both fall below the specified limits. Save the file as **Balance2.java** in the Chapter.05 folder on your Student Disk.

2. a. Write an application for a furniture company; the program determines the price of a table. Ask the user to choose 1 for pine, 2 for oak, or 3 for mahogany. The output is the name of the wood chosen as well as the price of the table. Pine tables cost $100, oak tables cost $225, and mahogany tables cost $310. If the user enters an invalid wood code, set the price to 0. Save the file as **Furniture.java** in the Chapter.05 folder on your Student Disk.

   b. Add a prompt to the application you wrote in Exercise 2a to ask the user to specify a (1) large or a (2) small table. Add $35 to the price of any large table. Save the file as **Furniture2.java** in the Chapter.05 folder on your Student Disk.

3. a. Write an application for a college's admissions office. Prompt the user for a student's numeric high school grade point average (for example, 3.2) and an admission test score from 0 to 100. Print the message "Accept" if the student has any of the following:

    » A grade point average of 3.0 or above and an admission test score of at least 60

    » A grade point average below 3.0 and an admission test score of at least 80

    If the student does not meet either of the qualification criteria, print "Reject". Save the file as **Admission.java** in the Chapter.05 folder on your Student Disk.

    b. Modify the application in Exercise 3a so that if a student enters a grade point average under 0 or over 4.0, or a test score under 0 or over 100, an error message appears instead of the "Accept" or "Reject" message. Save the file as **Admission2.java** in the Chapter.05 folder on your Student Disk.

4. a. Write an application that prompts an employee for an hourly pay rate and hours worked. Compute gross pay (hours times rate), withholding tax, and net pay (gross pay minus withholding tax). Withholding tax is computed as a percentage of gross pay based on the following:

Gross Pay ($)	Withholding Percentage
Up to and including 300.00	10
300.01 and up	12

    Save the file as **ComputeNet.java** in the Chapter.05 folder on your Student Disk.

    b. Modify the application you created in Exercise 4a using the following withholding percentage ranges:

Gross Pay ($)	Withholding Percentage
0 to 300.00	10
300.01 to 400.00	12
400.01 to 500.00	15
500.01 and over	20

    Save the file as **ComputeNet2.java** in the Chapter.05 folder on your Student Disk.

5. a. Write an application that prompts the user for two integers and then prompts the user to enter an option. If the choice is 1, add the two integers. If it is 2, subtract the second integer from the first; if it is 3, multiply the integers. Display the results of the arithmetic. Save the file as **Calculate.java** in the Chapter.05 folder on your Student Disk.

    b. Modify the Calculate application in Exercise 5a so the user can also enter 4 for divide. If the user enters 4 and the second integer entered is 0, display an error message because division by 0 is an illegal operation; otherwise, divide the first number by the second and display the results. Save the file as **Calculate2.java** in the Chapter.05 folder on your Student Disk.

6. a. Write an application for a lawn-mowing service. The lawn-mowing season lasts 20 weeks. The weekly fee for mowing a lot under 400 square feet is $25. The fee for a lot that is 400

square feet or more, but under 600 square feet, is $35 per week. The fee for a lot that is 600 square feet or over is $50 per week. Prompt the user for the length and width of a lawn, and then print the weekly mowing fee, as well as the 20-week seasonal fee. Save the file as **Lawn.java** in the Chapter.05 folder on your Student Disk.

b. To the Lawn application you created in Exercise 6a, add a prompt that asks the user whether the customer wants to pay (1) once, (2) twice, or (3) 20 times per year. If the user enters 1 for once, the fee for the season is simply the seasonal total. If the customer requests two payments, each payment is half the seasonal fee plus a $5 service charge. If the user requests 20 separate payments, add a $3 service charge per week. Display the number of payments the customer must make, each payment amount, and the total for the season. Save the file in the Chapter.05 folder on your Student Disk as **Lawn2.java**.

7. Write an application that asks a user to enter an IQ score. If the score is a number less than 0 or greater than 200, issue an error message; otherwise, issue an "above average", "average", or "below average" message for scores over, at, or under 100, respectively. Save the file as **IQ.java** in the Chapter.05 folder on your Student Disk.

8. Write an application that recommends a pet for a user based on the user's lifestyle. Prompt the user to enter whether he or she lives in a house, apartment, or dormitory (1, 2, or 3) and the number of hours the user is home during the average day. The user will select an hour category from a menu: (1) 18 or more; (2) 10 to 17; (3) 8 to 9; (4) 6 to 7; or (5) 0 to 5. Print your recommendation based on the following table:

Residence	Hours Home	Recommendation
House	18 or more	Pot-bellied pig
House	10 to 17	Dog
House	Fewer than 10	Snake
Apartment	10 or more	Cat
Apartment	Fewer than 10	Hamster
Dormitory	6 or more	Fish
Dormitory	Fewer than 6	Ant farm

Save the file as **PetAdvice.java** in the Chapter.05 folder on your Student Disk.

9. a. Write an application that displays a menu of three items in a restaurant as follows:

(1) Cheeseburger   4.99

(2) Pepsi   2.00

(3) Chips   0.75

Prompt the user to choose an item using the number (1, 2, or 3) that corresponds to the item, or to enter 0 to quit the application. After the user makes the first selection, if the choice is 0, display a bill of $0. Otherwise, display the menu again. The user should respond to this prompt with another item number to order or 0 to quit. If the user types 0, display the cost of the single requested item. If the user types 1, 2, or 3, add the cost of the second item to the first, and then display the menu a third time. If the user types 0 to quit, display the total cost of the two items; otherwise, display the total for all three selections. Save the file as **FastFood.java** in the Chapter.05 folder on your Student Disk.

b. Modify the application in Exercise 9a so that if the user makes a menu selection he or she has already made, ignore the selection—that is, do not add a second price for the same item to the total. The user still is allowed only three entries. Save the file as **FastFood2.java** in the Chapter.05 folder on your Student Disk.

10. a. Create a class named `Invoice` that holds an invoice number, balance due, and three fields representing the month, day, and year that the balance is due. Create a constructor that accepts values for all five data fields. Within the constructor, assign each argument to the appropriate field with the following exceptions:

   » If an invoice number is less than 1000, force the invoice number to 0.

   » If the month field is less than 1 or greater than 12, force the month field to 0.

   » If the day field is less than 1 or greater than 31, force the day field to 0.

   » If the year field is less than 2005 or greater than 2012, force the year field to 0.

   In the `Invoice` class, include a display method that displays all the fields on an `Invoice` object. Save the file as **Invoice.java** in the Chapter.05 folder on your Student Disk.

   b. Write an application containing a `main()` method that declares several `Invoice` objects, proving that all the statements in the constructor operate as specified. Save the file as **TestInvoice.java** in the Chapter.05 folder on your Student Disk.

   c. Modify the constructor in the `Invoice` class so that the day is not greater than 31, 30, or 28, depending on the month. Also, if the month is invalid, and thus forced to 0, also force the day to 0. Save the modified `Invoice` class as **Invoice2.java** in the Chapter.05 folder on your Student Disk. Then modify the `TestInvoice` class to create `Invoice2` objects. Create enough objects to test every decision in the constructor. Save this file as **TestInvoice2.java** in the Chapter.05 folder on your Student Disk.

   d. Modify the constructor in the `Invoice2` class so that if the year is 2008 or 2012 and the month is 2, the day is not greater than 29, accounting for leap year. Save the modified `Invoice2` class as **Invoice3.java** in the Chapter.05 folder on your Student Disk. Then modify the `TestInvoice2` class to create `Invoice3` objects, including at least one that tests the February 29th date. Save this file as **TestInvoice3.java** in the Chapter.05 folder on your Student Disk.

11. Use the Web to locate the lyrics to the traditional song "The Twelve Days of Christmas." The song contains a list of gifts received for the holiday. The list is cumulative so that as each "day" passes, a new verse contains all the words of the previous verse, plus a new item. Write an application that displays the words to the song starting with any day the user enters. (Hint: Use a `switch` statement with `cases` in descending day order and without any `break` statements so that the lyrics for any day repeat all the lyrics for previous days.) Save the file as **TwelveDays.java**.

DEBUGGING EXERCISES

Each of the following files in the Chapter.05 folder on your Student Disk has syntax and/or logic errors. In each case, determine the problem and fix the program. After you correct the errors, save each file using the same filename preceded with Fix. For example, save DebugFive1.java as FixDebugFive1.java.

a. DebugFive1.java

c. DebugFive3.java

b. DebugFive2.java

d. DebugFive4.java

CASE PROJECT

BARNHILL FASTENER COMPANY

Barnhill Fastener Company runs a small factory that makes several types of nuts and bolts. The company employs factory workers who are paid one of three hourly rates depending on skill level:

Skill Level	Hourly Pay Rate ($)
1	17.00
2	20.00
3	22.00

Each factory worker might work any number of hours per week; any hours over 40 are paid at one and one-half times the usual rate.

In addition, workers in skill levels 2 and 3 can elect the following insurance options:

Option	Explanation	Weekly Cost to Employee ($)
1	Medical insurance	32.50
2	Dental insurance	20.00
3	Long-term disability insurance	10.00

Also, workers in skill level 3 can elect to participate in the retirement plan at 3% of their gross pay.

Allen Branch, the factory manager, wants you to write an interactive Java payroll application that calculates the gross pay for a factory worker. The program prompts the user for skill level and hours worked, as well as appropriate insurance and retirement options for the employee's skill level category. The application displays: (1) the hours worked, (2) the hourly pay rate, (3) the regular pay for 40 hours, (4) the overtime pay, (5) the total of regular and overtime pay, and (6) the total itemized deductions. If the deductions exceed the gross pay, display an error message; otherwise, calculate and display (7) the net pay after all the deductions have been subtracted from the gross. Save the file as **Pay.java** in the Chapter.05 folder on your Student Disk.

GAME ZONE

1. In Chapter 1, you created a class called `RandomGuess`. In this game, players guess a number, the application generates a random number, and players determine whether they were correct. Now that you can make decisions, modify the application so it allows a player to enter a guess before the random number is displayed and then displays a message indicating whether the player's guess was correct, too high, or too low. Save the file as **RandomGuess2.java**. (After you finish Chapter 6, you will be able to modify the application so that the user can continue to guess until the correct answer is entered.)

2. Create a lottery game application. Generate three random numbers (see Appendix D for help in doing so), each between 0 and 9. Allow the user to guess three numbers. Compare each of the user's guesses to the three random numbers and display a message that includes the user's guess, the randomly determined three-digit number, and the amount of money the user has won as follows:

Matching Numbers	Award ($)
Any one matching	10
Two matching	100
Three matching, not in order	1000
Three matching in exact order	1,000,000
No matches	0

Make certain that your application accommodates repeating digits. For example, if a user guesses 1, 2, and 3, and the randomly generated digits are 1, 1, and 1, do not give the user credit for three correct guesses—just one. Save the file as **Lottery.java** in the Chapter.05 folder on your Student Disk.

3. In Chapter 3, you created a `Card` class. Modify the `Card` class so the `setValue()` method does not allow a `Card`'s value to be less than 1 or higher than 13. If the argument to `setValue()` is out of range, assign 1 to the `Card`'s value.

In Chapter 3, you also created a `PickTwoCards` application that randomly selects two playing cards and displays their values. In that application, all `Card` objects arbitrarily were assigned a suit represented by a single character, but they could have different values, and the player observed which of two `Card` objects had the higher value. Now, modify the application so the suit and the value both are chosen randomly. Using two `Card` objects, play a very simple version of the card game War. Deal two `Cards`—one for the computer and one for the player—and determine the higher card, then display a message indicating whether the cards are equal, the computer won, or the player won. (Playing cards are considered equal when they have the same value, no matter what their suit is.) For this game, assume the Ace (value 1) is low. Make sure that the two `Cards` dealt are not the same `Card`. For example, a deck cannot contain more than one `Card` representing the 2 of Spades. If two cards are chosen to have the same value, change the suit for one of them. Save the application as **War.java**. (After you learn about arrays in

Chapter 8, you will be able to create a more sophisticated War game in which you use an entire deck without repeating cards.)

4. In Chapter 4, you created a `Die` class from which you could instantiate an object containing a random value from 1 through 6. You also wrote an application that randomly "throws" two dice and displays their values. Modify the application so it determines whether the two dice are the same, the first has a higher value, or the second has a higher value. Save the application as **TwoDice2.java**.

5. In the game Rock Paper Scissors, two players simultaneously choose one of three options: rock, paper, or scissors. If both players choose the same option, then the result is a tie. However, if they choose differently, the winner is determined as follows:

» Rock beats scissors, because a rock can break a pair of scissors.
» Scissors beats paper, because scissors can cut paper.
» Paper beats rock, because a piece of paper can cover a rock.

Create a game in which the computer randomly chooses rock, paper, or scissors. Let the user enter a number 1, 2, or 3, each representing one of the three choices. Then, determine the winner. Save the application as **RockPaperScissors.java**. (In Chapter 7, you will modify the game so that the user enters a string for "rock", "paper", and "scissors", rather than just entering a number.)

UP FOR DISCUSSION

1. In this chapter, you learned how computer programs make decisions. Insurance companies use programs to make decisions about your insurability as well as the rates you will be charged for health and life insurance policies. For example, certain preexisting conditions may raise your insurance premiums considerably. Is it ethical for insurance companies to access your health records and then make insurance decisions about you?

2. Job applications are sometimes screened by software that makes decisions about a candidate's suitability based on keywords in the applications. For example, when a help-wanted ad lists "management experience," the presence of those exact words might determine which résumés are chosen for further scrutiny. Is such screening fair to applicants?

3. Medical facilities often have more patients waiting for organ transplants than there are available organs. Suppose you have been asked to write a computer program that selects which of several candidates should receive an available organ. What data would you want on file to use in your program, and what decisions would you make based on the data? What data do you think others might use that you would not use?

LOOPING

In this chapter, you will:

Learn about the loop structure
Use a `while` loop
Use shortcut arithmetic operators
Use a `for` loop
Learn how and when to use a `do...while` loop
Learn about nested loops
Understand how to improve loop performance

LEARNING ABOUT THE LOOP STRUCTURE

If making decisions is what makes programs seem smart, looping is what makes programs seem powerful. A **loop** is a structure that allows repeated execution of a block of statements. Within a looping structure, a Boolean expression is evaluated. If it is true, a block of statements called the **loop body** executes and the Boolean expression is evaluated again. As long as the expression is true, the statements in the loop body continue to execute. When the Boolean evaluation is false, the loop ends. Figure 6-1 shows a diagram of the logic of a loop.

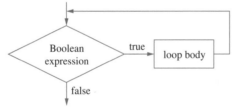

Figure 6-1 Flowchart of a loop structure

In Java, you can use several mechanisms to create loops. In this chapter, you will learn to use three types of loops:

» A while loop, in which the loop-controlling Boolean expression is the first statement in the loop

» A for loop, which is usually used as a concise format in which to execute loops

» A do...while loop, in which the loop-controlling Boolean expression is the last statement in the loop

USING A while LOOP TO CREATE A DEFINITE LOOP

You can use a **while loop** to execute a body of statements continually as long as the Boolean expression that controls entry into the loop continues to be true. In Java, a while loop consists of the keyword while followed by a Boolean expression within parentheses, followed by the body of the loop, which can be a single statement or a block of statements surrounded by curly braces.

You can use a while loop when you need to perform a task a predetermined number of times. A loop that executes a specific number of times is a **definite loop** or a counted loop.

To write a definite loop, you initialize a **loop control variable**, a variable whose value determines whether loop execution continues. While the loop control variable does not pass a limiting value, you continue to execute the body of the `while` loop. In the body of the loop, you must include a statement that alters the loop control variable. For example, the program segment shown in Figure 6-2 prints the series of integers 1 through 10. The variable `val` is the loop control variable—it starts the loop holding a value of 1, and while the value remains under 11, the `val` continues to print and be increased.

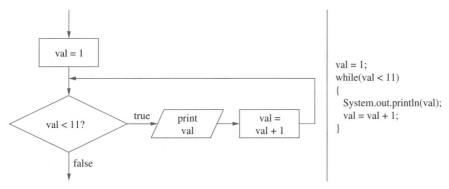

```
val = 1;
while(val < 11)
{
    System.out.println(val);
    val = val + 1;
}
```

Figure 6-2 A `while` loop that prints the integers 1 through 10

When you write applications containing loops, it is easy to make mistakes. For example, executing the code shown in Figure 6-3 causes the message "Hello" to display (theoretically) forever because there is no code to end the loop. A loop that never ends is called an **infinite loop**.

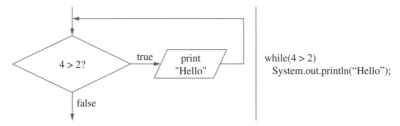

```
while(4 > 2)
    System.out.println("Hello");
```

Figure 6-3 A loop that displays "Hello" infinitely

> **NOTE** As an inside joke to programmers, the address of Apple Computer, Inc. is One Infinite Loop, Cupertino, California.

> **NOTE** An infinite loop might not actually execute infinitely. Depending on the tasks the loop performs, eventually the computer memory might be exhausted (literally and figuratively) and execution might stop. Also, it's possible that the processor has a time-out feature that forces the loop to end. Either way, and depending on your system, quite a bit of time could pass before the loop stops running.

In Figure 6-3, the expression `4 > 2` evaluates to `true`. You obviously never need to make such an evaluation, but if you do so in this `while` loop, the body of the loop is entered and "Hello" displays. Next, the expression is evaluated again. The expression `4 > 2` is still `true`, so the body is entered again. "Hello" displays repeatedly; the loop never finishes because `4 > 2` is never `false`.

» NOTE
On many keyboards, the Break key is also the Pause key.

It is a bad idea to intentionally write an infinite loop. However, even experienced programmers write them by accident. So, before you start writing loops, it is good to know how to exit from an infinite loop in the event you find yourself in the midst of one. You might suspect an infinite loop if the same output is displayed repeatedly, or if the screen simply remains idle for an extended period of time without displaying expected output. If you think your application is in an infinite loop, you can press and hold Ctrl, and then press C or Break; the looping program should terminate.

To prevent a `while` loop from executing infinitely, three separate actions must occur:

» A named loop control variable is initialized to a starting value.

» The loop control variable is tested in the `while` statement.

» If the test expression is `true`, the body of the `while` statement must take some action that alters the value of the loop control variable; the test of the `while` statement must eventually evaluate to `false` so that the loop can end.

All of these conditions are met by the example in Figure 6-4. First, a loop control variable `loopCount` is named and set to a value of 1. Second, the statement `while(loopCount < 3)` is tested. Third, the loop body is executed because the loop control variable `loopCount` is less than 3. Note that the loop body shown in Figure 6-4 consists of two statements made into a block by their surrounding curly braces. The first statement prints "Hello," and then the second statement adds 1 to `loopCount`. The next time `loopCount` is evaluated, it is 2. It is still less than 3, so the loop body executes again. "Hello" prints a second time, and `loopCount` becomes 3. Finally, because the expression `loopCount < 3` now evaluates to `false`, the loop ends. Program execution then continues with any subsequent statements.

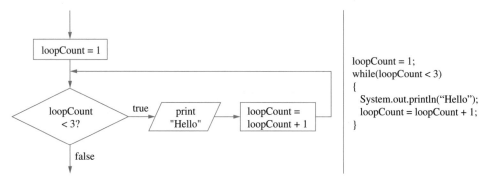

Figure 6-4 A `while` loop that prints "Hello" twice

» NOTE To an algebra student, a statement such as `loopCount = loopCount + 1;` looks wrong—a value can never be one more than itself. In algebra, the equal sign means equivalency. In Java, however, the equal sign assigns a value to the variable on the left. Therefore, `loopCount = loopCount + 1;` takes the value of `loopCount`, adds 1 to it, and then assigns the new value back into `loopCount`.

It is important that the loop control variable be altered within the body of the loop. Figure 6-5 shows the same code as in Figure 6-4, but the curly braces have been eliminated. In this case, the `while` loop stops at the semicolon that appears at the end of the "Hello" statement. Adding 1 to the `loopCount` is no longer part of a block that contains the loop, so the value of `loopCount` never changes and an infinite loop is created.

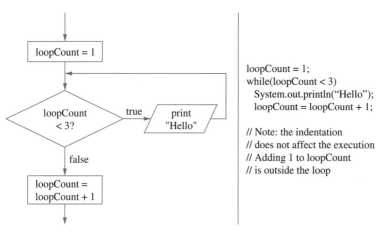

```
loopCount = 1;
while(loopCount < 3)
   System.out.println("Hello");
   loopCount = loopCount + 1;

// Note: the indentation
// does not affect the execution
// Adding 1 to loopCount
// is outside the loop
```

Figure 6-5 A `while` loop that prints "Hello" infinitely because `loopCount` is not altered in the loop body

As with the decision-making `if` statement that you learned about in Chapter 5, placement of the statement-ending semicolon is important when you work with the `while` statement. If a semicolon is mistakenly placed at the end of the partial statement `while (loopCount < 3);`, as shown in Figure 6-6, the loop is also infinite. This loop has an **empty body**, or a body with no statements in it. So, the Boolean expression is evaluated, and because it is `true`, the loop body is entered. Because the loop body is empty, no action is taken, and the Boolean expression is evaluated again. Nothing has changed, so it is still `true`, the empty body is entered, and the infinite loop continues.

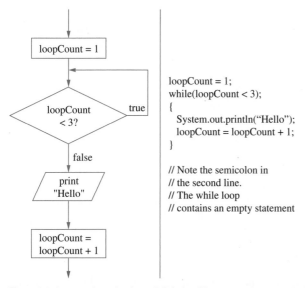

```
loopCount = 1;
while(loopCount < 3);
{
   System.out.println("Hello");
   loopCount = loopCount + 1;
}

// Note the semicolon in
// the second line.
// The while loop
// contains an empty statement
```

Figure 6-6 A `while` loop that loops infinitely with no output because the loop body is empty

It is very common to alter the value of a loop control variable by adding 1 to it, or **incrementing** the variable. However, not all loops are controlled by adding 1. The loop shown in

Figure 6-7 prints "Hello" twice, just as the loop in Figure 6-4 does, but its loop is controlled by subtracting 1 from a loop control variable, or **decrementing** it.

```
loopCount = 3;
while(loopCount > 1)
{
    System.out.println("Hello");
    loopCount = loopCount - 1;
}
```

Figure 6-7 A `while` loop that prints "Hello" twice, decrementing the `loopCount` variable in the loop body

In the program segment shown in Figure 6-7, the variable `loopCount` begins with a value of 3. The `loopCount` is greater than 1, so the loop body prints "Hello" and decrements `loopCount` to 2. The Boolean expression in the `while` loop is tested again. Because 2 is more than 1, "Hello" prints again and `loopCount` becomes 1. Now `loopCount` is not greater than 1, so the loop ends. There are many ways to execute a loop two times. For example, you can initialize a loop control variable to 10, and continue to print while the value is greater than 8, decreasing the value by 1 each time you pass through the loop. Similarly, you can initialize the loop control variable to 12, continue while it is greater than 2, and decrease the value by 5 each time. In general, you should not use such unusual methods to count repetitions because they simply make a program confusing. To execute a loop a specific number of times, the clearest and best method is to start the loop control variable at 0 or 1, stop when the loop control variable reaches the appropriate limit, and increment by 1 each time through the loop.

>> **NOTE**   When you first start programming, it seems reasonable to initialize counter values to 1, and that is a workable approach. However, many seasoned programmers start counter values at 0 because they are used to doing so when working with arrays. When you study arrays in Chapter 8, you will learn that their elements are numbered beginning with 0.

USING A while LOOP TO CREATE AN INDEFINITE LOOP

>> **NOTE**
A definite loop is a **counter-controlled loop**. An indefinite loop is an **event-controlled loop**; that is, an event occurs that determines whether the loop continues.

Within a loop, you are not required to alter the loop control variable by adding to it or subtracting from it. Often, the value of a loop control variable is not altered by arithmetic, but instead is altered by user input. For example, perhaps you want to continue performing some task as long as the user indicates a desire to continue. In this case, while you are writing the program, you do not know whether the loop eventually will be executed two times, 200 times, or at all. Unlike a loop that you program to execute a fixed number of times, a loop controlled by the user is a type of **indefinite loop** because you don't know how many times it will eventually loop.

Consider an application in which you ask the user for a bank balance and then ask whether the user wants to see the balance after interest has accumulated for each year. Each time the user chooses to continue, an increased balance appears, reflecting one more year of accumulated interest. When the user finally chooses to exit, the program ends. The program appears in Figure 6-8.

```
import javax.swing.JOptionPane;
public class BankBalance
{
    public static void main(String[] args)
    {
        int selection;
        String balanceString;
        double balance;
        int tempBalance;
        int year = 1;
        final double INT_RATE = 0.03;
        balanceString = JOptionPane.showInputDialog(null,
           "Enter initial bank balance");
        balance = Double.parseDouble(balanceString);
        selection = JOptionPane.showConfirmDialog(null,
           "Do you want to see next year's balance?");
        while(selection == JOptionPane.YES_OPTION)
        {
            balance = balance + balance * INT_RATE;
               // Note: the next two statements round the balance
            tempBalance = (int)(balance * 100);
            balance = tempBalance / 100.0;
            selection = JOptionPane.showConfirmDialog(null,
                "After " + year + " years at " +  INT_RATE +
                " interest rate, balance is $" + balance +
                "\nDo you want to see the balance at the end " +
                "\nof another year?");
            year = year + 1;
        }
        System.exit(0);
    }
}
```

Figure 6-8 The `BankBalance` application

The program shown in Figure 6-8 declares needed variables and a constant for a 3% interest rate, and then asks the user for a balance. The application uses an input dialog box containing Yes, No, and Cancel buttons to ask whether the user wants to see the balance after a year of interest has accumulated. As long as the user's selection is equivalent to the `JOptionPane.YES_OPTION`, the application continues to display increasing bank balances.

The loop in the application in Figure 6-8 begins with the line that contains:

```
while(selection == JOptionPane.YES_OPTION)
```

If the user selects any option other than Yes, the loop body never executes; instead, the next statement to execute is the `System.exit(0)` statement at the bottom of the application. However, if the user selects Yes, all five statements within the loop body execute. The application increases the balance by the interest rate value. Then, the balance times 100 is cast to an integer (for example, a calculated balance of 10.635 becomes 1063), and the result is divided by 100 (for example, 1063 becomes 10.63). The net effect of these two statements is to limit the number of decimal places in the balance to two. After these calculations, the application displays the new balance

» NOTE
You first learned about type casting in Chapter 2.

and asks whether the user wants another balance. The `year` variable increases and the loop body ends with a closing curly brace. After the loop body executes, control returns to the top of the loop, where the Boolean expression in the `while` loop is tested again. If the user selects Yes when presented with the last option, the loop is entered and the process begins again. Figure 6-9 shows the output of the `BankBalance` application after the user enters a $1000 starting balance and responds with Yes five times to the prompt for increased interest payments.

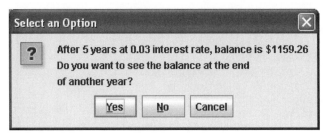

Figure 6-9 Output of the `BankBalance` application

Programmers commonly use indefinite loops when validating input data. **Validating data** is the process of ensuring that a value falls within a specified range. For example, suppose you require a user to enter a value no greater than 3. Figure 6-10 shows an application that does not progress past the data entry loop until the user enters a correct value. If the user enters 3 or less at the first prompt, the shaded loop never executes. However, if the user enters a number greater than 3, the shaded loop executes, providing the user with another chance to enter a correct value. While the user continues to enter incorrect data, the loop repeats.

```java
import javax.swing.*;
public class EnterSmallValue
{
    public static void main(String[] args)
    {
        int userEntry;
        String userString;
        userString = JOptionPane.showInputDialog(null,
          "Please enter an integer no higher than 3");
        userEntry = Integer.parseInt(userString);
        while(userEntry > 3)
        {
            userString = JOptionPane.showInputDialog(null,
                "The number you entered was too high\n" +
                "Please enter an integer no higher than 3");
            userEntry = Integer.parseInt(userString);
        }
        JOptionPane.showMessageDialog(null,
          "You entered " + userEntry);
        System.exit(0);
    }
}
```

Figure 6-10 The `EnterSmallValue` application

USING SHORTCUT ARITHMETIC OPERATORS

Programmers commonly need to increase the value of a variable in a program. As you saw in the previous section, many loops are controlled by continually adding 1 to some variable, or incrementing, as in `count = count + 1;`. Similarly, in the looping bank balance program shown in Figure 6-8, the program not only incremented the `year` variable by adding 1, but also increased a bank balance by an interest amount with the statement `balance = balance + balance * INT_RATE;`. In other words, the bank balance became its old value *plus* a new interest amount; the process of repeatedly increasing a value by some amount is known as **accumulating**.

Because increasing a variable is so common, Java provides you with several shortcuts for incrementing and accumulating. The statement `count += 1;` is identical in meaning to `count = count + 1`. The `+=` adds and assigns in one operation. Similarly, `balance += balance * INT_RATE;` increases a balance by the `INT_RATE` percentage. Besides using the shortcut operator `+=`, you can use `-=`, `*=`, and `/=`. Each of these operators is used to perform the operation and assign the result in one step. For example, `balanceDue -= payment` subtracts `payment` from `balanceDue` and assigns the result to `balanceDue`.

When you want to increase a variable's value by exactly 1, you can use two other shortcut operators—the **prefix** ++ (also known as the **prefix increment operator**), and the **postfix** ++ (also known as the **postfix increment operator**). To use a prefix ++, you type two plus signs before the variable name. The statement `someValue = 6;` followed by `++someValue;` results in `someValue` holding 7—one more than it held before you applied the ++. To use a postfix ++, you type two plus signs just after a variable name. The statements `anotherValue = 56; anotherValue++;` result in `anotherValue` containing 57. Figure 6-11 shows four ways you can increase a value by 1; each method produces the same result. You are never required to use shortcut operators; they are merely a convenience.

```
int value;
value = 24;
++value;  // Result - value is 25
value = 24;
value++;  // Result - value is 25
value = 24;
value = value + 1;   // Result - value is 25
value = 24;
value += 1;  // Result - value is 25
```

Figure 6-11 Four ways to add 1 to a value

» NOTE
You first learned about the term *unary* in Chapter 4. You use a unary minus sign preceding a value to make the value negative.

The prefix and postfix increment operators are unary operators because you use them with one value. Most arithmetic operators, such as those used for addition and multiplication, are **binary operators**—they operate on two values.

When you simply want to increase a variable's value by 1, there is no difference between using the prefix and postfix increment operators. For example, when value is set to 24 in Figure 6-11, both ++value and value++ result in value becoming 25; each operator results in increasing the variable by 1. However, these operators do function differently in terms of *when* the increment operation occurs. When you use the prefix ++, the result is calculated and stored, and then the variable is used. For example, if b = 4; and c = ++b;, the result is that both b and c hold the value 5. When you use the postfix ++, the variable is used, and then the result is calculated and stored. For example, if b = 4; and c = b++;, 4 is assigned to c, and then after the assignment, b is increased and takes the value 5. In other words, if b = 4;, the value of b++ is also 4, but after the statement is completed, the value of b is 5. If d = 8; and e = 8;, both ++d == 9 and e++ == 8 are true expressions.

Figure 6-12 shows an application that illustrates the difference between how the prefix and postfix increment operators work. Notice from the output in Figure 6-13 that when the prefix increment operator is used on myNumber, the value of myNumber increases from 17 to 18, and the result is stored in answer, which also becomes 18. After the value is reset to 17, the postfix increment operator is used; 17 is assigned to answer, and myNumber is incremented to 18.

```java
public class IncrementDemo
{
    public static void main(String[] args)
    {
        int myNumber, answer;
        myNumber = 17;
        answer = ++myNumber;
        System.out.println
            ("When myNumber is initialized to 17 and answer =
                ++myNumber");
        System.out.println("  myNumber is " + myNumber);
        System.out.println("  and answer is " + answer);
        myNumber = 17;
        answer = myNumber++;
        System.out.println
            ("When myNumber is initialized to 17 and answer =
                myNumber++");
        System.out.println("  myNumber is " + myNumber);
        System.out.println("  and answer is " + answer);
    }
}
```

Figure 6-12 The IncrementDemo application

Similar logic can be applied when you use the **prefix and postfix decrement operators**. For example, if b = 4; and c = b--;, 4 is assigned to c, and then after the assignment, b is decreased and takes the value 3. If b = 4; and c = --b;, b is decreased to 3 and 3 is assigned to c.

```
Command Prompt                                    _ □ ×
When myNumber is initialized to 17 and answer = ++myNumber
    myNumber is 18
    and answer is 18
When myNumber is initialized to 17 and answer = myNumber++
    myNumber is 18
    and answer is 17

C:\Java>
```

Figure 6-13 Output of the IncrementDemo application

USING A for LOOP

A **for loop** is a special loop that is used when a definite number of loop iterations is required. Although a while loop can also be used to meet this requirement, the for loop provides you with a shorthand notation for this type of loop. When you use a for loop, you can indicate the starting value for the loop control variable, the test condition that controls loop entry, and the expression that alters the loop control variable—all in one convenient place.

» NOTE
A for loop provides a convenient way to create a counter-controlled loop.

You begin a for loop with the keyword for followed by a set of parentheses. Within the parentheses are three sections separated by exactly two semicolons. The three sections are usually used for the following:

» Initializing the loop control variable

» Testing the loop control variable

» Updating the loop control variable

The body of the for statement follows the parentheses. As with an if statement or a while loop, you can use a single statement as the body of a for loop, or you can use a block of statements enclosed in curly braces. The for statement shown in Figure 6-14 produces the same output as the while statement shown previously in Figure 6-2—it prints the integers 1 through 10.

```
for(int val = 1; val < 11; ++val)
    System.out.println(val);
```

Figure 6-14 A for loop that prints the integers 1 through 10

> **» NOTE** The variable val did not have to be declared within the for statement. If val was declared earlier in the program block as int val; before the for statement begins, the for statement would be for(val = 1; val < 11; ++val). In other words, the for statement does not need to declare a variable; it can simply give a starting value to a previously declared variable. However, programmers frequently declare a variable within a for statement just for use within that loop.

Within the parentheses of the for statement shown in Figure 6-14, the first section prior to the first semicolon declares a variable named val and initializes it to 1. The program executes this statement once, no matter how many times the body of the for loop executes.

After initialization, program control passes to the middle, or test section, of the `for` statement. If the Boolean expression found there evaluates to `true`, the body of the `for` loop is entered. In the program segment shown in Figure 6-14, `val` is set to 1, so when `val < 11` is tested, it evaluates to `true`. The loop body prints the `val`. In this example, the loop body is a single statement, so no curly braces are needed. If you want multiple statements to execute within the loop, they have to be blocked within a pair of curly braces. This is the same technique you use to execute multiple statements that depend on an `if` or a `while`.

After the loop body executes, the final one-third of the `for` loop executes, and `val` is increased to 2. Following the third section in the `for` statement, program control returns to the second section, where `val` is compared to 11 a second time. Because `val` is still less than 11, the body executes: `val` (now 2) prints, and then the third, altering portion of the `for` loop executes again. The variable `val` increases to 3, and the `for` loop continues.

Eventually, when `val` is not less than 11 (after 1 through 10 have printed), the `for` loop ends, and the program continues with any statements that follow the `for` loop. Although the three sections of the `for` loop are most commonly used for initializing, testing, and incrementing, you can also perform the following tasks:

» Initialization of more than one variable by placing commas between the separate statements, as in the following:

```
for(g = 0, h = 1; g < 6; ++g)
```

» Performance of more than one test using AND or OR operators, as in the following:

```
for(g = 0; g < 3 && h > 1; ++g)
```

» Decrementation or performance of some other task, as in the following:

```
for(g = 5; g >= 1; --g)
```

> **NOTE** You can leave one or more portions of the `for` loop empty, although the two semicolons are still required as placeholders. For example, if `x` has been initialized in a previous program statement, you might write the following:
>
> ```
> for(; x < 10; ++x)...
> ```
>
> To someone reading your program, this technique at first glance is less clear than using all three sections of the `for` statement.

> **NOTE** Java 5 and 6 contain an enhanced `for` loop. You will learn about this loop in Chapter 8.

> **NOTE** In general, not only should you use the same loop control variable in all three parts of the `for` statement, you should also avoid altering it in the body of the loop. If a variable is altered both within the `for` statement and within the block it controls, it can be very difficult to follow the program's logic. This technique can also produce program bugs that are hard to find.

> **NOTE** Java also contains a built-in method to pause program execution. The `sleep()` method is part of the `Thread` class in the `java.lang` package.

Usually, you should use the `for` loop for its intended purpose—a shorthand way of programming a definite loop. Occasionally, you will encounter a `for` loop that contains no body, such as the following:

```
for(x = 0; x < 100000; ++x);
```

This kind of loop exists simply to use time—that is, to occupy the central processing unit for thousands of processing cycles—when a brief pause is desired during program execution, for example. As with `if` and `while` statements, usually you do not want to place a semicolon at the end of the `for` statement before the body of the loop.

LEARNING HOW AND WHEN TO USE A do...while LOOP

With all the loops you have written so far, the loop body might execute many times, but it is also possible that the loop will not execute at all. For example, recall the bank balance program that displays compound interest, part of which is shown in Figure 6-15.

```
selection = JOptionPane.showConfirmDialog(null,
        "Do you want to see next year's balance?");
while(selection == JOptionPane.YES_OPTION)
{
    balance = balance + balance * INT_RATE;
        // Note: the next two statements round the balance
    tempBalance = (int)(balance * 100);
    balance = tempBalance / 100.0;
    selection = JOptionPane.showConfirmDialog(null,
        "After " + year + " years at " +  INT_RATE +
        " interest rate, balance is $" + balance +
        "\nDo you want to see the balance at the end " +
        "\nof another year?");
    year = year + 1;
}
```

Figure 6-15 A loop from the `BankBalance` application

The program segment begins by showing the prompt "Do you want to see next year's balance?" in a dialog box. If the user does not respond by clicking Yes, the loop body never executes. The `while` loop checks a value at the "top" of the loop before the body has a chance to execute. Sometimes, you might need to ensure that a loop body executes at least one time. If so, you want to write a loop that checks at the "bottom" of the loop after the first iteration. The **do...while loop** checks the value of the loop control variable at the bottom of the loop after one repetition has occurred.

> **NOTE** A `while` loop is a **pretest loop**—one in which the loop control variable is tested before the loop body executes. The `do...while` loop is a **posttest loop**—one in which the loop control variable is tested after the loop body executes.

Figure 6-16 shows the general structure of a `do...while` loop. Notice that the loop body executes before the loop-controlling question is asked for the first time. Figure 6-17 shows a `do...while` loop that could be used in the `BankBalance` application. The loop starts with the keyword `do`. The body of the loop follows and is contained within curly braces. The first year's balance is output before the user has any option of responding. At the end of the loop, the user is prompted, "Do you want to see the balance at the end of another year?" Now the user has the option of seeing more balances, but the first display was unavoidable. The user's response is checked at the bottom of the loop; if it is Yes, the loop repeats.

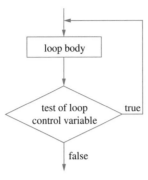

Figure 6-16 General structure of a do...while loop

```
do
{
    balance = balance + balance * INT_RATE;
        // Note: the next two statements round the balance
    tempBalance = (int)(balance * 100);
    balance = tempBalance / 100.0;
    selection = JOptionPane.showConfirmDialog(null,
        "After " + year + " years at " + INT_RATE +
    " interest rate, balance is $" + balance +
        "\nDo you want to see the balance at the end " +
        "\nof another year?");
    year = year + 1;
} while(selection == JOptionPane.YES_OPTION);
```

Figure 6-17 A do...while loop for the BankBalance application

In any situation in which you want to loop, you are never required to use a do...while loop. Within the bank balance example, you could achieve the same results as the logic shown in Figure 6-17 by unconditionally displaying the first year's bank balance once before starting the loop, prompting the user, and then starting a while loop that might not be entered. However, when you know you want to perform some task at least one time, the do...while loop is convenient.

> **» NOTE** When the body of a do...while loop contains a single statement, you do not need to use curly braces to block the statement. For example, the following loop correctly adds numberValue to total while total remains less than 200:
>
> ```
> do
>     total += numberValue;
> while (total < 200);
> ```
>
> Even though curly braces are not required in this case, many programmers recommend using them. Doing so prevents the third line of code from looking like it should begin a new while loop. Therefore, even though the result is the same, the following is less likely to be misunderstood by a reader:
>
> ```
> do
> {
>     total += numberValue;
> } while (total < 200);
> ```

LEARNING ABOUT NESTED LOOPS

Just as if statements can be nested, so can loops. You can place a while loop within a while loop, a for loop within a for loop, a while loop within a for loop, or any other combination. When loops are nested, each pair contains an **inner loop** and an **outer loop**. The inner loop must be entirely contained within the outer loop; loops can never overlap. Figure 6-18 shows a diagram in which the shaded loop is nested within another loop; the shaded area is the inner loop as well as the body of the outer loop.

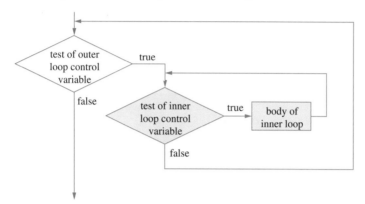

Figure 6-18 Nested loops

Suppose you want to display future bank balances for any number of years, but also for a variety of interest rates. Figure 6-19 shows an application that contains an indefinite outer loop controlled by the user's response to a question about viewing the next year's balance. Each time the user responds Yes to "Do you want to see next year's balance?", the outer loop body is entered. Within this outer loop, an inner definite loop displays balance values calculated with every interest rate from 1% through 5%. Only after the user has viewed each of the five interest rate calculations for a year (finishing the inner loop) does the program prompt the user about viewing a new year's values (starting another repetition of the outer loop).

When you use a loop within a loop, you should always think of the outer loop as the all-encompassing loop. When you describe the task at hand, you often use the word "each" when referring to the inner loop. For example, if you want to print three mailing labels each for 20 customers, the label variable would control the inner loop, as shown in the following code:

```
for(customer = 1; customer <= 20; ++customer)
    for(label = 1; label <= 3; ++label)
        printLabelMethod();
```

IMPROVING LOOP PERFORMANCE

Whether you decide to use a while, for, or do...while loop in an application, you can improve loop performance by making sure the loop does not include unnecessary operations or statements. For example, suppose a loop should execute while x is less than the sum of two integers, a and b. The loop could be written as:

```
while (x < a + b)
    // loop body
```

```
import javax.swing.JOptionPane;
public class BankBalanceVaryingInterest
{
    public static void main(String[] args)
    {
        int selection;
        String balanceString;
        double balance;
        int tempBalance;
        int year = 1;
        double interest;
        balanceString = JOptionPane.showInputDialog(null,
            "Enter initial bank balance");
        balance = Double.parseDouble(balanceString);
        selection = JOptionPane.showConfirmDialog(null,
            "Do you want to see next year's balance?");
        while(selection == JOptionPane.YES_OPTION)
        {
            for(interest = 0.02; interest <= 0.05; interest += 0.01)
            {
                balance = balance + balance * interest;
                tempBalance = (int)(balance * 100);
                balance = tempBalance / 100.0;
                JOptionPane.showMessageDialog(null,
                    "After " + year + " years at " + interest +
                    " interest rate, balance is $" + balance);
            }
            selection = JOptionPane.showConfirmDialog(null,
                "Do you want to see the balance at the end " +
                "\nof another year?");
            year = year + 1;
        }
        System.exit(0);
    }
}
```

Figure 6-19 The BankBalanceVaryingInterest class containing nested loops

> **» NOTE** In the code in Figure 6-19, values such as 0.02 (the starting interest rate in the for loop), 0.05 (the ending interest rate), and 0.01 (the step value) could all be stored as named constants. They were excluded from this example to reduce the number of code lines to read.

If this loop executes 1000 times, then the expression a + b is calculated 1000 times. Instead, if you use the following code, the results are the same, but the arithmetic is performed only once:

```
int sum = a + b;
while(x < sum)
    // loop body
```

Of course, if a or b is altered in the loop body, then a new sum must be calculated with every loop iteration. However, if the sum of a and b is fixed prior to the start of the loop, then writing the code the second way is far more efficient. As you become an experienced programmer, you should always be on the lookout for ways to improve program performance.

YOU DO IT

WRITING A LOOP TO VALIDATE DATA ENTRIES

In Chapter 5, you created a ChooseManager application. The application allowed the user to enter a 1 or 2 to select a private or corporate event to be held by Event Handlers Incorporated. The output was the name of the manager in charge of the event type. Next, you will improve the ChooseManager program so the user cannot make an invalid choice for the type of event—if the user does not enter a 1 or 2, the user will continue to be prompted until a valid selection is entered.

To improve the ChooseManager program to prevent invalid data entry:

1. Enter the first lines of the ChooseManager class. These statements are identical to those in the ChooseManager class you created in Chapter 5, so you can save time if you want by copying these lines of code from that file. The statements create a ChooseManager class and start a main() method that contains constants for the managers' names. The user is shown an input dialog box into which the user can enter a 1 or 2, representing a private or corporate event:

```java
import javax.swing.JOptionPane;
public class ChooseManager
{
  public static void main(String[] args)
  {
    String choiceString, chosenManager;
    int eventType;
    final String PRIV_MANAGER = "Dustin Britt";
    final String CORP_MANAGER = "Carmen Lindsey";
    choiceString = JOptionPane.showInputDialog(null,
      "What type of event are you scheduling?" +
      "\nEnter 1 for Private, 2 for Corporate");
    eventType = Integer.parseInt(choiceString);
```

2. Type the while loop that will continue to execute while the user's entry is not one of the two allowed event types. When the user's entry is not a 1 and not a 2, the user is informed of the error and is allowed to type a new choice:

```java
while(eventType != 1 && eventType != 2)
{
    choiceString = JOptionPane.showInputDialog(null,
      "Invalid entry. You must choose 1 or 2." +
      "\nEnter 1 for Private, 2 for Corporate");
    eventType = Integer.parseInt(choiceString);
}
```

3. On a new line, type the decision structure that sets the `chosenManager` variable. If the `eventType` is not 1, then it must be 2, or the program would still be executing the loop waiting for a 1 or 2 from the user:

```
if(eventType == 1)
   chosenManager = PRIV_MANAGER;
else
   chosenManager = CORP_MANAGER;
```

4. Display the manager for the chosen event type, and then exit the application:

```
JOptionPane.showMessageDialog(null,
    "Manager for this event will be " + chosenManager);
System.exit(0);
```

5. Add the closing curly brace for the `main()` method and the closing curly brace for the class. Save the file as **ChooseManager.java** in the Chapter.06 folder on your Student Disk.

6. Compile and execute the application. No matter how many invalid entries you make, the program continues to prompt you until you enter a 1 or 2 for the event type.

WORKING WITH PREFIX AND POSTFIX INCREMENT OPERATORS

Next, you will write an application that demonstrates how prefix and postfix operators are used in incrementation and how incrementing affects the expressions that contain these operators.

To demonstrate the effect of the prefix and postfix increment operators:

1. Open a new text file and begin a demonstration class named `DemoIncrement` by typing:

```
public class DemoIncrement
{
   public static void main(String[] args)
   {
```

2. On a new line, add a variable `v` and assign it a value of 4. Then declare a variable named `plusPlusV` and assign it a value of `++v` by typing:

```
int v = 4;
int plusPlusV = ++v;
```

3. The last statement, `int plusPlusV = ++v;` will increase `v` to 5, so before declaring a `vPlusPlus` variable to which you assign `v++`, reset `v` to 4 by typing:

```
v = 4;
int vPlusPlus = v++;
```

4. Add the following statements to print the three values:

```
System.out.println("v is " + v);
System.out.println("++v is " + plusPlusV);
System.out.println("v++ is " + vPlusPlus);
```

5. Add the closing curly brace for the `main()` method and the closing curly brace for the `DemoIncrement` class.

6. Save the file as **DemoIncrement.java** in the Chapter.06 folder on your Student Disk. Compile and execute the program. Your output should look like Figure 6-20.

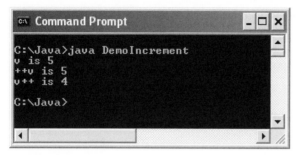

Figure 6-20 Output of the `DemoIncrement` class

7. To illustrate how comparisons are made, add a few more variables to the `DemoIncrement` program. Change the class name to **DemoIncrement2** and immediately save the file as **DemoIncrement2.java**.

8. Position the insertion point to the right of the last `println()` statement, and then press **Enter** to start a new line. Then add three new integer variables and two new Boolean variables. The first Boolean variable compares ++w to y; the second Boolean variable compares x++ to y:

```
int w = 17, x = 17, y = 18;
boolean compare1 = (++w == y);
boolean compare2 = (x++ == y);
```

9. Add the following statements to display the values stored in the `compare` variables:

```
System.out.println("First compare is " + compare1);
System.out.println("Second compare is " + compare2);
```

10. Save, compile, and run the program. The output appears in Figure 6-21. Make certain you understand why each statement displays the values it does.

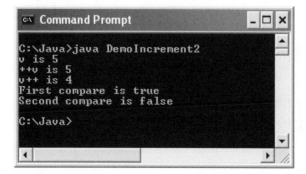

Figure 6-21 Output of the `DemoIncrement2` application

WORKING WITH DEFINITE LOOPS

Suppose you want to find all the numbers that divide evenly into 100. You want to write a definite loop—one that executes exactly 100 times. You can write a `for` loop that sets a variable to 1 and increments it to 100. Each of the 100 times through the loop, if 100 is evenly divisible by the variable, the application prints the number.

To write an application that finds the values that divide evenly into 100:

1. Open a new text file. Begin the application named `DivideEvenly` by typing the following code. Use a named constant for the 100 value and a variable named `var` that will hold, in turn, every value from 1 through 100:

```
public class DivideEvenly
{
 public static void main(String[] args)
 {
     final int NUMBER = 100;
     int var;
```

2. Type a statement that explains the purpose of the program:

```
System.out.print(NUMBER + " is evenly divisible by ");
```

3. Write the `for` loop that varies `var` from 1 through 100. With each iteration of the loop, test whether 100 % `var` is 0. If you divide 100 by a number and there is no remainder, the number goes into 100 evenly.

```
for(var = 1; var <= NUMBER; ++var)
   if(NUMBER % var == 0)
       System.out.print(var + " ");
       // Print the number and two spaces
```

4. Add an empty `println()` statement to advance the insertion point to the next line by typing the following:

```
System.out.println();
```

5. Type the closing curly braces for the `main()` method and the `DivideEvenly` class.

6. Save the program as **DivideEvenly.java** in the Chapter.06 folder on your Student Disk. Compile and run the program. Figure 6-22 shows the output.

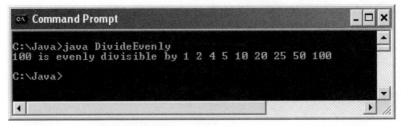

Figure 6-22 Output of the `DivideEvenly` application

WORKING WITH NESTED LOOPS

Suppose you want to know not just what numbers go evenly into 100, but also what numbers go evenly into every positive number, up to and including 100. You can write 99 more loops—one that shows the numbers that divide evenly into 1, another that shows the numbers that divide evenly into 2, and so on—or you can place the current loop inside a different, outer loop, as you will do next.

> **»NOTE** If you want to print divisors for each number from 1 to 100, the loop that varies the number to be divided is the outside loop. You need to perform 100 mathematical calculations on each number, so that constitutes the "smaller" or inside loop.

To create a nested loop to print even divisors for every number up to 100:

1. If necessary, open the file **DivideEvenly.java** in your text editor, change the class name to **DivideEvenly2**, and then save the class as **DivideEvenly2.java**.

2. You will create an outer loop that uses the variable `number` to test every number from 1 to 100, so change the declaration of the constant NUMBER to rename it more appropriately as LIMIT:

```
final int LIMIT = 100;
```

3. Add a new variable declaration:

```
int number;
```

4. Delete the following statement from the application. You have removed the NUMBER constant from the application, and you do not want the `number` value to precede the loop any longer; instead you will print a similar statement for each new tested `number` within the loop:

```
System.out.print(NUMBER + " is evenly divisible by ");
```

5. Replace the existing `for` loop with the following nested loop. The outer loop varies `number` from 1 to 100. For each number in the outer loop, the inner loop uses each positive integer from 1 up to the number, and tests whether it divides evenly into the number:

```
for(number = 1; number <= LIMIT; ++number)
{
    System.out.print(number + " is evenly divisible by ");
    for(var = 1; var <= number; ++var)
        if(number % var == 0)
            System.out.print(var + " ");
            // Print the number and two spaces
    System.out.println();
}
```

6. Make certain the file ends with three curly braces—one for the `for` outer loop that varies `number`, one for the `main()` method, and one for the class. The inner loop does not need curly braces because it contains a single output statement.

7. Save the file as **DivideEvenly2.java**, compile, and execute the application. When the output stops scrolling, it should look similar to Figure 6-23.

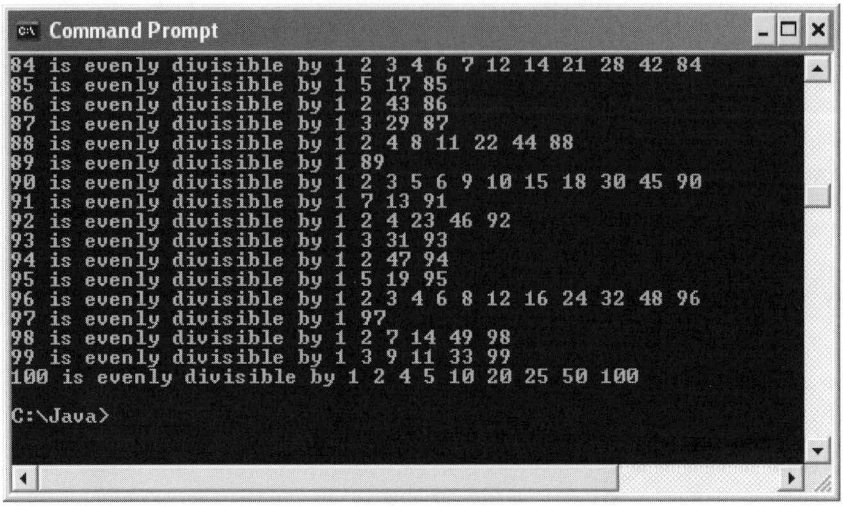

Figure 6-23 Output of the `DivideEvenly2` application when scrolling stops

USING A DO-NOTHING LOOP TO PAUSE PROGRAM EXECUTION

When the `DivideEvenly2` application executes, 100 lines of output display on the screen. But, as Figure 6-23 shows, many of the lines scroll so rapidly that you can't read them. It would help if you could stop the output after every 20 lines or so; then you would have time to read the messages. You will use the modulus operator for this task. You can test the outer loop variable to see if it is evenly divisible by 20; when it is (when `number` is 20, 40, 60, 80, and 100), you can pause program execution by executing a do-nothing loop for a few seconds.

To pause your program after every 20 lines of output:

1. Change the name of the `DivideEvenly2` class to **DivideEvenly3** and immediately save the file as **DivideEvenly3.java**.

2. At the end of the current list of variable and constant declarations, add a constant to hold the number of lines that will display at a time, as follows:

   ```
   final int LINES = 20;
   ```

3. Add a second constant that will control the timing of the pause:

   ```
   final int PAUSE_FACTOR = 80000;
   ```

4. After the last `println()` statement in the application, add a nested loop that does nothing but count to 80,000 eighty thousand times. This will cause the output to pause for a few seconds while you have a chance to read the lines just printed. When you execute this application, you might discover that you want to increase or decrease the number of loops executed to increase or decrease the length of time the output pauses before proceeding:

   ```
   if(number % LINES == 0)
       for(int x = 0; x < PAUSE_FACTOR; ++x)
           for(int y = 0; y < PAUSE_FACTOR; ++y);
   ```

226

5. Save, compile, and test the program. Expect a brief pause after every 20 lines of output. If the length of the pause between segments of output is longer or shorter than you like, increase or decrease the value of PAUSE_FACTOR and run the application again.

> **» NOTE** The amount of time "wasted" by the nested do-nothing loop varies based on the speed of your computer's processing unit. Java contains a pause() method that allows you to pause more accurately for a specific number of seconds; you will learn to use this method when you learn about exception handling in Chapter 15.

KEY TERMS

A **loop** is a structure that allows repeated execution of a block of statements.

A **loop body** is the block of statements that executes when the Boolean expression that controls the loop is true.

A **while loop** executes a body of statements continually as long as the Boolean expression that controls entry into the loop continues to be true.

A loop that executes a specific number of times is a **definite loop** or a counted loop.

A **loop control variable** is a variable whose value determines whether loop execution continues.

A loop that never ends is called an **infinite loop**.

An **empty body** is a block with no statements in it.

Incrementing a variable adds 1 to its value.

Decrementing a variable reduces its value by 1.

An **indefinite loop** is one in which the final number of loops is unknown.

A definite loop is a **counter-controlled loop**.

An indefinite loop is an **event-controlled loop**.

Validating data is the process of ensuring that a value falls within a specified range.

The process of repeatedly increasing a value by some amount is known as **accumulating**.

The **prefix ++**, also known as the **prefix increment operator**, adds 1 to a variable, then evaluates it.

The **postfix ++**, also known as the **postfix increment operator**, evaluates a variable, then adds 1 to it.

Binary operators operate on two values.

The **prefix and postfix decrement operators** subtract 1 from a variable. For example, if b = 4; and c = b--;, 4 is assigned to c, and then after the assignment, b is decreased and takes the value 3. If b = 4; and c = --b;, b is decreased to 3, and 3 is assigned to c.

A **for loop** is a special loop that can be used when a definite number of loop iterations is required.

The **do...while loop** executes a loop body at least one time; it checks the loop control variable at the bottom of the loop after one repetition has occurred.

A **pretest loop** is one in which the loop control variable is tested before the loop body executes.

A **posttest loop** is one in which the loop control variable is tested after the loop body executes.

An **inner loop** is contained entirely within another loop.

An **outer loop** contains another loop.

CHAPTER SUMMARY

» A loop is a structure that allows repeated execution of a block of statements. A loop that never ends is called an infinite loop. A loop that executes a specific number of times is a definite loop or counted loop. You can nest loops.

» Within a looping structure, a Boolean expression is evaluated, and if it is `true`, a block of statements called the loop body executes; then the Boolean expression is evaluated again.

» You can use a `while` loop to execute a body of statements continually while some condition continues to be `true`.

» To execute a `while` loop, you initialize a loop control variable, test it in a `while` statement, and then alter the loop control variable in the body of the `while` structure.

» The += operator adds and assigns in one operation.

» The prefix ++ and the postfix ++ increase a variable's value by 1. The prefix -- and postfix -- decrement operators reduce a variable's value by 1. When you use the prefix ++, the result is calculated and stored, and then the variable is used. When you use the postfix ++, the variable is used, and then the result is calculated and stored.

» Unary operators are used with one value. Most arithmetic operators are binary operators that operate on two values.

» The shortcut operators +=, -=, * =, and /= perform operations and assign the result in one step.

» A `for` loop initializes, tests, and increments in one statement. There are three sections within the parentheses of a `for` loop that are separated by exactly two semicolons.

» The `do...while` loop tests a Boolean expression after one repetition has taken place, at the bottom of the loop.

» You can improve loop performance by making sure the loop does not include unnecessary operations or statements.

REVIEW QUESTIONS

1. A structure that allows repeated execution of a block of statements is a _____ .

   a. cycle   c. ring

   b. loop   d. band

2. A loop that never ends is a(n) _____ loop.

   a. iterative   c. structured

   b. infinite   d. illegal

3. To construct a loop that works correctly, you should initialize a loop control _____ .

   a. variable   c. structure

   b. constant   d. condition

4. What is the output of the following code?

```
b = 1;
while (b < 4)
    System.out.print(b + " ");
```

a. 1

b. 1 2 3

c. 1 2 3 4

d. 1 1 1 1 1 1 ...

5. What is the output of the following code?

```
b = 1;
while (b < 4)
{
    System.out.print(b + " ");
    b = b + 1;
}
```

a. 1

b. 1 2 3

c. 1 2 3 4

d. 1 1 1 1 1 ...

6. What is the output of the following code?

```
e = 1;
while (e < 4);
    System.out.print(e + " ");
```

a. nothing

b. 1 1 1 1 1 1...

c. 1 2 3 4

d. 4 4 4 4 4 4 ...

7. If total = 100 and amt = 200, then after the statement total += amt, _____ .

a. total is equal to 200

b. total is equal to 300

c. amt is equal to 100

d. amt is equal to 300

8. The modulus operator % is a _____ operator.

a. unary

b. binary

c. tertiary

d. postfix

9. The prefix ++ is a _____ operator.

a. unary

b. binary

c. tertiary

d. postfix

10. If g = 5, then after h = ++g, the value of h is _____ .

a. 4

b. 5

c. 6

d. 7

11. If m = 9, then after n = m++, the value of n is _____ .

a. 8

b. 9

c. 10

d. 11

12. If `j` `=` `5` and `k` `=` `6`, then the value of `j++` `==` `k` is _____ .

    a. 5
    c. `true`
    b. 6
    d. `false`

13. You must always include _____ in a `for` loop's parentheses.

    a. two semicolons
    c. two commas
    b. three semicolons
    d. three commas

14. What does the following statement print?

    ```
    for(a = 0; a < 5; ++a)
        System.out.print(a + " ");
    ```

    a. 0 0 0 0 0
    c. 0 1 2 3 4 5
    b. 0 1 2 3 4
    d. nothing

15. What does the following statement print?

    ```
    for(b = 1; b > 3; ++b)
        System.out.print(b + " ");
    ```

    a. 1 1 1
    c. 1 2 3 4
    b. 1 2 3
    d. nothing

16. What does the following statement print?

    ```
    for(f = 1, g = 4; f < g; ++f, --g)
        System.out.print(f + " " + g + " ");
    ```

    a. 1 4 2 5 3 6 4 7...
    c. 1 4 2 3
    b. 1 4 2 3 3 2
    d. nothing

17. The loop that performs its conditional check at the bottom of the loop is a _____ loop.

    a. `while`
    c. `for`
    b. `do...while`
    d. `for...while`

18. What does the following program segment print?

    ```
    d = 0;
    do
    {
        System.out.print(d + " ");
        d++;
    } while (d < 2);
    ```

    a. 0
    c. 0 1 2
    b. 0 1
    d. nothing

19. What does the following program segment print?

```
for(f = 0; f < 3; ++f)
    for(g = 0; g < 2; ++g)
        System.out.print(f + " " + g + " ");
```

a. 0 0 0 1 1 0 1 1 2 0 2 1   c. 0 1 0 2 1 1 1 2

b. 0 1 0 2 0 3 1 1 1 2 1 3   d. 0 0 0 1 0 2 1 0 1 1 1 2 2 0 2 1 2 2

20. What does the following program segment print?

```
for(m = 0; m < 4; ++m);
    for(n = 0; n < 2; ++n);
        System.out.print(m + " " + n + " ");
```

a. 0 0 0 1 1 0 1 1 2 0 2 1 3 0 3 1   c. 4 2

b. 0 1 0 2 1 1 1 2 2 1 2 2   d. 3 1

EXERCISES

1. Write an application that prints all even numbers from 2 to 100 inclusive, and that starts a new line after every multiple of 20 (20, 40, 60, and 80). Save the file as **EvenNums.java** in the Chapter.06 folder on your Student Disk.

2. Write an application that asks a user to type 1, 2, 3, or 4. When the user types 4, the program ends. When the user types 1, 2, or 3, the program displays the message "Good job!" and then asks for another input. When the user types any other number, the application issues an error message and then asks for another input. Save the file as **Input123.java** in the Chapter.06 folder on your Student Disk.

3. Write an application that prints every integer value from 1 to 20 along with the squared value of each integer. Save the file as **TableOfSquares.java** in the Chapter.06 folder on your Student Disk.

4. Write an application that sums the integers from 1 to 50 (that is, $1 + 2 + 3 \ldots + 50$). Save the file as **Sum50.java** in the Chapter.06 folder on your Student Disk.

5. Write an application that shows the sum of 1 to n for every n from 1 to 50. That is, the program prints 1 (the sum of 1 alone), 3 (the sum of 1 and 2), 6 (the sum of 1, 2, and 3), 10 (the sum of 1, 2, 3, and 4), and so on. Save the file as **EverySum.java** in the Chapter.06 folder on your Student Disk.

6. Write an application that prints every perfect number from 1 through 1000. A perfect number is one that equals the sum of all the numbers that divide evenly into it. For example, 6 is perfect because 1, 2, and 3 divide evenly into it, and their sum is 6; however, 12 is not a perfect number because 1, 2, 3, 4, and 6 divide evenly into it, and their sum is greater than 12. Save the file as **Perfect.java** in the Chapter.06 folder on your Student Disk.

7. a. Write an application that calculates the amount of money earned on an investment, based on an 8% annual return. Prompt the user to enter an investment amount and the number of years for the investment. Display an error message if the user enters 0 for either value; otherwise, display the total amount (balance) for each year of the investment. Save the file as **Investment.java** in the Chapter.06 folder on your Student Disk.

   b. Modify the `Investment` application in Exercise 7a so the user also enters the interest rate. In addition to the error message that displays when the investment or term is 0, display an error message if the interest rate is 0. Save the file as **Investment2.java** in the Chapter.06 folder on your Student Disk.

8. Write an application that displays a series of at least four survey questions; the survey can be on any social or political topic you want, and each question should have at least three possible numeric-choice answers. At the end of the survey, use a dialog box to ask whether the user wants to (1) enter another set of responses to the same set of questions, or (2) quit. Continue to accept sets of responses until the user chooses to quit, and then display the results of the survey—for each question indicate how many users chose the first option, second option, and so on. Save the file as **Survey.java** in the Chapter.06 folder on your Student Disk.

9. a. Write an application that displays the results of a series of 10 coin tosses. Use the `Math.random()` function explained in Appendix D to generate a number between 0 and 1; you will use a statement similar to:

   ```
   result = Math.random();
   ```

   After each coin toss, display whether the toss represents "heads" or "tails." If the `result` is 0.5 or less, the result represents "heads"; otherwise, it represents "tails." After the 10 tosses are complete, display the percentages of heads and tails. Run the application several times until you are confident that the coin tosses occur randomly. Save the file as **FlipCoin.java** in the Chapter.06 folder on your Student Disk.

   b. Modify the application in Exercise 9a so that you generate 1000 coin tosses and keep track of the heads and tails. Do not display the coin toss result with each flip, but instead display percentages of the heads and tails after the 1000 coin tosses are complete. Save the file as **FlipCoin2.java** in the Chapter.06 folder on your Student Disk.

10. a. Create a class named `Purchase`. Each `Purchase` contains an invoice number, amount of sale, and amount of sales tax. Include set methods for the invoice number and sale amount. Within the `set()` method for the sale amount, calculate the sales tax as 5% of the sale amount. Also include a display method that displays a purchase's details. Save the file as **Purchase.java** in the Chapter.06 folder on your Student Disk.

    b. Create an application that declares a `Purchase` object and prompts the user for purchase details. When you prompt for an invoice number, do not let the user proceed until a number between 1000 and 8000 has been entered. When you prompt for a sale amount, do not proceed until the user has entered a non-negative value. After a valid `Purchase` object has been created, display the object's invoice number, sale amount, and sales tax. Save the file as **CreatePurchase.java** in the Chapter.06 folder on your Student Disk.

DEBUGGING EXERCISES

Each of the following files in the Chapter.06 folder on your Student Disk has syntax and/or logic errors. In each case, determine the problem and fix the program. After you correct the errors, save each file using the same filename preceded with Fix. For example, save DebugSix1.java as FixDebugSix1.java.

a. DebugSix1.java

b. DebugSix2.java

c. DebugSix3.java

d. DebugSix4.java

CASE PROJECT

MERCURY DELIVERIES

Mercury Deliveries, founded in 2001, operates a delivery service. The company wants you to write an object-oriented program for scheduling deliveries.

Create a `Delivery` class that contains fields to hold the following:

1. A delivery number that contains six digits assigned as follows:

   » The first digit represents the year; the company's first year, 2001, is 1. For example, for deliveries made in 2005, the first digit for all deliveries is 5.

   » The second and third digits represent the month. For example, a delivery in March 2008 begins with 803.

   » The last three digits represent the delivery number. For example, the 76th delivery in March 2008 has a complete delivery number of 803076.

2. A code representing the delivery area as follows:

   » 1—Local
   » 2—Long distance

3. A weight, in pounds, of the item to be delivered.

4. The fee for the delivery, as follows:

Distance	Weight	Fee ($)
1	Under 5 pounds	12.00
1	5 to 20 pounds	16.50
1	Over 20 pounds	22.00
2	Under 5 pounds	35.00
2	5 pounds or more	47.95

Create a constructor for the `Delivery` class that accepts arguments for the year, month, delivery number within the month, delivery distance code, and weight of the package. The constructor determines the six-digit delivery number and delivery fee. Also include a method that displays every `Delivery` object field. Save the file as **Delivery.java** in the Chapter.06 folder on your Student Disk.

Create an application that prompts the user for data for a delivery. Keep prompting the user for each of the following values until they are valid:

» A four-digit year between 2001 and 2009 inclusive

» A month between 1 and 12 inclusive

» A delivery number for the month between 1 and 999 inclusive

» A package weight between 0.10 pound and 100 pounds inclusive

» A delivery distance code that is either 1 or 2

When all the data entries are valid, construct a `Delivery` object, and then display its values. Save the file as **CreateDelivery.java** in the Chapter.06 folder on your Student Disk.

GAME ZONE

1. a. Write an application that creates a quiz. The quiz contains at least five questions about a hobby, popular music, astronomy, or any other personal interest. Each question should be a multiple-choice question with at least four options. When the user answers the question correctly, display a congratulatory message. If the user responds to a question incorrectly, display an appropriate message as well as the correct answer. At the end of the quiz, display the number of correct and incorrect answers, and the percentage of correct answers. Save the file as **Quiz.java** in the Chapter.06 folder on your Student Disk.

    b. Modify the `Quiz` application so that the user is presented with each question continually until it is answered correctly. Remove the calculation for percentage of correct answers—all users will have 100% correct by the time they complete the application. Save the file as **Quiz2.java** in the Chapter.06 folder on your Student Disk.

2. In Chapter 1, you created a class called `RandomGuess`. In this game, players guess a number, the application generates a random number, and players determine whether they were correct. In Chapter 5, you improved the application to display a message indicating whether the player's guess was correct, too high, or too low. Now, add a loop that continuously prompts the user for the number, indicating whether the guess is high or low, until the user enters the correct value. After the user correctly guesses the number, display a count of the number of attempts it took. Save the file as **RandomGuess3.java**.

3. In Chapter 4, you created a `Die` class from which you could instantiate an object containing a random value from 1 through 6. Now use the class to create a simple dice game in which the user chooses a number between 2 (the lowest total possible from two dice) and 12 (the highest total possible). The user "rolls" two dice up to three times. If the number chosen by the user comes up, the user wins and the game ends. If the number does not come up within three rolls, the computer wins. Save the application as **TwoDice3.java**.

4. a. Using the `Die` class you created in Chapter 4, create a version of the dice game Pig that a user can play against the computer. The object of the game is to be the first to score 100 points. The user and computer take turns rolling a pair of dice following these rules:

    » On a turn, each player "rolls" two dice. If no 1 appears, the dice values are added to a running total, and the player can choose whether to roll again or pass the turn to the other player.

» If a 1 appears on one of the dice, nothing more is added to the player's total and it becomes the other player's turn.

» If a 1 appears on both of the dice, not only is the player's turn over, but the player's entire accumulated score is reset to 0.

» In this version of the game, when the computer does not roll a 1 and can choose whether to roll again, generate a random value between 0 and 1, having the computer decide to continue when the value is 0.5 or more and decide to quit and pass the turn to the player when the value is not 0.5 or more.

Save the game as **PigDiceGame.java.**

b. Modify the `PigDiceGame` application so that if a player rolls a 1, not only does the player's turn end, but all the player's earned points during that round are eliminated. (Points from earlier rounds are not affected.) Save the game as **PigDiceGame2.java**.

UP FOR DISCUSSION

1. Suppose you wrote a program that you suspect is in an infinite loop because it keeps running for several minutes with no output and without ending. What would you add to your program to help you discover the origin of the problem?

2. Suppose that every employee in your organization has a seven-digit logon ID number they can use to retrieve their own personal information, some of which might be sensitive. For example, each employee has access to his own salary data and insurance claim information, but not to the information of others. Writing a loop would be useful to guess every combination of seven digits in an ID. Are there any circumstances in which you should try to guess another employee's ID number?

3. So far, you have created extremely simple games that rely on random number generation, but as you proceed through the chapters in this book, the games are becoming more complex. People can consume many hours playing computer games. Is there a point at which gaming interferes with family obligations or other parts of life? How many hours per week is too much? Do game developers have any obligation to make games less addictive?

7

CHARACTERS, STRINGS, AND THE STRINGBUFFER

In this chapter, you will:

Identify problems that can occur when you manipulate
   string data
Manipulate characters
Declare a `String` object
Compare `String` values
Use other `String` methods
Convert `Strings` to numbers
Learn about the `StringBuffer` class

JAVA ON THE JOB, SCENE 7

"What's the problem?" asks Lynn Greenbrier, your mentor at Event Handlers Incorporated, when she sees you frowning over a program at your desk.

"This program makes no sense," you say. "I'm typing a manager's name into an interactive application, comparing it to a stored name, and even though I know I'm typing the name correctly, the program tells me that I'm not!"

"Ahh, I understand your problem," Lynn says. "You need to learn more about objects in general and the `String` class in particular before you can work efficiently with `String` data like names and words."

IDENTIFYING PROBLEMS THAT CAN OCCUR WHEN YOU MANIPULATE STRING DATA

Manipulating characters and groups of characters provides some challenges for the beginning Java programmer. For example, consider the `TryToCompareStrings` application shown in Figure 7-1. The `main()` method declares a `String` named `aName` and assigns "Carmen" to it. The user is then prompted to enter a name. The application compares the two names using the equivalency operator (==) and displays one of two messages indicating whether the strings are equivalent. Figure 7-2 shows the execution of the application. When the user types "Carmen" as the value for `anotherName`, the application concludes that the two names are not equal.

```
import javax.swing.JOptionPane;
public class TryToCompareStrings
{
   public static void main(String[] args)
   {
      String aName = "Carmen";
      String anotherName;
      anotherName = JOptionPane.showInputDialog(null,
         "Enter your name");
      if(aName == anotherName)
         JOptionPane.showMessageDialog(null, aName +
         " equals " + anotherName);
      else
         JOptionPane.showMessageDialog(null, aName +
         " does not equal " + anotherName);
      System.exit(0);
   }
}
```

Figure 7-1 The `TryToCompareStrings` application

The application in Figure 7-1 seems to produce incorrect results. The problem stems from the fact that in Java `String` is a class, and each created `String` is a class object. As an object, a `String` variable name is not a simple data type—it is a **reference**; that is, a variable that holds a memory address. Therefore, when you compare two `String`s using the == operator, you are not comparing their values, but their computer memory locations.

Figure 7-2 Execution of the `TryToCompareStrings` application

Programmers want to compare the contents of memory locations (the values stored there) more frequently than they want to compare the locations themselves (the addresses). Fortunately, the creators of Java have provided three classes that you can use when working with character data; these classes provide you with many methods that make working with characters and strings easier:

» **Character**—A class whose instances can hold a single character value. This class also defines methods that can manipulate or inspect single-character data.

» **String**—A class for working with fixed-string data—that is, unchanging data composed of multiple characters.

» **StringBuffer**—A class for storing and manipulating changeable data composed of multiple characters.

MANIPULATING CHARACTERS

You learned in Chapter 2 that the `char` data type is used to hold any single character—for example, letters, digits, and punctuation marks. In addition to the primitive data type `char`, Java offers a `Character` class. The `Character` class contains standard methods for testing the values of characters. Table 7-1 describes many of the `Character` class methods. The methods that begin with "is", such as `isUpperCase()`, return a Boolean value that can be

Method	Description
`isUpperCase()`	Tests if character is uppercase
`toUpperCase()`	Returns the uppercase equivalent of the argument
`isLowerCase()`	Tests if character is lowercase
`toLowerCase()`	Returns the lowercase equivalent of the argument
`isDigit()`	Returns `true` if the argument is a digit (0–9) and `false` otherwise
`isLetter()`	Returns `true` if the argument is a letter and `false` otherwise
`isLetterOrDigit()`	Returns `true` if the argument is a letter or digit and `false` otherwise
`isWhitespace()`	Returns `true` if the argument is whitespace and `false` otherwise; this includes the space, tab, newline, carriage return, and form feed

Table 7-1 Commonly used methods of the `Character` class

used in comparison statements; the methods that begin with "to", such as toUpperCase(), return a character that has been converted to the stated format.

> **NOTE** The Character class is defined in java.lang and is automatically imported into every program you write. The Character class inherits from java.lang.Object. You will learn more about the Object class when you study inheritance concepts in Chapter 11.

Figure 7-3 contains an application that uses many of the methods shown in Table 7-1. The application declares a character variable named aChar and assigns the character 'C' to it. The application determines the attributes of the character and displays information about it. The output of the TestCharacter application is shown in Figure 7-4.

```
public class TestCharacter
{
  public static void main(String[] args)
  {
    char aChar = 'C';
    System.out.println("The character is " + aChar);
    if(Character.isUpperCase(aChar))
      System.out.println(aChar + " is uppercase");
    else
      System.out.println(aChar + " is not uppercase");
    if(Character.isLowerCase(aChar))
      System.out.println(aChar + " is lowercase");
    else
      System.out.println(aChar + " is not lowercase");
    aChar = Character.toLowerCase(aChar);
    System.out.println("After toLowerCase(), aChar is " + aChar);
    aChar = Character.toUpperCase(aChar);
    System.out.println("After toUpperCase(), aChar is " + aChar);
    if(Character.isLetterOrDigit(aChar))
      System.out.println(aChar + " is a letter or digit");
    else
      System.out.println(aChar +
        " is neither a letter nor a digit");
    if(Character.isWhitespace(aChar))
      System.out.println(aChar + " is whitespace");
    else
      System.out.println(aChar + " is not whitespace");
  }
}
```

Figure 7-3 The TestCharacter application

> **NOTE** You can tell that each of the Character class methods used in the TestCharacter application in Figure 7-3 is a static method because the method name is used without an object reference—you use only the class name, a dot, and the method name. You learned about the difference between static and instance methods in Chapter 3.

Figure 7-4 Output of the `TestCharacter` application

Notice in Figure 7-4 that when the character "C" is tested, you can see the following:

» The value returned by the `isUpperCase()` method is `true`.

» The value returned by the `isLowerCase()` method is `false`.

» The value returned by the `toLowerCase()` method is 'c'.

» The value returned by the `toUpperCase()` method is 'C'.

» The value returned by the `isLetterOrDigit()` method is `true`.

» The value returned by the `isWhitespace()` method is `false`.

DECLARING A `String` OBJECT

You learned in Chapter 1 that a sequence of characters enclosed within double quotation marks is a literal string. You have used many literal strings, such as "First Java application", and you have assigned values to `String` objects and used them within methods, such as `println()` and `showMessageDialog()`. A literal string is an unnamed object, or **anonymous object**, of the `String` class, and a **String variable** is simply a named object of the same class. The class `String` is defined in `java.lang.String`, which is automatically imported into every program you write.

When you declare a `String` variable, the `String` itself—that is, the series of characters contained in the `String`—is distinct from the variable you use to refer to it. You can create a `String` object by using the keyword `new` and the `String` constructor method, just as you would create an object of any other type. For example, the following statement defines an object named `aGreeting`, declares it to be of type `String`, and assigns an initial value of "Hello" to the `String`:

```
String aGreeting = new String("Hello");
```

The variable `aGreeting` stores a reference to a `String` object—it keeps track of where the `String` object is stored in memory. When you declare and initialize `aGreeting`, it links to the initializing `String` value. Alternatively, you can declare a `String` containing "Hello" with `String aGreeting = "Hello";`. Unlike other classes, the `String` class is special because you can create a `String` object without using the keyword `new` or explicitly calling the class constructor.

>> **NOTE** If you declare two String objects and initialize both to the same value, the value is stored only once in memory and the two object references hold the same memory address. Because the character string is stored just once, memory is saved.

COMPARING String VALUES

In Java, String is a class, and each created String is a class object. A String variable name is a reference; that is, a String variable name refers to a location in memory, rather than to a particular value.

The distinction is subtle, but when you declare a variable of a basic, primitive type, such as int x = 10;, the memory address where x is located holds the value 10. If you later assign a new value to x, the new value replaces the old one at the assigned memory address. For example, if you code x = 45;, then 45 replaces 10 at the address of x. When you declare a String, such as String aGreeting = "Hello";, aGreeting holds a memory address where the characters "Hello" are stored.

>> **NOTE**
In Chapter 2 you learned that programmers call unknown memory values "garbage."

The left side of Figure 7-5 shows a diagram of computer memory if aGreeting happens to be stored at memory address 10876 and the String "Hello" happens to be stored at memory address 26040. When you refer to aGreeting, you actually are accessing the address of the characters you want to use. (In the example in Figure 7-5, the memory location beginning at address 32564 has not yet been used and holds garbage values.)

If you subsequently assign a new value to aGreeting, such as aGreeting = "Bonjour";, the address held by aGreeting is altered; now, aGreeting holds a new address where the characters "Bonjour" are stored. As shown on the right side of Figure 7-5, "Bonjour" is an entirely new object created with its own location. The "Hello" String is still in memory, but aGreeting no longer holds its address. Eventually, a part of the Java system called the

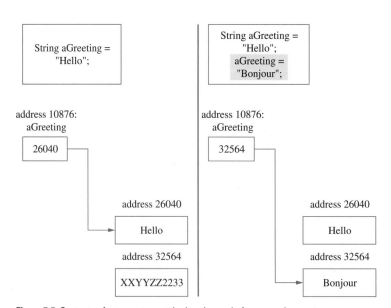

Figure 7-5 Contents of aGreeting at declaration and after an assignment

garbage collector discards the "Hello" characters. Strings, therefore, are never actually changed; instead, new Strings are created and String variables hold the new addresses. Strings and other objects that can't be changed are known as **immutable**.

Because String variables hold memory addresses, making simple comparisons between them often produces misleading results. For example, recall the TryToCompareStrings application in Figure 7-1. In this example, Java evaluates the String variables aName and anotherName as not equal because even though the variables contain the same series of characters, one set is assigned directly and the other is entered from the keyboard and stored in a different area of memory. When you compare Strings with the == operator, you are comparing their memory addresses, not their values.

Fortunately, the String class provides you with a number of useful methods. The String class **equals() method** evaluates the contents of two String objects to determine if they are equivalent. The method returns true if the objects have identical contents. For example, Figure 7-6 shows a CompareStrings application, which is identical to the TryToCompareStrings application in Figure 7-1 except for the shaded comparison. When a user runs the CompareStrings application and enters "Carmen" for the name, the output appears as shown in Figure 7-7.

```
import javax.swing.JOptionPane;
public class CompareStrings
{
    public static void main(String[] args)
    {
        String aName = "Carmen";
        String anotherName;
        anotherName = JOptionPane.showInputDialog(null,
            "Enter your name");
        if(aName.equals(anotherName))
            JOptionPane.showMessageDialog(null, aName +
            " equals " + anotherName);
        else
            JOptionPane.showMessageDialog(null, aName +
            " does not equal " + anotherName);
        System.exit(0);
    }
}
```

Figure 7-6 The CompareStrings application

Figure 7-7 Output of the CompareStrings application

Each `String` shown in Figure 7-6 (`aName` and `anotherName`) is an object of type `String`, so each `String` has access to the `String` class `equals()` method. If you analyze how the `equals()` method is used in the application in Figure 7-6, you can tell quite a bit about how the method was written by Java's creators:

» Because you use the `equals()` method with a `String` object and the method uses the unique contents of that object to make a comparison, you can tell that it is not a static method.

» Because the call to the `equals()` method can be used in an `if` statement, you can tell that it returns a Boolean value.

» Because you see a `String` used between the parentheses in the method call, you can tell that the `equals()` method takes a `String` argument.

So, the method header of the `equals()` method within the `String` class must be similar to the following:

```
public boolean equals(String s)
```

The only thing you do not know about the method header is the local name used for the `String` argument—it might be `s`, or it might be any other legal Java identifier. When you use a prewritten method such as `equals()`, you do not know how the code looks inside it. For example, you do not know whether the `equals()` method compares the characters in the `String`s from left to right or from right to left. All you know is that the method returns `true` if the two `String`s are completely equivalent and `false` if they are not.

Because both `aName` and `anotherName` are `String`s in the application in Figure 7-6, the `aName` object can call `equals()` with `aName.equals(anotherName)` as shown, or the `anotherName` object could call `equals()` with `anotherName.equals(aName)`. The `equals()` method can take either a variable `String` object or a literal string as its argument.

The `String` class **equalsIgnoreCase() method** is similar to the `equals()` method. As its name implies, this method ignores case when determining if two `String`s are equivalent. Thus, if you declare a `String` as `String aName = "Roger";`, then `aName.equals("roGER")` is `false`, but `aName.equalsIgnoreCase("roGER")` is `true`. This method is useful when users type responses to prompts in your programs. You cannot predict when a user might use the Shift key or the Caps Lock key during data entry. The `equalsIgnoreCase()` method allows you to test entered data without regard to capitalization.

When the `String` class **compareTo() method** is used to compare two `String`s, it provides additional information to the user in the form of an integer value. When you use `compareTo()` to compare two `String` objects, the method returns zero only if the two `String`s refer to the same value. If there is any difference between the `String`s, a negative number is returned if the calling object is "less than" the argument, and a positive number is returned if the calling object is "more than" the argument. `String`s are considered "less than" or "more than" each other based on their Unicode values; thus, "a" is less than "b", and "b" is less than "c". For example, if `aName` refers to "Roger", then `aName.compareTo("Robert");` returns a 5. The number is positive, indicating that

"Roger" is more than "Robert". This does not mean that "Roger" has more characters than "Robert"; it means that "Roger" is alphabetically "more" than "Robert". The comparison proceeds as follows:

» The R in "Roger" and the R in "Robert" are compared, and found to be equal.

» The o in "Roger" and the o in "Robert" are compared, and found to be equal.

» The g in "Roger" and the b in "Robert" are compared; they are different. The numeric value of g minus the numeric value of b is 5 (because g is five letters after b in the alphabet), so the `compareTo()` method returns the value 5.

>> **NOTE** Technically, the `equals()` method does not perform an alphabetical comparison with `String`s; it performs a **lexicographical comparison**—a comparison based on the integer Unicode values of the characters.

Often, you won't care what the specific return value of `compareTo()` is; you simply want to determine if it is positive or negative. For example, you can use a test such as `if(aWord. compareTo(anotherWord) < 0)...` to determine whether `aWord` is alphabetically less than `anotherWord`. If `aWord` is a `String` variable that refers to the value "hamster", and `anotherWord` is a `String` variable that refers to the value "iguana", the comparison `if(aWord.compareTo(anotherWord) < 0)` yields `true`.

USING OTHER String METHODS

A wide variety of additional `String` methods are available with the `String` class. The methods **toUpperCase()** and **toLowerCase()** convert any `String` to its uppercase or lowercase equivalent. For example, if you declare a `String` as `String aWord = "something";`, then the string "something" is created in memory and its address is assigned to `aWord`. The statement `aWord = aWord.toUpperCase()` creates "SOMETHING" in memory and assigns its address to `aWord`. Because `aWord` now refers to "SOMETHING," `aWord = aWord.toLowerCase()` alters `aWord` to refer to "something".

The **length() method** returns the length of a `String`. For example, the following statements result in the variable `len` holding the value 5:

```
String greeting = "Hello";
int len = greeting.length();
```

>> **NOTE** Methods that return information about an object are called **accessor methods**. The `length()` method is an example of an accessor method.

The **indexOf() method** determines whether a specific character occurs within a `String`. If it does, the method returns the position of the character; the first position of a `String` begins with zero. The return value is –1 if the character does not exist in the `String`. For example, in `String myName = "Stacy";`, the value of `myName.indexOf('a')` is 2, and the value of `myName.indexOf('q')` is –1.

The **charAt() method** requires an integer argument that indicates the position of the character that the method returns. For example, if `myName` is a `String` that refers to "Stacy", the value of `myName.charAt(0)` is 'S' and the value of `myName.charAt(1)` is 't'.

The **endsWith() method** and the **startsWith() method** each take a `String` argument and return `true` or `false` if a `String` object does or does not end or start with the specified argument. For example, if `String myName = "Stacy";`, then `myName.startsWith("Sta")` is `true`, and `myName.endsWith("z")` is `false`.

The **replace()** method allows you to replace all occurrences of some character within a String. For example, if String yourName = "Annette";, then String goofyName = yourName.replace('n', 'X'); assigns "AXXette" to goofyName.

Although not part of the String class, the **toString() method** is useful when working with String objects. It converts any object to a String. In particular, it is useful when you want to convert primitive data types to Strings. So, if you declare theString and someInt = 4;, as follows, then after the following statements, theString refers to "4":

```
String theString;
int someInt = 4;
theString = Integer.toString(someInt);
```

» NOTE
In Chapter 12, you will learn more about the toString() method and how to construct your own versions for classes you create.

If you declare another String and a double as follows, then after the following statements, aString refers to "8.25":

```
String aString;
double someDouble = 8.25;
aString = Double.toString(someDouble);
```

Another method is available to convert any primitive type to a String. You can join a simple variable to a String, creating a longer String—a process called **concatenation**. For example, if you declare a variable as int myAge = 25;, the following statement results in aString referring to "My age is 25":

```
String aString = "My age is " + myAge;
```

Similarly, if you write the following, then anotherString refers to "12.34":

```
String anotherString;
float someFloat = 12.34f;
anotherString = "" + someFloat;
```

The Java interpreter first converts the float 12.34f to a String "12.34" and adds it to the null String "".

» NOTE The toString() method is not part of the String class; it is a method included in Java that you can use with any type of object. You have been using toString() throughout this book without knowing it. When you use print() and println(), their arguments are automatically converted to Strings if necessary. You don't need import statements to use toString() because it is part of java.lang, which is imported automatically. Because the toString() method you use with println() takes arguments of any primitive type, including int, char, double, and so on, it is a working example of polymorphism.

You already know that you can concatenate Strings with other Strings or values by using a plus sign (+); you have used this approach in methods such as println() and showMessageDialog() since Chapter 1. For example, you can print a firstName, a space, and a lastName with the following statement:

```
System.out.println(firstName + " " + lastName);
```

In addition, you can extract part of a String with the **substring() method**, and use it alone or concatenate it with another String. The substring() method takes two integer arguments—a start position and an end position—that are both based on the fact that a String's first position is position zero. The length of the extracted substring is the difference between the second integer and the first integer; if you write the method without a second integer, the substring extends to the end of the original string.

For example, the application in Figure 7-8 prompts the user for a customer's first and last names. The application then extracts these names so that a friendly business letter can be constructed. After the application prompts the user to enter a name, a loop control variable is initialized to 0. While the variable remains less than the length of the entered name, each character is compared to the space character. When a space is found, two new strings are created. The first, firstName, is the substring of the original entry from position 0 to the location where the space was found. The second, familyName, is the substring of the original entry from the position after the space to the end of the string. Once the first and last names have been created, the loop control variable is set to the length of the original string so the loop will exit and proceed to the display of the friendly business letter. Figure 7-9 shows the data entry screen as well as the output letter created.

> **>> NOTE** To keep the example simple, the BusinessLetter application in Figure 7-8 displays a letter for just one customer. An actual business application would most likely allow a clerk to enter dozens or even hundreds of customer names and store them in a data file for future use. You will learn to store data permanently in files in Chapter 16. For now, just concentrate on the string-handling capabilities of the application.

```java
import javax.swing.*;
public class BusinessLetter
{
    public static void main(String[] args)
    {
        String name;
        String firstName = "";
        String familyName = "";
        int x;
        char c;
        name = JOptionPane.showInputDialog(null,
            "Please enter customer's first and last name");
        x = 0;
        while(x < name.length())
        {
            if(name.charAt(x) == ' ')
            {
                firstName = name.substring(0, x);
                familyName = name.substring(x + 1, name.length());
                x = name.length();
            }
            ++x;
        }
        JOptionPane.showMessageDialog(null,
            "Dear " + firstName +
            ",\nI am so glad we are on a first name basis" +
            "\nbecause I would like the opportunity to" +
            "\ntalk to you about an affordable insurance" +
            "\nprotection plan for the entire " + familyName +
            "\nfamily. Call A-One Family Insurance today" +
            "\nat 1-800-555-9287.");
        System.exit(0);
    }
}
```

Figure 7-8 The BusinessLetter application

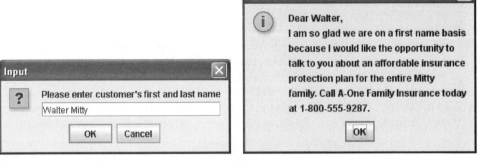

Figure 7-9 Typical execution of the `BusinessLetter` application

CONVERTING Strings TO NUMBERS

If a `String` contains all numbers, as in "649," you can convert it from a `String` to a number so you can use it for arithmetic, or use it like any other number. For example, suppose you ask a user to enter a salary in an input dialog box. When you accept input using `showInputDialog()`, the accepted value is always a `String`. To be able to use the value in arithmetic statements, you must convert the `String` to a number.

To convert a `String` to an integer, you use the **Integer class**, which is part of `java.lang` and is automatically imported into programs you write. The `Integer` class is an example of a wrapper. A **wrapper** is a class or object that is "wrapped around" a simpler element; the `Integer` wrapper class contains a simple integer and useful methods to manipulate it. You have already used the **parseInt() method**, which is part of the `Integer` class; it takes a `String` argument and returns its integer value. For example, `int anInt = Integer.parseInt("649");` stores the numeric value 649 in the variable `anInt`. You can then use the integer value just as you would any other integer.

> **NOTE** The word "parse" in English means "to resolve into component parts," as when you parse a sentence. In Java, to parse a `String` means to break down its separate characters into a numeric format.

Alternatively, you can use the `Integer` class `valueOf()` method to convert a `String` to an `Integer` class object, and then use the `Integer` class `intValue()` method to extract the simple integer from its wrapper class. The `ConvertStringToInteger` application in Figure 7-10 shows how you can accomplish the conversion. When the user enters a `String` in the `showInputDialog()` method, the `String` is stored in `stringHours`. The application then uses the `valueOf()` method to convert the `String` to an `Integer` object, and uses the `intValue()` method to extract the integer. When the user enters "35" as the `String`, it is converted to a number that can be used in a mathematical statement, and the output appears as expected; this output is shown in Figure 7-11.

It is also easy to convert a `String` object to a `double` value. You must use the **Double class**, which, like the `Integer` class, is a wrapper class and is imported into your programs automatically. A method of the `Double` class is the **parseDouble() method**, which takes a `String` argument and returns its `double` value. For example, `double doubleValue =`

```
import javax.swing.JOptionPane;
public class ConvertStringToInteger
{
    public static void main(String[] args)
    {
        String stringHours;
        int hours;
        Integer integerHours;
        final double PAY_RATE = 12.25;
        stringHours = JOptionPane.showInputDialog(null,
            "How many hours did you work this week?");
        integerHours = Integer.valueOf(stringHours);
        hours = integerHours.intValue();
        JOptionPane.showMessageDialog(null, "You worked " +
            hours + " hours at $" + PAY_RATE + " per hour" +
            "\nThat's $" + (hours * PAY_RATE));
        System.exit(0);
    }
}
```

Figure 7-10 The ConvertStringToInteger application

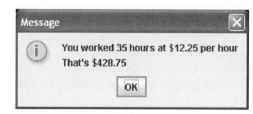

Figure 7-11 Typical execution of the ConvertStringToInteger application

Double.parseDouble("147.82"); stores the numeric value 147.82 in the variable doubleValue.

To convert a String containing "147.82" to a double, you can also use the following code:

```
String stringValue = new String("147.82");
Double tempValue = Double.valueOf(stringValue);
double value = tempValue.doubleValue();
```

The stringValue is passed to the Double.valueOf() method, which returns a Double object. The doubleValue() method is used with the tempValue object; this method returns a simple double that is stored in value.

> **NOTE** Besides Double and Integer, other wrapper classes such as Float and Long also provide valueOf() methods that convert Strings to the wrapper types. Additionally, the classes provide parseFloat() and parseLong() methods, respectively.

> **NOTE**
> The methods parseInt() and parseDouble() are newer than the valueOf() methods, and many programmers prefer to use them when writing new applications.

LEARNING ABOUT THE
StringBuffer CLASS

In Java, the value of a `String` is fixed after the `String` is created; `String`s are immutable, or unchangeable. When you write `someString = "Hello";` and follow it with `someString = "Goodbye";`, you have neither changed the contents of computer memory at the address represented by `someString` nor eliminated the characters "Hello". Instead, you have stored "Goodbye" at a new computer memory location and stored the new address in the `someString` variable. If you want to modify `someString` from "Goodbye" to "Goodbye Everybody", you cannot add a space and "Everybody" to the `someString` that contains "Goodbye". Instead, you must create an entirely new `String`, "Goodbye Everybody", and assign it to the `someString` address.

To circumvent these limitations, you can use the `StringBuffer` class. You use the `StringBuffer` class, an alternative to the `String` class, when you know a `String` will be modified; usually, you can use a `StringBuffer` object anywhere you would use a `String`. Like the `String` class, the `StringBuffer` class is part of the `java.lang` package and is automatically imported into every program.

You can create a `StringBuffer` object that contains a `String` with a statement such as `StringBuffer eventString = new StringBuffer("Hello there");`. When you create a `String`, you have the option of omitting the keyword `new`, but when you initialize a `StringBuffer` object you must use the keyword `new`, the constructor name, and an initializing value between the constructor's parentheses. You can create an empty `StringBuffer` variable using a statement such as `StringBuffer uninitializedString = null;`. The variable does not refer to anything until you initialize it with a defined `StringBuffer` object. Generally, when you create a `String` object, sufficient memory is allocated to accommodate the number of Unicode characters in the string. A `StringBuffer` object, however, contains a memory block called a **buffer**, which might or might not contain a `String`. Even if it does contain a `String`, the `String` might not occupy the entire buffer. In other words, the length of a `String` can be different from the length of the buffer. The actual length of the buffer is the **capacity** of the `StringBuffer` object.

You can change the length of a `String` in a `StringBuffer` object with the **setLength()** **method**. The **length property** is an attribute of the `StringBuffer` class that identifies the number of characters in the `String` contained in the `StringBuffer`. When you increase a `StringBuffer` object's length to be longer than the `String` it holds, the extra characters contain '\u0000'. If you use the `setLength()` method to specify a length shorter than its `String`, the string is truncated.

To find the capacity of a `StringBuffer` object, you use the **capacity() method**. For example, the `StringBufferDemo` application in Figure 7-12 demonstrates the `StringBuffer` `capacity()` method. The application creates a `nameString` object containing the seven characters "Barbara". The capacity of the `StringBuffer` object is obtained and stored in an integer variable named `nameStringCapacity` and printed. Figure 7-13 shows the `StringBuffer` capacity is 23, which is 16 characters more than the length of the string "Barbara". When you create a `StringBuffer` object, its capacity is the length of the `String` contained in `StringBuffer`, plus 16. The "extra" 16 positions allow for reasonable modification of the `StringBuffer` object after creation without allocating any new memory locations.

```
import javax.swing.JOptionPane;
public class StringBufferDemo
{
    public static void main(String[] args)
    {
        StringBuffer nameString = new StringBuffer("Barbara");
        int nameStringCapacity = nameString.capacity();
        System.out.println("Capacity of nameString is " +
            nameStringCapacity);
        StringBuffer addressString = null;
        addressString = new
            StringBuffer("6311 Hickory Nut Grove Road");
        int addStringCapacity = addressString.capacity();
        System.out.println("Capacity of addressString is " +
            addStringCapacity);
        nameString.setLength(20);
        System.out.println("The name is " + nameString + "end");
        addressString.setLength(20);
        System.out.println("The address is " + addressString);
    }
}
```

Figure 7-12 The `StringBufferDemo` application

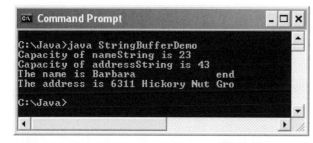

Figure 7-13 Output of the `StringBufferDemo` application

》NOTE The creators of Java chose 16 characters as the "extra" length for a `StringBuffer` object because 16 characters fully occupy four bytes of memory. As you work more with computers in general and programming in particular, you will notice that storage capacities are almost always created in exponential values of 2—for example, 4, 8, 16, 32, 64, and so on.

In the application in Figure 7-12, the `addressString` variable is created as `StringBuffer` `addressString = null;`. The variable does not refer to anything until it is initialized with the defined `StringBuffer` object:

```
addressString = new StringBuffer("6311 Hickory Nut Grove Road");
```

The capacity of this new `StringBuffer` object is shown in Figure 7-13 as the length of the string plus 16, or 43.

In the application shown in Figure 7-12, the length of each of the `String`s is changed to 20 using the `setLength()` method. The application prints the expanded `nameString` and "end", so you can see in the output that there are 13 extra spaces at the end of the String. The application also prints the truncated addressString so that you can see the effect of reducing its length to 20.

Using StringBuffer objects provides improved computer performance over String objects because you can insert or append new contents into a StringBuffer. In other words, unlike immutable Strings, the ability of StringBuffers to be modified makes them more efficient when you know string contents will change.

The StringBuffer class provides you with four constructors. Three of them are introduced in the following list:

» public StringBuffer() constructs a StringBuffer with no characters and a default size of 16 characters.
» public StringBuffer(int capacity) constructs a StringBuffer with no characters and a capacity specified by the parameter.
» public StringBuffer(String s) contains the same characters as those stored in the String object s. (The capacity of the StringBuffer is the length of the String argument you provide, plus 16 additional characters.)

> **NOTE** The fourth StringBuffer constructor uses an argument of CharSequence. CharSequence is another Java class; it is an interface that holds a sequence of char values. You will learn to create interfaces in Chapter 12.

The **append() method** lets you add characters to the end of a StringBuffer object. For example, if a StringBuffer object is declared as StringBuffer someBuffer = new StringBuffer("Happy");, the statement someBuffer.append(" birthday") alters someBuffer to refer to "Happy birthday".

The **insert() method** lets you add characters at a specific location within a StringBuffer object. For example, if someBuffer refers to "Happy birthday", then someBuffer.insert (6, "30th "); alters the StringBuffer to contain "Happy 30th birthday". The first character in the StringBuffer object occupies position zero. To alter just one character in a StringBuffer, you can use the **setCharAt() method**, which allows you to change a character at a specified position within a StringBuffer object. This method requires two arguments: an integer position and a character. If someBuffer refers to "Happy 30th birthday", then someBuffer.setCharAt(6,'4'); changes the someBuffer value into a 40th birthday greeting.

One way you can extract a character from a StringBuffer object is to use the charAt() method. The **charAt() method** accepts an argument that is the offset of the character position from the beginning of a String and returns the character at that position. If you declare the following:

```
StringBuffer text = new StringBuffer("Java Programming");
```

then text.charAt(5) refers to the character "P".

> **NOTE** If you try to use an index that is less than 0 or greater than the index of the last position in the StringBuffer object, you cause an error known as an exception and your program terminates.

YOU DO IT

USING `String` CLASS METHODS

To demonstrate the use of the `String` methods, you will create an application that asks a user for a name and then "fixes" the name so that the first letter of each new word is upper-case, whether the user entered the name that way or not.

To create the name-repairing application:

1. Open a new text file in your text editor. Enter the following first few lines of a `RepairName` program. The program declares several variables, including two strings that will refer to a name: one will be "repaired" with correct capitalization; the other will be saved as the user entered it so it can be displayed in its original form at the end of the program. After declaring the variables, prompt the user for a name:

```
import javax.swing.*;
public class RepairName
{
    public static void main(String[] args)
    {
        String name, saveOriginalName;
        int stringLength;
        int i;
        char c;
        name = JOptionPane.showInputDialog(null,
            "Please enter your first and last name");
```

2. Store the name entered in the `saveOriginalName` variable. Next, calculate the length of the name the user entered, then begin a loop that will examine every character in the name. The first character of a name is always capitalized, so when the loop control variable `i` is 0, the character in that position in the name string is extracted and converted to its uppercase equivalent. Then the name is replaced with the uppercase character appended to the remainder of the existing name.

```
        saveOriginalName = name;
        stringLength = name.length();
        for(i=0; i < stringLength; i++)
        {
            c = name.charAt(i);
            if(i == 0)
            {
                c = Character.toUpperCase(c);
                name = c + name.substring(1, stringLength);
            }
```

3. After the first character in the name is converted, the program looks through the rest of the name, testing for spaces and capitalizing every character that follows a space. When a space is found at position `i`, `i` is increased, the next character is extracted from the name,

the character is converted to its uppercase version, and a new name string is created using the old string up to the current position, the newly capitalized letter, and the remainder of the name string. The `if...else` ends and the `for` loop ends.

```
else
    if(name.charAt(i) == ' ')
    {
        ++i;
        c = name.charAt(i);
        c = Character.toUpperCase(c);
        name = name.substring(0, i) + c +
            name.substring(i + 1, stringLength);
    }
}
```

4. After every character has been examined, display the original and repaired names and exit the program.

```
JOptionPane.showMessageDialog(null, "Original name was " +
    saveOriginalName + "\nRepaired name is " + name);
System.exit(0);
    }
}
```

5. Save the application as **RepairName.java** in the Chapter.07 folder on your Student Disk, and then compile and run the program. Figure 7-14 shows the result after a user enters a name using all lowercase characters. Make certain you understand how all the `String` methods contribute to the success of this program.

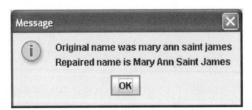

Figure 7-14 Output of the `RepairName` application

CONVERTING A `String` TO AN INTEGER

When planning an event, Event Handlers Incorporated must know how many guests to expect. Next, you will prompt the user for the number of guests, read characters from the keyboard, store the characters in a `String`, and then convert the `String` to an integer.

To create a program that accepts integer input:

1. Open a new text file in your text editor. Type the statement **import javax.swing.*;**, press **Enter**, and then enter the following first few lines of a `NumberInput` class that will accept string input:

```
public class NumberInput
{
    public static void main(String[] args)
    {
```

2. Declare the following variables for the input String and the resulting integer:

```
String inputString;
int inputNumber;
```

3. Declare a constant that holds the maximum number of guests. If a party has more guests than the maximum, an extra charge is incurred:

```
final int MAX_GUESTS = 100;
```

4. Enter the following input dialog box statement that stores the user keyboard input in the String variable inputString:

```
inputString = JOptionPane.showInputDialog(null,
    "Enter the number of guests at your event");
```

5. Use the following Integer.parseInt() method to convert the input String to an integer. Then use the integer in a numeric decision that displays a message dialog box when the number of guests entered is greater than 100:

```
inputNumber = Integer.parseInt(inputString);
if(inputNumber > MAX_GUESTS)
    JOptionPane.showMessageDialog(null,
        "A surcharge will apply!");
```

6. Enter the closing statement **System.exit(0);**, press **Enter**, and then enter the final two closing curly braces for the program.

7. Save the program as **NumberInput.java** in the Chapter.07 folder on your Student Disk, and then compile and test the program. Even though the user enters a String, it can be compared successfully to a numeric value because it was converted using the parseInt() method.

USING StringBuffer METHODS

To use StringBuffer methods:

1. Open a new text file and type the following first lines of a DemoStringBuffer class:

```
public class DemoStringBuffer
{
    public static void main(String[] args)
    {
```

2. Use the following code to create a StringBuffer variable, and then call a print() method (that you will create in Step 7) to print the StringBuffer:

```
StringBuffer str = new StringBuffer("singing");
print(str);
```

3. Enter the following append() method to add characters to the existing StringBuffer and print it again:

```
str.append(" in the dead of ");
print(str);
```

4. Enter the following `insert()` method to insert characters, print, insert additional characters, and print the `StringBuffer` again:

```
str.insert(0, "Black");
print(str);
str.insert(5, "bird ");
print(str);
```

5. Add one more `append()` and `print()` combination:

```
str.append("night");
print(str);
```

6. Add a closing curly brace for the `main()` method.

7. Enter the following `print()` method that prints `StringBuffer` objects:

```
public static void print(StringBuffer s)
{
    System.out.println(s);
}
```

8. Type the closing curly brace for the class, and then save the file as **DemoStringBuffer.java** in the Chapter.07 folder on your Student Disk. Compile and execute, and then compare your output to Figure 7-15.

Figure 7-15 Output of the `DemoStringBuffer` application

KEY TERMS

A **reference** is a variable that holds a memory address.

The **Character class** is one whose instances can hold a single character value. This class also defines methods that can manipulate or inspect single-character data.

The **String class** is for working with fixed-string data—that is, unchanging data composed of multiple characters.

The **StringBuffer class** is for storing and manipulating changeable data composed of multiple characters. It is an alternative to the `String` class when you know a `String` will be modified.

An **anonymous object** is an unnamed object.

A **String variable** is a named object of the `String` class.

Immutable objects cannot be changed.

The String class **equals() method** evaluates the contents of two String objects to determine if they are equivalent.

The String class **equalsIgnoreCase() method** is similar to the equals() method. As its name implies, it ignores case when determining if two Strings are equivalent.

The String class **compareTo() method** is used to compare two Strings; the method returns zero only if the two Strings refer to the same value. If there is any difference between the Strings, a negative number is returned if the calling object is "less than" the argument, and a positive number is returned if the calling object is "more than" the argument.

A **lexicographical comparison** is based on the integer Unicode values of characters.

The String class **toUpperCase() method** converts any String to its uppercase equivalent.

The String class **toLowerCase() method** converts any String to its lowercase equivalent.

The String class **length() method** returns the length of a String.

Accessor methods return information about an object.

The String class **indexOf() method** determines whether a specific character occurs within a String. If it does, the method returns the position of the character; the first position of a String begins with zero. The return value is –1 if the character does not exist in the String.

The String class **charAt() method** requires an integer argument that indicates the position of the character that the method returns.

The String class **endsWith() method** takes a String argument and returns true or false if a String object does or does not end with the specified argument.

The String class **startsWith() method** takes a String argument and returns true or false if a String object does or does not start with the specified argument.

The String class **replace() method** allows you to replace all occurrences of some character within a String.

The **toString() method** converts any object to a String.

Concatenation is the process of joining a variable to a string to create a longer string.

The **substring() method** allows you to extract part of a String.

The **Integer class** is a wrapper class that contains a simple integer and useful methods to manipulate it.

A **wrapper** is a class or object that is "wrapped around" a simpler element.

The Integer class **parseInt() method** takes a String argument and returns its integer value.

The **Double class** is a wrapper class that contains a simple double and useful methods to manipulate it.

The Double class **parseDouble() method** takes a String argument and returns its double value.

A **buffer** is a block of memory.

The **capacity** of a StringBuffer object is the actual length of the buffer, as opposed to that of the string contained in the buffer.

The `StringBuffer` class **setLength() method** changes the length of the characters in the `String` in a `StringBuffer` object.

The **length property** is an attribute of the `StringBuffer` class that identifies the number of characters in the `String` contained in the `StringBuffer`.

The `StringBuffer` class **capacity() method** returns the actual length, or capacity, of the `StringBuffer` object.

The `StringBuffer` class **append() method** lets you add characters to the end of a `StringBuffer` object.

The `StringBuffer` class **insert() method** lets you add characters at a specific location within a `StringBuffer` object.

The `StringBuffer` class **setCharAt() method** allows you to change a character at a specified position within a `StringBuffer` object.

The `StringBuffer` class **charAt() method** accepts an argument that is the offset of the character position from the beginning of a `String` and returns the character at that position.

CHAPTER SUMMARY

» `String` variables are references.
» The `Character` class is one whose instances can hold a single character value. This class also defines methods that can manipulate or inspect single-character data.
» A sequence of characters enclosed within double quotation marks is a literal string. You can create a `String` object by using the keyword `new` and the `String` constructor method. Unlike other classes, you can also create a `String` object without using the keyword `new` or explicitly calling the class constructor.
» Each `String` is a class object. `String`s are never changed; they are immutable. Useful `String` class methods include the `equals()` method. The `compareTo()`, `toUpperCase()`, `toLowerCase()`, `indexOf()`, `endsWith()`, and `startsWith()` methods provide useful `String` information and manipulation.
» The `toString()` method converts any object to a `String`. You can join `String`s with other `String`s or values by using a plus sign (+); this process is called concatenation. You can extract part of a `String` with the `substring()` method, which takes two arguments—a start and end position—both of which are based on the fact that a `String`'s first position is position zero.
» If a `String` contains appropriate characters, you can convert it to a number. The `Integer.parseInt()` method takes a `String` argument and returns its integer value. The `Integer.valueOf()` method converts a `String` to an `Integer` object; the `intValue()` method converts an `Integer` object to an `int` variable. The `Double.parseDouble()` method takes a `String` argument and returns its `double` value. The `Double.valueOf()` method converts a `String` to a `Double` object; the `doubleValue()` method converts a `Double` object to a `double` variable.
» You can use the `StringBuffer` class to improve performance when a string's contents must change. You can insert or append new contents into a `StringBuffer`.

REVIEW QUESTIONS

1. A sequence of characters enclosed within double quotation marks is a _____.

   a. symbolic string

   b. literal string

   c. prompt

   d. command

2. To create a `String` object, you can use the keyword _____ before the constructor call, but you are not required to use this format.

   a. `object`

   b. `create`

   c. `char`

   d. `new`

3. A `String` variable name is a _____.

   a. reference

   b. value

   c. constant

   d. literal

4. The term that programmers use to describe objects that cannot be changed is _____.

   a. irrevocable

   b. nonvolatile

   c. immutable

   d. stable

5. Suppose you declare two `String` objects as:

   ```
   String word1 = new String("happy");
   String word2;
   ```

   When you ask a user to enter a value for `word2`, if the user types "happy", the value of `word1 == word2` is _____.

   a. `true`

   b. `false`

   c. illegal

   d. unknown

6. If you declare two `String` objects as:

   ```
   String word1 = new String("happy");
   String word2 = new String("happy");
   ```

   the value of `word1.equals(word2)` is _____.

   a. `true`

   b. `false`

   c. illegal

   d. unknown

7. The method that determines whether two `String` objects are equivalent, regardless of case, is _____.

   a. `equalsNoCase()`

   b. `toUpperCase()`

   c. `equalsIgnoreCase()`

   d. `equals()`

8. If a `String` is declared as:

   ```
   String aStr = new String("lima bean");
   then aStr.equals("Lima Bean"); is _____.
   ```

   a. `true`   c. illegal

   b. `false`   d. unknown

9. If you create two `String` objects:

   ```
   String name1 = new String("Jordan");
   String name2 = new String("Jore");
   ```

   then `name1.compareTo(name2)` has a value of _____.

   a. `true`   c. –1

   b. `false`   d. 1

10. If `String myFriend = new String("Ginny");`, which of the following has the value 1?

    a. `myFriend.compareTo("Gabby");`

    b. `myFriend.compareTo("Gabriella");`

    c. `myFriend.compareTo("Ghazala");`

    d. `myFriend.compareTo("Hammie");`

11. If `String movie = new String("West Side Story");`, the value of `movie.indexOf('s')` is _____.

    a. `true`   c. 2

    b. `false`   d. 3

12. The `String` class `replace()` method replaces _____.

    a. a `String` with a character

    b. one `String` with another `String`

    c. one character in a `String` with another character

    d. every occurrence of a character in a `String` with another character

13. The `toString()` method converts a(n) _____ to a `String`.

    a. `char`   c. `float`

    b. `int`   d. all of the above

14. Joining `Strings` with a '+' is called _____.

    a. chaining   c. linking

    b. parsing   d. concatenation

15. The first position in a String _____ .
    a. must be alphabetic
    b. must be uppercase
    c. is position zero
    d. is ignored by the compareTo() method

16. The method that extracts a string from within another string is _____ .
    a. extract()   c. substring()
    b. parseString()   d. append()

17. The method parseInt() converts a(n) _____ .
    a. integer to a String   c. Double to a String
    b. integer to a Double   d. String to an integer

18. The difference between int and Integer is _____ .
    a. int is a primitive type; Integer is a class
    b. int is a class; Integer is a primitive type
    c. nonexistent; both are primitive types
    d. nonexistent; both are classes

19. For an alternative to the String class, and so you can change a String's contents, you can use _____ .
    a. char   c. StringBuffer
    b. StringHolder   d. StringMerger

20. Unlike when you create a String, when you create a StringBuffer, you must use the keyword _____ .
    a. buffer   c. null
    b. new   d. class

EXERCISES

1. Write an application that concatenates the following three Strings: "Event Handlers is dedicated ", "to making your event ", and "a most memorable one." Print each String and the concatenated String. Save the file as **JoinStrings.java** in the Chapter.07 folder on your Student Disk.

2. a. Write an application that counts the total number of vowels contained in the String "Event Handlers is dedicated to making your event a most memorable one." Save the file as **CountVowels.java** in the Chapter.07 folder on your Student Disk.

   b. Write an application that counts the total number of vowels contained in a String entered by the user. Save the file as **CountVowels2.java** in the Chapter.07 folder on your Student Disk.

3. a. Write an application that counts the total number of letters contained in the String "Event Handlers Incorporated, 8900 U.S. Highway 14, Crystal Lake, IL 60014". Save the file as **CountLetters.java** in the Chapter.07 folder on your Student Disk.

   b. Write an application that counts the total number of letters contained in a String entered by the user. Save the file as **CountLetters2.java** in the Chapter.07 folder on your Student Disk.

4. a. Write an application that counts the total number of whitespaces contained in a String. Save the file as **CountWhitespaces.java** in the Chapter.07 folder on your Student Disk.

   b. Write an application that counts the total number of whitespaces contained in a String entered by the user. Save the file as **CountWhitespaces2.java** in the Chapter.07 folder on your Student Disk.

5. Write an application that demonstrates that when two identical names are compared and the case differs, the equals() method returns false, but the equalsIgnoreCase() method returns true. Save the file as **ComparisonCase.java** in the Chapter.07 folder on your Student Disk.

6. Write an application that demonstrates conditions under which the compareTo() method returns a positive number, a negative number, and a zero when used to compare two Strings. Save the file as **CompareStringValues.java** in the Chapter.07 folder on your Student Disk.

7. Write an application that demonstrates each of the following methods, based on the statement String dedicate = "Dedicated to making your event a most memorable one";.
   » indexOf('D')
   » charAt(15)
   » endsWith(one)
   » replace('a', 'A')

   Save the file as **Demonstrate.java** in the Chapter.07 folder on your Student Disk.

8. Create a class that holds three initialized StringBuffer objects: your first name, middle name, and last name. Create three new StringBuffer objects as follows:
   » An object named entireName that refers to your three names, separated by spaces
   » An object named lastFirst that refers to your last name, a comma, a space, and your first name, in that order
   » An object named signature that refers to your first name, a space, your middle initial (not the entire name), a period, a space, and your last name

   Display all three objects. Save the file as **Buffer.java** in the Chapter.07 folder on your Student Disk.

9. Write an application that determines whether a phrase entered by the user is a palindrome. A palindrome is a phrase that reads the same backward and forward without regarding capitalization or punctuation. For example, "Dot saw I was Tod", "Was it a car or

a cat I saw?", and "Madam, I'm Adam" are palindromes. Save the file as **Palindrome.java** in the Chapter.07 folder on your Student Disk.

10. Write an application that prompts a user for a full name and street address and constructs an ID from the user's initials and numeric part of the address. For example, the user William Henry Harrison who lives at 34 Elm would have an ID of WHH34, whereas user Addison Mitchell who lives at 1778 Monroe would have an ID of AM1778. Save the file as **ConstructID.java** in the Chapter.07 folder on your Student Disk.

11. Write an application that accepts a user's password from the keyboard. When the entered password is less than six characters, more than 10 characters, or does not contain at least one letter and one digit, prompt the user again. When the user's entry meets all the password requirements, prompt the user to reenter the password, and do not let the user continue until the second password matches the first one. Save the file as **Password.java** in the Chapter.07 folder on your Student Disk.

DEBUGGING EXERCISES

Each of the following files in the Chapter.07 folder on your Student Disk has syntax and/or logic errors. In each case, determine the problem and fix the program. After you correct the errors, save each file using the same filename preceded with Fix. For example, DebugSeven1.java will become FixDebugSeven1.java.

a. DebugSeven1.java   c. DebugSeven3.java

b. DebugSeven2.java   d. DebugSeven4.java

CASE PROJECT

THE TAX ADVANTAGE COMPANY

The Tax Advantage Company provides free tax preparation services to people who need help calculating their personal taxes. You have been asked to write a Java application that will calculate an estimated tax for a taxpayer, based on keyboard responses.

Create a `TaxReturn` class with fields that hold a taxpayer's Social Security number, last name, first name, street address, city, state, zip code, annual income, marital status, and tax liability. Include a constructor that requires arguments that provide values for all the fields other than the tax liability. The constructor calculates the tax liability based on annual income and the percentages in the following table.

| | Marital status | |
Income ($)	Single	Married
0–20,000	15%	15%
20,001–50,000	22%	20%
50,001 and over	30%	28%

In the `TaxReturn` class, also include a display method that displays all the `TaxReturn` data. Save the file as **TaxReturn.java** in the Chapter.07 folder on your Student Disk.

Create an application that prompts a user for the data needed to create a TaxReturn. Continue to prompt the user for data as long as any of the following are true:

» The Social Security number is not in the correct format, with digits and dashes in the appropriate positions; for example, 999-99-9999.

» The zip code is not five digits.

» The marital status does not begin with one of the following: "S", "s", "M", or "m".

» The annual income is negative.

After all the input data is correct, create a TaxReturn object and then display its values. Save the file as **PrepareTax.java** in the Chapter.07 folder on your Student Disk.

GAME ZONE

1. a. In Chapter 3, you designed a Card class. The class holds fields that contain a Card's value and suit. Currently, the suit is represented by a single character (s, h, d, or c). Modify the class so that the suit is a string ("Spades", "Hearts", "Diamonds", or "Clubs"). Also, add a new field to the class to hold the string representation of a Card's rank based on its value. Within the Card class setValue() method, besides setting the numeric value, also set the string rank value as follows:

Numeric value	String value for rank
1	"Ace"
2 through 10	"2" through "10"
11	"Jack"
12	"Queen"
13	"King"

»NOTE
Recall that in this version of War, you assume that the Ace is the lowest-valued card.

b. In Chapter 5, you created a War Card game that randomly selects two cards (one for the player and one for the computer) and declares a winner (or a tie). Modify the game to set each Card's suit as the appropriate string, then execute the game using the newly modified Card class. Figure 7-16 shows four typical executions. Save the game as **War2.java**.

Figure 7-16 Four typical executions of the War2 game

2. In Chapter 5, you created a Rock Paper Scissors game. In the game, a player entered a number to represent one of the three choices. Make the following improvements to the game:

    » Allow the user to enter a string ("rock", "paper", or "scissors") instead of a digit.

    » Make sure the game works correctly whether the player enters a choice in uppercase or lowercase letters, or a combination of the two.

    » To allow for player misspellings, accept the player's entry as long as the first two letters are correct. (In other words, if a player types "scixxrs", you will accept it as "scissors" because at least the first two letters are correct.)

    » When the player does not type at least the first two letters of the choice correctly, reprompt the player and continue to do so until the player's entry contains at least the first two letters of one of the options.

    » Allow 10 complete rounds of the game. At the end, display counts of the number of times the player won, the number of times the computer won, and the number of tie games.

    Save the file as **RockPaperScissors2.java**.

3. Create a simple guessing game, similar to Hangman, in which the user guesses letters and then attempts to guess a partially hidden phrase. Display a phrase in which some of the letters are replaced by asterisks; for example, "G* T***" (for "Go Team"). Each time the user guesses a letter, either place the letter in the correct spot (or spots) in the phrase and display it again, or tell the user the guessed letter is not in the phrase. Display a congratulatory message when the entire correct phrase has been deduced. Save the game as **SecretPhrase.java.** In Chapter 8, you will modify this program so that instead of presenting the user with the same phrase every time the game is played, the program will randomly select the phrase from a list of phrases.

4. Eliza is a famous 1966 computer program written by Joseph Weizenbaum. It imitates a psychologist (more specifically, a Rogerian therapist) by rephrasing many of a patient's statements as questions and posing them to the patient. This type of therapy (sometimes called nondirectional) is often parodied in movies and television shows, in which the therapist does not even have to listen to the patient, but gives "canned" responses that lead the patient from statement to statement. For example, when the patient says, "I am having trouble with my brother," the therapist might say, "Tell me more about your brother." If the patient says, "I dislike school," the therapist might say, "Why do you say you dislike school?" Eliza became a milestone in the history of computers because it was the first time a computer programmer attempted to create the illusion of human-to-human interaction.

    Create a simple version of Eliza by allowing the user to enter statements continually until the user quits by typing "Goodbye". After each statement, have the computer make one of the following responses:

    » If the user entered the word "my" (for example, "I am having trouble with my brother"), respond with "Tell me more about your" and insert the noun in question—for example, "Tell me more about your brother".

» If the user entered a strong word, such as "love" or "hate", respond with, "You seem to have strong feelings about that".

» Add a few other appropriate responses of your choosing.

» In the absence of any of the preceding inputs, respond with a random phrase from the following: "Please go on", "Tell me more", or "Continue".

Save the file as **Eliza.java.**

>> **NOTE** When you search for a word in the user's entry, make sure it is truly the word and not just letters hidden within another word. For example, when searching for "my", make sure it is not hidden in "dum*my*".

UP FOR DISCUSSION

1. Read the description of the Eliza program in the preceding Game Zone exercise. Is it ethical to make people think they are talking to another human when they are not? Does it make a difference if they find the program to be helpful? Would you mind if a Help facility for some software you were using was a machine instead of a person? Have you ever been embarrassed when you thought you were talking to a human but later found out you were not? (For example, have you ever started to respond on the phone only to realize you are listening to an answering machine greeting rather than a person?)

2. Read the description of the Eliza program in the preceding Game Zone exercise. Robots can be programmed to respond to humans in very "natural" ways. A famous author, Isaac Asimov, proposed three laws of robotics, and later added a "zeroth" law. What are these four laws? Do you agree with them? Would you add more?

3. If you are completing all the programming exercises at the ends of the chapters in this book, you are getting a sense of the considerable amount of work that goes into a complex professional program. How would you feel if someone copied your work without compensating you? Investigate the magnitude of software piracy in our society. What are the penalties for illegally copying software? Are there circumstances under which it is acceptable to copy a program? If a friend asked you to make a copy of a program for him, would you? What should be done about the problem of software piracy, if anything?

ARRAYS

DECLARING AND INITIALIZING AN ARRAY

While completing the first five chapters in this book, you stored values in variables. In those early chapters, you simply stored a value and used it, usually only once, but never more than a few times. In Chapter 6, you created loops that allow you to "recycle" variables and use them many times; that is, after creating a variable, you can assign a value, use the value, and then, in successive cycles through the loop, reuse the variable as it holds different values.

At times, however, you might encounter situations in which storing just one value at a time in memory does not meet your needs. For example, a sales manager who supervises 20 employees might want to determine whether each employee has produced sales above or below the average amount. When you enter the first employee's sales figure into an application, you can't determine whether it is above or below average because you don't know the average until you have all 20 figures. Unfortunately, if you assign 20 sales figures to the same variable, when you assign the figure for the second employee, it replaces the figure for the first employee.

A possible solution is to create 20 separate employee sales variables, each with a unique name, so you can store all the sales until you can determine an average. A drawback to this method is that if you have 20 different variable names to be assigned values, you need 20 separate assignment statements. For 20 different variable names, the statement that calculates total sales will be unwieldy, such as:

```
total = firstAmt + secondAmt + thirdAmt+ ...
```

This method might work for 20 salespeople, but what if you have 10,000 salespeople?

The best solution is to create an array. An **array** is a named list of data items that all have the same type. You declare an array variable in the same way you declare any simple variable, but you insert a pair of square brackets after the type. For example, to declare an array of double values to hold sales figures for salespeople, you can write the following:

```
double[] salesFigure;
```

Similarly, to create an array of integers to hold student ID numbers, you can write the following:

```
int[] idNum;
```

> **NOTE** You can also declare an array variable by placing the square brackets after the array name, as in `double salesFigure[];`. This format is familiar to C and C++ programmers, but the preferred format among Java programmers is to place the brackets following the variable type and before the variable name, as in `double[] salesFigure;`. This format emphasizes that the data type of `salesFigure` is an array of `doubles` and not simply a `double`.

After you create an array variable, you still need to reserve memory space. You use the same procedure to create an array that you use to create an object. Recall that when you create a class named `Employee`, you can declare an `Employee` object with a declaration such as:

```
Employee oneWorker;
```

However, that declaration does not actually create the `oneWorker` object. You create the `oneWorker` object when you use the keyword `new` and the constructor method, as in:

```
oneWorker = new Employee();
```

Similarly, declaring an array and reserving memory space for it are two distinct processes. To reserve memory locations for 20 `salesFigure` objects, you declare the array variable with:

```
double[] salesFigure;
```

Then you create the array with:

```
salesFigure = new double[20];
```

Just as with objects, you can declare and create an array in one statement with the following:

```
double[] salesFigure = new double[20];
```

> **» NOTE** In Java, the size of an array is never declared in brackets following the array name, as in `double salesFigure[20]`. That syntax is used in C++, but it causes a compiler error in Java.

> **» NOTE** Other languages, such as Visual Basic, BASIC, and COBOL, use parentheses rather than brackets to refer to individual array elements. By using brackets, the creators of Java made it easier for you to distinguish array names from methods.

The statement `double[] salesFigure = new double[20];` reserves 20 memory locations for 20 `salesFigure` values. You can distinguish each `salesFigure` from the others with a subscript. A **subscript** is an integer contained within square brackets that indicates one of an array's variables, or **elements**. In Java, any array's elements are numbered beginning with zero, so you can legally use any subscript from 0 through 19 when working with an array that has 20 elements. In other words, the first `salesFigure` array element is `salesFigure[0]` and the last `salesFigure` element is `salesFigure[19]`. Figure 8-1 shows how the array of 20 sales figures appears in computer memory.

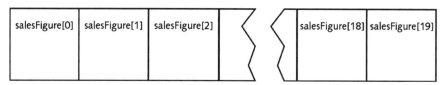

Figure 8-1 An array of 20 `salesFigure` items in memory

It is common to forget that the first element in an array is element 0, especially if you know another programming language in which the first array element is element 1. Making this mistake means you will be "off by one" in your use of any array.

» NOTE To remember that array elements begin with element 0, it might help if you think of the first array element as being "zero elements away from" the beginning of the array, the second element as being "one element away from" the beginning of the array, and so on.

When you work with any individual array element, you treat it no differently than you would treat a single variable of the same type. For example, to assign a value to the first `salesFigure` in an array, you use a simple assignment statement, such as the following:

```
salesFigure[0] = 2100.00;
```

To print the last `salesFigure` in an array of 20, you write:

```
System.out.println(salesFigure[19]);
```

» NOTE
Providing values for all the elements in an array is called **populating the array**.

INITIALIZING AN ARRAY

A variable that has a primitive type, such as `int`, holds a value. A variable with a reference type, such as an array, holds a memory address where a value is stored.

Array names represent computer memory addresses; that is, array names contain references, as do all Java objects. When you declare an array name, no computer memory address is assigned to it. Instead, the array variable name has the special value `null`, or Unicode value '\u0000'. When you declare `int[] someNums;`, the variable `someNums` has a value of `null`.

When you use the keyword `new` to define an array, the array name acquires an actual memory address value. For example, when you define `someNums` in the following statement, a memory address is assigned:

```
int[] someNums = new int[10];
```

When you declare `int[] someNums = new int[10];`, each element of `someNums` has a value of 0 because `someNums` is a numeric array. (Each element in a `double` or `float` array is assigned 0.0.) By default, `char` array elements are assigned '\u0000' and `boolean` array elements automatically are assigned the value `false`.

You already know how to assign a different value to a single element of an array, as in:

```
someNums[0] = 46;
```

You can also assign nondefault values to array elements upon creation. To initialize an array, you use a list of values separated by commas and enclosed within curly braces. For example, if you want to create an array named `tenMult` and store the first six multiples of 10 within the array, you can declare `tenMult` as follows:

```
int[] tenMult = {10, 20, 30, 40, 50, 60};
```

When you initialize an array by giving it values upon creation, you do not give the array a size—the size is assigned based on the number of values you place in the initializing list. For example, the `tenMult` array just defined has a size of 6. Also, when you initialize an array, you do not need to use the keyword `new`; instead, new memory is assigned based on the length of the list of provided values.

» NOTE In Java, you do not usually use a semicolon after a closing curly brace, such as at the end of a method body. However, every statement in Java requires a semicolon, and an array initialization is a statement. Remember to type the semicolon after the closing brace at the end of an array's initialization list.

> **NOTE** In Java, you cannot directly initialize part of an array. For example, you cannot create an array of 10 elements and initialize only five; you must either initialize every element or none of them.

USING SUBSCRIPTS WITH AN ARRAY

If you treat each array element as an individual entity, there isn't much of an advantage to declaring an array over declaring individual **scalar** (primitive) variables, such as int, double, or char. The power of arrays becomes apparent when you begin to use subscripts that are variables, rather than subscripts that are constant values.

For example, suppose you declare an array of five integers that holds quiz scores, such as the following:

```
int[] scoreArray = {2, 14, 35, 67, 85};
```

You might want to perform the same operation on each array element, such as increasing each score by a constant amount. To increase each scoreArray element by three points, for example, you can write the following:

```
scoreArray[0] += 3;
scoreArray[1] += 3;
scoreArray[2] += 3;
scoreArray[3] += 3;
scoreArray[4] += 3;
```

With five scoreArray elements, this task is manageable, requiring only five statements. However, you can reduce the amount of program code needed by using a variable as the subscript. Then, you can use a loop to perform arithmetic on each array element, as in the following example:

```
for(sub = 0; sub < 5; ++sub)
    scoreArray[sub] += 3;
```

The variable sub is set to 0, and then it is compared to 5. Because the value of sub is less than 5, the loop executes and 3 is added to scoreArray[0] . Then, the variable sub is incremented and it becomes 1, which is still less than 5, so when the loop executes again, scoreArray[1] is increased by 3, and so on. A process that took five statements now takes only one. In addition, if the array had 100 elements, the first method of increasing the array values by 3 in separate statements would result in 95 additional statements. The only changes required using the second method would be to change the array size to 100 by inserting additional initial values for the scores, and to change the middle portion of the for statement to compare sub to 100 instead of to 5. The loop to increase 100 separate scores by 3 each is:

```
for(sub = 0; sub < 100; ++sub)
    scoreArray[sub] += 3;
```

When an application contains an array and you want to use every element of the array in some task, it is common to perform loops that vary the loop control variable from 0 to one less than the size of the array. For example, if you get input values for the elements in the array, alter every value in the array, sum all the values in the array, or display every element in the array, you need to perform a loop that executes the same number of times as there are elements. When there are 10 array elements, the subscript varies from 0 through 9; when there are 800 elements, the subscript varies from 0 through 799. Therefore, in an application that includes an array, it is convenient to declare a symbolic constant equal to the size of the array and use the symbolic constant as a limiting value in every loop that processes the array. That way, if the array size changes in the future, you need to modify only the value stored in the symbolic constant, and you do not need to search for and modify the limiting value in every loop that processes the array.

For example, if you declare a symbolic constant as:

```
final int NUMBER_OF_SCORES = 5;
```

the following two loops are identical:

```
for(sub = 0; sub < 5; ++sub)
    scoreArray[sub] += 3;
for(sub = 0; sub < NUMBER_OF_SCORES; ++sub)
    scoreArray[sub] += 3;
```

» NOTE
You learned about symbolic constants and the conventions used in naming them in Chapter 4. In Java, it is conventional to use all uppercase characters in constant identifiers.

The second format has two advantages. First, by using the symbolic constant, NUMBER_OF_SCORES, the reader understands that you are processing every array element for the size of the entire array. If you use the number 5, the reader must look back to the array declaration to confirm that 5 represents the full size of the array. Second, if the array size changes because you remove or add scores, you change the symbolic constant value only once, and all loops that use the constant are automatically altered to perform the correct number of repetitions.

As another option, you can use a field (instance variable) that is automatically assigned a value for every array you create; the length **field** contains the number of elements in the array. For example, when you declare the following, the field scoreArray.length is assigned the value 5:

```
int[] scoreArray = new int[5];
```

Therefore, you can use the following loop to add 3 to every array element:

```
for(sub = 0; sub < scoreArray.length; ++ sub)
    scoreArray[sub] += 3;
```

» NOTE
An instance variable or object field such as length is also called a **property** of the object.

Later, if you modify the size of the array and recompile the program, the value in the length field of the array changes appropriately. When you work with array elements, it is always better to use a symbolic constant or the length field when writing a loop that manipulates an array.

» NOTE A frequent programmer error is to attempt to use length as an array method, referring to scoreArray.length(). However, length is not an array method; it is a field.

In Chapter 6, you learned to use the for loop. Java 5 and 6 also support an **enhanced for loop**. This loop allows you to cycle through an array without specifying the starting and ending points for the loop control variable. For example, you can use either of the following statements to display every element in an array named scoreArray:

```
for(int sub = 0; sub < scoreArray.length; ++ sub)
    System.out.println(scoreArray[sub]);
for(int val : scoreArray)
    System.out.println(val);
```

In the second code line, `val` is defined to be the same type as the array named following the colon. Within the loop, `val` takes on, in turn, each value in the array.

DECLARING AN ARRAY OF OBJECTS

Just as you can declare arrays of integers or `doubles`, you can declare arrays that hold elements of any type, including objects. For example, assume you create the `Employee` class shown in Figure 8-2. This class has two data fields (`empNum` and `empSal`), a constructor, and a get method for each field.

```java
public class Employee
{
    private int empNum;
    private double empSal;
    Employee (int e, double s)
    {
        empNum = e;
        empSal = s;
    }
    public int getEmpNum()
    {
        return empNum;
    }
    public double getSalary()
    {
        return empSal;
    }
}
```

Figure 8-2 The `Employee` class

You can create separate `Employee` objects with unique names, such as either of the following:

```java
Employee painter, electrician, plumber;
Employee firstEmployee, secondEmployee, thirdEmployee;
```

However, in many programs it is far more convenient to create an array of `Employee` objects. An array named `emp` that holds seven `Employee` objects is defined as:

```java
Employee[] emp = new Employee[7];
```

Alternatively, if you have declared a symbolic constant such as `final int NUM_EMPLOYEES = 7;`, you can write the following:

```java
Employee[] emp = new Employee[NUM_EMPLOYEES];
```

These statements reserve enough computer memory for seven `Employee` objects named `emp[0]` through `emp[6]`. However, the statements do not actually construct those `Employee` objects; instead, you must call the seven individual constructors. According to the class definition shown in Figure 8-2, the `Employee` constructor requires two arguments: an employee number and a salary. If you want to number your `Employees` 101, 102, 103, and so on, and start each `Employee` at a salary of $6.35, the loop that constructs seven `Employee` objects is as follows:

```
final double PAYRATE = 6.35;
for(int x = 0; x < NUM_EMPLOYEES; ++x)
    emp[x] = new Employee(101 + x, PAYRATE);
```

As x varies from 0 through 6, each of the seven emp objects is constructed with an employee number that is 101 more than x, and each of the seven emp objects holds the same salary of $6.35, as assigned in the constant `PAYRATE`.

> **》》NOTE** Unlike the `Employee` class in Figure 8-2, which contains a constructor with arguments, some classes contain only the automatically supplied default constructor and others contain an explicitly written constructor that requires no arguments. In either of these cases, if a class has only a default constructor, you must still call the constructor using the keyword `new` for each declared array element.

To use a method that belongs to an object that is part of an array, you insert the appropriate subscript notation after the array name and before the dot that precedes the method name. For example, to print data for seven `Employees` stored in the emp array, you can write the following:

```
for(int x = 0; x < NUM_EMPLOYEES; ++x)
    System.out.println (emp[x] .getEmpNum() + " " + emp[x] .getSalary());
```

Pay attention to the syntax of the `Employee` objects' method calls, such as `emp[x].getEmpNum()`. Although you might be tempted to place the subscript at the end of the expression after the method name—as in `emp.getEmpNum[x]` or `emp.getEmpNum()[x]` —you cannot; the values in x (0 through 6) refer to a particular emp, each of which has access to a single `getEmpNum()` method. Placement of the bracketed subscript so it follows emp means the method "belongs" to a particular emp.

SEARCHING AN ARRAY FOR AN EXACT MATCH

When you want to determine whether a variable holds one of many valid values, one option is to use a series of `if` statements to compare the variable to a series of valid values. Suppose that a company manufactures 10 items. When a customer places an order for an item, you need to determine whether the item number on the order form is valid. If valid item numbers are sequential, such as 101 through 110, the following simple `if` statement that uses a logical AND can verify the order number and set a Boolean field to `true`:

```
final int LOW = 101;
final int HIGH = 110;
boolean validItem = false;
if(itemOrdered >= LOW && itemOrdered <= HIGH)
    validItem = true;
```

If the valid item numbers are nonsequential—for example, 101, 108, 201, 213, 266, 304, and so on—you can code the following deeply nested `if` statement or a lengthy OR comparison to determine the validity of an item number:

```
if(itemOrdered == 101)
    validItem = true;
else if(itemOrdered == 108)
    validItem = true;
else if(itemOrdered == 201)
    validItem = true;
// and so on
```

Instead of a long series of `if` statements, a more elegant solution is to compare the `itemOrdered` variable to a list of values in an array, a process called **searching an array**. You can initialize the array with the valid values with the following statement:

```
int[] validValues = { 101, 108, 201, 213, 266,
    304, 311, 409, 411, 412};
```

> **▶▶ NOTE** From earlier in this chapter, recall that when you initialize an array with 10 values using this technique, exactly 10 array elements are created in memory, and their subscripts are 0 through 9.

After the list of valid values is set up, you can use a `for` statement to loop through the array, and set a Boolean variable to `true` when a match is found:

```
for(int x = 0; x < validValues.length; ++x)
{
    if(itemOrdered == validValues[x])
        validItem = true;
}
```

This simple `for` loop replaces the long series of `if` statements; it checks the `itemOrdered` value against each of the 10 array values in turn. Also, if a company carries 1000 items instead of 10, nothing changes in the `for` statement—the value of `validValues.length` is updated automatically.

As an added bonus, if you set up another parallel array with the same number of elements and corresponding data, you can use the same subscript to access additional information. A **parallel array** is one with the same number of elements as another, and for which the values in corresponding elements are related. For example, if the 10 items your company carries have 10 different prices, you can set up an array to hold those prices as follows:

```
double[] prices = { 0.29, 1.23, 3.50, 0.69...};
```

The prices must appear in the same order as their corresponding item numbers in the `validValues` array. Now, the same `for` loop that finds the valid item number also finds the price, as shown in the application in Figure 8-3. In the shaded portion of the code, notice that when the ordered item's number is found in the `validValues` array, the `itemPrice` value is "pulled" from the `prices` array. In other words, if the item number is found in the second position in the `validValues` array, you can find the correct price in the second position in the `prices` array. Figure 8-4 shows the output of the application when a user requests item 409.

```
import javax.swing.*;
public class FindPrice
{
    public static void main(String[] args)
    {
        final int NUMBER_OF_ITEMS = 10;
        int[] validValues = {101,  108,  201,  213,  266,
            304,  311,  409,  411,  412};
        double[] prices = {0.29,  1.23,  3.50,  0.69,  6.79,
            3.19,  0.99,  0.89,  1.26,  8.00};
        String strItem;
        int itemOrdered;
        double itemPrice = 0.0;
        boolean validItem = false;
        strItem = JOptionPane.showInputDialog(null,
            "Enter the item number you want to order");
        itemOrdered = Integer.parseInt(strItem);
        for (int x = 0; x < NUMBER_OF_ITEMS; ++x)
        {
            if(itemOrdered == validValues[x] )
            {
                validItem = true;
                itemPrice = prices[x] ;
            }
        }
        if(validItem)
            JOptionPane.showMessageDialog(null, "The price for item " +
                itemOrdered + " is $" + itemPrice);
        else
            JOptionPane.showMessageDialog(null,
                "Sorry - invalid item entered");
        System.exit(0);
    }
}
```

Note If you initialize parallel arrays, it is convenient to use spacing so that the values that correspond to each other visually align on the screen or printed page.

Figure 8-3 The `FindPrice` application that accesses information in parallel arrays

Figure 8-4 Output of the `FindPrice` application after the user enters 409 for an item

Note Instead of parallel arrays containing item numbers and prices, you might prefer to create a class named `Item` in which each instance contains two fields—`itemOrdered` and `itemPrice`. Then you could create a single array of objects that encapsulate item numbers and prices. There are almost always multiple ways to approach programming problems.

Within the code shown in Figure 8-3, you compare every `itemOrdered` with each of the 10 `validValues`. Even when an `itemOrdered` is equivalent to the first value in the `validValues` array (101), you always make nine additional cycles through the array. On each of these nine additional cycles, the comparison between `itemOrdered` and `validValues[x]` is always `false`. As soon as a match for an `itemOrdered` is found, it is most efficient to break out of the `for` loop early. An easy way to accomplish this is to set x to a high value within the block of statements executed when there is a match. Then, after a match, the `for` loop does not execute again because the limiting comparison (x < NUMBER_OF_ITEMS) is surpassed. Figure 8-5 shows this loop.

```
for (int x = 0; x < NUMBER_OF_ITEMS; ++x)
{
    if(itemOrdered == validValues[x])
    {
        validItem = true;
        itemPrice = prices[x] ;
        x = NUMBER_OF_ITEMS;
    }
}
```

Figure 8-5 A `for` loop with an early exit

> **NOTE** In an array with many possible matches, it is most efficient to place the more common items first, so they are matched right away. For example, if item 311 is ordered most often, place 311 first in the `validValues` array, and its price ($0.99) first in the `prices` array.

> **NOTE** In Figure 8-5, instead of the statement that sets x to 10 (the value of NUMBER_OF_ITEMS) when a match is found, in its place within the `for` loop you could insert a `break` statement. However, many programmers feel that breaking out of a `for` loop early, whether you do it by setting a variable's value or by using a `break` statement, disrupts the loop flow and makes the code harder to understand. If you (or your instructor) agree with this philosophy, consider using a method that employs a `while` statement, as described next.

You can choose to forgo the `for` loop entirely, and as an alternative use a `while` loop to search for a match. Using this approach, you set a subscript to zero, and while the `itemOrdered` is not equal to a value in the array, you increase the subscript and keep looking. You search only while the subscript remains lower than the number of elements in the array. If the subscript increases to 10, you never found a match in the 10-element array. If the loop ends before the subscript reaches 10, you found a match and the correct price can be assigned to the `itemPrice` variable. Figure 8-6 shows a loop that uses this programming approach.

```
x = 0;
while(x < NUMBER_OF_ITEMS && itemOrdered != validValues[x] )
    ++x;
if(x != NUMBER_OF_ITEMS)
{
    validItem = true;
    itemPrice = prices[x] ;
}
```

Figure 8-6 A `while` loop with an early exit

SEARCHING AN ARRAY FOR A RANGE MATCH

Searching an array for an exact match is not always practical. Suppose your company gives customer discounts based on the quantity of items ordered. Perhaps no discount is given for any order of fewer than a dozen items, but there are increasing discounts available for orders of increasing quantities, as shown in Table 8-1.

Total Quantity Ordered	Discount
1 to 12	None
13 to 49	10%
50 to 99	14%
100 to 199	18%
200 or more	20%

Table 8-1 Discount table

One awkward programming option is to create a single array to store the discount rates. You could use a variable named numOfItems as a subscript to the array, but the array would need hundreds of entries, as in the following example:

```
double[] discount = { 0, 0, 0, 0, 0, 0, 0, 0,
    0, 0, 0, 0, 0, 0.10, 0.10, 0.10 ...};
```

When numOfItems is 3, for example, discount[numOfItems], or discount[3], is 0. When numOfItems is 14, discount[numOfItems], or discount[14], is 0.10. Because a customer might order thousands of items, the discount array would need to be ridiculously large to hold an exact value for each possible order.

> **NOTE** Notice that 13 zeroes are listed in the discount array in the preceding example. The first array element has a zero subscript (and a zero discount for zero items). The next 12 discounts (1 through 12 items) are also discounts of zero.

A better option is to create parallel arrays and perform a **range match**, in which you compare a value to the endpoints of numerical ranges to find the category in which a value belongs. For example, one array can hold the five discount rates, and the other array can hold five discount range limits. The Total Quantity Ordered column in Table 8-1 shows five ranges. If you use only the first figure in each range, you can create an array that holds five low limits:

```
int[] discountRangeLimit= { 1, 13, 50, 100, 200 };
```

A parallel array can hold the five discount rates:

```
double[] discountRate = { 0, 0.10, 0.14, 0.18, 0.20 };
```

Then, starting at the last discountRangeLimit array element, for any numOfItems greater than or equal to discountRangeLimit[4], the appropriate discount is discount[4]. In other words, for any numOrdered less than discountRangeLimit[4], you should decrement the subscript and look in a lower range. Figure 8-7 shows an application that uses the parallel arrays, and Figure 8-8 shows the output when a user enters an order for 54 items.

```
import javax.swing.*;
public class FindDiscount
{
    public static void main(String[] args)
    {
        final int NUM_RANGES = 5;
        int[] discountRangeLimit = {    1,    13,    50,   100,   200};
        double[] discountRate =     {0.00, 0.10, 0.14, 0.18, 0.20};
        double customerDiscount;
        String strNumOrdered;
        int numOrdered;
        int sub = NUM_RANGES - 1;
        strNumOrdered = JOptionPane.showInputDialog(null,
            "How many items are ordered? ");
        numOrdered = Integer.parseInt(strNumOrdered);
        while(sub >= 0 && numOrdered < discountRangeLimit[sub] )
            --sub;
        customerDiscount = discountRate[sub] ;
        JOptionPane.showMessageDialog(null, "Discount rate for " +
            numOrdered + " items is " + customerDiscount);
        System.exit(0);
    }
}
```

Figure 8-7 The `FindDiscount` class

Figure 8-8 Output of the `FindDiscount` class when the user enters 54

>> **NOTE** In the `while` loop in the application in Figure 8-7, `sub` is required to be greater than or equal to 0 before the second half of the statement that compares `numOrdered` to `discountRangeLimit[sub]` executes. It is a good programming practice to ensure that a subscript to an array does not fall below zero, causing a run-time error. This would happen if a user entered a value of less than 1 for `numOrdered`.

PASSING ARRAYS TO METHODS

You have already seen that you can use any individual array element in the same manner as you use any single variable of the same type. That is, if you declare an integer array as int[ ] someNums = new int[12] ;, you can subsequently print someNums[0] , or increment someNums[1] , or work with any element just as you do for any integer. Similarly, you can pass a single array element to a method in exactly the same manner as you pass a variable.

Examine the PassArrayElement application class shown in Figure 8-9 and the output shown in Figure 8-10. The application creates an array of four integers and prints them. Then,

```
public class PassArrayElement
{
    public static void main(String[] args)
    {
        final int NUM_ELEMENTS = 4;
        int[] someNums = { 5, 10, 15, 20};
        int x;
        System.out.print("At start of main: ");
        for(x = 0; x < NUM_ELEMENTS; ++x)
            System.out.print(" " + someNums[x]);
        System.out.println();
        for(x = 0; x < NUM_ELEMENTS; ++x)
            methodGetsOneInt(someNums[x]);
        System.out.print("At end of main: ");
        for(x = 0; x < NUM_ELEMENTS; ++x)
            System.out.print(" " + someNums[x]);
        System.out.println();
    }
    public static void methodGetsOneInt(int one)
    {
        System.out.print("At start of method one is: " + one);
        one = 999;
        System.out.println(" and at end of method one is: " + one);
    }
}
```

Figure 8-9 The `PassArrayElement` class

Figure 8-10 Output of the `PassArrayElement` application

the application calls the `methodGetsOneInt()` method four times, passing each element in turn. The method prints the number, changes the number to 999, and then prints the number again. Finally, back in the `main()` method, the four numbers are printed again.

As you can see in Figure 8-10, the four numbers that were changed in the `methodGetsOneInt()` method remain unchanged back in `main()` after the method executes. The variable named `one` is local to the `methodGetsOneInt()` method, and any changes to variables passed into the method are not permanent and are not reflected in the array in the `main()` program. Each variable named `one` in the `methodGetsOneInt()` method holds only a copy of the array element passed into the method. The individual array elements are **passed by value**; that is, a copy of the value is made and used within the receiving method. When any primitive type (boolean, char, byte, short, int, long, float, or double) is passed to a method, the value is passed.

The outcome is quite different when you pass an array (that is, pass its name) to a method. Arrays, like all nonprimitive objects, are **reference types**; this means that the object actually holds a memory address where the values are stored and the receiving method gets a copy of the array's actual memory address. Therefore, the receiving method has access to, and the ability to alter, the original values in the array elements in the calling method. The class shown in Figure 8-11 creates an array of four integers. After the integers print, the array name (its address) is passed to a method named methodGetsArray(). Within the method, the numbers print, which shows that they retain their values from main(), but then the value 888 is assigned to each number. Even though the methodGetsArray() method is a void

```java
public class PassArray
{
    public static void main(String[] args)
    {
        final int NUM_ELEMENTS = 4;
        int[] someNums = {5, 10, 15, 20};
        int x;
        System.out.print("At start of main: ");
        for(x = 0; x < NUM_ELEMENTS; ++x)
            System.out.print(" " + someNums[x] );
        System.out.println();
        methodGetsArray(someNums, NUM_ELEMENTS);
        System.out.print("At end of main: ");
        for(x = 0; x < NUM_ELEMENTS; ++x)
            System.out.print(" " + someNums[x] );
        System.out.println();
    }
    public static void methodGetsArray(int arr[], int numEls)
    {
        int x;
        System.out.print("At start of method arr holds: ");
        for(x = 0; x < numEls; ++x)
            System.out.print(" " + arr[x] );
        System.out.println();
        for(x = 0; x < numEls; ++x)
            arr[x] = 888;
        System.out.print(" and at end of method arr holds: ");
        for(x = 0; x < numEls; ++x)
            System.out.print(" " + arr[x] );
        System.out.println();
    }
}
```

Figure 8-11 The PassArray class

>> **NOTE** Instead of passing the array size to the methodGetsArray() method in Figure 8-11, you could use the array's length field within the method. For example, each for loop in the method could be written as follows:

```java
for(x = 0; x < arr.length; ++x)
```

method—meaning nothing is returned to the `main()` method—when the program prints the array for the second time within `main()`, all of the values have been changed to 888, as you can see in the output in Figure 8-12. Because the method receives a reference to the array, the `methodGetsArray()` method "knows" the address of the array declared in `main()` and makes its changes directly to the original array that was declared in the `main()` method.

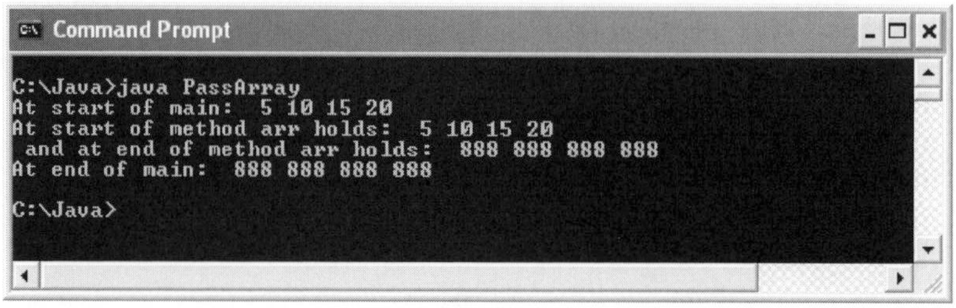

Figure 8-12 Output of the `PassArray` application

> ▶▶ **NOTE** In some other languages, notably C and C++, you can choose to pass variables to methods by value or reference. In Java, you cannot make this choice. Primitive type variables are always passed by value. When you pass an object, a copy of the reference to the object is always passed.

CREATING ARRAYS OF `Strings`

As with any other object, you can create an array of `Strings`. For example, you can store three company department names as follows:

```
String[] deptName = { "Accounting", "Human Resources", "Sales"};
```

You can access these department names like any other array object. For example, you can use the following code to print the list of `Strings` stored in the `deptName` array:

```
for(int a = 0; a < deptName.length; ++a)
    System.out.println(deptName[a] );
```

> ▶▶ **NOTE** Notice that `deptName.length;` refers to the length of the array `deptName` (three elements) and not to the length of any `String` objects stored in the `deptName` array. Each `String` object has access to a `length()` method that returns the length of a `String`. For example, if `deptName[0]` is "Accounting", `deptName[0].length()` is 10 because "Accounting" contains 10 characters.

In Chapter 7, you learned about methods for comparing characters and comparing strings. You determined whether they were the same and, if they were different, which one was considered larger. With arrays, you often want to know whether a certain character or string can be found within the elements of the array. For example, does the letter 'z' appear in an array of characters, or does the name "John" appear in the array of first names? The idea is to search the array to see if you can find an exact match. The `SearchList` application in Figure 8-13 shows an example of such a search. The user enters a department name, and the application provides a message indicating whether the `String` was found. Figure 8-14 shows the output when the user enters "Sales".

```
import javax.swing.*;
public class SearchList
{
    public static void main(String[] args)
    {
        String[] deptName = { "Accounting", "Human Resources", "Sales"};
        String dept;
        int x;
        boolean deptWasFound = false;
        dept = JOptionPane.showInputDialog(null,
            "Enter a department name");
        for(x = 0; x < deptName.length; ++x)
            if(dept.equals(deptName[x] ))
                deptWasFound = true;
        if(deptWasFound)
            JOptionPane.showMessageDialog(null, dept +
                " was found in the list");
        else
            JOptionPane.showMessageDialog(null, dept +
                " was not found in the list");
        System.exit(0);
    }
}
```

Figure 8-13 The SearchList class

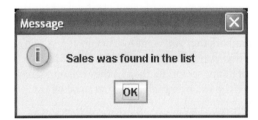

Figure 8-14 Output of the SearchList application when the user enters "Sales"

SORTING ARRAY ELEMENTS

Sorting is the process of arranging a series of objects in some logical order. When you place objects in order, beginning with the object that has the lowest value, you are sorting in **ascending** order; conversely, when you start with the object that has the largest value, you are sorting in **descending** order.

The simplest possible sort involves two values that are out of order. To place the values in order, you must swap the two values. Suppose that you have two variables—valA and valB— and further suppose that valA = 16 and valB = 2. To exchange the values of the two variables, you cannot simply use the following code:

```
valA = valB; // 2 goes to valA
valB = valA; // 2 goes to valB
```

If `valB` is 2, after you execute `valA = valB;`, both variables hold the value 2. The value 16 that was held in `valA` is lost. When you execute the second assignment statement, `valB = valA;`, each variable still holds the value 2.

The solution that allows you to retain both values is to employ a variable to hold `valA`'s value temporarily during the swap:

```
temp = valA; // 16 goes to temp
valA = valB; // 2 goes to valA
valB = temp; // 16 goes to valB
```

Using this technique, `valA`'s value (16) is assigned to the `temp` variable. The value of `valB` (2) is then assigned to `valA`, so `valA` and `valB` are equivalent. Then, the `temp` value (16) is assigned to `valB`, so the values of the two variables finally are swapped.

If you want to sort any two values, `valA` and `valB`, in ascending order so that `valA` is always the lower value, you use the following `if` statement to make the decision whether to swap. If `valA` is more than `valB`, you want to switch the values. If `valA` is not more than `valB`, you do not want to switch the values.

```
if(valA > valB)
{
    temp = valA;
    valA = valB;
    valB = temp;
}
```

Sorting two values is a fairly simple task; sorting more values (`valC`, `valD`, `valE`, and so on) is more complicated. Without the use of an array, sorting a series of numbers is a daunting task; the task becomes manageable when you know how to use an array.

As an example, you might have a list of five numbers that you want to place in ascending numerical order. One approach is to use a method popularly known as a bubble sort. In a **bubble sort**, you continue to compare pairs of items, swapping them if they are out of order, so that the smallest items "bubble" to the top of the list, eventually creating a sorted list.

To use a bubble sort, you place the original, unsorted values in an array, such as the following:

```
int[] someNums = { 88, 33, 99, 22, 54};
```

You compare the first two numbers; if they are not in ascending order, you swap them. You compare the second and third numbers; if they are not in ascending order, you swap them. You continue down the list. Generically, for any `someNums[x]`, if the value of `someNums[x]` is larger than `someNums[x + 1]`, you want to swap the two values.

With the numbers 88, 33, 99, 22, and 54, the process proceeds as follows:

» Compare 88 and 33. They are out of order. Swap them. The list becomes 33, 88, 99, 22, 54.

» Compare the second and third numbers in the list—88 and 99. They are in order. Do nothing.

» Compare the third and fourth numbers in the list—99 and 22. They are out of order. Swap them. The list becomes 33, 88, 22, 99, 54.

» Compare the fourth and fifth numbers—99 and 54. They are out of order. Swap them. The list becomes 33, 88, 22, 54, 99.

When you reach the bottom of the list, the numbers are not in ascending order, but the largest number, 99, has moved to the bottom of the list. This feature gives the bubble sort its name—the "heaviest" value has sunk to the bottom of the list as the "lighter" values have bubbled to the top.

Assuming b and temp both have been declared as integer variables, the code so far is as follows:

```
for(b = 0; b < someNums.length - 1; ++b)
    if(someNums[b] > someNums[b + 1])
    {
        temp = someNums[b];
        someNums[b] = someNums[b + 1];
        someNums[b + 1] = temp;
    }
```

Notice that the for statement tests every value of b from 0 through 3. The array someNums contains five integers. The subscripts in the array range in value from 0 through 4. Within the for loop, each someNums[b] is compared to someNums[b + 1], so the highest legal value for b is 3 when array element b is compared to array element b + 1. For a sort on any size array, the value of b must remain less than the array's length minus 1.

The list of numbers that began as 88, 33, 99, 22, 54 is currently 33, 88, 22, 54, 99. You must perform the entire comparison-swap procedure again.

» Compare the first two values—33 and 88. They are in order; do nothing.
» Compare the second and third values—88 and 22. They are out of order. Swap them so the list becomes 33, 22, 88, 54, 99.
» Compare the third and fourth values—88 and 54. They are out of order. Swap them so the list becomes 33, 22, 54, 88, 99.
» Compare the fourth and fifth values—88 and 99. They are in order; do nothing.

After this second pass through the list, the numbers are 33, 22, 54, 88, and 99—close to ascending order, but not quite. You can see that with one more pass through the list, the values 22 and 33 will swap, and the list is finally placed in order. To fully sort the worst-case list, one in which the original numbers are descending (as out-of-ascending order as they could possibly be), you need to go through the list four times, making comparisons and swaps. At most, you always need to pass through the list as many times as its length minus one. Figure 8-15 shows the entire procedure.

```
for(a = 0; a < someNums.length - 1; ++a)
    for(b = 0; b < someNums.length - 1; ++b)
        if(someNums[b] > someNums[b+ 1])
        {
            temp = someNums[b];
            someNums[b] = someNums[b + 1];
            someNums[b + 1] = temp;
        }
```

Figure 8-15 Ascending bubble sort of the someNums array elements

▶▶ NOTE To place the list in descending order, you need to make only one change in the code in Figure 8-15: You change the greater-than sign (>) in `if(someNums[b] > someNums[b + 1])` to a less-than sign (<).

When you use a bubble sort to sort any array into ascending order, the largest value "falls" to the bottom of the array after you have compared each pair of values in the array one time. The second time you go through the array making comparisons, there is no need to check the last pair of values. The largest value is guaranteed to already be at the bottom of the array. You can make the sort process even more efficient by using a new variable for the inner `for` loop and reducing the value by one on each cycle through the array. Figure 8-16 shows how you can use a new variable named `comparisonsToMake` to control how many comparisons are made in the inner loop during each pass through the list of values to be sorted. The `comparisonsToMake` value is decremented by 1 on each pass through the list.

```
int comparisonsToMake = someNums.length - 1;
for(a = 0; a < someNums.length - 1; ++a)
{
    for(b = 0; b < comparisonsToMake; ++b)
    {
        if(someNums[b] > someNums[b + 1])
        {
            temp = someNums[b];
            someNums[b] = someNums[b + 1];
            someNums[b + 1] = temp;
        }
    }
    --comparisonsToMake;
}
```

Figure 8-16 More efficient ascending bubble sort of the `someNums` array elements

SORTING ARRAYS OF OBJECTS

You can sort arrays of objects in much the same way that you sort arrays of primitive types. The major difference occurs when you make the comparison that determines whether you want to swap two array elements. When you construct an array of the primitive element type, you compare the two array elements to determine whether they are out of order. When array elements are objects, you usually want to sort based on a particular object field.

Assume you have created a simple `Employee` class, as shown in Figure 8-17. (Figure 8-2 showed a different, briefer `Employee` class. The class shown in the following figure contains more fields and methods.) The class holds four data fields, a constructor, and get and set methods for the fields.

You can write a program that contains an array of `Employee` objects using the following statement:

```
Employee[] someEmps = new Employee[5];
```

Assume that after you assign employee numbers and salaries to the `Employee` objects, you want to sort the `Employees` in `salary` order. You can pass the array and its length to a

```
public class Employee
{
    private int empNum;
    private String lastName;
    private String firstName;
    private double salary;
    public int getEmpNum()
    {
        return empNum;
    }
    public void setEmpNum(int emp)
    {
        empNum = emp;
    }
    public String getLastName()
    {
        return lastName;
    }
    public void setLastName(String name)
    {
        lastName = name;
    }
    public String getFirstName()
    {
        return firstName;
    }
    public void setFirstName(String name)
    {
        firstName = name;
    }
    public double getSalary()
    {
        return salary;
    }
    public void setSalary(double sal)
    {
        salary = sal;
    }
}
```

Figure 8-17 An expanded Employee class

bubbleSort() method that is prepared to receive Employee objects. Figure 8-18 shows the method.

>> **NOTE** Instead of passing the variable len to the bubbleSort() method, you could compute highSubscript as array.length - 1.

>> **NOTE** Instead of comparing the return values of the getSalary() method for Employee objects, you could write a compareTo() method for the Employee class that compares two Employee salary values. You always have multiple options for solving programming problems.

```
public static void bubbleSort(Employee[] array, int len)
{
    int a, b;
    Employee temp;
    int highSubscript = len - 1;
    for(a = 0; a < highSubscript; ++a)
     for(b = 0; b < highSubscript; ++b)
       if(array[b].getSalary() > array[b + 1].getSalary())
       {
           temp = array[b];
           array[b] = array[b + 1];
           array[b + 1] = temp;
       }
}
```

Figure 8-18 The `bubbleSort()` method that sorts `Employee` objects by their salaries

Examine Figure 8-18 carefully and notice that the `bubbleSort()` method is similar to the `bubbleSort()` method you use for an array of any primitive type, but there are three major differences:

» The `bubbleSort()` method header shows that it receives an array of type `Employee`.

» The `temp` variable created for swapping is type `Employee`. The `temp` variable will hold an `Employee` object, not just one number or one field.

» The comparison for determining whether a swap should occur uses method calls to the `getSalary()` method to compare the returned salary for each `Employee` object in the array with the salary of the adjacent `Employee` object.

> **NOTE** It is important to note that even though only employee salaries are compared, you do not just swap employee salaries. You do not want to substitute one employee's salary for another's. Instead, you swap each `Employee` object's `empNum` and `salary` as a unit.

USING TWO-DIMENSIONAL AND MULTIDIMENSIONAL ARRAYS

When you declare an array such as `int[] someNumbers = new int[3];`, you can envision the three declared integers as a column of numbers in memory, as shown in Figure 8-19. In other words, you can picture the three declared numbers stacked one on top of the next. An array that you can picture as a column of values, and whose elements you can access using a single subscript, is a **one-dimensional** or **single-dimensional array**.

Java also supports two-dimensional arrays. **Two-dimensional arrays** have two or more columns of values, as shown in Figure 8-20. It is easiest to picture two-dimensional arrays as having both rows and columns. You must use two subscripts when you access an element in a two-dimensional array. When mathematicians use a two-dimensional array, they often call it a **matrix** or a **table**; you might have used a two-dimensional array called a spreadsheet.

When you declare a one-dimensional array, you type a set of square brackets after the array type. To declare a two-dimensional array, you type two sets of brackets after the array type.

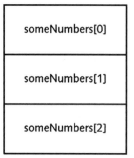

Figure 8-19 View of a single-dimensional array in memory

>> NOTE
You can think of the single dimension of a single-dimensional array as the height of the array.

someNumbers[0, 0]	someNumbers[0, 1]	someNumbers[0, 2]	someNumbers[0, 3]
someNumbers[1, 0]	someNumbers[1, 1]	someNumbers[1, 2]	someNumbers[1, 3]
someNumbers[2, 0]	someNumbers[2, 1]	someNumbers[2, 2]	someNumbers[2, 3]

Figure 8-20 View of a two-dimensional array in memory

>> NOTE
You can think of the two dimensions of a two-dimensional array as height and width.

For example, the array in Figure 8-20 can be declared as the following, creating an array named someNumbers that holds three rows and four columns:

```
int[][] someNumbers = new int[3][4];
```

Just as with a one-dimensional array, if you do not provide values for the elements in a two-dimensional numerical array, the values default to zero. You can assign other values to the array elements later. For example, someNumbers[0][0] = 14; assigns the value 14 to the element of the someNumbers array that is in the first column of the first row. Alternatively, you can initialize a two-dimensional array with values when it is created. For example, the following code assigns values to someNumbers when it is created:

```
int[][] someNumbers = {{ 8, 9, 10, 11},
                       { 1, 3, 12, 15},
                       { 5, 9, 44, 99} };
```

>> NOTE
You do not need to place each row of values for a two-dimensional array on its own line. However, doing so makes the positions of values easier to understand.

The someNumbers array contains three rows and four columns. You contain the entire set of values within a pair of curly braces. The first row of the array holds the four integers 8, 9, 10, and 11. Notice that these four integers are placed within their own set of curly braces to indicate that they constitute one row, or the first row, which is row 0. Similarly, 1, 3, 12, and 15 make up the second row (row 1), which you reference with the subscript 1. Next, 5, 9, 44, and 99 are the values in the third row (row 2), which you reference with the subscript 2. The value of someNumbers[0][0] is 8. The value of someNumbers[0][1] is 9. The value of someNumbers[2][3] is 99. The value within the first set of brackets following the array name always refers to the row; the value within the second brackets refers to the column.

As an example of how useful two-dimensional arrays can be, assume you own an apartment building with four floors—a basement, which you refer to as floor zero, and three other floors numbered one, two, and three. In addition, each of the floors has studio (with no bedroom) and one- and two-bedroom apartments. The monthly rent for each type of apartment is different—the higher the floor, the higher the rent (the view is better), and the rent is higher for apartments with more bedrooms. Table 8-2 shows the rental amounts.

Floor	Zero Bedrooms	One Bedroom	Two Bedrooms
0	400	450	510
1	500	560	630
2	625	676	740
3	1000	1250	1600

Table 8-2 Rents charged (in dollars)

To determine a tenant's rent, you need to know two pieces of information: the floor on which the tenant rents an apartment and the number of bedrooms in the apartment. Within a Java program, you can declare an array of rents using the following code:

```
int[][] rents = { { 400, 450, 510},
                  { 500, 560, 630},
                  { 625, 676, 740},
                  { 1000, 1250, 1600} };
```

Assume you declare two integers to hold the floor number and bedroom count, as in the following statement:

```
int floor, bedrooms;
```

Then any tenant's rent can be referred to as rents[floor][bedrooms].

When you pass a two-dimensional array to a method, you include the appropriate number of bracket pairs in the method header. For example, the following method headers accept two-dimensional arrays of ints, doubles, and Employees, respectively:

```
public static void displayScores(int[][] scoresArray)
public static boolean areAllPricesHigh(double[][] prices)
public static double computePayrollForAllEmployees(Employee[][] staff)
```

In each case, notice that the brackets indicating the array in the method header are empty. There is no need to insert numbers into the brackets because each passed array name is a starting memory address. The way you manipulate subscripts within the method determines how rows and columns are accessed.

Besides one- and two-dimensional arrays, Java also supports **multidimensional arrays** with more than two dimensions. For example, if you own an apartment building with a number of floors and different numbers of bedrooms available in apartments on each floor, you can use a two-dimensional array to store the rental fees. If you own several apartment buildings, you might want to employ a third dimension to store the building number. An expression such as rents[building][floor][bedrooms] refers to a specific rent figure for a building whose building number is stored in the `building` variable and whose floor and bedroom numbers are stored in the `floor` and `bedrooms` variables. Specifically, `rents[5][1][2]` refers to a two-bedroom apartment on the first floor of building 5. When you are programming in Java, you can use four, five, or more dimensions in an array. As long as you can keep track of the order of the variables needed as subscripts, and as long as you don't exhaust your computer's memory, Java lets you create arrays of any size.

USING THE Arrays CLASS

When you fully understand the power of arrays, you will want to use them to store all kinds of objects. Frequently, you will want to perform similar tasks with different arrays—for example, filling them with values and sorting their elements. Java provides an **Arrays class**, which contains many useful methods for manipulating arrays. Table 8-3 shows some of the useful methods of the `Arrays` class. For each method listed in the left column of the table, `type` stands for a data type; an overloaded version of each method exists for each appropriate data type. For example, there is a version of the `sort()` method to sort `int`, `double`, `char`, `byte`, `float`, `long`, `short`, and `Object` arrays.

> **▶▶NOTE**
> You will learn about the `Object` class in Chapter 12.

Method	Purpose
`static int binarySearch(type [] a, type key)`	Searches the specified array for the specified key value using the binary search algorithm
`static boolean equals(type[] a, type[] a2)`	Returns `true` if the two specified arrays of the same type are equal to one another
`static void fill (type[] a, type val)`	Assigns the specified value to each element of the specified array
`static void sort (type[] a)`	Sorts the specified array into ascending numerical order
`static void sort(type[] a, int fromIndex, int toIndex)`	Sorts the specified range of the specified array into ascending numerical order

Table 8-3 Useful methods of the `Arrays` class

The methods in the `Arrays` class are `static` methods, which means you use them with the class name without instantiating an `Arrays` object. The `ArraysDemo` application in Figure 8-21 provides a demonstration of how some of the methods in the `Arrays` class can be used. In the `ArraysDemo` class, the `myScores` array is created to hold five integers. Then, a message and the array reference are passed to a `display()` method. The first line of the output in Figure 8-22 shows that the original array is filled with 0s at creation. After the first display, the `Arrays.fill()` method is called in the first shaded statement in Figure 8-21. Because the arguments are the name of the array and the number 8, when the array is displayed a second time the output is all 8s. In the application, two of the array elements are changed to 6 and 3,

> **▶▶NOTE**
> The `Arrays` class is located in the `java.util` package, so you can use the `import` statement `import java.util.*;` to access it.

```
import java.util.*;
public class ArraysDemo
{
    public static void main(String[] args)
    {
        int[] myScores = new int[5];
        display("Original array:              ", myScores);
        Arrays.fill(myScores, 8);
        display("After filling with 8s:       ", myScores);
        myScores[2] = 6;
        myScores[4] = 3;
        display("After changing two values:  ", myScores);
        Arrays.sort(myScores);
        display("After sorting:               ", myScores);
    }

    public static void display(String message, int[] array)
    {
        int sz = array.length;
        System.out.print(message);
        for(int x = 0; x < sz; ++x)
            System.out.print(array[x] + " ");
        System.out.println();
    }
}
```

Figure 8-21 The `ArraysDemo` application

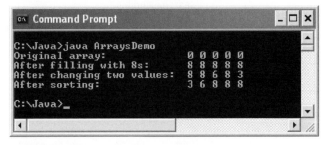

Figure 8-22 Output of the `ArraysDemo` application

and the array is displayed again. Finally, in the second shaded statement, the `Arrays.sort()` method is called. The output in Figure 8-22 shows that when the `display()` method executes the fourth time, the array elements have been sorted in ascending order.

The `Arrays` class `binarySearch()` methods provide convenient ways to search through sorted lists of values of various data types. It is important that the list be in order before you use it in a call to `binarySearch()`; otherwise, the results are unpredictable. You do not have to understand how a binary search works to use the `binarySearch()` method, but basically the operation takes place as follows:

» You have a sorted array and an item for which you are searching within the array. Based on the array size, you determine the middle position. (In an array with an even number of elements, this can be either of the two middle positions.)

» You compare the item you are looking for with the element in the middle position of the array and decide whether your item is above that point in the array—that is, whether your item's value is less than the middle-point value.

» If it is above that point in the array, you next find the middle position of the top half of the array; if it is not above that point, you find the middle position of the bottom half. Either way, you compare your item with that of the new middle position and divide the search area in half again.

» Ultimately, you find the element or determine that it is not in the array.

» **NOTE** Programmers often refer to a binary search as a "divide and conquer" procedure. If you have ever played a game in which you tried to guess what number someone was thinking, you might have used a similar technique.

Figure 8-23 contains an `ArraysDemo2` application that verifies a letter grade entered by the user. The array `grades` holds five values in ascending order. The user enters a grade that is extracted from the first `String` position using the `String` class `charAt()` method. Next, the array of valid characters and the user-entered character are passed to the `Arrays.binarySearch()` method. If the character is found in the array, its position is returned. If the character is not found in the array, a negative integer is returned and the application displays an error message. Figure 8-24 shows the output when the user enters an 'A'; the character is found in position 0 in the array.

» **NOTE** The negative integer returned by the `binarySearch()` method when the value is not found is the negative equivalent of the array size. In most applications, you do not care about the exact value returned when there is no match, but only whether it is negative.

```java
import java.util.*;
import javax.swing.*;
public class ArraysDemo2
{
    public static void main(String[] args)
    {
        char[] grades = {'A', 'B', 'C', 'D', 'F'};
        String entry;
        char myGrade;
        int position;
        entry = JOptionPane.showInputDialog(null,
            "Enter student grade");
        myGrade = entry.charAt(0);
        position = Arrays.binarySearch(grades, myGrade);
        if(position >= 0)
            JOptionPane.showMessageDialog(null, "Position of " +
                myGrade + " is " + position);
        else
            JOptionPane.showMessageDialog(null, "Invalid grade");
        System.exit(0);
    }
}
```

Figure 8-23 The `ArraysDemo2` application

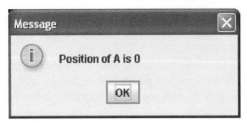

Figure 8-24 Output of the `ArraysDemo2` application when user enters 'A'

> **»NOTE** The `sort()` and `binarySearch()` methods in the `Arrays` class are very useful and allow you to achieve results by writing many fewer instructions than if you had to write the methods yourself. This does not mean you wasted your time reading about sorting and searching methods earlier in this chapter. The more completely you understand how arrays can be manipulated, the more useful, efficient, and creative your future applications will be.

YOU DO IT

CREATING AND POPULATING AN ARRAY

In this section, you will create a small array to see how arrays are used. The array will hold salaries for four categories of employees.

To create a program that uses an array:

1. Open a new text file in your text editor.

2. Begin the class that demonstrates how arrays are used by typing the following class and `main()` headers and their corresponding opening curly braces:

```
public class DemoArray
{
    public static void main(String[] args)
    {
```

3. On a new line, declare and create an array that can hold four double values by typing the following:

```
double[] salary = new double[4];
```

4. One by one, assign four values to the four salary array elements by typing the following:

```
salary[0] = 6.25;
salary[1] = 6.55;
salary[2] = 10.25;
salary[3] = 16.85;
```

5. To confirm that the four values have been assigned, print the salaries, one by one, using the following code:

```
System.out.println("Salaries one by one are:");
System.out.println(salary[0]);
System.out.println(salary[1]);
System.out.println(salary[2]);
System.out.println(salary[3]);
```

6. Add the two closing curly braces that end the main() method and the DemoArray class.

7. Save the program as **DemoArray.java** in the Chapter.08 folder on your Student Disk.

8. Compile and run the program. The program's output appears in Figure 8-25.

```
C:\Java>java DemoArray
Salaries one by one are:
6.25
6.55
10.25
16.85

C:\Java>
```

Figure 8-25 Output of the DemoArray application

INITIALIZING AN ARRAY

Next, you will alter your DemoArray program to initialize the array of doubles, rather than declaring the array and assigning values later.

To initialize an array of doubles:

1. Open the **DemoArray.java** file in your text editor. Immediately save the file as **DemoArray2.java**. Change the class name to **DemoArray2**. Delete the statement that declares the array of four doubles named salary, and then replace it with the following initialization statement:

```
double[] salary = {6.25, 6.55, 10.25, 16.85};
```

2. Delete the following four statements that individually assign the values to the array:

```
salary[0] = 6.25; salary[1] = 6.55; salary[2] = 10.25;
    salary[3] = 16.85;
```

3. Save the file (as **DemoArray2.java**), compile, and test the application. The values that are output are the same as those shown for the DemoArray application in Figure 8-25.

USING A for LOOP TO ACCESS ARRAY ELEMENTS

Next, you will modify the DemoArray2 program to use a for loop with the array.

To use a for loop with the array:

1. Open the **DemoArray2.java** file in your text editor. Immediately save the file as **DemoArray3.java**. Change the class name to **DemoArray3**. Delete the four println() statements that print the four array values, and then replace them with the following for loop:

```
for(int x = 0; x < salary.length; ++x)
    System.out.println(salary[x]);
```

2. Save the program (as **DemoArray3.java**), compile, and run the program. Again, the output is the same as that shown in Figure 8-25.

CREATING PARALLEL ARRAYS TO ELIMINATE NESTED `if` STATEMENTS

Next, you will create an `Event` class for Event Handlers Incorporated. The class contains three data fields: an integer representing the type of event, a `double` representing the rate that is charged for the event, and a `String` that holds the event manager's name. The class also contains methods to get and set the field values. You will create a constructor that bases field values on data stored in parallel arrays.

To create the `Event` class:

1. Open a new file in your text editor and create the `Event` class, as shown in Figure 8-26. Alternatively, open the **Event.java** class file you created and stored in the Chapter.05 folder on your Student Disk—it should look just like Figure 8-26. Save the file as **Event.java** in the Chapter.08 folder on your Student Disk.

```
public class Event
{
    private int typeOfEvent;
    private double rate;
    private String manager;
    public int getType()
    {
        return typeOfEvent;
    }
    public double getRate()
    {
        return rate;
    }
    public String getManager()
    {
        return manager;
    }
    public void setType(int eventType)
    {
        typeOfEvent = eventType;
    }
    public void setRate(double eventRate)
    {
        rate = eventRate;
    }
    public void setManager(String managerName)
    {
        manager = managerName;
    }
}
```

Figure 8-26 The `Event` class

2. Add a constructor to the `Event` class. Position the insertion point after the third field declaration (`manager`), press **Enter** to start a new line, and add the following constructor. The constructor requires an argument for the event type; the constructor uses it to determine

the rate charged and the manager's name for the event. Table 8-4 shows the appropriate values based on the event type. Although with only three event types it would be possible to make assignments using nested `if` statements, the constructor will use arrays to hold the possible field values. That way, when event types are added in the future, the only necessary change will be to add the data that corresponds to the new type of event. Also notice two features when you examine the constructor code:

» The event types are 1, 2, and 3, but arrays begin with element 0, so the 0 position of the `rateSchedule` and `managerList` arrays is reserved for error codes—a rate of 0 and a manager name of "X".

» Then, if the event code passed to the constructor is too high, it is forced to 0 before the arrays are accessed to assign rates and manager names.

Event Type Code	Event Type	Manager	Rate ($)
1	Private	Dustin Britt	47.99
2	Corporate	Carmen Lindsey	75.99
3	Non-profit	Robin Armanetti	40.99

Table 8-4 Events, managers, and rates charged per person

```
public Event(int eType)
{
    double[] rateSchedule = {0.0, 47.99, 75.99, 40.99};
    String[] managerList = {"X", "Dustin Britt",
        "Carmen Lindsey", "Robin Armanetti"};
    typeOfEvent = eType;
    if(eType > rateSchedule.length)
        eType = 0;
    rate = rateSchedule[eType];
    manager = managerList[eType];
}
```

3. Save the file (as **Event.java**) and compile it.

CREATING AN APPLICATION WITH AN ARRAY OF OBJECTS

Next, you will create an application that can hold an array of Event class objects.

To create an application that holds an array of objects:

1. Open a new text file in your text editor to create an `EventArray` application.

2. Type the following class header, the `main()` method header, and their opening curly braces:

```
public class EventArray
{
    public static void main(String[] args)
    {
```

3. Declare an array of five `Event` objects using the following code. You also declare an integer that can be used as a subscript:

```
Event[] someEvents = new Event[5];
int x;
```

4. Enter the following `for` loop that calls the `Event` constructor five times, making each `Event` type 1:

```
for(x = 0; x < someEvents.length; ++x)
   someEvents[x] = new Event(1);
```

5. To confirm that the `Event` objects have been created, print their values by typing the following:

```
for(x = 0; x < someEvents.length; ++x)
   System.out.println(someEvents[x].getType() +
      " " + someEvents[x].getRate() +
      " " + someEvents[x].getManager());
```

6. Add the two curly braces that end the `main()` method and the class definition.

7. Save the program as **EventArray.java** in the Chapter.08 folder. Compile and run the application. Figure 8-27 shows the program's output.

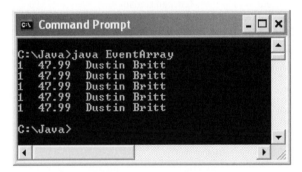

Figure 8-27 Output of the `EventArray` application

CREATING AN INTERACTIVE APPLICATION THAT CREATES AN ARRAY OF OBJECTS

An array of five `Event` objects—each of which has the same event type and fee—is not very interesting or useful. Next, you will create an `EventArray2` application that creates the events interactively so that each event possesses unique properties.

To create an interactive `EventArray2` program:

1. Open a new file in your text editor and enter the following code to begin the class. The `main()` method contains an array of `Strings` describing the event types and two more `Strings`; the first of these `Strings` is used to construct a `choicesString` prompt, and the second is used to accept the user's response from the keyboard. In addition, you include an integer to hold the selected event number, an array of five `Event` objects, and an integer to be used as a subscript when accessing arrays:

```
import javax.swing.*;
public class EventArray2
{
    public static void main(String[] args)
    {
```

```
String[] eventTypes = {"", "Private", "Corporate",
    "Non-profit"};
String choicesString = "";
String strSelectedEvent;
int selectedEvent;
Event[] someEvents = new Event[5];
int x;
```

2. Add a `for` loop that builds the `String` to be used as part of the prompt for the user, listing the available choices for event types. Instead of this loop, you could declare a `String` as `"1 Private\n2 Corporate\n3 Non-profit"` and the results would be identical. However, by creating the `String` in a loop, you avoid being required to change this prompt if the event type codes and names are altered in the future. Also notice that this loop begins with `x = 1` because you do not want to display the 0 option:

```
for(x = 1; x < eventTypes.length; ++x)
    choicesString = choicesString + "\n" + x + " " +
        eventTypes[x];
```

3. The next `for` loop executes one time for each `Event` object that is instantiated. It prompts the user, converts the user's choice to an integer, forces the choice to 0 if it is invalid, and finally creates the object:

```
for(x = 0; x < someEvents.length; ++x)
{
    strSelectedEvent = JOptionPane.showInputDialog(null,
        "Event #" + (x + 1) +
        " Enter the number for the type of event you want" +
        choicesString);
    selectedEvent = Integer.parseInt(strSelectedEvent);
    if (selectedEvent < 1 || selectedEvent > 3)
        selectedEvent = 0;
    someEvents[x] = new Event(selectedEvent);
}
```

4. The last `for` loop lists the details of each created `Event`:

```
for(x = 0; x < someEvents.length; ++x)
    System.out.println(someEvents[x].getType() +
        " " + eventTypes[someEvents[x].getType()] +
        " " + someEvents[x].getRate() +
        " " + someEvents[x].getManager());
```

5. Add **System.exit(0);** and the two closing curly braces—one for the `main()` method and the other for the class.

6. Save the file as **EventArray2.java** in the Chapter.08 folder on your Student Disk. Compile and execute the application. Provide an event number at each prompt and confirm that the correct objects are created. For example, Figure 8-28 shows the output when the user enters 0, 1, 2, 3, and 4 in that order for the event types. Notice that the last event type has been forced to 0 because an invalid entry (4) was made.

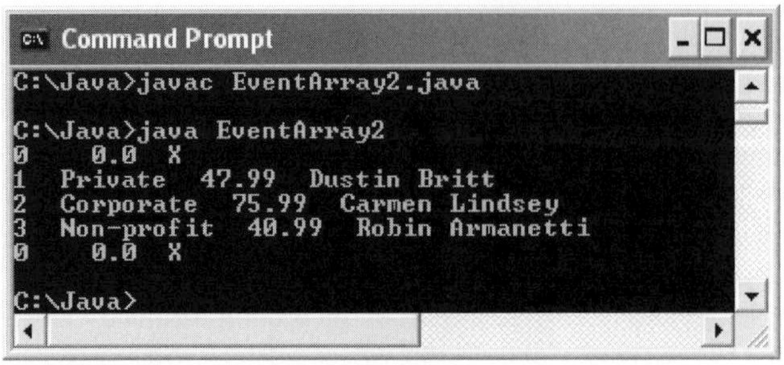

Figure 8-28 Output of the `EventArray2` application

PASSING AN ARRAY TO A METHOD

Next, you will add a new method to the `EventArray2` application that increases the rate for each `Event`. This application demonstrates that changes made to a passed array within a method permanently affect values in the array.

To add a new method to the `EventArray2` class:

1. In your text editor, open the **EventArray2.java** file from the Chapter.08 folder on your Student Disk, if it is not already open. Immediately save the file as **EventArray3.java**. Change the class name to match the filename.

   Just before the closing curly brace for the class, add the following method that accepts three arguments—an array of `Event` objects, the number of elements in the array, and an amount by which each `Event` rate should be increased. Within the method, each array element is processed in a `for` loop. With each element, you use the `getRate()` method of the `Event` class to retrieve the `Event` current rate, add a fixed amount to it, and return the sum to the class field using the `Event` class `setRate()` method.

   ```java
   public static void increaseFees(Event[] e, int num, double
       increaseAmt)
   {
       int x;
       for(x = 0; x < num; ++x)
           e[x].setRate(e[x].getRate() + increaseAmt);
   }
   ```

2. After the final `for` loop in the existing class, and just before `System.exit(0);`, add the following statement, which calls the `increaseFees()` method, passing the array of `Event` objects, the number of array elements, and a flat $100.00 per event increase:

   ```java
   increaseFees(someEvents, someEvents.length, 100.00);
   ```

NOTE
If you do not want to type this last `println()` statement, you can simply use your text editor's copy function to copy the identical statement that already exists within the program.

3. On the next lines, add a statement that heads the list of `Events` after the increases have taken place, and then displays all the `Event` details in a loop.

   ```java
   System.out.println("After increases: ");
   for(x = 0; x < someEvents.length; ++x)
       System.out.println(someEvents[x].getType() +
           " " + eventTypes[someEvents[x].getType()] +
           " " + someEvents[x].getRate() +
           " " + someEvents[x].getManager());
   ```

300

4. Save the file (as **EventArray3.java**) and compile and execute the program. The output appears as shown in Figure 8-29 after the user enters 1, 2, 3, 2, and 1 as Event choices. Notice that the changes you made to each Event in the method persist when the Event array is displayed in the main() method.

Figure 8-29 Output of the EventArray3 application

USING Arrays CLASS METHODS

Next, you will create an application for Event Handlers Incorporated that demonstrates several Arrays class methods. The application will allow the user to enter the menu of entrees that are available for the day. Then, it will present the menu to the user, allow a request, and indicate whether the requested item is on the menu.

To write an application that uses Arrays class methods:

1. Open a new file in your text editor and type the import statements you need to create an application that will use JOptionPane and the Arrays classes:

```
import java.util.*;
import javax.swing.*;
```

2. Add the first few lines of the MenuSearch application class:

```
public class MenuSearch
{
    public static void main(String[] args)
    {
```

3. Declare an array to hold the day's menu choices; the user is allowed to enter up to 10 entrees. Also declare two Strings—one to hold the user's current entry and the other to accumulate the entire menu list as it is entered. The two String variables are initialized to empty Strings using quotation marks; if you do not initialize these Strings, you receive a compiler error because you might attempt to display them without having entered a legitimate value. Also, declare an integer to use as a subscript for the array, another to hold

the number of menu items entered, and a third to hold the highest allowable subscript, which is 1 less than the array size:

```
String[] menuChoices = new String[10];
String entry= "", menuString = "";
int x = 0;
int numEntered;
int highestSub = menuChoices.length - 1;
```

4. Use the `Arrays.fill()` method to fill the menu array with "Z" characters. You do this so that when you perform a search later, actual values will be stored in any unused menu positions. If you ignore this step and fill less than half the array, your search method might generate an error:

```
Arrays.fill(menuChoices, "ZZZZZZZ");
```

5. Display an input dialog box into which the user can enter a menu item. Allow the user to quit before entering 10 items by typing "zzz". (Using a value such as "zzz" is a common programming technique to check for the user's desire to stop entering data. If the data items are numeric instead of text, you might use a value such as 999. Values the user enters that are not "real" data, but just signals to stop, are often called **dummy values**.) After the user enters the first menu item, the application enters a loop that continues to add the entered item to the menu list, increase the subscript, and prompt for a new menu item. The loop continues while the user has not entered "zzz" and the subscript has not exceeded the allowable limit. When the loop ends, save the number of menu items entered:

```
menuChoices[x] = JOptionPane.showInputDialog(null,
    "Enter an item for today's menu, or zzz to quit:");
while(!menuChoices[x].equals("zzz") && x < highestSub)
{
    menuString = menuString + menuChoices[x] + "\n";
    ++x;
    if(x < highestSub)
        menuChoices[x] = JOptionPane.showInputDialog(null,
            "Enter an item for today's menu, or zzz to quit");
}
numEntered = x;
```

6. When the menu is complete, display it for the user and allow the user to make a request:

```
entry = JOptionPane.showInputDialog(null,
    "Today's menu is:\n" + menuString + "Please make a selection:");
```

7. Sort the array from index position 0 to numEntered so that it is in ascending order prior to using the `binarySearch()` method. If you do not sort the array, the result of the `binarySearch()` method is unpredictable. You could sort the entire array, but it is more efficient to sort only the elements that hold actual menu items:

```
Arrays.sort(menuChoices, 0, numEntered);
```

8. Use the `Arrays.binarySearch()` method to search for the requested entry in the previously sorted array. If the method returns a non-negative value that is less than the

numEntered value, display the message "Excellent choice"; otherwise, display an error message:

```
x = Arrays.binarySearch(menuChoices, entry);
if(x >= 0 && x < numEntered)
    JOptionPane.showMessageDialog(null, "Excellent choice");
else
    JOptionPane.showMessageDialog(null,
        "Sorry - that item is not on tonight's menu");
```

9. Add the statement that exits the application, as well as the closing curly braces for the main() method and the class:

```
System.exit(0);
    }
}
```

10. Save the file as **MenuSearch.java** in the Chapter.08 folder on your Student Disk. Compile and execute the application. When prompted, enter as many menu choices as you want, and enter "zzz" when you want to quit data entry. When prompted again, enter a menu choice and observe the results. Figure 8-30 shows a typical menu as it is presented to the user, and the results after the user makes a valid choice.

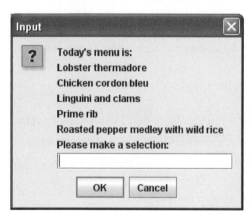
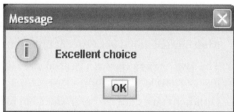

Figure 8-30 Typical execution of the MenuSearch application

KEY TERMS

An **array** is a named list of data items that all have the same type.

A **subscript** is an integer contained within square brackets that indicates one of an array's variables, or elements.

An **element** is one variable or object in an array.

Providing values for all the elements in an array is called **populating the array**.

Scalar variables are simple, primitive variables, such as int, double, or char.

The **length field** contains the number of elements in an array.

An object's instance variable or field is also called a **property** of the object.

The **enhanced for loop** allows you to cycle through an array without specifying the starting and ending points for the loop control variable.

Searching an array is the process of comparing a value to a list of values in an array, looking for a match.

A **parallel array** is one with the same number of elements as another, and for which the values in corresponding elements are related.

A **range match** is the process of comparing a value to the endpoints of numerical ranges to find a category in which the value belongs.

When a variable is **passed by value** to a method, a copy is made in the receiving method.

Arrays are **reference types**, meaning that the object actually holds a memory address where the values are stored.

Sorting is the process of arranging a series of objects in some logical order.

When you place objects in order, beginning with the object that has the lowest value, you are sorting in **ascending** order.

When you place objects in order, beginning with the object that has the highest value, you are sorting in **descending** order.

A **bubble sort** is a type of sort in which you continue to compare pairs of items, swapping them if they are out of order, so that the smallest items "bubble" to the top of the list, eventually creating a sorted list.

A **one-dimensional array** or **single-dimensional array** contains one column of values; you access its elements using a single subscript.

Two-dimensional arrays have two or more columns of values, and you must use two subscripts to access an element.

When mathematicians use a two-dimensional array, they often call it a **matrix** or a **table**.

Multidimensional arrays contain two or more dimensions.

The Java **Arrays class** is a built-in class that contains many useful methods for searching, filling, comparing, and sorting arrays.

Dummy values are not "real" data, but just signals to stop data entry.

CHAPTER SUMMARY

» An array is a named list of data items that all have the same type. You declare an array variable in the same way you declare any simple variable, but you insert a pair of square brackets after the type. To reserve memory space for an array, you use the keyword `new`. You use a subscript contained within square brackets to refer to one of an array's variables, or elements. In Java, any array's elements are numbered beginning with zero.

» Array names represent computer memory addresses; that is, when array names are passed to a method, the method receives the memory address of the array. When you declare an array name, no computer memory address is assigned to it. Instead, the array variable name has the special value `null`, or Unicode value '\u0000'. When you declare int[] someNums;, the variable someNums has a value of null. When you use the keyword new, as in int[] someNums = new int[10];, then someNums has an actual memory address value. Each element of someNums has a value of 0 because someNums is a numeric array. By default, character array elements are assigned '\u0000'. Boolean array elements automatically are assigned false. You can assign nondefault values to array elements upon creation. To initialize an array, you use a list of values separated by commas and enclosed within curly braces.

» You can shorten many array-based tasks by using a variable as a subscript. When an application contains an array, it is common to perform loops that execute from 0 to one less than the size of the array. The length field is an automatically created field that is assigned to every array; it contains the number of elements in the array.

» Just as you can declare arrays of integers or doubles, you can declare arrays that hold elements of any type, including objects. To use a method that belongs to an object that is part of an array, you insert the appropriate subscript notation after the array name and before the dot that precedes the method name.

» By looping through an array and making comparisons, you can search an array to find a match to a value. You can use a parallel array with the same number of elements to hold related elements.

» You perform a range match by placing end values of a numeric range in an array and making greater-than or less-than comparisons.

» You can pass a single array element to a method in exactly the same manner as you would pass a simple variable, and the array receives a copy of the passed value. However, arrays, like all objects, are reference types; this means that when an array name is passed to a method, the method receives a copy of the array's actual memory address and has access to the values in the original array.

» As with any other object, you can create an array of Strings.

» Sorting is the process of arranging a series of objects in some logical order. When you place objects in order, beginning with the object that has the lowest value, you are sorting in ascending order; conversely, when you start with the object that has the largest value, you are sorting in descending order. A bubble sort is a type of sort in which you continue to compare pairs of items, swapping them if they are out of order, so that the smallest items "bubble" to the top of the list, eventually creating a sorted list.

» You can sort arrays of objects in much the same way that you sort arrays of primitive types. The major difference occurs when you make the comparison that determines whether you want to swap two array elements. When array elements are objects, you usually want to sort based on a particular object field.

» An array that you can picture as a column of values, and whose elements you can access using a single subscript, is a one-dimensional or single-dimensional array. Two-dimensional arrays have both rows and columns. You must use two subscripts when you access an element in a two-dimensional array. When you declare a one-dimensional array, you type a set of square brackets after the array type. To declare a two-dimensional array, you type two sets of brackets after the array type.

» The Java Arrays class contains many useful methods for searching, comparing, filling, and sorting arrays.

REVIEW QUESTIONS

1. An array is a list of data items that _____.
   a. all have the same type   c. all are integers
   b. all have different names   d. all are `null`

2. When you declare an array, _____.
   a. you always reserve memory for it in the same statement
   b. you might reserve memory for it in the same statement
   c. you cannot reserve memory for it in the same statement
   d. your ability to reserve memory for it in the same statement depends on the type of the array

3. You reserve memory locations for an array when you _____.
   a. declare the array name
   b. use the keyword `new`
   c. use the keyword `mem`
   d. explicitly store values within the array elements

4. For how many integers does the following statement reserve room?
   ```
   int[] value = new int[34];
   ```
   a. 0   c. 34
   b. 33   d. 35

5. A(n) _____ contained within square brackets is used to indicate one of an array's elements.
   a. character   c. `int`
   b. `double`   d. `String`

6. If you declare an array as follows, how do you indicate the final element of the array?
   ```
   int[] num = new int[6];
   ```
   a. num[0]   c. num[5]
   b. num[1]   d. impossible to tell

7. If you declare an integer array as follows, what is contained in the element num[2]?
   ```
   int[] num = { 101, 202, 303, 404, 505, 606};
   ```
   a. 101   c. 303
   b. 202   d. impossible to tell

8. Array names represent _____ .

   a. values   c. references

   b. functions   d. allusions

9. Unicode value '\u0000' is also known as _____ .

   a. nil   c. nada

   b. void   d. null

10. When you initialize an array by giving it values upon creation, you _____ .

   a. do not explicitly give the array a size

   b. must also give the array a size

   c. must make all the values zero, blank, or `false`

   d. must make certain each value is different from the others

11. Assume an array is declared as follows. Which of the following statements correctly assigns the value 100 to each of the four array elements?

```
int[] num = new int[4];
```

   a. `for (x = 0; x < 3; ++x) num[x] = 100;`

   b. `for (x = 0; x < 4; ++x) num[x] = 100;`

   c. `for (x = 1; x < 4; ++x) num[x] = 100;`

   d. `for (x = 1; x < 5; ++x) num[x] = 100;`

12. If a class named `Student` contains a method `setID()` that takes an `int` argument and you write an application in which you create an array of 20 `Student` objects named `scholar`, which of the following statements correctly assigns an ID number to the first `Student scholar`?

   a. `Student[0].setID(1234);`

   b. `scholar[0].setID(1234);`

   c. `Student.setID[0](1234);`

   d. `scholar.setID[0](1234);`

13. In which of the following situations would setting up parallel arrays be most useful?

   a. You need to look up an employee's ID number to find the employee's last name.

   b. You need to calculate interest earned on a savings account balance.

   c. You need to store a list of 20 commonly misspelled words.

   d. You need to determine the shortest distance between two points on a map.

14. When you pass an array element to a method, the method receives _____ .

   a. a copy of the array

   b. the address of the array

   c. a copy of the value in the element

   d. the address of the element

15. When you pass an array to a method, the method receives _____ .

   a. a copy of the array

   b. a copy of the first element in the array

   c. the address of the array

   d. nothing

16. When you place objects in order beginning with the object with the highest value, you are sorting in _____ order.

   a. acquiescing   c. demeaning

   b. ascending   d. descending

17. Using a bubble sort involves _____ .

   a. comparing parallel arrays

   b. comparing each array element to the average

   c. comparing each array element to the adjacent array element

   d. swapping every array element with its adjacent element

18. Which array types cannot be sorted?

   a. arrays of characters

   b. arrays of `Strings`

   c. arrays of objects

   d. You can sort all of these array types.

19. When array elements are objects, you usually want to sort based on a particular _____ of the object.

   a. field   c. name

   b. method   d. type

20. The following defines a _____ array:

   ```
   int[][] nums={{ 1, 2}, { 3, 4}, { 5, 6}};
   ```

   a. one-dimensional   c. three-dimensional

   b. two-dimensional   d. six-dimensional

EXERCISES

1. Write an application that can hold five integers in an array. Display the integers from first to last, and then display the integers from last to first. Save the file as **IntArray.java** in the Chapter.08 folder on your Student Disk.

2. Write an application that prompts the user to make a choice for a pizza size—S, M, L, or X—and then displays the price as $6.99, $8.99, $12.50, or $15.00, accordingly. Display an error message if the user enters an invalid pizza size. Save the file as **PizzaChoice.java** in the Chapter.08 folder on your Student Disk.

3. a. Create a class named `Taxpayer`. Data fields for `Taxpayer` include Social Security number (use an `int` for the type, and do not use dashes within the Social Security number) and yearly gross income. Methods include a constructor that requires values for both data fields, and two methods that each return one of the data field values. Write an application named `UseTaxpayer` that declares an array of 10 `Taxpayer` objects. Set each Social Security number to 999999999 and each gross income to zero. Display the 10 `Taxpayer` objects. Save the files as **Taxpayer.java** and **UseTaxpayer.java** in the Chapter.08 folder on your Student Disk.

   b. Modify your `UseTaxpayer` application so each `Taxpayer` has a successive Social Security number from 1 through 10 and a gross income that ranges from $10,000 to $100,000, increasing by $10,000 for each successive `Taxpayer`. Save the file as **UseTaxpayer2.java** in the Chapter.08 folder on your Student Disk.

4. Create an application containing an array that stores 20 prices, such as $2.34, $7.89, $1.34, and so on. The application should (1) display the sum of all the prices, (2) display all values less than $5.00, (3) calculate the average of the prices, and (4) display all values that are higher than the calculated average value. Save the file as **Prices.java** in the Chapter.08 folder on your Student Disk.

5. a. Create a `CollegeCourse` class. The class contains fields for the course ID (for example, "CIS 210"), credit hours (for example, 3), and a letter grade (for example, 'A'). Include `get()` and `set()` methods for each field. Create a `Student` class containing an ID number and an array of five `CollegeCourse` objects. Create a `get()` and `set()` method for the `Student` ID number. Also create a `get()` method that returns one of the `Student`'s `CollegeCourses`; the method takes an integer argument and returns the `CollegeCourse` in that position (0 through 4). Next, create a `set()` method that sets the value of one of the `Student`'s `CollegeCourses`; the method takes two arguments—a `CollegeCourse` and an integer representing the `CollegeCourse`'s position (0 through 4). Save the files as **CollegeCourse.java** and **Student.java** in the Chapter.08 folder on your Student Disk.

   b. Write an application that prompts a professor to enter grades for five different courses each for 10 students. Prompt the professor to enter data for one student at a time, including student ID and course data for five courses. Use prompts containing the number of the student whose data is being entered and the course number—for example, "Enter ID for student #s", where s is an integer from 1 through 10, indicating the student, and "Enter course ID #n", where n is an integer from 1 through 5, indicating the course number. Verify that the professor enters only A, B, C, D, or F for the grade value for each course. Save the file as **InputGrades.java** in the Chapter.08 folder on your Student Disk.

6. Write an application in which the user can enter a date using digits and slashes (for example, "2/4/2009"), and receive output that displays the date with the month as a word (such as "February 4, 2009"). Allow for the fact that the user might or might not precede a month or day number with a zero (for example, the user might type "02/04/2009" or "2/4/2009"). Do not allow the user to enter an invalid date, defined as one for which the month is less than 1 or more than 12, or one for which the day number is less than 1 or greater than the number of days in the specified month. Also display the date's ordinal position in the year; for example, 2/4 is the 35th day. In this application, use your knowledge of arrays to store the month names, as well as values for the number of days in each month so that you can calculate the number of days that have passed. Figure 8-31 shows the output when the user has entered 2/4/2009. Save the application as **ConvertDate.java**.

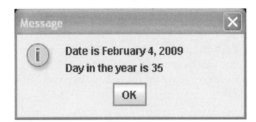

Figure 8-31 Typical execution of `ConvertDate` application

» NOTE When determining whether a date is valid and when calculating the number of days that have passed, remember that some years are leap years. In a leap year, February 29th is added to the calendar. A leap year is any year that is evenly divisible by 4, unless the year is also evenly divisible by 100. So 1904 and 2004 were both leap years, but 1900 was not a leap year. Another exception occurs when a year is evenly divisible by 400—the year is a leap year. Therefore, 2000 was a leap year, but 2100 will not be one.

7. a. Write an application that stores vowels (a, e, i, o, and u) in an array. Ask the user to enter a character. Then, the program should indicate whether the entered character is a lowercase vowel. Save the file as **VowelArray.java** in the Chapter.08 folder on your Student Disk.

   b. Modify the `VowelArray` application so that uppercase vowels are also recognized as vowels. Save the file as **VowelArray2.java** in the Chapter.08 folder on your Student Disk.

8. Write an application that allows a user to enter the names and phone numbers of up to 20 friends. Continue to prompt the user for names and phone numbers until the user enters "zzz" or has entered 20 names, whichever comes first. When the user is finished entering names, produce a count of how many names were entered, but make certain not to count the application-ending dummy "zzz" entry. Then display the names. Ask the user to type one of the names and display the corresponding phone number. Save the application as **PhoneBook.java** in the Chapter.08 folder on your Student Disk.

9. Store 20 employee ID numbers in an integer array and 20 corresponding employee last names in a `String` array. Use dialog boxes to accept an ID number, and display the appropriate last name. Save the application as **EmployeeIDArray.java** in the Chapter.08 folder on your Student Disk.

10. Create an array of `String`s, each containing one of the top 10 reasons that you like Java. Prompt a user to enter a number from 1 to 10, convert the number to an integer, and then use the integer to display one of the reasons. Save the application as **JavaArray.java** in the Chapter.08 folder on your Student Disk.

11. Create an array of five `String`s containing the first names of people in your family. Write a program that counts and displays the total number of vowels (both uppercase and lowercase) in all five `String`s that you entered. Save the file as **Vowels.java** in the Chapter.08 folder on your Student Disk.

12. Write an application containing three parallel arrays that hold 10 elements each. The first array holds four-digit student ID numbers, the second holds first names, and the third holds the students' grade point averages. Use dialog boxes to accept a student ID number and display the student's first name and grade point average. If a match is not found, display an appropriate message and allow the user to search for a new ID number. Save the file as **StudentIDArray.java** in the Chapter.08 folder on your Student Disk.

13. A personal phone directory contains room for first names and phone numbers for 30 people. Assign names and phone numbers for the first 10 people. Prompt the user for a name, and if the name is found in the list, display the corresponding phone number. If the name is not found in the list, prompt the user for a phone number, and add the new name and phone number to the list. Continue to prompt the user for names until the user enters "quit". After the arrays are full (containing 30 names), do not allow the user to add new entries. Save the file as **PhoneNumbers.java** in the Chapter.08 folder on your Student Disk.

14. a. Write an application containing an array of 15 `double` values. Include a method to sort and display the values in ascending order. Compile, run, and check the results. Save the file as **SortDoubles.java** in the Chapter.08 folder on your Student Disk.

    b. Modify the `SortDoubles` application to prompt the user whether to view the list in ascending or descending order. Save the file as **SortDoublesWithOption.java** in the Chapter.08 folder on your Student Disk.

15. a. Create a class named `LibraryBook` that contains fields to hold methods for setting and getting a `LibraryBook`'s title, author, and page count. Save the file as **LibraryBook.java** in the Chapter.08 folder on your Student Disk.

    b. Write an application that instantiates five `LibraryBook` objects and prompts the user for values for the data fields. Then prompt the user to enter which field the `LibraryBook`s should be sorted by—title, author, or page count. Perform the requested sort procedure and display the `LibraryBook` objects. Save the file as **LibraryBookSort.java** in the Chapter.08 folder on your Student Disk.

16. Write an application that stores at least four different course names and meeting days and times in a two-dimensional array. Allow the user to enter a course name (such as "CIS 110") and display the day of the week and time that the course is held (such as "Th 3:30"). If the course does not exist, display an error message. Save the file as **Schedule.java** in the Chapter.08 folder on your Student Disk.

DEBUGGING EXERCISES

Each of the following files in the Chapter.08 folder on your Student Disk has syntax and/or logic errors. In each case, determine the problem and fix the program. After you correct the errors, save each file using the same filename preceded with Fix. For example, DebugEight1.java will become FixDebugEight1.java.

a. DebugEight1.java   c. DebugEight3.java

b. DebugEight2.java   d. DebugEight4.java

CASE PROJECT

CURL UP AND DYE SALON

The Curl Up and Dye Salon offers a variety of salon services for its customers. Jane Fields, the owner, has contracted to have you write a program that allows reports to be output, sorted by each type of service offered. Table 8-5 shows the various services, service prices, and service times.

Service	Price ($)	Time (Minutes)
Cut	8.00	15
Shampoo	4.00	10
Manicure	18.00	30
Style	48.00	55
Permanent	18.00	35
Trim	6.00	5

Table 8-5 Salon services, prices, and times

Create a class for services offered by a salon. Data fields include a String to hold the service description (for example, "Cut", "Shampoo", or "Manicure"), a double to hold the price, and an integer to hold the average number of minutes it takes to perform the service. The class name is Service. Include a constructor that requires arguments for all three data fields and three get methods that each return one of the data field's values.

Write an application named SalonReport that contains an array to hold six Service objects and fill it with the data from Table 8-5. Include methods to sort the array in ascending order by price of service, time it takes to perform the service, and in alphabetical order by service description.

Prompt the user for the preferred sorting method, and offer three choices: sort by description, price, or time. Depending on the user's input, display the results.

Save the files as **Service.java** and **SalonReport.java** in the Chapter.08 folder on your Student Disk.

GAME ZONE

1. Write an application that contains an array of 10 multiple-choice quiz questions related to your favorite hobby. Each question contains three answer choices. Also create an array that holds the correct answer to each question—A, B, or C. Display each question and verify that the user enters only A, B, or C as the answer—if not, keep prompting the user until a valid response is entered. If the user responds to a question correctly, display "Correct!"; otherwise, display "The correct answer is" and the letter of the correct answer. After the user answers all the questions, display the number of correct and incorrect answers. Save the file as **Quiz.java** in the Chapter.08 folder on your Student Disk.

2. a. In Chapter 4, you created a `Die` application that randomly "throws" five dice for the computer and five dice for the player. The application displays the values. Modify the application to decide the winner based on the following hierarchy of `Die` values. Any higher combination beats a lower one; for example, five of a kind beats four of a kind.

   » Five of a kind
   » Four of a kind
   » Three of a kind
   » A pair

   For this game, the dice values do not count; for example, if both players have three of a kind, it's a tie, no matter what the values of the three dice are. Additionally, the game does not recognize a full house (three of a kind plus two of a kind). Figure 8-32 shows three successive sample executions. Save the application as **FiveDice2.java**.

   b. Improve the `FiveDice2` game so that when both players have the same combination of dice, the higher value wins. For example, two 6's beats two 5's. Figure 8-33 shows three successive example executions. Save the application as **FiveDice3.java**.

3. a. In Chapter 7, you modified a previously created `Card` class so that each `Card` would hold the name of a suit ("Spades", "Hearts", "Diamonds", or "Clubs") as well as a value ("Ace", "King", "Queen", "Jack", or a number value). Now, create an array of 52 `Card` objects, assigning a different value to each `Card`, and display each `Card`. Save the application as **FullDeck.java.**

   b. In Chapter 7, you created a `War2` card game that randomly selects two `Card` objects (one for the player and one for the computer) and declares a winner or a tie based on the card values. Now create a game that plays 26 rounds of War, dealing a full deck with no repeated cards. Some hints:

   » Start by creating an array of all 52 playing cards, as in Exercise 3a.
   » Select a random number for the deck position of the player's first card and assign the card at that array position to the player.

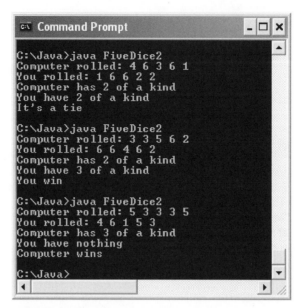

Figure 8-32 Typical executions of `FiveDice2` application

Figure 8-33 Typical executions of `FiveDice3` application

» Move every higher-positioned card in the deck "down" one to fill in the gap. In other words, if the player's first random number is 49, select the card at position 49, move the card that was in position 50 to position 49, and move the card that was in position 51 to position 50. Only 51 cards remain in the deck after the player's first card is dealt, so the available-card array is smaller by one.

» In the same way, randomly select a card for the computer and "remove" the card from the deck.

» Display the values of the player's and computer's cards, compare their values, and determine the winner.

» When all the cards in the deck are exhausted, display a count of the number of times the player wins, the number of times the computer wins, and the number of ties.

Save the game as **War3.java**.

4. In Chapter 7, you created a Secret Phrase game similar to Hangman, in which the user guesses letters in a partially hidden phrase in an attempt to determine the complete phrase. Modify the program so that:

» The phrase to be guessed is selected randomly from a list of at least 10 phrases.

» The clue is presented to the user with asterisks replacing letters to be guessed, but with spaces in the appropriate locations. For example, if the phrase to be guessed is "No man is an island," then the user sees the following as a first clue:

** *** ** ** ******

The spaces provide valuable clues as to where individual words start and end.

» Make sure that when a user makes a correct guess, all the matching letters are filled in, regardless of case.

Save the game as **SecretPhrase2.java.**

5. Create a guessing game called "Does It Have Legs?", in which you think of an animal and the computer tries to guess what it is. The game continually becomes "smarter" as you play because you teach it how to become more specific with its questions. For example, a typical game session might proceed as follows:

Computer: Does the animal you are thinking of have legs?
Player: Yes.
Computer: Is it a dog?
Player: Yes.
Computer: Yay! I win. Do you want to play again?
Player: Yes.
Computer: Does the animal you are thinking of have legs?
Player: Yes.
Computer: Is it a dog?
Player: No.
Computer: I give up. What was your animal?
Player: Horse.
Computer: Type a question for which the answer is Yes for Dog but No for Horse.
Player: Does it live in the house?
Computer: Do you want to play again?
Player: Yes.
Computer: Does the animal you are thinking of have legs?
Player: Yes.
Computer: Does it live in the house?
Player: No.
Computer: Is it a Horse?
Player: No.

Computer: I give up. What was your animal?
Player: Cow.
Computer: Type a question for which the answer is Yes for Horse but No for Cow.
Player: Do people ride it?
Computer: Do you want to play again?
Player: Yes.
Computer: Does the animal you are thinking of have legs?
Player: Yes.
Computer: Does it live in the house?
Player: No.
Computer: Do people ride it?
Player: No.
Computer: Is it a Cow?
Player: Yes.
Computer: Yay! I win. Do you want to play again?
Player: No.

(Hint: You might want to look up "binary trees" on the Internet as a method to organize this application.)

Save the application as **DoesItHaveLegs.java**.

6. a. Create a Tic Tac Toe game. In this game, two players alternate placing X's and O's into a grid until one player has three matching symbols in a row, either horizontally, vertically, or diagonally. Create a game in which the user is presented with a three-by-three grid containing the digits 1 through 9, similar to the first window shown in Figure 8-34. When the user chooses a position by typing a number, place an X in the appropriate spot. For example, after the user chooses 3, the screen looks like the second window in Figure 8-34. Generate a random number for the position where the computer will place an O. Do not allow the player or the computer to place a symbol where one has already been placed. When either the player or computer has three symbols in a row, declare a winner; if all positions have been exhausted and no one has three symbols in a row, declare a tie. Save the game as **TicTacToe.java.**

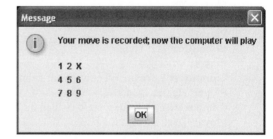

Figure 8-34 Typical execution of TicTacToe

b. In the `TicTacToe` application in Exercise 6a, the computer's selection is chosen randomly. Improve the `TicTacToe` game so that when the computer has two O's in any row, column, or diagonal, it selects the winning position for its next move rather than selecting a position randomly. Save the improved game as **TicTacToe2.java**.

UP FOR DISCUSSION

1. A train schedule is an everyday, real-life example of an array. Think of at least four more.

2. In the "You Do It" section, an array is used to hold a restaurant menu. Where else do you use menus?

3. This chapter discusses sorting data. Suppose you are hired by a large hospital to write a program that displays lists of potential organ recipients. The hospital's doctors will consult this list if they have an organ that can be transplanted. You are instructed to sort potential recipients by last name and display them sequentially in alphabetical order. If more than 10 patients are waiting for a particular organ, the first 10 patients are displayed; the user can either select one of these or move on to view the next set of 10 patients. You worry that this system gives an unfair advantage to patients with last names that start with A, B, C, and D. Should you write and install the program? If you do not, many transplant opportunities will be missed while the hospital searches for another programmer to write the program.

4. This chapter discusses sorting data. Suppose your supervisor asks you to create a report that lists all employees sorted by salary. Suppose you also know that your employer will use this report to lay off the highest-paid employee in each department. Would you agree to write the program? Instead, what if the report's purpose was to list the worst performer in each department in terms of sales? What if the report grouped employees by gender? What if the report grouped employees by race? Suppose your supervisor asks you to sort employees by the dollar value of medical insurance claims they have in a year, and you fear the employer will use the report to eliminate workers who are driving up the organization's medical insurance costs. Do you agree to write the program even if you know that the purpose of the report is to eliminate workers?

9

APPLETS

In this chapter, you will:

Learn about applets
Write an HTML document to host an applet
Understand where applets fit in the class hierarchy
Create a `JApplet` containing an `init()` method
Change a `JLabel's` font
Add `JTextField` and `JButton` components
   to a `JApplet`
Learn about event-driven programming
Add and remove `JApplet` components
Understand the `JApplet` life cycle
Use additional methods, such as `setLocation()` and
   `setEnabled()`

"It seems like I've learned a lot," you tell Lynn Greenbrier during a coffee break at Event Handlers Incorporated. "I can use variables, make decisions, write loops, and use arrays."

"Yes, you've come a long way," Lynn agrees.

"But at the same time," you continue, "I feel like I know next to nothing. When I visit the simplest Web site, it looks far more sophisticated than my most advanced application. There is color and movement. There are buttons to click and boxes where I can type responses to questions. Nothing I've done even approaches that."

"But you have a good foundation in Java programming," Lynn says. "Now you can put all that knowledge to work. By adding a few new objects to your repertoire, and by learning a little about applets, you can comfortably enter the world of interactive Web programming."

INTRODUCING APPLETS

You have written many Java applications. After you write the source code for a Java application, you do the following:

» Save the application with a .java file extension.
» Compile the application into bytecode using the `javac` command. The bytecode is stored in a file with a .class file extension.
» Use the `java` command to interpret and execute the .class file.

As you know, applications are stand-alone programs that execute beginning with their `main()` methods. In contrast, **applets** are Java programs that are called from within another application. Frequently, an applet is run from a Web page. An applet is displayed as a rectangular area. It can contain any number of components, such as buttons, text fields, and pictures. Often, an applet can respond to user-initiated events, such as mouse clicks or keyboard presses. Many of an applet's behaviors come from a Java class named `JApplet`. Other behaviors are written by the programmer.

>> **NOTE** When programmers say that many of an applet's behaviors come from a Java class named `JApplet`, they mean that the behaviors are inherited. You will learn more about inheritance in Chapter 11.

Writing an applet requires four major steps:

» Setting up a layout for the applet
» Creating components and adding them to the applet
» Arranging for listeners to listen for events generated by users who interact with the applet's components
» Writing methods to respond when the events occur

In addition, you must write a document to host the applet.

WRITING AN HTML DOCUMENT TO HOST AN APPLET

You run applets within a page on the Internet or an intranet. You can also run an applet on a local computer from within another program called **Applet Viewer**, which comes with the Java Software Development Kit (SDK). To view an applet, it must be called from within another document written in HTML. **HTML**, or **Hypertext Markup Language**, is a simple language used to create Web pages for the Internet. HTML contains many commands that allow you to format text on a Web page, import graphic images, and link your page to other Web pages. When you create an applet, you do the following:

» Write the applet in Java, and save it with a .java file extension, just as when you write a Java application.

» Compile the applet into bytecode using the `javac` command, just as when you write a Java application.

» Write an HTML document that includes a statement to call your compiled Java class.

» Load the HTML document into a Web browser (such as Netscape Navigator or Microsoft Internet Explorer), or run the Applet Viewer program, which in turn uses the HTML document.

»NOTE Newer browsers, such as Netscape 7 or later, directly support Java applets. If you have an older browser, you need the Java Plug-In, which is automatically installed with the Java SDK.

Java in general and applets in particular are popular topics among programmers, partly because users can execute applets using a Web browser on the Internet. A **Web browser** is a program that allows you to display HTML documents on your computer screen. Web documents often contain Java applets.

»NOTE Because applets are sent over the Internet and run from other applications, applet code is not trusted. **Untrusted code** carries the possibility of doing harm. For example, a malicious programmer might try to include code that contains a virus, reads data from your files, establishes a network connection to an unwanted host, or performs other dangerous or undesirable tasks. Therefore, applet code runs in a constrained area called a sandbox. A **sandbox** is a safe area in which a program can run, much like a real sandbox is an area in a yard where children can play safely.

Fortunately, to run a Java applet, you don't need to learn the entire HTML language; you need to learn only two pairs of HTML commands, called **tags**. The tag that begins every HTML document is **<html>**. Like all tags, this tag is surrounded by angle brackets. The `html` within the tag is an HTML keyword that specifies that an HTML document follows the keyword. The tag that ends every HTML document is **</html>**. Placing a backslash before any tag indicates that the tag is the ending half of a pair of tags. The following is the simplest HTML document you can write:

```
<html>
</html>
```

NOTE Unlike Java, HTML is not case sensitive, so you can use `<HTML>` in place of `<html>`. However, this book uses the all-lowercase convention when displaying HTML code. With the growing importance of XML and XHTML, many programmers recommend putting all tags in lowercase because XML and XHTML are case sensitive, even though HTML is not.

The simple HTML document, containing just the pair of `html` tags, begins and ends and does nothing in between; you can create an analogous situation in a Java method by typing an opening curly brace and following it immediately with the closing curly brace. HTML documents generally contain more statements. For example, to run an applet from within an HTML document, you add an `<object>` and `</object>` tag pair. Usually, you place three attributes within the `<object>` tag: `code`, `width`, and `height`. **Attributes**, sometimes referred to as arguments, promote activity or describe the features of the tag; with arguments, the HTML tag can do something in a certain way. Note the following example:

```
<object code = "AClass.class" width = 300 height = 200> </object>
```

The three `object` tag attributes in the previous example are described with their corresponding arguments in the following list:

- `code` = is followed by the name of the compiled applet you are calling.
- `width` = is followed by the width of the applet on the screen.
- `height` = is followed by the height of the applet on the screen.

The name of the applet you call must be a compiled Java applet (with a .class file extension). The width and height of an applet are measured in pixels. **Pixels** are the picture elements, or tiny dots of light, that make up the image on your video monitor. For monitors that display 800 pixels horizontally and 600 pixels vertically, a statement such as `width = 400 height = 300` creates an applet that occupies approximately one-fourth of most screens (half the height and half the width).

NOTE SVGA monitors commonly display 800 x 600 pixels, 1024 x 768 pixels, or higher. If you want most users to see larger applets without scrolling, the maximum size of your applets should be 760 x 520 pixels. The standard 600 x 400 pixels was used to support the older 640 x 480 VGA monitors and is currently considered out of date. Keep in mind that the browser's menu bar and screen elements (such as the toolbar and the scroll bars) take up some of the screen viewing area for an applet.

NOTE Instead of the `<object>` and `</object>` tag pair, you can use the tag set `<applet>` and `</applet>` in your HTML applet host documents. The World Wide Web Consortium recommends using `object` rather than `applet` because it is more general and includes new and future media types, as well as applets. For more information, including definitions and recommendations for using all the other HTML tags, visit *http://www.w3.org.*

Figure 9-1 shows the HTML file that could be used to run a `JApplet` named `JHello`. The applet will be 450 pixels wide by 200 pixels tall.

```
<html>
<object code = "JHello.class" width = 450 height = 200>
</object>
</html>
```

Figure 9-1 The JHello.html file

NOTE In Figure 9-1, the JHello.class file resides in the same folder as the HTML file, so no path is necessary in the object code statement. Later in this chapter, you will learn how to create the JHello class.

RUNNING AN APPLET

You can run an applet in one of two ways—by using a Web browser or by using the `appletviewer` command. To run an applet in a Web browser, such as Microsoft Internet Explorer or Netscape, you click File on the menu bar, click Open or Open Page, and type the complete path for the HTML document that you created. After you press Enter, the applet appears on your screen.

You can also view your applet using the `appletviewer` command. The **appletviewer command** is part of the SDK that provides a convenient environment in which to test your applets. In the "You Do It" exercises at the end of this chapter, you will test your applets using this command.

To run the applet using the `appletviewer` command, you type "appletviewer" at the command line, followed by the full HTML filename, including the extension. When you press Enter, the Applet Viewer window opens and displays the applet.

> **NOTE** You do not have to connect to the Internet to run an applet in your browser; you can simply use the browser locally.

NOTE When you save an HTML file, you can use .html or .htm as a file extension. In some older versions of DOS and Windows, filename extensions were not allowed to be more than three characters. Most current Web browsers and servers accept files with .htm and .html extensions. Examples in this book use the four-character .html extension.

UNDERSTANDING WHERE APPLETS FIT IN THE CLASS HIERARCHY

To write an applet, you must learn only a few additions and changes to writing a Java application. In addition to what you learned about creating applets in the beginning of this chapter, you must also do the following to write an applet:

» Include `import` statements to ensure that necessary classes are available.
» Learn to use some user interface (**UI**) components, such as buttons and text fields, and applet methods.
» Learn to use the keyword `extends`.

You have already used `import` statements such as `javax.swing.JOptionPane` and `java.util.GregorianCalendar` to access classes within your applications. You imported these classes so you would not have to write them yourself; they were prewritten because other programmers frequently need the same types of objects. Similarly, Java's creators fashioned an applet class named `JApplet` that you can import using the statement `import javax.swing.JApplet;`. Like the `JOptionPane` class that you have been using to display dialog boxes throughout this book, **JApplet** is a `Swing` class from which you can instantiate an applet. **Swing components** are UI elements such as dialog boxes and buttons; you can usually recognize their names because they begin with J.

> **NOTE** Swing components were named after a musical style that was popular in the 1940s.

NOTE In early versions of Java, components had simple names, such as `Applet` and `Button`. The components created from these original classes did not have a consistent appearance when used with different browsers and operating systems. When Java's creators designed new, improved classes, they needed new names for the classes, so they used a J in front of each new class name. Hence, `Swing` components have names like `JApplet`, `JButton`, `JScrollbar`, `JOptionPane`, and so on.

> **NOTE** The Swing classes are part of a more general set of UI programming capabilities that are collectively referred to as the **Java Foundation Classes**, or **JFC**. JFC includes Swing component classes and selected classes from the java.awt package.

> **NOTE** When you import Swing classes, you use the javax.swing package instead of java.swing. The "x" originally stood for "extension," so named because the Swing classes were an extension of the original Java language specifications.

A JApplet is a Component, and it is also a Container. **Component** is the name of a class that defines objects you can display on a screen. **Container** is a class that defines Components that do more than ordinary Components—they can hold and display other Components. Every Container is a Component, but every Component is not a Container; only some are. Every JApplet is a Container and therefore is also a Component. In Java, every JApplet, Container, and Component is also an Object. Object is a class to which all objects belong. Figure 9-2 shows the relationship among JApplet, Container, Component, and Object.

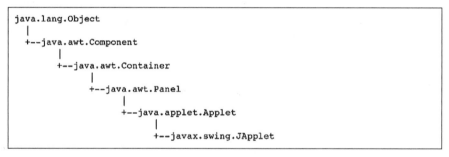

```
java.lang.Object
    |
    +--java.awt.Component
            |
            +--java.awt.Container
                    |
                    +--java.awt.Panel
                            |
                            +--java.applet.Applet
                                    |
                                    +--javax.swing.JApplet
```

Figure 9-2 Inheritance hierarchy of the JApplet class

Figure 9-2 shows an **inheritance hierarchy chart**—a chart of the parent-child relationships among classes. You will learn much more about inheritance in Chapter 11; for now, just realize that you can use the term "is a(n)" to describe each step in the relationship—that is, a JApplet "is a" Container, a Container "is a" Component, and a Component "is an" Object. When a poodle "is a" dog and a dog "is an" animal, you understand that not only do poodles have all the attributes and behaviors of dogs, but that they also have all the attributes and behaviors of animals. In the same way, JApplets can do everything that Containers, Components, and Objects can do. The JApplet class extends the capabilities of those classes, and any JApplet you create extends the capabilities of the JApplet class. If the JApplet class were not already written, you would have to write more than 200 methods to give your JApplet all the capabilities of the built-in JApplet class. When you create an application, you follow any needed import statements with a class header, such as public class AClass. Applets begin the same way as Java applications, but they must also include the words extends JApplet. The keyword extends indicates that your applet builds on, or inherits, the traits of the JApplet class.

> **NOTE** Although you acquire many methods that are already created when you use the JApplet class, you also can add any of your own methods, just as you can within Java applications.

CREATING A JApplet CONTAINING AN init() METHOD

The JApplet class provides four methods that are invoked by a Web browser when the browser runs an applet. In an application, the main() method calls other methods that you write. In contrast, an applet does not contain a main() method. With an applet, the browser calls several methods automatically at different times. The following four methods are included in every applet:

» public void init()

» public void start()

» public void stop()

» public void destroy()

» NOTE
Later in this chapter, you will learn that these four methods constitute the life cycle of an applet.

If you fail to write one or more of these methods, Java creates them for you. The methods Java creates have opening and closing curly braces only—in other words, they are empty. To create a Java application that does anything useful, you must code statements within at least one of these methods.

For example, you can create a JApplet using only the init() method. The **init() method** is the first method called in any applet. You use it to perform initialization tasks, such as setting variables to initial values or placing applet components on the screen. You must code the init() method's header as follows:

```
public void init()
```

One of the components you might want to place on the screen in a JApplet is a JLabel. **JLabel** is a built-in Java Swing class that holds text you can display within an applet. The inheritance hierarchy of the JLabel class is shown in Figure 9-3.

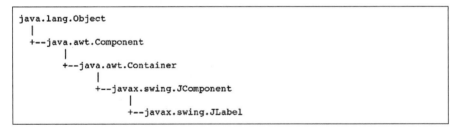

```
java.lang.Object
    |
    +--java.awt.Component
            |
            +--java.awt.Container
                    |
                    +--javax.swing.JComponent
                            |
                            +--javax.swing.JLabel
```

Figure 9-3 The JLabel class inheritance hierarchy

Available constructors for the JLabel class include the following:

» JLabel() creates a JLabel instance with no image and with an empty string for the title.

» JLabel(Icon image) creates a JLabel instance with the specified image.

» JLabel(Icon image, int horizontalAlignment) creates a JLabel instance with the specified image and horizontal alignment.

» JLabel(String text) creates a JLabel instance with the specified text.

» JLabel(String text, Icon icon, int horizontalAlignment) creates a JLabel instance with the specified text, image, and horizontal alignment.

» JLabel(String text, int horizontalAlignment) creates a JLabel instance with the specified text and horizontal alignment.

For example, you can create a JLabel named greeting that holds the words "Hello. Who are you?" by writing the following statement:

```
JLabel greeting = new JLabel("Hello. Who are you?");
```

You then can add the greeting object to an applet within its init() method using the **add() method**. In general, a Swing Container must use a **content pane**, which is a window to which components can be added. The content pane is an object of the Container class that is included in the java.awt package. A Container content pane object can be created using the **getContentPane() method**. To create a Container object named con, the syntax is:

```
Container con = getContentPane();
```

> **NOTE** A JApplet automatically creates a content pane. When you call getContentPane(), you are not creating it, but "getting" a reference to it. As an alternative in an applet, you could use the this reference with the getContentPane() call, as in the following:
>
> ```
> Container con = this.getContentPane();
> ```
>
> The getContentPane() call gets the container for *this* JApplet.

> **NOTE** Starting with Java 5, you can add write statements that add components directly to a JApplet instead of explicitly using the getContentPane() method call. You will learn more about the ramifications of using this technique in Chapter 13.

The statement JLabel greeting = new JLabel(); creates a JLabel. You add the greeting object to the content pane with the following statement:

```
con.add(greeting);
```

Figure 9-4 shows the JApplet that displays "Hello. Who are you?" on the screen. Figure 9-5 shows how the applet appears on your screen.

```java
import javax.swing.*;
import java.awt.*;
public class JHello extends JApplet
{
    Container con = getContentPane();
    JLabel greeting = new JLabel("Hello. Who are you?");
    public void init()
    {
        con.add(greeting);
    }
}
```

Figure 9-4 The JHello JApplet

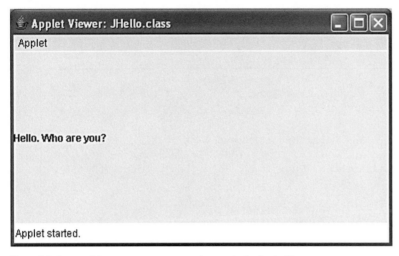

Figure 9-5 Output of the `JHello` `JApplet` when run in the Applet Viewer

CHANGING A `JLabel`'s FONT

If you use the Internet and a Web browser to visit Web sites, you probably are not very impressed with the simple applet displayed in Figure 9-5. You might think that the string "Hello. Who are you?" is pretty plain and lackluster. Fortunately, Java provides you with a **Font class** from which you can create an object that holds typeface and size information. The **setFont() method** requires a `Font` object argument. To construct a `Font` object, you need three arguments: typeface, style, and point size.

The **typeface argument** to the `Font` constructor is a `String` representing a font. Common fonts are Arial, Helvetica, Courier, and Times New Roman. The typeface argument in the `Font` constructor is only a request; the system on which your applet runs might not have access to the requested font, and if necessary, it substitutes a default font. The **style argument** applies an attribute to displayed text and is one of three values: `Font.PLAIN`, `Font.BOLD`, or `Font.ITALIC`. The **point size argument** is an integer that represents about 1/72 of an inch. Printed text is usually about 12 point; a headline might be 30 point.

> **»NOTE** In printing, point size defines a measurement between lines of text in a single-spaced text document. The point size is based on typographic points, which are approximately 1/72 of an inch. Java adopts the convention that one point on a display is equivalent to one unit in user coordinates. For more information, see the `Font` documentation at *http://java.sun.com.*

To give a `JLabel` object a new font, you can create a `Font` object, as in the following:

```
Font headlineFont = new Font("Helvetica", Font.BOLD, 36);
```

The typeface name is a `String`, so you must enclose it in double quotation marks when you use it to declare the `Font` object. Then, you use the `setFont()` method to assign the `Font` to a `JLabel` with a statement such as:

```
greeting.setFont(headlineFont);
```

Figure 9-6 shows a modified `JHello` applet named `JHello2`. This applet contains a `Font` object that is applied to the greeting. Figure 9-7 shows how the `JApplet` looks when displayed using the Applet Viewer.

```java
import javax.swing.*;
import java.awt.*;
public class JHello2 extends JApplet
{
    Container con = getContentPane();
    JLabel greeting = new JLabel("Hello. Who are you?");
    Font headlineFont = new Font("Helvetica", Font.BOLD, 36);
    public void init()
    {
        greeting.setFont(headlineFont);
        con.add(greeting);
    }
}
```

Figure 9-6 The `JHello2` `JApplet`

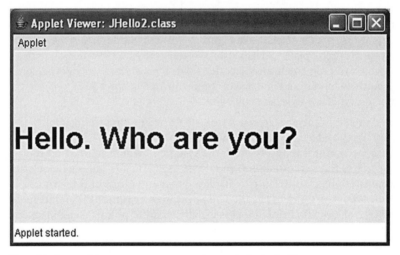

Figure 9-7 Output of the `JHello2` `JApplet` when run in the Applet Viewer

ADDING `JTextField` AND `JButton` COMPONENTS TO A `JApplet`

In addition to including `JLabel` objects, `JApplets` often contain other window features, such as `JTextField`s and `JButton`s. A **JTextField** is a component into which a user can type a single line of text data. (Text data comprises any characters you can enter from the keyboard, including numbers and punctuation.) The inheritance hierarchy of the `JTextField` class is shown in Figure 9-8.

```
java.lang.Object
    |
  +--java.awt.Component
          |
        +--java.awt.Container
                |
              +--javax.swing.JComponent
                      |
                    +--javax.swing.text.JTextComponent
                            |
                          +--javax.swing.JTextField
```

Figure 9-8 The JTextField class inheritance hierarchy

Typically, a user types a line into a JTextField and then presses Enter on the keyboard or clicks a button with the mouse to enter the data. You can construct a JTextField object using one of several constructors:

» public JTextField() constructs a new JTextField.

» public JTextField(int columns) constructs a new, empty JTextField with a specified number of columns.

» public JTextField(String text) constructs a new JTextField initialized with the specified text.

» public JTextField(String text, int columns) constructs a new JTextField initialized with the specified text and columns.

For example, to provide a JTextField for a user to answer the "Who are you?" question, you can code the following to provide a JTextField that is empty and displays approximately 10 characters:

```
JTextField answer = new JTextField(10);
```

To add the JTextField named answer to the Container named con within the JApplet, you write:

```
con.add(answer);
```

> » **NOTE** The number of characters a JTextField can display depends on the font being used and the actual characters typed. For example, in most fonts, 'w' is wider than 'i', so a JTextField of size 10 using the Arial font can display 24 'i' characters, but only eight 'w' characters.

> » **NOTE** Try to anticipate how many characters your users might enter when you create a JTextField. The user can enter more characters than those that display, but the extra characters scroll out of view. It can be disconcerting to try to enter data into a field that is not large enough. It is usually better to overestimate the size of a user text field.

Several other methods are available for use with JTextFields. The **setText() method** allows you to change the text in a JTextField (or other Component) that has already been created, as in the following:

```
answer.setText("Thank you");
```

After a user has entered text in a JTextField, you can clear it out with a statement such as:

```
answer.setText("");
```

The **getText()** **method** allows you to retrieve the `String` of text in a `JTextField` (or other `Component`), as in:

```
String whatDidTheySay = answer.getText();
```

When a user encounters a `JTextField` you have placed within an applet, the user must position the mouse pointer in the `JTextField` and click to get an insertion point. When the user clicks within the `JTextField`, the `JTextField` has **keyboard focus**, which means that the next entries from the keyboard are entered at that location. When you want the insertion point to appear automatically within the `JTextField` without requiring the user to click in it first, you can use the **requestFocus()** **method**. For example, if you have added a `JTextField` named `answer` to an applet, `answer.requestFocus()` causes the insertion point to appear within the `JTextField`, and the user can begin typing immediately without moving the mouse. In addition to saving the user some time and effort, `requestFocus()` is useful when you have several `JTextField`s and you want to direct the user's attention to a specific one. At any time, only one component within a window can have the keyboard focus.

When a `JTextField` has the capability of accepting keystrokes, the `JTextField` is **editable**. If you do not want the user to be able to enter data in a `JTextField`, you can use the **setEditable()** **method** to change the editable status of a `JTextField`. For example, if you want to give a user only one chance to answer a question correctly, you can prevent the user from replacing or editing the characters in the `JTextField` by using the following statement:

```
answer.setEditable(false);
```

If conditions change, and you want the user to be able to edit the `JTextField`, use the following statement:

```
answer.setEditable(true);
```

ADDING JButtons

A **JButton** is a `Component` the user can click with a mouse to make a selection. A `JButton` is even easier to create than a `JTextField`. There are five `JButton` constructors:

» `public JButton()` creates a button with no set text.
» `public JButton(Icon icon)` creates a button with an icon of type `Icon` or `ImageIcon`.
» `public JButton(String text)` creates a button with text.
» `public JButton(String text, Icon icon)` creates a button with initial text and an icon of type `Icon` or `ImageIcon`.
» `public JButton(Action a)` creates a button in which properties are taken from the `Action` supplied. (`Action` is a Java class.)

The inheritance hierarchy of the `JButton` class is shown in Figure 9-9.

To create a `JButton` with the label "Press when ready", you write the following:

```
JButton readyJButton = new JButton("Press when ready");
```

To add the `JButton` to a `Container` named `con` in an applet, you write:

```
con.add(readyJButton);
```

```
java.lang.Object
   |
  +--java.awt.Component
        |
       +--java.awt.Container
             |
            +--javax.swing.JComponent
                  |
                 +--javax.swing.AbstractButton
                       |
                      +--javax.swing.JButton
```

Figure 9-9 The JButton class inheritance hierarchy

You can change a JButton's label with the **setLabel() method**, as in:

```
readyJButton.setLabel("Don't press me again!");
```

You can get the JLabel and assign it to a String object with the **getLabel() method**, as in:

```
String whatsOnJButton = readyJButton.getLabel();
```

> **» NOTE**
> Your programs are more user-friendly when the label on a JButton describes its function for the user.

> **» NOTE** As with JTextField components, you can use the requestFocus() method with JButton components. The surface of the button that has the keyboard focus appears with an outline so it stands out from the other JButtons.

ADDING MULTIPLE COMPONENTS TO A JApplet

When you add more than one component to a JApplet, you must take special actions so that the components don't hide each other. For example, Figure 9-10 shows a JApplet to which a JLabel and a JTextField have been added. Figure 9-11 shows the executed JApplet. The applet appears to be blank because within the JHello3 applet, the JLabel (named greeting) is placed in the Container, and then the JTextField (named answer) is placed on top of it, completely hiding the JLabel.

```
import javax.swing.*;
import java.awt.*;
public class JHello3 extends JApplet
{
    JLabel greeting = new JLabel("Hello. Who are you? ");
    Font headlineFont = new Font("Helvetica", Font.BOLD, 36);
    JTextField answer = new JTextField(10);
    public void init()
    {
        Container con = getContentPane();
        greeting.setFont(headlineFont);
        con.add(greeting);
        con.add(answer);
    }
}
```

Figure 9-10 The JHello3 JApplet

> **» NOTE** In the JHello3 class in Figure 9-10, notice that the Container that holds the content pane is declared within the init() method. In the earlier examples in this chapter, JHello and JHello2, the Container for the content pane was declared above the init() method. That technique would also work in JHello3. When you declare an object at the start of a class before any methods, all the methods in the class can use the object. When you declare an object within a method, the object is local to that method, and only that method can use it. Because each example program shown so far in this chapter has only one method, init(), the Container could have been declared in either location in each example, producing identical results.

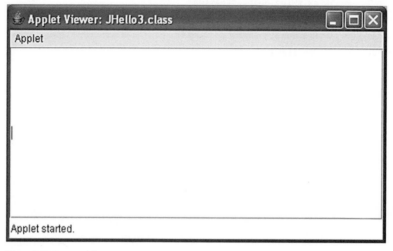

Figure 9-11 Output of the JHello3 JApplet when run in the Applet Viewer; the JTextField obscures the JLabel

In the JHello4 applet shown in Figure 9-12, the positions of the statements that add the JLabel and JTextField to the ContentPane have been reversed, causing the opposite effect, as you can see in Figure 9-13. In this case, the JTextField is placed in the JApplet first, and the subsequent placement of the JLabel completely obscures the JTextField.

```java
import javax.swing.*;
import java.awt.*;
public class JHello4 extends JApplet
{
    Container con = getContentPane();
    JLabel greeting = new JLabel("Hello. Who are you?");
    Font headlineFont = new Font("Helvetica", Font.BOLD, 36);
    JTextField answer = new JTextField(10);
    public void init()
    {
        greeting.setFont(headlineFont);
        con.add(answer);
        con.add(greeting);
    }
}
```

Figure 9-12 The JHello4 JApplet

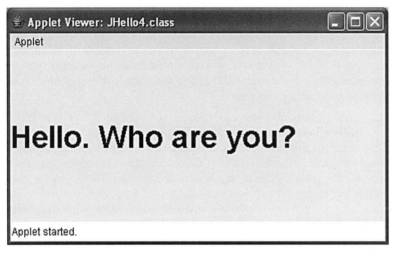

Figure 9-13 Output of the JHello4 JApplet when run in the Applet Viewer; the JLabel obscures the JTextField

To place multiple components at a specified position in a container so they do not hide each other, you must use a **layout manager**—a class that controls component positioning. The normal (default) behavior of a JApplet is to use a layout format named BorderLayout. A **BorderLayout**, created by using the BorderLayout class, divides a container into five regions: north, south, east, west, and center, as shown in Figure 9-14.

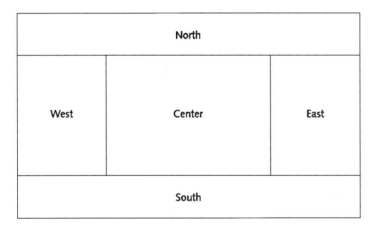

Figure 9-14 Position of regions in a BorderLayout

You create a BorderLayout object using the BorderLayout() or BorderLayout(int, int) constructor methods. The following statement creates a BorderLayout object named border:

```
BorderLayout border = new BorderLayout();
```

To create a BorderLayout object named borderWithGap with a horizontal gap of five pixels and a vertical gap of 10 pixels between components, you can use the statement:

```
BorderLayout borderWithGap = new BorderLayout(5, 10);
```

The components in the north, south, east, and west areas take up as much space as needed; the center uses whatever space is left over.

》 NOTE
You will learn more about layout managers in Chapter 14.

When components use `BorderLayout`, as `Container`s in `JApplet`s do, components are placed in the center region. This means that when you add multiple components to a `JApplet`, the components all lie in the center and appear to be on top of each other, so you can only see the most recently added component.

When you use a `FlowLayout` instead of a `BorderLayout`, components do not lie on top of each other. Instead, the **flow layout manager** places components in a row, and when a row is filled, it automatically spills components into the next row. By default, the components in each row are centered. In the `FlowLayout` class, three constants are defined that specify how components are positioned in each row of their container. These constants are `FlowLayout.LEFT`, `FlowLayout.RIGHT`, and `FlowLayout.CENTER`. For example, to create a layout manager named `flow` that positions the components to the right rather than in the center by default, you can use the following statement:

```
FlowLayout flow = new FlowLayout(FlowLayout.RIGHT);
```

Then, the layout of a `Container` named `con` can be set to the newly created `FlowLayout` using the statement:

```
con.setLayout(flow);
```

A more compact syntax that combines the two statements into one is:

```
con.setLayout(new FlowLayout(FlowLayout.RIGHT);
```

When you use this option, the `FlowLayout` is constructed, but unnamed.

Figure 9-15 shows a `JApplet` to which three components—a `JLabel`, a `JTextField`, and a `JButton`—have been added. Because this `JApplet` uses a `FlowLayout` layout manager, all the components are viewable, as shown in the output in Figure 9-16.

```
import javax.swing.*;
import java.awt.*;
public class JHello5 extends JApplet
{
    Container con = getContentPane();
    JLabel greeting = new JLabel("Hello. Who are you?");
    Font headlineFont = new Font("Helvetica", Font.BOLD, 36);
    JTextField answer = new JTextField(10);
    JButton pressMe = new JButton("Press me");
    public void init()
    {
        greeting.setFont(headlineFont);
        con.add(greeting);
        con.add(answer);
        con.add(pressMe);
        con.setLayout(new FlowLayout());
    }
}
```

Figure 9-15 The `JHello5` `JApplet`

Figure 9-16 Output of the `JHello5` `JApplet`, using a `FlowLayout`, when run in the Applet Viewer

LEARNING ABOUT EVENT-DRIVEN PROGRAMMING

An **event** occurs when someone using your applet takes action on a component, such as clicking the mouse on a `JButton` object. In an **event-driven program**, the user might initiate any number of events in any order. For example, if you use a word-processing program, you have dozens of choices at your disposal at any moment in time. You can type words, select text with the mouse, click a button to change text to bold, click a button to change text to italic, choose a menu item, and so on. With each word-processing document you create, you choose options in any order that seems appropriate at the time. The word-processing program must be ready to respond to any event you initiate.

Within an event-driven program, a component on which an event is generated is the **source** of the event. A button that a user can click is an example of a source; a text field that a user can use to enter text is another source. An object that is interested in an event is a **listener**. Not all objects can receive all events—you probably have used programs in which clicking many areas of the screen has no effect. If you want an object, such as your applet, to be a listener for an event, you must register the object as a listener for the source.

> **» NOTE**
> A source object and a listener object can be the same object. For example, you might program a `JButton` to change its own label when a user clicks it.

Newspapers around the world register with news services, such as the Associated Press or United Press International. The news services maintain a list of subscribers and send each one a story when important national or international events occur. Similarly, a Java component source object (such as a button) maintains a list of registered listeners and notifies all registered listeners (such as an applet) when any event occurs, such as a mouse click. When the listener "receives the news," an event-handling method that is part of the listener object responds to the event.

To respond to user events within any `JApplet` you create, you must do the following:

» Prepare your `JApplet` to accept event messages.

» Tell your `JApplet` to expect events to happen.

» Tell your `JApplet` how to respond to events.

PREPARING YOUR JApplet TO ACCEPT EVENT MESSAGES

» NOTE
In Chapter 12, you will learn to create and implement your own interfaces.

You prepare your JApplet to accept mouse events by importing the java.awt.event package into your program and adding the phrase implements ActionListener to the class header. The java.awt.event package includes event classes with names such as ActionEvent, ComponentEvent, and TextEvent. ActionListener is an **interface**, or a class containing a set of specifications for methods that you can use. Implementing ActionListener provides you with standard event method specifications that allow your applet to work with ActionEvents, which are the types of events that occur when a user clicks a button.

» NOTE You can identify interfaces such as ActionListener because they use the keyword implements. Interfaces are implemented, not imported or extended. In ordinary language, an item that is implemented is put into service, or used. Implementation has a similar meaning when applied to interfaces. In contrast, packages that are imported are brought into an application, and classes that are added onto are extended.

TELLING YOUR JApplet TO EXPECT EVENTS TO HAPPEN

You tell your applet to expect ActionEvents with the **addActionListener() method**. If you have declared a JButton named aButton and you want to perform an action when a user clicks aButton, aButton is the source of a message, and you can think of your applet as a target to which to send a message. You learned in Chapter 4 that the this reference means "this current method," so the code aButton.addActionListener(this); causes any ActionEvent messages (button clicks) that come from aButton to be sent to "this current object."

» NOTE Not all Events are ActionEvents with an addActionListener() method. For example, KeyListeners have an addKeyListener() method and FocusListeners have an addFocusListener() method. Additional event types and methods are covered in more detail in Chapters 13 and 14.

TELLING YOUR JApplet HOW TO RESPOND TO EVENTS

The ActionListener interface contains the **actionPerformed(ActionEvent e) method** specification. When a JApplet has registered as a listener with a Component such as a JButton, and a user clicks the JButton, the actionPerformed() method executes. You must explicitly write the actionPerformed() method, which contains a header and a body, like all methods. You use the following header, in which e is any name you choose for the Event (the JButton click) that initiated the notification of the ActionListener (which is the JApplet):

```
public void actionPerformed (ActionEvent e)
```

The body of the method contains any statements that you want to execute when the action occurs. You might want to perform mathematical calculations, construct new objects, produce output, or execute any other operation. For example, Figure 9-17 shows a JApplet containing an actionPerformed() method that produces a line of output at the operating system prompt. Within the actionPerformed() method that executes when the user clicks the pressMe JButton, the String that a user has typed into the JTextField is stored in the name variable. The name is then used as part of the output at the command line. Figure 9-18 shows the output when the user enters "Ryan" into the JTextField and clicks the button.

When more than one component is added and registered to an applet, it might be necessary to determine which component was used. For example, in the JHello6 JApplet in Figure 9-17, you might want the user to be able to either click the button or press Enter in the JTextField to view the displayed message. In that case, you would designate both the pressMe button and

```
import javax.swing.*;
import java.awt.*;
import java.awt.event.*;
public class JHello6 extends JApplet implements ActionListener
{
    Container con = getContentPane();
    JLabel greeting = new JLabel("Hello. Who are you?");
    Font headlineFont = new Font("Helvetica", Font.BOLD, 36);
    JTextField answer = new JTextField(10);
    JButton pressMe = new JButton("Press me");
    public void init()
    {
        greeting.setFont(headlineFont);
        con.add(greeting);
        con.add(answer);
        con.add(pressMe);
        con.setLayout(new FlowLayout());
        pressMe.addActionListener(this);
    }
    public void actionPerformed(ActionEvent e)
    {
        String name = answer.getText();
        System.out.println("You pressed the button, " + name);
    }
}
```

Figure 9-17 The JHello6 class that produces output when the user clicks the JButton

Figure 9-18 Output of the JHello6 JApplet when the user enters "Ryan" into the JTextField and clicks the JButton

the answer text field to be message sources by using the addActionListener() method with each, as follows:

```
pressMe.addActionListener(this);
answer.addActionListener(this);
```

These two statements make the JApplet (this) the receiver of messages. The JApplet has only one actionPerformed() method, so it is the method that executes when either the pressMe button or the answer text field sends a message. To determine the source of the event, you can use the getSource() method of the sent object to determine which component generated the event. For example, within a method with the header public void actionPerformed(ActionEvent e), e is an ActionEvent. ActionEvent (and other event classes) are part of the java.awt.event package and are subclasses of the EventObject class. To determine what object generated the ActionEvent, you can use the following statement:

```
Object source = e.getSource();
```

If a JApplet contains two JButtons named option1 and option2, you can use the following decision structure to take different courses of action based on the button that is clicked:

```
void actionPerformed(ActionEvent e)
{
    Object source = e.getSource();
    if (source == option1)
        //execute these statements when user clicks option1
    else
        //execute these statements when user clicks any other option
}
```

> **NOTE** Every object is an Object; that is, every instance of a JButton, JTextField, or other object you create can be stored as an instance of the class named Object. You will learn more about the Object class in Chapter 12.

You can also use the instanceof keyword inside an event-handling method to determine the source of the event. The instanceof keyword is used when it is necessary to know only the component's type, rather than what component triggered the event. For example, if you want to take some action when a user enters data into any JTextField, you could use the following method format:

```
void actionPerformed(ActionEvent e)
{
    Object source = e.getSource();
    if (source instanceof JTextField)
    {
        //execute these statements when any JTextField
        //generates the event
    }
}
```

ADDING AND REMOVING JApplet COMPONENTS

A JApplet that produces output on the command-line screen is not very exciting. Naturally, you want to make changes as various events occur. For example, rather than using a System.out.println statement when the user clicks an applet button, you might want to add new components to the applet itself. One approach is to create a new JLabel that you can add to the applet with the add() method after the user enters a name. The

JApplet in Figure 9-19 shows how you can declare a new, empty JLabel with the first shaded statement:

```
JLabel personalGreeting = new JLabel("");
```

The shaded code in the actionPerformed() method shows that after the user clicks the button, the name is retrieved from the text field. Then, you can use the setText() method to set the JLabel text for personalGreeting to "Hello, " + name, and add it to the JApplet's Container. Figure 9-20 shows the JApplet after the user enters "Lindsey".

```
import javax.swing.*;
import java.awt.*;
import java.awt.event.*;
public class JHello7 extends JApplet implements ActionListener
{
    JLabel greeting = new JLabel("Hello. Who are you?");
    Font headlineFont = new Font("Helvetica", Font.BOLD, 36);
    JTextField answer = new JTextField(10);
    JButton pressMe = new JButton("Press me");
    JLabel personalGreeting = new JLabel("");
    Container con = getContentPane();
    public void init()
    {
        greeting.setFont(headlineFont);
        personalGreeting.setFont(headlineFont);
        con.add(greeting);
        con.add(answer);
        con.add(pressMe);
        con.setLayout(new FlowLayout());
        pressMe.addActionListener(this);
        answer.addActionListener(this);
    }
    public void actionPerformed(ActionEvent e)
    {
        String name = answer.getText();
        personalGreeting.setText("Hello, " + name);
        con.add(personalGreeting);
        validate();
    }
}
```

Figure 9-19 The JHello7 class that adds a JLabel when the user clicks the JButton

In the actionPerformed() method in Figure 9-19, the final statement is validate(). Invoking the **validate() method** after adding one or more JComponents to an applet ensures that the Components draw themselves on the screen.

>> **NOTE**
The validate() method is complex. Even the online Java documentation at *http://java. sun.com* refers to its performance as "voodoo."

>> **NOTE** It isn't necessary to call the validate() method every time you add a JComponent to an applet. For example, when you add components in the init() or start() methods, you do not have to call validate(). When you add components in other methods (frequently event-handling methods), you must call validate().

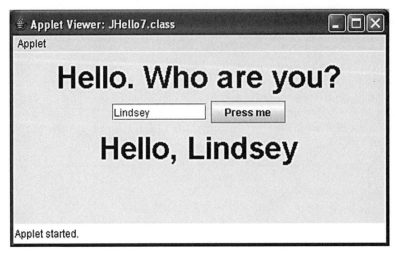

Figure 9-20 Output of the `JHello7` `JApplet` when the user enters "Lindsey" into the `JTextField` and clicks the `JButton`

If you can add components to an applet, you should also be able to remove them; you do so with the **remove() method**. For example, after a user enters a name into the `JTextField`, you might not want the user to use the `JTextField` or its `JButton` again, so you can remove them from the applet. To use the `remove()` method, you place the component's name within the parentheses. Figure 9-21 shows the revised `actionPerformed()` method for the `JHello` applet in which the `JButton` and `JTextField` are removed when the user clicks the `JButton`. Figure 9-22 shows the result when the user enters "Lindsey".

```
public void actionPerformed(ActionEvent e)
{
    remove(pressMe);
    remove(answer);
    String name = answer.getText();
    personalGreeting.setText("Hello, " + name);
    con.add(personalGreeting);
    validate();
}
```

Figure 9-21 Revised `actionPerformed()` method that removes components

>> NOTE In the `actionPerformed()` method in Figure 9-21, if you add the `personalGreeting` before removing the `JButton` and `JTextField`, the placement of the components is different because the button and field occupy space on the applet surface. You can experiment with the `JHello8` applet (which is not shown in this chapter, but is available on your Student Disk) to see how the order of statements that add and remove components affects the display.

>> NOTE As with adding components, when you change the appearance of an applet screen by removing components, you should always subsequently call the `validate()` method.

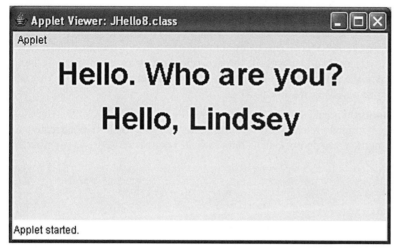

Figure 9-22 Output of applet containing revised `actionPerformed()` method

UNDERSTANDING THE JApplet LIFE CYCLE

Applets are popular because they are easy to use in a Web page. Because applets execute in a browser, the `JApplet` class contains methods that are automatically called by the browser. Earlier in this chapter, you learned the names of four of these methods: `init()`, `start()`, `stop()`, and `destroy()`.

» NOTE
In Chapter 10, you will learn about another automatically called method named `paint()`.

You have already seen many examples of `JApplet`s containing `init()` methods. When you write a method that has the same method header as an automatically provided method, you replace or **override** the original version. When a Web page containing a `JApplet` is loaded in the browser, or when you run the `appletviewer` command within an HTML document that calls a `JApplet`, the applet's `init()` method executes—either your version (if you have written one) or the automatically provided `init()` method (if you have not). You should write your own `init()` method when you have any initialization tasks to perform, such as setting up user interface components.

> **» NOTE** When you override a method, you create your own version that Java uses, instead of using the automatically supplied version with the same name. It is not the same as overloading a method, which is writing several methods that have the same name but take different arguments. You learned about overloading methods in Chapter 4.

The **start() method** executes after the `init()` method, and it executes again every time the applet becomes active after it has been inactive. For example, if you run a `JApplet` using the `appletviewer` command and then minimize the Applet Viewer window, the `JApplet` becomes inactive. When you restore the window, the `JApplet` becomes active again. On the Internet, users can leave a Web page, visit another page, and then return to the first site. Again, the `JApplet` becomes inactive and then active. When you write your own `start()` method, you must include any actions you want your `JApplet` to take when a user revisits the JApplet. For example, you might want to resume some animation that you suspended when the user left the applet.

When a user leaves a Web page (perhaps by minimizing a window or traveling to a different Web page), the **stop() method** is invoked. You override the existing empty stop() method only if you want to take some action when a JApplet is no longer visible. You don't usually need to write your own stop() methods.

The **destroy() method** is called when the user closes the browser or Applet Viewer. Closing the browser or Applet Viewer releases any resources the JApplet might have allocated. As with the stop() method, you do not usually have to write your own destroy() methods.

> **»» NOTE** Advanced Java programmers override the stop() and destroy() methods when they want to add instructions to "suspend a thread," or stop a chain of events that were started by a JApplet but which are not yet completed.

Every JApplet has the same life cycle outline, as shown in Figure 9-23. When the applet executes, the init() method runs, followed by the start() method. If the user leaves the JApplet's page, the stop() method executes. When the user returns, the start() method executes. The stop() and start() sequence might continue any number of times until the user closes the browser (or Applet Viewer), which invokes the destroy() method.

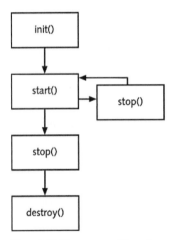

Figure 9-23 The JApplet life cycle

USING ADDITIONAL APPLET METHODS

You can use nearly 200 additional methods to manipulate Components within JApplets. You can read the definitions for each of these methods at the *http://java.sun.com* Web site. You will also learn about several more of these methods and their related Components in Chapters 13 and 14. Two methods, setLocation() and setEnabled(), are discussed here to provide examples of operations you might perform on applet components.

USING THE setLocation() METHOD

Although you must learn more about Java before you can change the initial placement of components when you use the add() method in a JApplet, you can use the `setLocation()` method to change the location of a component at a later time. The **setLocation() method** allows you to place a component at a specific location within the Applet Viewer window.

Any applet window consists of a number of horizontal and vertical pixels on the screen. You set the pixel values in the HTML document you write to test the `JApplet`. Any component you place on the screen has a horizontal, or **x-axis**, position as well as a vertical, or **y-axis**, position in the window. The upper-left corner of any display is position 0,0. The first, or **x-coordinate**, value increases as you travel from left to right across the window. The second, or **y-coordinate**, value increases as you travel from top to bottom.

For example, to position a `JLabel` object named `someLabel` at the upper-left corner of a window, you write `someLabel.setLocation(0,0);`. If a window is 200 pixels wide by 100 pixels tall, you can place a `Button` named `pressMe` in the approximate center of the window with the following statement:

```
pressMe.setLocation(100,50);
```

The coordinate arguments can be numeric constants or variables. Figure 9-24 illustrates the screen coordinate positions.

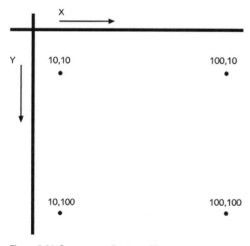

Figure 9-24 Screen coordinate positions

> **NOTE** When you use `setLocation()`, the upper-left corner of the component is placed at the specified x- and y-coordinates. If a window is 100 by 100 pixels, `aButton.setLocation(100,100);` places the `JButton` outside the window, where you cannot see the component.

The `setLocation()` method can seem difficult to use at first because it works correctly only when it is used after the layout manager has finished positioning all the applet components (or in cases where no layout manager is functioning). For example, Figure 9-25 shows a `JHello9` applet with one shaded addition to the `actionPerformed()` method from Figure 9-21. After the components have all been removed or placed, the `personalGreeting` is relocated to position 10, 150, which is in the lower-left area of the applet surface. Figure 9-26 shows the

```
import javax.swing.*;
import java.awt.*;
import java.awt.event.*;
public class JHello9 extends JApplet implements ActionListener
{
    JLabel greeting = new JLabel("Hello. Who are you?");
    Font headlineFont = new Font("Helvetica", Font.BOLD, 36);
    JTextField answer = new JTextField(10);
    JButton pressMe = new JButton("Press me");
    JLabel personalGreeting = new JLabel("");
    Container con = getContentPane();
    public void init()
    {
        greeting.setFont(headlineFont);
        personalGreeting.setFont(headlineFont);
        con.add(greeting);
        con.add(answer);
        con.add(pressMe);
        con.setLayout(new FlowLayout());
        pressMe.addActionListener(this);
        answer.addActionListener(this);
    }
    public void actionPerformed(ActionEvent e)
    {
        remove(pressMe);
        remove(answer);
        String name = answer.getText();
        personalGreeting.setText("Hello, " + name);
        con.add(personalGreeting);
        validate();
        personalGreeting.setLocation(10, 150);
    }
}
```

Figure 9-25 The `JHello9` applet containing a `setLocation()` method call

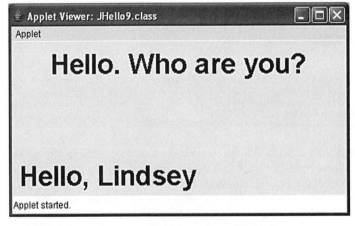

Figure 9-26 Output of `JHello9` applet after user enters "Lindsey"

result after the user enters a name. Notice the position of the greeting compared to that shown in Figure 9-22 before the setLocation() method was included.

USING THE setEnabled() METHOD

You probably have used computer programs in which a component becomes disabled or unusable. For example, a JButton might become dim and unresponsive when the programmer no longer wants you to have access to the JButton's functionality. You can use the **setEnabled() method** to make a component unavailable and then make it available again in turn. The setEnabled() method takes an argument of true if you want to enable a component, or false if you want to disable a component.

»NOTE
In Java, when you create a Component, it is enabled by default.

For example, you can see that in the actionPerformed() method in Figure 9-27, the JButton and JTextField from the JHello applet are disabled instead of removed. Figure 9-28 shows the results of a typical execution. You can see that the two components are dimmed rather than removed, as they were in the output in Figure 9-26.

```java
public void actionPerformed(ActionEvent e)
{
    pressMe.setEnabled(false);
    answer.setEnabled(false);
    String name = answer.getText();
    personalGreeting.setText("Hello, " + name);
    con.add(personalGreeting);
    validate();
    personalGreeting.setLocation(10, 150);
}
```

Figure 9-27 An actionPerformed() method that disables components

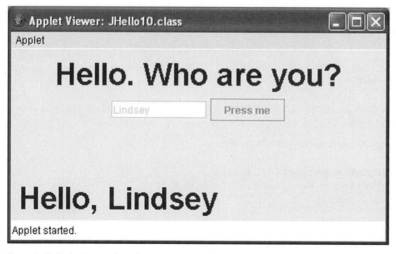

Figure 9-28 Typical execution of JHello applet using method in Figure 9-27

YOU DO IT

CREATING AN HTML DOCUMENT TO HOST AN APPLET

In this section, you create a simple HTML document that you will use to display the applet you will create in the next section. You will name the applet JGreet, and it will occupy a screen area of 450 by 200 pixels.

To create an HTML document to host an applet:

1. Open a new file in your text editor. Type the opening HTML tag:

   ```
   <html>
   ```

2. On the next line, type the opening object tag that contains the applet's name and dimensions:

   ```
   <object code = "JGreet.class" width = 450 height = 200>
   ```

3. On the next line, type the applet's closing tag:

   ```
   </object>
   ```

4. On the next line, type the closing HTML tag:

   ```
   </html>
   ```

5. Save the file as **TestJGreet.html** in the Chapter.09 folder on your Student Disk. Just as when you create a Java application, be certain that you save the file as text only. The .html file extension is required and makes the file easy to identify as an HTML file. If you are using Notepad or another text editor, you can enclose the filename in quotation marks to save the .html file extension, as in "C:\Java\Chapter.09\TestJGreet.html".

CREATING AND RUNNING A JApplet

Next, you will create the JGreet applet for which you prepared the HTML document.

To create and run the JGreet applet:

1. Open a new text file in your text editor. Enter the following import statements you need for the JApplet. You need the javax.swing package because it defines JApplet, and you need the java.awt package because it defines Container.

   ```
   import javax.swing.*;
   import java.awt.*;
   ```

2. Next, enter the JGreet JApplet. It contains a Container that holds a JLabel. The init() method adds the JLabel to the Container.

   ```
   public class JGreet extends JApplet
   {
      Container con = getContentPane();
      JLabel greeting = new JLabel("Greetings!");
      public void init()
      {
         con.add(greeting);
      }
   }
   ```

3. Save the file as **JGreet.java** in the Chapter.09 folder on your Student Disk.

4. Compile the class using the command **javac JGreet.java**. If necessary, correct any errors and compile again.

5. At the command line, type **appletviewer TestJGreet.html**, and then press **Enter**. The applet appears on your screen, as shown in Figure 9-29.

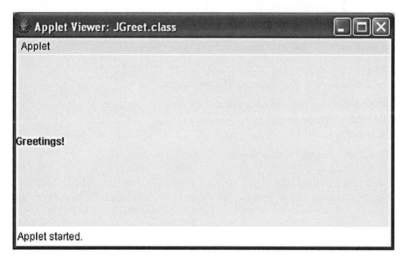

Figure 9-29 The JGreet JApplet

6. Use the mouse pointer to drag any corner of the Applet Viewer window to resize it. Notice that if you widen the window by dragging its right border to the right, the window is redrawn on the screen and the JLabel is automatically repositioned to remain centered within the window. If you narrow the window by dragging its right border to the left, the JLabel eventually becomes partially obscured when the window becomes too narrow for the display.

> **»NOTE** If your operating system does not allow you to make the window narrow enough to obscure part of the greeting, make the string in the label longer—for example, "Greetings to you and all your family!" Recompile the applet and then use the appletviewer command to execute the HTML document again. The string displayed will be long enough for you to observe the effects when you narrow the width of the window.

7. Close the Applet Viewer by clicking the **Close button** in the upper-right corner of the window.

RUNNING A JApplet IN YOUR WEB BROWSER
To run the applet using your Web browser:

1. Open any Web browser, such as Microsoft Internet Explorer or Netscape. You do not have to connect to the Internet; you will use the browser locally.

2. Click **File** on the menu bar, click **Open** or **Open Page**, type the complete path for the HTML document that you created to access JGreet.class (for example, **C:\Java\Chapter.09\TestJGreet.html**), and then press **Enter**. The applet should appear in the browser on your screen. If you receive an error message, verify that the path and spelling of the HTML file are correct.

> **»NOTE**
> If you do not have a Web browser installed on your computer, skip to the end of Step 3.

3. Click the **Close button** in the upper-right corner of the browser to close your Web browser.

CHANGING A JLabel's FONT

Next, you will change the font of the text in your `JGreet` applet.

To change the appearance of the greeting in the `JGreet` applet:

1. Open the **JGreet.java** file in your text editor, and change the class name to `JGreet2`. Immediately save the file using the filename **JGreet2.java**.

2. Position the insertion point at the end of the line that declares the greeting `JLabel`, and then press **Enter** to start a new line of text. Declare a `Font` object named `bigFont` by typing the following:

```
Font bigFont = new Font("Times Roman", Font.ITALIC, 24);
```

3. Place the insertion point to the right of the opening curly brace of the `init()` method, and then press **Enter** to start a new line. Set the `greeting` font to `bigFont` by typing the following:

```
greeting.setFont(bigFont);
```

4. Save the file (using the filename JGreet2.java).

5. At the command line, compile the program, and correct any errors if necessary.

6. Open the **TestJGreet.html** document you created earlier, change the class named in the `object code` statement to **JGreet2.class**, and save the file as **TestJGreet2.html**.

7. Execute the **appletviewer TestJGreet2.html** command. Figure 9-30 shows the output. The greeting appears in a large, italicized font style.

8. Close the Applet Viewer window.

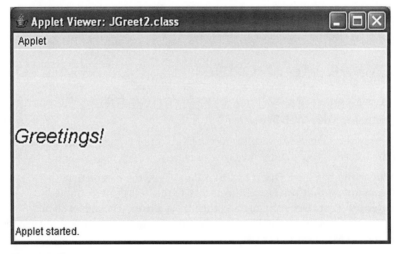

Figure 9-30 The `JGreet2` `JApplet`

ADDING MULTIPLE COMPONENTS TO A JApplet

Next, you will add two JLabels, two JTextFields, and a JButton to your JApplet.

To add multiple components to the JGreet2 JApplet:

1. Open the **JGreet2.java** file in your text editor and change the class name to **JGreet3**. Immediately save the file as **JGreet3.java**.

2. Position the insertion point at the end of the line that defines the bigFont Font object, and then press **Enter** to start a new line of text. Declare two JLabels, two empty JTextFields, and a JButton with the label "View Greeting" by typing the following:

```
JLabel firstLabel = new JLabel("Please enter your first name:");
JLabel lastLabel = new JLabel("Please enter your last name:");
JTextField firstField = new JTextField("",10);
JTextField lastField = new JTextField("",10);
JButton viewButton = new JButton("View Greeting");
```

3. Set the new layout manager to a flow layout with the following statement:

```
FlowLayout flow = new FlowLayout();
```

4. Within the init() method, position the insertion point at the end of the statement con.add(greeting);, press **Enter** to start a new line, and type **con.setLayout(flow);**.

5. Add all the newly created components to the applet by typing the following:

```
con.add(firstLabel);
con.add(firstField);
con.add(lastLabel);
con.add(lastField);
con.add(viewButton);
```

6. On the next line, request focus for the first-name text field by typing:

```
firstField.requestFocus();
```

7. Save the file (as JGreet3.java) and compile it.

8. Open the **TestJGreet2.html** document you created earlier, and change the class name in the object code statement to **JGreet3.class**. Save the file as **TestJGreet3.html**. Execute the **appletviewer TestJGreet3.html** command. The output is shown in Figure 9-31. Confirm that you can type characters into the JTextFields and that you can click the JButton using the mouse. You haven't coded any action to take place as a result of a JButton click yet, but the components should function.

9. Close the Applet Viewer window.

MAKING THE JApplet's BUTTON RESPOND TO EVENTS

Next, you will make your applet an event-driven program by adding functionality to the applet. When the user enters a name and clicks the JButton, the JApplet displays a personalized greeting.

To add functionality to your JApplet:

1. Open the **JGreet3.java** file in your text editor and change the class name to **JGreet4**. Immediately save the file as **JGreet4.java**.

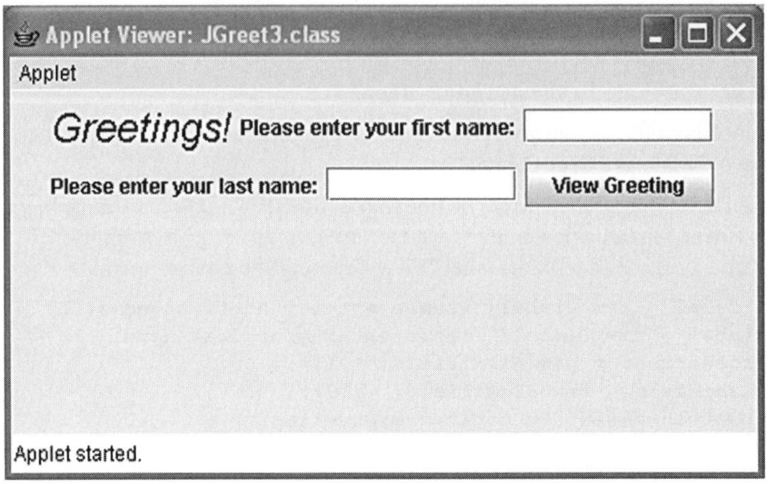

Figure 9-31 The `JGreet3` `JApplet`

2. Add a third `import` statement to your program by typing the following:

```
import java.awt.event.*;
```

3. Position the insertion point at the end of the class header `public class JGreet4 extends JApplet`, press the **Spacebar**, and then type:

```
implements ActionListener
```

4. Position the insertion point at the end of the statement in the `init()` method that adds the `viewButton` to the `JApplet`, and press **Enter**. Prepare your `JApplet` for `JButton`-sourced events by typing the following statement:

```
viewButton.addActionListener(this);
```

5. Position the insertion point to the right of the closing curly brace for the `init()` method, and then press **Enter**. Add the following `actionPerformed()` method that follows the `init()` method but comes before the closing brace for the `JGreet4` class. In the method, declare two `Strings`—one to hold the user's first name and another for the last name—and then use the `getText()` method on the `JTextFields` to retrieve values for these `Strings`. Using the `Strings`, display a personalized question for the user.

```
public void actionPerformed(ActionEvent thisEvent)
{
    String firstName = firstField.getText();
    String lastName = lastField.getText();
    greeting.setText("How are you, " + firstName + " " +
        lastName + "?");
}
```

6. Save the file (as JGreet4.java) and compile the program. Edit the file **TestJGreet3.html** to change the class reference to **JGreet4.class**, and then save the file as **TestJGreet4.html**. Run the applet using the **appletviewer TestJGreet4.html** command.

7. Type your name in the `JTextField`s and then click the **View Greeting** button. The personalized message should appear, similar to the one in Figure 9-32.

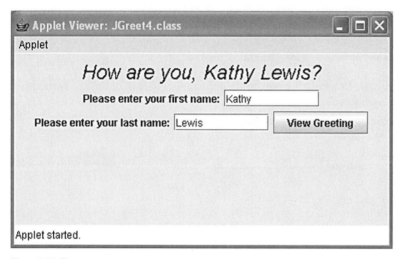

8. Drag the mouse to highlight the first or last name (or both) in the Applet Viewer window, and then type a different name. Click the **View Greeting** button. A greeting that uses the new name appears.

9. Close the Applet Viewer window.

UNDERSTANDING THE APPLET LIFE CYCLE

To demonstrate the life cycle methods in action, you can write a `JApplet` that overrides all four methods—`init()`, `start()`, `stop()`, and `destroy()`. When you run this applet, you can observe the number of times each method executes.

To demonstrate the life cycle of a `JApplet`:

1. Open a new text file in your text editor, and then type the following `import` statements:

```
import javax.swing.*;
import java.awt.*;
import java.awt.event.*;
```

2. To make the `JApplet` include a `JButton` that the user can click, and to implement an `ActionListener`, type the following header for a `JLifeCycle` applet:

```
public class JLifeCycle extends JApplet implements ActionListener
```

3. Press **Enter**, type the opening curly brace for the class, and then press **Enter** again to start a new line.

4. Declare the following six `JLabel` objects, which display each of the six methods that execute during the lifetime of the applet:

```
JLabel messageInit = new JLabel("init ");
JLabel messageStart = new JLabel("start ");
```

```
JLabel messageDisplay = new JLabel ("display ");
JLabel messageAction = new JLabel ("action ");
JLabel messageStop = new JLabel ("stop ");
JLabel messageDestroy = new JLabel ("destroy ");
```

5. Declare a JButton by typing the following:

```
JButton pressButton = new JButton ("Press");
```

6. Declare six integers that hold the number of occurrences of each of the six methods by typing the following code:

```
int countInit, countStart, countDisplay, countAction,
    countStop, countDestroy;
```

7. Start the init() method by adding a container and flow layout manager with the following statements:

```
public void init()
{
    Container con = getContentPane();
    con.setLayout (new FlowLayout());
```

8. Add the following statements, which add 1 to countInit, place the components within the applet, and then call the display() method:

```
    ++countInit;
    con.add(messageInit);
    con.add(messageStart);
    con.add(messageDisplay);
    con.add(messageAction);
    con.add(messageStop);
    con.add(messageDestroy);
    con.add(pressButton);
    pressButton.addActionListener(this);
    display();
}
```

9. Add the following start() method, which adds 1 to countStart and calls display():

```
public void start()
{
    ++countStart;
    display();
}
```

10. Add the following display() method, which adds 1 to countDisplay, displays the name of each of the six methods with the current count, and indicates how many times the method has executed:

```
public void display()
{
    ++countDisplay;
    messageInit.setText("init " + countInit);
    messageStart.setText("start " + countStart);
```

```
    messageDisplay.setText("display " + countDisplay);
    messageAction.setText("action " + countAction);
    messageStop.setText("stop " + countStop);
    messageDestroy.setText("destroy " + countDestroy);
}
```

11. Add the following `stop()` and `destroy()` methods, which each add 1 to the appropriate counter and call `display()`:

```
public void stop()
{
    ++countStop;
    display();
}
public void destroy()
{
    ++countDestroy;
    display();
}
```

12. When the user clicks `pressButton`, the following `actionPerformed()` method executes; it adds 1 to `countAction` and displays it:

```
public void actionPerformed(ActionEvent e)
{
    Object source = e.getSource();
    if(source == pressButton)
    {
        ++countAction;
        display();
    }
}
```

13. Add the closing curly brace for the class. Save the file as **JLifeCycle.java** in the Chapter.09 folder on your Student Disk. If necessary, compile, correct any errors, and compile again.

Take a moment to examine the code you created for JLifeCycle.java. Each method adds 1 to one of the six counters, but you never explicitly call any of the methods except `display()`; each of the other methods is called automatically. Next, you will create an HTML document so you can test JLifeCycle.java.

To create an HTML document to test JLifeCycle.java:

1. Open a new text file in your text editor, and then enter the following HTML code:

```
<html>
<object code = "JLifeCycle.class" width = 460 height = 100>
</object>
</html>
```

2. Save the file as **TestJLifeCycle.html** in the Chapter.09 folder on your Student Disk.

3. Run the HTML document using the following command:

```
appletviewer TestJLifeCycle.html
```

Figure 9-33 shows the output. When the applet begins, the `init()` method is called, so 1 is added to `countInit`. The `init()` method calls `display()`, so 1 is added to `countDisplay`. Immediately after the `init()` method executes, the `start()` method is executed, and 1 is added to `countStart`. The `start()` method calls `display()`, so 1 more is added to `countDisplay`. The first time you see the applet, `countInit` is 1, `countStart` is 1, and `countDisplay` is 2. The methods `actionPerformed()`, `stop()`, and `destroy()` have not yet been executed.

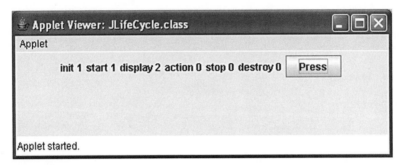

Figure 9-33 The `JLifeCycle` `JApplet` when it first executes

4. Click the **Minimize** button to minimize the Applet Viewer window, and then click the **Taskbar** button to restore it. The applet now looks like Figure 9-34. The `init()` method still has been called only once, but when you minimized the applet, the `stop()` method executed, and when you restored it, the `start()` method executed. Therefore, `countStop` is now 1 and `countStart` has increased to 2. In addition, because `start()` and `stop()` call `display()`, `countDisplay` is increased by two and now holds the value 4.

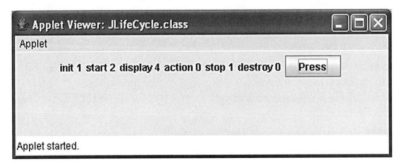

Figure 9-34 The `JLifeCycle` `JApplet` after minimizing and restoring

5. Minimize and restore the Applet Viewer window again. Now, the `stop()` method has executed twice, the `start()` method has executed three times, and the `display()` method has executed a total of six times, as shown in Figure 9-35.

6. Click the **Press** button. The count for the `actionPerformed()` method is now 1, and `actionPerformed()` calls `display()`, so `countDisplay` is now 7, as shown in Figure 9-36.

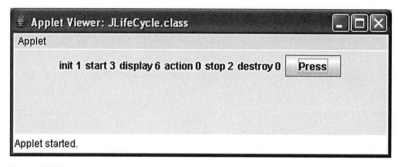

Figure 9-35 The `JLifeCycle` `JApplet` after minimizing and restoring twice

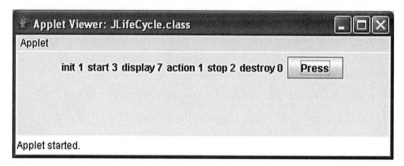

Figure 9-36 The `JLifeCycle` `JApplet` after minimizing and restoring twice, and then pressing the button

7. Continue to minimize, maximize, and click the **Press** button. Note the changes that occur with each activity until you can correctly predict the outcome. Notice that the `destroy()` method is not executed until you close the applet, and then it is too late to observe an increase in `countDestroy`.

8. Close the Applet Viewer.

KEY TERMS

Applets are Java programs that are called from within another application.

A program called **Applet Viewer**, which comes with the Java SDK, allows you to view applets without using a Web browser.

HTML, or **Hypertext Markup Language**, is a simple language used to create Web pages for the Internet.

A **Web browser** is a program that allows you to display HTML documents on your computer screen.

Untrusted code carries the possibility of doing harm.

A **sandbox** is a safe area in which a program can run without causing harm to other areas of a system.

Tags are HTML commands.

The tag that begins every HTML document is **<html>**.

The tag that ends every HTML document is **</html>**.

Attributes, sometimes referred to as arguments, promote activity or describe the features of an HTML tag.

Pixels are the picture elements, or tiny dots of light, that make up the image on your video monitor.

The **appletviewer command** is part of the Java SDK that provides a convenient environment in which to test your applets.

UI components are user interface components, such as buttons and text fields, with which the user can interact.

JApplet is a Swing class from which you can instantiate an applet.

Swing components are UI elements such as dialog boxes and buttons; you can usually recognize their names because they begin with J.

The **Java Foundation Classes**, or **JFC**, are a set of classes that provide UI capabilities to Java applications and applets.

Component is the name of a class that defines objects you can display on a screen.

Container is a class that defines Components that can hold and display other Components.

An **inheritance hierarchy chart** depicts the parent-child relationships among classes.

The **init() method** is the first method called in any applet.

JLabel is a built-in Java Swing class that holds text you can display within an applet.

You can add objects to an applet using the **add() method**.

A **content pane** is a window to which components can be added.

A Container content pane object can be created using the **getContentPane() method**.

The **Font class** is a class from which you can create an object that holds typeface and size information.

The **setFont() method** assigns a font to an object.

The **typeface argument** to the Font constructor is a String representing a font.

The **style argument** to the Font constructor applies an attribute to displayed text and is one of three values: Font.PLAIN, Font.BOLD, or Font.ITALIC.

The **point size argument** to the Font constructor is an integer that represents approximately 1/72 of an inch.

A **JTextField** is a component into which a user can type a single line of text data.

The **setText() method** allows you to change the text in a Component that has already been created.

The **getText() method** allows you to retrieve the String of text in a Component.

When a Component has **keyboard focus**, the next entries from the keyboard are entered at that location.

When you want the insertion point to appear automatically within a JTextField or other Component without requiring the user to click in it first, you can use the **requestFocus() method**.

When a JTextField has the capability of accepting keystrokes, it is **editable**.

If you do not want the user to be able to enter data in a JTextField, you can use the **setEditable() method** to change the editable status of a JTextField.

A **JButton** is a Component the user can click with a mouse to make a selection.

You can change a JButton's label with the **setLabel() method**.

You can retrieve a JButton's label and assign it to a String object with the **getLabel() method**.

A **layout manager** is a class that controls component positioning.

A **BorderLayout**, created by using the BorderLayout class, divides a container into five regions: north, south, east, west, and center.

The **flow layout manager** places components in a row, and when a row is filled it automatically spills components into the next row.

An **event** occurs when a user takes action on a component.

In an **event-driven program**, actions occur in the order determined by a user triggering events.

Within an event-driven program, a component on which an event is generated is the **source** of the event.

Within an event-driven program, an object that is interested in an event is a **listener**.

An **interface** is a class containing a set of specifications for methods that you can use.

You tell your applet to expect ActionEvents with the **addActionListener() method**.

The ActionListener interface contains the **actionPerformed(ActionEvent e) method** specification. This method executes when a user takes action on a Component for which the applet is registered as a listener.

Invoking the **validate() method** after adding one or more Components to an applet ensures that the Components draw themselves onscreen.

To remove components from an applet, you use the **remove() method**.

When you write a method that has the same method header as an automatically provided method, you replace or **override** the original version.

In an applet, the **start() method** executes after the init() method, and it executes again every time the applet becomes active after it has been inactive.

In an applet, when a user leaves a Web page (perhaps by minimizing a window or traveling to a different Web page), the **stop() method** is invoked.

Within an applet, the **destroy() method** is called when the user closes the browser or Applet Viewer.

The **setLocation() method** allows you to place a component at a specific location within the Applet Viewer window.

The **x-axis** defines a horizontal position in a window.

The **y-axis** defines a vertical position in a window.

The **x-coordinate** value increases as you travel from left to right across a window.

The **y-coordinate** value increases as you travel from top to bottom in a window.

You can use the `setEnabled()` **method** to make a component unavailable and then make it available again in turn.

CHAPTER SUMMARY

» Applets are programs that are called from within another application. Frequently, an applet is run from a Web page. An applet is displayed as a rectangular area. It can contain any number of components, such as buttons, text fields, and pictures. Often, an applet can respond to user-initiated events, such as button clicks.

» You run applets within a Web page or within another program called Applet Viewer, which comes with the Java Software Development Kit (SDK). An applet must be called from within an HTML document.

» A `JApplet` object extends the capabilities of the `Container`, `Component`, and `Object` classes.

» Every `JApplet` contains four automatically created methods—`init()`, `start()`, `stop()`, and `destroy()`. You use the `init()` method to perform initialization tasks. For example, you can add a `Component`, such as a `JLabel`, to a `ContentPane` `Container` within a `JApplet`. To give a `JLabel` object a new font, you can create a `Font` object and then use the `setFont()` method to assign the `Font` to a `JLabel`.

» A `JTextField` is a `Component` into which a user can type a single line of text data. Typically, a user types a line into a `JTextField` and then inputs the data by pressing Enter on the keyboard or clicking a `JButton` with the mouse. A `JButton` is a `Component` a user can click with a mouse to make a selection. To place multiple components at specified positions in a container so they do not hide each other, you must use a layout manager.

» An event occurs when a `JApplet`'s user takes action on a component, such as using the mouse to click a `JButton` object. Within an event-driven program, a component on which an event is generated is the source of the event. An object that is interested in an event is a listener.

» To respond to user events within any `JApplet` you create, you must prepare your applet to accept event messages, tell your applet to expect events to happen, and then tell your applet how to respond to events. Adding `implements ActionListener` to an applet's class header prepares a `JApplet` to receive event messages.

» You can add `JComponents` to `JApplets` and remove `JComponents` from `JApplets` using the `add()` and `remove()` methods. When you change the appearance of an applet screen by adding or removing components, you should always call the `validate()` method.

» Every `JApplet` has the same life cycle outline. When the applet executes, the `init()` method runs, followed by the `start()` method. If the user leaves the `JApplet`'s page, the `stop()` method executes. When the user returns, the `start()` method executes. The `stop()` and `start()` sequence might continue any number of times until the user closes the browser (or Applet Viewer), which invokes the `destroy()` method.

» The `setLocation()` method allows you to place a component at a specific location within an Applet Viewer window. When you include x- and y-coordinates within the `setLocation()` method, the upper-left corner of the component is placed at the specified location. You can use the `setEnabled()` method to make a component unavailable and then make it available again in turn.

REVIEW QUESTIONS

1. A program that allows you to display HTML documents on your computer screen is a _____ .

    a. search engine   c. browser

    b. compiler   d. server

2. The name of any applet called using `code` within an HTML document must use the extension _____ .

    a. .exe   c. .java

    b. .code   d. .class

3. A `JApplet` is a(n) _____ .

    a. `Container`   c. `Object`

    b. `Component`   d. all of the above

4. The first method called in any `JApplet` is the _____ method.

    a. `init()`   c. `begin()`

    b. `start()`   d. `main()`

5. A `JTextField` is a `Swing` component _____ .

    a. into which a user can type a single line of text data

    b. into which a user can type multiple lines of text data

    c. that automatically has focus when the applet runs

    d. whose text cannot be changed

6. The Swing `add()` method _____ .

    a. adds two integers

    b. adds a component directly to the `JApplet`

    c. places a component within a container

    d. places a text value within an applet component

7. The `start()` method called in any `JApplet` is called _____ .

a. as the first method when an applet starts

b. when the user closes the browser

c. when a user revisits an applet

d. when a user leaves a Web page

8. A `Font` object contains all of the following arguments except _____ .

a. language

b. typeface

c. style

d. point size

9. To respond to user events within a `JApplet`, you must _____ .

a. prepare the applet to accept event messages

b. import the `java.applet.*` package

c. tell your applet how to respond to events

d. accomplish both a and c

10. The constructor `public JButton("4")` creates _____ .

a. four `JButton`s

b. a `JButton` four pixels wide

c. a `JButton` four characters wide

d. a `JButton` with a "4" on it

11. One occasion on which an event occurs is when a _____ .

a. component requests focus

b. component is enabled

c. component sets text

d. button is clicked

12. `ActionListener` is an example of a(n) _____ .

a. import

b. applet

c. interface

d. component

13. When an applet is registered as a listener with a `JButton` and a user clicks the `JButton`, the method that executes is _____ .

a. `buttonPressed()`

b. `addActionListener()`

c. `start()`

d. `actionPerformed()`

14. When you write a method that has the same method header as an automatically provided method, you _____ the original version.

   a. destroy   c. call

   b. override   d. copy

15. Which of the following statements creates a `JLabel` that says "Welcome"?

   a. `JLabel = new JLabel("Welcome");`

   b. `JLabel aLabel = JLabel("Welcome");`

   c. `aLabel = new JLabel("Welcome");`

   d. `JLabel aLabel = new JLabel("Welcome");`

16. Which of the following statements correctly creates a `Font` object?

   a. `Font aFont = new Font("TimesRoman", Font.ITALIC, 20);`

   b. `Font aFont = new Font(30, "Helvetica", Font.ITALIC);`

   c. `Font aFont = new Font(Font.BOLD,"Helvetica", 24);`

   d. `Font aFont = new Font(22, Font.BOLD,"TimesRoman");`

17. The method that positions a component within an applet is _____ .

   a. `position()`   c. `location()`

   b. `setPosition()`   d. `setLocation()`

18. In a window that is 200 x 200 pixels, position 10,190 is nearest to the _____ corner.

   a. upper-left   c. lower-left

   b. upper-right   d. lower-right

19. An object's _____ method can be used to determine the component that sends an event to a method.

   a. `getSource()`

   b. `instanceof()`

   c. both of the above

   d. none of the above

20. Which of the following statements disables a component named `someComponent`?

   a. `someComponent.setDisabled();`

   b. `someComponent.setDisabled(true);`

   c. `someComponent.disable();`

   d. `someComponent.setEnabled(false);`

EXERCISES

For each JApplet you create in the following exercises, create an HTML host document named **Test** plus the JApplet name. For example, the host document for the **JNumberOne.java** file is named **TestJNumberOne.html**.

1. Create a JApplet with a JButton labeled "Who's number one?" When the user clicks the button, display your favorite sports team in a large font. Save the file as **JNumberOne.java**.

2. a. Create a JApplet that asks a user to enter a password into a JTextField and to then press Enter. Compare the password to "Rosebud"; if it matches exactly, display "Access Granted". If not, display "Access Denied". Save the file as **JPasswordA.java**.

   b. Modify the password applet in Exercise 2a to ignore differences in case between the typed password and "Rosebud". Save the file as **JPasswordB.java**.

   c. Modify the password applet in Exercise 2b to compare the password to a list of five valid passwords: "Rosebud", "Redrum", "Jason", "Surrender", or "Dorothy". Save the file as **JPasswordC.java**.

3. Create a JApplet that contains a JLabel and JButton. When the user clicks the JButton, change the font typeface, style, and size on the JLabel. Save the file as **JChangeFont.java**.

4. Create a JApplet that contains a JButton and a JTextField. When the user clicks the JButton, display "Today is", the date, and the time in the JTextField. Save the file as **JDateAndTime.java**.

5. Create a JApplet that contains two JTextFields, a JButton, and three JLabels. When the user types an employee's first and last names (separated by a space) in a JTextField, the employee's job title displays in a second JTextField. Include two JLabels to describe the JTextFields used for data entry, and include a third JLabel that holds the employee's title or an error message if no match is found for the employee. Use parallel arrays to store the employees' names and job titles. Save the file as **JEmployeeTitle.java**.

6. Create a JApplet that contains two parallel arrays containing at least five employees' names and jobs. Allow the user to enter either a title or a name and to click a JButton to display the other. Include a JLabel to describe each JTextField. Save the file as **JEmployeeTitle2.java**.

7. Create a JApplet that initially displays a single JButton. When the user clicks the JButton, display a JLabel that prompts the user to enter an integer, a JTextField into which the user can type the integer, and a second JButton containing the text "Double me". When the user clicks the second button, the integer is doubled and the answer is displayed in the JTextField. Save the file as **JDouble.java**.

8. Create a JApplet that prompts the user to enter two integers into two separate JTextFields. When the user clicks a JButton, the sum of the integers is displayed in a JLabel you add to the JApplet. Save the file as **JAdd.java**.

9. Create a JApplet named JDivide that allows the user to enter two integers in two separate JTextFields. The user can click a JButton to divide the first integer by the second integer and display the result. If the user attempts division by 0, display an error message. Save the file as **JDivide.java**.

10. a. Create a payroll JApplet named JCalculatePay that allows the user to enter two double values—hours worked and an hourly rate. When the user clicks a JButton, gross pay is calculated. Display the result in a JTextField that appears on the screen only after the user clicks the JButton. Save the file as **JCalculatePay.java**.

    b. Modify the payroll applet created in Exercise 10a so that federal withholding tax is subtracted from gross pay based on the following table:

Income ($)	Withholding %
0 to 99.99	10
100.00 to 299.99	15
300.00 to 599.99	21
600.00 and up	28

    Save the file as **JCalculatePay2.java**.

11. a. Create a conversion JApplet that prompts the user to enter a distance in miles in a JTextField, and then converts miles to kilometers and displays the result in a JTextField as "XX.XX kilometers", where XX.XX is the number of kilometers. A mile is 1.6 kilometers. Save the file as **JConversion.java**.

    b. Modify the JApplet you created in Exercise 11a so that the user can enter a value into either the miles JTextField or the kilometers JTextField, and can choose either of two JButtons—one that converts miles to kilometers or one that converts kilometers to miles. Save the file as **JConversion2.java**.

12. Create a JApplet that calculates the current balance in a checking account and displays it in a JTextField. The user enters the beginning balance, check amounts, and deposit amounts in separate JTextFields that are identified with appropriate JLabels. After the user clicks a button to make the applet calculate the current balance, reposition the JTextFields and JLabels so that the beginning balance appears on the first line, the check and deposit amounts appear on the second line, and the new balance appears on the third line. Save the file as **JCalculateBalance.java**.

DEBUGGING EXERCISES

Each of the following files in the Chapter.09 folder on your Student Disk has syntax and/or logic errors. In each case, determine the problem and fix the program. After you correct the errors, save each file using the same filename preceded with Fix. For example, DebugNine1.java will become FixDebugNine1.java. You can test each applet with the TestFixDebugNine1.html through TestFixDebugNine4.html files on your Student Disk.

   a. DebugNine1.java   c. DebugNine3.java

   b. DebugNine2.java   d. DebugNine4.java

CASE PROJECT

EVENT HANDLERS INCORPORATED

Event Handlers Incorporated wants you to create a `JPartyPlanner` applet that lets a user estimate the cost of an event hosted by the company. Event Handlers uses a sliding fee scale so that the per-guest cost decreases as the total number of invited guests increases. Table 9-1 shows the fee structure.

Number of Guests	Cost per Guest ($)
1 to 24	27
25 to 49	25
50 to 99	22
100 to 199	19
200 to 499	17
500 to 999	14
1000 and over	11

Table 9-1 Cost per guest for events

The applet lets the user enter a number of anticipated guests. The user can click either of two `JButtons`—one to display the fee per person and another to display the fee for the event (the cost per person times the number of guests). The user can continue to request fees for a different number of guests and view the results for any length of time before making another request or leaving the page. When the user leaves the page, erase the last number of requested guests and ensure that the next user starts fresh with a blank `JTextField` that holds the number of guests. Save the file as **JPartyPlanner.java** in the Chapter.09 folder on your Student Disk.

GAME ZONE

1. In Chapter 2, you created a *Mad Libs*® game in which the user entered several words out of context that were then inserted into a rhyme or story, producing humorous effects. Modify the game so it becomes an applet. In turn, prompt the user for each required word. After all the words are entered, display the completed rhyme or story. Figure 9-37 shows the screens displayed during a typical execution. Save the applet as **JMadLib.java**. Create an HTML document to execute the applet and save it as **JMadLib.html**.

2. In Chapter 5, you created a Rock Paper Scissors game. Now create it as a `JApplet` in which the user can click one of three buttons labeled "Rock", "Paper", or "Scissors". The computer's choice is still randomly generated. Figure 9-38 shows a typical start-up screen, how it might look after the user selects "Paper" once, and how it might look after the user selects "Paper" again. Save the applet as **JRockPaperScissors.java**. Create an HTML file to execute the applet and save it as **JRockPaperScissors.html**.

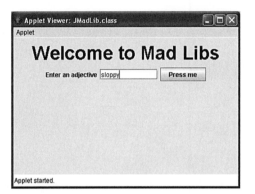

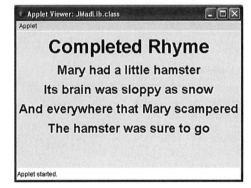

Figure 9-37 Typical execution of `JMadLib` applet

3. In Chapter 8, you created a Secret Phrase game in which the user guesses a randomly selected secret phrase by entering one letter at a time. Now, create an applet that plays the game, allowing users to choose a letter by selecting one of 26 buttons. (*Hint*: Consider creating an array of buttons rather than 26 individually named buttons.)

   Disable a letter button once it has been guessed, and after the puzzle is complete, disable all the letters. Figure 9-39 shows a typical execution at (1) the start of the applet; (2) after

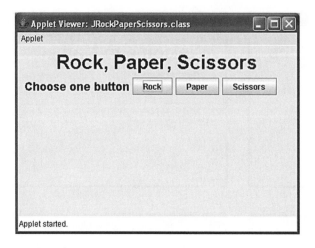

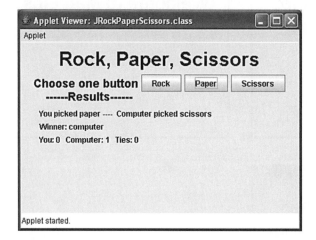

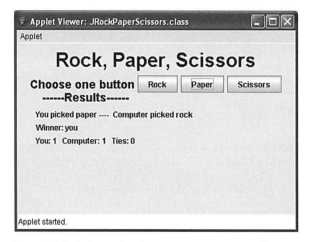

Figure 9-38 Typical execution of JRockPaperScissors applet

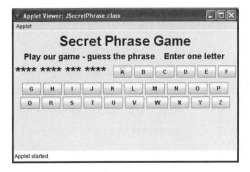

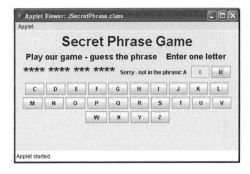

Figure 9-39 Typical execution of `JSecretPhrase` applet

the user has guessed an "A", which is not in the phrase; (3) after the user has guessed a "W", which is in the phrase; and (4) after the user has completed the puzzle. Save the applet as **JSecretPhrase.java**. Create an HTML file to execute the applet and save it as **JSecretPhrase.html**.

4. In earlier chapters, you created and used a `Card` class in which each object represents a playing `Card`, and in Chapter 8 you constructed a deck of 52 unique `Cards`. Create a `JApplet` that uses such a deck. Start the player with a $10 stake. Randomly deal a card to the computer and allow the player to make one of four bets:

  » $5 that the player's card will be higher than the computer's card

  » $10 that the player's card will be higher than the computer's card

  » $5 that the player's card will be lower than the computer's card

  » $10 that the player's card will be lower than the computer's card

After the player makes a bet, deal the player's card and add or subtract the correct amount from the player's winnings based on the results. When the computer's and player's cards are the same value, the computer wins. The game ends when the first of these events happens:

  » The player goes broke (the winnings go to 0 or below).

  » The player wins $100.

  » All 52 cards are exhausted without a winner.

As shown in Figure 9-40, when the player is making a bet, enable four betting buttons. After the player makes a bet, disable the betting buttons while the player examines the

Figure 9-40 Typical execution of JCardBet applet

outcome, and enable an OK button. When the player indicates he is ready to resume play by clicking OK, disable the OK button and enable the four betting buttons. Save the game as **JCardBet.java**. Create an HTML file to execute the applet and save it as **JCardBet.html**.

5. In Chapter 8, you created a Tic Tac Toe game in which you used a two-dimensional array of characters to hold Xs and Os for a player and the computer. Now create a Tic Tac Toe JApplet that uses an array of nine JButtons to represent the Tic Tac Toe grid. When the user clicks a JButton, if the button has not already been taken, place an X on the button and then allow the computer to place an O on a different button. Announce the winner when either the computer or the player achieves three marks in sequence, or announce that the game was a tie. Figure 9-41 shows a typical game in progress and after the player has won. Save the game as **JTicTacToe.java**. Create an HTML file to execute the applet and save it as **JTicTacToe.html**.

Figure 9-41 Typical execution of `JTicTacToe` applet

UP FOR DISCUSSION

1. Why are applets not as popular in the programming community as applications?

2. Think of some practice or position to which you are opposed. For example, you might have objections to organizations on the far right or left politically. Now suppose such an organization offered you twice your annual salary to create Web sites for them. Would you do it? Is there a price at which you would do it? What if the organization was not so extreme, but featured products you found mildly distasteful? What if the Web site you designed was not objectionable, but the parent company's policies were objectionable? For example, if you are opposed to smoking, is there a price at which you would design a Web site for a tobacco company, even if the Web site simply displayed sports scores without promoting smoking directly?

3. Suppose you have learned a lot about programming from your employer. Is it ethical for you to use this knowledge to start your own home-based programming business on the side? Does it matter whether you are in competition for the same clients as your employer? Does it matter whether you use just your programming expertise or whether you also use information about clients' preferences and needs gathered from your regular job? Suppose you know your employer is overcharging clients and you can offer the same services for less money; does this alter your opinion?

10

GRAPHICS

In this chapter, you will:

Learn about the `paint()` and `repaint()` methods
Use the `drawString()` method to draw `String`s using
  various fonts and colors
Create `Graphics` and `Graphics2D` objects
Draw lines and shapes
Learn more about fonts and methods you can use
  with them
Draw with Java 2D graphics
Add sound, images, and simple animation to `JApplet`s

LEARNING ABOUT THE paint() AND repaint() METHODS

In Chapter 9, you learned about four methods contained in every JApplet: init(), start(), stop(), and destroy(). If you don't write these methods, Java provides you with a "do nothing" copy—a default copy that contains no statements. You can, however, override any of these automatically supplied methods by writing your own versions.

> **NOTE** You cannot see the copies of the automatically provided JApplet methods; they work behind the scenes. They are similar to how a default constructor exists in classes in which you do not write statements to provide a constructor instantiation.

In addition to the four methods listed above, a fifth method is automatically supplied within every JApplet. The **paint() method** runs when Java displays your applet. You can write your own paint() method to override the default one whenever you want to paint graphics, such as shapes, on the screen. As with init(), start(), stop(), and destroy() methods, if you don't write a paint() method, you get an automatic version from Java. The paint() method executes automatically every time you minimize, maximize, or resize the Applet Viewer window.

The paint() method header is:

```
public void paint(Graphics g)
```

> **NOTE**
> You learned about the basic structure of JApplets in Chapter 9.

> **NOTE**
> The update() method clears the Component's background as well as calls the paint() method.

The header indicates that the method requires a Graphics object argument; here, it is named g, but you can use any legal identifier. You don't usually call the paint() method directly. Instead, you call the **repaint() method**, which you can use when a window needs to be updated, such as when it contains new images or you have moved a new object onto the screen. The Java system calls the repaint() method when it needs to update a window, or you can call it yourself—in either case, repaint() creates a Graphics object for you. The repaint() method calls another method named update(), which calls the paint() method. The series of events is best described with an example. Figure 10-1 shows a JDemoPaint applet with a Container that contains a JButton. The init() method gets a content pane, adds the button to it, and prepares the applet to receive messages from the button.

In the JDemoPaint applet in Figure 10-1, the actionPerformed() method executes when the user presses the JButton. It contains a single statement—a call to repaint(), which is unseen in the JApplet and which automatically calls the paint() method.

```
import javax.swing.*;
import java.awt.*;
import java.awt.event.*;
public class JDemoPaint extends JApplet implements ActionListener
{
    Container con = getContentPane();
    JButton pressButton = new JButton("Press");
    public void init()
    {
        con.setLayout(new FlowLayout());
        con.add(pressButton);
        pressButton.addActionListener(this);
    }
    public void paint(Graphics g)
    {
        super.paint(g);
        System.out.println("In paint method");

    }
    public void actionPerformed(ActionEvent e)
    {
        repaint();
    }
}
```

Figure 10-1 The JDemoPaint JApplet

>> **NOTE** In Figure 10-1, the shaded code in the paint() method is super.paint(g);. This statement is a call to the paint() method that is part of JDemoPaint's parent class (JApplet), and it passes the local Graphics object (named g) to this method. Although this JApplet and others in this chapter will work without this statement, omitting it causes errors in more complicated applets. In Chapter 11, you will learn more about the super() method. For now, you can get in the habit of including this method call as the first statement in any JApplet's paint() method, using whatever local name you have declared for your paint() method's Graphics argument.

>> **NOTE** Starting with Java 5, you can add write statements that add components directly to a JApplet instead of explicitly using the getContentPane() method call, as shown in Figure 10-1. However, until you learn more about the ramifications of using this simplified technique in Chapter 13, this book shows applet examples that add buttons, labels, and other components using the contentPane() call.

>> **NOTE** It is usually best to avoid combining drawing on an applet with placing components (such as buttons) on it, as in Figure 10-1. For one thing, it is difficult to predetermine where components will be placed. In this example, a button is placed on the applet along with the drawn string so that you can take action to illustrate when paint() is called. In Chapter 14, you will learn to place components in their own panels within an applet; this helps you place components more accurately.

The paint() method in the JDemoPaint JApplet overrides the automatically supplied paint() method. The paint() method displays a line of output at the command line—it announces that the paint() method is executing. Figure 10-2 shows an HTML document that could host the JApplet.

>> **NOTE** If you call repaint() alone in a JApplet, then the entire applet is repainted. This might cause unnecessary paint processing if only part of the JApplet has changed. If you call repaint() with a component, as in pressButton.repaint(), then only that component is repainted.

```
<html>
<object code = "JDemoPaint.class" width = 100 height = 100>
</object>
</html>
```

Figure 10-2 The TestJDemoPaint HTML document

When the JApplet in Figure 10-1 starts, the paint() method executes automatically, so the message "In paint method" appears on the command line. When the user clicks the pressButton in the applet, the actionPerformed() method calls the repaint() method, and the repaint() method calls the update() method, which then calls the paint() method, so a second message appears on the command line. If the user minimizes the Applet Viewer window and then restores it, or reduces the size of the window by dragging its border, an "In paint method" message appears on the command line. Figure 10-3 shows the JApplet after the user has taken several actions.

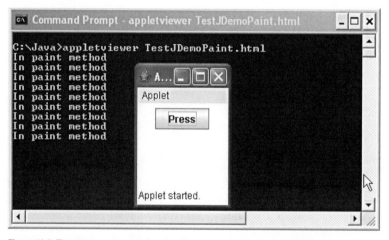

Figure 10-3 The JDemoPaint applet after the user clicks the button several times

> **NOTE** The repaint() method only requests that Java repaint the screen. If a second request to repaint() occurs before Java can carry out the first request, Java executes only the last repaint() method.

> **NOTE** Before the built-in update() method calls paint(), it fills in the entire applet with its background color. Then it calls the paint() method to redraw the contents. The effect is that components are "erased" before being redrawn. (This is the reason you need to call repaint() with the button in the paint() method in Figure 10-1.) If you want to avoid this step, you can override the update() method so it calls paint() directly, as in the following example:
>
> ```
> public void update(Graphics g)
> {
>     paint(g);
> }
> ```

USING THE drawString() METHOD TO DRAW Strings

The **drawString() method** allows you to draw a String in a JApplet window. The drawString() method requires three arguments: a String, an x-axis coordinate, and a y-axis coordinate.

You are already familiar with x- and y-axis coordinates because you used them with the setLocation() method for components in Chapter 9. However, there is a minor difference in how you place components using the setLocation() method and how you place Strings using the drawString() method. When you use x- and y-coordinates with components, such as JLabels, the upper-left corner of the component is placed at the coordinate position. When you use x- and y-coordinates with drawString(), the lower-left corner of the String appears at the coordinates. Figure 10-4 shows the positions of a JLabel placed at the coordinates 30, 10 and a String placed at the coordinates 10, 30.

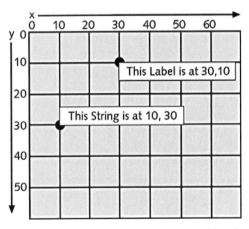

Figure 10-4 Placement of String and JLabel objects in an applet

The drawString() method is a member of the Graphics class, so you need to use a Graphics object to call it. Recall that the paint() method header shows that the method receives a Graphics object from the update() method. If you use drawString() within paint(), the Graphics object you name in the header is available to you. For example, if you write a paint() method with the header public void paint(Graphics brush), you can draw a String within your paint() method by using a statement such as:

```
brush.drawString("Hi", 50, 80);
```

USING THE setFont() METHOD

You can improve the appearance of strings drawn using Graphics objects by using the **setFont() method**. The setFont() method requires a Font object, which as you recall, you create with a statement such as:

```
Font someFont = new Font("TimesRoman", Font.BOLD, 16);
```

» NOTE
You learned about the Font object when you changed a JLabel's font in Chapter 9.

Then, you can instruct a Graphics object to use the font by using it as the argument in a setFont() method. For example, if a Graphics object is named artist and a Font object is named someFont, the font is set to someFont with the following:

```
artist.setFont(someFont);
```

Figure 10-5 shows an applet that uses the setFont() method with a Graphics object named brush. When the paint() method executes, the automatically created brush object is assigned the bigFont and then used to draw the hello string at position 10, 100. Figure 10-6 shows the output.

```
import javax.swing.*;
import java.awt.*;
public class JDemoFont extends JApplet
{
    Font bigFont = new Font("Helvetica", Font.ITALIC, 48);
    String hello = "Hello";
    public void paint(Graphics brush)
    {
        super.paint(brush);
        brush.setFont(bigFont);
        brush.drawString(hello, 10, 100);
    }
}
```

Figure 10-5 The JDemoFont JApplet

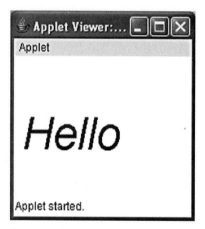

Figure 10-6 Output of the JDemoFont JApplet

USING COLOR

You can designate a Graphics color with the **setColor() method**. The Color class contains 13 constants, which are shown in Table 10-1. You can use any of these constants as an argument to the setColor() method. For example, you can instruct a Graphics object named brush to apply green paint by using the following statement:

```
brush.setColor(Color.GREEN);
```

Until you change the color, subsequent graphics output appears as green.

> **» NOTE** Java constants are usually written in all uppercase letters, as you learned in Chapter 4. However, Java's creators declared two constants for every color in the Color class—an uppercase version, such as BLUE, and a lowercase version, such as blue. Earlier versions of Java contained only the lowercase Color constants. (The uppercase Color constants use an underscore in DARK_GRAY and LIGHT_GRAY; the lowercase versions are a single word: darkgray and lightgray.)

BLACK	GREEN	RED
BLUE	LIGHT_GRAY	WHITE
CYAN	MAGENTA	YELLOW
DARK_GRAY	ORANGE	
GRAY	PINK	

Table 10-1 Color class constants

You can also create your own Color object with the following statement:

```
Color someColor = new Color(r, g, b);
```

In this statement, r, g, and b are numbers representing the intensities of red, green, and blue you want in your color. The numbers can range from 0 to 255, with 0 being the darkest shade of the color and 255 being the lightest. (You might expect 0 to represent the lightest shade, but it does not.) For example, the following statement produces a dark purple color that has red and blue components, but no green.

```
Color darkPurple = new Color(100, 0, 100);
```

You can create more than 16 million custom colors using this approach.

You can discover the red, green, or blue components of any existing color with the methods getRed(), getGreen(), and getBlue(). Each of these methods returns an integer. For example, you can discover the amount of red in MAGENTA by printing the value of Color.MAGENTA.getRed();.

> **» NOTE**
> Some computers cannot display each of the 16 million possible colors. Each computer displays the closest color it can.

In addition to changing the color of Strings that you display, you can change the background color of your applet. For example, if an applet contains a content pane named con, then the following statement changes the applet's color to pink:

```
con.setBackground(Color.PINK);
```

You do not need a Graphics object to change the applet's background color; the JApplet itself (its content pane) changes colors.

> **» NOTE** Because this book is printed in only two colors, you can't see the full effect of setting JApplets' colors in the figures. However, when you work through the "You Do It" exercises later in this chapter, you can observe the effect of color changes on your own monitor.

CREATING Graphics AND Graphics2D OBJECTS

When you call the paint() method from within an applet, you can use the automatically created Graphics object that is passed to it, but you can also instantiate your own Graphics or Graphics2D objects. For example, you might want to use a Graphics object when some action occurs, such as a mouse event. Because the actionPerformed() method does not supply you with a Graphics object automatically, you can create your own.

For example, to display a string when the user clicks a JButton, you can code an actionPerformed() method such as the following:

```
public void actionPerformed(ActionEvent e)
{
    Graphics draw = getGraphics();
    draw.drawString("You clicked the button!", 50, 100);
}
```

This method instantiates a Graphics object named draw. (You can use any legal Java identifier.) The getGraphics() method provides the draw object with Graphics capabilities. Then, the draw object can employ any of the Graphics methods you have learned, such as setFont(), setColor(), and drawString().

> **» NOTE** Notice that when you create the draw object, you are not calling the Graphics constructor directly. (The name of the Graphics constructor is Graphics(), not getGraphics().) This operation is similar to the way you call getContentPane(). You are not allowed to call the Graphics or ContentPane constructors because those classes are abstract classes. You will learn about abstract classes in Chapter 12.

> **» NOTE** If you call getGraphics() in an applet or for a frame that is not visible, you receive a NullPointerException and the applet will not execute.

DRAWING LINES AND SHAPES

> **» NOTE**
> Any line or shape is drawn in the current color you set with the setColor() method. When you do not set a color, lines are drawn in black by default.

Just as you can draw Strings using a Graphics object and the drawString() method, Java provides you with several methods for drawing a variety of lines and geometric shapes.

You can use the **drawLine() method** to draw a straight line between any two points on the screen. The drawLine() method takes four arguments: the x- and y-coordinates of the line's starting point and the x- and y-coordinates of the line's ending point. For example, if you create a Graphics object named pen, then the following statement draws a straight line that slants down and to the right, from position 10, 10 to position 100, 200, as shown in Figure 10-7.

```
pen.drawLine(10, 10, 100, 200);
```

Because you can start at either end when you draw a line, an identical line is created with the following:

```
pen.drawLine(100, 200, 10, 10);
```

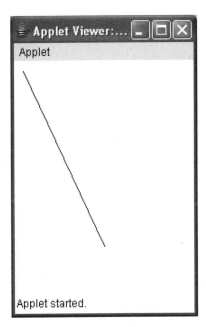

Figure 10-7 A line created with the `drawLine()` method

You can use the **drawRect() method** and **fillRect() method**, respectively, to draw the outline of a rectangle or to draw a solid, or filled, rectangle. Each of these methods requires four arguments. The first two arguments represent the x- and y-coordinates of the upper-left corner of the rectangle. The last two arguments represent the width and height of the rectangle. For example, the following statement draws a short, wide rectangle that begins at position 20, 100, and is 200 pixels wide by 10 pixels tall:

```
drawRect(20, 100, 200, 10);
```

The **clearRect() method** also requires four arguments and draws a rectangle. The difference between using the `drawRect()` and `fillRect()` methods and the `clearRect()` method is that the first two methods use the current drawing color, whereas the `clearRect()` method draws what appears to be an empty or "clear" rectangle. For example, the `JDemoRectangles` program shown in Figure 10-8 produces the `JApplet` shown in Figure 10-9. First, the `init()` method sets the background color to blue and sets the layout manager. Then, the `paint()` method sets the drawing color to red, draws a filled rectangle in red, and draws a smaller, "clear" rectangle within the boundaries of the filled rectangle.

You can create rectangles with rounded corners when you use the **drawRoundRect() method**. The `drawRoundRect()` method requires six arguments. The first four arguments match the four arguments required to draw a rectangle: the x- and y-coordinates of the upper-left corner, the width, and the height. The two additional arguments represent the arc width and height associated with the rounded corners (an **arc** is a portion of a circle). If you assign zeros to the arc coordinates, the rectangle is not rounded; instead, the corners are square. At the other extreme, if you assign values to the arc coordinates that are at least the width and height of the rectangle, the rectangle is so rounded that it is a circle. The `paint()`

```
import javax.swing.*;
import java.awt.*;
public class JDemoRectangles extends JApplet
{
    Container con = getContentPane();
    public void init()
    {
        con.setBackground(Color.BLUE);
        con.setLayout(new FlowLayout());
    }
    public void paint(Graphics gr)
    {
        super.paint(gr);
        gr.setColor(Color.RED);
        gr.fillRect(20, 20, 120, 120);
        gr.clearRect(49, 40, 50, 50);
    }
}
```

Figure 10-8 The JDemoRectangles JApplet

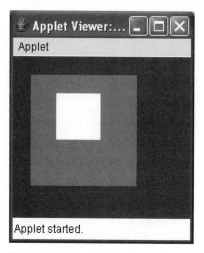

Figure 10-9 Output of the JDemoRectangles JApplet

>> **NOTE** A rectangle created with the clearRect() method is not really "clear"; that is, it is not transparent. When you create a rectangle, you do not see objects that might be hidden behind it.

method in Figure 10-10 draws four rectangles with increasingly large corner arcs. The first rectangle is drawn at coordinates 20, 20, and the horizontal coordinate is increased by 100 for each subsequent rectangle. Each rectangle is the same width and height, but each set of arc values becomes larger, producing rectangles that are not rounded, slightly rounded, very rounded, and completely rounded in sequence. Figure 10-11 shows the program's output. Notice that a rectangle with the same height and width is a square, and a completely rounded square is actually a circle.

```
import javax.swing.*;
import java.awt.*;
public class JDemoRoundRectangles extends JApplet
{
    public void paint(Graphics gr)
    {
        super.paint(gr);
        int x = 20;
        int y = 20;
        int width = 80, height = 80;
        gr.drawRoundRect(x, y, width, height, 0, 0);
        x += 100;
        gr.drawRoundRect(x, y, width, height, 20, 20);
        x += 100;
        gr.drawRoundRect(x, y, width, height, 40, 40);
        x += 100;
        gr.drawRoundRect(x, y, width, height, 80, 80);
    }
}
```

Figure 10-10 The JDemoRoundRectangles JApplet

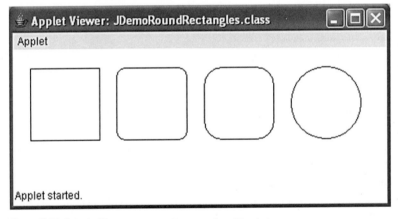

Figure 10-11 Output of the JDemoRoundRectangles JApplet

> **NOTE** As with the fillRect() method, you can use the fillRoundRect() method to create a filled, rounded rectangle. However, as of Java 6.0 (internal version number 1.6), there is no clearRoundRect() method.

DRAWING OVALS

It is possible to draw an oval using the drawRoundRect() or fillRoundRect() methods, but it is usually easier to use the **drawOval()** and **fillOval() methods**. The drawOval() and fillOval() methods both draw ovals using the same four arguments that rectangles use. When you supply drawOval() or fillOval() with x- and y-coordinates for the upper-left corner and width and height measurements, you can picture an imaginary rectangle that uses the four arguments. The oval is then placed within the rectangle so it touches the rectangle at the center of each of the rectangle's sides. For example, suppose you create a `Graphics` object named `tool` and draw a rectangle with:

```
tool.drawRect(50, 50, 100, 60);
```

and then you create an oval with the same coordinates:

```
tool.drawOval(50, 50, 100, 60);
```

The output appears as shown in Figure 10-12, with the oval edges just skimming the rectangle's sides.

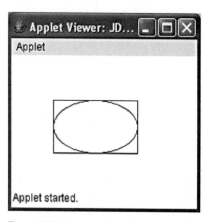

>> **NOTE**
If you draw a rectangle with identical height and width, you draw a square. If you draw an oval with identical height and width, you draw a circle.

Figure 10-12 Demonstration of the `drawOval()` method

DRAWING ARCS

In Java, you can draw an arc using the `Graphics` **drawArc() method**. To use the `drawArc()` method, you provide six arguments:

» The x-coordinate of the upper-left corner of an imaginary rectangle that represents the bounds of the imaginary circle that contains the arc

» The y-coordinate of the same point

» The width of the imaginary rectangle that represents the bounds of the imaginary circle that contains the arc

» The height of the same imaginary rectangle

» The beginning arc position

» The arc angle

Arc positions and angles are measured in degrees; there are 360 degrees in a circle. The zero-degree position for any arc is the three o'clock position, as shown in Figure 10-13. The other 359 degree positions increase as you move counterclockwise around an imaginary circle, so 90 degrees is at the top of the circle in the twelve o'clock position, 180 degrees is opposite the starting position at nine o'clock, and 270 degrees is at the bottom of the circle in the six o'clock position.

The arc angle is the number of degrees over which you want to draw the arc, traveling counterclockwise from the starting position. For example, you can draw a half circle by indicating an arc angle of 180 degrees, or a quarter circle by indicating an arc angle of 90 degrees. If you

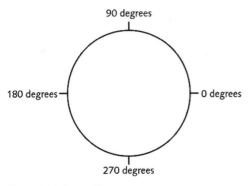

Figure 10-13 Arc positions

want to travel clockwise from the starting position, you express the degrees as a negative number. Just as when you draw a line, when drawing any arc you can take one of two approaches: either start at point A and travel to point B, or start at point B and travel to point A. For example, to create an arc object named halfArc that looks like the top half of a circle, the following statements produce identical results:

```
halfArc.drawArc(x, y, w, h, 0, 180);
halfArc.drawArc(x, y, w, h, 180, -180);
```

The first statement starts an arc at the three o'clock position and travels 180 degrees counter-clockwise to the nine o'clock position. The second statement starts at nine o'clock and travels clockwise to three o'clock.

The **fillArc() method** creates a solid arc. The arc is drawn, and two straight lines are drawn from the arc endpoints to the center of the imaginary circle whose perimeter the arc occupies. For example, the following two statements together produce the output shown in Figure 10-14:

```
solidArc.fillArc(10, 50, 100, 100, 20, 320);
solidArc.fillArc(200, 50, 100, 100, 340, 40);
```

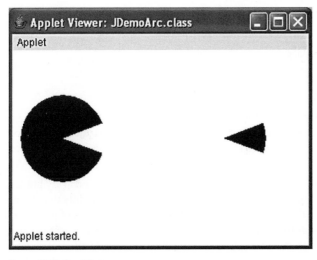

Figure 10-14 Two filled arcs

Each of the two arcs is in a circle that has a size of 100 by 100. The first arc almost completes a full circle, starting at position 20 (near two o'clock) and ending 320 degrees around the circle (at position 340, near four o'clock). The second filled arc more closely resembles a pie slice, starting at position 340 and extending 40 degrees to end at position 20.

CREATING THREE-DIMENSIONAL RECTANGLES

The `draw3DRect()` method is a minor variation on the `drawRect()` method. You use the **`draw3DRect()` method** to draw a rectangle that appears to have "shadowing" on two of its edges—the effect is that of a rectangle that is lit from the upper-left corner and slightly raised or slightly lowered. The `draw3DRect()` method requires a fifth argument in addition to the x- and y-coordinates and width and height required by the `drawRect()` method. The fifth argument is a Boolean value, which is `true` if you want the raised rectangle effect (darker on the right and bottom) and `false` if you want the lowered rectangle effect (darker on the left and top). There is also a **`fill3DRect()` method** for creating filled three-dimensional rectangles. For example, the `JApplet` in Figure 10-15 creates two filled, 3D rectangles in pink. You can see that the effect on the output in Figure 10-16 is very subtle; the shadowing is only one pixel wide.

NOTE The three-dimensional methods work well only with lighter drawing colors.

NOTE In the "You Do It" exercises at the end of this chapter, you will create a 3D rectangle for which the three-dimensional shading is more dramatic.

```
import javax.swing.*;
import java.awt.*;
public class JDemo3DRectangles extends JApplet
{
   public void paint(Graphics gr)
   {
      super.paint(gr);
      int width = 60, height = 80;
      gr.setColor(Color.PINK);
      gr.fill3DRect(20, 20, width, height, true);
      gr.fill3DRect(120, 20, width, height, false);
   }
}
```

Figure 10-15 The `JDemo3DRectangles JApplet`

CREATING POLYGONS

When you want to create a shape that is more complex than a rectangle, you can use a sequence of calls to the `drawLine()` method, or you can use the **`drawPolygon()` method** to draw complex shapes. The `drawPolygon()` method requires three arguments: two integer arrays and a single integer.

The first integer array holds a series of x-coordinate positions, and the second array holds a series of corresponding y-coordinate positions. These positions represent points that are connected to form the polygon. The third integer argument is the number of pairs of points you want to connect. If you don't want to connect all the points represented by the array values, you can assign this third argument integer a value that is smaller than the number of elements

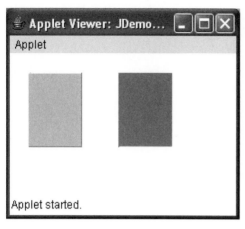

Figure 10-16 Output of the `JDemo3DRectangles` JApplet

in each array. However, an error occurs if the third argument is a value higher than the available number of coordinate pairs.

For example, examine the code shown in Figure 10-17, which is a `JApplet` that has one task—to draw a star-shaped polygon. Two parallel arrays are assigned x- and y-coordinates; the `paint()` method draws the polygon. The program's output appears in Figure 10-18.

```
import javax.swing.*;
import java.awt.*;
public class JStar extends JApplet
{
    public void paint(Graphics gr)
    {
        super.paint(gr);
        int xPoints[]  =  { 42,  52,  72,  52,   60,  40,  15,   28,  9,   32,  42};
        int yPoints[]  =  { 38,  62,  68,  80,  105,  85, 102,   75, 58,   60,  38};
        gr.drawPolygon(xPoints,  yPoints,  xPoints.length);
    }
}
```

Figure 10-17 The `JStar` JApplet

> **NOTE** In Chapter 8, you learned that you can use `length` for the length of an array. Rather than using a constant integer value, such as 11, in the call to `drawPolygon()` in Figure 10-17, it is convenient to use the length of one of the coordinate point arrays, as in `xPoints.length`.

You can use the **`fillPolygon()` method** to draw a solid shape. The major difference between the `drawPolygon()` and `fillPolygon()` methods is that if the beginning and ending points used with the `fillPolygon()` method are not identical, the two endpoints are connected by a straight line before the polygon is filled with color.

Rather than providing the `fillPolygon()` method with three arguments, you can also create a `Polygon` object and pass the constructed object as a single argument to the `fillPolygon()`

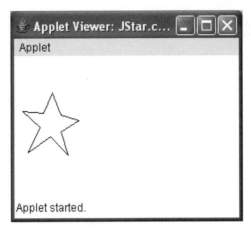

Figure 10-18 Output of the `JStar` `JApplet`

method. The `Polygon` constructor requires an array of x-coordinates, an array of y-coordinates, and a size. For example, you can create a filled polygon using the following statements:

```
Polygon someShape = new Polygon(xPoints, yPoints, xPoints.length);
gr.fillPolygon(someShape);
```

These statements have the same result as the following:

```
gr.fillPolygon(xPoints, yPoints, xPoints.length);
```

In addition, you can instantiate an empty `Polygon` object (with no points) using the following statement:

```
Polygon someFutureShape = new Polygon();
```

You use the **addPoint() method** in statements such as the following to add points to the polygon later:

```
someFutureShape.addPoint(100, 100);
someFutureShape.addPoint(150, 200);
someFutureShape.addPoint(50, 250);
```

It is practical to use `addPoint()` instead of coding the point values when you want to write a program in which you calculate points later in the program or in which the user enters polygon point values. Whether the user does so from the keyboard or with a mouse, you can continue to add points to the polygon indefinitely.

COPYING AN AREA

After you create a graphics image, you might want to create copies of the image. For example, you might want a company logo to appear several times in an applet. Of course, you can redraw the picture, but you can also use the **copyArea() method** to copy any rectangular area to a new location. The `copyArea()` method requires six parameters:

 » The x- and y-coordinates of the upper-left corner of the area to be copied

 » The width and height of the area to be copied

 » The horizontal and vertical displacement of the destination of the copy

For example, the following line of code causes a Graphics object named gr to copy an area 20 pixels wide by 30 pixels tall from the upper-left corner of your JApplet (coordinates 0, 0) to an area that begins 100 pixels to the right and 50 pixels down:

```
gr.copyArea(0, 0, 20, 30, 100, 50);
```

LEARNING MORE ABOUT FONTS AND METHODS YOU CAN USE WITH THEM

As you add more components in your JApplet, positioning becomes increasingly important. In particular, when you draw Strings using different fonts and you do not place the Strings correctly, they overlap and become impossible to read. In addition, even when you define a font such as the following, you have no guarantee that the font will be available on every computer that runs your applet:

```
Font myFont = new Font("TimesRoman", Font.PLAIN, 10);
```

If your user's computer does not have the requested font loaded, Java chooses a default replacement font, so you are never completely certain how your output will look. Fortunately, Java provides many useful methods for obtaining information about the fonts you use.

▶▶ NOTE
The number of available fonts varies greatly among operating systems. The most common default font is Serif.

You can discover the fonts that are available on your system by using the **getAllFonts()** **method**, which is part of the GraphicsEnvironment class defined in the java.awt package. The GraphicsEnvironment class describes the collection of Font objects and GraphicsDevice objects available to a Java application on a particular platform. The getAllFonts() method returns an array of String objects that are the names of available fonts. For example, the following statements declare a GraphicsEnvironment object named ge, and then use the object with the getAvailableFontFamilyNames() method to store the font names in a string array:

```
GraphicsEnvironment ge =
    GraphicsEnvironment.getLocalGraphicsEnvironment();
String[] fontnames = ge.getAvailableFontFamilyNames();
```

Notice in the preceding example that you can't instantiate the GraphicsEnvironment object directly. Instead, you must get a reference object to the current computer environment by calling the static getLocalGraphicsEnvironment() method. Figure 10-19 shows a JApplet that lists all the available font names on the computer on which the applet was executed. After the GraphicsEnvironment object is created and the getAvailableFontFamilyNames() method is used to retrieve the array of font names, the names are displayed on the screen using a for loop in which the horizontal coordinate where each font String is drawn is increased by a fixed value, so that four columns are displayed equally spaced across the JApplet surface. After four columns are displayed, the horizontal coordinate is set back to 10 and the vertical coordinate is increased so that the next four columns are displayed below the previous set of columns. The output for one specific computer is shown in Figure 10-20.

```
import javax.swing.*;
import java.awt.*;
public class JFontList extends JApplet
{
    public void paint(Graphics gr)
    {
        super.paint(gr);
        int i, x, y = 10;
        final int VERTICAL_SPACE = 15;
        final int HORIZONTAL_SPACE = 180;
        GraphicsEnvironment ge =
            GraphicsEnvironment.getLocalGraphicsEnvironment();
        String[] fontnames = ge.getAvailableFontFamilyNames();
        for (i = 0; i < fontnames.length; i += 4)
        {
            x = 10;
            gr.drawString(fontnames[ i], x, y);
            if(i+1 < fontnames.length)
                gr.drawString(fontnames[ i+1], x += HORIZONTAL_SPACE, y);
            if(i+2 < fontnames.length)
                gr.drawString(fontnames[ i+2], x += HORIZONTAL_SPACE, y);
            if(i+3 < fontnames.length)
                gr.drawString(fontnames[ i+3], x += HORIZONTAL_SPACE, y);
            y = y + VERTICAL_SPACE;
        }
    }
}
```

Figure 10-19 The JFontList JApplet

DISCOVERING SCREEN STATISTICS USING THE Toolkit CLASS

Frequently, before you can determine the best Font size to use, it is helpful to know statistics about the screen on which the Font will be displayed. You can discover the resolution and screen size on your system by using the getScreenResolution() and getScreenSize() methods, which are part of the Toolkit class.

The **getDefaultToolkit() method** provides information about the system in use. The **getScreenResolution() method** returns the number of pixels as an integer. You can create a Toolkit object and get the screen resolution using the following code:

```
Toolkit tk = Toolkit.getDefaultToolkit();
int resolution = tk.getScreenResolution();
```

The Dimension class is useful for representing the width and height of a user interface component, such as a JApplet or a JButton. The Dimension class has three constructors:

» The Dimension() method creates an instance of Dimension with a width of zero and a height of zero.

» Dimension(Dimension d) creates an instance of Dimension whose width and height are the same as for the specified dimension.

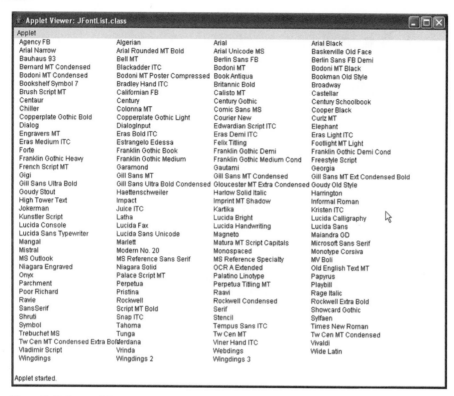

Figure 10-20 Output of the JFontList JApplet

» Dimension(int width, int height) constructs a Dimension and initializes it to the specified width and height.

The **getScreenSize() method**, a member of the Toolkit object, returns an object of type Dimension, which specifies the width and height of the screen in pixels. Knowing the number of pixels for the width and height of your display is useful to set the coordinates for the position, width, and height of a window. For example, the following code stores the width and height of a screen in separate variables:

```
Toolkit tk = Toolkit.getDefaultToolkit();
Dimension screen = tk.getScreenSize();
int width = screen.width;
int height = screen.height;
```

DISCOVERING FONT STATISTICS

Typesetters and desktop publishers measure the height of every font in three parts: leading, ascent, and descent. **Leading** is the amount of space between baselines. **Ascent** is the height of an uppercase character from a baseline to the top of the character. **Descent** measures the part of characters that "hang below" the baseline, such as the tails on the lowercase letters g and j. The **height of a font** is the sum of the leading, ascent, and descent. Figure 10-21 shows each of these measurements.

Leading is pro-
nounced "ledding."

Figure 10-21 Parts of a font's height

You can discover a font's height by first using the Graphics class **getFontMetrics() method** to return a FontMetrics object, and then by using one of the following FontMetrics class methods with the object to return one of a Font's statistics:

» public int getLeading()

» public int getAscent()

» public int getDescent()

» public int getHeight()

>> **NOTE** Another method, getLineMetrics(), is available in Java 5.0 and later versions. It is more complicated to use, but returns similar font statistics. For more details, see *http://java.sun.com*.

Each of these methods returns an integer value representing the font size in points (one point measures 1/72 of an inch) of the requested portion of the Font object. For example, if you define a Font object named myFont and a Graphics object named paintBrush, you can set the current font for the Graphics object by using the following statements:

```
paintBrush.setFont(myFont);
int heightOfFont = paintBrush.getFontMetrics().getHeight();
```

Then, the heightOfFont variable holds the total height of myFont characters.

>> **NOTE** Notice the object-dot-method-dot-method construction of the getHeight() statement. You can also write two statements if that approach is clearer to you. The first statement declares a FontMetrics object:

```
FontMetrics fmObject = paintBrush.getFontMetrics();
```

The second statement assigns a value to heightOfFont:

```
int heightOfFont = fmObject.getHeight();
```

When you define a Font object, you use point size. However, when you use the FontMetrics get methods, the sizes are returned in pixels.

A practical use for discovering the height of a font is to space Strings correctly as you display them. For example, instead of placing every String in a series vertically equidistant from the previous String with a statement such as:

```
pen.drawString("Some string", x, y += INCREASE);
```

(where INCREASE is always the same), you can make the actual increase in the vertical position dependent on the font. If you code the following, you are assured that each String has enough room, and appears regardless of which font is currently in use by the Graphics pen object:

```
pen.drawString("Some string",
    x,  y += pen.getFontMetrics().getHeight());
```

When you create a String, you know how many characters are in the String. However, you cannot be certain which font Java will use or substitute, and because fonts have different measurements, it is difficult to know the exact width of the String in a JApplet. Fortunately, the FontMetrics class contains a **stringWidth() method** that returns the integer width of a String. As an argument, the stringWidth() method requires the name of a String. For example, if you create a String named myString, you can retrieve the width of myString with the following code:

```
int width = gr.getFontMetrics().stringWidth(myString);
```

DRAWING WITH JAVA 2D GRAPHICS

Drawing operations earlier in this chapter were called using a Graphics object—either an automatically generated one that was passed to the paint() method or one the programmer instantiated. In addition, you can call drawing operations using a Graphics2D object. The advantage of using Java 2D is the higher-quality, two-dimensional (2D) graphics, images, and text it provides. The 2D classes don't replace the existing java.awt classes; you can still use the other classes and applications that use them.

> **NOTE**
> This book cannot cover all of the Graphics2D capabilities. For more information, visit *http://java.sun. com.*

Features of some of the 2D classes include:

» Fill patterns, such as gradients
» Strokes that define the width and style of a drawing stroke
» Anti-aliasing, a graphics technique for producing smoother screen graphics

Graphics2D is found in the java.awt package. A Graphics2D object is produced by casting, or converting and promoting, a Graphics object. For example, in a paint() method that automatically receives a Graphics object, you can cast the object to a Graphics2D object using the following code:

```
public void paint(Graphics pen)
{
    Graphics2D newpen = (Graphics2D)pen;
```

The process of drawing with Java 2D objects includes:

» Specifying the rendering attributes
» Setting a drawing stroke
» Creating objects to draw

SPECIFYING THE RENDERING ATTRIBUTES

The first step in drawing a 2D object is to specify how a drawn object is rendered. Whereas drawings that are not 2D can only use the attribute Color, with 2D you can designate other attributes, such as line width and fill patterns. You specify 2D colors by using the setColor() method, which works like the Graphics method of the same name. Using a Graphics2D object, you can set the color to black using the following code:

```
gr2D.setColor(Color.BLACK);
```

Fill patterns control how a drawing object is filled in. In addition to using a solid color, 2D fill patterns can be a gradient fill, a texture, or even a pattern that you devise. A fill pattern is created by using the setPaint() method of Graphics2D with a fill pattern object as the only argument. Classes from which you can construct a fill pattern include `Color`, `TexturePaint`, and `GradientPaint`.

A **gradient fill** is a gradual shift from one color at one coordinate point to a different color at a second coordinate point. If the color shift occurs once between the points—for example, slowly changing from yellow to red—you are using an **acyclic gradient**, one that does not cycle between the colors. If the shift occurs repeatedly, such as from yellow to red and back to yellow again, you are using a **cyclic gradient**, one that does cycle between the colors.

Figure 10-22 shows a `JApplet` that demonstrates acyclic and cyclic gradient fills. The first highlighted `setPaint()` method call sets a gradient that begins at coordinates 10, 20 in `LIGHT_GRAY` and ends at coordinates 180, 100 in `DARK_GRAY`. The last argument to the `GradientPaint()` constructor is `false`, indicating an acyclic gradient. After the `Graphics2D` object's paint is applied, a filled rectangle is drawn over the same area. These statements produce the rectangle on the left in Figure 10-23 that gradually shifts from light gray to dark gray,

```java
import javax.swing.*;
import java.awt.*;
import java.awt.geom.*;
public class JGradient extends JApplet
{
    public void paint(Graphics gr)
    {
        super.paint(gr);
        int x = 10, y = 20, x2 = 180, y2 = 100;
        Graphics2D gr2D = (Graphics2D)gr;
        gr2D.setPaint(new GradientPaint(x, y, Color.LIGHT_GRAY,
            x2, y2, Color.DARK_GRAY, false));
        gr2D.fill(new Rectangle2D.Double(x, y, x2, y2));
        x = 210;
        gr2D.setPaint(new GradientPaint(x, y, Color.LIGHT_GRAY,
            x2, y2, Color.DARK_GRAY, true));
        gr2D.fill(new Rectangle2D.Double(x, y, x2, y2));
    }
}
```

Figure 10-22 The `JGradient` JApplet

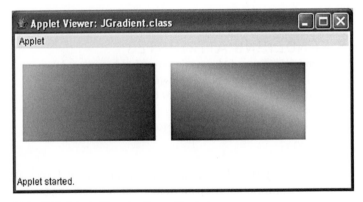

Figure 10-23 Output of the `JGradient` JApplet

moving down and to the right. The second highlighted `setPaint()` statement in Figure 10-22 establishes a new gradient beginning farther to the right. In this statement, the final argument to `GradientPaint()` is `true`, creating a cyclic gradient. As you can see on the right side in Figure 10-23, this rectangle's shading changes gradually across its surface.

> **» NOTE** Later in this chapter, you will learn about the `Rectangle2D.Double` class used to create the rectangles in this `JApplet`.

SETTING A DRAWING STROKE

All lines in non-2D graphics operations are drawn as solid, with square ends and a line width of one pixel. With the 2D methods, the drawing line is a **stroke**, which represents a single movement as if you were using a drawing tool, such as a pen or a pencil. In Java 2D, you can change a stroke's width using the **setStroke() method**. `Stroke` is actually an interface; the class that defines line types and implements the `Stroke` interface is named **BasicStroke**. A `BasicStroke` constructor takes three arguments:

» A `float` value representing the line width
» An `int` value determining the type of cap decoration at the end of a line
» An `int` value determining the style of juncture between two line segments

`BasicStroke` class variables determine the endcap and juncture style arguments. **Endcap styles** apply to the ends of lines that do not join with other lines, and include `CAP_BUTT`, `CAP_ROUND`, and `CAP_SQUARE`. **Juncture styles**, for lines that join, include `JOIN_MITER`, `JOIN_ROUND`, and `JOIN_BEVEL`.

The following statements create a `BasicStroke` object and make it the current stroke:

```
BasicStroke aLine = new BasicStroke(1.0f,
    BasicStroke.CAP_ROUND, BasicStroke.JOIN_ROUND);
```

Figure 10-24 shows a `JApplet` that draws a rectangle using a very wide stroke. The highlighted statement sets the `BasicStroke` width to 15 pixels using round endcap and juncture parameters. Figure 10-25 shows the drawn rectangle.

> **» NOTE** In Chapter 2, you learned that a constant value such as 1.0 is a `double` by default. You place an "f" after a floating-point constant to indicate that it is a `float` rather than a `double`.

```
import javax.swing.*;
import java.awt.*;
import java.awt.geom.*;
public class JStroke extends JApplet
{
    public void paint(Graphics gr)
    {
        super.paint(gr);
        Graphics2D gr2D = (Graphics2D)gr;
        BasicStroke aStroke = new BasicStroke(15.0f,
            BasicStroke.CAP_ROUND, BasicStroke.JOIN_ROUND);
        gr2D.setStroke(aStroke);
        gr2D.draw(new Rectangle2D.Double(10, 20, 100, 100));
    }
}
```

Figure 10-24 The `JStroke` JApplet

Figure 10-25 Output of the JStroke JApplet

CREATING OBJECTS TO DRAW

After you have created a Graphics2D object and specified the rendering attributes, you can create different objects to draw. Objects that are drawn in Java 2D are first created by defining them as geometric shapes using the java.awt.geom package classes. You can define the shape of lines, rectangles, ovals, and arcs; after you define the shape, you use it as an argument to the draw() or fill() methods. The Graphics2D class does not have different methods for each shape you can draw.

LINES

Lines are created using the Line2D.Float class or the Line2D.Double class. Both of these classes have a constructor that takes four arguments. The arguments are the x- and y-coordinates of the two endpoints of the line. For example, to create a line from the endpoint (60, 5) to the endpoint (13, 28), you could write the following:

```
Line2D.Float line = new Line2D.Float(60F, 5F, 13F, 28F);
```

It is also possible to create lines based on points. You can use the Point2D.Float or Point2D.Double class to create points that have both an x- and y-coordinate. For example, you could create two Point2D.Float points using the following code:

```
Point2D.Float pos1 = new Point2D.Float(60, 5);
Point2D.Float pos2 = new Point2D.Float(13, 28);
```

Then, the code to create a line might be:

```
Line2D.Float line = new Line2D.Float (pos1, pos2);
```

RECTANGLES

You can create rectangles by using a Rectangle2D.Float or a Rectangle2D.Double class. As with the Line and Point classes, these two classes are distinguished by the type of arguments used in their constructors—float or double. Rectangle2D.Float and Rectangle2D.Double can each be created using four arguments representing the x-coordinate, y-coordinate, width, and height. For example, the code to create a Rectangle2D.Float object named rect at (10, 10) with a width of 50 and height of 40 is:

```
Rectangle2D.Float rect = new Rectangle2D.Float(10F, 10F, 50F, 40F);
```

OVALS

You can create `Oval` objects with the `Ellipse2D.Float` or `Ellipse2D.Double` class. The `Ellipse2D.Float` constructor requires four arguments representing the x-coordinate, y-coordinate, width, and height. The code to create an `Ellipse2D.Float` object named `ell` at (10, 73) with a width of 40 and height of 20 is:

```
Ellipse2D.Float ell = new Ellipse2D.Float(10F, 73F, 40F, 20F);
```

ARCS

You can create arcs with the `Arc2D.Float` or `Arc2D.Double` class. The `Arc2D.Float` constructor takes seven arguments. The first four arguments represent the x-coordinate, y-coordinate, width, and height that apply to the ellipse of which the arc is a part. The remaining three arguments are as follows:

» The starting position of the arc

» The number of degrees it travels

» An integer indicating how it is closed

The starting position is expressed in degrees, like the `Graphics` class `drawArc()` method; for example, 0 is the three o'clock position. The number of degrees traveled by the arc is specified in a counterclockwise direction using positive numbers. The final argument uses one of the three class fields:

» `Arc2D.PIE` connects the arc to the center of an ellipse and looks like a pie slice.

» **`Arc2D.CHORD`** connects the arc's endpoints with a straight line.

» `Arc2D.OPEN` is an unclosed arc.

To create an `Arc2D.Float` object named `ac` at (10, 133) with a width of 30 and height of 33, a starting degree of 30, 120 degrees traveled, and using the class variable `Arc2D.PIE`, you use the following statement:

```
Arc2D.Float ac = new Arc2D.Float(10,133,30,33,30,120,Arc2D.PIE);
```

POLYGONS

You create a `Polygon` object by defining movements from one point to another. The movement that creates a polygon is a `GeneralPath` object; the `GeneralPath` class is found in the `java.awt.geom` package.

» The statement `GeneralPath pol = new GeneralPath();` creates a `GeneralPath` object named `pol`.

» The `moveTo()` method of `GeneralPath` is used to create the beginning point of the polygon. Thus, the statement `pol.moveTo(10F, 193F);` starts the polygon named `pol` at the coordinates (10, 193).

» The `lineTo()` method is used to create a line that ends at a new point. The statement `pol.lineTo(25F,183F);` creates a second point using the arguments of 25 and 183 as the x- and y-coordinates of the new point.

» The statement `pol.lineTo(100F, 223F);` creates a third point. The `lineTo()` method can be used to connect the current point to the original point. Alternatively, you can use the `closePath()` method without any arguments.

ADDING SOUND, IMAGES, AND SIMPLE ANIMATION TO JApplets

Java 2D supports sound using methods from the `Applet` class (rather than `JApplet`). You can use these methods to retrieve and play sound files that use various sound formats. These formats include the Windows Wave file format (.wav), Sun Audio file format (.au), and Music and Instrument Digital Interface file format (.midi or .mid).

The simplest way to retrieve and play a sound is to use the `play()` method of the `Applet` class. The **play() method** retrieves and plays the sound as soon as possible after it is called. The `play()` method takes one of two forms:

» `play()` with one argument—The argument is a Uniform Resource Locator (URL) object that loads and plays an audio clip when both the URL object and the audio clip are stored at the same URL.

» `play()` with two arguments—The first argument is a URL object, and the second argument is a folder path name, which loads and plays the audio file. The first argument is often a call to a `getCodeBase()` method or `getDocumentBase()` method to retrieve the URL object; the second argument is the name of the audio clip within the folder path that is stored at that URL.

> **>> NOTE** The `<object>` tag was introduced in Chapter 9 to run an applet from within an HTML document using the attributes `code`, `height`, and `width`. The `getCodeBase()` and `getDocumentBase()` methods are `Applet` methods. By using these methods when loading sound or images, you make it possible for the applet to work even if you move it to another Web server.

Used with the `codebase` attribute, which indicates the filename of the applet's main class file, the `getCodeBase()` and `getDocumentBase()` methods direct the browser to look in a different folder for the applet and other files it uses. This is necessary when the desired files are in a different location than the Web page containing the applet. By calling `getCodeBase()` in an applet, you get a URL object that represents the folder in which the applet's class file is stored. For example, the following statement retrieves and plays the event.au sound file, which is stored in the same place as the applet:

```
play(getCodeBase(), "event.au");
```

> **>> NOTE** The `getDocumentBase()` method returns an absolute URL naming the directory of the document in which the applet is stored. It is sometimes used instead of `getCodeBase()` as a matter of preference. An applet is restricted to reading files only from the server that hosts it.

To play a sound more than once, or to start or stop the sound, you must load the sound into an `AudioClip` object using the applet's `newAudioClip()` method. `AudioClip` is part of the `java.awt.Applet` class and must be imported into your program. Like the `play()` method, the `getAudioClip()` method can take one or two arguments. The first argument (or only argument, if there is only one) is a URL argument that identifies the sound file; the second argument is a folder path reference needed for locating the file.

The following statement loads the sound file from the previous example into the clip object:

```
AudioClip aClip = newAudioClip(getCodeBase(), "audio/event.au");
```

Here, the sound file reference indicates that the event.au sound file is in the audio folder. After you have created an `AudioClip` object, you can use the `play()` method to call and play the sound, the `stop()` method to halt the playback, and the `loop()` method to play the sound repeatedly.

> **NOTE** Multiple AudioClip items can play at the same time, and the resulting sound is mixed together to produce a composite.

ADDING IMAGES

An **image** is a likeness of a person or thing. Images abound on the Internet in all shapes, colors, and sizes. Image formats supported by Java include:

» Graphics Interchange Format (GIF), which can contain a maximum of 256 different colors

» Joint Photographic Experts Group (JPEG), which is commonly used to store photographs, and is a more sophisticated way to represent a color image

» Portable Network Graphics (PNG), which is more flexible than the GIF format and stores images in a lossless form. (PNG was originally designed to be a portable image storage form for computer-originated images.)

> **NOTE** **Lossless data compression** is a set of rules that allows an exact replica of data to be reconstructed from a compressed version. If you have ever worked with a .zip file, you have worked with lossless data compression.

The Image class provides many of Java's image capabilities; this class loads images that have been stored in one of the allowed Image formats. The Image class, which you can find in the java.awt package, is an abstract class. An **abstract** class is one from which you cannot create any objects but which you can use as an interface or from which you can inherit. Because Image is abstract, you must create Image objects indirectly using the getImage() method.

> **NOTE** You will learn about abstract classes in detail in Chapter 12.

To declare an Image with the name eventLogo, you use the declaration Image eventLogo;. The getImage() method is used to load an Image into the named Image in the applet. Like the AudioClip method used for loading sound, one version of the getImage() method can take up to two arguments—a location where the image is stored and its filename. For example, you can create and load the Image named eventLogo with a statement such as the following:

```
eventLogo = getImage(getCodeBase(),"event.gif");
```

You can use the applet paint() method to display Image object images. The drawImage() method is a Graphics method that uses the following four arguments:

» The first argument is a reference to the Image object in which the image is stored.
» The second argument is the x-coordinate where the image appears on the applet.
» The third argument is the y-coordinate where the image appears on the applet.
» The fourth argument is a reference to an ImageObserver object.

An ImageObserver object can be any object that implements the ImageObserver interface. Because the Component class implements the ImageObserver interface, all Components, including JApplets, inherit this implementation. Usually, the ImageObserver object is the object on which the image appears—in this case, the JApplet. Recall from Chapter 4 that the this reference refers to the current object using a method. Frequently, with the drawImage() method, you use the this reference to indicate that you want the Image drawn on the current JApplet. For example, the code to display the eventLogo image in the upper-left corner of the JApplet is as follows:

```
g.drawImage(eventLogo, 0, 0, this);
```

You can use an overloaded version of the Graphics method drawImage() to output a scaled image. This method takes six arguments. Notice that the first three arguments are the same as those for the four-argument version of the drawImage() method. In the overloaded version:

» The first argument is a reference to the Image object in which the image is stored.

» The second argument is the x-coordinate where the image appears on the applet.

» The third argument is the y-coordinate where the image appears on the applet.

» The fourth argument is the width of the scaled object.

» The fifth argument is the height of the scaled object.

» The sixth argument uses the this reference to implement the ImageObserver object.

For example, the following code displays the eventLogo image at coordinates 0, 120, using the full width of the JApplet, but 100 pixels less than the height:

```
g.drawImage(eventLogo, 0, 120, getWidth(), getHeight() -100, this);
```

» NOTE In the preceding drawImage() method call, you could write this.getWidth() and this.getHeight() to achieve the same results. The this reference is to the current JApplet.

Figure 10-26 shows a JApplet that draws an image three times. The JEventImage JApplet uses an image file named event.gif, which holds a logo that is originally 300 pixels wide by 40 pixels high. Within the paint() method in the JApplet, the image is drawn first in its "natural," or original, size in the upper-left corner. Then, it is redrawn 50 pixels lower, using a size of 600 by 80—twice its original size. Finally, it is drawn again at location 0, 120 to be 100 pixels narrower than the JApplet and 120 pixels shorter. The output of the JEventImage applet is shown in Figure 10-27.

```
import java.awt.*;
import java.applet.*;
import javax.swing.*;
public class JEventImage extends JApplet
{
    Image eventLogo;
    public void init()
    {
        eventLogo = getImage(getCodeBase(), "event.gif");
    }
    public void paint(Graphics g)
    {
        super.paint(g);
        // Draw image at its natural size 300 X 40
        g.drawImage(eventLogo, 0, 0, this);
        // Draw the image scaled - twice as large
        g.drawImage(eventLogo, 0, 50, 600, 80, this);
        // Draw the image 100 pixels narrower than the JApplet
        //      and 120 pixels shorter
        g.drawImage(eventLogo, 0, 120, (getWidth() - 100),
            (getHeight() - 120), this);
    }
}
```

Figure 10-26 The JEventImage JApplet

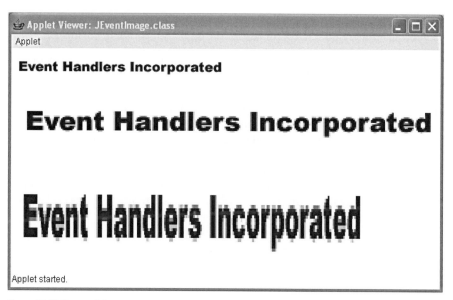

Figure 10-27 Output of the JEventImage JApplet

> **»NOTE** In Figure 10-27, notice that the Image contains whitespace surrounding the letters; for example, the letters in the third displayed image are not 120 pixels shorter than the JApplet, but the entire Image is, including the whitespace above and below the letters. If you want, you can examine the original event.gif file in the Chapter.10 folder on your Student Disk.

USING ImageIcons

You can also use the ImageIcon class to create images in your applications and applets. In general, working with the ImageIcon class is simpler than working with Image. You can use all the Image methods with an ImageIcon, plus many additional methods. Unlike the Image class, you can create ImageIcon objects directly. Also, unlike Images, you can place an ImageIcon on a Component, such as a JPanel, JLabel, or JButton. For example, the following statements create a JButton that contains a picture of an arrow:

```
ImageIcon arrowPicture = new ImageIcon("arrow.gif");
JButton arrowButton = new JButton(arrowPicture);
```

> **»NOTE** Behind the scenes, each ImageIcon object uses an Image object to hold the image data and a MediaTracker object to keep track of the image's loading status. As you are aware if you have visited many Web pages, some images can require a good deal of time to load. To improve performance, the Image get() methods return immediately while the image continues to load, so that your application does not have to wait before performing other operations.

You can also use the paintIcon() method to display ImageIcon images. This method requires four arguments:

» The first argument is a reference to the Component on which the image appears—this in the following example.

» The second argument is a reference to the Graphics object used to render the image—g in the following example.

» The third argument is the x-coordinate for the upper-left corner of the image.

» The fourth argument is the y-coordinate for the upper-left corner of the image.

The code to display the arrowPicture ImageIcon using the paintIcon() method is:

```
arrowPicture.paintIcon(this, g, 180, 0);
```

You can retrieve an ImageIcon's width and height with methods named getIconWidth() and getIconHeight(); each returns an integer. Figure 10-28 shows an example of how you can manipulate an ImageIcon's width and height to achieve display effects. In the JBear JApplet, an ImageIcon is created using a .gif file. In the init() method, the width and height of the ImageIcon are stored in variables named width and height. In the actionPerformed() method, the width and height of the image are doubled with every button click. Figure 10-29 shows the JApplet when it starts, after the user has clicked the button once, and after the user has clicked the button twice.

```
import java.awt.*;
import java.awt.event.*;
import javax.swing.*;
public class JBear extends JApplet implements ActionListener
{
    private ImageIcon image = new ImageIcon("bear.gif");
    private JButton closerButton = new JButton("Oh my!");
    private int width, height;
    Container con = getContentPane();
    public void init()
    {
        con.setLayout(new FlowLayout());
        closerButton.addActionListener(this);
        con.add(closerButton);
        width = image.getIconWidth();
        height = image.getIconHeight();
    }
    public void actionPerformed(ActionEvent event)
    {
        width = width * 2;
        height = height * 2;
        repaint();
    }
    public void paint(Graphics g)
    {
        super.paint(g);
        g.drawImage(image.getImage(), 0, 0, width, height, this);

    }
}
```

Figure 10-28 The JBear JApplet

» NOTE If you eliminate the call to super.paint() as the first statement in the paint() method in Figure 10-28, the previous bear image remains on the screen "behind" the newer, larger one.

Figure 10-29 Output of the `JBear` `JApplet`

In the `paint()` method in the `JBear` `JApplet`, notice that the `drawImage()` method uses the `getImage()` method with the image in the following statement:

```
g.drawImage(image.getImage(), 0, 0, width, height, this);
```

An `ImageIcon` cannot be drawn to scale, but an `Image` can, so you use the `getImage()` method to return a scalable `Image` reference.

YOU DO IT

UNDERSTANDING THE `paint()` AND `repaint()` METHODS

In the next steps, you will create a `JApplet` that helps you observe when various `JApplet` methods execute.

To demonstrate how the `paint()` and `repaint()` methods operate:

1. Open a new text file in your text editor.

2. Type the following first few lines of a `JApplet` named `JDemoPaint`:

```
import javax.swing.*;
import java.awt.*;
import java.awt.event.*;
public class JDemoPaint extends JApplet
   implements ActionListener
{
```

3. The only component in this applet is a `JButton` that you can create by typing the following code on the next line:

```
JButton pressButton = new JButton("Press");
```

4. Type the following init() method, which initializes a Container named con, sets the con layout to FlowLayout, and adds pressButton to con:

```
public void init()
{
    Container con = getContentPane();
    con.setLayout(new FlowLayout());
    con.add(pressButton);
    pressButton.addActionListener(this);
}
```

5. Override the paint() method by typing the following code, so it displays a message on the screen every time it executes:

```
public void paint(Graphics g)
{
    super.paint(g);
    System.out.println("in paint method");
}
```

6. Call the repaint() method when the user clicks the JButton by typing the following:

```
public void actionPerformed(ActionEvent e)
{
    Object source = e.getSource();
    if(source == pressButton)
    {
        repaint();
    }
}
```

7. Add the closing curly brace for the class, and then save the file as **JDemoPaint.java** in the Chapter.10 folder on your Student Disk. Compile the JApplet using the **javac JDemoPaint.java** command.

8. Open a new text file and then create the following HTML document to host the JApplet:

```
<html>
<object code = "JDemoPaint.class" width = 100 height = 100>
</object>
</html>
```

9. Save the file as **TestJDemoPaint.html** in the Chapter.10 folder on your Student Disk, and then type **appletviewer TestJDemoPaint.html** at the command prompt to run the JApplet using the file. Be certain you can view the command line and the JApplet on your screen. When the JApplet starts, the paint() method executes automatically, so the message "in paint method" appears on the command line. Click the **pressButton** in the JApplet. The actionPerformed() method calls the repaint() method, and the repaint() method calls the update() method, which then calls the paint() method, so a second message appears on the command line. Minimize the Applet Viewer window and then restore it. Reduce the size of the window by dragging its border. With each action, an "in paint method" message appears on the command line, demonstrating all the conditions under which the paint() method executes.

10. Close the Applet Viewer window.

USING THE drawString() METHOD

In the next steps, you will write a JApplet that uses the drawString() method.

To use the drawString() method to place a String within a JApplet:

1. Open a new text file and begin a class definition for a JDemoGraphics class by typing the following:

```
import javax.swing.*;
import java.awt.*;
import java.awt.event.*;
public class JDemoGraphics extends JApplet
{
```

2. Declare a String to hold the company name for Event Handlers Incorporated by typing the following:

```
String companyName = new String("Event Handlers Incorporated");
```

3. Type the following paint() method that calls the super() method and uses a Graphics object to draw the companyName String. Then, add the closing curly brace for the class:

```
    public void paint(Graphics gr)
    {
        super.paint(gr);
        gr.drawString(companyName, 10, 100);
    }
}
```

4. Save the file as **JDemoGraphics.java** in the Chapter.10 folder on your Student Disk, and then compile at the command prompt using the **javac** command.

5. Open a new text file and create the following HTML document for the JDemoGraphics class:

```
<html>
<object code = "JDemoGraphics.class" width = 420 height = 300>
</object>
</html>
```

6. Save the file as **TestJDemoGraphics.html** in the Chapter.10 folder on your Student Disk, and use the **appletviewer TestJDemoGraphics.html** command to run the program. The program's output appears in Figure 10-30.

7. Close the Applet Viewer window.

USING FONTS AND COLORS

Next, you will use your knowledge of fonts and colors to set the color and font style of a JApplet.

To add a Font and Color to your JDemoGraphics class:

1. Open the **JDemoGraphics.java** text file in your text editor and rename the class **JDemoGraphics2**.

2. Just after the companyName declaration, add a Font object by typing the following:

```
Font bigFont = new Font("Helvetica", Font.ITALIC, 24);
```

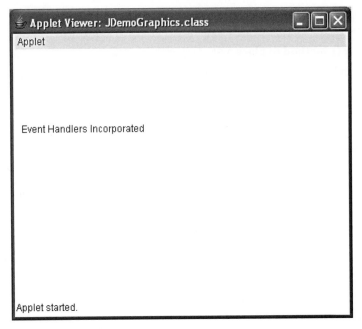

Figure 10-30 Output of the JDemoGraphics JApplet

3. For the first two statements in the paint() method after the opening curly brace, type the following statements so the gr object uses the bigFont object and the color magenta:

```
gr.setFont(bigFont);
gr.setColor(Color.MAGENTA);
```

4. Following the existing drawString() method call, type the following lines to change the color and add another call to the drawString() method:

```
gr.setColor(Color.BLUE);
gr.drawString(companyName, 40, 140);
```

5. Save the file as **JDemoGraphics2.java** in the Chapter.10 folder on your Student Disk, and compile at the command prompt using the **javac** command. Modify the **TestJDemoGraphics.html** document for use with the JDemoGraphics2 applet, and then save it as **TestJDemoGraphics2.html**. Use the **appletviewer TestJDemoGraphics2.html** command to run the program. The program's output appears in Figure 10-31. Although the figure is shown in black and white in this book, notice that the Strings on your screen display as magenta and blue text.

> **» NOTE** The fonts that appear in your JApplet might be different, depending on your computer's installed fonts. You can view a list of available fonts on your computer by executing an applet similar to the JFontList applet shown in Figure 10-19.

6. Close the Applet Viewer window.

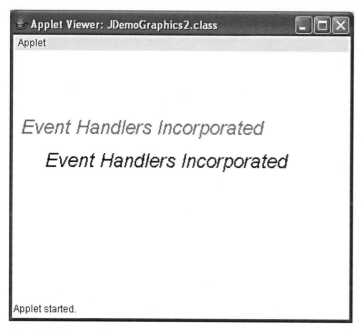

Figure 10-31 Output of the `JDemoGraphics2` JApplet

WORKING WITH COLOR

Next, you will use the methods for getting and setting colors to display several hundred colors in a `JApplet`.

To create a demonstration program that displays several hundred colors:

1. Open a new text file in your text editor.

2. Type the following `import` statements, a class header for a `JDemoColor` program, and the opening curly brace:

```
import javax.swing.*;
import java.awt.*;
public class JDemoColor extends JApplet
{
```

3. Define a small font by typing the following code:

```
Font littleFont = new Font("Helvetica", Font.ITALIC, 6);
```

4. Add the following `paint()` method with five integer variables—r, g, b, x, and y:

```
public void paint(Graphics gr)
{
    super.paint(gr);
    int r, g, b;
    int x = 0, y = 0;
```

5. Set the `Graphics` object font by typing:

```
gr.setFont(littleFont);
```

6. Declare constants to hold the number of characters displayed horizontally and the height of the gap between horizontal rows:

```
final int CHARS_PER_LINE = 400;
final int VERT_GAP = 10;
```

7. Create a `for` loop in which the red component varies from 255 down to 0 in decrements of 20. Within the red `for` loop, vary the intensity of green, and within the green `for` loop, vary the intensity of blue. Although you won't get every possible combination of components, you get a wide variety:

```
final int HIGH = 255;
final int DECREMENT = 20;
for(r = HIGH; r >= 0; r -= DECREMENT)
    for(g = HIGH; g >= 0; g -= DECREMENT)
        for(b = HIGH; b >= 0; b -= DECREMENT)
        {
```

8. Within the body of the innermost `for` loop, create a new color, set the color, and draw an X. After the X is drawn, increase the x-axis coordinate by 5. When the value of x approaches the horizontal limit of the `JApplet`—that is, when it passes 400 or so—increase y and reset x to 0. To accomplish this processing, type the following code:

```
Color variety = new Color(r, g, b);
gr.setColor(variety);
gr.drawString("X", x, y);
x += 5;
if (x >= CHARS_PER_LINE)
{
    x = 0;
    y += VERT_GAP;
}//end if
}//end for
}//end paint()
}//end JDemoColor class
```

9. Save the file as **JDemoColor.java** in the Chapter.10 folder on your Student Disk, and then compile at the command prompt using the **javac** command. Modify the **TestJDemoGraphics2.html** document for use with the `JDemoColor` class and save it as **TestJDemoColor.html**. When you run the `JApplet`, you should see it filled with hundreds of small Xs in many different colors.

10. Close the Applet Viewer window.

CREATING YOUR OWN Graphics OBJECT

Next, you will create a `Graphics` object named pen and use the object to draw a `String` on the screen. The text of the `String` will appear to move each time a `JButton` is clicked.

To write a JApplet in which you create your own Graphics object:

1. Open a new text file in your text editor, and type the following `import` statements for the `JApplet`:

```
import javax.swing.*;
import java.awt.*;
import java.awt.event.*;
```

2. Start typing the following JApplet that uses the mouse and defines a String, a JButton, a Font, and three integers—two to hold x- and y-coordinates and one to act as a constant size to measure the gap between lines displayed on the screen:

```
public class JDemoCreateGraphicsObject extends JApplet
  implements ActionListener
{
    String companyName = new String("Event Handlers Incorporated");
    JButton moveButton = new JButton("Move It");
    Font helv12Font = new Font("Helvetica", Font.ITALIC, 12);
    int x = 10, y = 50;
    final int GAP = 20;
```

3. Type the following init() method, which changes the background color and sets the layout of the Container, adds the JButton, and prepares the JApplet to listen for JButton events:

```
public void init()
{
    Container con = getContentPane();
    con.setBackground(Color.YELLOW);
    con.setLayout(new FlowLayout() );
    con.add(moveButton);
    moveButton.addActionListener(this);
}
```

4. Within the actionPerformed() method, you can create a Graphics object and use it to draw the String on the screen. Each time a user clicks the JButton, the x- and y-coordinates both increase, so a copy of the company name appears slightly below and to the right of the previous company name. Type the following code to accomplish this processing:

```
public void actionPerformed(ActionEvent e)
{
    Object source = e.getSource();
    if (source == moveButton)
    {
        Graphics pen = getGraphics();
        pen.setFont(helv12Font);
        pen.setColor(Color.MAGENTA);
        pen.drawString(companyName, x += GAP, y += GAP);
    }//end if
}//end actionPerformed()
}//end JDemoCreateGraphicsObject class
```

5. Save the file as **JDemoCreateGraphicsObject.java** in the Chapter.10 folder on your Student Disk, and then compile at the command prompt using the **javac** command.

6. Modify the **TestJDemoGraphics2.html** document for use with the JDemoCreateGraphicsObject class, and save it as **TestJDemoCreateGraphicsObject.html** in the Chapter.10 folder on your Student Disk. Use the **appletviewer TestJDemoCreateGraphicsObject.html** command to run the program. Click the **moveButton** several times to see the String message appear and move on the screen.

7. When you finish clicking the moveButton, close the Applet Viewer window.

EXAMINING SCREEN COORDINATES

If you run JDemoCreateGraphicsObject and click the JButton enough times, the "Event Handlers Incorporated" String appears to march off the bottom of the JApplet. Every time you click the JButton, the x- and y-coordinates used by drawString() increase. You can prevent this error by checking the screen coordinates' values to see if they exceed the applet's dimensions.

To avoid the error of exceeding the applet viewing area:

1. Open the **JDemoCreateGraphicsObject** file and change the class name to **JDemoCreateGraphicsObject2**.

2. Because you add 20 to the x variable each time you draw the String within the applet, you can ensure that the String appears only 12 times by preventing the x-coordinate from exceeding a value of 250. Create a constant to hold this limit by adding the following, just after the declaration of GAP:

```
final int LIMIT = GAP * 12;
```

3. Position the insertion point to the right of the statement pen.setColor (Color.MAGENTA); in the actionPerformed() method, and then press **Enter** to start a new line. Type the following if statement to check the x-coordinate value:

```
if(x < LIMIT)
```

4. Position the insertion point to the right of the following line, and press **Enter**.

```
pen.drawString(companyName, x += GAP, y += GAP);
```

5. On the new line, type the following else statement that disables the JButton after the x-coordinate becomes too large:

```
else
 moveButton.setEnabled(false);
```

6. Save the file as **JDemoCreateGraphicsObject2.java** in the Chapter.10 folder on your Student Disk, and compile at the command prompt using the **javac** command. Modify the **TestJDemoCreateGraphicsObject.html** document for use with the JDemoCreateGraphicsObject2 class, and save it as **TestJDemoCreateGraphicsObject2.html** in the Chapter.10 folder on your Student Disk. Use the **appletviewer TestJDemoCreateGraphicsObject2.html** command to run the program. Now when you click the moveButton, until the company name moves to x-coordinate 250, the JButton is disabled and the company name no longer violates the applet size limits.

7. Close the Applet Viewer window.

CREATING A DRAWING

Next, you will add a simple line drawing to the JDemoCreateGraphicsObject2 program. The drawing will appear after the user clicks the JButton enough times to increase the x-coordinate to 250, which disables the JButton.

To add a line drawing to a JApplet:

1. Open the **JDemoCreateGraphicsObject2** file and rename the class **JDemoCreateGraphicsObject3**.

2. Replace the current `if...else` structure that tests whether x is less than `LIMIT` (250) in the `actionPerformed()` method with the following code that tests the value of x, and either draws the company name or disables the `JButton` and draws a logo. Set the drawing color to black, and create a simple drawing of the Event Handlers Incorporated logo, which is two overlapping balloons with strings attached:

```
if(x < LIMIT)
{
    pen.drawString(companyName, x += GAP, y += GAP);
}
else
{
    moveButton.setEnabled(false);
    pen.setColor(Color.BLACK);
    pen.drawOval(50, 170, 70, 70);
    pen.drawLine(85, 240, 110, 300);
    pen.drawOval(100, 170, 70, 70);
    pen.drawLine(135, 240, 110, 300);
}
```

3. Save the file as **JDemoCreateGraphicsObject3.java** in the Chapter.10 folder on your Student Disk, and compile at the command prompt using the **javac** command. Modify the **TestJDemoCreateGraphicsObject2.html** document for use with the JDemoCreateGraphicsObject3 class, and save it as **TestJDemoCreateGraphicsObject3.html** in the Chapter.10 folder on your Student Disk.

4. Execute the `JApplet` using the `appletviewer` command. After the company name moves to the x-coordinate with the `LIMIT` value (250), the `JButton` is disabled and the balloon drawing appears, as shown in Figure 10-32.

5. Close the Applet Viewer window.

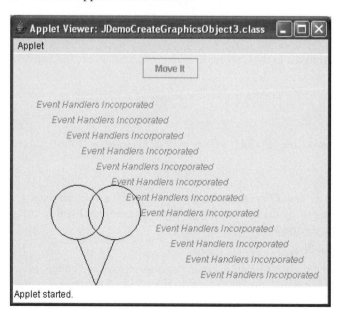

Figure 10-32 The `JDemoCreateGraphicsObject3` JApplet after the `JButton` is disabled

COPYING AN AREA

Next, you will learn how to copy an area containing a logo that you want to appear several times on a JApplet. By copying, you do not have to re-create the logo each time.

To copy an area:

1. Open a new text file in your text editor, and then enter the beginning statements for a JApplet that uses the copyArea() method:

```
import javax.swing.*;
import java.awt.*;
public class JThreeStars extends JApplet
{
```

2. Add the following statements, which create a polygon in the shape of a star:

```
int xPoints[] = {42, 52, 72, 52,
                 60, 40, 15, 28, 9, 32, 42};
int yPoints[] = {38, 62, 68, 80,
                 105, 85, 102, 75, 58, 60, 38};
Polygon aStar =
 new Polygon(xPoints, yPoints, xPoints.length);
```

3. Add the following paint() method, which sets a color, draws a star, and then draws two additional, identical stars:

```
    public void paint(Graphics star)
    {
        super.paint(star);
        star.setColor(Color.RED);
        star.drawPolygon(aStar);
        star.copyArea(0, 0, 75, 105, 80, 40);
        star.copyArea(0, 0, 75, 105, 40, 150);
    }
}
```

4. Save the file as **JThreeStars.java** in the Chapter.10 folder on your Student Disk, and then compile the program.

5. Open a new file in your text editor, and then enter the following HTML document to test the JApplet:

```
<html>
<object code = "JThreeStars.class" width = 220 height = 300>
</object>
</html>
```

6. Save the HTML document as **TestJThreeStars.html** in the Chapter.10 folder on your Student Disk, and then run it using the **appletviewer TestJThreeStars.html** command. The output should look like Figure 10-33.

7. Close the Applet Viewer window.

8. Modify the program to add more stars in any location you choose, save and compile the program, and then run the HTML document to confirm that the stars are copied to your desired locations.

9. Close the Applet Viewer window.

Figure 10-33 Output of the JThreeStars JApplet

USING FontMetrics METHODS TO COMPARE FONTS

Next, you will write a JApplet to demonstrate FontMetrics methods. You will create three Font objects and display their metrics.

To demonstrate FontMetrics methods:

1. Open a new text file in your text editor, and then enter the first few lines of the JDemoFontMetrics program:

```
import javax.swing.*;
import java.awt.*;
public class JDemoFontMetrics extends JApplet
{
```

2. Type the following code to create a String and a few fonts to use for demonstration purposes:

```
String companyName =
    new String("Event Handlers Incorporated");
Font courierItalic   =
    new Font("Courier", Font.ITALIC, 16),
    timesPlain = new Font("TimesRoman", Font.PLAIN, 16),
    helvetBold = new Font("Helvetica", Font.BOLD, 16);
```

3. Add the following code to define four integer variables to hold the four font measurements, and two integer variables to hold the current horizontal and vertical output positions within the JApplet:

```
int ascent, descent, height, leading;
int x = 10, y = 15;
```

4. Within the JApplet, you will draw Strings for output that you position 40 pixels apart vertically on the screen. At the end of the applet, the Strings that hold the statistics will be 15 pixels apart. Type the following statements to create constants to hold these vertical increase values:

```
final int INCREASE_SMALL = 15;
final int INCREASE_LARGE = 40;
```

5. Add the following statements to start writing a paint() method. Within the method, you set the Font to courierItalic, draw the companyName String to show a working example of the font, and then call a displayMetrics() method that you will write in Step 6. Pass the Graphics object to the displayMetrics() method, so the displayMetrics() method can discover the sizes associated with the current font. Perform the same three steps using the timesPlain and helvetBold fonts.

```
public void paint(Graphics pen)
{
    super.paint(pen);
    pen.setFont(courierItalic);
    pen.drawString(companyName, x, y);
    displayMetrics(pen);
    pen.setFont(timesPlain);
    pen.drawString(companyName, x, y += INCREASE_LARGE);
    displayMetrics(pen);
    pen.setFont(helvetBold);
    pen.drawString(companyName, x, y += INCREASE_LARGE);
    displayMetrics(pen);
}
```

6. Next, add the header and opening curly brace for the displayMetrics() method. The method will receive a Graphics object from the paint() method. Add the following statements to call the four getFontMetrics() methods to obtain values for the leading, ascent, descent, and height variables:

```
public void displayMetrics(Graphics metrics)
{
    leading = metrics.getFontMetrics().getLeading();
    ascent = metrics.getFontMetrics().getAscent();
    descent = metrics.getFontMetrics().getDescent();
    height = metrics.getFontMetrics().getHeight();
```

7. Add the following four drawString() statements to display the values. Use the expression y += INCREASE to change the vertical position of each String by the INCREASE constant.

```
    metrics.drawString("Leading is " + leading,
        x, y += INCREASE_SMALL);
    metrics.drawString("Ascent is " + ascent,
        x, y += INCREASE_SMALL);
```

```
    metrics.drawString("Descent is " + descent,
        x, y += INCREASE_SMALL);
    metrics.drawString("Height is " + height,
        x, y += INCREASE_SMALL);
    }
}
```

8. Save the file as **JDemoFontMetrics.java** in the Chapter.10 folder on your Student Disk, and then compile it using the **javac** command.

9. Open a new text file in your text editor, and then enter the following HTML document to host the JDemoFontMetrics JApplet:

```
<html>
<object code = "JDemoFontMetrics.class" width = 400     height = 350>
</object>
</html>
```

10. Save the HTML document as **TestJDemoFontMetrics.html** in the Chapter.10 folder on your Student Disk. At the command prompt, type **appletviewer TestJDemoFontMetrics.html**. Your output should look like Figure 10-34. Notice that even though each Font object was constructed with a size of 16, the individual statistics vary for each Font object.

11. Close the Applet Viewer window.

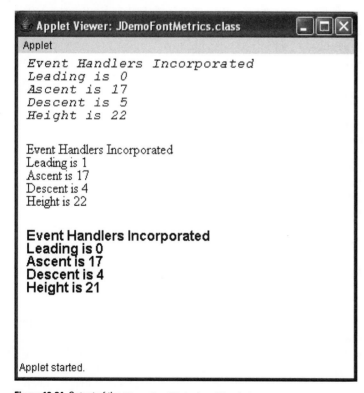

Figure 10-34 Output of the JDemoFontMetrics JApplet

USING FontMetrics METHODS TO PLACE A BORDER AROUND A String

Next, you will use the FontMetrics methods to draw a rectangle around a String. Instead of guessing at appropriate pixel positions, you can use the height and width of the String to create a box with borders placed symmetrically around the String.

To draw a rectangle around a String:

1. Open a new file in your text editor and enter the first few lines of a JBoxAround JApplet:

```
import javax.swing.*;
import java.awt.*;
public class JBoxAround extends JApplet
{
```

2. Enter the following statements to add a String, a Font, and variables to hold the font metrics and x- and y-coordinates:

```
String companyName =
    new String("Event Handlers Incorporated");
Font serifItalic = new Font("Serif", Font.ITALIC, 20);
int leading, ascent, height, width;
int x = 40, y = 60;
```

3. Create the following named constant that holds a number of pixels indicating the dimensions of the rectangle that you draw around the String:

```
static final int BORDER = 5;
```

4. Add the following paint() method, which sets the font, draws the String, and obtains the font metrics:

```
public void paint(Graphics gr)
{
    super.paint(gr);
    gr.setFont(serifItalic);
    gr.drawString(companyName, x, y);
    leading = gr.getFontMetrics().getLeading();
    ascent = gr.getFontMetrics().getAscent();
    height = gr.getFontMetrics().getHeight();
    width = gr.getFontMetrics().stringWidth(companyName);
```

5. Draw a rectangle around the String using the following drawRect() method. In Figure 10-35, the x- and y-coordinates of the upper-left edge are set at 40 – BORDER, 60 – (ascent + leading + BORDER). The proper width and height are then determined to draw a uniform rectangle around the string.

The values of the x- and y-coordinates used in the drawString() method indicate the left side of the baseline of the first character in the String. You want to position the upper-left corner of the rectangle five pixels to the left of the String, so the first argument to drawRect() is 5 less than x, or x – BORDER. The second argument to drawRect() is the y-coordinate of the String minus the ascent of the String, minus the leading of the String, minus 5, or y – (ascent + leading + BORDER). The final two arguments to drawRect() are the width and height of the rectangle. The width is the String's width plus five pixels on the left and five pixels on the right. The height of the rectangle is the `String`'s height, plus five pixels above the `String` and five pixels below the `String`.

```
gr.drawRect(x - BORDER, y - (ascent + leading + BORDER),
    width + 2 * BORDER,  height + 2 * BORDER);
repaint ();
   }
}
```

6. Save the file as **JBoxAround.java** in the Chapter.10 folder on your Student Disk, and then compile it using the **javac** command.

7. Open a new text file in your text editor, and then enter the following HTML document to host the applet:

```
<html>
<object code = "JBoxAround.class" width = 400 height = 120>
</object>
</html>
```

8. Save the HTML document as **TestJBoxAround.html** in the Chapter.10 folder on your Student Disk, and then run the program using the **appletviewer TestJBoxAround.html** command. Your output should look like Figure 10-35.

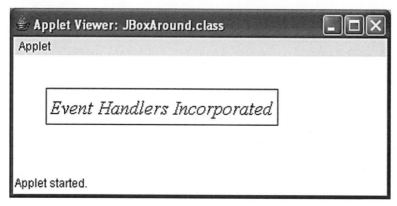

Figure 10-35 Output of the `JBoxAround JApplet`

9. Close the Applet Viewer window, and then experiment with changing the contents of the `String` and the size of the `BORDER` constant. Confirm that the rectangle is drawn symmetrically around any `String` object. When you finish, close the Applet Viewer window.

USING DRAWING STROKES

Next, you will create a line with a drawing stroke to illustrate how it can have different end types and juncture types where lines intersect.

To create a line with a drawing stroke:

1. Open a new file in your text editor, and then enter the first few lines of a `J2DLine` JApplet. (Note that you are importing the `java.awt.geom` package.)

```
import javax.swing.*;
import java.awt.*;
```

```
import java.awt.geom.*;
public class J2DLine extends JApplet
{
```

2. Enter the following statements to create a `paint()` method, create a `Graphics` environment `gr`, and cast the `Graphics` environment to a `Graphics2D` environment `gr2D`. Create x and y points with the `Point2D.Float` class.

```
public void paint(Graphics gr)
{
    super.paint(gr);
    Graphics2D gr2D = (Graphics2D)gr;
    Point2D.Float pos1 = new Point2D.Float(50, 10);
    Point2D.Float pos2 = new Point2D.Float(13, 28);
```

3. Create a `BasicStroke` object, and then create a drawing stroke named `aLine`. Note that the line width is set to 15 pixels and the endcap style and juncture style are set to `CAP_ROUND` and `JOIN_ROUND`, respectively.

```
BasicStroke aLine = new BasicStroke(15.0f,
    BasicStroke.CAP_ROUND, BasicStroke.JOIN_ROUND);
```

4. Add the following code to create a line between the points `pos1` and `pos2`, and draw the line:

```
        gr2D.setStroke(aLine);
            Line2D.Float line = new Line2D.Float(pos1, pos2);
        gr2D.draw(line);
        repaint();
    }
}
```

5. Save the file as **J2DLine.java** in the Chapter.10 folder on your Student Disk, and then compile it using the **javac** command.

6. Open a new file in your text editor, and then enter the following HTML document to host the applet:

```
<html>
<object code = "J2DLine.class" width = 50 height = 50>
</object>
</html>
```

7. Save the HTML document as **TestJ2DLine.html** in the Chapter.10 folder on your Student Disk, and then run the program using the **appletviewer TestJ2DLine.html** command. Your output should look like Figure 10-36.

ADDING DIMENSIONS TO DRAWINGS

Earlier in this chapter, Figure 10-15 showed a `JDemo3DRectangles` class that displayed rectangles with a very narrow, one-pixel wide, three-dimensional shading. To create an effect with more pronounced depth, you can layer multiple rectangles.

Figure 10-36 Output of the J2DLine JApplet

To create a dramatic three-dimensional effect:

1. Open a new file in your text editor and start the following JDemo3DRectangles2 JApplet.

```
import javax.swing.*;
import java.awt.*;
public class JDemo3DRectangles2 extends JApplet
{
```

2. Add a paint() method that contains a loop that draws 10 consecutive pink rectangles, each one pixel to the left and higher than the previous one.

```
public void paint(Graphics gr)
{
    super.paint(gr);
    int width = 60, height = 80;
    int x;
    int y;
    gr.setColor(Color.PINK);
    for(x = 30, y = 30;   x > 20;  --x, --y)
       gr.fill3DRect(x, y, width, height, true);
}
```

3. Add a closing curly brace for the class.

4. Save the file as **JDemo3DRectangles2.java** in the Chapter.10 folder on your Student Disk, and then compile it using the **javac** command.

5. Open a new file in your text editor and then enter the following HTML document to host the applet:

```
<html>
<object code = "JDemo3DRectangles2.class" width = 150 height = 150>
</object>
</html>
```

6. Save the HTML document as **TestJDemo3DRectangles2.html** in the Chapter.10 folder on your Student Disk, and then run the program using the **appletviewer** command. Your output should look like Figure 10-37.

Figure 10-37 Output of the `JDemo3DRectangles2` JApplet

WORKING WITH SHAPES

Next, you will use the Java 2D drawing object types to create a `JApplet` that illustrates sample rectangles, ovals, arcs, and polygons.

To create the `JShapes2D` JApplet:

1. Open a new file in your text editor, and then enter the first few lines of a `JShapes2D` JApplet:

```
import javax.swing.*;
import java.awt.*;
import java.awt.geom.*;
public class JShapes2D extends JApplet
{
```

2. Enter the following statements to create a `paint()` method, create a `Graphics` environment `gr`, and cast the `Graphics` environment to a `Graphics2D` environment `gr2D`:

```
public void paint(Graphics gr)
{
    super.paint(gr);
    Graphics2D gr2D = (Graphics2D)gr;
```

3. Create two `Rectangle2D.Float` objects named `rect` and `rect2`. Draw the `rect` object and fill the `rect2` object:

```
Rectangle2D.Float rect = new Rectangle2D.Float(10F, 10F, 40F,
    20F);
Rectangle2D.Float rect2 = new Rectangle2D.Float(10F, 40F, 40F,
    20F);
gr2D.draw(rect);
gr2D.fill(rect2);
```

4. Create two `Ellipse2D.Float` objects named `ellipse` and `ellipse2`. Draw the `ellipse` object and fill the `ellipse2` object:

```
Ellipse2D.Float ellipse = new Ellipse2D.Float(10F, 73F, 40F, 20F);
```

```
Ellipse2D.Float ellipse2 = new Ellipse2D.Float(10F, 103F, 40F, 20F);
gr2D.draw(ellipse);
gr2D.fill(ellipse2);
```

5. Create two `Arc2D.Float` objects named `ac` and `ac2`. Draw the `ac` object and fill the `ac2` object:

```
Arc2D.Float ac = new Arc2D.Float(10, 133, 30, 33, 30, 120,
    Arc2D.PIE);
Arc2D.Float ac2 = new Arc2D.Float(10, 163, 30, 33, 30, 120,
    Arc2D.PIE);
gr2D.draw(ac);
gr2D.fill(ac2);
```

6. Create a new `GeneralPath` object named `pol`. Set the starting point of the polygon and create two additional points. Use the `closePath()` method to close the polygon by connecting the current point to the starting point. Draw the `pol` object:

```
        GeneralPath pol = new GeneralPath();
        pol.moveTo(10F, 193F);
        pol.lineTo(25F, 183F);
        pol.lineTo(100F, 223F);
        pol.closePath();
        gr2D.draw(pol);
    }
}
```

7. Save the file as **JShapes2D.java** in the Chapter.10 folder on your Student Disk, and then compile it using the **javac** command.

8. Open a new file in your text editor, and then enter the following HTML document to host the applet:

```
<html>
<object code = "JShapes2D.class" width = 250 height = 150>
</object>
</html>
```

9. Save the HTML document as **TestJShapes2D.html** in the Chapter.10 folder on your Student Disk, and then run the program using the **appletviewer TestJShapes2D.html** command. Your output should look like Figure 10-38.

PLAYING SOUNDS

Next, you will use the `loop()` method and an `AudioClip` to play a sound continually in an applet. You will also create and add a `Graphics2D` object.

To play a sound and add a `Graphics2D` object in a `JApplet` for Event Handlers Incorporated:

1. Open a new file in your text editor, and then enter the first few lines of the `JEventSound` `JApplet`:

```
import java.awt.*;
import java.applet.*;
import javax.swing.*;
public class JEventSound extends JApplet
{
```

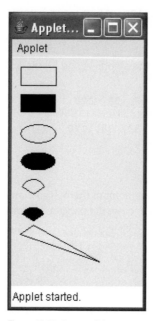

Figure 10-38 Output of the JShapes2D JApplet

2. Enter the following statement to declare an `AudioClip` object named `sound`:

```
AudioClip sound;
```

3. Create the `init()` method and an `AudioClip` object to play the event.au sound file by entering the following code:

```
public void init()
{
    sound = getAudioClip(getCodeBase(),"event.au");
}
```

4. Create the following `start()` method. This method uses the `loop()` method to play the event.au sound file continually:

```
public void start()
{
    sound.loop();
}
```

5. Create the following `stop()` method to halt the event.au sound file.

```
public void stop()
{
    sound.stop();
}
```

6. Create a `Graphics` object using `paint(Graphics g)`, and then use a cast to change the graphics context to a `Graphics2D` object. Use the `drawString()` method to create a message that appears on the screen while the `JApplet` plays. Add a closing curly brace for the class.

```
    public void paint(Graphics g)
    {
        super.paint(g);
        Graphics2D g2D = (Graphics2D)g;
        g2D.drawString("Playing Event Handlers Inc. Event sounds ...",
            10, 10);
    }
}
```

7. Save the file as **JEventSound.java** in the Chapter.10 folder on your Student Disk, and then compile it using the **javac** command.

8. Open a new file in your text editor, and then enter the following HTML document to test the JApplet:

```
<html>
<object code = "JEventSound.class" width = 300 height = 50>
</object>
</html>
```

9. Save the HTML document as **TestJEventSound.html** in the Chapter.10 folder on your Student Disk, and then run it using the **appletviewer TestJEventSound.html** command. The output should look like Figure 10-39. If speakers are installed on your system, and they are on, you should also be able to hear sound playing continuously.

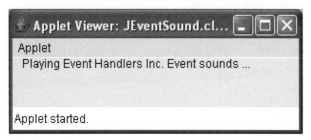

Figure 10-39 Output of the JEventSound JApplet

CREATING A JApplet THAT INCLUDES CHANGES CAUSED BY A JButton CLICK

Next, you will create a JApplet for Event Handlers Incorporated that contains a graphical representation of the current day, date, and time, which changes when the user clicks a JButton. In addition, a sound plays while the message "It's time to party. . ." appears under the graphical time representation. An image of a banner of the Event Handlers company name appears under the message.

To create the JGregorianTime applet:

1. Open a new text file, and enter the first few lines of the JGregorianTime JApplet:

```
import java.applet.*;
import java.awt.*;
```

```
import java.awt.event.*;
import java.util.*;
import javax.swing.*;
public class JGregorianTime extends JApplet
    implements ActionListener
{
```

2. Add the following statements to create an `AudioClip` named `sound`, a new `Color` named `tan`, an empty `String` named `lastTime`, and an `ImageIcon` named `eventLogo`:

```
private AudioClip sound;
private Color tan = new Color(255, 204, 102);
private String lastTime = "";
private ImageIcon eventLogo;
```

3. Add the following statement to create a `JButton` for the user to click:

```
JButton pressMe = new JButton("Press Me");
```

4. Begin the `init()` method, and enter the following statements to add a sound object and `ImageIcon` object:

```
public void init()
{
    sound = getAudioClip(getCodeBase(),"event.au");
    eventLogo = new ImageIcon("event.gif");
```

> **NOTE** Make sure the event.au and event.gif files on your Student Disk are copied to the default folder in which you save this program. If these files are not in the default folder, you will not hear the music or see the banner. Also, you will not hear the music unless the system's speakers are turned on.

5. Add the following statements to create a `Container` named `con`, set its background color to blue, and change the default layout from `BorderLayout` to `FlowLayout`:

```
Container con = getContentPane();
con.setBackground(Color.BLUE);
con.setLayout(new FlowLayout());
```

6. Add the following statements, which add the `JButton` named `pressMe` to the container and register the applet as a listener for `pressMe`. Then, add the closing curly brace to the `init()` method:

```
    con.add(pressMe);
    pressMe.addActionListener(this);
}
```

7. Begin the `paint()` method and cast the `Graphics` context to `Graphics2D`. Create a font named `monoFont` and set the font of the `Graphics2D` object to `monoFont`. (Note the syntax for setting `monoFont` in a `Graphics2D` environment.)

```
public void paint(Graphics g)
{
    super.paint(g);
    Graphics2D g2D = (Graphics2D)g;
    Font monoFont = new Font("Monospaced", Font.BOLD, 20);
    g2D.setFont(monoFont);
```

8. Create a `GregorianCalendar` object named `day`, create a `String` named `time` using the `getTime()` method, and then convert the result using the `toString()` method.

```
GregorianCalendar day = new GregorianCalendar();
String time = day.getTime().toString();
```

9. Use the `setColor()` method and `drawString()` method to set the color and draw the `Strings` `lastTime` and `time`. (Note that when the animation starts, the `String` `lastTime` is empty.) Set the `g2D` object's color to tan (the custom color you created), and then draw the `time` `String`. Finally, reference the `String` `lastTime` to the `String` `time`:

```
g2D.setColor(Color.BLUE);
g2D.drawString(lastTime, 5, 75);
g2D.setColor(tan);
g2D.drawString(time, 5, 75);
lastTime = time;
```

10. Add the `ImageIcon` `eventLogo` to the `paint()` method below the graphic representation of the day, date, and time. Add the `drawString()` method under the `eventLogo` Image to display the string "It's time to party . . . ". Add a `repaint()` method so that the `JButton` is redrawn each time the `paint()` method is called, and then add the closing curly brace to the `paint()` method:

```
    eventLogo.paintIcon(this, g, 50, 120);
    g2D.drawString("It's time to party...", 50, 100);
}
```

11. Add the `JApplet`'s `start()` and `stop()` methods. Add the `loop()` method to the applet's `start()` method to play the sound continually. Then, add the `stop()` method to the applet's `stop()` method:

```
public void start()
{
    sound.loop();
}
public void stop()
{
    sound.stop();
}
```

12. At this point, the `JApplet` is almost completed. You still must add the `actionPerformed()` method that executes when the user clicks the `JButton`. The only task performed by the method is to call the `repaint()` method. Add the following method to your applet. Then, add the closing curly braces for the `actionPerformed()` method and the class:

```
    public void actionPerformed(ActionEvent e)
    {
        Object source = e.getSource();
        if(source == pressMe)
            repaint();
    }
}
```

13. Save the file as **JGregorianTime.java** in the Chapter.10 folder on your Student Disk, and then compile it using the **javac** command.

14. Open a new file in your text editor, and then enter the code for an HTML document to host the applet:

```
<html>
<object code = "JGregorianTime.class" width = 400 height = 200>
</object>
</html>
```

15. Save the HTML document as **TestJGregorianTime.html** in the Chapter.10 folder on your Student Disk, and then run it using the **appletviewer TestJGregorianTime.html** command. The output appears on the first screen in Figure 10-40. Wait at least a couple of seconds, click the **pressMe** button, and observe the time changes. The second screen in Figure 10-40 shows the output of the program after the JButton has been clicked several seconds later.

16. Close the Applet Viewer window.

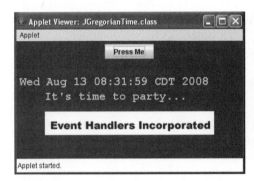

Figure 10-40 Output of the JGregorianTime JApplet

CHANGING A JApplet's OUTPUT BY CHANGING THE DRAWING COLOR

You can show text that changes by displaying an updated String with successive clicks of a JButton. Figure 10-41 shows a JApplet that contains two Strings—string1 holds a company's name, and string2 holds the company's phone number. The actionPerformed() method associated with a button repaints the applet. The action within the paint() method that seems to cause animation is shaded in Figure 10-41. Each time the user clicks the button, the string that was previously drawn in black is redrawn in white. The result is similar to using white liquid correction fluid on a typed, white paper—it writes over the previously drawn black string so it seems to disappear. Then, if the showString currently is the company name string, it is changed to hold the phone number, and if the showString is the phone number, it is changed to hold the company name. The drawing color is changed to BLACK, and the new string is displayed. Similarly, each time a string change is made, a different one of the two images is displayed. Figure 10-42 shows the output of the JMessages JApplet before and after the user clicks the button. Notice how the displayed image changes as well as the string message.

```
import java.applet.*;
import java.awt.*;
import java.awt.event.*;
import java.util.*;
import javax.swing.*;
public class JMessages extends JApplet implements ActionListener
{
    private Image image1;
    private Image image2;
    JButton pressMe = new JButton("Press Me");
    String showString;
    String string1 = "Empire Enterprises - Call today";
    String string2 = "1-800-555-8921";
    public void init()
    {
        image1 = getImage(getCodeBase(), "up1.gif");
        image2 = getImage(getCodeBase(), "down1.gif");
        Container con = getContentPane();
        con.setBackground(Color.WHITE);
        con.setLayout(new FlowLayout());
        con.add(pressMe);
        pressMe.addActionListener(this);
        showString = string2;
    }
    public void paint(Graphics g)
    {
        super.paint(g);
        Graphics2D g2D = (Graphics2D)g;
        Font arialFont = new Font("Arial", Font.BOLD, 26);
        g2D.setFont(arialFont);
        g2D.setColor(Color.WHITE);
        g2D.drawString(showString, 15, 100);
        if(showString.equals(string1))
        {
            showString = string2;
            g.drawImage(image1, 200, 150, this);
        }
        else
        {
            showString = string1;
            g.drawImage(image2, 200, 150, this);
        }
        g2D.setColor(Color.BLACK);
        g2D.drawString(showString, 15, 100);

    }
    public void actionPerformed(ActionEvent e)
    {
        repaint();
    }
}
```

Figure 10-41 The JMessages JApplet

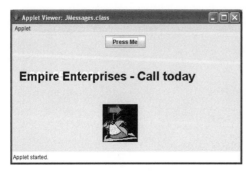

Figure 10-42 Output of the JMessages JApplet before and after clicking the button

To observe the JMessages JApplet in action:

1. Open your text editor, and open the **JMessages.java** JApplet from the Chapter.10 folder on your Student Disk.

2. Compile the JApplet using the **javac** command.

3. Examine the **TestJMessages.html** document that is in the Chapter.10 folder on your Student Disk. Execute this file using the **appletviewer** command. Confirm that your output is similar to Figure 10-42.

KEY TERMS

The **paint() method** runs when Java displays your JApplet. You can write your own paint() method to override the automatically supplied one whenever you want to paint graphics, such as shapes, on the screen.

You call the **repaint() method** when a window needs to be updated, such as when it contains new images. The repaint() method calls another method named update(), which calls the paint() method.

The **drawString() method** allows you to draw a String in a JApplet window.

The **setFont() method** changes the Font of a String displayed in the Graphics environment.

You can designate a Graphics color with the **setColor() method**.

The **drawLine() method** draws a straight line between any two points on the screen.

The **drawRect() method** draws the outline of a rectangle.

The **fillRect() method** draws a solid, or filled, rectangle.

The **clearRect() method** draws a rectangle using the background color to create what appears to be an empty or "clear" rectangle.

The **drawRoundRect() method** draws rectangles with rounded corners.

An **arc** is a portion of a circle.

The **drawOval() method** draws an oval.

The **fillOval() method** draws a solid, filled oval.

The **drawArc() method** draws an arc.

The **fillArc()** **method** creates a solid arc.

You use the **draw3DRect()** **method** to draw a rectangle that appears to have "shadowing" on two of its edges—the effect is that of a rectangle that is lit from the upper-left corner and slightly raised or slightly lowered.

You use the **fill3DRect()** **method** to create filled, three-dimensional rectangles.

The **drawPolygon()** **method** draws complex shapes. The drawPolygon() method requires three arguments: two integer arrays that hold x- and y-coordinate positions for the points in the polygon, and a single integer that holds the number of points to connect.

The **fillPolygon()** **method** draws a solid shape.

You use the **addPoint()** **method** to add points to a Polygon object.

The **copyArea()** **method** copies any rectangular area to a new location.

You can discover the fonts that are available on your system by using the **getAllFonts()** **method**.

The **getDefaultToolkit()** **method** provides information about the system in use.

The **getScreenResolution()** **method** returns the screen resolution on the current system.

The **getScreenSize()** **method** returns the screen size as a Dimension object.

Leading is one of three measures of a Font's height; it is the amount of space between baselines.

Ascent is one of three measures of a Font's height; it is the height of an uppercase character from a baseline to the top of the character.

Descent is one of three measures of a Font's height; it measures the part of characters that "hang below" the baseline, such as the tails on the lowercase letters g and j.

The **height of a font** is the sum of its leading, ascent, and descent.

You can discover a Font's height by using the Graphics class **getFontMetrics()** **method** to return a FontMetrics object, and then using one of the following: public int getLeading(), public int getAscent(), public int getDescent(), or public int getHeight().

The FontMetrics class contains a **stringWidth()** **method** that returns the integer width of a String.

Fill patterns control how a drawing object is filled in.

A **gradient fill** is a gradual shift from one color at one coordinate point to a different color at a second coordinate point.

An **acyclic gradient** is a fill pattern in which a color shift occurs once between two points.

A **cyclic gradient** is a fill pattern in which a shift between colors occurs repeatedly between two points.

A **stroke** is a line-drawing feature in Java 2D that represents a single movement as if you were using a drawing tool, such as a pen or a pencil.

The **setStroke()** **method** changes a stroke's width in Java 2D.

BasicStroke is the class that defines line types and implements the Stroke interface.

Endcap styles apply to the ends of lines that do not join with other lines, and include CAP_BUTT, CAP_ROUND, and CAP_SQUARE.

Juncture styles, for lines that join, include JOIN_MITER, JOIN_ROUND, and JOIN_BEVEL.

The **play() method** of the Applet class retrieves and plays sounds.

An **image** is a likeness of a person or thing.

Lossless data compression is a set of rules that allows an exact replica of data to be reconstructed from a compressed version.

An **abstract** class is one from which you cannot create any objects, but from which you can inherit.

CHAPTER SUMMARY

» The paint() method executes automatically every time you minimize, maximize, or resize a JApplet that is running. The paint() method header is public void paint(Graphics g), requiring a Graphics object argument that is usually supplied by the repaint() method.

» The drawString() method allows you to draw a String in a JApplet window. The drawString() method requires three arguments: a String, an x-axis coordinate, and a y-axis coordinate. You can improve the appearance of strings drawn using Graphics objects by using the setFont() and setColor() methods.

» When you call the paint() method from within an applet, you can use the automatically created Graphics object that is passed to it, but you can also instantiate your own Graphics or Graphics2D objects.

» Java provides several methods for drawing a variety of lines and geometric shapes. You can use the drawLine(), drawRect(), and fillRect() methods, respectively, to draw lines, the outline of a rectangle, and a solid, or filled, rectangle. The clearRect() method uses the current background color to draw what appears to be an empty or "clear" rectangle. You can create rectangles with rounded corners when you use the drawRoundRect() method. The drawOval(), fillOval(), drawArc(), and fillArc() methods create ovals, solid ovals, arcs, and solid arcs, respectively. You use the draw3DRect() and fill3DRect() methods to draw rectangles that appear to have three-dimensional shadowing. When you want to create a shape that is more complex than a rectangle, you can use a sequence of calls to the drawLine() method, or you can use the drawPolygon() method to draw complex shapes. You can use the fillPolygon() method to draw a solid shape. You can also use the copyArea() method to copy any rectangular area to a new location.

» You can discover the fonts that are available on your system by using the getAllFonts() method, which is part of the GraphicsEnvironment class defined in the java.awt package. You can discover the resolution and screen size on your system by using the getScreenResolution() and getScreenSize() methods, which are part of the Toolkit class.

» Leading is the amount of space between baselines. Ascent is the height of an uppercase character from a baseline to the top of the character. Descent measures the part of characters that "hang below" the baseline, such as the tails on the lowercase letters g and j. The height of a font is the sum of the leading, ascent, and descent. You can discover a font's height by first using the Graphics class getFontMetrics() method to return a FontMetrics object, and then by using FontMetrics class methods with the object to return one of a Font's statistics.

» The advantage of using Java 2D is the higher-quality, two-dimensional (2D) graphics, images, and text it provides. A Graphics2D object is produced by casting, or converting and promoting, a Graphics object. The process of drawing with Java 2D objects includes specifying the rendering attributes, setting a drawing stroke, and creating objects to draw.

» Java 2D supports sound using methods from the Applet class (rather than JApplet). You can use methods that retrieve and play sound files that use various sound formats.

» An image is a likeness of a person or thing. The Image class provides many of Java's image capabilities; this class loads images that have been stored in one of the allowed Image formats. The ImageIcon class can also be used to create images in your applications and applets. You can use all the Image methods with an ImageIcon, plus many additional methods. Unlike the Image class, you can create ImageIcon objects directly. Also, unlike Images, you can place an ImageIcon on a Component, such as a JPanel, JLabel, or JButton.

REVIEW QUESTIONS

1. The method that calls the paint() method for you is _____ .

   a. callPaint()

   b. repaint()

   c. requestPaint()

   d. draw()

2. The paint() method header requires a(n) _____ argument.

   a. void   c. String

   b. int   d. Graphics

3. The statement g.drawString(someString, 50, 100); places someString's _____ corner at position 50, 100.

   a. upper-left   c. upper-right

   b. lower-left   d. lower-right

4. If you use the setColor() method to change a Graphics object's color to yellow, _____ .

   a. the next output from the object always appears in yellow

   b. all output from the object for the remainder of the method always appears in yellow

   c. all output from the object for the remainder of the applet always appears in yellow

   d. all output from the object appears in yellow until you change the color

5. The correct statement to instantiate a `Graphics` object named `picasso` is _____ .

    a. `Graphics picasso;`

    b. `Graphics picasso = new Graphics();`

    c. `Graphics picasso = getGraphics();`

    d. `Graphics picasso = getGraphics(new);`

6. The statement `g.drawRoundRect(100, 100, 100, 100, 0, 0);` draws a shape that looks most like a _____ .

    a. square

    b. round-edged rectangle

    c. circle

    d. straight line

7. If you draw an oval with the same value for width and height, you draw a(n) _____ .

    a. circle   c. rounded square

    b. square   d. ellipsis

8. The zero-degree position for any arc is at the _____ o'clock position.

    a. three   c. nine

    b. six   d. twelve

9. The method you use to create a solid arc is _____ .

    a. `solidArc()`

    b. `fillArc()`

    c. `arcSolid()`

    d. `arcFill()`

10. You use the _____ method to copy any rectangular area to a new location.

    a. `copyRect()`

    b. `copyArea()`

    c. `repeatRect()`

    d. `repeatArea()`

11. The measurement of an uppercase character from the baseline to the top of the character is its _____ .

    a. ascent   c. leading

    b. descent   d. height

12. To be certain that a vertical series of Strings has enough room to appear in an applet, you use which of the following statements?

    a. g.drawString("Some string",

        x, y += g.getFontMetrics().getHeight());

    b. g.drawString("Some string",

        x, y += g.getFontMetrics().getLeading());

    c. g.drawString("Some string", x,

        y += g.getFontMetrics().getAscent());

    d. g.drawString("Some string",

        x, y += g.getFontMetrics().getDescent());

13. You can discover the fonts that are available on your system by using the _____ .

    a. getAllFonts() method of the GraphicsEnvironment class

    b. getAllFonts() method of the Graphics class

    c. setAllFonts() method of the GraphicsEnvironment class

    d. getAllFonts() method of the ImageEnvironment class

14. The getScreenResolution() method and getScreenSize() method _____ .

    a. both return the number of pixels as an int type

    b. return the number of pixels as an int type and an object of type Dimension, respectively

    c. both return an object of type Dimension

    d. return the number of pixels as a double type and an object of type Dimension, respectively

15. A Graphics2D object is produced by _____ .

    a. the setGraphics2D() method

    b. the Graphics2D newpen = Graphics2D() statement

    c. the Graphics2D = Graphics(g) statement

    d. casting a Graphics object

16. The process of drawing with Java 2D objects includes _____ .

    a. specifying the rendering attributes

    b. setting a drawing stroke

    c. both of the above

    d. none of the above

17. A gradient fill is a gradual change in _____ .

    a. color

    b. font size

    c. drawing style

    d. line thickness

18. After the `getAudioClip()` method retrieves a sound object named `mysound`, the _____ plays a sound continually in a `JApplet`.

  a. `mysound.music()` method

  b. `mysound.play()` method

  c. `mysound.loop()` method

  d. `mysound.continuous()` method

19. The _____ is particularly useful for loading an image into either an applet or application.

  a. `Image` class

  b. `ImageLogo` class

  c. `ImageIcon` class

  d. `GetImage` class

20. Showing successive images on the screen is called _____ .

  a. action-oriented

  b. object-oriented

  c. animation

  d. volatility

EXERCISES

For each applet you create in the following exercises, create an HTML host document named **Test** plus the applet name.

1. Write a `JApplet` that displays your first name in every even-numbered font size from 4 through 24. Save the `JApplet` as **JFontSizeDemo.java**.

2. Write a `JApplet` that displays your name in blue the first time the user clicks a `JButton`. The second time the user clicks the `JButton`, make the first name seem to disappear. (*Hint:* Redraw it using the background color.) At the same time, draw your first name again in a larger font in dark gray. Save the `JApplet` as **JBlueGray.java**.

3. Write a `JApplet` that displays eight nested rectangles, like those in Figure 10-43. You may use only one `drawRect()` statement in the program. (*Hint*: Use it in a loop.) Save the `JApplet` as **JNestedBoxes.java**.

4. Write a `JApplet` that displays 15 nested circles, like those in Figure 10-44. You may use only one `drawOval()` statement in the program. Save the `JApplet` as **JNestedCircles.java**.

5. Write a `JApplet` that displays diagonal lines in a square, like those in Figure 10-45. Save the `JApplet` as **JDiagonalLines.java**.

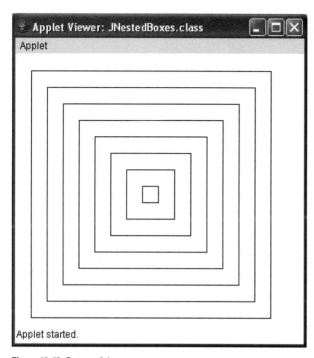

Figure 10-43 Output of the JNestedBoxes JApplet

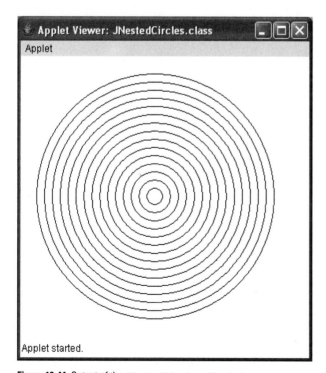

Figure 10-44 Output of the JNestedCircles JApplet

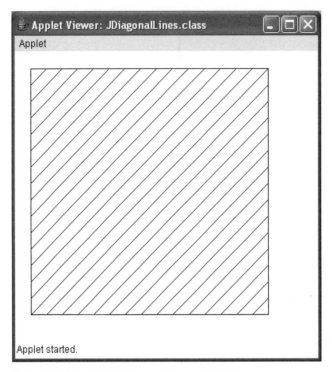

Figure 10-45 Output of the JDiagonalLines JApplet

6. Write a JApplet that displays a form for creating an e-mail directory. The form should contain three JLabels that describe three JTextFields for first name, last name, and e-mail address. After the user enters the third item (an e-mail address) and presses Enter, the JApplet should display the information that was entered. Use the drawString() method to display a heading line, such as "The e-mail information you entered is: ", followed by the e-mail information. Save the JApplet as **JEmailForm.java**.

7. a. Write a JApplet that displays a yellow smiling face on the screen. Save the JApplet as **JSmileFace.java**.

   b. Add a JButton to the JSmileFace JApplet so the smile changes to a frown when the user clicks the JButton. Save the JApplet as **JSmileFace2.java**.

8. a. Use polygons and lines to create a graphics image that looks like a fireworks display. Write a JApplet that displays the fireworks. Save the JApplet as **JFireworks.java**.

   b. Add a JButton to the JFireworks JApplet. Do not show the fireworks until the user clicks the JButton. Save the JApplet as **JFireworks2.java**.

9. a. Write a JApplet to display your name. Place boxes around your name at intervals of 10, 20, 30, and 40 pixels. Save the JApplet as **JBorders.java**.

   b. Make each of the four borders in the JBorders.java applet display a different color. Save the JApplet as **JBorders2.java**.

10. Create a `JApplet` and use `JOptionPane.showInputDialog()` boxes to prompt the user to enter his or her name and weight in pounds. After the name and weight are entered, use `Graphics2D` methods to display the user's name and weight, with the weight displayed in pounds, ounces, kilograms, and metric tons on separate lines. Use the following conversion factors:

    » 1 pound = 16 ounces
    » 1 kilogram = 1 pound / 2.204623
    » 1 metric ton = 1 pound / 2204.623

    Save the `JApplet` as **JCalculateWeight.java**.

11. Write a `JApplet` that uses the `Graphics2D` environment to create a `GeneralPath` object. Use the `GeneralPath` object to create the outline of your favorite state. Display the state name at the approximate center of the state boundaries. Save the `JApplet` as **JFavoriteState.java**.

12. Write a `JApplet` that draws a realistic-looking stop sign. Save the `JApplet` as **JStopSign.java**.

13. Write a `JApplet` that uses the `ImageIcon` class to place image icon objects on four `JButtons`. Download any free JPG or GIF files from the Internet; if necessary, reduce the size of the images to approximately 30 by 30 pixels. Alternatively, you can use the four files named up.jpg, down.jpg, left.jpg, and right.jpg on your Student Disk. Each time a `JButton` is clicked, display a different message below the `JButtons`. Save the `JApplet` as **JButtonIcons.java**.

14. Create a `JApplet` that paints an `ImageIcon` the first time its `paint()` method is called, and then randomly draws small, filled ovals in the background color over the image each time a `JButton` is clicked. The resulting effect is that the image seems to be erased by an increasing number of small, overlapping ovals. For example, if you place an `ImageIcon` at the coordinates contained in variables named `startPosX` and `startPosY`, you can create a series of 10-by-10 filled ovals placed randomly on the `ImageIcon`'s surface using the following `for` loop:

```
for(int count = 0; count < 20; ++count)
{
    int x = (int) (Math.random() * imageWidth) + startPosX;
    int y = (int) (Math.random() * imageHeight) + startPosY;
    g.fillOval(x, y, 10, 10);
}
```

    Save your `JApplet` as **JEraseImage.java**.

15. Create a `JApplet` for Business Associates, a consulting firm whose motto is "Let Business Associates take care of your business." Include two `JButtons`—clicking one `JButton` plays the tune "Taking Care of Business" continuously, and clicking the other stops the music. You can find the business.mid file on your Student Disk. Save the `JApplet` as **JBusiness.java**.

DEBUGGING EXERCISES

Each of the following files in the Chapter.10 folder on your Student Disk has syntax and/or logic errors. In each case, determine the problem and fix the program. After you correct the errors, save each file using the same filename preceded with Fix. For example, DebugTen1.java will become FixDebugTen1.java. You can test each applet with the appropriate TestDebugTen.html file on your Student Disk. Remember to change the Java class file referenced in the HTML document to match the DebugTen applet on which you are working.

a. DebugTen1.java

c. DebugTen3.java

b. DebugTen2.java

d. DebugTen4.java

CASE PROJECT

THE PARTY PLANNERS

The Party Planners organization in your town is sponsoring a contest to see who can program the best Java JApplet to be used as an advertisement for its party events. You can download sound clips and graphics images from the Internet to use in your program. Create a JApplet named JPartyPlanners and an HTML test file to run the JApplet.

GAME ZONE

1. In Chapter 9, you created a Tic Tac Toe game. Now add a graphic that displays a large letter representing the winning player. Draw a large X, O, or, in case of a tie, an overlapping X and O in different colors. Save the game as **JTicTacToe2.java**. Create an HTML document to host the applet and save it as **JTicTacToe2.html**.

2. Create a JApplet that plays a card game named Lucky Seven. In real life, the game can be played with seven cards, each containing a number from 1 through 7, that are shuffled and dealt number-side down. To start the game, a player turns over any card. The exposed number on the card determines the position (reading from left to right) of the next card that must be turned over. For example, if the player turns over the first card and its number is 7, the next card turned must be the seventh card (counting from left to right). If the player turns over a card whose number denotes a position that was already turned, the player loses the game. If the player succeeds in turning over all seven cards, the player wins.

   Instead of cards, you will use seven buttons labeled 1 through 7 from left to right. Randomly associate one of the seven values 1 through 7 with each button. (In other words, the associated value might or might not be equivalent to the button's labeled value.) When the player clicks a button, reveal the associated hidden value. If the value represents the position of a button already clicked, the player loses. If the revealed number represents an available button, force the user to click it —that is, do not take any action until the user clicks the correct button. After a player clicks a button, remove the button from play. (After you remove a button, you can call repaint() to ensure that the image of the button is removed.)

   For example, a player might click Button 7, revealing a 4. Then the player clicks Button 4, revealing a 2. Then the player clicks Button 2, revealing a 7. The player loses because Button 7 is already "used."

Save the game as **JLuckySeven.java**. Create an HTML file to execute the applet and save it as **JLuckySeven.html**.

3. In Chapter 9, you created a `JSecretPhrase` applet in which the user clicks lettered buttons to fill in a target phrase. Now, make this game more like the traditional letter-guessing game Hangman by drawing a "hanged" person piece by piece with each missed letter. For example, when the user chooses a correct letter, place it in the appropriate position or positions in the phrase, but the first time the user chooses a letter that is not in the target phrase, draw a head for the "hanged" man. The second time the user makes an incorrect guess, add a torso. Continue with arms and legs. If the complete body is drawn before the user has guessed all the letters in the phrase, display a message indicating that the player has lost the game. If the user completes the phrase before all the body parts are drawn, display a message that the player has won. Save the game as **JSecretPhrase2.java**. Create an HTML document to host the applet and save it as **TestJSecretPhrase2.html**.

4. In Chapter 9, you created an applet that lets the user play Rock Paper Scissors against the computer. Using `2DGraphics`, add simple drawings to the applet that represent the user's choice. For the choice of "rock," use an ellipse; for "paper," use a rectangle; and for "scissors," create a simple image from two lines and two circles. Add the appropriate image each time the player makes a selection; make sure the old image is completely erased before displaying the new one. Save the game as **JRockPaperScissors2.java**. Create an HTML document to host the applet and save it as **TestJRockPaperScissors2.html**.

UP FOR DISCUSSION

1. Making exciting and professional-looking applets becomes easier once you learn to include graphics images. You can copy graphics images from many locations on the Web. Should there be any restrictions on what graphics you use? Does it make a difference if you are writing programs for your own enjoyment as opposed to putting them on the Web where others can see them? Is using photographs different from using drawings? Does it matter if the photographs contain recognizable people? Would you impose any restrictions on images posted to your organization's Web site?

2. Should you be allowed to store computer games on your computer at work? If so, should you be allowed to play the games during working hours? If so, should there be any restrictions on when you can play them?

3. Suppose you discover a way to breach security in a Web site so that its visitors might access information that belongs to the company for which you work. Should you be allowed to publish your findings? Should you notify the organization? Should the organization pay you a reward for discovering the breach? If they did, would this encourage you to search for more potential security violations? Suppose the newly available information on the Web site is relatively innocuous—for example, office telephone numbers of company executives. Next, suppose that the information is more sensitive—for example, home telephone numbers for the same executives. Does this make a difference?

INTRODUCTION
TO INHERITANCE

In this chapter, you will:

Learn about the concept of inheritance

Extend classes

Override superclass methods

Understand how constructors are called during inheritance

Use superclass constructors that require arguments

Access superclass methods

Learn about information hiding

Use methods you cannot override

JAVA ON THE JOB, SCENE 11

"You look exhausted," Lynn Greenbrier says one Friday afternoon.

"I am," you reply. "Now that I know some Java, I am writing programs for several departments in the company. It's fun, but it's a lot of work, and the worst thing is that I seem to do the same work over and over."

"What do you mean?" Lynn asks.

"Well, the Event Planning Department asked me to develop several classes that will hold information for every event type handled by Event Handlers. There are weekday and weekend events, events with or without dinners, and events with or without guest speakers. Sure, these various types of events have differences, but all events have many things in common, such as an event number and a number of guests."

"I see," Lynn says. "So you'd like to create a class based on an existing class, just by adding the specific new components needed by the new class. You want to avoid rewriting components that you already created."

"Exactly," you say. "But, because I can't do that, I'll have to get back to work."

"Go home and relax," Lynn says. "On Monday morning, I'll teach you how to use inheritance to solve these problems."

LEARNING ABOUT THE CONCEPT OF INHERITANCE

In Java and all object-oriented languages, **inheritance** is a mechanism that enables one class to inherit, or assume, both the behavior and the attributes of another class. Inheritance is the principle that allows you to apply your knowledge of a general category to more specific objects. You are familiar with the concept of inheritance from all sorts of nonprogramming situations.

>> **NOTE** In Chapter 3, you first learned about inheritance, in which a class object can inherit all the attributes of an existing class. You can create a functional new class simply by indicating how it is different from the class from which it is derived.

When you use the term *inheritance*, you might think of genetic inheritance. You know from biology that your blood type and eye color are the product of inherited genes; you can say that many facts about you—your attributes, or "data fields"—are inherited. Similarly, you often can credit your behavior to inheritance. For example, your attitude toward saving money might be the same as your grandma's, and the odd way that you pull on your ear when you are tired might match what your Uncle Steve does—thus, your methods are inherited, too.

You might also choose plants and animals based on inheritance. You plant impatiens next to your house because of your shady street location; you adopt a Doberman pinscher because you need a watchdog. Every individual plant and pet has slightly different characteristics, but within a species, you can count on many consistent inherited attributes and behaviors. Similarly, the classes you create in object-oriented programming languages can inherit data and methods from existing classes. When you create a class by making it inherit from another class, you are provided with data fields and methods automatically.

Beginning with the first chapter of this book, you have been creating classes and instantiating objects that are members of those classes. Programmers and analysts sometimes use a graphical language to describe classes and object-oriented processes; this **Unified Modeling Language** (**UML**) consists of many types of diagrams.

For example, consider the simple `Employee` class shown in Figure 11-1. The class contains two data fields, `empNum` and `empSal`, and four methods, a get and set method for each field. Figure 11-2 shows a UML class diagram for the `Employee` class. A **class diagram** is a visual tool that provides you with an overview of a class. It consists of a rectangle divided into three sections—the top section contains the name of the class, the middle section contains the names and data types of the attributes, and the bottom section contains the methods. Only the method return type, name, and arguments are provided in the diagram—the instructions that make up the method body are omitted.

```
public class Employee
{
    private int empNum;
    private double empSal;
    public int getEmpNum()
    {
        return empNum;
    }
    public double getEmpSal()
    {
        return empSal;
    }
    public void setEmpNum(int num)
    {
        empNum = num;
    }
    public void setEmpSal(double sal)
    {
        empSal = sal;
    }
}
```

Figure 11-1 The `Employee` class

```
Employee
-empNum : int
-empSal : double
+getEmpNum : int
+getEmpSal : double
+setEmpNum(int num) : void
+setEmpSal(double sal) : void
```

Figure 11-2 The `Employee` class diagram

>> **NOTE** By convention, a class diagram contains the data type following each attribute or method, as shown in Figure 11-2. A minus sign (–) is inserted in front of each `private` field or method, and a plus sign (+) is inserted in front of each `public` field or method.

After you create the Employee class, you can create specific Employee objects, such as the following:

```
Employee receptionist = new Employee();
Employee deliveryPerson = new Employee();
```

These Employee objects can eventually possess different numbers and salaries, but because they are Employee objects, you know that each Employee has *some* number and salary.

Suppose you hire a new Employee named serviceRep. Suppose further that a serviceRep object requires an employee number and a salary, but a serviceRep object also requires a data field to indicate territory served. You can create a class with a name such as EmployeeWithTerritory, and provide the class three fields (empNum, empSal, and empTerritory) and six methods (get and set methods for each of the three fields). However, when you do this, you are duplicating much of the work that you have already done for the Employee class. The wise, efficient alternative is to create the class EmployeeWithTerritory so it inherits all the attributes and methods of Employee. Then, you can add just the one field and two methods that are additions within EmployeeWithTerritory objects. Figure 11-3 shows a class diagram of this relationship; the arrow that extends from the EmployeeWithTerritory class and points to the Employee class shows the inheritance relationship.

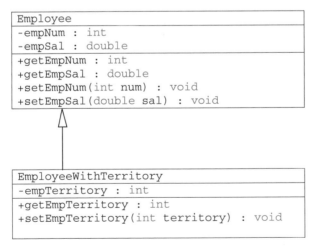

Figure 11-3 Class diagram showing the relationship between Employee and EmployeeWithTerritory

When you use inheritance to create the `EmployeeWithTerritory` class, you:

» Save time because the `Employee` fields and methods already exist

» Reduce errors because the `Employee` methods already have been used and tested

» Reduce the amount of new learning required to use the new class, because you have used the `Employee` methods on simpler objects and already understand how they work

The ability to use inheritance in Java makes programs easier to write, less error-prone, and more quickly understood. Besides creating `EmployeeWithTerritory`, you can also create several other specific `Employee` classes (perhaps `EmployeeEarningCommission`, including a commission rate, or `DismissedEmployee`, including a reason for dismissal). By using inheritance, you can develop each new class correctly and more quickly.

> **» NOTE** The concept of inheritance is useful because it makes class code reusable. Each method already written and tested in the original class becomes part of the new class that inherits it.

> **» NOTE** In Chapter 4, you learned about the `GregorianCalendar` class. It descends from a more general class named `Calendar`.

A class that is used as a basis for inheritance, such as `Employee`, is a **base class**. When you create a class that inherits from a base class (such as `EmployeeWithTerritory`), it is a **derived class**. When considering two classes that inherit from each other, you can tell which is the base class and which is the derived class by using the two classes in a sentence with the phrase "is a(n)." A derived class always "is a" case or example of the more general base class. For example, a `Tree` class can be a base class to an `Evergreen` class. An `Evergreen` "is a" `Tree`, so `Tree` is the base class; however, it is not true for all `Tree`s that "a `Tree` is an `Evergreen`." Similarly, an `EmployeeWithTerritory` "is an" `Employee`—but not the other way around—so `Employee` is the base class.

> **» NOTE** Do not confuse "is a" situations with "has a" situations. For example, you might create a `Business` class that contains an array of `Department` objects; in turn, each `Department` object might contain an array of `Employee` objects. You would not say "A department is a business," but that "a business *has* departments." Therefore, this relationship is not inheritance; it is **composition**—the relationship in which a class contains one or more members of another class, when those members would *not* continue to exist without the object that contains them. (For example, if a `Business` closes, its `Department`s do too.) Similarly, you would not say "an employee is a department", but that "a department *has* employees." This relationship is not inheritance either; it is a specific type of composition known as **aggregation**—the relationship in which a class contains one or more members of another class, when those members would continue to exist without the object that contains them. (For example, if a business or department closed, the employees would continue to exist.)

You can use the terms **superclass** and **subclass** as synonyms for base class and derived class, respectively. Thus, `Evergreen` can be called a subclass of the `Tree` superclass. You can also use the terms **parent class** and **child class**. An `EmployeeWithTerritory` is a child to the `Employee` parent. Use the pair of terms with which you are most comfortable; all of these terms are used interchangeably throughout this book.

As an alternative way to discover which of two classes is the base class or subclass, you can try saying the two class names together. When people say their names together, they state the more specific name before the all-encompassing family name, as in "Ginny Kroening." Similarly, with classes, the order that "makes more sense" is the child-parent order. "Evergreen Tree" makes more sense than "Tree Evergreen," so `Evergreen` is the child class.

Finally, you can usually distinguish superclasses from their subclasses by size. Although it is not required, in general a subclass is larger than a superclass because it usually has additional fields and methods. A subclass description might look small, but any subclass contains all the fields and methods of its superclass, as well as the new, more specific fields and methods you add to that subclass.

EXTENDING CLASSES

You use the keyword **extends** to achieve inheritance in Java. For example, the following class header creates a superclass-subclass relationship between `Employee` and `EmployeeWithTerritory`:

```
public class EmployeeWithTerritory extends Employee
```

Each `EmployeeWithTerritory` automatically receives the data fields and methods of the superclass `Employee`; you then add new fields and methods to the newly created subclass. Figure 11-4 shows an `EmployeeWithTerritory` class.

```
public class EmployeeWithTerritory extends Employee
{
    private int empTerritory;
    public int getEmpTerritory()
    {
        return empTerritory;
    }
    public void setEmpTerritory(int num)
    {
        empTerritory = num;
    }
}
```

Figure 11-4 The `EmployeeWithTerritory` class

» NOTE You used the phrase `extends JApplet` throughout Chapters 9 and 10. Every `JApplet` that you write is a child of the `JApplet` class.

You can write a statement that instantiates an object, such as the following:

```
EmployeeWithTerritory northernRep = new EmployeeWithTerritory();
```

Then you can use any of the next statements to get field values for the `northernRep` object:

```
northernRep.getEmpNum();
northernRep.getEmpSal();
northernRep.getEmpTerritory();
```

The `northernRep` object has access to all three get methods—two methods that it inherits from `Employee` and one method that belongs to `EmployeeWithTerritory`.

Similarly, after the `northernRep` object is declared, any of the following statements are legal:

```
northernRep.setEmpNum(915);
northernRep.setEmpSal(210.00);
northernRep.setEmpTerritory(5);
```

The `northernRep` object has access to all the parent `Employee` class set methods, as well as its own class's new set method.

Inheritance is a one-way proposition; a child inherits from a parent, not the other way around. When you instantiate an `Employee` object, as in `Employee aClerk = new Employee();`, the `Employee` object does not have access to the `EmployeeWithTerritory` methods. `Employee` is the parent class, and `aClerk` is an object of the parent class. It makes sense that a parent class object does not have access to its child's data and methods. When you create the parent class, you do not know how many future subclasses it might have or what their data or methods might look like.

In addition, subclasses are more specific. An `Orthodontist` class and `Periodontist` class are children of the `Dentist` parent class. You do not expect all members of the general parent class `Dentist` to have the `Orthodontist`'s `applyBraces()` method or the `Periodontist`'s `deepClean()` method. However, `Orthodontist` objects and `Periodontist` objects have access to the more general `Dentist` methods `conductExam()` and `billPatients()`.

In Chapter 9, you learned that you can use the `instanceof` keyword inside an event-handling method to determine the source of the event. For example, to determine whether any `JButton` generated an event, you could write:

```
if(objectThatCausedEvent instanceof JButton)...
```

Similarly, every child class is an instance of its parent. For example, if the `Orthodontist` class inherits from `Dentist`, and `myOrthodontist` is an `Orthodontist` object, then both of the following are true:

```
myOrthodontist instanceof Dentist
myOrthodontist instanceof Orthodontist
```

OVERRIDING SUPERCLASS METHODS

When you create a subclass by extending an existing class, the new subclass contains data and methods that were defined in the original superclass. In other words, any child class object has all the attributes of its parent. Sometimes, however, the superclass data fields and methods are not entirely appropriate for the subclass objects; in these cases, you want to override the parent class methods.

When you use the English language, you often use the same method name to indicate diverse meanings. For example, if you think of `MusicalInstrument` as a class, you can think of `play()` as a method of that class. If you think of various subclasses such as `Guitar` and `Drum`, you know that you carry out the `play()` method quite differently for each subclass. Using the same method name to indicate different implementations is called **polymorphism**, a term that means "many forms"—many different forms of action take place, even though you use the same word to describe the action. In other words, many forms of the same word exist, depending on the object associated with the word.

>> **NOTE** You first learned the term *polymorphism* in Chapter 1. Polymorphism is one of the basic principles of object-oriented programming. If a programming language does not support polymorphism, the language is not considered object-oriented.

For example, suppose you create an `Employee` superclass containing data fields such as `firstName`, `lastName`, `socialSecurityNumber`, `dateOfHire`, `rateOfPay`, and so on, and the methods contained in the `Employee` class include the usual collection of get and set methods. If your usual time period for payment to each `Employee` object is weekly, your `printRateOfPay()` method might include a statement such as:

```
System.out.println("Pay is " + rateOfPay + " per week");
```

Imagine your company has a few `Employees` who are not paid weekly. Maybe some are paid by the hour, and others are `Employees` whose work is contracted on a job-to-job basis. Because each `Employee` type requires different paycheck-calculating procedures, you might want to create subclasses of `Employee`, such as `HourlyEmployee` and `ContractEmployee`.

When you call the `printRateOfPay()` method for an `HourlyEmployee` object, you want the display to include the phrase "per hour", as in "Pay is $8.75 per hour." When you call the `printRateOfPay()` method for a `ContractEmployee`, you want to include "per contract", as in "Pay is $2000 per contract." Each class—the `Employee` superclass and the two subclasses—requires its own `printRateOfPay()` method. Fortunately, if you create separate `printRateOfPay()` methods for each class, the objects of each class use the appropriate method for that class. When you create a method in a child class that has the same name and argument list as a method in its parent class, you **override the method** in the parent class. When you use the method name with a child object, the child's version of the method is used.

>> NOTE
You first saw the term *override* in Chapter 4, when you learned that a variable declared within a block overrides another variable with the same name declared outside the block.

>> NOTE It is important to note that each subclass method overrides any method in the parent class that has both the same name and argument list. If the parent class method has the same name but a different argument list, the subclass method does not override the parent class version; instead, the subclass method overloads the parent class method and any subclass object has access to both versions. You learned about overloading methods in Chapter 4.

If you could not override superclass methods, you could always create a unique name for each subclass method, such as `printRateOfPayForHourly()`, but the classes you create are easier to write and understand if you use one reasonable name for methods that do essentially the same thing. Because you are attempting to print the rate of pay for each object, `printRateOfPay()` is an excellent method name for all the object types.

>> NOTE You have already overridden methods in your `JApplets`. When you write your own `init()` or `start()` method within an applet, you are overriding the automatically supplied superclass version you acquire when you use the phrase `extends JApplet`.

Object-oriented programmers use the term *polymorphism* when discussing any operation that has multiple meanings. For example, the plus sign (+) is polymorphic because you can use it to add integers or `doubles`, to concatenate strings, or to indicate a positive value. As another example, methods with the same name but different argument lists are polymorphic because the method call operates differently depending on the arguments. When Java developers refer to polymorphism, they most often mean **subtype polymorphism**—the ability of one method name to work appropriately for different subclass objects of the same parent class.

UNDERSTANDING HOW CONSTRUCTORS ARE CALLED DURING INHERITANCE

When you create any object, as in the following statement, you are calling a class constructor method that has the same name as the class itself:

```
SomeClass anObject = new SomeClass();
```

When you instantiate an object that is a member of a subclass, you are actually calling at least two constructors: the constructor for the base class and the constructor for the extended, derived class. When you create any subclass object, the superclass constructor must execute first, and *then* the subclass constructor executes.

> **NOTE** In Chapter 12, you will learn that every Java object automatically is a child of a class named Object. So, when you instantiate any object, you call its constructor and Object's constructor, and when you create parent and child classes of your own, the child classes use three constructors.

When a superclass contains a default constructor and you instantiate a subclass object, the execution of the superclass constructor often is transparent—that is, nothing calls attention to the fact that the superclass constructor is executing. However, you should realize that when you create an object such as the following (where HourlyEmployee is a subclass of Employee), *both* the Employee() and HourlyEmployee() constructors execute.

```
HourlyEmployee clerk = new HourlyEmployee();
```

For example, Figure 11-5 shows three classes. The class named ASuperClass has a constructor that displays a message. The class named ASubClass descends from ASuperClass, and its constructor displays a different message. The DemoConstructors class instantiates one object of type ASubClass. Figure 11-6 shows the output when DemoConstructors executes. You can see that when DemoConstructors instantiates the ASubClass object, the parent class constructor executes first, displaying its message, and then the child class constructor executes. Even though only one object is created, two constructors execute.

```java
public class ASuperClass
{
    public ASuperClass()
    {
        System.out.println("In superclass constructor");
    }
}
public class ASubClass extends ASuperClass
{
    public ASubClass()
    {
        System.out.println("In subclass constructor");
    }
}
public class DemoConstructors
{
    public static void main(String[] args)
    {
        ASubClass child = new ASubClass();
    }
}
```

Figure 11-5 Three classes that demonstrate constructor calling when a subclass object is instantiated

Of course, most constructors perform many more tasks than printing a message to inform you that they exist. When constructors initialize variables, you usually want the superclass

Figure 11-6 Output of the `DemoConstructors` application

constructor to take care of initializing the data fields that originate in the superclass. Usually, the subclass constructor only needs to initialize the data fields that are specific to the subclass.

USING SUPERCLASS CONSTRUCTORS THAT REQUIRE ARGUMENTS

> **»NOTE**
> Don't forget that a class can have many constructors. As soon as you create at least one constructor for a class, you can no longer use the automatically supplied version.

When you create a class and do not provide a constructor, Java automatically supplies you with a default constructor—one that never requires arguments. When you write your own constructor, you replace the automatically supplied version. Depending on your needs, a constructor you create for a class might require arguments. When you use a class as a superclass and the class has only constructors that require arguments, you must be certain that any subclasses provide the superclass constructor with the arguments it needs.

When a superclass has a default constructor, you can create a subclass with or without its own constructor. This is true whether the default constructor is the automatically supplied one or one you have written. However, when a superclass contains only constructors that require arguments, you must include at least one constructor for each subclass you create. Your subclass constructors can contain any number of statements, but the first statement within each constructor must call the superclass constructor. When a superclass requires parameters upon instantiation, even if you have no other reason to create a subclass constructor, you must write the subclass constructor so it can call its superclass's constructor.

> **»NOTE** If a superclass has multiple constructors but one is a default constructor, you do not have to create a subclass constructor unless you want to. If the subclass contains no constructor, all subclass objects use the superclass default constructor when they are instantiated.

The format of the statement that calls a superclass constructor is:

```
super(list of arguments);
```

The keyword **super** always refers to the superclass of the class in which you use it.

If a superclass contains only constructors that require arguments, you must create a subclass constructor, but the subclass constructor does not necessarily have to have arguments of its own. For example, suppose that you create an `Employee` class with a constructor that requires three arguments—a character, a `double`, and an integer—and you create an `HourlyEmployee` class that is a subclass of `Employee`. The following code shows a valid constructor for `HourlyEmployee`:

```
public HourlyEmployee()
{
    super('P', 12.35, 40);
    // Other statements can go here
}
```

This version of the HourlyEmployee constructor requires no arguments, but it passes three arguments to its superclass constructor. A different HourlyEmployee constructor can require arguments. It could then pass the appropriate arguments to the superclass constructor. For example:

```
public HourlyEmployee(char dept, double rate, int hours)
{
    super(dept, rate, hours);
    // Other statements can go here
}
```

>> NOTE Although it seems that you should be able to use the superclass constructor name to call the superclass constructor—for example, Employee()—Java does not allow this. You must use the keyword super.

ACCESSING SUPERCLASS METHODS

Earlier in this chapter, you learned that a subclass could contain a method with the same name and arguments (the same signature) as a method in its parent class. When this happens, using the subclass method overrides the superclass method. However, you might want to use the superclass method within a subclass. If so, you can use the keyword super to access the parent class method.

For example, examine the Customer class in Figure 11-7 and the PreferredCustomer class in Figure 11-8. A Customer has an idNumber and balanceOwed. In addition to these fields, a PreferredCustomer receives a discountRate. In the PreferredCustomer display() method, you want to display all three fields—idNumber, balanceOwed, and discountRate. Because two-thirds of the code to accomplish the display has already been written for the Customer class, it is convenient to have the PreferredCustomer display() method use its parent's version of the display() method before printing its own discount rate. Figure 11-9 shows a brief application that displays one object of each class, and Figure 11-10 shows the output.

```
public class Customer
{
    private int idNumber;
    private double balanceOwed;
    public Customer(int id, double bal)
    {
        idNumber = id;
        balanceOwed = bal;
    }
    public void display()
    {
        System.out.println("Customer #" + idNumber +
            " Balance $" + balanceOwed);
    }
}
```

Figure 11-7 The Customer class

```
public class PreferredCustomer extends Customer
{
    double discountRate;
    public PreferredCustomer(int id, double bal, double rate)
    {
        super(id, bal);
        discountRate = rate;
    }
    public void display()
    {
        super.display();
        System.out.println("Discount rate is " + discountRate);
    }
}
```

Figure 11-8 The PreferredCustomer class

```
public class TestCustomers
{
    public static void main(String[] args)
    {
        Customer oneCust = new Customer(124, 123.45);
        PreferredCustomer onePCust = new
            PreferredCustomer(125, 3456.78, 0.15);
        oneCust.display();
        onePCust.display();
    }
}
```

Figure 11-9 The TestCustomers application

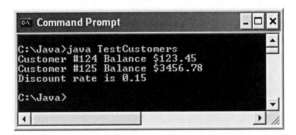

Figure 11-10 Output of the TestCustomers application

> **NOTE** You can use the keyword this as the opposite of super. For example, if a superclass and its subclass each have a method named someMethod(), within the subclass, super.someMethod() refers to the superclass version of the method. Both someMethod() and this.someMethod() refer to the subclass version.

LEARNING ABOUT INFORMATION HIDING

The Student class shown in Figure 11-11 is an example of a typical Java class. Within the Student class, as with most Java classes, the keyword private precedes each data field, and the keyword public precedes each method. In fact, the four get and set methods are public within the Student class specifically because the data fields are private. Without the public get and set methods, there would be no way to access the private data fields.

```java
public class Student
{
    private int idNum;
    private double gpa;
    public int getIdNum()
    {
        return idNum;
    }
    public double getGpa()
    {
        return gpa;
    }
    public void setIdNum(int num)
    {
        idNum = num;
    }
    public void setGpa(double gradePoint)
    {
        gpa = gradePoint;
    }
}
```

Figure 11-11 The Student class

When an application is a client of the Student class (that is, it instantiates a Student object), the client cannot directly alter the data in any private field. For example, when you write a main() method that creates a Student as:

```java
Student someStudent = new Student();
```

you cannot change the Student's idNum with a statement such as:

```java
someStudent.idNum = 812;
```

The idNum of the someStudent object is not accessible in the main() method that uses the Student object because idNum is private. Only methods that are part of the Student class itself are allowed to alter Student data. To alter a Student's idNum, you must use a public method, as in the following:

```java
someStudent.setIdNum(812);
```

The concept of keeping data private is known as **information hiding**. When you employ information hiding, your data can be altered only by the methods you choose and only in ways that you can control. For example, you might want the setIdNum() method to check to make certain the `idNum` is within a specific range of values. If a class other than the `Student` class could alter `idNum`, `idNum` could be assigned a value that the `Student` class couldn't control.

When a class serves as a superclass to other classes you create, your subclasses inherit all the data and methods of the superclass. The methods in a subclass can use all of the data fields and methods that belong to its parent, with one exception: `private` members of the parent class are not accessible within a child class's methods. If you could use `private` data outside its class, you would lose the advantages of information hiding. For example, if you want the `Student` class data field `idNum` to be `private`, you don't want any outside classes using the field. If a new class could simply extend your `Student` class and get to its data fields without going through the proper channels, information hiding would not be operating.

》 NOTE If the members of a base class don't have an explicit modifier, their access modifier is `package` by default. Such base class members cannot be accessed within a child class unless the two classes are in the same package. You will learn about packages in Chapter 12.

Sometimes, you want to access parent class data from within a subclass. For example, suppose you create two child classes—`PartTimeStudent` and `FullTimeStudent`—that extend the `Student` class. If you want the subclass methods to be able to directly access `idNum` and `gpa`, these data fields cannot be `private`. However, if you don't want other, nonchild classes to access these data fields, they cannot be `public`. To solve this problem, you can create the fields using the modifier `protected`. Using the keyword **protected** provides you with an intermediate level of security between `public` and `private` access. If you create a `protected` data field or method, it can be used within its own class or in any classes extended from that class, but it cannot be used by "outside" classes. In other words, `protected` members are those that can be used by a class and its descendants.

》 NOTE A child class can always access its parent's `private` data fields by using `public` methods defined in the parent class, just as any other class can. You only need to make parent class fields `protected` if you want child classes to be able to access `private` data directly.

USING METHODS YOU CANNOT OVERRIDE

The three types of methods that you cannot override in a subclass are:

» `static` methods
» `final` methods
» Methods within `final` classes

A SUBCLASS CANNOT OVERRIDE `static` METHODS IN ITS SUPERCLASS

A subclass cannot override methods that are declared `static` in the superclass. In other words, a subclass cannot override a class method—a method you use without instantiating an object. A subclass can *hide* a `static` method in the superclass by declaring a `static` method in the subclass with the same signature as the `static` method in the superclass; then, you can call the new `static` method from within the subclass or in another class by using a subclass object. However, this `static` method that hides the superclass `static` method cannot access the parent method using the `super` object.

Figure 11-12 shows a `BaseballPlayer` class that contains a single `static` method named
`printOrigins()`. Figure 11-13 shows a `ProfessionalBaseballPlayer` class that extends
the `BaseballPlayer` class to provide a salary. Within the `ProfessionalBaseballPlayer`
class, an attempt is made to override the `printOrigins()` method to display the general
Abner Doubleday message about baseball as well as the more specific message about professional baseball. However, the compiler returns the error message shown in Figure 11-14—you
cannot override a `static` method with a nonstatic method.

```
public class BaseballPlayer
{
    private int jerseyNumber;
    private double battingAvg;
    public static void printOrigins()
    {
        System.out.println("Abner Doubleday is often " +
            "credited with inventing baseball");
    }
}
```

Figure 11-12 The `BaseballPlayer` class

```
public class ProfessionalBaseballPlayer extends BaseballPlayer
{
    double salary;
    public void printOrigins()
    {
        super.printOrigins();
        System.out.println("The first professional " +
            "major league baseball game was played in 1871");
    }
}
```

Figure 11-13 The `ProfessionalBaseballPlayer` class attempting to override the parent's `static` method

Figure 11-14 Error message when compiling the `ProfessionalBaseballPlayer` class in Figure 11-13

Figure 11-15 shows a second version of the `ProfessionalBaseballPlayer` class. In this
version, the `printOrigins()` method has been changed to `static`. Figure 11-16 shows the
error message that displays, proving that the parent class method is not overridden.

```
public class ProfessionalBaseballPlayer extends BaseballPlayer
{
    double salary;
    public static void printOrigins()
    {
        super.printOrigins();
        System.out.println("The first professional " +
            "major league baseball game was played in 1871");
    }
}
```

Figure 11-15 The `ProfessionalBaseballPlayer` class attempting to reference `super`

```
Command Prompt                                                    _ □ ×

C:\Java>javac ProfessionalBaseballPlayer.java
ProfessionalBaseballPlayer.java:6: non-static variable super cannot be reference
d from a static context
        super.printOrigins();
        ^
1 error

C:\Java>
```

Figure 11-16 Error message when compiling the `ProfessionalBaseballPlayer` class in Figure 11-15

Finally, Figure 11-17 shows a `ProfessionalBaseballPlayer` class that compiles without error. Its `printOrigins()` method is `static`. Because this method has the same name as the parent class method, when you use the name with a child class object, this method hides the original. However, it does not override the original, or the `super` call in the version of the method in Figure 11-15 would have compiled without error. If you want the `ProfessionalBaseballPlayer` class to display information about baseball in general as well as professional baseball in particular, you can do either of the following:

» You can display both messages from within a child class method with `println()` statements.

» You can use the parent class name, a dot, and the method name. Although a child class cannot inherit its parent's `static` methods, it can access its parent's `static` methods the same way any other class can.

```
public class ProfessionalBaseballPlayer extends BaseballPlayer
{
    double salary;
    public static void printOrigins()
    {
        BaseballPlayer.printOrigins();
        System.out.println("The first professional " +
            "major league baseball game was played in 1871");
    }
}
```

Figure 11-17 The `ProfessionalBaseballPlayer` class

Figure 11-18 shows a class that creates a `ProfessionalBaseballPlayer` and tests the method; Figure 11-19 shows the output.

```
public class TestProPlayer
{
    public static void main(String[] args)
    {
        ProfessionalBaseballPlayer aYankee =
            new ProfessionalBaseballPlayer();
        aYankee.printOrigins();
    }
}
```

Figure 11-18 The `TestProPlayer` class

Figure 11-19 Output of the `TestProPlayer` application

A SUBCLASS CANNOT OVERRIDE final METHODS IN ITS SUPERCLASS

A subclass cannot override methods that are declared `final` in the superclass. For example, consider the `BasketballPlayer` and `ProfessionalBasketballPlayer` classes in Figures 11-20 and 11-21, respectively. When you attempt to compile the `ProfessionalBasketballPlayer` class, you receive the error message in Figure 11-22, because the class cannot override the `final` `printMessage()` method in the parent class.

```
public class BasketballPlayer
{
    private int jerseyNumber;
    public final void printMessage()
    {
        System.out.println("Michael Jordan is the " +
            "greatest basketball player - and that is final");
    }
}
```

Figure 11-20 The `BasketballPlayer` class

```
public class ProfessionalBasketballPlayer extends BasketballPlayer
{
    double salary;
    public void printMessage()
    {
        System.out.println("I have nothing to say");
    }
}
```

Figure 11-21 The `ProfessionalBasketballPlayer` class that attempts to override a `final` method

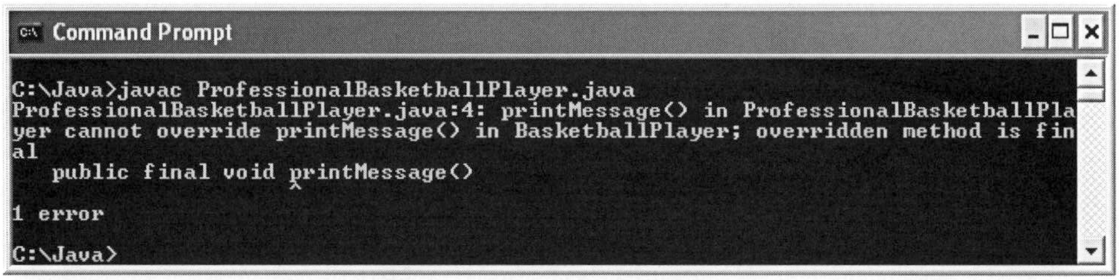

```
Command Prompt                                                    _ □ ×

C:\Java>javac ProfessionalBasketballPlayer.java
ProfessionalBasketballPlayer.java:4: printMessage() in ProfessionalBasketballPla
yer cannot override printMessage() in BasketballPlayer; overridden method is fin
al
    public final void printMessage()
                      ^
1 error

C:\Java>
```

Figure 11-22 Error message when compiling the `ProfessionalBasketballPlayer` class in Figure 11-21

> **▶▶ NOTE** If you make the `printMessage()` method `final` in the `ProfessionalBasketballPlayer` class in Figure 11-21, you receive the same compiler error message as shown in Figure 11-22. If you make the `printMessage()` method `static` in the `ProfessionalBasketballPlayer` class, the class does not compile, but you do receive an additional error message.

In Chapter 4, you learned that you can use the keyword `final` when you want to create a constant, as in `final double TAXRATE = .065;`. You can also use the `final` modifier with methods when you don't want the method to be overridden—that is, when you want every child class to use the original parent class version of a method.

In Java, all instance method calls are **virtual method calls** by default—that is, the method used is determined when the program runs because the type of the object used might not be known until the method executes. For example, with the following method you can pass in a `BasketballPlayer` object, or any object that is a child of `BasketballPlayer`, so the "actual" type of the argument `bbplayer`, and which version of `printMessage()` to use, is not known until the method executes.

```
public void display(BasketballPlayer bbplayer)
{
    bbplayer.printMessage();
}
```

In other words, the version of `printMessage()` that is called is not determined when the program is compiled; it is determined when the method call is made. An advantage to making a method `final` is that the compiler knows there will be only one version of the method—the parent class version—and so the compiler *does* know which method version will be used—the only version.

Because a `final` method's definition can never change—that is, can never be overridden with a modified version—the compiler can optimize a program's performance by removing the calls to `final` methods and replacing them with the expanded code of their definitions at each method call location. This process is called **inlining** the code. You are never aware that inlining is taking place; the compiler chooses to use this procedure to save the overhead of calling a method, and this makes the program run faster. The compiler chooses to inline a `final` method only if it is a small method that contains just one or two lines of code.

A SUBCLASS CANNOT OVERRIDE METHODS IN A `final` SUPERCLASS

Finally, you can declare a class to be `final`. When you do, all of its methods are `final`, regardless of which access modifier precedes the method name. A `final` class cannot be a parent. Figure 11-23 shows two classes: a `HideAndGoSeekPlayer` class that is a `final` class because of the word `final` in the class header, and a `ProfessionalHideAndGoSeekPlayer` class that attempts to extend the `final` class, adding a salary field. Figure 11-24 shows the error message generated when you try to compile the `ProfessionalHideAndGoSeekPlayer` class.

» NOTE
Java's Math class, which you learned about in Chapter 4, is an example of a final class.

```java
public final class HideAndGoSeekPlayer
{
    private int count;
    public void printRules()
    {
        System.out.println("You have to count to " + count +
            " before you start looking for hiders");
    }
}
public final class ProfessionalHideAndGoSeekPlayer
    extends HideAndGoSeekPlayer
{
    private double salary;
}
```

Figure 11-23 The `HideAndGoSeekPlayer` and `ProfessionalHideAndGoSeekPlayer` classes

```
C:\Java>javac ProfessionalHideAndGoSeekPlayer.java
ProfessionalHideAndGoSeekPlayer.java:2: cannot inherit from final HideAndGoSeekP
layer
    extends HideAndGoSeekPlayer
            ^
1 error

C:\Java>
```

Figure 11-24 Error message when compiling the `ProfessionalHideAndGoSeekPlayer` class in Figure 11-23

» NOTE A subclass is required to override methods that are declared abstract in the superclass (or the subclass itself must be abstract). You will learn about abstract classes and methods in Chapter 12.

YOU DO IT

In this section, you create a working example of inheritance. To see the effects of inheritance, you create this example in four stages:

» First, you create a general `Event` class for Event Handlers Incorporated. This `Event` class is small—it holds just one data field and two methods.

» After you create the general `Event` class, you write an application to demonstrate its use.

» Then, you create a more specific `DinnerEvent` subclass that inherits the attributes of the `Event` class.

» Finally, you modify the demonstration application to add an example using the `DinnerEvent` class.

CREATING A SUPERCLASS AND AN APPLICATION TO USE IT

To create the general Event class:

1. Open a new file in your text editor, and enter the following first few lines for a simple `Event` class. The class hosts one integer data field—the number of guests expected at the event:

```java
import javax.swing.*;
public class Event
{
    private int eventGuests;
```

2. To the `Event` class, add the following method that displays the number of `eventGuests`:

```java
public void displayEventGuests()
{
    JOptionPane.showMessageDialog(null, "Event guests: " +
        eventGuests);
}
```

3. Add a second method that prompts the user for the number of guests, temporarily stores the response in the `guestsString` field, and then uses the `parseInt()` method to convert the number to an integer to be stored in the class `eventGuests` field:

```java
public void setEventGuests()
{
    char inChar;
    String guestsString = new String("");
    guestsString = JOptionPane.showInputDialog(null,
        "Enter the number of guests at your event ");
    eventGuests = Integer.parseInt(guestsString);
}
```

4. Add the closing curly brace for the class, then save the file as **Event.java** in the Chapter.11 folder on your Student Disk. At the command prompt, compile the class using the **javac Event.java** command. If necessary, correct any errors and compile again.

Now that you have created a class, you can use it in an application or an applet. A very simple application creates an `Event` object, calls the method to set a value for the data field, and displays the results.

To write a simple application that uses the `Event` class:

1. Open a new file in your text editor.

2. Write a `UseSimpleEvent` application that has one method—a `main()` method. Enter the following `main()` method, which declares an `Event` object, supplies it with a value, and then displays the value:

```
public class UseSimpleEvent
{
    public static void main(String[] args)
    {
        Event anEvent = new Event();
        anEvent.setEventGuests();
        anEvent.displayEventGuests();
        System.exit(0);
    }
}
```

3. Save the file as **UseSimpleEvent.java** in the Chapter.11 folder on your Student Disk. Compile the class using the **javac UseSimpleEvent.java** command. After the class compiles without errors, run the application by typing **java UseSimpleEvent**. When the program executes, type **30** and press **Enter**. The application's output appears in Figure 11-25. Click **OK** to dismiss the dialog box.

Figure 11-25 Execution of the `UseSimpleEvent` application

CREATING A SUBCLASS AND AN APPLICATION TO USE IT

Next, you create a class named `DinnerEvent`. A `DinnerEvent` "is a" type of `Event` at which dinner is served, so `DinnerEvent` is a child class of `Event`.

To create a `DinnerEvent` class that extends `Event`:

1. Open a new file in your text editor, and type the first few lines for the `DinnerEvent` class:

```
import javax.swing.*;
public class DinnerEvent extends Event
{
```

2. A `DinnerEvent` contains a number of guests, but you do not have to define the variable here. The variable is already defined in `Event`, which is the superclass of this class. You only need to add any variables that are particular to a `DinnerEvent`. Enter the following

code to add an integer to hold the dinner menu choices, which are 1 or 2 for beef or chicken, respectively:

```
int dinnerChoice;
```

3. The `Event` class already contains methods to set and print the number of guests, so `DinnerEvent` only needs methods to print and set the `dinnerChoice` variable. To keep this example simple, you do not validate the input character to ensure that it is 1 or 2; you can add this improvement to the method later. The `displayDinnerChoice()` method assumes that if the choice is not beef, it must be chicken. Type the `displayDinnerChoice()` method as follows:

```
public void displayDinnerChoice()
{
    if(dinnerChoice == 1)
        JOptionPane.showMessageDialog(null,
            "Dinner choice is beef");
    else
        JOptionPane.showMessageDialog(null,
            "Dinner choice is chicken");
}
```

4. Enter the following `setDinnerChoice()` method, which prompts the user for the choice of entrees at the event, and then adds a closing curly brace for the class:

```
public void setDinnerChoice()
{
    String choice;
    choice = JOptionPane.showInputDialog(null,
        "Enter dinner choice\n1 for beef, 2 for chicken");
    dinnerChoice = Integer.parseInt(choice);
}
}
```

5. Save the file as **DinnerEvent.java** in the Chapter.11 folder on your Student Disk, and then compile it.

Now, you can modify the `UseSimpleEvent` application so that it creates a `DinnerEvent` as well as a plain `Event`.

To modify the `UseSimpleEvent` application:

1. Open the **UseSimpleEvent.java** file in your text editor. Change the class name from `UseSimpleEvent` to **UseDinnerEvent**.

2. The application uses dialog boxes, so add an `import` line as follows:

```
import javax.swing.*;
```

3. Position the insertion point at the end of the line that constructs `anEvent` (the first statement within the `main()` method), and then press **Enter** to start a new line. Type the following statement so that when you run the application, you know that you are using the `Event` class to create the event:

```
JOptionPane.showMessageDialog(null, "Creating an event");
```

4. Position the insertion point at the end of the line that displays the event guests (just before the `System.exit(0)` call), and then press **Enter** to start a new line. Add the following two new statements—one constructs a `DinnerEvent`, and the other displays a message so that when you run the application you understand you are creating a `DinnerEvent`:

```
DinnerEvent aDinnerEvent = new DinnerEvent();
JOptionPane.showMessageDialog(null,
    "Creating an event with dinner");
```

5. Add the following method calls to set the number of guests and dinner choice for the `DinnerEvent` object. Even though the `DinnerEvent` class does not contain a `setEventGuests()` method, its parent class (`Event`) does, so `aDinnerEvent` can use the `setEventGuests()` method.

```
aDinnerEvent.setEventGuests();
aDinnerEvent.setDinnerChoice();
```

6. Enter the following code to call the methods that display the entered data:

```
aDinnerEvent.displayEventGuests();
aDinnerEvent.displayDinnerChoice();
```

7. Save the file as **UseDinnerEvent.java** in the Chapter.11 folder on your Student Disk. Compile the class and run it using the values shown in Figure 11-26. The `DinnerEvent` object successfully uses the data field and methods of its superclass, as well as its own data field and methods.

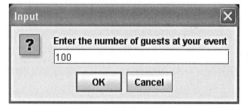

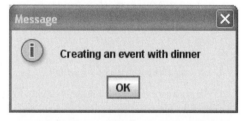

Figure 11-26 Execution of the `UseDinnerEvent` application (*continued*) ▶

Figure 11-26 Execution of the `UseDinnerEvent` application

CREATING A SUBCLASS METHOD THAT OVERRIDES A SUPERCLASS METHOD

Next, you create two methods with the same name, `displayPricingInfo()`, with one version in the `Event` superclass and another in the `DinnerEvent` subclass. When you call the `displayPricingInfo()` method, the correct version executes based on the object you use.

To add a `displayPricingInfo()` method to the `Event` class:

1. In your text editor, open the **Event.java** file in the Chapter.11 folder on your Student Disk. Change the class name from `Event` to `EventWithInfo` because this new class contains a method that allows you to display pricing information for an event. Save the file as **EventWithInfo.java** in the Chapter.11 folder on your Student Disk. In addition to providing a descriptive name, changing the class name serves another purpose. By giving the class a new name, you retain the original class on your disk so you can study the differences later.

2. Position the insertion point at the end of the line that contains the closing curly brace for the `setEventGuests()` method, and then press **Enter** to start a new line.

3. Enter the following `displayPricingInfo()` method:

```
public void displayPricingInfo()
{
    JOptionPane.showMessageDialog(null,
        "Events cost $100 per hour\n" +
        "There is a three-hour minimum");
}
```

4. Save the file and then compile it.

To demonstrate that a subclass method overrides a superclass method with the same signature:

1. Open the **DinnerEvent.java** file in the Chapter.11 folder. Change the class name from `DinnerEvent` to `DinnerEventWithInfo`, and change the class from which it extends—`Event`—to **EventWithInfo**. Save the file as **DinnerEventWithInfo.java** in the Chapter.11 folder on your Student Disk.

2. Because dinner events have a different pricing schedule than "ordinary" events, you override the parent class `displayPricingInfo()` method within the child class. Position your insertion point at the end of the line that contains the closing curly brace for the `setDinnerChoice()` method, and then press **Enter** to start a new line of text. Add the following `displayPricingInfo()` method to this class.

```
public void displayPricingInfo()
{
    JOptionPane.showMessageDialog(null,
        "Dinner events cost $85 per hour\n" +
        "Plus the cost of the meals\n" +
        "There is a four-hour minimum");
}
```

3. Save the file and then compile it.

You just created an `EventWithInfo` class that contains a `displayPricingInfo()` method. Then, you extended the class by creating a `DinnerEventWithInfo` subclass containing a method with the same name. Now, you will write an application demonstrating that the correct method executes, depending on the object.

To create an application demonstrating that the correct `displayPricingInfo()` method executes, depending on the object:

1. Open a new file in your text editor, and then enter the first few lines of a `UseEventWithInfo` class:

```
import javax.swing.*;
public class UseEventWithInfo
{
    public static void main(String[] args)
    {
```

2. Enter the following code to create two objects—an `EventWithInfo` and a `DinnerEventWithInfo`:

```
EventWithInfo anEvent = new EventWithInfo();
DinnerEventWithInfo aDinnerEvent = new DinnerEventWithInfo();
```

3. Enter the code to call the `displayPricingInfo()` method with each object type, then add the `System.exit(0);` command and the closing curly braces for the `main()` method and the class:

```
        anEvent.displayPricingInfo();
        aDinnerEvent.displayPricingInfo();
        System.exit(0);
    }
}
```

4. Save the file as **UseEventWithInfo.java** in the Chapter.11 folder on your Student Disk. Compile and run the application. The output looks like Figure 11-27. Each type of object

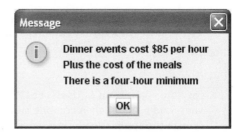

Figure 11-27 Execution of the `UseEventWithInfo` application

uses the method appropriate for that type; the child class method has successfully overridden the parent class method.

UNDERSTANDING THE ROLE OF CONSTRUCTORS IN INHERITANCE

Next, you add a constructor to the `EventWithInfo` class that you created for Event Handlers Incorporated. When you instantiate a subclass object, the superclass constructor executes before the subclass constructor executes.

To demonstrate that instantiating a subclass object calls the superclass constructor:

1. Open the **EventWithInfo.java** file in your text editor. Use your text editor's Save As command to save the file as **EventWithConstructor.java** in the Chapter.11 folder on your Student Disk. Be certain to change the class name from `EventWithInfo` to `EventWithConstructor`.

2. Position the insertion point to the right of the statement that declares the `eventGuests` data field, and then press **Enter** to start a new line. Type a constructor for the `EventWithConstructor` class that does nothing other than display a message indicating it is working:

```
EventWithConstructor()
{
    System.out.println("Creating an Event");
}
```

3. Save the file and compile it.

4. In your text editor, open the **DinnerEventWithInfo.java** file from the Chapter.11 folder on your Student Disk. Change the class header so that both the class name and the parent class name read as follows:

```
public class DinnerEventWithConstructor extends EventWithConstructor
```

5. Save the file as **DinnerEventWithConstructor.java** in the Chapter.11 folder on your Student Disk, and then compile it. In your text editor, open a new file so you can write an application to demonstrate the use of the base class constructor with an extended class object. This application only creates one child class object:

```
public class UseEventWithConstructor
{
    public static void main(String[] args)
    {
        DinnerEventWithConstructor aDinnerEvent =
            new DinnerEventWithConstructor();
    }
}
```

6. Save the application as **UseEventWithConstructor.java** in the Chapter.11 folder on your Student Disk, then compile and run it. The output is shown in Figure 11-28. Even though the application only creates one subclass object (and no superclass objects) and the subclass contains no constructor of its own, the superclass constructor executes.

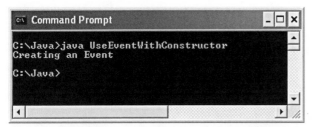

Figure 11-28 Output of the UseEventWithConstructor application

UNDERSTANDING INHERITANCE WHEN THE SUPERCLASS REQUIRES CONSTRUCTOR ARGUMENTS

Next, you modify the EventWithConstructor class so that its constructor requires an argument. Then, you will observe that a subclass without a constructor cannot compile.

To demonstrate how inheritance works when a superclass constructor requires an argument:

1. Open the **EventWithConstructor.java** file in your text editor, and then change the class name to **EventWithConstructorArg**.

2. Replace the existing constructor with a new version that requires an argument, which it uses to set the number of guests who will attend an event:

```
EventWithConstructorArg(int numGuests)
{
    eventGuests = numGuests;
}
```

3. Save the file as **EventWithConstructorArg.java** in the Chapter.11 folder on your Student Disk, and then compile it.

Next, you modify the DinnerEventWithConstructor class so it inherits from EventWithConstructorArg.

To create the child class:

1. Open the **DinnerEventWithConstructor.java** file in your text editor.

2. Change the class header as follows so that the name of the class is DinnerEventWithConstructorArg, and thus inherits from EventWithConstructorArg:

```
public class DinnerEventWithConstructorArg extends
    EventWithConstructorArg
```

3. Save the file as **DinnerEventWithConstructorArg.java** in the Chapter.11 folder on your Student Disk, and then compile it. An error message appears, as shown in Figure 11-29. When you attempt to compile the subclass, a call is made to the superclass constructor, but because this constructor requires a passed parameter, the compile fails.

To correct the error:

1. Open the **DinnerEventWithConstructorArg.java** file in your text editor, if it is not still open.

Figure 11-29 Error message generated when compiling the `DinnerEventWithConstructorArg` class

2. Place the insertion point after the declaration of the `dinnerChoice` field.

3. Press **Enter** to start a new line, and insert a constructor for the class as follows:

```
DinnerEventWithConstructorArg(int numGuests)
{
    super(numGuests);
}
```

4. Save the file and compile it. This time, the compile is successful because the subclass calls its parent's constructor, passing along an integer value. Note that the `DinnerEventWithConstructorArg` subclass constructor is not required to receive an integer argument, although in this example it does. For example, it would be acceptable to create a subclass constructor that required no arguments but passed a constant (for example, 0) to its parent. Similarly, the subclass constructor could require several arguments and pass one of them to its parent. The requirement is not that the subclass constructor must have the same number or types of parameters as its parent; the only requirement is that the subclass constructor calls `super()` and passes to the parent what it needs to execute.

Now, you can create an application to demonstrate creating parent and child class objects when the parent constructor needs an argument.

To create the application:

1. Open a new file in your text editor, and then enter the following first few lines of an application that demonstrates creating superclass and subclass objects using the classes you just created:

```
public class UseEventsWithConstructorArg
{
    public static void main(String[] args)
    {
```

2. Enter the following code to create two objects: an `EventWithConstructorArg` object with 45 guests and a `DinnerEventWithConstructorArg` object with 65 guests.

```
EventWithConstructorArg anEvent = new EventWithConstructorArg(45);
DinnerEventWithConstructorArg aDinnerEvent = new
    DinnerEventWithConstructorArg(65);
```

3. Add the following statements to display guest values for each object, and then add the `System.exit(0);` statement (because the application used GUI objects). Also add closing curly braces for the method and the class:

```
        anEvent.displayEventGuests();
        aDinnerEvent.displayEventGuests();
        System.exit(0);
    }
}
```

4. Save the file as **UseEventsWithConstructorArg.java** in the Chapter.11 folder on your Student Disk, and then compile and execute the application. The output appears in Figure 11-30. Each object is correctly initialized because the superclass constructor was correctly called in each case.

Figure 11-30 Output of the UseEventsWithConstructorArg application

ACCESSING AN OVERRIDDEN SUPERCLASS METHOD FROM WITHIN A SUBCLASS

When a subclass contains a method with the same signature as a method in the parent class, and you then use the method name with a subclass object, the subclass version of the method executes. If you want to access the superclass version of the method instead, you must use the keyword super. To demonstrate, you will create a simple subclass that has a method with the same name and argument list as a method that is part of its superclass.

To create an application that demonstrates accessing a superclass method from within a subclass:

1. Open a new file in your text editor, and then create the following parent class with a single method:

```
public class AParentClass
{
    private int aVal;
    public void displayClassName()
    {
        System.out.println("AParentClass");
    }
}
```

2. Save the file as **AParentClass.java** in the Chapter.11 folder on your Student Disk, and then compile it.

3. Open a new text file and create the following child class that inherits from the parent. The child class has one method. The method has the same signature as the parent's method, but the child class can call the parent's method without conflict by using the keyword super.

```
public class AChildClass extends AParentClass
{
    public void displayClassName()
    {
        System.out.println("I am AChildClass");
        System.out.print("My parent is ");
        super.displayClassName();
    }
}
```

4. Save the file as **AChildClass.java** in the Chapter.11 folder on your Student Disk, and then compile it.

5. Finally, open a new text file and enter the following demonstration application to show that the child class can call its parent's method:

```
public class DemoSuper
{
    public static void main(String[] args)
    {
        AChildClass child = new AChildClass();
        child.displayClassName();
    }
}
```

6. Save the file as **DemoSuper.java** in the Chapter.11 folder on your Student Disk, and then compile and execute the application. As the output in Figure 11-31 shows, even though the child and parent classes have methods with the same name, the child class can use the parent class method correctly by employing the keyword `super`.

Figure 11-31 Output of the DemoSuper application

>> **NOTE** If you omit the keyword `super` within the `displayClassName()` method in `AChildClass`, you cause an infinite loop because the `displayClassName()` method calls itself. In other words, each time `displayClassName()` executes, it starts executing again when it gets to the third statement. The method executes repeatedly until an error message is finally generated.

UNDERSTANDING THE protected ACCESS MODIFIER

Next, you create a superclass with a `protected` field using the `protected` access modifier with a data field. This allows you to access the field directly within a subclass method.

To create a superclass with a protected field:

1. In your text editor, open the **Event.java** file. For simplicity, you can use the file that you created before adding constructors. Change the class name to **EventWithProtectedData**.

2. Change the modifier on the `eventGuests` field from `private` to **protected**.

3. Save the file as **EventWithProtectedData.java** in the Chapter.11 folder on your Student Disk, and then compile it.

4. Open the **DinnerEvent.java** file. Change its name and its parent's name so the class header reads as follows:

```
public class DinnerEventWithProtectedData extends
    EventWithProtectedData
```

5. Assume that Event Handlers Incorporated requires at least 10 guests for an event with dinner, but that there is no minimum guest number for other event types. To ensure that dinner events (unlike "plain" events) have at least 10 guests, the subclass `setEventGuests()` method overrides the `setEventGuests()` method in the superclass. The subclass version of the method calls the superclass method, but if the user does not enter a guest number of at least 10, the subclass method continues to call the superclass method until a suitable value is entered.

6. To create the subclass `setEventGuests()` method, position the insertion point at the end of the closing curly brace of the `setDinnerChoice()` method, press **Enter** to start a new line, and type the following method. This method first calls the parent class method, and then, while the number of guests is below the minimum required for dinner, continues to display an error message and to recall the parent class `setEventGuests()` method:

```
public void setEventGuests()
{
    super.setEventGuests();
    while(eventGuests < 10)
    {
        JOptionPane.showMessageDialog(null,
            "Dinner events require at least 10 guests");
        super.setEventGuests();
    }
}
```

> **» NOTE** If `eventGuests` had not been made protected (that is, if it was still `private`), you would need to use a method with a name such as `public int getEventGuests()` to access its value.

7. Save the file as **DinnerEventWithProtectedData.java** in the Chapter.11 folder on your Student Disk, and then compile it.

8. Next, create a simple application to test these classes. Open a new file in your text editor and enter the following demonstration application, which creates a `DinnerEventWithProtectedData` object and sets and displays its number of guests:

```
public class UseProtectedEvent
{
    public static void main(String[] args)
    {
        DinnerEventWithProtectedData aDinnerEvent =
            new DinnerEventWithProtectedData();
        aDinnerEvent.setEventGuests();
        aDinnerEvent.displayEventGuests();
        System.exit(0);
    }
}
```

9. Save the file as **UseProtectedEvent.java** in the Chapter.11 folder on your Student Disk. Compile and execute the class. When you run the application, make several attempts to set the number of dinner guests to values of less than 10. The application continues to prompt you until your guest number meets the required minimum. Sample output appears in Figure 11-32.

Figure 11-32 Series of dialog boxes that display when a user executes the `UseProtectedEvent` application

KEY TERMS

In Java, **inheritance** is a mechanism that enables one class to inherit, or assume, both the behavior and the attributes of another class.

The **Unified Modeling Language** (**UML**) is a graphical language used by programmers and analysts to describe classes and object-oriented processes.

A **class diagram** is a visual tool that provides you with an overview of a class. It consists of a rectangle divided into three sections—the top section contains the name of the class, the middle section contains the names and data types of the attributes, and the bottom section contains the methods.

A class that is used as a basis for inheritance is a **base class**.

A class that inherits from a base class is a **derived class**.

Composition is the relationship in which one class contains or has one or more members of another class that would not continue to exist without the object that contains them.

Aggregation is a type of composition in which a class contains or has one or more members of another class that would continue to exist without the object that contains them.

You can use the terms **superclass** and **subclass** as synonyms for base class and derived class.

You can also use the terms **parent class** and **child class** as synonyms for base class and derived class.

You use the keyword **extends** to achieve inheritance in Java.

Using the same method name to indicate different implementations is called **polymorphism**.

You **override a method** in a parent class when you create a method in a child class that has the same name and argument list as a method in its parent class.

Subtype polymorphism is the ability of one method name to work appropriately for different subclasses of a parent class.

The keyword **super** always refers to the superclass of the class in which you use it.

Information hiding is the concept of keeping data private.

Using the keyword **protected** provides you with an intermediate level of security between `public` and `private` access. `Protected` members are those that can be used by a class and its descendants.

Virtual method calls are those in which the method used is determined when the program runs, because the type of the object used might not be known until the method executes. In Java, all instance method calls are virtual calls by default.

Inlining the code is an automatic process that optimizes performance. Because a `final` method's definition can never be overridden, the compiler can optimize a program's performance by removing the calls to `final` methods and replacing them with the expanded code of their definitions at each method call location.

CHAPTER SUMMARY

» In Java, inheritance is a mechanism that enables one class to inherit both the behavior and the attributes of another class. When you use inheritance, you save time because the original fields and methods already exist, have been tested, and are familiar to you. A class that is used as a basis for inheritance is a base class. A class you create that inherits from a base class is called a derived class. You can use the terms *superclass* and *subclass* as synonyms for base class and derived class; you can also use the terms *parent class* and *child class*.

» You use the keyword `extends` to achieve inheritance in Java. A parent class object does not have access to its child's data and methods, but when you create a subclass by extending an existing class, the new subclass contains data and methods that were defined in the original superclass.

» Sometimes, superclass data fields and methods are not entirely appropriate for the subclass objects. Polymorphism is the act of using the same method name to indicate different implementations. You use polymorphism when you override a superclass method in a subclass by creating a method with the same name and argument list.

» When you instantiate an object that is a member of a subclass, you are actually calling at least two constructors: the constructor for the base class and the constructor for the extended, derived class. When you create any subclass object, the superclass constructor must execute first, and *then* the subclass constructor executes. When a superclass contains a default constructor, the execution of the superclass constructor when a subclass object is instantiated often is transparent.

» When a superclass contains only constructors that require arguments, you must include at least one constructor for each subclass you create. Your subclass constructors can contain any number of statements, but the first statement within each constructor must call the superclass constructor. When a superclass requires parameters upon instantiation, even if you have no other reason to create a subclass constructor, you must write the subclass constructor so it can call its superclass's constructor. The format of the statement that calls a superclass constructor is `super(list of arguments);`.

» If you want to use a superclass method within a subclass, you can use the keyword `super` to access the parent class method.

» The concept of keeping data private is known as information hiding. When you employ information hiding, your data can be altered only by the methods you choose and only in ways that you can control. When a class serves as a superclass to other classes you create, the subclasses inherit all the data and methods of the superclass. The methods in a subclass can use all of the data fields and methods that belong to its parent, with one exception: `private` members of the parent class are not accessible with a child class's methods. Using the keyword `protected` provides you with an intermediate level of security between `public` and `private` access. If you create a `protected` data field or method, it can be used within its own class or in any classes extended from that class, but it cannot be used by "outside" classes. In other words, `protected` members are those that can be used by a class and its descendants.

» A subclass cannot override methods that are declared `static` in the superclass. In other words, a subclass cannot override a class method. A subclass can *hide* a `static` method in the superclass by declaring a `static` method in the subclass with the same signature as the `static` method in the superclass; then, you can call the new `static` method from within the subclass or in another class by using a subclass object. However, this `static` method that hides the superclass `static` method cannot access the parent method using the `super` object. A subclass cannot override methods that are declared `final` in the superclass or methods declared within a `final` class.

REVIEW QUESTIONS

1. As an alternative way to discover which of two classes is the base class or subclass, _____ .

   a. look at the class size

   b. try saying the two class names together

   c. use polymorphism

   d. Both a and b are correct.

2. Employing inheritance reduces errors because _____ .

   a. the new classes have access to fewer data fields

   b. the new classes have access to fewer methods

   c. you can copy methods that you already created

   d. many of the methods you need have already been used and tested

3. A base class can also be called a _____ .

   a. child class   c. derived class

   b. subclass   d. superclass

4. Which of the following choices is the best example of a parent class/child class relationship?

   a. `Rose/Flower`   c. `Dog/Poodle`

   b. `Present/Gift`   d. `Sparrow/Bird`

5. The Java keyword that creates inheritance is _____ .

   a. `static`   c. `extends`

   b. `enlarge`   d. `inherits`

6. A class named `Building` has a `public`, nonstatic method named `getFloors()`. If `School` is a child class of `Building`, and `modelHigh` is an object of type `School`, which of the following statements is valid?

   a. `Building.getFloors();`

   b. `School.getFloors();`

   c. `modelHigh.getFloors();`

   d. All of the previous statements are valid.

7. Which of the following statements is false?

   a. A child class inherits from a parent class.

   b. A parent class inherits from a child class.

   c. Both of the preceding statements are false.

   d. Neither a nor b is false.

8. When a subclass method has the same name and argument types as a superclass method, the subclass method can _____ the superclass method.

   a. override   c. overload

   b. overuse   d. overcompensate

9. When you instantiate an object that is a member of a subclass, the _____ constructor executes first.

   a. subclass   c. extended class

   b. child class   d. parent class

10. The keyword `super` always refers to the _____ of the class in which you use it.

   a. child class

   b. derived class

   c. subclass

   d. parent class

11. If a superclass constructor requires arguments, its subclass _____ .

   a. must contain a constructor

   b. must not contain a constructor

   c. must contain a constructor that requires arguments

   d. must not contain a constructor that requires arguments

12. If a superclass constructor requires arguments, any constructor of its subclasses must call the superclass constructor _____ .

    a. as the first statement

    b. as the last statement

    c. at some time

    d. multiple times if multiple arguments are involved

13. A child class `Motorcycle` extends a parent class `Vehicle`. Each class constructor requires one `String` argument. The `Motorcycle` class constructor can call the `Vehicle` class constructor with the statement _____ .

    a. `Vehicle("Honda");`

    b. `Motorcycle("Harley");`

    c. `super("Suzuki");`

    d. none of the above

14. In Java, the concept of keeping data private is known as _____ .

    a. polymorphism

    b. information hiding

    c. data deception

    d. concealing fields

15. If you create a data field or method that is _____, it can be used within its own class or in any classes extended from that class.

    a. `public`   c. `private`

    b. `protected`   d. both a and b

16. Within a subclass, you cannot override _____ methods.

    a. `public`   c. `static`

    b. `private`   d. constructor

17. You call a `static` method using _____ .

    a. the name of its class, a dot, and the method name

    b. the name of the class's superclass, a dot, and the method name

    c. the name of an object in the same class, a dot, and the method name

    d. either a or b

18. You use a _____ method access modifier when you create methods for which you want to prevent overriding in extended classes.

    a. `public`   c. `final`

    b. `protected`   d. subclass

19. A compiler can decide to _____ a `final` method—that is, determine the code of the method call when the program is compiled.

    a. duplicate   c. redline

    b. inline   d. beeline

20. When a parent class contains a `static` method, child classes _____ override it.

    a. frequently   c. must

    b. seldom   d. cannot

EXERCISES

1. Create a class named `Book` that contains data fields for the title and number of pages. Include get and set methods for these fields. Next, create a subclass named `Textbook`, which contains an additional field that holds a grade level for the `Textbook` and additional methods to get and set the grade level field. Write an application that demonstrates using objects of each class. Save the files as **Book.java**, **Textbook.java**, and **DemoBook.java**.

2. Create a class named `Square` that contains data fields for `height`, `width`, and `surfaceArea`, and a method named `computeSurfaceArea()`. Create a child class named `Cube`. `Cube` contains an additional data field named `depth`, and a `computeSurfaceArea()` method that overrides the parent method. Write an application that instantiates a `Square` object and a `Cube` object and displays the surface areas of the objects. Save the files as **Cube.java**, **Square.java**, and **DemoSquare.java**.

3. Create a class named `Order` that performs order processing of a single item. The class has five fields: customer name, customer number, quantity ordered, unit price, and total price. Include set and get methods for each field except the total price field. The set methods prompt the user for values for each field. This class also needs a method to compute the total price (quantity times unit price) and a method to display the field values. Create a subclass named `ShippedOrder` that overrides `computePrice()` by adding a shipping and handling charge of $4.00. Write an application named `UseOrder` that instantiates an object of each of these classes. Prompt the user for data for the `Order` object, and display the results; then prompt the user for data for the `ShippedOrder` object, and display the results. Save the files as **Order.java**, **ShippedOrder.java**, and **UseOrder.java**.

4. a. Create a class named `Year` that contains a data field that holds the number of days in a year. Include a get method that displays the number of days and a constructor that sets the number of days to 365. Create a subclass named `LeapYear`. `LeapYear`'s constructor overrides `Year`'s constructor and sets the number of days to 366. Write an application named `UseYear` that instantiates one object of each class and displays their data. Save the files as **Year.java**, **LeapYear.java**, and **UseYear.java**.

   b. Add a method named `daysElapsed()` to the `Year` class you created in Exercise 4a. The `daysElapsed()` method accepts two arguments representing a month and a day; it returns an integer indicating the number of days that have elapsed since January 1 of that year. For example, on March 3 in nonleap years, 61 days have elapsed (31 in January, 28 in February, and 2 in March). Create a daysElapsed() method for the LeapYear class that overrides the method in the Year class. For example, on March 3 in a LeapYear, 62 days have elapsed (31 in January, 29 in February, and 2 in March). Write an application named UseYear2 that prompts the user for a month and day, and calculates the days elapsed in a Year and in a LeapYear. Save the files as **Year2.java**, **LeapYear2.java**, and **UseYear2.java**.

5. Create a class named HotelRoom that includes an integer field for the room number and a double field for the nightly rental rate. Include get methods for these fields and a constructor that requires an integer argument representing the room number. The constructor sets the room rate based on the room number; rooms numbered 299 and below are $69.95 per night, and others are $89.95 per night. Create an extended class named Suite whose constructor requires a room number and adds a $40 surcharge to the regular hotel room rate, which again is based on the room number. Write an application named UseHotelRoom that creates an object of each class, and demonstrate that all the methods work correctly. Save the files as **HotelRoom.java**, **Suite.java**, and **UseHotelRoom.java**.

6. Create a class named Package with data fields for weight in ounces, shipping method, and shipping cost. The shipping method is a character: 'A' for air, 'T' for truck, or 'M' for mail. The Package class contains a constructor that requires arguments for weight and shipping method. The constructor calls a calculateCost() method that determines the shipping cost based on the following table:

Weight (oz.)	Air ($)	Truck ($)	Mail ($)
1 to 8	2.00	1.50	.50
9 to 16	3.00	2.35	1.50
17 and over	4.50	3.25	2.15

The Package class also contains a display() method that displays the values in all four fields. Create a subclass named InsuredPackage that adds an insurance cost to the shipping cost based on the following table:

Shipping Cost Before Insurance ($)	Additional Cost ($)
0 to 1.00	2.45
1.01 to 3.00	3.95
3.01 and over	5.55

Write an application named UsePackage that instantiates at least three objects of each type (Package and InsuredPackage) using a variety of weights and shipping method codes. Display the results for each Package and InsuredPackage. Save the files as **Package.java**, **InsuredPackage.java**, and **UsePackage.java**.

7. Create a class named CarRental that contains fields that hold a renter's name, zip code, size of the car rented, daily rental fee, length of rental in days, and total rental fee. The

class contains a constructor that requires all the rental data except the daily rate and total fee, which are calculated based on the size of the car: economy at $29.99 per day, midsize at $38.99 per day, or full size at $43.50 per day. The class also includes a display() method that displays all the rental data. Create a subclass named LuxuryCarRental. This class sets the rental fee at $79.99 per day and prompts the user to respond to the option of including a chauffeur at $200 more per day. Override the parent class display() method to include chauffeur fee information. Write an application named UseCarRental that prompts the user for the data needed for a rental and creates an object of the correct type. Display the total rental fee. Save the files as **CarRental.java**, **LuxuryCarRental.java**, and **UseCarRental.java**.

8. Create a class named CollegeCourse that includes data fields that hold the department (for example, "ENG"), the course number (for example, 101), the credits (for example, 3), and the fee for the course (for example, $360). All of the fields are required as arguments to the constructor, except for the fee, which is calculated at $120 per credit hour. Include a display() method that displays the course data. Create a subclass named LabCourse that adds $50 to the course fee. Override the parent class display() method to indicate that the course is a lab course and to display all the data. Write an application named UseCourse that prompts the user for course information. If the user enters a class in any of the following departments, create a LabCourse: BIO, CHM, CIS, or PHY. If the user enters any other department, create a CollegeCourse that does not include the lab fee. Then display the course data. Save the files as **CollegeCourse.java**, **LabCourse.java**, and **UseCourse.java**.

9. Create a class named Vehicle that acts as a superclass for vehicle types. The Vehicle class contains private variables for the number of wheels and the average number of miles per gallon. The Vehicle class also contains a constructor with integer arguments for the number of wheels and average miles per gallon, and a toString() method that returns a String containing these values. Create two subclasses, Car and MotorCycle, that extend the Vehicle class. Each subclass contains a constructor that accepts the miles-per-gallon value as an argument and forces the number of wheels to the appropriate value—2 for a MotorCycle and 4 for a Car. Write a UseVehicle class to instantiate the two Vehicle objects and print the objects' values. Save the files as **Vehicle.java**, **Car.java**, **MotorCycle.java**, and **UseVehicle.java**.

DEBUGGING EXERCISES

Each of the following files in the Chapter.11 folder on your Student Disk has syntax and/ or logic errors. In each case, determine the problem and fix the program. After you correct the errors, save each file using the same filename preceded with Fix. For example, DebugEleven1.java will become FixDebugEleven1.java.

a. DebugEleven1.java

b. DebugEleven2.java

c. DebugEleven3.java

d. DebugEleven4.java

e. Eight other Debug files in the Chapter.11 folder; these files are used by the DebugEleven exercises

CASE PROJECT

BELLMONT COLLEGE

Bellmont College wants you to develop a set of classes for them to use in various student service and personnel applications. Classes you need to design include the following:

» Person—A Person contains a first name, last name, street address, zip code, and phone number. The class also includes a method that sets each data field, using a series of dialog boxes and a display method that displays all of a Person's information on a single line at the command line on the screen.

» CollegeEmployee—CollegeEmployee descends from Person. A CollegeEmployee also includes a Social Security number, an annual salary, and a department name, as well as methods that override the Person methods to accept and display all CollegeEmployee data.

» Faculty—Faculty descends from CollegeEmployee. This class also includes a Boolean field that indicates whether the Faculty member is tenured, as well as methods that override the CollegeEmployee methods to accept and display this additional piece of information.

» Student—Student descends from Person. In addition to the fields available in Person, a Student contains a major field of study and a grade point average, as well as methods that override the Person methods to accept and display these additional facts.

Write an application named CollegeList that declares an array of four "regular" CollegeEmployees, three Faculty, and seven Students. Prompt the user to specify which type of person's data will be entered ('C', 'F', or 'S'), or allow the user to quit ('Q'). While the user chooses to continue (that is, does not quit), accept data entry for the appropriate type of Person. If the user attempts to enter data for more than four CollegeEmployees, three Faculty, or seven Students, display an error message. When the user quits, display a report on the screen listing each group of Persons under the appropriate heading "College Employees," "Faculty," or "Students." If the user has not entered data for one or more types of Persons during a session, display an appropriate message under the appropriate heading.

Save the files as **Person.java**, **CollegeEmployee.java**, **Faculty.java**, **Student.java**, and **CollegeList.java** in the Chapter.11 folder on your Student Disk.

GAME ZONE

1. a. Create an Alien class. Include at least three protected data members of your choice, such as the number of eyes the Alien has. Include a constructor that requires a value for each data field and a toString() method that returns a String containing a complete description of the Alien. Save the file as **Alien.java**.

    b. Create two classes—Martian and Jupiterian—that descend from Alien. Supply each with a constructor that sets the Alien data fields with values you choose. For example, you can decide that a Martian has four eyes but a Jupiterian has only two. Also create a draw() method for each child class. The draw() method accepts a Graphics object and x- and y- starting coordinates. The method draws the Aliens in any way you choose, using lines, ovals, rectangles, and so on. Using the drawString() method, include a description that names each drawing. Save the files as **Martian.java** and **Jupiterian.java**.

c. Create an application that instantiates one `Martian` and one `Jupiterian`. Call the `toString()` method with each object and display the results. Save the application as **CreateAliens.java**.

d. Create an applet that instantiates a `Martian` and a `Jupiterian`. In the applet's `paint()` method, draw each type of `Alien`. Save the file as **JDemoAliens.java**. Also create an HTML document to host the applet. Save the file as **TestJDemoAliens.html**. Figure 11-33 shows some sample `Aliens`, but your `Aliens` might look very different.

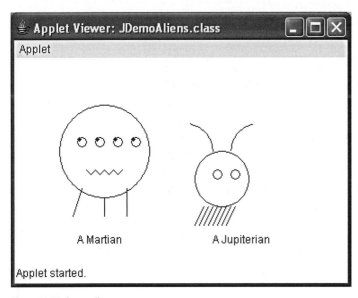

Figure 11-33 Some aliens

e. Create an applet containing an Alien Hunt game. Place eight numbered buttons in the applet. Randomly assign `Martians` to six of the buttons and `Jupiterians` to two. (*Hint:* You do not need to create an `Alien` array; you can simply create an array that randomly contains 0s and 1s, representing `Martians` and `Jupiterians`.) The object of the game is to find all the `Martians` before finding both `Jupiterians`. When a user clicks a button, display the `Alien` represented by the button. If the user clicks two `Jupiterians` before clicking six `Martians`, the player loses the game. When this happens, display two `Jupiterians` and a message telling the user that Earth has been destroyed. Disable any button after it has been selected. Save the game as **JAlienHunt.java**. Also create an HTML document to host the applet. Save the file as **TestJAlienHunt.html**.

2. a. In Chapter 4, you created a `Die` class that you can use to instantiate objects that hold one of six values. Modify this class so its value field is `protected` instead of `private`. This will allow a child class to access the value. Save the file as **Die.java**.

b. Create a `GraphicDie` class that descends from `Die` but adds a `drawDie()` method that draws a representation of the die on the screen. Design the method so it accepts a `Graphics` object as well as x- and y-coordinate positions where the drawing should be placed. Create the drawing of a `Die` based on its value and using the `drawRect()` and `fillOval()` methods. Save the file as **GraphicDie.java**.

c. Create a `JGraphicDie` JApplet that instantiates a `GraphicDie` object. In the JApplet's `paint()` method, pass the method's `Graphics` object and two values to the `GraphicDie`

object's `drawDie()` method. Save the file as **JGraphicDie.java**. Also, create an HTML document to host the applet. Save the file as **TestJGraphicDie.html**.

d. In Chapter 8, you created a `FiveDice3` game in which a player's random roll of five dice is compared to the computer's roll and a winner is determined. Now create an applet that plays the game. At each roll, initiated by a player's button click, display the player's five dice and the computer's five dice. Save the file as **JFiveDice.java**. Also, create an HTML document to host the applet. Save the file as **TestJFiveDice.html**. Figure 11-34 shows a typical game.

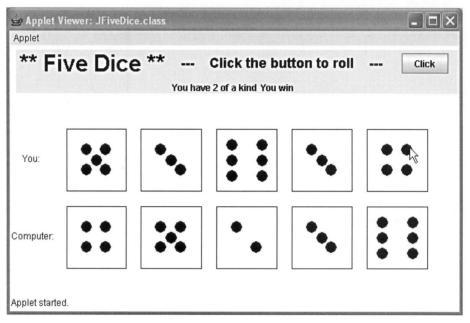

Figure 11-34 The `JFiveDice` applet

UP FOR DISCUSSION

1. In this chapter, you learned the difference between `public`, `private`, and `protected` class members. Some programmers are opposed to classifying class members as `protected`. Why do they feel that way? Do you agree with them?

2. Some programmers argue that, in general, superclasses are larger than subclasses. Others argue that, in general, subclasses are larger. How can both be correct?

3. Playing computer games has been shown to increase the level of dopamine in the human brain. High levels of this substance are associated with addiction to drugs. Suppose you work for a game manufacturer that decides to research how its games can produce more dopamine in the brains of players. Would you support the company's decision?

4. In the case problem at the end of this chapter, you store an employee's Social Security number. Besides using it for tax purposes, many organizations also use this number as an identification number. Is this a good idea? Is a Social Security number unique?

12

ADVANCED INHERITANCE CONCEPTS

In this chapter, you will:

Create and use abstract classes
Use dynamic method binding
Use a superclass as a method parameter
Create arrays of subclass objects
Use the `Object` class and its methods
Use inheritance to achieve good software design
Create and use interfaces
Create and use packages

> ## JAVA ON THE JOB, SCENE 12
>
> "Inheritance sure makes my programming job easier," you tell Lynn Greenbrier over a frosty lemonade at the Event Handlers Incorporated company picnic.
>
> "So, everything is going well, I take it?" asks Lynn.
>
> "It is," you say, "but I'm ready to learn more. What else can you tell me about inheritance?"
>
> "Enjoy the picnic for today," Lynn says. "On Monday morning, I'll teach you about superclass arrays that can use subclass methods, interfaces, and packages. Then you will be an inheritance pro."

CREATING AND USING ABSTRACT CLASSES

Developing new classes is easier after you understand the concept of inheritance. When you use a class as a basis from which to create extended child classes, the child classes are more specific than their parent. When you create a child class, it inherits all the general attributes you need; thus, you must create only the new, more specific attributes. For example, a SalariedEmployee and an HourlyEmployee are more specific than an Employee. They can inherit general Employee attributes, such as an employee number, but they add specific attributes, such as pay-calculating methods.

Notice that a superclass contains the features that are shared by its subclasses. For example, the attributes of the Dog class are shared by every Poodle and Spaniel. The subclasses are more specific examples of the superclass type; they add more features to the shared, general features. Conversely, when you examine a subclass, you see that its parent is more general and less specific; for example, Animal is more general than Dog.

> **NOTE** Recall from Chapter 11 that a child class contains all the members of its parent, whether those members are public, protected, or private. However, a child object cannot directly access a private member inherited from a parent.

> **NOTE**
> Nonabstract classes from which objects can be instantiated are called concrete classes. Before this chapter, all the classes you created were nonabstract.

Sometimes, a parent class is so general that you never intend to create any specific instances of the class. For example, you might never create an object that is "just" an Employee; each Employee is more specifically a SalariedEmployee, HourlyEmployee, or ContractEmployee. A class such as Employee that you create only to extend from, but not to instantiate objects from, is an abstract class. An **abstract class** is one from which you cannot create any concrete objects, but from which you can inherit. Abstract classes usually have one or more empty abstract methods. You use the keyword abstract when you declare an abstract class.

> **NOTE**
> In other programming languages, such as C++, abstract classes are known as virtual classes.

> **NOTE** In Chapter 4, you worked with the GregorianCalendar class. GregorianCalendar is a concrete class that extends the abstract class Calendar. In other words, there are no "plain" Calendar objects.

> **NOTE** In Chapter 11, you learned that you can create final classes if you do not want other classes to be able to extend them. Classes that you declare to be abstract are the opposite; your only purpose in creating them is to enable other classes to extend them.

You cannot create instances of abstract classes by using the `new` operator; you create abstract classes simply to provide a superclass from which other objects can inherit. Abstract classes are like regular classes because they have data and methods, but they are different in that they usually contain at least one abstract method. An **abstract method** has no body—no curly braces and no method statements. When you create an abstract method, you provide the keyword `abstract` and the header, including the method type, name, and arguments, but the declaration ends there—you do not provide any statements within the method, but you do include a semicolon at the end of the declaration. When you create a subclass that inherits an abstract method from a parent, either the new method must itself be abstract, or you must provide the actions, or implementation, for the inherited method. It's important to understand that you are required to code a subclass method to override the empty superclass method that is inherited.

>> **NOTE** If you provide an empty method within an abstract class, the method is an abstract method even if you do not explicitly use the keyword `abstract` when defining the method.

>> **NOTE** Programmers of an abstract class can include two method types: (1) nonabstract methods such as those you create in any class, which are implemented in the abstract class and are simply inherited by its children; and (2) methods that are abstract and must be implemented by its children.

>> **NOTE** If you attempt to instantiate an object from an abstract class, you receive an error message from the compiler that you have committed an `InstantiationError`.

Suppose you want to create classes to represent different animals, such as `Dog` and `Cow`. You can create a generic abstract class named `Animal` so you can provide generic data fields, such as the animal's name, only once. An `Animal` is generic, but all specific `Animal`s make a sound; the actual sound differs from `Animal` to `Animal`. If you code an empty `speak()` method in the abstract `Animal` class, you require all future `Animal` subclasses to code a `speak()` method that is specific to the subclass. Figure 12-1 shows an abstract `Animal` class containing a data field for the name, `getAnimalName()` and `setAnimalName()` methods, and an abstract `speak()` method.

```
public abstract class Animal
{
    private String nameOfAnimal;
    public abstract void speak();
    public String getAnimalName()
    {
        return nameOfAnimal;
    }
    public void setAnimalName(String name)
    {
        nameOfAnimal = name;
    }
}
```

Figure 12-1 The abstract `Animal` class

The `Animal` class in Figure 12-1 is declared as `abstract`. You cannot place a statement such as `Animal myPet = new Animal("Murphy");` within another class, because a class that attempts to instantiate an `Animal` object does not compile. `Animal` is an abstract class, so no `Animal` objects can exist.

>> **NOTE** If you declare any method to be an abstract method, you must also declare its class to be abstract.

You create an abstract class such as Animal only so you can extend it. For example, because a dog is an animal, you can create a Dog class as a child class of Animal. Figure 12-2 shows a Dog class that extends Animal.

```
public class Dog extends Animal
{
    public void speak()
    {
        System.out.println("Woof!");
    }
}
```

Figure 12-2 The Dog class

>> **NOTE** The speak() method within the Dog class is required because the abstract, parent Animal class contains an abstract speak() method. You can code any statements you want within the Dog speak() method, but the speak() method must exist. Remember, you cannot instantiate an Animal object; however, instantiating a Dog object is perfectly legal because Dog is not an abstract class. When you code Dog myPet = new Dog("Murphy");, you create a Dog object. Then, when you code myPet.speak();, the correct Dog speak() method executes.

>> **NOTE** If you do not provide a subclass method to override a superclass abstract method, you cannot instantiate any subclass objects. In this case, you must also declare the subclass itself to be abstract. Then, you can extend the subclass into sub-subclasses in which you write code for the method.

The classes in Figures 12-3 and 12-4 also inherit from the Animal class. Figure 12-5 contains a UseAnimals application; the output in Figure 12-6 shows that when you create Dog, Cow, and Snake objects, each is an Animal with access to the Animal class getAnimalName() and setAnimalName() methods, and each uses its own speak() method appropriately. In Figure 12-6, notice how the myDog.getAnimalName() and myDog.speak() method calls produce different output from when the same method names are used with myCow and mySnake.

```
public class Cow extends Animal
{
    public void speak()
    {
        System.out.println("Moo!");
    }
}
```

Figure 12-3 The Cow class

```
public class Snake extends Animal
{
    public void speak()
    {
        System.out.println("Ssss!");
    }
}
```

Figure 12-4 The Snake class

```
public class UseAnimals
{
    public static void main(String[] args)
    {
        Dog myDog = new Dog();
        Cow myCow = new Cow();
        Snake mySnake = new Snake();
        myDog.setAnimalName("My dog Murphy");
        myCow.setAnimalName("My cow Elsie");
        mySnake.setAnimalName("My snake Sammy");
        System.out.print(myDog.getAnimalName() + " says ");
        myDog.speak();
        System.out.print(myCow.getAnimalName() + " says ");
        myCow.speak();
        System.out.print(mySnake.getAnimalName() + " says ");
        mySnake.speak();
    }
}
```

Figure 12-5 The UseAnimals application

Figure 12-6 Output of the UseAnimals application

»NOTE In Chapter 11, you learned that using the same method name to indicate different implementations is called polymorphism. Using polymorphism, one method name causes different actions for different types of objects.

USING DYNAMIC METHOD BINDING

When you create a superclass and one or more subclasses, each object of each subclass "is a" superclass object. Every SalariedEmployee "is an" Employee; every Dog "is an" Animal. (The opposite is not true. Superclass objects are not members of any of their subclasses. An Employee is not a SalariedEmployee. An Animal is not a Dog.) Because every subclass object "is a" superclass member, you can convert subclass objects to superclass objects.

As you are aware, when a superclass is abstract, you cannot instantiate objects of the superclass; however, you can indirectly create a reference to a superclass abstract object. A reference is not an object, but it points to a memory address. When you create a reference, you do not use the keyword new to create a concrete object; instead, you create a variable name in which you can hold the memory address of a concrete object. So, although a reference to an abstract superclass object is not concrete, you can store a concrete subclass object there.

For example, if you create an `Animal` class, as shown previously in Figure 12-1, and various sub-classes, such as `Dog`, `Cow`, and `Snake`, as shown in Figures 12-2 through 12-4, you can create an application containing a generic `Animal` reference variable into which you can assign any of the concrete `Animal` child objects. Figure 12-7 shows an `AnimalReference` application, and Figure 12-8 shows its output. The variable `ref` is a type of `Animal`. No superclass `Animal` object is created (none can be); instead, `Dog` and `Cow` objects are created using the `new` keyword. When the `Cow` object is assigned to the `Animal` reference, the `ref.speak()` method call results in "Moo!"; when the `Dog` object is assigned to the `Animal` reference, the method call results in "Woof!"

```java
public class AnimalReference
{
    public static void main(String[] args)
    {
        Animal ref;
        ref = new Cow();
        ref.speak();
        ref = new Dog();
        ref.speak();
    }
}
```

Figure 12-7 The `AnimalReference` application

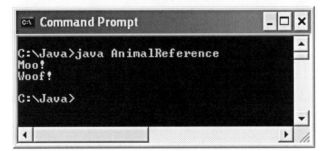

Figure 12-8 Output of the `AnimalReference` application

> **»NOTE** Recall from Chapter 11 that you can use the `instanceof` keyword to determine whether an object is an instance of any class in its hierarchy. For example, using the `Animal` and `Dog` classes, both of the following statements are true if `myPoodle` is a `Dog` object:
>
>   myPoodle instanceof Animal
>   myPoodle instanceof Dog

The application in Figure 12-7 demonstrates polymorphic behavior. The same statement, `ref.speak();`, repeats after `ref` is set to each new animal type. Each call to the `speak()` method results in different output. Each reference "chooses" the correct `speak()` method based on the type of animal referenced. This flexible behavior is most useful when you pass references to methods; you will learn more about this in the next section. In Chapter 11, you learned that in Java all instance method calls are virtual method calls by default—that is, the method that is used is determined when the program runs, because the type of the object used might not be known until the method executes. An application's ability to select the correct subclass method is known as **dynamic method binding**. When the application executes, the correct method is attached (or bound) to the application based on the current, changing context (dynamically).

> **»NOTE**
> Dynamic method binding is also called late binding. The opposite of dynamic method binding is static (fixed) method binding. Dynamic method binding makes programs flexible; however, static method binding operates more quickly.

USING A SUPERCLASS AS A METHOD PARAMETER

Dynamic method binding is most useful when you want to create a method that has one or more parameters that might be one of several types. For example, the shaded header for the `talkingAnimal()` method in Figure 12-9 accepts any type of `Animal` argument.

```java
public class TalkingAnimalDemo
{
    public static void main(String[] args)
    {
        Dog dog = new Dog();
        Cow cow = new Cow();
        dog.setAnimalName("Ginger");
        cow.setAnimalName("Molly");
        talkingAnimal(dog);
        talkingAnimal(cow);
    }
    public static void talkingAnimal(Animal animal)
    {
        System.out.println("Come one come all");
        System.out.println
            ("See the amazing talking animal!");
        System.out.println(animal.getAnimalName() +
            " says");
        animal.speak();
        System.out.println("***************");
    }
}
```

Figure 12-9 The `TalkingAnimalDemo` class

The method can be used in programs that contain `Dog` objects, `Cow` objects, or objects of any other class that descends from `Animal`. The application in Figure 12-9 passes first a `Dog` and then a `Cow` to the method. The output in Figure 12-10 shows that the method works correctly no matter which type of `Animal` descendant it receives.

Figure 12-10 Output of `TalkingAnimalDemo` application

CREATING ARRAYS OF SUBCLASS OBJECTS

>>NOTE
In Chapter 8, you learned that all elements in a single array must be of the same type.

You might want to create a superclass reference and treat subclass objects as superclass objects, so that you can create an array of different objects that share the same ancestry. For example, even though `Employee` is an abstract class, and every `Employee` object is either a `SalariedEmployee` or an `HourlyEmployee` subclass object, it can be convenient to create an array of generic `Employee` references. Likewise, an `Animal` array might contain individual elements that are `Dog`, `Cow`, or `Snake` objects. As long as every `Employee` subclass has access to a `calculatePay()` method, or every `Animal` subclass has access to a `speak()` method, you can manipulate an array of superclass objects by invoking the appropriate method for each subclass member.

The following statement creates an array of three `Animal` references:

```
Animal[] ref = new Animal[ 3 ];
```

The statement reserves enough computer memory for three `Animal` objects named `ref[0]`, `ref[1]`, and `ref[2]`. The statement does not actually instantiate `Animals`; `Animals` are abstract and cannot be instantiated. The statement simply reserves memory for three `Animal` object references. If you instantiate three `Animal` subclass objects, you can place references to those objects in the `Animal` array, as Figure 12-11 illustrates. Figure 12-12 shows the output of the `AnimalArrayDemo` application. The array of three references is used to access each appropriate `speak()` method.

```
public class AnimalArrayDemo
{
    public static void main(String[] args)
    {
        Animal[] ref = new Animal[ 3 ];
        ref[0] = new Dog();
        ref[1] = new Cow();
        ref[2] = new Snake();
        for(int x = 0; x < 3; ++x)
            ref[x] .speak();
    }
}
```

Figure 12-11 The `AnimalArrayDemo` application

>> **NOTE** In the `AnimalArrayDemo` application in Figure 12-11, a new instance of the `Dog` class is assigned to the first `Animal` reference, and then new instances of `Cow` and `Snake` are assigned to the second and third array elements. After the objects are in the array, you can manipulate them like any other array objects. For example, you can use a `for` loop and a subscript to get each individual reference to `speak()`.

Figure 12-12 Output of the `AnimalArrayDemo` application

>> **NOTE** When you create an array of any type of objects, concrete or abstract, you are not actually constructing those objects. Instead, you are creating space for references to objects that are not yet instantiated.

USING THE Object CLASS AND ITS METHODS

Every class in Java is actually a subclass, except one. When you define a class, if you do not explicitly extend another class, your class is an extension of the Object class. The **Object class** is defined in the java.lang package, which is imported automatically every time you write a program; it includes methods that you can use or override as you see fit.

USING THE toString() METHOD

The Object class **toString() method** converts an Object into a String that contains information about the Object. If you do not create a toString() method for a class, you can use the superclass version of the toString() method. For example, examine the Dog class originally shown in Figure 12-2 and repeated in Figure 12-13. Notice that it does not contain a toString() method and that it extends the Animal class. Examine the Animal parent class

```
public abstract class Animal
{
    private String nameOfAnimal;
    public abstract void speak();
    public String getAnimalName()
    {
        return nameOfAnimal;
    }
    public void setAnimalName(String name)
    {
        nameOfAnimal = name;
    }
}

public class Dog extends Animal
{
    public void speak()
    {
        System.out.println("Woof!");
    }
}

public class DisplayDog
{
    public static void main(String[] args)
    {
        Dog myDog = new Dog();
        String dogString = myDog.toString();
        System.out.println(dogString);
    }
}
```

Figure 12-13 The DisplayDog application

originally shown in Figure 12-1 and repeated in Figure 12-13. Notice that it also does not define a toString() method. Yet, when you write the DisplayDog application in Figure 12-13, it uses a toString() method with a Dog object in the shaded statement. The class compiles correctly, converts the Dog object to a String, and produces the output shown in Figure 12-14.

The output of the DisplayDog application in Figure 12-14 is not very useful. It consists of the class name of which the object is an instance (Dog), the at sign (@), and a hexadecimal (base 16) number that represents a unique identifier for every object in the current application.

Figure 12-14 Output of the DisplayDog application

Instead of using the automatic `toString()` method with your classes, it is usually more useful to write your own overloaded version of the `toString()` method that displays some or all of the data field values for the object with which you use it. A good `toString()` method can be very useful in debugging a program. If you do not understand why a class is behaving as it is, you can display the `toString()` value and examine its contents. For example, Figure 12-15 shows a `BankAccount` class that contains a mistake in the shaded line—the `BankAccount` balance value is set to the account number instead of the balance amount. Of course, if you made such a mistake within one of your own classes, there would be no shading or comment to help you find the mistake. In addition, a useful `BankAccount` class would be much larger, so the mistake would be more difficult to locate. However, when you ran programs containing `BankAccount` objects, you would notice that the balances of your `BankAccounts` were incorrect. To help you discover why, you could create a short application like the `TestBankAccount` class in Figure 12-16. This application uses the `BankAccount` class `toString()` method to display the relevant details of a `BankAccount` object. The output of the `TestBankAccount` application appears in Figure 12-17.

```
public class BankAccount
{
    private int acctNum;
    private double balance;
    public BankAccount(int num, double bal)
    {
        acctNum = num;
        balance = num; // Mistake! Should be balance = bal
    }
    public String toString()
    {
        String info = "BankAccount acctNum = " + acctNum +
            "   Balance = $" + balance;
        return info;
    }
}
```

Figure 12-15 The `BankAccount` class

```
public class TestBankAccount
{
    public static void main(String[] args)
    {
        BankAccount myAccount = new BankAccount(123, 4567.89);
        System.out.println(myAccount.toString());
    }
}
```

Figure 12-16 The `TestBankAccount` application

Figure 12-17 Output of the `TestBankAccount` application

From the output in Figure 12-17, you can see that the account number and balance have the same value, and this knowledge might help you to pin down the location of the incorrect statement in the `BankAccount` class. Of course, you do not have to use a method named `toString()` to discover a `BankAccount`'s attributes. If the class had methods such as `getAcctNum()` and `getBalance()`, you could use them to create a similar application. The advantage of creating a `toString()` method for your classes is that `toString()` is Java's universal name for a method that converts an object's relevant details into `String` format. Because `toString()` originates in the `Object` class, you can be assured that `toString()` compiles with any object whose details you want to see, even if the method has not been rewritten for the subclass in question. In addition, as you write your own applications and use classes written by others, you can hope that those programmers have overridden `toString()` to provide useful information.

USING THE `equals()` METHOD

The `Object` class also contains an **`equals()` method** that takes a single argument, which must be the same type as the type of the invoking object, as in the following example:

```
if(someObject.equals(someOtherObjectOfTheSameType))
    System.out.println("The objects are equal");
```

> **NOTE** Other classes, such as the `String` class, also have their own `equals()` methods that overload the `Object` class method. You first used the `equals()` method to compare `String` objects in Chapter 7. Two `String` objects were considered equal only if their `String` contents were identical.

The `Object` class `equals()` method returns a `boolean` value indicating whether the objects are equal. This `equals()` method considers two objects of the same class to be equal only if they have the same hash code; in other words, they are equal only if one is a reference to the other. For example, two `BankAccount` objects named `myAccount` and `yourAccount` are not automatically equal, even if they have the same account numbers and balances; they are equal only if they have the same memory address. If you want to consider two objects to be equal only when one is a reference to the other, you can use the built-in `Object` class `equals()` method. However, if you want to consider objects to be equal based on their contents, you must write your own `equals()` method for your classes.

> **NOTE** When you want to compare the contents of two objects, you do not have to overload the `Object` class `equals()` method. Instead, you can write a method with a unique name, such as `areTheyEqual()` or `areContentsSame()`. However, users of your classes will appreciate that you use the expected, usual, and conventional identifiers for your methods.

>> **NOTE** Java's `Object` class contains a public method named `hashCode()` that returns an integer representing the hash code. Discovering this number is of little use to you. However, whenever you override the `equals()` method in a professional class, you generally want to override the `hashCode()` method as well, because equal objects should have equal hash codes. See the documentation at *http://java.sun.com* for more details.

The application shown in Figure 12-18 instantiates two `BankAccount` objects, using the `BankAccount` class in Figure 12-15. The `BankAccount` class does not include its own `equals()` method, so it does not override the `Object equals()` method. Thus, the application in Figure 12-18 produces the output in Figure 12-19. Even though the two `BankAccount` objects have the same account numbers and balances, the `BankAccounts` are not considered equal because they do not have the same memory address.

```
public class CompareAccounts
{
    public static void main(String[] args)
    {
        BankAccount acct1 = new BankAccount(1234, 500.00);
        BankAccount acct2 = new BankAccount(1234, 500.00);
        if(acct1.equals(acct2))
            System.out.println("Accounts are equal");
        else
            System.out.println("Accounts are not equal");
    }
}
```

Figure 12-18 The `CompareAccounts` application

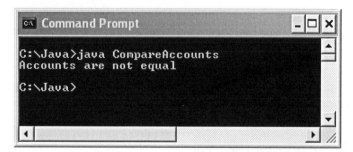

```
C:\Java>java CompareAccounts
Accounts are not equal

C:\Java>
```

Figure 12-19 Output of the `CompareAccounts` application

If your intention is that within applications, two `BankAccount` objects with the same account number and balance are equal, and you want to use the `equals()` method to make the comparison, you must write your own `equals()` method within the `BankAccount` class. For example, Figure 12-20 shows a new version of the `BankAccount` class containing a shaded `equals()` method. When you reexecute the `CompareAccounts` application in Figure 12-18, the result appears as in Figure 12-21. The two `BankAccount` objects are equal because their account numbers and balances match. Because the `equals()` method in Figure 12-20 is part of the `BankAccount` class, within the method, the object that calls the method is held by the `this` reference. That is, in the application in Figure 12-18, `acct1` becomes the `this` reference in the `equals()` method, so the fields `acctNum` and `balance` refer to `acct1` object values.

In the `CompareAccounts` application, `acct2` is the parameter to the `equals()` method. That is, within the `equals()` method, `acct2` becomes `secondAcct`, and the `secondAcct.acctNum` and `secondAcct.balance` refer to `acct2`'s values.

```
public class BankAccount
{
    private int acctNum;
    private double balance;
    public BankAccount(int num, double bal)
    {
        acctNum = num;
        balance = num; // Mistake! Should be balance = bal
    }
    public String toString()
    {
        String info = "BankAccount acctNum = " + acctNum +
            "     Balance = $" + balance;
        return info;
    }
    public boolean equals(BankAccount secondAcct)
    {
        boolean result;
        if(acctNum == secondAcct.acctNum &&
                balance == secondAcct.balance)
            result = true;
        else
            result = false;
        return result;
    }
}
```

Figure 12-20 The `BankAccount` class containing its own `equals()` method

》NOTE
You can determine when objects are equal based on any criteria that suit your needs.

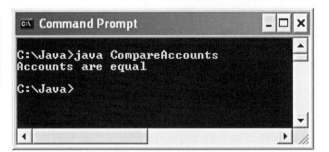

Figure 12-21 Output of the `CompareAccounts` application after adding an overloaded `equals()` method to the `BankAccount` class

》NOTE You might decide to consider two `BankAccount` objects equal if their account numbers match, disregarding their balances. If so, you simply change the `if` clause in the `equals()` method to the following:

```
if(acctNum == secondAcct.acctNum)
```

» NOTE If you change a class (such as changing `BankAccount` by adding a new method), not only must you recompile the class, you must also recompile any client applications (such as `CompareAccounts`) so the newly updated class can be relinked to the application and so the clients include the new features of the altered class. If you execute the `CompareAccounts` application but do not recompile `BankAccount`, the application continues to use the previously compiled version of the class.

USING INHERITANCE TO ACHIEVE GOOD SOFTWARE DESIGN

When an automobile company designs a new car model, the company does not build every component of the new car from scratch. The company might design a new feature completely from scratch; for example, at some point someone designed the first air bag. However, many of a new car's features are simply modifications of existing features. The manufacturer might create a larger gas tank or more comfortable seats, but even these new features still possess many properties of their predecessors in the older models. Most features of new car models are not even modified; instead, existing components, such as air filters and windshield wipers, are included on the new model without any changes.

Similarly, you can create powerful computer programs more easily if many of their components are used either "as is" or with slight modifications. Inheritance does not enable you to write programs that you could not write if inheritance did not exist. If Java did not allow you to extend classes, you *could* create every part of a program from scratch. Inheritance simply makes your job easier. Professional programmers constantly create new class libraries for use with Java programs. Having these classes available makes programming large systems more manageable.

You have already used many "as is" classes, such as `String` and `JApplet`. In these cases, your programs were easier to write than if you had to write these classes yourself. Now that you have learned about inheritance, you have gained the ability to modify existing classes. When you create a useful, extendable superclass, you and other future programmers gain several advantages:

» Subclass creators save development time because much of the code needed for the class has already been written.

» Subclass creators save testing time because the superclass code has already been tested and probably used in a variety of situations. In other words, the superclass code is reliable.

» Programmers who create or use new subclasses already understand how the superclass works, so the time it takes to learn the new class features is reduced.

» When you create a new subclass in Java, neither the superclass source code nor the superclass bytecode is changed. The superclass maintains its integrity.

When you consider classes, you must think about the commonalities between them; then you can create superclasses from which to inherit. You might be rewarded professionally when you see your own superclasses extended by others in the future.

CREATING AND USING INTERFACES

Some object-oriented programming languages, such as C++, allow a subclass to inherit from more than one parent class. For example, you might create an `InsuredItem` class that contains data fields pertaining to each possession for which you have insurance. Data fields might include the name of the item, its value, the insurance policy type, and so on. You might also create an `Automobile` class that contains data fields such as vehicle identification number, make, model, and year. When you create an `InsuredAutomobile` class for a car rental agency, you might want to include `InsuredItem` information and methods, as well as `Automobile` information and methods. It would be convenient to inherit from both the `InsuredItem` and `Automobile` classes. The capability to inherit from more than one class is called **multiple inheritance**.

Many programmers consider multiple inheritance to be a difficult concept, and when inexperienced programmers use it they encounter many problems. Programmers have to deal with the possibility that variables and methods in the parent classes might have identical names, which creates conflict when the child class uses one of the names. Also, you have already learned that a child class constructor must call its parent class constructor. When there are two or more parents, this task becomes more complicated—to which class should `super()` refer when a child class has multiple parents? For all of these reasons, multiple inheritance is prohibited in Java.

>> **NOTE** In Java, a class can inherit from a superclass that has inherited from another superclass—this represents single inheritance with multiple generations. What Java does not allow is for a class to inherit directly from two or more parents.

Java, however, does provide an alternative to multiple inheritance—an interface. An **interface** looks much like a class, except that all of its methods (if any) are implicitly `public` and `abstract`, and all of its data items (if any) are implicitly `public`, `static`, and `final`. An interface is a description of what a class does, but not how it is done; it declares method headers, but not the instructions within those methods. When you create a class that uses an interface, you include the keyword `implements` and the interface name in the class header. This notation requires class objects to include code for every method in the interface that has been implemented. Whereas using `extends` allows a subclass to use nonprivate, nonoverridden members of its parent's class, `implements` requires the subclass to implement its own version of each method.

>> **NOTE** In English, an interface is a device or a system that unrelated entities use to interact. Within Java, an interface provides a way for unrelated objects to interact with each other. An interface is analogous to a protocol, which is an agreed-on behavior. In some respects, an `Automobile` can behave like an `InsuredItem`, and so can a `House`, a `TelevisionSet`, and a `JewelryPiece`.

As an example, recall the `Animal` and `Dog` classes from earlier in this chapter. Figure 12-22 shows these classes, with `Dog` inheriting from `Animal`.

You can create a `Worker` interface (stored in its own file), as shown in the shaded statements in Figure 12-22. For simplicity, this example gives the `Worker` interface a single method named `work()`. When any class implements `Worker`, it must also include a `work()` method.

The `WorkingDog` class in Figure 12-23 extends `Dog` and implements `Worker`. A `WorkingDog` contains a data field that a "regular" `Dog` does not—an integer that holds hours of training received. The `WorkingDog` class also contains get and set methods for this field. Because the `WorkingDog` class implements the `Worker` interface, it also contains a `work()` method that calls the `Dog` `speak()` method, and then produces two more lines of output—a statement about working and the number of training hours.

```
public abstract class Animal
{
    private String nameOfAnimal;
    public abstract void speak();
    public String getAnimalName()
    {
        return nameOfAnimal;
    }
    public void setAnimalName(String name)
    {
        nameOfAnimal = name;
    }
}
public class Dog extends Animal
{
    public void speak()
    {
        System.out.println("Woof!");
    }
}
public interface Worker
{
    public void work();
}
```

Figure 12-22 The `Animal` and `Dog` classes and a `Worker` interface

```
public class WorkingDog extends Dog implements Worker
{
    private int hoursOfTraining;
    public void setHoursOfTraining(int hrs)
    {
        hoursOfTraining = hrs;
    }
    public int getHoursOfTraining()
    {
        return hoursOfTraining;
    }
    public void work()
    {
        speak();
        System.out.println("I am a dog who works");
        System.out.println("I have " + hoursOfTraining +
            " hours of professional training!");
    }
}
```

Figure 12-23 The `WorkingDog` class

»NOTE   As you know from many classes you have seen in this chapter and in Chapter 11, a class can extend another without implementing any interfaces. A class can also implement an interface even though it does not extend any other class. When a class both extends and implements, like the WorkingDog class, by convention the implements clause follows the extends clause in the class header.

The DemoWorkingDogs application in Figure 12-24 instantiates two WorkingDog objects. Each object can use the following methods:

» The setAnimalName() and getAnimalName() methods that WorkingDog inherits from the Animal class

» The speak() method that WorkingDog inherits from the Dog class

» The setHoursOfTraining() and getHoursOfTraining() methods contained within the WorkingDog class

» The work() method that the WorkingDog class was required to contain when it used the phrase implements Worker; the work() method also calls the speak() method contained in the Dog class

```
public class DemoWorkingDogs
{
    public static void main(String[] args)
    {
        WorkingDog aSheepHerder = new WorkingDog();
        WorkingDog aSeeingEyeDog = new WorkingDog();
        aSheepHerder.setAnimalName("Simon, the Border Collie");
        aSeeingEyeDog.setAnimalName("Sophie, the German Shepherd");
        aSheepHerder.setHoursOfTraining(40);
        aSeeingEyeDog.setHoursOfTraining(300);

        System.out.println(aSheepHerder.getAnimalName() + " says ");
        aSheepHerder.speak();
        aSheepHerder.work();
        System.out.println(); // prints a blank line for readability

        System.out.println(aSeeingEyeDog.getAnimalName() + " says ");
        aSeeingEyeDog.speak();
        aSeeingEyeDog.work();
    }
}
```

Figure 12-24 The DemoWorkingDogs application

Figure 12-25 shows the output when the DemoWorkingDogs application executes. Each Animal knows how to "work"—that is, each can execute the work() method contained in the implemented interface. Of course, the WorkingDog class was not required to implement the Worker interface; instead, it could have just contained a work() method that all WorkingDog objects could use. If WorkingDog was the only class that would ever use work(), such an approach would probably be the best course of action. However, if many classes will be Workers—that is, require a work() method—they all can implement work(). If you are already familiar with the Worker interface and its method, when you glance at a class definition for a WorkingHorse, WorkingBird, or Employee and see that it implements Worker, you do not have to guess at the name of the method that shows the work the class objects perform.

Command Prompt

```
C:\Java>java DemoWorkingDogs
Simon, the Border Collie says
Woof!
Woof!
I am a dog who works
I have 40 hours of professional training!

Sophie, the German Shepherd says
Woof!
Woof!
I am a dog who works
I have 300 hours of professional training!

C:\Java>
```

Figure 12-25 Output of the DemoWorkingDogs application

>> **NOTE** Notice that when a class implements another, it represents a situation similar to inheritance. Just as a WorkingDog "is a" Dog and "is an" Animal, so too it "is a" Worker. When a class implements an interface, it is promising to "take care of" all the methods listed in the interface class. Either the class must implement all the methods declared in the interface (and any interfaces that the interface itself inherits from), or the class must be declared abstract so that other classes that inherit from it can implement the methods.

Abstract classes and interfaces are similar in that you cannot instantiate concrete objects from either one. Abstract classes differ from interfaces because abstract classes can contain nonabstract methods, but all methods within an interface must be abstract. A class can inherit from only one abstract superclass, but it can implement any number of interfaces.

Beginning programmers sometimes find it difficult to decide when to create an abstract superclass and when to create an interface. Remember, you create an abstract class when you want to provide data or methods that subclasses can inherit, but at the same time these subclasses maintain the ability to override the inherited methods.

Suppose you create a CardGame class to use as a base class for different card games. It contains four methods named shuffle(), deal(), displayRules(), and keepScore(). The shuffle() method works the same way for every CardGame, so you write the statements for shuffle() within the superclass, and any CardGame objects you create later inherit shuffle(). The methods deal(), displayRules(), and keepScore() operate differently for every subclass, so you force CardGame children to contain instructions for those methods by leaving them empty in the superclass. The CardGame class, therefore, should be an abstract superclass. When you write classes named Hearts, Solitaire, and Poker, you extend the CardGame parent class, inherit the shuffle() method, and write code within the deal(), displayRules(), and keepScore() methods for each specific child.

You create an interface when you know what actions you want to include, but you also want every user to separately define the behavior that must occur when the method executes. Suppose you create a MusicalInstrument class to use as a base for different musical instrument object classes such as Piano, Violin, and Drum. The parent MusicalInstrument class contains methods such as playNote() and outputSound() that apply to every instrument, but you want to implement these methods differently for each type of instrument. By making MusicalInstrument an interface, you require every subclass to code all the methods.

> **NOTE** An interface specifies only the messages to which an object can respond; an abstract class can include methods that contain the actual behavior the object performs when those messages are received.

You also create an interface when you want a class to implement behavior from more than one parent. For example, suppose that you want to create an interactive NameThatInstrument card game in which you play an instrument sound from the computer speaker, and ask players to identify the instrument they hear by clicking one of several cards that display instrument images. This game class could not extend from two classes, but it could extend from CardGame and implement MusicalInstrument.

> **NOTE** You used prewritten interfaces earlier in this book. For example, in Chapters 9 and 10, when you wanted a user to be able to initiate actions using a JButton, you implemented the ActionListener interface, which provided the means to respond to ActionEvents. When you implemented ActionListener, you had to include an actionPerformed() method, which is an abstract method in the ActionPerformed interface. You will use more interfaces in future chapters.

> **NOTE** When you create a class and use the implements clause to implement an interface, but fail to code one of the interface's methods, the compiler error generated indicates that you must declare your class to be abstract. If you want your class to be used only for extending, you can make it abstract. However, if your intention is to create a class from which you can instantiate objects, do not make it abstract. Instead, find out which methods from the interface you have failed to implement within your class and code those methods.

> **NOTE** Java has many built-in interfaces with names such as Serializable, Runnable, Externalizable, and Cloneable. See the documentation at *http://java.sun.com* for more details.

CREATING INTERFACES TO STORE RELATED CONSTANTS

Interfaces can contain data fields, but they must be public, static, and final. It makes sense that interface data must be public because interface methods cannot contain method bodies; and without method bodies, you have no way to retrieve private data. It also makes sense that the data fields in an interface are static because you cannot create interface objects. Finally, it makes sense that interface data fields are final because, without methods containing bodies, you have no way, other than at declaration, to set the data fields' values, and you have no way to change them.

Your purpose in creating an interface containing constants is to provide a set of data that a number of classes can use without having to redeclare the values. For example, the interface class in Figure 12-26 provides a number of constants for a pizzeria. Any class written for the pizzeria can implement this interface and use the permanent values. Figure 12-27 shows an example of one application that uses each value, and Figure 12-28 shows the output. The application in Figure 12-27 only needs a declaration for the current special price; all the constants, such as the name of the pizzeria, are retrieved from the interface.

```
public interface PizzaConstants
{
    public static final int SMALL_DIAMETER = 12;
    public static final int LARGE_DIAMETER = 16;
    public static final double TAX_RATE = 0.07;
    public static final String COMPANY = "Antonio's Pizzeria";
}
```

Figure 12-26 The PizzaConstants interface

```
public class PizzaDemo implements PizzaConstants
{
    public static void main(String[] args)
    {
        double specialPrice = 11.25;
        System.out.println("Welcome to " + COMPANY);
        System.out.println("We are having a special offer:\na " +
            SMALL_DIAMETER + " inch pizza with four ingredients\nor a " +
            LARGE_DIAMETER +
            " inch pizza with one ingredient\nfor only $" + specialPrice);
        System.out.println("With tax, that is only $" +
            (specialPrice + specialPrice * TAX_RATE));
    }
}
```

Figure 12-27 The `PizzaDemo` application

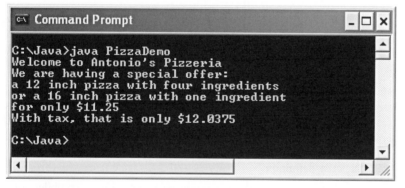

Figure 12-28 Output of the `PizzaDemo` application

CREATING AND USING PACKAGES

Throughout most of this book, you have imported packages into your programs. You learned in Chapter 4 that the `java.lang` package is automatically imported into every program you write. You have explicitly imported packages such as `java.util` and `javax.swing`. A **package** is a named collection of classes; when you create your own classes, you can place them in packages so that you or other programmers can easily import related classes into new programs. When you create a number of classes that inherit from each other, as well as multiple interfaces that you want to implement with these classes, you often will find it convenient to place these related classes in a package.

>>NOTE
A package is often called a **class library** or a **library of classes**.

>>NOTE Creating packages encourages others to reuse software because it makes it convenient to import many related classes at once. Creating packages also helps avoid naming conflicts—different programmers might create classes with the same name, but they are contained in different packages. Class naming conflicts are sometimes called **collisions**.

> **» NOTE** Because of packages, you can create a class without worrying that its name already exists in Java. For example, you can create a class named `Font` and place it in a package named `com.course.display`. To use each class, you can use the complete name, or **fully qualified name**. The fully qualified name of your `Font` class is `com.course.display.Font`, and the fully qualified name of the built-in `Font` class is `java.awt.Font`.

> **» NOTE** In Chapter 3, you learned that if you do not use one of the three access modifiers `public`, `private`, or `protected` for a class, then it has default access and is accessible to any class in the same package.

When you create classes for others to use, you most often do not want to provide the users with your source code in the files with .java extensions. You expend significant effort developing workable code for your programs, and you do not want other programmers to be able to copy your programs, make minor changes, and market the new product themselves. Rather, you want to provide users with the compiled files with the .class extensions. These are the files the user needs to run the program you have developed. Likewise, when other programmers use the classes you have developed, they need only the completed compiled code to import into their programs. The .class files are the files you place in a package so other programmers can import them.

> **» NOTE** In the Java programming language, a package or class library is often delivered to users as a **Java ARchive (JAR) file**. JAR files compress the data they store, which reduces the size of archived class files. The JAR format is based on the popular Zip file format.

> **» NOTE**
> The package statement, import statements, and comments are the only statements that appear outside class definitions in Java program files.

You can include a package statement at the beginning of your class file to place the compiled code into the indicated folder. For example, when it appears at the beginning of a class file, the statement `package com.course.animals;` indicates that the compiled file should be placed in a folder named com.course.animals. That is, the compiled file should be stored in the animals subfolder inside the course subfolder inside the com subfolder (or com\course\animals). The pathname can contain as many levels as you want. Within the file, the package statement must appear outside the class definition.

When you compile a file that you want to place in a package, you must use a compiler option with the `javac` command. The `-d` option indicates that you want to place the generated .class file in a folder. For example, the following command indicates that the compiled Animal.java file should be placed in the root directory of drive C:

> **» NOTE**
> If you do not specify a package for a class, it is placed in an unnamed **default package**.

```
javac -d C:\ Animal.java
```

If the `Animal` class file contains the statement `package com.course.animals;`, the Animal.class file is placed in C:\com\course\animals. If any of these subfolders do not exist, Java creates them. Similarly, if you package the compiled files for Dog.java, Cow.java, and so on, future programs need only use the following statement to be able to use all the related classes:

```
import com.course.animals.*
```

The wildcard format is known as a **type-import-on-demand declaration**. Alternatively, you can list each class separately, as in the following two statements:

```
import com.course.Dog;
import com.course.Cow;
```

Usually, if you want to use only one or two classes in a package, you use separate import statements for each class. Using the fully qualified name is the most precise method and provides documentation by explicitly listing all imported classes at the top of the source code file. However, if you want to use many classes in a package, it takes less typing to import the entire package, even if there are some classes you will not use.

>>NOTE The d in the -d compiler option stands for directory, which is another name for folder.

>>NOTE You cannot import more than one package in one statement; for example, if multiple packages are stored in a folder named com, you cannot import them with the statement `import com.*`. The import statement only imports files from one folder at a time.

Because Java is used extensively on the Internet, it is important to give every package a unique name. Sun Microsystems, the creator of Java, has defined a package-naming convention in which you use your Internet domain name in reverse order. For example, if your domain name is course.com, you begin all of your package names with com.course. Subsequently, you organize your packages into reasonable subfolders. Using this convention ensures that your package names do not conflict with those of any other Java code providers.

>>NOTE If a class is not `public`, it can be used only by other classes within the same package.

YOU DO IT

CREATING AN ABSTRACT CLASS

In this section, you will create an abstract `Entertainment` class for Event Handlers Incorporated. The `Entertainment` class holds data about entertainment acts that customers can hire to perform at their events. The class includes fields for the name of the act and for the fee charged for providing the act. `Entertainment` is an abstract class; there will never be a "plain" `Entertainment` object. You will create two subclasses, `MusicalEntertainment` and `OtherEntertainment`; these more specific classes include different methods for calculating the entertainment act's fee (musical acts are paid by the performance; other acts are paid by the hour), as well as different methods for displaying data.

To create an abstract `Entertainment` class:

1. Open a new file in your text editor and enter the following first few lines to begin creating an abstract `Entertainment` class:

```
import javax.swing.*;
public abstract class Entertainment
{
```

2. Define the two data fields that hold the entertainer's name and fee as `protected` rather than `private`, because you want child classes to be able to access the fields when the fee is set and when the fields are shown on the screen. Define the fields as follows:

```
protected String entertainer;
protected int fee;
```

3. The `Entertainment` constructor calls two methods. The first method accepts the entertainer's name from the keyboard. The second method sets the entertainer's fee.

```
public Entertainment()
{
    setEntertainerName();
    setEntertainmentFee();
}
```

4. Include the following two get methods that return the values for the entertainer's name and the act's fee:

```
public String getEntertainerName()
{
    return entertainer;
}
public double getEntertainmentFee()
{
    return fee;
}
```

5. Enter the following setEntertainerName() method, which is a data-entry method that prompts the user for the name of an entertainment act and assigns the entered String to the entertainer field.

```
public void setEntertainerName()
{
    entertainer = JOptionPane.showInputDialog
        (null, "Enter name of entertainer ");
}
```

6. The setEntertainmentFee() method is an abstract method. Each subclass you eventually create that represents different entertainment types will have a different fee schedule. Type the abstract method definition and the closing curly brace for the class:

```
    public abstract void setEntertainmentFee();
}
```

7. Save the file as **Entertainment.java** in the Chapter.12 folder on your Student Disk. At the command prompt, compile the file using the **javac** command.

EXTENDING AN ABSTRACT CLASS

You just created an abstract class, but you cannot instantiate any objects from this class. Rather, you must extend this class to be able to create any Entertainment-related objects. Next, you will create a MusicalEntertainment class that extends the Entertainment class. This new class is concrete; that is, you can create actual MusicalEntertainment class objects.

To create the MusicalEntertainment class:

1. Open a new file in your text editor, and then type the following, including a header for a MusicalEntertainment class that is a child of the Entertainment class:

```
import javax.swing.*;
public class MusicalEntertainment extends Entertainment
{
```

2. Add the definition of a music type field that is specific to musical entertainment by typing the following code:

```
private String typeOfMusic;
```

3. The MusicalEntertainment constructor must call its parent's constructor. It also uses the following method that sets the music type in which the entertainer specializes:

```
public MusicalEntertainment()
{
    super();
    setTypeOfMusic();
}
```

4. Enter the following `setTypeOfMusic()` method, which asks for user input:

```
public void setTypeOfMusic()
{
    typeOfMusic = JOptionPane.showInputDialog
        (null, "What kind of music does this act play? ");
}
```

5. Event Handlers Incorporated charges a flat rate of $600 per event for musical entertainment. Add the following `setEntertainmentFee()` method to your program:

```
public void setEntertainmentFee()
{
    fee = 600;
}
```

6. Add the following `toString()` method that you can use when you want to convert the details of a `MusicalEntertainment` object into a `String`, so you can easily and efficiently display the contents of the object. Add the closing curly brace for the class.

> **NOTE** In Chapter 7, you first used the automatically included `toString()` method that converts objects to `Strings`. Now, you are overriding that method for this class by writing your own version.

```
public String toString()
{
    return(entertainer + " features " + typeOfMusic +
        " music; the fee is $ " + fee + " per event.");
}
}
```

7. Save the file as **MusicalEntertainment.java** in the Chapter.12 folder on your Student Disk, and then compile the file.

EXTENDING AN ABSTRACT CLASS WITH A SECOND SUBCLASS

Event Handlers Incorporated classifies all nonmusical entertainment acts, such as clowns, jugglers, and stand-up comics, as `OtherEntertainment`. The `OtherEntertainment` class inherits from `Entertainment`, just as the `MusicalEntertainment` class does. Whereas the `MusicalEntertainment` class requires a data field to hold the type of music played by the act, the `OtherEntertainment` class requires a field for the type of act. Other differences lie in the content of the prompt within the `setTypeOfAct()` method and in the handling of fees. Event Handlers Incorporated charges $50 per hour for nonmusical acts, so both the `setEntertainmentFee()` and `toString()` methods differ from those in the `MusicalEntertainment` class.

Next, you will create an `OtherEntertainment` class to implement the abstract method `setEntertainmentFee()`.

To create the `OtherEntertainment` class file:

1. Open a new file in your text editor, and then type the following first lines of the `OtherEntertainment` class:

```
import javax.swing.*;
public class OtherEntertainment extends Entertainment
{
```

2. Create the following `String` variable to hold the type of entertainment act (such as comedian):

```
private String typeOfAct;
```

3. Enter the following code so the `OtherEntertainment` class constructor calls the parent constructor, and then calls its own method to set the act type:

```
public OtherEntertainment()
{
    super();
    setTypeOfAct();
}
```

4. Enter the following `setTypeOfAct()` method:

```
public void setTypeOfAct()
{
    typeOfAct = JOptionPane.showInputDialog
        (null, "What type of act is this? ");
}
```

5. The fee for nonmusical acts is $50 per hour, so add the following `setEntertainmentFee()` method:

```
public void setEntertainmentFee()
{
    fee = 50;
}
```

6. Enter the following `toString()` method and add the closing curly brace for the class:

```
public String toString()
{
    return(entertainer + " is a " + typeOfAct +
        "; the fee is $ " + fee + " per hour.");
}
}
```

7. Save the file as **OtherEntertainment.java** in the Chapter.12 folder on your Student Disk, and then compile the class.

INSTANTIATING OBJECTS FROM SUBCLASSES

Next, you will create a program that instantiates concrete objects from each of the two child classes you just created.

To create an application that demonstrates using the `MusicalEntertainment` and `OtherEntertainment` classes:

1. Open a new file in your text editor, and then enter the `DemoEntertainment` class header, opening curly brace, `main()` method header, and its opening curly brace as follows:

```
import javax.swing.*;
public class DemoEntertainment
{
    public static void main(String[] args)
    {
```

2. Enter the following statement that prompts the user to enter a musical act description. Then instantiate a `MusicalEntertainment` object.

```
JOptionPane.showMessageDialog (null,
    "You will be asked to enter a musical act description");
MusicalEntertainment anAct = new MusicalEntertainment();
```

3. Enter the following similar statements for a nonmusical act:

```
JOptionPane.showMessageDialog (null,
    "You will be asked to enter a nonmusical act description");
OtherEntertainment anotherAct = new OtherEntertainment();
```

4. Enter the following lines to display the contents of the two objects and exit. Add the closing curly brace for the `main()` method and for the class:

```
        JOptionPane.showMessageDialog(null,
            "\nDescription of entertainment acts:\n" +
            anAct.toString() + "\n" + anotherAct.toString());
        System.exit(0);
    }
}
```

5. Save the file as **DemoEntertainment.java** in the Chapter.12 folder on your Student Disk, and then compile it. After you compile the class with no errors (using **javac DemoEntertainment.java**), run this application using the **java DemoEntertainment** command. When the application prompts you, enter the name of a musical act, a type of music, the name of a nonmusical act, and the type of act. Figure 12-29 shows a sample execution.

Figure 12-29 Typical execution of the `DemoEntertainment` application (*continued*)

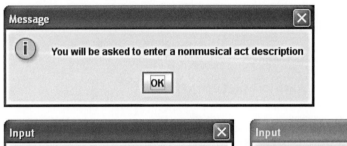

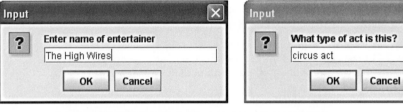

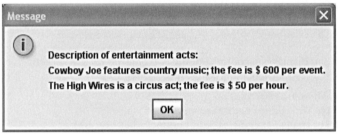

Figure 12-29 Typical execution of the DemoEntertainment application

USING OBJECT REFERENCES

Next, you will write an application for Event Handlers Incorporated in which you create an array of Entertainment references. Within the application, you assign MusicalEntertainment objects and OtherEntertainment objects to the same array. Then, because the different object types are stored in the same array, you can easily manipulate them by using a for loop.

To write an application that uses an Entertainment array:

1. Open a new file in your text editor, and then enter the following first few lines of the EntertainmentDataBase program:

```
import javax.swing.*;
public class EntertainmentDataBase
{
    public static void main(String[] args)
    {
```

2. Create the following array of six Entertainment references and an integer subscript to use with the array:

```
Entertainment[] actArray = new Entertainment[6];
int x;
```

3. Enter the following for loop that prompts you to select whether to enter a musical or non-musical entertainment act. Based on user input, instantiate either a MusicalEntertainment or an OtherEntertainment object.

```
for(x = 0; x < actArray.length; ++x)
{
    String userEntry;
    int actType;
    userEntry = JOptionPane.showInputDialog(null,
        "Please select the type of\n " +
        "act you want to enter: \n1 - Musical act\n" +
        " 2 - Any other type of act");
    actType = Integer.parseInt(userEntry);
    if(actType == 1)
        actArray[x] = new MusicalEntertainment();
    else
        actArray[x] = new OtherEntertainment();
}
```

4. After entering the information for all the acts, display the array contents by typing the following code. First create a `StringBuffer` to hold the list of acts. Then, in a `for` loop, build an output `String` by repeatedly adding a newline character and an act from the array to the `StringBuffer` object. Display the constructed `StringBuffer` in a dialog box. Then type the exit call and the closing curly braces for the `main()` method and for the class:

```
StringBuffer actsString = new StringBuffer();
for(x = 0; x < actArray.length; ++x)
{
    actsString.append("\n");
    actsString.append(actArray[x].toString());
}
JOptionPane.showMessageDialog(null,
    "Our available entertainment selections include:\n" +
    actsString);
System.exit(0);
}
}
```

5. Save the file as **EntertainmentDataBase.java** in the Chapter.12 folder on your Student Disk, and then compile it. Run the application, entering several acts of your choice. Figure 12-30 shows typical output.

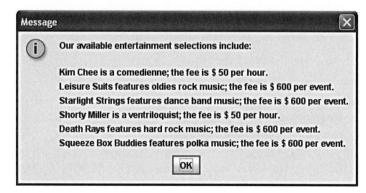

Figure 12-30 Output of the `EntertainmentDataBase` application

OVERRIDING THE Object CLASS equals() METHOD

Next, you will add an equals() method to the Event Handlers Incorporated Entertainment class. The built-in equals() method would determine that two acts were equal only if they had the same hash code; the new version of the method will consider two Entertainment acts equal when they have the same act name. You will use the equals() method in the EntertainmentDataBase program to compare each new Entertainment act to every act residing in the database. Your improved application will not allow two acts to have the same name.

To add an equals() method to the Entertainment class:

1. Open the **Entertainment.java** file in your text editor, and change the constructor and the class name to **Entertainment2**.

2. Position your insertion point after the closing curly brace of the Entertainment2 constructor, and then press **Enter** to start a new line.

Type the equals() method as follows:

```
public boolean equals(Entertainment2 act)
{
    boolean result;
    if(entertainer.equals(act.entertainer))
        result = true;
    else
        result = false;
    return result;
}
```

> **NOTE** As a briefer alternative, you can write the Entertainment2 class equals() method as follows:
>
> ```
> public boolean equals(Entertainment2 act)
> {
>     return entertainer.equals(act.entertainer);
> }
> ```
>
> In this condensed version of the method, the two entertainer String values are compared within the return statement. The comparison returns a boolean value that is simply returned by the method instead of being used in an if statement. This format and the format that uses the if statement are both acceptable—use the one that is clearer to you. Almost every Java program offers multiple ways to achieve the same result.

3. Save the file as **Entertainment2.java**, and then compile it using the **javac** command.

ELIMINATING DUPLICATE USER ENTRIES

Next, you will modify the EntertainmentDataBase program so the user cannot enter Entertainment objects with the same entertainer names.

To modify the EntertainmentDataBase class:

1. Open the **EntertainmentDataBase.java** file in your text editor, and then save it as **EntertainmentNoDuplicates.java**. Change the class name in the file from EntertainmentDataBase to **EntertainmentNoDuplicates**.

2. Change the Entertainment[] actArray = new Entertainment[6]; statement to the following, because you just updated the Entertainment class to an Entertainment2 class containing an equals() method:

```
Entertainment2[] actArray = new Entertainment2[6];
```

3. In the `if` statement that tests the selected act, change `actArray[x] =`
`new MusicalEntertainment();` and `actArray[x]  = new OtherEntertainment();`
to the following two statements, respectively, and then save the file:

```
actArray[x] = new MusicalEntertainment2();
actArray[x] = new OtherEntertainment2();
```

4. Open the **MusicalEntertainment** file and change the names of both the class and the constructor to **MusicalEntertainment2**. Change the class that this class extends to **Entertainment2**. Save the file as **MusicalEntertainment2.java**, and then compile it.

5. Open the **OtherEntertainment** file and change the names of both the class and the constructor to **OtherEntertainment2**. Change the class that this class extends to **Entertainment2**. Save the file as **OtherEntertainment2.java**, and then compile it.

> **»NOTE**   You must change the names of the MusicalEntertainment and OtherEntertainment files so that the new files, MusicalEntertainment2 and OtherEntertainment2, now extend Entertainment2. When the `equals()` method in the `Entertainment2` class receives an object to compare, it must be of the same type as `Entertainment2`.

6. Open the **EntertainmentNoDuplicates** file if necessary, position your insertion point at the end of the line that reads `actArray[x]  = new OtherEntertainment2();`, and press **Enter** to start a new line. Just before the closing curly brace for the `for` loop that controls data entry, add the following additional `for` loop that compares the most recently entered `actArray` element with all previously entered `actArray` elements. If the new element equals any previously entered `Entertainment` act, issue an error message and reduce the subscript by one. Reducing the subscript ensures that the next act you enter overwrites the duplicate act.

```
for(int y = 0; y < x; ++y)
    if(actArray[x].equals(actArray[y]))
    {
        JOptionPane.showMessageDialog(null,
            "Sorry, you entered a duplicate act");
        --x;
    }
```

7. Save the file, compile it using the **javac** command, and then execute the application. When you see the prompts, enter any appropriate data. Be certain that you repeat an entertainer's name for several of the prompts. Each time you repeat a name, you see an error message and get another opportunity to enter an act. The application does not end until you enter six acts with unique names.

CREATING A PACKAGE

Next, you will place some of the Event Handlers Incorporated classes into a package. Because Event Handlers Incorporated sponsors a Web site at *eventhandlers.com*, you will use the com.eventhandlers package.

To place three of your classes for Event Handlers Incorporated into a package:

1. Open the **Entertainment.java** file in your text editor.

2. For the first line in the file, insert the following statement:

```
package com.eventhandlers.entertainment;
```

3. Save the file as **C:\Entertainment.java**. Notice that you are saving this file in the root directory of your disk, and not in the Chapter.12 folder. Because Java uses the dot (period) to separate folder names for packages, you cannot use a dot within a folder name.

> **NOTE** Note that your drive letter might vary. For example, if you are working in a school lab, you might be required to save your files to a floppy disk, Zip disk, or network drive. The rest of these steps assume you are working from the C drive, but change the storage drive letter if necessary.

> **NOTE**
> To change to the command prompt for the root directory on your Student Disk, type cd\ at the command prompt.

4. At the command line for the root directory on the C drive, compile the file using the command **javac -d C:\ Entertainment.java**. (Be certain that you type a space between the backslash that follows the drive name and the filename **Entertainment.java**.) Java creates a folder named com\eventhandlers\entertainment on your hard drive. The compiled **Entertainment.class** file is placed in this folder.

> **NOTE** If you see a list of compile options when you try to compile the file, you did not type a space between C:\ and Entertainment.java. Repeat Step 4 to compile again.

5. Examine the folders on your Student Disk, using any operating system program with which you are familiar. For example, if you are compiling at the DOS command line, type **dir C:** at the command-line prompt to view the folders stored in the root directory. You can see that Java created a folder named com. (If you have too many files and folders stored, it might be difficult to locate the com folder. If so, type **dir C:\com*.*** to see all files and folders that begin with "com".)

Alternatively, in a Windows operating system you can double-click **My Computer**, double-click the appropriate storage device, and locate the com folder. Within the com folder is an eventhandlers folder, and within eventhandlers is an entertainment folder. The **Entertainment.class** file is within the entertainment subfolder, and not in the same folder as the .java source file where it ordinarily would be placed.

> **NOTE** If Java did not create a com folder on your Student Disk, you probably did not compile the file at the command prompt for the root directory. Repeat Steps 4 and 5, but be certain that you first change to the command prompt for the root directory.

> **NOTE**
> If you don't want to delete the Entertainment.java file, you don't have to. If you want, you can move it to the Chapter.12 folder on your Student Disk and overwrite the existing file.

6. You could now delete the copy of the **Entertainment.java** file from the root directory of your Student Disk. There is no further need for this source file because the compiled .class file is stored in the com\eventhandlers\entertainment folder. Don't delete your original code that is still in the Chapter.12 folder on your Student Disk; you might want to retain a copy of the code for modification later.

7. Open the **MusicalEntertainment.java** file in your text editor. For the first line in the file, insert the following statement:

```
package com.eventhandlers.entertainment;
```

8. Save the file in the root directory as **C:\MusicalEntertainment.java**. At the command line for the root directory on your Student Disk, compile the file using the command **javac -d C:\ MusicalEntertainment.java**. (Be certain that you type a space between the backslash that follows the drive name and the MusicalEntertainment.java filename.) Then delete the **MusicalEntertainment.java** source file from the root directory on your Student Disk (not from the Chapter.12 folder—you want to retain a copy of your original code).

9. Repeat Steps 7 and 8 to perform the same operations using the **OtherEntertainment.java** file.

10. Open the **EntertainmentDataBase.java** file in your text editor. For the first line in the file, insert the following statements:

```
import com.eventhandlers.entertainment.Entertainment;
import com.eventhandlers.entertainment.MusicalEntertainment;
import com.eventhandlers.entertainment.OtherEntertainment;
```

11. Save the file as **C:\EntertainmentDataBase.java**. Compile the file at the C:\> prompt using the **javac EntertainmentDataBase.java** command, and then run the program at the C:\> prompt using the **java EntertainmentDataBase** command. The program's output should be the same as it was before you added the import statements.

12. Examine the contents of your Student Disk again. The only .class file in the root directory of your Student Disk is the EntertainmentDataBase.class file. Because this file imports the class files from the com.eventhandlers.entertainment package, your program recognizes the `Entertainment`, `MusicalEntertainment`, and `OtherEntertainment` classes, even though neither their .java files nor their .class files are in the same folder with the `EntertainmentDataBase`.

Placing the `Entertainment`-related class files in a folder is not required for the `EntertainmentDataBase` program to execute correctly; you ran it in exactly the same manner before you learned about creating packages. The first time you executed the `EntertainmentDataBase`, all the files you used (source files as well as .class compiled files) were in the Chapter.12 folder on your Student Disk. If you distribute that folder to clients, they have access to all the code you have written.

After placing the class files in a package, you could import the package into the `EntertainmentDataBase` program and run the program from a separate folder. The folder with the three .class files is the only folder you would want to distribute to programmers who use your `Entertainment` classes to write programs similar to `EntertainmentDataBase`. Placing classes in packages gives you the ability to more easily isolate and distribute files.

KEY TERMS

An **abstract class** is one from which you cannot create any concrete objects, but from which you can inherit. Abstract classes usually have one or more empty abstract methods.

An **abstract method** is declared with the keyword `abstract`. It is a method with no body—no curly braces and no method statements—just a return type, a method name, an optional argument list, and a semicolon. You are required to code a subclass method to override the empty superclass method that is inherited.

Dynamic method binding is the ability of an application to select the correct subclass method when the program executes.

The **Object class** is defined in the `java.lang` package, which is imported automatically every time you write a program; it includes methods that you can use or override. When you define a class, if you do not explicitly extend another class, your class is an extension of the `Object` class.

The `Object` class **toString() method** converts an `Object` into a `String` that contains information about the `Object`.

A **hash code** is a calculated number used to identify an object.

The `Object` class **`equals()` method** takes a single argument, which must be the same type as the type of the invoking object, and returns a Boolean value indicating whether the objects are equal. This `equals()` method considers two objects of the same class to be equal only if they have the same memory address; in other words, they are equal only if one is a reference to the other.

Multiple inheritance is the capability to inherit from more than one class.

An **interface** looks much like a class, except that all of its methods must be abstract and all of its data (if any) must be `static final`; it declares method headers, but not the instructions within those methods.

A **package** is a named collection of classes.

A package is often called a **class library** or a **library of classes**.

Collision is a term that describes a class naming conflict.

A **fully qualified name** includes the entire hierarchy in which a class is stored.

A **Java ARchive (JAR) file** compresses the stored data.

If you do not specify a package for a class, it is placed in an unnamed **default package**.

A **type-import-on-demand declaration** is an import statement that uses the wildcard format to import a package in an application.

CHAPTER SUMMARY

» A class that you create only to extend from, but not to instantiate from, is an abstract class. Usually, abstract classes contain abstract methods—methods with no method statements. You must code a subclass method to override any inherited abstract superclass method.

» When you create a superclass and one or more subclasses, each object of the subclass "is a" superclass object. Because every subclass object "is a" superclass member, you can convert subclass objects to superclass objects. The ability of a program to select the correct subclass method is known as dynamic method binding.

» Dynamic method binding is most useful when you want to create a method that has one or more parameters that might be one of several types. You can also create an array of superclass object references but store subclass instances in it.

» When you create a useful, extendable superclass, you save development time because much of the code needed for the class has already been written. In addition, you save testing time and, because the superclass code is reliable, you reduce the time it takes to learn the new class features. You also maintain superclass integrity.

» An interface is similar to a class, but all of its methods are implicitly `public` and `abstract`, and all of its data (if any) is implicitly `public`, `static`, and `final`. When you create a class that uses an interface, you include the keyword `implements` and the interface name in the class header. This notation serves to require class objects to include code for all the methods in the interface.

» Abstract classes and interfaces are similar in that you cannot instantiate concrete objects from either. Abstract classes differ from interfaces because abstract classes can contain nonabstract methods, but all methods within an interface must be abstract. A class can inherit from only one abstract superclass, but it can implement any number of interfaces.

» You can place classes in packages so you or other programmers can easily import related classes into new classes. The convention for naming packages uses Internet domain names in reverse order to ensure that your package names do not conflict with those of any other Internet users.

REVIEW QUESTIONS

1. Parent classes are _____ than their child classes.

   a. less specific

   b. more specific

   c. easier to understand

   d. more cryptic

2. Abstract classes differ from other classes in that you _____ .

   a. must not code any methods within them

   b. must instantiate objects from them

   c. cannot instantiate objects from them

   d. cannot have data fields within them

3. Abstract classes can contain _____ .

   a. abstract methods

   b. nonabstract methods

   c. both of the above

   d. none of the above

4. An abstract class `Product` has two subclasses, `Perishable` and `NonPerishable`. None of the constructors for these classes requires any arguments. Which of the following statements is legal?

   a. `Product myProduct = new Product();`

   b. `Perishable myProduct = new Product();`

   c. `NonPerishable myProduct = new NonPerishable();`

   d. none of the above

5. An abstract class `Employee` has two subclasses, `Permanent` and `Temporary`. The `Employee` class contains an abstract method named `setType()`. Before you can instantiate `Permanent` and `Temporary` objects, which of the following statements must be true?

   a. You must code statements for the `setType()` method within the `Permanent` class.

   b. You must code statements for the `setType()` method within both the `Permanent` and `Temporary` classes.

   c. You must not code statements for the `setType()` method within either the `Permanent` or `Temporary` class.

   d. You can code statements for the `setType()` method within the `Permanent` class or the `Temporary` class, but not both.

6. When you create a superclass and one or more subclasses, each object of the subclass _____ superclass object.

   a. overrides the   c. "is not a"

   b. "is a"   d. is a new

7. Which of the following statements is true?

   a. Superclass objects are members of their subclass.

   b. Superclasses can contain abstract methods.

   c. You can create an abstract class object using the `new` operator.

   d. An abstract class cannot contain an abstract method.

8. When you create a _____ in Java, you create a variable name in which you can hold the memory address of an object.

   a. field   c. recommendation

   b. pointer   d. reference

9. An application's ability to select the correct subclass method to execute is known as _____ method binding.

   a. polymorphic   c. early

   b. dynamic   d. intelligent

10. Which statement creates an array of five reference objects of an abstract class named `Currency`?

    a. `Currency[] = new Currency[5];`

    b. `Currency[] currencyref = new Currency[5];`

    c. `Currency[5] currencyref = new Currency[5];`

    d. `Currency[5] = new Currency[5];`

11. You _____ override the `toString()` method in any class you create.

    a. cannot

    b. can

    c. must

    d. must implement `StringListener` to

12. The `Object` class `equals()` method takes _____ .

    a. no arguments

    b. one argument

    c. two arguments

    d. as many arguments as you need

13. Assume the following statement appears in a working Java program:

    ```
    if(thing.equals(anotherThing)) x = 1;
    ```

    You know that _____ .

    a. `thing` is an object of the `Object` class

    b. `anotherThing` is the same type as `thing`

    c. Both of the above are correct.

    d. None of the above are correct.

14. The `Object` class `equals()` method considers two objects of the same class to be equal if they have the same _____ .

    a. value in all data fields

    b. value in any data field

    c. data type

    d. memory address

15. Java subclasses have the ability to inherit from _____ parent class(es).

    a. one   c. multiple

    b. two   d. no

16. The alternative to multiple inheritance in Java is known as a(n) _____ .

    a. superobject

    b. abstract class

    c. interface

    d. none of the above

17. When you create a class that uses an interface, you include the keyword _____ and the interface's name in the class header.

    a. `interface`

    b. `implements`

    c. `accouterments`

    d. `listener`

18. You can instantiate concrete objects from a(n) _____ .

    a. abstract class

    b. interface

    c. either a or b

    d. neither a nor b

19. In Java, a class can _____ .

    a. inherit from one abstract superclass at most

    b. implement one interface at most

    c. both a and b

    d. neither a nor b

20. When you want to provide some data or methods that subclasses can inherit, but you want the subclasses to override some specific methods, you should write a(n) _____ .

    a. abstract class

    b. interface

    c. final superclass

    d. concrete object

EXERCISES

1. a. Create an abstract class named `Book`. Include a `String` field for the book's title and a `double` field for the book's price. Within the class, include a constructor that requires the book title and add two get methods—one that returns the title and one that returns the price. Include an abstract method named `setPrice()`. Create two child classes of `Book` called `Fiction` and `NonFiction`. Each must include a `setPrice()` method that sets the price for all `Fiction` Books to $24.99 and for all `NonFiction` Books to $37.99. Write a constructor for each subclass, and include a call to `setPrice()` within each. Write an application demonstrating that you can create both a `Fiction` and a `NonFiction` Book, and display their fields. Save the files as **Book.java**, **Fiction.java**, **NonFiction.java**, and **UseBook.java**.

    b. Write an application named `BookArray` in which you create an array that holds 10 `Books`, some `Fiction` and some `NonFiction`. Using a `for` loop, display details about all 10 books. Save the file as **BookArray.java**.

2. a. Create an abstract class named `Account` for a bank. Include an integer field for the account number and a `double` field for the account balance. Also include a constructor that requires an account number and that sets the balance to 0.0. Include a set method for the balance. Also include two abstract get methods—one for each field. Create two child classes of `Account`: `Checking` and `Savings`. Within the `Checking` class, the get method displays the `String` "Checking Account Information", the account number, and the balance. Within the `Savings` class, add a field to hold the interest rate, and require the `Savings` constructor to accept an argument for the value of the interest rate. The `Savings` get method displays the `String` "Savings Account Information", the account number, the balance, and the interest rate. Write an application that demonstrates you can instantiate and display both `Checking` and `Savings` objects. Save the files as **Account.java**, **Checking.java**, **Savings.java**, and **DemoAccounts.java**.

    b. Write an application named `AccountArray` in which you enter data for a mix of 10 `Checking` and `Savings` accounts. Use a `for` loop to display the data. Save the file as **AccountArray.java**.

3. Create an abstract `Auto` class with fields for the car make and price. Include get and set methods for these fields; the `setPrice()` method is abstract. Create two subclasses for individual automobile makers (for example, Ford or Chevy), and include appropriate `setPrice()` methods in each subclass (for example, $20,000 or $22,000). Finally, write an application that uses the `Auto` class and subclasses to display information about different cars. Save the files as **Auto.java**, **Ford.java**, **Chevy.java**, and **UseAuto.java**.

4. Create an abstract `Division` class with fields for a company's division name and account number, and an abstract `display()` method. Use a constructor in the superclass that requires values for both fields. Create two subclasses named `InternationalDivision` and `DomesticDivision`. The `InternationalDivision` includes a field for the country in which the division is located and a field for the language spoken; its constructor requires both. The `DomesticDivision` includes a field for the state in which the division is located; a value for this field is required by the constructor. Write an application named `UseDivision` that creates `InternationalDivision` and `DomesticDivision` objects for two different companies and displays information about them. Save the files as **Division.java**, **InternationalDivision.java**, **DomesticDivision.java**, and **UseDivision.java**.

5. Write an application named `UseChildren` that creates and displays at least two `Child` objects—one `Male` and one `Female`. `Child` is an abstract class and `Male` and `Female` are subclasses. The `Child` class contains fields that hold the name, gender, and age of a child. The `Child` class constructor requires a name and a gender. The `Child` class also contains two abstract methods named `setAge()` and `display()`. The `Male` and `Female` subclass constructors require only a name; they pass the name and appropriate gender to the `Child`. The subclass constructors also prompt the user for an age using the `setAge()` method, and display the `Child`'s data using the `display()` method. Save the files as **Child.java**, **Male.java**, **Female.java**, and **UseChildren.java**.

6. Create a class named `NewspaperSubscriber` with fields for a subscriber's street address and the subscription rate. Include get and set methods for the subscriber's street address, and include get and set methods for the subscription rate. The set method for the rate is abstract. Include an `equals()` method that indicates two `Subscribers` are equal if they have the same street address. Create child classes named `SevenDaySubscriber`, `WeekdaySubscriber`, and `WeekendSubscriber`. Each child class constructor sets the rate as follows: `SevenDaySubscribers` pay $4.50 per week, `WeekdaySubscribers` pay $3.50 per week, and `WeekendSubscribers` pay $2.00 per week. Each child class should include a `toString()` method that returns the street address, rate, and service type. Write an application named `Subscribers` that prompts the user for the subscriber's street address and requested service, and then creates the appropriate object based on the service type. Do not let the user enter more than one subscription type for any given street address. Save the files as **NewspaperSubscriber.java**, **WeekdaySubscriber.java**, **WeekendSubscriber.java**, **SevenDaySubscriber.java**, and **Subscribers.java**.

7. a. Create an interface named `Turner`, with a single method named `turn()`. Create a class named `Leaf` that implements `turn()` to print "Changing colors". Create a class named `Page` that implements `turn()` to print "Going to the next page". Create a class named `Pancake` that implements `turn()` to print "Flipping". Write an application named `DemoTurners` that creates one object of each of these class types and demonstrates the

turn() method for each class. Save the files as **Turner.java**, **Leaf.java**, **Page.java**, **Pancake.java**, and **DemoTurners.java**.

b. Think of two more objects that use turn(), create classes for them, and then add objects to the DemoTurners application, renaming it **DemoTurners2.java**. Save the files, using the names of new objects that use turn().

8. Write an application named UseInsurance that uses an abstract Insurance class and Health and Life subclasses to display different types of insurance policies and the cost per month. The Insurance class contains a String representing the type of insurance and a double that holds the monthly price. The Insurance class constructor requires a String argument indicating the type of insurance, but the Life and Health class constructors require no arguments. The Insurance class contains a get method for each field; it also contains two abstract methods named setCost() and display(). The Life class setCost() method sets the monthly fee to $36, and the Health class sets the monthly fee to $196. Write an application named UseInsurance that prompts the user for the type of insurance to be displayed, and then create the appropriate object. Save the files as **Life.java**, **Health.java**, **Insurance.java**, and **UseInsurance.java**.

9. Write an application named UseLoan that uses an abstract class named PersonalLoan and subclasses to display two different types of loans—home and car—and the cost per month for each. Each of the subclasses contains a constructor that sets the cost per month based on the loan type, after prompting the user for at least one data-entry item that is used in the cost-determining decision. (For example, with a car loan, you might ask the age of the car, or whether it is a sports car.) Include an abstract toString() method in the PersonalLoan class that constructs a String containing all the relevant data. Prompt the user for the type of insurance, and then create and display the appropriate object. Save the files as **PersonalLoan.java**, **CarLoan.java**, **HomeLoan.java**, and **UseLoan.java**.

10. Create an abstract class called GeometricFigure. Each figure includes a height, a width, a figure type, and an area. Include an abstract method to determine the area of the figure. Create two subclasses called Square and Triangle. Create an application that demonstrates creating objects of both subclasses, and store them in an array. Save the files as **GeometricFigure.java**, **Square.java**, **Triangle.java**, and **UseGeometric.java**.

11. Modify Exercise 10, adding an interface called SidedObject that contains a method called printSides(); this method displays the number of sides the object possesses. Modify the GeometricFigure subclasses to include the use of the interface to print the number of sides of the figure. Create an application that demonstrates the use of both subclasses. Save the files as **GeometricFigure2.java**, **Square2.java**, **Triangle2.java**, **SidedObject.java**, and **UseGeometric2.java**.

12. Create an interface called Player. The interface has an abstract method called play() that displays a message describing the meaning of "play" to the class. Create classes called Child, Musician, and Actor that all implement Player. Create an application that

demonstrates the use of the classes. Save the files as **Player.java**, **Child.java**, **Actor.java**, **Musician.java**, and **UsePlayer.java**.

13. Create an abstract class called `Student`. The `Student` class includes a name and a Boolean value representing full-time status. Include an abstract method to determine the tuition, with full-time students paying a flat fee of $2000 and part-time students paying $200 per credit hour. Create two subclasses called `FullTime` and `PartTime`. Create an application that demonstrates how to create objects of both subclasses. Save the files as **Student.java**, **FullTime.java**, **PartTime.java**, and **UseStudent.java**.

14. Create a `Building` class and two subclasses, `House` and `School`. The `Building` class contains fields for square footage and stories. The `House` class contains additional fields for number of bedrooms and baths. The `School` class contains additional fields for number of classrooms and grade level (for example, elementary or junior high). All the classes contain appropriate get and set methods. Place the `Building`, `House`, and `School` classes in a package named com.course.buildings. Create an application that declares objects of each type and uses the package. Save the necessary files as **Building.java**, **House.java**, **School.java**, and **CreateBuildings.java**.

DEBUGGING EXERCISES

Each of the following files in the Chapter.12 folder on your Student Disk has syntax and/or logic errors. In each case, determine the problem and fix the program. After you correct the errors, save each file using the same filename preceded with Fix. For example, DebugTwelve1.java will become FixDebugTwelve1.java.

a. DebugTwelve1.java

b. DebugTwelve2.java

c. DebugTwelve3.java

d. DebugTwelve4.java

e. Three other Debug files in the Chapter.12 folder

CASE PROJECT

SANCHEZ CONSTRUCTION LOAN CO.

Sanchez Construction Loan Co. makes small loans for construction projects, up to a maximum of $100,000. There are two categories of `Loans`—those to businesses and those to individual applicants.

Write an application that tracks all new construction loans. The application must also calculate the total amount owed at the due date (original loan amount + loan fee). The application should include the following classes:

» Loan—A public abstract class that implements the `LoanConstants` interface. A `Loan` includes a loan number, customer last name, amount of loan, interest rate, and term. The constructor requires data for each of the fields except interest rate. Do not allow loan amounts over $100,000. Force any loan term that is not one of the three defined in the LoanConstants class to a short-term, one-year loan. Create a toString() method that displays all the loan data.

» LoanConstants—A public interface class. LoanConstants includes constant values for short-term (one year), medium-term (three years), and long-term (five years) loans. It also contains constants for the company name and the maximum loan amount.

» BusinessLoan—A public class that extends Loan. The BusinessLoan constructor sets the interest rate to 1% over the current prime interest rate.

» PersonalLoan—A public class that extends Loan. The PersonalLoan constructor sets the interest rate to 2% over the current prime interest rate.

» CreateLoans—An application that creates an array of five Loans. Prompt the user for the current prime interest rate. Then, in a loop, prompt the user for a loan type and all relevant information for that loan. Store the created Loan objects in the array. When data entry is complete, display all the loans.

Save the files in the Chapter.12 folder on your Student Disk.

GAME ZONE

1. In Chapter 11, you created an Alien class as well as two descendant classes, Martian and Jupiterian. Because you never create any "plain" Alien objects, alter the Alien class so it is abstract. Verify that the Martian and Jupiterian classes can still inherit from Alien and that the JDemoAliens applet still works correctly. Save the altered Alien file as **Alien.java**.

2. a. Create an abstract CardGame class similar to the one described in this chapter. The class contains a "deck" of 52 playing cards that uses the Card class you developed in Chapter 9. It also contains an integer field that holds the number of cards dealt to a player in a particular game. The class contains a constructor that initializes the deck of cards with appropriate values (e.g., "King of Hearts"), and a shuffle() method that randomly arranges the positions of the Cards in the array. The class also contains two abstract methods: displayDescription(), which displays a brief description of the game in child classes, and deal(), which deals the appropriate number of Card objects to one player of a game. Save the file as **CardGame.java**.

   b. Create two child classes that extend CardGame. You can choose any games you prefer. For example, you might create a Poker class or a Bridge class. Create a constructor for each child class that initializes the field that holds the number of cards dealt to the correct value. (For example, in standard poker, a player receives five cards, but in bridge, a player receives 13.) Create an appropriate displayDescription() and deal() method for each child class. Save each file using an appropriate name—for example, **Poker.java** or **Bridge.java**.

   c. Create an application that instantiates one object of each game type and demonstrates that the methods work correctly. Save the application as **PlayCardGames.java**.

UP FOR DISCUSSION

1. Programming sometimes can be done from a remote location. For example, as a professional programmer, you might be able to work from home. Does this appeal to you? What are the advantages and disadvantages? If you have other programmers working for you, would you allow them to work from home? Would you require any "face time"—that is, time in the office with you or other workers?

2. Programming sometimes can be done from a remote location. For example, your organization might contract with programmers who live in another country, where wages are considerably lower than in the United States. Do you have any objections to employers using these workers? If not, what objections do you think others might have?

3. Suppose your organization hires programmers to work in another country. Suppose you also discover that working conditions there are not the same as in your country. For example, the buildings in which the workers do their jobs might not be subject to the same standards for ventilation and fire codes as the building where you work. Is your company under any obligation to change the working conditions?

13

UNDERSTANDING SWING COMPONENTS

USING THE JFrame CLASS

>> **NOTE**
Although applets always contain UI components, applications also can contain UI components.

Computer programs usually are more user-friendly (and more fun to use) when they contain user interface (UI) components such as buttons, check boxes, and menus. In Chapter 9, you learned how to add a few UI components to an applet; in this chapter, you will learn how to add several more components to applets and applications.

You already know that you do not need to create UI components from scratch; Java's creators packaged `Swing` components such as `JButton` and `JLabel` for you to use in your UI applications. Each `Swing` component is a descendant of a `JComponent`, which in turn inherits from the `java.awt.Container` class. You insert the import statement `import javax.swing.*;` at the beginning of your Java program files so you can take advantage of the `Swing` UI components and their methods.

>> **NOTE**
Components are also called controls or widgets, which stands for windows gadgets.

>> **NOTE** Almost all `Swing` components are said to be **lightweight components** because they are written completely in Java and do not have to rely on the code written to run the local operating system. This means the components are not "weighed down" by having to interact with the operating system (for example, Windows or Macintosh) in which the application is running. Some `Swing` components, such as `JFrame`s, are called **heavyweight components** because they do require interaction with the local operating system.

>> **NOTE** A lightweight component reuses the native (original) window of its closest heavyweight ancestor; a heavyweight component has its own opaque native window.

When you use `Swing` components, you usually place them in containers. A **container** is a type of component that holds other components so you can treat a group of them as a single entity.

Containers are defined in the `Container` class. Often, a container takes the form of a window that you can drag, resize, minimize, restore, and close.

As you know from reading Chapters 11 and 12, all Java classes are subclasses; they all descend from the `Object` class. The `Component` class is a child of the `Object` class, and the `Container` class is a child of the `Component` class. Therefore, every `Container` object "is a" `Component`, and every `Component` object (including every `Container`) "is an" `Object`. You have created many `Container` objects to hold your `JApplets'` content panes.

The `Container` class is also a parent class, and the `Window` class is a child of `Container`. However, Java programmers rarely use `Window` objects because the `Window` subclass `Frame` and its child, the `Swing` component **JFrame**, both allow you to create more useful objects. `Window` objects do not have title bars or borders, but `JFrame` objects do. Figure 13-1 shows the `JFrame`'s inheritance tree.

```
java.lang.Object
  !--java.awt.Component
        !--java.awt.Container
              !--java.awt.Window
                    !--java.awt.Frame
                          !--javax.swing.JFrame
```

Figure 13-1 Relationship of the `JFrame` class to its ancestors

> **NOTE** Recall that the `Object` class is defined in the `java.lang` package, which is imported automatically every time you write a Java program. However, its descendants shown in Figure 13-1 are not automatically imported.

> **NOTE** The only heavyweight components used in Swing are `swing.JFrame`, `swing.JDialog`, `swing.JWindow`, `swing.JApplet`, `awt.Component`, `awt.Container`, and `awt.JComponent`.

You usually create a `JFrame` so that you can place other objects within it for display. The `JFrame` class has four constructors:

» `JFrame()` constructs a new frame that initially is invisible and has no title.

» `JFrame(String title)` creates a new, initially invisible `JFrame` with the specified title.

» `JFrame(GraphicsConfiguration gc)` creates a `JFrame` in the specified `GraphicsConfiguration` of a screen device with a blank title.

» `JFrame(String title, GraphicsConfiguration gc)` creates a `JFrame` with the specified title and the specified `GraphicsConfiguration` of a screen.

> **NOTE** You will learn about the `GraphicsConfiguration` class as you continue to study Java.

You can construct a `JFrame` as you do other objects, using the class name, an identifier, the assignment operator, the `new` operator, and a constructor call. For example, the following two statements construct two `JFrames`: one with the title "Hello" and another with no title:

```
JFrame firstFrame = new JFrame("Hello");
JFrame secondFrame = new JFrame();
```

After you create a `JFrame` object, you can use the now-familiar object-dot-method format you have used with other objects to call methods that manipulate a `JFrame`'s features. Table 13-1 describes some useful `JFrame` class methods. For example, the following statements set the

Method	Purpose
`void setTitle(String)`	Sets a `JFrame`'s title using the `String` argument
`void setSize(int, int)`	Sets a `JFrame`'s size in pixels with the width and height as arguments
`void setSize(Dimension)`	Sets a `JFrame`'s size using a `Dimension` class object; the `Dimension(int, int)` constructor creates an object that represents both a width and a height
`String getTitle()`	Returns a `JFrame`'s title
`void setResizable (boolean)`	Sets the `JFrame` to be resizable by passing `true` to the method, or sets the `JFrame` not to be resizable by passing `false` to the method
`boolean isResizable()`	Returns `true` or `false` to indicate whether the `JFrame` is resizable
`void setVisible (boolean)`	Sets a `JFrame` to be visible using the `boolean` argument `true` and invisible using the `boolean` argument `false`
`void setBounds(int, int, int, int)`	Overrides the default behavior for the `JFrame` to be positioned in the upper-left corner of the computer screen's desktop. The first two arguments are the horizontal and vertical positions of the `JFrame`'s upper-left corner on the desktop. The final two arguments set the width and height.

Table 13-1 Useful methods inherited by the `JFrame` class

> **NOTE** The methods in Table 13-1 represent only a small portion of the available methods you can use with a `JFrame`. Each of the methods listed in Table 13-1 is inherited from either `JFrame`'s `Component` or `Frame` parent class. These classes contain many useful methods in addition to the few listed here. You can read the documentation for all the methods at *http://java.sun.com*.

`firstFrame` object's size to 200 pixels horizontally by 100 pixels vertically, and set the `JFrame`'s title to display a `String` argument:

```
firstFrame.setSize(200, 100);
firstFrame.setTitle("My frame");
```

Figure 13-2 shows an application that creates a small, empty `JFrame`; the resulting `JFrame` shown in Figure 13-3 resembles frames that you have probably seen when using different UI programs you have purchased. One reason to use similar frame objects in your own programs is that your program's user is already familiar with the frame environment. When users see frames on their computer screens, they expect to see a title bar at the top containing text information (such as "First frame"). Users also expect to see Minimize, Maximize or Restore, and Close buttons in the frame's upper-right corner. Most users assume that they can change

```
import javax.swing.*;
public class JFrame1
{
    public static void main(String[] args)
    {
        JFrame aFrame = new JFrame("First frame");
        aFrame.setSize(200, 100);
        aFrame.setVisible(true);
    }
}
```

Figure 13-2 The `JFrame1` application

>> **NOTE** In the application in Figure 13-2, all three statements are important. After you instantiate `aFrame`, if you do not use `setVisible(true)`, you do not see the `JFrame`, and if you do not set its size, you see only the title bar of the `JFrame` because the `JFrame` size is 0 × 0 by default.

>> **NOTE** In the application in Figure 13-2, you might prefer to use named constants for the `JFrame` dimensions rather than the literal constants 200 and 100. That way, your intentions are more obvious to someone reading your program. The following examples use this approach.

Figure 13-3 Output of the `JFrame1` application

>> **NOTE** It might seem unusual that the default state for a `JFrame` is invisible. However, consider that you might want to construct a `JFrame` in the background while other actions are occurring and that you might want to make it visible later, when appropriate (for example, after the user has taken an action such as selecting an option). To make a frame visible, some Java programmers use the `show()` method instead of the `setVisible()` method.

a frame's size by dragging its border or reposition the frame on their screen by dragging the frame's title bar to a new location. The `JFrame` in Figure 13-3 has all of these capabilities.

When a user closes a `JFrame` by clicking the Close button in the upper-right corner, the default behavior is for the `JFrame` to become hidden and for the application to keep running. This makes sense when there are other tasks for the program to complete after the main frame is closed—for example, displaying additional frames, closing open data files, or printing an activity report. However, when a `JFrame` serves as a `Swing` application's main user interface (as happens frequently in interactive programs), you usually want the program to exit when the user clicks Close. To change this behavior, you can call a `JFrame`'s `setDefaultCloseOperation()` method and use one of the following four values as an argument:

» `JFrame.EXIT_ON_CLOSE` exits the program when the `JFrame` is closed. This value is used in Figure 13-4 and other examples in this chapter.

» `WindowConstants.DISPOSE_ON_CLOSE` closes the frame, disposes of the `JFrame` object, and keeps running the application.

```
import javax.swing.*;
import java.awt.*;
public class JFrame2
{
    public static void main(String[] args)
    {
        final int FRAME_WIDTH = 200;
        final int FRAME_HEIGHT = 100;
        JFrame aFrame = new JFrame("Second frame");
        aFrame.setSize(FRAME_WIDTH, FRAME_HEIGHT);
        aFrame.setVisible(true);
        aFrame.setDefaultCloseOperation(JFrame.EXIT_ON_CLOSE);
        JLabel label = new JLabel("Hello");
        Container con = aFrame.getContentPane();
        con.setLayout(new FlowLayout());
        con.add(label);
    }
}
```

Figure 13-4 The `JFrame2` class

»NOTE

JApplet, JFrame, JPanel, and JWindow are similar in that all can contain other components.

» `WindowConstants.DO_NOTHING_ON_CLOSE` keeps the `JFrame` and continues running. In other words, it disables the Close button.

» `WindowConstants.HIDE_ON_CLOSE` closes the `JFrame` and continues running; this is the default operation that you frequently want to override.

»NOTE Each of the four usable `setDefaultCloseOperation()` arguments represents an integer; for example, the value of `JFrame.EXIT_ON_CLOSE` is 3. However, it is easier to remember the constant names than the numeric values they represent, and it makes it easier for other programmers to understand your intentions if you use the named constant identifier.

When you want to add components to a `JFrame`, you can get a reference to the `JFrame`'s automatically created content pane, much as you do with a `JApplet`. For example, Figure 13-4 shows an application in which a frame is created and its size, visibility, and close operation are set. Then a `JLabel` is created and the `getContentPane()` method gets a reference to the content pane, as shown in the shaded statement. The layout is set and the label is added to the content pane. Figure 13-5 shows the output.

»NOTE In Java version 5 and later, you can create the `JFrame2` application without using the `getContentPane()` method. You will learn more about content panes later in this chapter.

Figure 13-5 Output of the `JFrame2` application

CUSTOMIZING A JFrame's APPEARANCE

The appearance of the frames in Figures 13-3 and 13-5 is provided by the operating system in which the program is running (in this case, Windows). For example, the coffee-cup icon in the frame's title bar and the Minimize, Restore, and Close buttons look and act as they do in other Windows applications. The icon and buttons are known as **window decorations**; by default, window decorations are supplied by the operating system. However, you can request that Java's look and feel provide the decorations for a frame. A **look and feel** is the default appearance and behavior of any user interface.

Optionally, you can set a JFrame's look and feel using the setDefaultLookAndFeelDecorated() method. For example, Figure 13-6 shows an application in which this method is called. Figure 13-6 differs from Figure 13-4 only in the shaded areas, which show the class name, the text in the title bar, and the look-and-feel statement. Figure 13-7 shows the output. If you compare the frame in Figure 13-5 with the one in Figure 13-7, you can see that Java's look and feel has similar features to that of Windows, but their appearance is different.

> **NOTE** You might decide to use the setDefaultLookAndFeelDecorated() method call in all your applications that contain JFrames. To keep the examples simpler, this book usually omits the statement and uses the look and feel of the default operating system.

```
import javax.swing.*;
import java.awt.*;
public class JFrame3
{
    public static void main(String[] args)
    {
        final int FRAME_WIDTH = 200;
        final int FRAME_HEIGHT = 100;
        JFrame.setDefaultLookAndFeelDecorated(true);
        JFrame aFrame = new JFrame("Third frame");
        aFrame.setSize(FRAME_WIDTH, FRAME_HEIGHT);
        aFrame.setVisible(true);
        aFrame.setDefaultCloseOperation(JFrame.EXIT_ON_CLOSE);
        JLabel label = new JLabel("Hello");
        Container con = aFrame.getContentPane();
        con.setLayout(new FlowLayout());
        con.add(label);
    }
}
```

Figure 13-6 The JFrame3 class

> **NOTE** You can provide a custom icon for a frame instead of using your operating system's default icon or the Java look-and-feel icon. For details, go to *http://java.sun.com* and search for "How to Make Frames".

Figure 13-7 Output of the `JFrame3` application

»NOTE Look-and-feel is a legal issue because some software companies claim that competitors are infringing on their copyright protection by copying the look and feel of their products. As of this writing, the courts have not made a definitive ruling on this matter.

EXTENDING THE JFrame CLASS

You can instantiate a simple `JFrame` object within an application's `main()` method, a `JApplet`'s `init()` method, or any other method of any class you write. Alternatively, you can create your own class that descends from the `JFrame` class. The advantage to creating a child class of `JFrame` is that you can set the `JFrame`'s properties within your object's constructor method; then, when you create your `JFrame` child object, it is automatically endowed with the features, such as size, that you have specified.

You already know that you create a child class by using the keyword `extends` in the class header, followed by the parent class name. You also know that you can call the parent class's constructor method using the keyword `super`. For example, the `JMyFrame` class in Figure 13-8 extends `JFrame`. Within the `JMyFrame` constructor, the `super()` `JFrame` constructor is called; it accepts a `String` argument to use as the `JFrame`'s title. (Alternatively, the `setTitle()` method could have been used.) The `JMyFrame` constructor also sets the size, visibility, and default close operation for every `JMyFrame`. Each of the methods—`setSize()`, `setVisible()`, and `setDefaultCloseOperation()`—appears in the constructor in Figure 13-8 without an object, because the object is the current `JMyFrame` being constructed. Each of the three methods could be preceded with a `this` reference with exactly the same

```
import javax.swing.*;
public class JMyFrame extends JFrame
{
    final int WIDTH = 400;
    final int HEIGHT = 120;
    public JMyFrame()
    {
        super("This is my frame");
        setSize(WIDTH, HEIGHT);
        setVisible(true);
        setDefaultCloseOperation(JFrame.EXIT_ON_CLOSE);
    }
}
```

Figure 13-8 The `JMyFrame` class

meaning. That is, within the JMyFrame constructor, the following two statements have identical meanings:

```
setSize(WIDTH, HEIGHT);
this.setSize(WIDTH, HEIGHT);
```

Each statement sets the size of "this" current JMyFrame instance.

Figure 13-9 shows an application that declares two JMyFrame objects. Each has the same set of attributes, determined by the JMyFrame constructor. When you execute the application in Figure 13-9, the two JMyFrame objects display with the second one on top of, or obscuring, the first. Figure 13-10 shows the output of the CreateTwoJMyFrameObjects application after the top JMyFrame has been dragged to partially expose the bottom one.

```
public class CreateTwoJMyFrameObjects
{
    public static void main(String[] args)
    {
        JMyFrame myFrame = new JMyFrame();
        JMyFrame mySecondFrame = new JMyFrame();
    }
}
```

Figure 13-9 The CreateTwoJMyFrameObjects application

>> **NOTE** You could use the setBounds() method with one of the JMyFrame objects in the application in Figure 13-9 so that you don't have to move the second JMyFrame object to view the first. See Table 13-1 for details. The Object class also includes a setLocation() method you can use with a JFrame. To use this method, you provide horizontal and vertical position values as method arguments.

Figure 13-10 Output of the CreateTwoJMyFrameObjects application after dragging the top frame

>> **NOTE** You exit the application when you click the Close button on either of the two JMyFrame objects shown in Figure 13-10. Each object has the same default close operation because each uses the same constructor that specifies this operation. To allow only one JMyFrame to control the program's exit, you could use the setDefaultCloseOperation() method with one or both of the objects in the application to change its close behavior. For example, you could use DISPOSE_ON_CLOSE to dismiss one of the frames but keep the application running.

USING THE JPanel CLASS

The simplest Swing container is the **JPanel**—it is a plain, borderless surface that can hold lightweight UI components. Figure 13-11 shows the inheritance hierarchy of the JPanel class. You can see that every JPanel is a Container; you use a JPanel to hold other UI components, such as JButtons, JCheckBoxes, or even other JPanels.

```
java.lang.Object
  !--java.awt.Component
       !--java.awt.Container
            !--javax.swing.JComponent
                 !--javax.swing.JPanel
```

Figure 13-11 The inheritance hierarchy of the `JPanel` class

To add a component to a `JPanel`, you call the container's `add()` method, using the component as the argument. For example, Figure 13-12 shows the code that creates a `JFrameWithPanels` class that extends `JFrame`. A `JButton` is added to a `JPanel` named `pane`, and two more `JButtons` are added to another `JPanel` named `pane2`. Then, `pane` and `pane2` are added to the `JFrame`'s content pane. Figure 13-13 shows an application that creates one instance of `JFrameWithPanels`, and Figure 13-14 shows the output, in which two `JPanels` have been added to the `JFrame`. Because this application uses the `setBackground()` method to make each `JPanel`'s background blue, you can see where one panel ends and the other begins. The upper `JPanel` contains a single `JButton` and the lower one contains two `JButtons`.

```java
import javax.swing.*;
import java.awt.*;
public class JFrameWithPanels extends JFrame
{
    final int SIZE = 150;
    JButton button1 = new JButton("One");
    JButton button2 = new JButton("Two");
    JButton button3 = new JButton("Three");
    public JFrameWithPanels()
    {
        super("JFrame with Panels");
        setDefaultCloseOperation(JFrame.EXIT_ON_CLOSE);
        JPanel pane = new JPanel();
        JPanel pane2 = new JPanel();
        Container con = getContentPane();
        con.setLayout(new FlowLayout());
        con.add(pane);
        con.add(pane2);
        pane.add(button1);
        pane.setBackground(Color.BLUE);
        pane2.add(button2);
        pane2.add(button3);
        pane2.setBackground(Color.BLUE);
        setSize(SIZE, SIZE);
        setVisible(true);
    }
}
```

Figure 13-12 The `JFrameWithPanels` class

```
public class CreateJFrameWithPanels
{
    public static void main(String[] args)
    {
        JFrameWithPanels panel = new JFrameWithPanels();
    }
}
```

Figure 13-13 The `CreateJFrameWithPanels` application

Figure 13-14 Output of the `CreateJFrameWithPanels` application

In the `JFrame` shown in Figure 13-14, the buttons are not functional—nothing happens when a user clicks them. To create a class that responds to user-initiated events, you use an event listener.

UNDERSTANDING Swing EVENT LISTENERS

Classes that respond to user-initiated events, such as button clicks, must implement an interface that deals with, or handles, the events. These interfaces are called **event listeners**, and you first learned about them in Chapter 9 when you used the `ActionListener` interface with `JButton` objects. Many types of listeners exist in Java, and each of these listeners can handle a specific event type. A class can implement as many event listeners as it needs—for example, a class might need to respond to both mouse and keyboard events, so you might implement `ActionListener` and `KeyListener` interfaces. Table 13-2 lists some event listeners and the types of events for which they are used.

An event occurs every time a user types a character or clicks a mouse button. Any object can be notified of an event as long as it implements the appropriate interface and is registered as an event listener on the appropriate event source. For example, in Chapter 9 you used `JApplet`s in which the `JApplet` listened to, and was notified of, events generated by a `JButton` source. You learned that you establish a relationship between a `JButton` and its `JApplet` using the `addActionListener()` method. Similarly, you can create relationships between other `Swing` components and the classes that react to users' manipulations of them. In Table 13-3, each component listed on the left is associated with a method on the right. For example, when you want a `JCheckBox` to respond to a user's clicks, you can use the

Listener	Type of Events	Example
ActionListener	Action events	Button clicks
AdjustmentListener	Adjustment events	Scroll bar moves
ChangeListener	Change events	Slider is repositioned
FocusListener	Keyboard focus events	Text field gains or loses focus
ItemListener	Item events	Check box changes status
KeyListener	Keyboard events	Text is entered
MouseListener	Mouse events	Mouse clicks
MouseMotionListener	Mouse movement events	Mouse rolls
WindowListener	Window events	Window closes

Table 13-2 Alphabetical list of some event listeners

Components	Associated Listener-Registering Methods
JButton, JCheckBox, JComboBox, JTextField, and JRadioButton	addActionListener()
JScrollBar	addAdjustmentListener()
All Swing components	addFocusListener(), addKeyListener(), addMouseListener(), and addMouseMotionListener()
JButton, JCheckBox, JComboBox, and JRadioButton	addItemListener()
All JWindow and JFrame components	addWindowListener()
JSlider and JCheckBox	addChangeListener()

Table 13-3 Some Swing components and their associated listener-registering methods

> **NOTE** You learned about some of the components listed in Table 13-3 (such as JButton) in previous chapters. You will learn about others (such as JCheckBox) later in this chapter.

addItemListener() method to register the JCheckBox as the type of object that can create an ItemEvent. The argument you place within the parentheses of the call to the addItemListener() method is the object that should respond to the event—perhaps a JApplet or a JFrame that contains the JCheckBox that generates the event. The format is:

```
theSourceOfTheEvent.addListenerMethod (theClassThatShouldRespond);
```

> **NOTE** Any event source can have multiple listeners registered on it. Conversely, a single listener can register with multiple event sources. In other words, a single instance of JCheckBox might generate ItemEvents and FocusEvents, and a single instance of the JFrame class might respond to ActionEvents generated by a JButton and ItemEvents generated by a JCheckBox.

The class of the object that responds to an event must contain a method that accepts the event object created by the user's action. In other words, when you register a component (such as a JFrame) to be a listener for events generated by another component (such as a JCheckBox), you must write a method that reacts to any generated event. You cannot choose your own name for the reacting methods—specific methods react to specific event types. Table 13-4 lists just some of the methods that react to events.

Listener	Method
ActionListener	actionPerformed(ActionEvent)
AdjustmentListener	adjustmentValueChanged(AdjustmentEvent)
FocusListener	focusGained(FocusEvent) and
	focusLost(FocusEvent)
ItemListener	itemStateChanged(ItemEvent)

Table 13-4 Selected methods that respond to events

>> **NOTE** Each listener in Table 13-4 is associated with only one or two methods. Other listeners, such as KeyListener and MouseListener, are associated with multiple methods. You will learn how to use these more complicated listeners in Chapter 14.

Until you become familiar with the event-handling model, it can seem quite confusing. You will learn more about the event model in Chapter 14. For now, remember these points:

» When you declare a class that handles an event, you create the class to either implement a listener interface or extend a class that implements a listener interface. For example, if a JFrame named MyFrame needs to respond to a user's clicks on a JCheckBox, you would write the following class header:

```
public class MyFrame extends JFrame
    implements ItemListener
```

» Register an instance of the event handler class as a listener for one or more components. For example, if MyFrame contains a JCheckBox named myCheckBox, you would code:

```
myCheckBox.addItemListener(this);
```

The this reference is to the class in which myCheckBox is declared—in this case, MyFrame.

» Write a method that accepts the generated event and reacts to it. For example:

```
public void itemStateChanged(ItemEvent event)
{
    // code that executes whenever the event occurs
}
```

>> **NOTE** If you fail to include an actionPerformed() method in a program that implements ActionListener, the program does not compile.

If more than one component generates an event, you usually want to figure out which component generated the specific event. For example, if an application contains two buttons, you usually need to know which one a user clicked so you can decide which action to take. Each action's automatically called method listed in Table 13-4 contains an event argument that contains information about the object that caused the event. For example, if you code a method header as follows, then anInterestingEvent is an object that contains event details:

```
public void itemStateChanged(ItemEvent anInterestingEvent)
```

You can use the getSource() method to determine the component that sent the event. For example, the following actionPerformed() method gets the source of the event and then compares it to a JButton named oneButton, which takes one action if the JButton is the source of the event and a different action if some other component is the source of the event.

```
public void actionPerformed(ActionEvent event)
{
    Object source = event.getSource();
    if(source == oneButton)
        //take some action
    else
        //take some other action
}
```

USING THE JCheckBox CLASS

A **JCheckBox** consists of a label positioned beside a square; you can click the square to display or remove a check mark. Usually, you use a JCheckBox to allow the user to turn an option on or off. For example, Figure 13-15 shows the code for an application that uses four JCheckBoxes, and Figure 13-16 shows the output. The inheritance hierarchy of the JCheckBox class is shown in Figure 13-17; frequently used JCheckBox methods appear in Table 13-5.

```
import java.awt.*;
import javax.swing.*;
import java.awt.event.*;
public class CheckBoxDemonstration extends JFrame implements
    ItemListener
{
    FlowLayout flow = new FlowLayout();
    JLabel label = new JLabel("What would you like to drink?");
    JCheckBox coffee = new JCheckBox("Coffee", false);
    JCheckBox cola = new JCheckBox("Cola", false);
    JCheckBox milk = new JCheckBox("Milk", false);
    JCheckBox water = new JCheckBox("Water", false);
    String output, insChosen;
    JPanel panel = new JPanel();
    Container con;
    public CheckBoxDemonstration()
    {
        super("CheckBox Demonstration");
        setDefaultCloseOperation(JFrame.EXIT_ON_CLOSE);
        con = getContentPane();
        con.add(panel);
        panel.setLayout(flow);
        label.setFont(new Font("Arial", Font.ITALIC, 22));
        coffee.addItemListener(this);
```

Figure 13-15 The CheckBoxDemonstration class (*continued*) ▶

```
        cola.addItemListener(this);
        milk.addItemListener(this);
        water.addItemListener(this);
        panel.add(label);
        panel.add(coffee);
        panel.add(cola);
        panel.add(milk);
        panel.add(water);
    }
    public static void main(String[] arguments)
    {
        final int FRAME_WIDTH = 350;
        final int FRAME_HEIGHT = 120;
        CheckBoxDemonstration frame =
            new CheckBoxDemonstration();
        frame.setSize(FRAME_WIDTH, FRAME_HEIGHT);
        frame.setVisible(true);
    }
    public void itemStateChanged(ItemEvent check)
    {
        // Actions based on choice go here
    }
}
```

Figure 13-15 The CheckBoxDemonstration class

>> **NOTE** In Figure 13-15, the JLabel and JCheckBox objects are added to a JPanel and the JPanel is added to the Container that serves as the content pane. Alternatively, the JLabel and JCheckBoxes could have been added directly to the Container without using a JPanel. The examples in this chapter will continue to use a JPanel to hold the applications' components, so that modifications can be made more easily by adding more JPanels to the root Container.

>> **NOTE** As yet another option, the JLabel and JCheckBoxes in the JCheckBoxDemonstration class could have been added directly to the JFrame without using a Container. You will learn more about this approach later in this chapter.

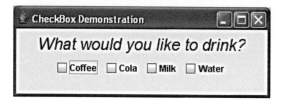

Figure 13-16 Output of the CheckBoxDemonstration class

```
java.lang.Object
  !--java.awt.Component
        !--java.awt.Container
              !--javax.swing.JComponent
                    !--javax.swing.AbstractButton
                          !--javax.swing.JToggleButton
                                !--javax.swing.JCheckBox
```

Figure 13-17 The inheritance hierarchy of the JCheckBox class

Method	Purpose
void setText(String)	Sets the text for the JCheckBox
String getText()	Returns the JCheckBox text
void setSelected(boolean)	Sets the state of the JCheckBox to true for selected or false for unselected
boolean isSelected()	Gets the current state (checked or unchecked) of the JCheckBox

Table 13-5 Frequently used JCheckBox methods

Several constructors can be used with JCheckBoxes. When you construct a JCheckBox, you can choose whether to assign it a label; you can also decide whether the JCheckBox appears selected (JCheckBoxes start unselected by default). The following statements create four JCheckBox objects—one with no label and unselected, two with labels and unselected, and one with a label and selected.

```
» JCheckBox box1 = new JCheckBox();
        // No label, unselected
» JCheckBox box2 = new JCheckBox("Check here");
        // Label, unselected
» JCheckBox box3 = new JCheckBox("Check here", false);
        // Label, unselected
» JCheckBox box4 = new JCheckBox("Check here", true);
        // Label, selected
```

If you do not initialize a JCheckBox with a label and you want to assign one later, or if you want to change an existing label, you can use the setText() method, as in the following example:

```
box1.setText("Check this box now");
```

You can set the state of a JCheckBox with the setSelected() method; for example, you can use the following statement to ensure that box1 is unchecked:

```
box1.setSelected(false);
```

The isSelected() method is most useful in Boolean expressions, as in the following example, which adds one to a voteCount variable if box2 is currently checked.

```
if(box2.isSelected())
    ++voteCount;
```

When the status of a JCheckBox changes from unchecked to checked (or from checked to unchecked), an ItemEvent is generated and the itemStateChanged() method executes. You can use the getItem() method to determine which object generated the event and the getStateChange() method to determine whether the event was a selection or a deselection. The getStateChange() method returns an integer that is equal to one of two class variables—ItemEvent.SELECTED or ItemEvent.DESELECTED. For example, in Figure 13-18 the itemStateChanged() method calls the getItem() method, which returns the object named source. Then, the value of source is tested in an if statement to determine if it is equivalent to a JCheckBox object named checkBox. If the two objects are equal, the code determines whether the checkBox was selected or deselected, and in each case appropriate actions are taken.

```
public void itemStateChanged(ItemEvent e)
{
    Object source = e.getItem();
    if(source == checkBox)
    {
        int select = e.getStateChange();
        if(select == ItemEvent.SELECTED)
            // statements that execute when the box is checked
        else
            // statements that execute when the box is unchecked
    }
    else
    {
        // statements that execute when the source of the event is
        // some component other than the checkBox object
    }
}
```

Figure 13-18 Using the `itemStateChanged()` method

USING THE ButtonGroup CLASS

Sometimes, you want options to be mutually exclusive—that is, you want the user to be able to select only one of several choices. When you create a **ButtonGroup**, you can group several components, such as JCheckBoxes, so a user can select only one at a time. When you group JCheckBox objects, all of the other JCheckBoxes are automatically turned off when the user selects any one check box. The inheritance hierarchy for the ButtonGroup class is shown in Figure 13-19. You can see that ButtonGroup descends directly from the Object class.

> **» NOTE**
> Even though it does not begin with a "J", the ButtonGroup class is part of the javax.swing package.

```
java.lang.Object
  !--java.swing.ButtonGroup
```

Figure 13-19 The inheritance hierarchy for the ButtonGroup class

> **» NOTE** A group of JCheckBoxes in which a user can select only one at a time also acts like a set of radio buttons (for example, those used to select preset radio stations on an automobile radio), which you can create using the JRadioButton class. The JRadioButton class is very similar to the JCheckBox class, and you might prefer to use it when you have a list of mutually exclusive user options. Each class is used to present a user with options that can be selected or not. It makes sense to use ButtonGroups with items that can be selected (that is, those that use an isSelected() method). You can find more information about the JRadioButton class at *http://java.sun.com*.

To create a ButtonGroup and then add a JCheckBox, you must perform three steps:

> **» NOTE**
> If you create a ButtonGroup but forget to add the JCheckBox objects to it, then the objects act as individual, nonexclusive check boxes.

» Create a ButtonGroup, such as `ButtonGroup aGroup = new ButtonGroup();`.
» Create a JCheckBox, such as `JCheckBox aBox = new JCheckBox();`.
» Add aBox to aGroup with `aGroup.add(aBox);`.

You either can create a ButtonGroup and then create the individual JCheckBox objects, or you can create the JCheckBoxes and then create the ButtonGroup.

> **» NOTE** If you assign the true state to multiple JCheckBoxes within a group, each new true assignment negates the previous one because only one box can be selected within a group.

A user can set one of the JCheckBoxes within a group to "on" by clicking it with the mouse, or you can select a JCheckBox within a ButtonGroup with a statement such as aGroup.setSelected(aBox);. You can determine which, if any, of the JCheckBoxes in a ButtonGroup is selected using the isSelected() method.

» NOTE Each individual JCheckBox object has access to every JCheckBox class method, regardless of whether the JCheckBox is part of a ButtonGroup.

» NOTE After a JCheckBox in a ButtonGroup has been selected, one in the group will always be selected. In other words, you cannot "clear the slate" for all the items that are members of a ButtonGroup. You could cause all the JCheckBoxes in a ButtonGroup to initially *appear* unselected by adding one JCheckBox that is not visible (by using the setVisible() method). Then, you could use the setSelected() method to select the invisible JCheckBox, and all the others would appear to be deselected.

USING THE JComboBox CLASS

A **JComboBox** is a component that combines two features: a display area showing an option and a list box containing additional options. (A list box is also known as a combo box or a drop-down list.) The display area contains either a button that a user can click or an editable field into which the user can type. When a JComboBox appears on the screen, a default option displays. When the user clicks the JComboBox, a list of alternative items drops down; if the user selects one, it replaces the box's displayed item. Figure 13-20 shows a JComboBox as it looks when first displayed and as it looks after a user clicks it. The inheritance hierarchy of the JComboBox class is shown in Figure 13-21.

Figure 13-20 A JComboBox before and after the user clicks it

```
java.lang.Object
  !--java.awt.Component
       !--java.awt.Container
            !--javax.swing.JComponent
                 !--javax.swing.JComboBox
```

Figure 13-21 The inheritance hierarchy of the JComboBox class

You can build a JComboBox by using a constructor with no arguments and then adding items (for example, Strings) to the list with the addItem() method. The following statements create a JComboBox named majorChoice containing three options from which a user can choose:

```
JComboBox majorChoice = new JComboBox();
majorChoice.addItem("English");
majorChoice.addItem("Math");
majorChoice.addItem("Sociology");
```

Alternatively, you can construct a JComboBox using an array of Objects as the constructor argument; the Objects in the array become the listed items within the JComboBox. For example, the following code creates the same majorChoiceJComboBox as the preceding code:

```
String[] majorArray = { "English", "Math", "Sociology"};
JComboBox majorChoice = new JComboBox(majorArray);
```

>> **NOTE** Users often expect to view JComboBox options in alphabetical order. If it makes sense for your application, consider displaying your options this way. Another reasonable approach is to place the most frequently selected options first.

Table 13-6 lists some methods you can use with a JComboBox object. For example, you can use the setSelectedItem() or setSelectedIndex() method to choose one of the items in a JComboBox to be the initially selected item. You also can use the getSelectedItem() or getSelectedIndex() method to discover which item is currently selected.

Method	Purpose
void addItem(Object)	Adds an item to the list
void removeItem(Object)	Removes an item from the list
void removeAllItems()	Removes all items from the list
Object getItemAt(int)	Returns the list item at the index position specified by the integer argument
int getItemCount()	Returns the number of items in the list
int getMaximumRowCount()	Returns the maximum number of items the combo box can display without a scroll bar
int getSelectedIndex()	Returns the position of the currently selected item
Object getSelectedItem()	Returns the currently selected item
Object[] getSelectedObjects()	Returns an array containing selected Objects
void setEditable(boolean)	Sets the field to be editable or not editable
void setMaximumRowCount(int)	Sets the number of rows in the combo box that can display at one time
void setSelectedIndex(int)	Selects the index at the position indicated by the argument
void setSelectedItem(Object)	Sets the selected item in the combo box display area to be the Object argument

Table 13-6 Some JComboBox class methods

You can treat the list of items in a JComboBox object as an array; the first item is at position 0, the second at position 1, and so on. It is convenient to use the getSelectedIndex() method to determine the list position of the currently selected item; then, you can use the index to access corresponding information stored in a parallel array. For example, if a JComboBox named historyChoice has been filled with a list of historical events, such as "Declaration of Independence", "Pearl Harbor", and "Man walks on moon", after the user chooses one of the historical events, you can code the following:

```
int positionOfSelection = historyChoice.getSelectedIndex();
```

The variable `positionOfSelection` now holds the position of the selected item, and you can use the `positionOfSelection` variable to access an array of dates so you can display the date that corresponds to the selected historical event. For example, if you declare the following, then `dates[ positionOfSelection]` holds the year for the selected historical event:

```
int[] dates = { 1776, 1941, 1969 };
```

>> **NOTE** A `JComboBox` does not have to hold `String`s; it can hold an array of `Object`s. Instead of using parallel arrays to store historical events and dates, you could design a `HistoricalEvent` class that encapsulates `String`s for the event and `int`s for the date.

In addition to `JComboBox`es for which users click items presented in a list, you can create `JComboBox`es into which users type text. To do this, you use the `setEditable()` method. A drawback to using an editable `JComboBox` is that the text a user types must exactly match an item in the list box. If the user misspells the selection or uses the wrong case, no valid value is returned from the `getSelectedIndex()` method. You can use an `if` statement to test the value returned from `getSelectedIndex()`; if it is negative, the selection did not match any items in the `JComboBox` and you can issue an appropriate error message.

CREATING `JScrollPanes`

When components in a `Swing` UI require more display area than they have been allocated, you can use a `JScrollPane` container to hold the components. A **JScrollPane** provides scroll bars along the side or bottom of a pane, or both, so that the user can scroll initially invisible parts of the pane into view. Figure 13-22 displays the inheritance hierarchy of the `JScrollPane` class.

```
java.lang.Object
  !--java.awt.Component
      !--java.awt.Container
          !--javax.swing.JComponent
              !--javax.swing.JScrollPane
```

Figure 13-22 The inheritance hierarchy of the `JScrollPane` class

The `JScrollPane` constructor takes one of four forms:

» `JScrollPane()` creates an empty `JScrollPane` in which both horizontal and vertical scroll bars appear when needed.

» `JScrollPane(Component)` creates a `JScrollPane` that displays the contents of the specified component.

» `JScrollPane(Component, int, int)` creates a `JScrollPane` that displays the specified component and includes both vertical and horizontal scroll bar specifications.

» `JScrollPane(int, int)` creates a `JScrollPane` with both vertical and horizontal scroll bar specifications.

When you create a simple scroll pane using the constructor that takes no arguments, as in the following example, horizontal and vertical scroll bars appear only if they are needed—that is, if the contents of the pane cannot be fully displayed without them:

```
JScrollPane aScrollPane = JScrollPane();
```

To force the display of a scroll bar, you can use class variables defined in the ScrollPaneConstants class, as follows:

```
ScrollPaneConstants.HORIZONTAL_SCROLLBAR_AS_NEEDED
ScrollPaneConstants.HORIZONTAL_SCROLLBAR_ALWAYS
ScrollPaneConstants.HORIZONTAL_SCROLLBAR_NEVER
ScrollPaneConstants.VERTICAL_SCROLLBAR_AS_NEEDED
ScrollPaneConstants.VERTICAL_SCROLLBAR_ALWAYS
ScrollPaneConstants.VERTICAL_SCROLLBAR_NEVER
```

For example, the following code creates a scroll pane that displays an image named picture, a vertical scroll bar, and no horizontal scroll bar:

```
JScrollPane scroll = new JScrollPane(picture,
    ScrollPaneConstants.VERTICAL_SCROLLBAR_ALWAYS,
    ScrollPaneConstants.HORIZONTAL_SCROLLBAR_NEVER);
```

Figure 13-23 shows a JScrollDemo class in which a label with a large font is added to a panel. The scroll pane named scroll includes the panel and two scroll bars. The size of the

```java
import javax.swing.*;
import java.awt.*;
public class JScrollDemo extends JFrame
{
    JPanel panel = new JPanel();
    JScrollPane scroll = new JScrollPane(panel,
        ScrollPaneConstants.VERTICAL_SCROLLBAR_ALWAYS,
        ScrollPaneConstants.HORIZONTAL_SCROLLBAR_ALWAYS);
    JLabel label = new JLabel("Event Handlers Incorporated");
    Font bigFont = new Font("Arial", Font.PLAIN, 20);
    Container con;
    public JScrollDemo()
    {
        super("JScrollDemo");
        setDefaultCloseOperation(JFrame.EXIT_ON_CLOSE);
        con = getContentPane();
        label.setFont(bigFont);
        con.add(scroll);
        panel.add(label);
    }
    public static void main(String[] args)
    {
        final int WIDTH = 180;
        final int HEIGHT = 100;
        JScrollDemo aFrame = new JScrollDemo();
        aFrame.setSize(WIDTH, HEIGHT);
        aFrame.setVisible(true);
    }
}
```

Figure 13-23 The JScrollDemo application

> **» NOTE** The application in Figure 13-23 introduces you to a new concept. In previous examples, this book has used separate files to store classes from which you instantiate objects and classes that are the applications that instantiate the objects. The class in Figure 13-23 does both—it creates the `JScrollDemo` class from which the scrollable frame is created, and it also includes a `static main()` method that is used to demonstrate the creation of a class object. If you find this format convenient, you can use it when testing your own classes.

> **» NOTE**
> The viewable area in a `JScrollPane` is called a **viewport**.

Figure 13-24 Output of the `JScrollDemo` application

`JScrollDemo` object is purposely set small enough (180×100) so that only part of the label is visible at a time. A user would slide the scroll bars to view the entire "Event Handlers Incorporated" label. Figure 13-24 shows the output.

UNDERSTANDING WHEN TO USE `getContentPane()`

> **» NOTE**
> You first learned about content panes in Chapter 9. You have been using them with all your applets and frames.

In versions prior to Java 5, you could not add components directly to a `JFrame` or `JApplet`. Instead, if you wanted to add a `Component` to one of these `Container`s, you had to call the `getContentPane()` method to get a reference to the `Container`'s content pane. For example, to add a `JButton` named `button` to a `JFrame`, you wrote code similar to the following:

```
Container con = getContentPane();
con.add(button);
```

> **» NOTE** Besides `JFrame` and `JApplet`, the `Container`s for which you previously needed to call `getContentPane()` included `JDialog`, `JWindow`, and `JInternalFrame`.

Alternatively, you could have used an anonymous `Container` as the content pane, as in either of the following examples:

```
getContentPane().add(button);
this.getContentPane().add(button);
```

> **» NOTE**
> In the second example, `this` refers to the current `JFrame` or `JApplet`.

When you use Java 5 or later, you are allowed to add `Component`s directly to `JFrame`s and `JApplet`s without explicitly calling `getContentPane()`. You also can use the `remove()` and `setLayout()` methods without an explicit call to `getContentPane()`. For example, the class in Figure 13-25 creates a `JFrame` like the ones you have created throughout this chapter. The `getContentPane()` method assigns a reference to a `Container` named `con`, and the `Container` reference is used later with the `setLayout()` and `add()` methods.

```
import java.awt.*;
import javax.swing.*;
public class JFrameWithContentCall extends JFrame
{
    final int SIZE = 180;
    Container con = getContentPane();
    JButton button = new JButton("Press Me");
    public JFrameWithContentCall()
    {
        super("Frame");
        setSize(SIZE, SIZE);
        setVisible(true);
        con.setLayout(new FlowLayout());
        con.add(button);
    }
}
```

Figure 13-25 The `JFrameWithContentCall` class

NOTE To keep the example simple in Figure 13-25, the default close operation was not set and the button was not assigned any tasks.

Figure 13-26 contains a similar class to the one in Figure 13-25. The only changes are:

» The class and constructor name are different (these changes are both shaded in Figure 13-26).

» The shaded portions of the class in Figure 13-25 (the parts that refer to the `Container` named `con`) have been removed.

```
import java.awt.*;
import javax.swing.*;
public class JFrameWithoutContentCall extends JFrame
{
    final int SIZE = 180;
    JButton button = new JButton("Press Me");
    public JFrameWithoutContentCall()
    {
        super("Frame");
        setSize(SIZE, SIZE);
        setVisible(true);
        setLayout(new FlowLayout());
        add(button);
    }
}
```

Figure 13-26 The `JFrameWithoutContentCall` class

NOTE In versions of Java prior to version 5, the `JFrameWithoutContentCall` class in Figure 13-26 will not compile; an explicit call to `getContentPane()` is required.

Figure 13-27 shows an application that creates one instance of each of the frames. When the application executes and the top frame is dragged away from the bottom one, the output looks like Figure 13-28. The two frames are identical.

```
public class TestFramesWithAndWithout
{
    public static void main(String[] args)
    {
        JFrameWithContentCall f1 =
            new JFrameWithContentCall();
        JFrameWithoutContentCall f2 =
            new JFrameWithoutContentCall();
    }
}
```

Figure 13-27 The `TestFramesWithAndWithout` application

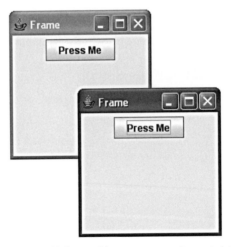

Figure 13-28 Output of the `TestFramesWithAndWithout` application

In Java 5 and later, it is convenient that when you call add(button) from within the JFrameWithoutContentCall class, you do not have to create the Container object con. In the newer versions of Java, in effect, you are calling this.getContentPane().add(button), but you are allowed to write the statement more simply. The same is true for any calls to the setLayout() and remove() methods.

Although it is convenient not to have to declare a Container, call getContentPane(), and use the container's name, a problem arises when you want to use methods other than add(), remove(), and setLayout(). For example, Figures 13-29 and 13-30 show classes whose only modifications from the earlier versions are new class and constructor names and new shaded setBackground() statements, which are intended to set the background color of the frame to blue.

```
import java.awt.*;
import javax.swing.*;
public class JFrameWithContentCall2 extends JFrame
{
    final int SIZE = 180;
    Container con = getContentPane();
    JButton button = new JButton("Press Me");
    public JFrameWithContentCall2()
    {
        super("Frame");
        setSize(SIZE, SIZE);
        setVisible(true);
        con.setLayout(new FlowLayout());
        con.add(button);
        con.setBackground(Color.BLUE);
    }
}
```

Figure 13-29 The JFrameWithContentCall2 class

```
import java.awt.*;
import javax.swing.*;
public class JFrameWithoutContentCall2 extends JFrame
{
    final int SIZE = 180;
    JButton button = new JButton("Press Me");
    public JFrameWithoutContentCall2()
    {
        super("Frame");
        setSize(SIZE, SIZE);
        setVisible(true);
        setLayout(new FlowLayout());
        add(button);
        setBackground(Color.BLUE);
    }
}
```

Figure 13-30 The JFrameWithoutContentCall2 class

When you create an instance of each revised frame, as in Figure 13-31, the frame that uses the content pane displays a blue background, but the one that does not use an explicit call to getContentPane() retains the default light gray background. The output is shown in Figure 13-32.

```
public class TestFramesWithAndWithout2
{
    public static void main(String[] args)
    {
        JFrameWithContentCall2 f1 =
            new JFrameWithContentCall2();
        JFrameWithoutContentCall2 f2 =
            new JFrameWithoutContentCall2();
    }
}
```

Figure 13-31 The TestFramesWithAndWithout2 class

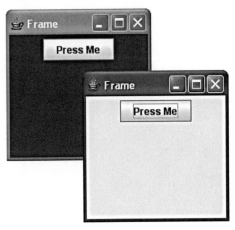

Figure 13-32 Output of the `TestFramesWithAndWithout2` application

In Figure 13-32, the second `JFrame` does not appear in blue because the `setBackground()` method cannot be used without a content pane reference. Therefore, when you create a `JFrame` or `JApplet` and want to use methods other than `add()`, `setLayout()`, and `remove()` with them, you either must declare a `Container` reference, as in the `JFrameWithContentCall2` class in Figure 13-29, or you must use an explicit call to `getContentPane()` when using the methods that require them. For example, you could replace the call to `setBackground()` in the `JFrameWithoutContentCall2` application with the following statement:

```
getContentPane().setBackground(Color.BLUE);
```

If you are using Java 5 or later and writing an application that does not use any methods requiring the explicit call to `getContentPane()`, then you should use the simpler method. Many examples in this book continue to use the explicit call to `getContentPane()` for two reasons: (1) to continue to remind you that the content pane exists even when an explicit call is not required, and (2) so that the examples work correctly even if you use an older version of Java.

YOU DO IT

CREATING A JFrame

In this section, you will create a `JFrame` object that appears on the screen.

To create a JFrame object:

1. Open a new file in your text editor.

2. Type the following statement to import the `java.swing` classes:

   `import javax.swing.*;`

3. On the next lines, type the following class header for the `JDemoFrame` class and its opening curly brace:

   `public class JDemoFrame`
   `{`

4. On the next lines, type the following `main()` method header and its opening curly brace:

```
public static void main(String[] args)
{
```

5. Within the body of the `main()` method, enter the following code to declare a `JFrame` with a title, set its size, and make it visible. If you neglect to set a `JFrame`'s size, you see only the title bar of the `JFrame` (because the size is 0 × 0 by default); if you neglect to make the `JFrame` visible, you do not see anything. Add two closing curly braces—one for the `main()` method and one for the `JDemoFrame` class.

```
        JFrame aFrame = new JFrame("This is a frame");
        final int WIDTH = 200;
        final int HEIGHT = 250;
        aFrame.setSize(WIDTH, HEIGHT);
        aFrame.setVisible(true);
    }
}
```

6. Save the file as **JDemoFrame.java** in the Chapter.13 folder on your Student Disk. Compile the class using the **javac** command, then run the program using the **java** command. The output looks like Figure 13-33—an empty `JFrame` with a title bar, a little taller than it is wide.

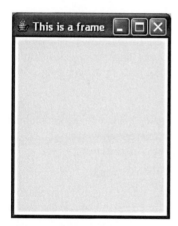

Figure 13-33 Output of the `JDemoFrame` application

7. The `JFrame` has all the properties of frames you have seen in applications you have used. For example, click the `JFrame`'s **Minimize** button, and the `JFrame` minimizes to an icon on the Windows taskbar.

8. Click the `JFrame`'s **icon** on the taskbar. The `JFrame` returns to its previous size.

9. Click the `JFrame`'s **Maximize** button. The `JFrame` fills the screen.

10. Click the `JFrame`'s **Restore** button. The `JFrame` returns to its original size.

11. Position your mouse pointer on the `JFrame`'s title bar, and then drag the `JFrame` to a new position on your screen.

12. Click the `JFrame`'s **Close** button. The `JFrame` disappears or hides. The default behavior of a `JFrame` is simply to hide when the user clicks the Close button—not to end the program.

13. To end the program and return control to the command line, click the Command Prompt window and then press **Ctrl+C**.

> **» NOTE** In Chapter 6, you learned to press Ctrl+C to stop a program that contains an infinite loop. This situation is similar—you want to stop a program that does not have a way to end automatically.

ENDING AN APPLICATION WHEN A JFrame CLOSES

Next, you will modify the JDemoFrame program so that the application ends when the user clicks the JDemoFrame Close button.

To modify the application so it ends when the user clicks the JDemoFrame Close button:

1. Within the JDemoFrame class file, change the class name to JDemoFrameThatCloses.

2. Add a new line of code as the final executable statement within the main() method, as follows:

```
aFrame.setDefaultCloseOperation(JFrame.EXIT_ON_CLOSE);
```

3. Save the file as **JDemoFrameThatCloses.java** in the Chapter.13 folder on your Student Disk.

4. Compile and execute the application.

5. When the JFrame appears on your screen, confirm that it still has Minimize, Maximize, and Restore capabilities. Then click the JFrame's **Close** button. The JFrame closes, and the command prompt returns as the program relinquishes control to the operating system.

ADDING COMPONENTS TO A JFrame

Next, you will create a Swing application that displays a JFrame that holds a JPanel containing some components: a JLabel, JTextField, and JButton. This exercise shows that you can add components to a JPanel in an application just as easily as you can add them to an applet.

To create a JFrame that displays three components within a JPanel:

1. Open a new file in your text editor, then type the following first few lines of an application. The import statements make the Swing and AWT components available and the class header indicates that the class is a JFrame. The class contains several components: a label, field, and button. Each of these components will be contained in a panel that will be placed in the frame's content pane.

```
import javax.swing.*;
import java.awt.*;
public class JFrameWithComponents extends JFrame
{
    JLabel label = new JLabel("Enter your name");
    JTextField field = new JTextField(12);
    JButton button = new JButton("OK");
    JPanel panel = new JPanel();
    Container con;
```

2. In the JFrameWithComponents constructor, set the JFrame title to "Frame with Components" and the default close operation to exit the program when the JFrame is

closed. Get the content pane, add the panel to it, and add the label, field, and button to the panel.

```
public JFrameWithComponents()
{
    super("Frame with Components");
    setDefaultCloseOperation(JFrame.EXIT_ON_CLOSE);
    con = getContentPane();
    con.add(panel);
    panel.add(label);
    panel.add(field);
    panel.add(button);
}
```

3. Add a closing curly brace for the class, and then save the file as **JFrameWithComponents.java** in the Chapter.13 folder on your Student Disk.

4. Compile the class and correct any errors.

5. Next, write an application that creates a new `JFrameWithComponents` named `aFrame`, sizes it using the `setSize()` method, and then sets its visible property to `true`.

```
import javax.swing.*;
public class CreateJFrameWithComponents
{
    public static void main(String[] args)
    {
        JFrameWithComponents aFrame =
            new JFrameWithComponents();
        final int WIDTH = 350;
        final int HEIGHT = 100;
        aFrame.setSize(WIDTH, HEIGHT);
        aFrame.setVisible(true);
    }
}
```

6. Save the file as **CreateJFrameWithComponents.java** in the Chapter.13 folder on your Student Disk. Compile the file using the **javac** command, and then execute the application. The output is shown in Figure 13-34.

Figure 13-34 Output of the `CreateJFrameWithComponents` application

7. Click the `JButton`. It acts like a button should—that is, it appears to be pressed when you click it, but nothing happens because you have not yet written instructions for the button clicks to execute.

8. Close the application.

ADDING FUNCTIONALITY TO A JButton

Next, you will add functionality to the JButton that you created in the JFrameWithComponents class.

To create an application with a functional JButton:

1. Open the **JFrameWithComponents.java** file. Immediately save the file as **JChangeMessage.java** in the Chapter.13 folder on your Student Disk.

2. After the existing import statements at the top of the file, add the following import statement that will allow event handling:

   ```
   import java.awt.event.*;
   ```

3. Change the class name to JChangeMessage to match the new filename. Also change the constructor method header to match the new class name. Within the constructor, change the string argument to the super() method from "Frame with Components" to "Change Message".

4. After extends JFrame at the end of the JChangeMessage class header, add the following phrase so that the class can respond to ActionEvents:

   ```
   implements ActionListener
   ```

5. Register the JChangeMessage class as a listener for events generated by either the button or the text field by adding the following statements at the end of, but within, the JChangeMessage() constructor:

   ```
   button.addActionListener(this);
   field.addActionListener(this);
   ```

6. Just prior to the closing curly brace for the class, add the following actionPerformed() method. The method changes the button label from "OK" to "Done" whenever the user clicks the button or presses Enter in the text field.

   ```
   public void actionPerformed(ActionEvent e)
   {
       button.setText("Done");
   }
   ```

7. Just after the actionPerformed() method, and just before the closing curly brace for the class, add a main() method to the class so that you can instantiate a JChangeMessage object for demonstration purposes.

   ```
   public static void main(String[] args)
   {
       JChangeMessage aFrame = new JChangeMessage();
       final int WIDTH = 250;
       final int HEIGHT = 100;
       aFrame.setSize(WIDTH, HEIGHT);
       aFrame.setVisible(true);
   }
   ```

8. Save the file, then compile and execute it. The output again looks like Figure 13-34, which shows the output of the CreateJFrameWithComponents program. The label, text field, and button are still shown; the only difference is the text displayed in the title bar.

9. Type a name in the text field and then click the **OK** button. Its text changes to "Done" and its size increases slightly because the label "Done" requires more space than the label "OK". The output looks like Figure 13-35.

Figure 13-35 Output of the `JChangeMessage` application after the user clicks the "OK" button

10. Close the application and then execute it again. This time, enter a name in the text field and press **Enter**. Again, the button text changes, showing that the `actionPerformed()` method reacts to actions that take place on either the button or the text field.

11. Close the application.

DISTINGUISHING EVENT SOURCES

Next, you will modify the `actionPerformed()` method of the `JChangeMessage` class so that different results will occur depending on which action a user takes.

1. Open the **JChangeMessage.java** file in your text editor if the file is not still open. Immediately save the file as **JChangeMessage2.java**.

2. Change the class name and the constructor name to match the new filename by adding **2** to each name.

3. In the `main()` method, change the statement that instantiates the `JFrame` object to the following:

```
JChangeMessage2 aFrame = new JChangeMessage2();
```

4. Within the `actionPerformed()` method, you can use the named `ActionEvent` argument and the `getSource()` method to determine the source of the event. Using an `if` statement, you can take different actions when the argument represents different sources. For example, you can change the label in the frame to indicate the event's source. Change the `actionPerformed()` method to:

```
public void actionPerformed(ActionEvent e)
{
    Object source = e.getSource();
    if(source == button)
        label.setText("You clicked the button");
    else
        label.setText("You pressed Enter");
}
```

5. Save the file (as JChangeMessage2.java), then compile and execute it. Type a name, press **Enter** or click the button, and notice the varying results in the frame's label. For example, Figure 13-36 shows the application after the user has typed a name and pressed Enter.

6. Close the application.

Figure 13-36 JChangeMessage2 output after user has typed a name and pressed Enter

INCLUDING JCheckBoxes IN AN APPLICATION

Next, you will create an interactive program that Event Handlers Incorporated clients can use to determine an event's price. The base price of an event is $300, and a user can choose from several options. Holding the event on a weekend adds $100 to the price, hosting over 200 guests adds $200, and including live entertainment adds $400. A guest can select none, some, or all of these premium additions. Each time the user changes the option package, the event price is recalculated.

To write a Swing application that includes three JCheckBox objects used to determine an event's price:

1. Open a new file in your text editor, then type the following first few lines of a Swing application that demonstrates the use of a JCheckBox. Note that the JCheckBoxEventPriceCalculator class implements the ItemListener interface:

```
import javax.swing.*;
import java.awt.*;
import java.awt.event.*;
public class JCheckBoxEventPriceCalculator extends
      JFrame implements ItemListener
{
```

2. Declare the named constants that hold the base price for an event and the premium amounts for holding the event on a weekend, having over 200 guests, and including live entertainment. Also include a variable that holds the total price of the event, and initialize it to the value of the base price. Later, depending on the user's selections, premium fees might be added to totalPrice, making it more than BASE_PRICE.

```
final int BASE_PRICE = 300;
final int WEEKEND_PREMIUM = 100;
final int GUEST_PREMIUM = 200;
final int ENTERTAINMENT_PREMIUM = 400;
int totalPrice = BASE_PRICE;
```

3. Declare three JCheckBox objects. Each is labeled with a String that contains a description of the option and the cost of the option. Each JCheckBox starts unchecked or deselected.

```
JCheckBox weekendBox = new JCheckBox
      ("Weekend premium $" + WEEKEND_PREMIUM, false);
JCheckBox guestBox = new
      JCheckBox("Over 200 guests $" + GUEST_PREMIUM, false);
JCheckBox entertainBox = new JCheckBox
      ("Live entertainment $" + ENTERTAINMENT_PREMIUM, false);
```

4. Include JLabels to hold user instructions and information and a JTextField in which to display the total price:

```
JLabel eventHandlersLabel = new JLabel
    ("Event Handlers Incorporated");
JLabel ePrice = new JLabel("The price for your event is");
JTextField totPrice = new JTextField(10);
JLabel optionExplainLabel = new JLabel
    ("Base price for an event is $"
    + BASE_PRICE + ".");
JLabel optionExplainLabel2 = new JLabel
    ("Check the options you want.");
```

5. Add a JPanel and a Container that will serve as a reference to the content pane:

```
JPanel panel = new JPanel();
Container con;
```

6. Begin the JCheckBoxEventPriceCalculator class constructor. Include instructions to set the title by passing it to the JFrame parent class constructor, and to set the default close operation. Get the content pane and add the JPanel to it, then add all the necessary components to the JPanel.

```
public JCheckBoxEventPriceCalculator()
{
        super("Event Price Estimator");
        setDefaultCloseOperation(JFrame.EXIT_ON_CLOSE);
        con = getContentPane();
        con.add(panel);
        panel.add(eventHandlersLabel);
        panel.add(optionExplainLabel);
        panel.add(optionExplainLabel2);
        panel.add(weekendBox);
        panel.add(guestBox);
        panel.add(entertainBox);
        panel.add(ePrice);
        panel.add(totPrice);
```

7. Continue the constructor by setting the text of the totPrice JTextField to display a dollar sign and the totalPrice value. Register the class as a listener for events generated by each of the three JCheckBoxes. Finally, add a closing curly brace for the constructor.

```
        totPrice.setText("$" + totalPrice);
        weekendBox.addItemListener(this);
        guestBox.addItemListener(this);
        entertainBox.addItemListener(this);
}
```

8. Add a main() method that creates an instance of the JFrame and sets its size and visibility.

```
public static void main(String[] args)
{
    JCheckBoxEventPriceCalculator aFrame =
        new JCheckBoxEventPriceCalculator();
```

```
        final int WIDTH = 300;
        final int HEIGHT = 250;
        aFrame.setSize(WIDTH, HEIGHT);
        aFrame.setVisible(true);
    }
```

9. Begin the itemStateChanged() method that executes when the user selects or dese-lects a JCheckBox. Use the appropriate methods to determine which JCheckBox is the source of the current ItemEvent and whether the event was generated by selecting a JCheckBox or by deselecting one.

```
public void itemStateChanged(ItemEvent event)
{
    Object source = event.getSource();
    int select = event.getStateChange();
```

10. Write a nested if statement that tests whether the source is equivalent to the weekendBox, guestBox, or, by default, the entertainBox. In each case, depending on whether the event was a selection or deselection, add or subtract the corresponding pre-mium fee from the totalPrice. Display the total price in the JTextField and add two closing curly braces—one for the method and one for the class.

```
        if(source == weekendBox)
            if(select == ItemEvent.SELECTED)
                totalPrice += WEEKEND_PREMIUM;
            else
                totalPrice -= WEEKEND_PREMIUM;
        else if(source == guestBox)
        {
            if(select == ItemEvent.SELECTED)
                totalPrice += GUEST_PREMIUM;
            else
                totalPrice -= GUEST_PREMIUM;
        }
        else       // if(source == entertainBox) by default
            if(select == ItemEvent.SELECTED)
                totalPrice += ENTERTAINMENT_PREMIUM;
            else
                totalPrice -= ENTERTAINMENT_PREMIUM;
            totPrice.setText("$" + totalPrice);
    }
}
```

11. Save the file as **JCheckBoxEventPriceCalculator.java** in the Chapter.13 folder on your Student Disk. Compile and execute the application. The output appears in Figure 13-37 with the base price initially set to $300.

12. Select the **Weekend premium** JCheckBox and note the change in the total price of the event. Experiment with selecting and deselecting options to ensure that the price changes correctly. For example, Figure 13-38 shows the Event Price Estimator with the weekend and entertainment options selected, adding a total of $500 to the initial $300 base price.

13. Close the application.

Figure 13-37 Initial output of the `JCheckBoxEventPriceCalculator` application

Figure 13-38 Output of the `JCheckBoxEventPriceCalculator` application after the user has made selections

CREATING A ButtonGroup

Next, you will create an application that contains a `ButtonGroup`. Event Handlers Incorporated has decided to base event prices strictly on the number of guests: $1300, $2400, or $6000 for groups of 1–100, 101–200, or over 200, respectively. The user must choose a guest number category to see an event's price. A `ButtonGroup` is appropriate because the options are mutually exclusive; you would not want a user to be able to select two or three categories.

To write an application that uses a ButtonGroup:

1. Open a new file in your text editor and type the first few lines needed for a `JButtonGroupDemo` class, as follows:

```
import javax.swing.*;
import java.awt.*;
import java.awt.event.*;
public class JButtonGroupDemo extends JFrame
   implements ItemListener
{
```

2. Declare three named constants to hold the event prices for the three categories, and three
   JCheckBoxes from which the user can select the party size. Make the first JCheckBox
   the default option by using true in its constructor call.

```
int PREMIUM1 = 1300;
int PREMIUM2 = 2400;
int PREMIUM3 = 6000;
JCheckBox guestBox1 = new JCheckBox
      ("1 - 100 guests $" + PREMIUM1, true);
JCheckBox guestBox2 = new JCheckBox
      ("101 - 200 guests $" + PREMIUM2, false);
JCheckBox guestBox3 = new JCheckBox
      ("over 200 guests $" + PREMIUM3, false);
```

3. Create some JLabels that explain the application's purpose and a JTextField in which
   to display the price for the selected guest option. Also create a Container reference for
   the content pane and a JPanel to hold the application's components.

```
JLabel eventHandlersLabel = new
JLabel("Event Handlers Incorporated");
JLabel ePrice = new
     JLabel(" The price for your event is");
JTextField totPrice = new JTextField(10);
JLabel optionExplainLabel = new JLabel
     ("Check the number of guests at your event");
Container con;
JPanel panel = new JPanel();
```

4. Begin to create the JButtonGroupDemo constructor. Set the title, set the close operation,
   get the content pane, and add the JPanel to the content pane.

```
public JButtonGroupDemo()
{
    super("Event Price Estimator");
    setDefaultCloseOperation(JFrame.EXIT_ON_CLOSE);
    con = getContentPane();
    con.add(panel);
```

5. Write statements that add each of the components—the JLabels, JCheckBoxes, and
   JTextField—to the JPanel. Also create a ButtonGroup named guestGroup and
   add the three JCheckBoxes to the group. This ensures that only one of the three
   JCheckBoxes can be selected at a time.

```
    panel.add(eventHandlersLabel);
    panel.add(optionExplainLabel);
    panel.add(guestBox1);
    panel.add(guestBox2);
    panel.add(guestBox3);
    ButtonGroup guestGroup = new ButtonGroup();
    guestGroup.add(guestBox1);
    guestGroup.add(guestBox2);
```

```
guestGroup.add(guestBox3);
panel.add(ePrice);
panel.add(totPrice);
```

6. Set the text of the `totPrice` field so that when the application begins, it holds the first guest premium amount by default. Use the `addItemListener()` method to register the class as a listener to events generated by each of the check boxes. Include a closing curly brace for the constructor method.

```
totPrice.setText("$" + PREMIUM1);
guestBox1.addItemListener(this);
guestBox2.addItemListener(this);
guestBox3.addItemListener(this);
}
```

7. Write a `main()` method that declares a `JButtonGroupDemo` object, sets its size, and makes it visible.

```
public static void main(String[] args)
{
    JButtonGroupDemo aFrame = new JButtonGroupDemo();
    final int WIDTH = 300;
    final int HEIGHT = 250;
    aFrame.setSize(WIDTH, HEIGHT);
    aFrame.setVisible(true);
}
```

8. Write an `itemStateChanged()` method that executes when a user clicks any of the three `JCheckBoxes`. Use a nested `if` statement with the `isSelected()` method to determine which of the three `JCheckBoxes` in the `ButtonGroup` is selected, and set the text of the `totPrice` field with the appropriate price.

```
public void itemStateChanged(ItemEvent event)
{
    if(guestBox1.isSelected())
        totPrice.setText("$" + PREMIUM1);
    else if(guestBox2.isSelected())
        totPrice.setText("$" + PREMIUM2);
    else // if(guestBox3.isSelected())
        totPrice.setText("$" + PREMIUM3);
}
```

9. Add a closing curly brace for the class, and then save the file as **JButtonGroupDemo.java** in the Chapter.13 folder on your Student Disk.

   Compile and execute the application. The output looks like Figure 13-39. By default, the first `JCheckBox` is checked; it indicates that 1 to 100 guests are selected and that the event price is $1300. If you click either of the remaining `JCheckBoxes`, the first box becomes deselected and the total price changes.

10. Continue to click the check boxes and observe the application's behavior. Then close the application.

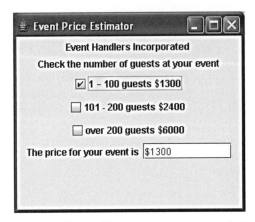

Figure 13-39 Output of the `JButtonGroupDemo` application

CREATING AN APPLICATION CONTAINING MULTIPLE UI OBJECTS

Next, you will create an application for Event Handlers Incorporated that allows the user to choose a number of options and calculate the per-person price for an event. The application combines many of the `Swing` UI components you learned to use in this chapter. The application contains `JCheckBoxes`, a `ButtonGroup`, a `JComboBox`, and several other components.

To write an application containing many `Swing` components:

1. Open a new file in your text editor, then add the necessary import statements and class header for the `JEventPriceEstimator` class:

```
import javax.swing.*;
import java.awt.*;
import java.awt.event.*;
public class JEventPriceEstimator extends JFrame
    implements ItemListener
{
```

2. Declare a number of constants and variables to use in the program. All customers are charged a base price of $20 for a chicken dinner. Users can choose to add cocktail service, one of two additional entrees, and a party favor. The prices of the favors are stored in an array. Other variables are used to hold the selected favor price and the total price after users have made their selections.

```
final int COCKTAIL_PRICE = 15;
final int CHICKEN_PRICE = 0, BEEF_PRICE = 8, FISH_PRICE = 5;
final int[] FAVOR_PRICE = {0,1,2,4,6};
int favPrice = 0;
final int BASE_PRICE = 20;
int totalPrice = BASE_PRICE;
```

3. Declare `JCheckBoxes` for the optional cocktail service and the three entrees:

```
JCheckBox cocktailBox = new
    JCheckBox("Cocktails $" + COCKTAIL_PRICE, false);
```

```
JCheckBox chickenBox = new
   JCheckBox("Chicken $" + CHICKEN_PRICE, true);
JCheckBox beefBox = new
   JCheckBox("Beef $" + BEEF_PRICE, false);
JCheckBox fishBox = new
   JCheckBox("Fish $" + FISH_PRICE, false);
```

4. Declare a `JLabel` describing the party favor option, and then declare an array of `Strings` that holds the favor names. Each `String` is composed of a text portion and the value of the corresponding favor price. Then create a `JComboBox` using the array of `Strings` as the constructor argument.

```
JLabel favorLabel = new
   JLabel("Party favors: Make a selection");
String[] favorNames = {"None $" + FAVOR_PRICE[0],
   "Hat $" + FAVOR_PRICE[1],
   "Streamers $" + FAVOR_PRICE[2],
   "Noise makers $" + FAVOR_PRICE[3],
   "Helium balloons $" + FAVOR_PRICE[4]};
JComboBox favorBox = new JComboBox(favorNames);
```

5. Add the remaining `JLabel` and `JTextField` components the application requires:

```
JLabel eventHandlersLabel = new JLabel("Event Handlers
   Incorporated");
JLabel ePrice = new JLabel(" Per-person event price estimate");
JTextField totPrice = new JTextField(10);
JTextField message = new JTextField(30);
JLabel optionExplainLabel = new JLabel
      ("Base price for dinner with chicken entree is $"
      + BASE_PRICE + ".");
JLabel optionExplainLabel2 = new JLabel
      ("Optionally, you can choose to serve cocktails");
JLabel optionExplainLabel3 = new JLabel
      ("and change the entree to beef or fish");
```

6. Add a `Container` that will hold the content pane and a `JPanel` into which all the components can be placed.

```
Container con;
JPanel panel = new JPanel();
```

7. Create a constructor for the `JEventPriceEstimator` class. The constructor sets the `JFrame`'s title and close operation, gets the content pane reference, and adds a `JPanel` to it. The three entrees are stored as a group so that a user can select only one at a time. Every component is added to the `JPanel`, and the class is registered as a listener for all the components that might generate an event.

```
public JEventPriceEstimator()
{
   super("Event Price Estimator");
   setDefaultCloseOperation(JFrame.EXIT_ON_CLOSE);
   con = getContentPane();
   con.add(panel);
```

```
        ButtonGroup dinnerGroup = new ButtonGroup();
        dinnerGroup.add(chickenBox);
        dinnerGroup.add(beefBox);
        dinnerGroup.add(fishBox);
        panel.add(cocktailBox);
        panel.add(chickenBox);
        panel.add(beefBox);
        panel.add(fishBox);
        panel.add(favorLabel);
        panel.add(favorBox);
        panel.add(eventHandlersLabel);
        panel.add(optionExplainLabel);
        panel.add(optionExplainLabel2);
        panel.add(optionExplainLabel3);
        panel.add(ePrice);
        panel.add(totPrice);
        panel.add(message);
        totPrice.setText("$" + totalPrice);
        cocktailBox.addItemListener(this);
        chickenBox.addItemListener(this);
        beefBox.addItemListener(this);
        fishBox.addItemListener(this);
        favorBox.addItemListener(this);
    }
```

8. The `main()` method for the class declares a `JEventPriceEstimator` object and sets its size and visibility.

```
public static void main(String[] args)
{
    final int WIDTH = 400;
    final int HEIGHT = 250;
    JEventPriceEstimator aFrame = new
        JEventPriceEstimator();
    aFrame.setSize(WIDTH, HEIGHT);
    aFrame.setVisible(true);
}
```

9. When an event is generated, the `itemStateChanged()` method executes. Begin the method by determining the event's source and state. Then set a message informing the user whether a change was made to the cocktail selection, dinner selection, or party favor selection. In addition, if the selection is a party favor selection, determine the price of the favor selected.

```
public void itemStateChanged(ItemEvent event)
{
    Object source = event.getSource();
    int select = event.getStateChange();
    if(source == cocktailBox)
        if(select == ItemEvent.SELECTED)
            message.setText("Action: Cocktails selected");
        else
            message.setText("Action: Cocktails deselected");
```

```
    else if(source == favorBox)
    {
        int favNum = favorBox.getSelectedIndex();
        favPrice = FAVOR_PRICE[favNum];
        message.setText("Action: Favor selection changed: $" +
            favPrice + " added");
    }
    else
        message.setText("Action: Meal change made");
```

10. Compute the event's per-person total price by adding the selected favor price (which might be $0) to the base price. Then, if chicken is not the selected entree (if it is beef or fish), add the upgraded meal price. If cocktail service is selected, add its price. Set the value of the field that displays the total price and add a closing curly brace for the method.

```
    totalPrice = BASE_PRICE + favPrice;
    if(beefBox.isSelected())
        totalPrice += BEEF_PRICE;
    else if(fishBox.isSelected())
        totalPrice += FISH_PRICE;
    if(cocktailBox.isSelected())
        totalPrice += COCKTAIL_PRICE;
    totPrice.setText("$" + totalPrice);
}
```

11. Add a closing curly brace for the class, and then save the file as **JEventPriceEstimator.java** in the Chapter.13 folder on your Student Disk.

12. Compile and execute the program. Confirm that each UI component operates as you would expect. For example, Figure 13-40 shows the application after the user has made a beef selection and is about to make a party favor selection from the JComboBox.

13. Close the application.

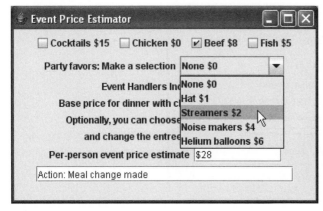

Figure 13-40 Execution of the JEventPriceEstimator application

MODIFYING A JComboBox TO ACCEPT KEYBOARD INPUT

Next, you will modify the JEventPriceEstimator application to allow the user to make a choice by entering the text of a list item.

To make a choice by entering the text of a list item:

1. Open the **JEventPriceEstimator.java** file if it is not still open on your screen, and immediately save it as **JEventPriceEstimator2.java** in the Chapter.13 folder on your Student Disk. Change the class name to **JEventPriceEstimator2** in four locations—in the class header, in the constructor method header, and two times in the declaration of the JEventPriceEstimator object in the main() method.

2. Modify the JComboBox so the user can type the name of a favor instead of simply choosing one from a list. The favor name the user types must match one of the items in the list exactly, so, because the user should not be expected to know each favor's price, eliminate the prices from the array of Strings that forms the list of favor names. Within the declaration section of the JEventPriceEstimator2 class, change the statement that declares the favorNamesString array to the following:

   ```
   String[] favorNames = {"None", "Hat", "Streamers",
       "Noise makers", "Helium balloons"};
   ```

3. Within the JEventPriceEstimator2 constructor, place your insertion point at the end of the statement that adds the favorBox to the panel (panel.add(favorBox);), and press **Enter** to insert a new line. Set the favorBox to be editable by typing:

   ```
   favorBox.setEditable(true);
   ```

   This is the statement that allows a user to type in the JComboBox's display field.

4. Save the file, then compile and execute it. When the application appears, delete the default contents of the JComboBox text field ("None"), and type **Hat**. (Be certain to use a capital H.) Press **Enter**. Your output looks like Figure 13-41—the Hat option is selected, and its price ($1) is added to the event total.

5. Delete the text entry **Hat**, replace it with **Disposable camera**, and then press **Enter**. As Figure 13-42 shows, a number of error messages are displayed at the command line because

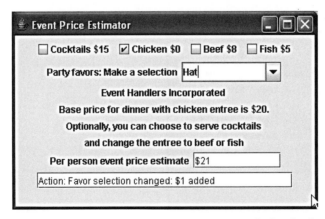

Figure 13-41 Output of the JEventPriceEstimator2 application after the user types "Hat" in the JComboBox

Figure 13-42 Error messages generated by an invalid party favor selection in the `JEventPriceEstimator2` application

"Disposable camera" does not exactly match any items in the list, making the subscript used with the `favorPrice` array invalid. The number of error statements in Figure 13-42 appears overwhelming. However, if you examine the first messages, you can see that the error was generated by an array index out of bounds within the `itemStateChanged()` method.

6. Close the application.

PREVENTING THE OUT OF BOUNDS ERROR
WITH AN EDITABLE `JComboBox`

In the next steps, you will prevent the error that occurred in the previous section when you typed an unfound item into the editable `JComboBox`.

To prevent a user's invalid entry from generating an error when using an editable `JComboBox` object:

1. Open the **JEventPriceEstimator2.java** file if it is not still open. Immediately save it as **JEventPriceEstimator3.java** in the Chapter.13 folder on your Student Disk. Change the class name to **JEventPriceEstimator3** in four locations—in the class header, in the constructor method header, and two times in the declaration of the JEventPriceEstimator object in the main() method.

2. The error generated by the application in the previous set of steps occurs because the getSelectedIndex() method does not return a valid value to use as a subscript with the favorPrice array. To prevent generating the error messages, you can replace two statements—the one that sets the favPrice (favPrice = FAVOR_PRICE[favNum] ;) and the one that sets the text of the message to "Action: Favor selection changed". Instead, use the following if statement that tests the value of the favNum subscript. If favNum is negative—that is, if the user does not type an option that matches one in the list—set the message text to "Sorry - no such option". Otherwise, determine the correct favPrice as before.

```
if(favNum < 0)
   message.setText("Sorry - no such option");
else
{
   favPrice = FAVOR_PRICE[favNum];
   message.setText
      ("Action: Favor selection changed: $" +
      favPrice + " added");
}
```

3. Save the file, then compile and execute it. When the frame appears on the screen, type an invalid favor name into the JComboBox, and then press **Enter**. Figure 13-43 shows the output when the user types "Name tag". Instead of generating multiple command-line error messages, the message in the frame displays "Sorry – no such option". The user now can type a new option or click the JComboBox to display the list box from which a valid selection can be made.

4. Close the application.

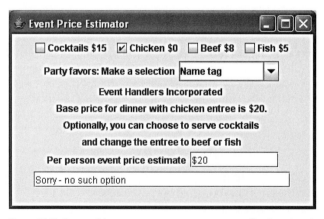

Figure 13-43 Output of the JEventPriceEstimator3 application when the user types an unfound party favor

KEY TERMS

Lightweight components are written completely in Java and do not have to rely on the local windowing platform in which the application is running. This means the components are not "weighed down" by having to interact with the local windowing system.

Heavyweight components require interaction with the local windowing system.

A **container** is a type of component that holds other components so you can treat a group of them as a single entity.

A **JFrame** is a Swing component into which you place objects for display.

Window decorations are the icons and buttons that are part of a window or frame.

A **look and feel** is the default appearance and behavior of any user interface.

A **JPanel** is a plain, borderless surface that can hold lightweight UI components.

Event listeners are interfaces that are implemented by classes that respond to user-initiated events.

A **JCheckBox** consists of a label positioned beside a square; you can click the square to display or remove a check mark.

A **ButtonGroup** can group several components, such as JCheckBoxes, so a user can select only one at a time.

A **JComboBox** is a component that combines two features: a display area showing an option and a list box containing additional options.

A **JScrollPane** provides scroll bars along the side or bottom of a pane, or both, so that the user can scroll initially invisible parts of the pane into view.

A **viewport** is the viewable area in a JScrollPane.

CHAPTER SUMMARY

» A JFrame is a Swing Container that resembles a Window but has a title bar and borders, as well as the ability to be resized, minimized, restored, and closed; you usually create a JFrame so that you can place other objects within it for display. A JFrame's default behavior is to become hidden when the user clicks the Close button; to change this behavior, you can call a JFrame's setDefaultCloseOperation() method.

» Instead of using the decorations for a JFrame provided by the operating system, you can request that Java's look and feel provide them.

» The advantage of creating a child class of JFrame is that you can set the JFrame's properties within your object's constructor method; then, when you create your JFrame child object, it is automatically endowed with the features, such as size, that you have specified.

» The simplest `Swing` container is the `JPanel`—it is a plain, borderless surface that can hold UI components.

» Classes that respond to user-initiated events, such as button clicks, must implement an interface called a listener that deals with, or handles, the events. Many types of listeners exist in Java, and each of these listeners can handle a specific event type. Any object can be notified of an event generated by a component as long as it implements the appropriate interface and is registered as an event listener on the appropriate event source. The class of the object that responds to an event must contain a method that accepts the event object created by the user's action. Each action's automatically called method contains an event argument that contains information about the object that caused the event; you can use the `getSource()` method to determine the component that sent the event.

» A `JCheckBox` consists of a label positioned beside a square; you can click the square to display or remove a check mark. Usually, you use a `JCheckBox` to allow the user to turn an option on or off. You can use the `setText()` and `setSelected()` methods, respectively, to change the label and state of a `JCheckBox`. When the status of a `JCheckBox` changes from unchecked to checked, or from checked to unchecked, an `ItemEvent` is generated and the `itemStateChanged()` method executes.

» When you create a `ButtonGroup`, you can group several components, such as `JCheckBoxes`, so a user can select only one at a time. To create a `ButtonGroup` and then add a `JCheckBox`, you must create a `ButtonGroup`, create a `JCheckBox`, and use the `add()` method to add the `JCheckBox` to the `ButtonGroup`. A user can set one of the `JCheckBoxes` within a group to "on" by clicking it with the mouse, or you can select a `JCheckBox` within a `ButtonGroup` with a statement such as `aGroup.setSelected(aBox);`. You can determine which, if any, of the `JCheckBoxes` in a `ButtonGroup` is selected by using the `isSelected()` method.

» A `JComboBox` is a component that combines two features: a display area showing an option and a list box containing additional options. You can build a `JComboBox` by using a constructor with no arguments, and then adding items to the list with the `addItem()` method. Alternatively, you can construct a `JComboBox` using an array of `Objects` as the constructor argument; the `Objects` in the array become the listed items within the `JComboBox`. You can use the `setSelectedItem()` or `setSelectedIndex()` method to choose one of the items in a `JComboBox`; you can also use the `getSelectedItem()` or `getSelectedIndex()` method to discover which item is currently selected. You can treat the list of items in a `JComboBox` object as an array.

» A `JScrollPane` provides scroll bars along the side or bottom of a pane, or both, so that the user can scroll initially invisible parts of a pane into view. When you create a simple scroll pane using a constructor that takes no arguments, horizontal and vertical scroll bars appear only if they are needed—that is, if the contents of the pane cannot be fully displayed without them. To force the display of a scroll bar, you can use one of the class variables defined in the `ScrollPaneConstants` class.

» When you use Java 5 or later, you can use `add()`, `remove()`, and `setLayout()` directly with `JFrames` and `JApplets` without explicitly calling `getContentPane()`.

REVIEW QUESTIONS

1. The type of Java component that holds other components is a member or child class of the _____ class.

   a. `Component`

   b. `Container`

   c. `Object`

   d. `Jar`

2. A programmer might prefer using a `JFrame` instead of a `Window` because, unlike a window, a `JFrame` _____ .

   a. can hold other objects

   b. can be made visible

   c. can have descendants

   d. has a title bar and border

3. The statement `JFrame myFrame = new JFrame();` creates a `JFrame` that is _____ .

   a. invisible and has no title

   b. invisible and has a title

   c. visible and has no title

   d. visible and has a title

4. To create a `JFrame` named `aFrame` that is 300 pixels wide by 200 pixels tall, you can _____ .

   a. use the declaration `JFrame aFrame = new JFrame(300, 200);`

   b. declare a `JFrame` named `aFrame`, and then code `aFrame.setSize(300, 200);`

   c. declare a `JFrame` named `aFrame`, and then code `aFrame.setBounds(300, 200);`

   d. use any of the above

5. When a user closes a `JFrame`, the default behavior is for _____ .

   a. the `JFrame` to close and the application to keep running

   b. the `JFrame` to become hidden and the application to keep running

   c. the `JFrame` to close and the application to exit

   d. nothing to happen

6. An advantage of extending the `JFrame` class is _____ .

   a. you can set the child class properties within the class constructor method

   b. there is no other way to cause an application to close when the user clicks a `JFrame`'s Close button

   c. there is no other way to make a `JFrame` visible

   d. all of the above

7. A JPanel is a _____ .

   a. component that holds other components

   b. Swing component

   c. Container

   d. all of the above

8. When you want a JPanel to hold components, you must use the method _____ .

   a. setPanel()   c. add()

   b. setContainer()   d. addContent()

9. A class that must respond to button clicks must implement a(n) _____ .

   a. ButtonListener

   b. ItemListener

   c. ClickListener

   d. ActionListener

10. A class can implement _____ .

    a. one listener

    b. two listeners

    c. as many listeners as it needs

    d. any number of listeners as long as they are not conflicting listeners

11. Which of the following could be registered as a listener for ItemEvents?

    a. a JApplet   c. a JPanel

    b. a JFrame   d. any of the above

12. When you write a method that reacts to JCheckBox changes, you name the method _____ .

    a. itemStateChanged()

    b. actionPerformed()

    c. checkBoxChanged()

    d. any legal identifier you choose

13. If a class contains two components that might each generate a specific event type, you can determine which component caused the event by using the _____ method.

    a. addActionListener()

    b. getSource()

    c. whichOne()

    d. identifyOrigin()

14. The declaration `JCheckBox myChoice = new JCheckBox();` creates a `JCheckBox` that is _____ .

 a. unlabeled and unselected

 b. unlabeled and selected

 c. labeled and unselected

 d. labeled and selected

15. To group several components, such as `JCheckBox`es, so that a user can select only one at a time, you create a _____ .

 a. `JCheckBoxGroup`   c. `JButtonGroup`

 b. `CheckBoxGroup`   d. `ButtonGroup`

16. Suppose you have declared a `ButtonGroup` named `threeOptions` and added three `JCheckBox`es named `box1`, `box2`, and `box3` to it. If you code `threeOptions.setSelected(box1);`, then `threeOptions.setSelected(box2);`, and then `threeOptions.setSelected(box3);`, the selected box(es) are _____ .

 a. `box1`   c. `box3`

 b. `box2`   d. all of the above

17. A component that combines a display area that shows an option with a list box containing additional options is a _____ .

 a. `JDropList`   c. `JDisplay`

 b. `JComboBox`   d. `JListBox`

18. In the statement `JComboBox optionBox = new JComboBox(options);`, the data type of the argument `options` must be _____ .

 a. an integer holding the number of options

 b. an array of option `Object`s

 c. either a or b

 d. neither a nor b

19. Suppose you have created a `JScrollPane` as `JScrollPane aPane = new JScrollPane();`. In `aPane`, scroll bars appear _____ .

 a. horizontally

 b. both horizontally and vertically

 c. only if needed to display the contents

 d. always

20. A `JScrollPane` can contain _____ .

 a. a horizontal scroll bar   c. an invisible scroll bar

 b. a diagonal scroll bar   d. all of the above

EXERCISES

1. Write an application that displays a `JFrame` containing the words to any well-known nursery rhyme. Save the file as **JNurseryRhyme.java**.

2. Create an application with a `JFrame` that holds five labels describing reasons that a customer might not buy your product (for example, "Too expensive"). Every time the user clicks a `JButton`, remove one of the negative reasons. Save the file as **JDemoResistance.java**.

3. Write an application for a construction company to handle a customer's order to build a new home. Use separate `ButtonGroups` to allow the customer to select one of four models (the Aspen, $100,000; the Brittany, $120,000; the Colonial, $180,000; or the Dartmoor, $250,000), the number of bedrooms (two, three, or four; each bedroom adds $10,500), and a garage (zero-, one-, two-, or three-car; each car adds $7775). Save the file as **JMyNewHome.java**.

4. a. Write an application for a video store. Place the names of 10 of your favorite movies in a combo box. Let the user select the movie that he wants to rent. Charge $2.00 for most movies, $1.00 for two movies you don't like very much, and $3.00 for your personal favorite movie. Display the rental fee. Save the file as **JVideo.java**.

   b. Change the `JVideo` application to include an editable combo box. Allow the user to type the name of the movie to rent. Display an appropriate error message if the desired movie is not available. Save the file as **JVideo2.java**.

5. Design an application for a pizzeria. The user makes pizza order choices from list boxes, and the application displays the price. The user can choose a pizza size of small ($7), medium ($9), large ($11), or extra large ($14) and one of any number of toppings. There is no additional charge for cheese, but any other topping adds $1 to the base price. Offer at least five different topping choices. Save the file as **JPizza.java**.

6. Write an application that allows a user to select a favorite basketball team from a list box. Include at least five teams in the list, and display the chosen team in a text field after the user makes a selection. Save the file as **JBasketball.java**.

7. Write an application that allows the user to choose insurance options in `JCheckBoxes`. Use a `ButtonGroup` to allow the user to select only one of two insurance types—HMO (health maintenance organization) or PPO (preferred provider organization). Use regular (single) `JCheckBoxes` for dental insurance and vision insurance options; the user can select one option, both options, or neither option. As the user selects each option, display its name and price in a text field; the HMO costs $200 per month, the PPO costs $600 per month, the dental coverage adds $75 per month, and the vision care adds $20 per month. When a user deselects an item, make the text field blank. Save the file as **JInsurance.java**.

8. a. Search the Java Web site at *http://java.sun.com* for information on how to use a `JTextArea`, its constructors, and its `setText()` and `append()` methods. Write an application that

allows the user to select options for a dormitory room. Use `JCheckBoxes` for options such as private room, Internet connection, cable TV connection, microwave, refrigerator, and so on. When the application starts, use a text area to display a message listing the options that are not yet selected. As the user selects and deselects options, add appropriate messages to the common text area so it accumulates a running list that reflects the user's choices. Save the file as **JDorm.java**.

  b. Modify the `JDorm` application so that instead of a running list of the users' choices, the application displays only the current choices. Save the file as **JDorm2.java**.

9. a. Search the Java Web site at *http://java.sun.com* for information on how to use a `JTextArea`, its constructors, and its `setText()` and `append()` methods. Write an application for the WebBuy Company that allows a user to compose the three parts of a complete e-mail message: the "To:", "Subject:", and "Message:" text. The "To:" and "Subject:" text areas should provide a single line for data entry. The "Message:" area should allow multiple lines of input and be able to scroll if necessary to accommodate a long message. The user clicks a button to send the e-mail message. When the message is complete and the Send button is clicked, the application displays "Mail has been sent!" on a new line in the message area. Save the file as **JEMail.java**.

  b. Modify the `JEMail` application to include a Clear button that the user can click at any time to clear the "To:", "Subject:", and "Message:" fields. Save the file as **JEMail2.java**.

DEBUGGING EXERCISES

Each of the following files in the Chapter.13 folder on your Student Disk has syntax and/ or logic errors. In each case, determine the problem and fix the program. After you correct the errors, save each file using the same filename preceded with Fix. For example, DebugThirteen1.java will become FixDebugThirteen1.java.

  a. DebugThirteen1.java

  b. DebugThirteen2.java

  c. DebugThirteen3.java

  d. DebugThirteen4.java

CASE PROJECT

KOCH'S COTTAGES

Create an application for Koch's Cottages—a weekend getaway resort that rents cottages and boats to use on the local lake. The application allows users to compute the price of their vacations. Include mutually exclusive check boxes to select a one-bedroom cottage at $600 per week or a two-bedroom cottage at $850 per week. The user also can choose rowboat rental at $60 per week. Include labels as appropriate to explain the application's functionality. Save the file as **JCottageFrame.java** in the Chapter.13 folder on your Student Disk.

GAME ZONE

1. Create a quiz game that displays, in turn, five questions about any topic of your choice. All five questions should have the same three possible multiple-choice answers. For example, you might ask questions about U.S. state trivia for which the correct response to each question is either California, Florida, or New York. After each question is displayed, allow the user to choose one, two, or all three answers by selecting JCheckBoxes. In other words, if the user is sure of an answer, he will select just one box, but if he is uncertain, he might select two or three boxes. When the user is ready to submit the answer(s), he clicks a button. If the user's answer to the question is correct and he has selected just one box, award 5 points. If the user is correct but has selected two boxes, award 2 points. If the user has selected all three boxes, award 1 point. If the user has selected fewer than three boxes but is incorrect, the user receives 0 points. A total of 25 points is possible. If the user has accumulated more than 21 points at the end of the quiz, display the message "Fantastic!". If the user has accumulated more than 15 points, display the message "Very good", and if the user has accumulated fewer points, display "OK". Save the file as **HedgeYourBet.java**.

2. In Chapter 5, you created a lottery game application. Create a similar game using check boxes. For this game, generate six random numbers, each between 0 and 30 inclusive. Allow the user to choose six check boxes to play the game. (Do not allow the user to choose more than six boxes.) After the player has chosen six numbers, display the randomly selected numbers, the player's numbers, and the amount of money the user has won, as follows:

Matching Numbers	Award ($)
Three matches	100
Four matches	10,000
Five matches	50,000
Six matches	1,000,000
Zero, one, or two matches	0

Save the file as **JLottery2.java.**

3. a. Create a game called Last Man Standing in which the objective is to select the last remaining JCheckBox. The game contains 10 JCheckBoxes. The player can choose one, two, or three boxes, then clicks a JButton to indicate the turn is complete. The computer then randomly selects one, two, or three JCheckBox objects. When the last JCheckBox is selected, display a message indicating the winner. Save the game as **LastManStanding.java**.

   b. In the current version of the Last Man Standing game, the computer might randomly make strategic mistakes. For example, when only two JCheckBox objects are left, the computer might randomly choose to check only one, allowing the player to check the last one and win. Modify the game to make it as smart as possible, using a random value for the number of the computer's selections only when there is no superior alternative. Save the improved game as **SmarterLastManStanding.java**.

UP FOR DISCUSSION

1. Suppose you are asked to create a Web application that allows users to play online gambling games in which they can win and lose real money after providing a credit card number. Would you want to work on such a site? Would you impose any restrictions on users' losses or the amount of time they can play in a day? If your supervisors asked you to create a Web site that would be so engaging that gamblers would not want to leave it, would you agree to write the application? If a family member of an addicted gambler contacted you (as the webmaster of the site) and asked that their relative be barred from further gambling, would you block the user?

2. Would you ever use a computer dating site? Would you go on a date with someone you met over the Web? What precautions would you take before such a date?

3. At least one lawsuit has been filed by a Web user who claims a Web site discriminated against him on the basis of marital status. The Web site is a dating service that does not allow married participants. How do you feel about this case?

14

USING LAYOUT MANAGERS AND EVENTS

In this chapter, you will:

Learn about layout managers
Use JPanels to increase layout options
Understand events and event handling
Use the AWTEvent class methods
Handle mouse events

JAVA ON THE JOB, SCENE 14

You have been developing Java applets and applications at Event Handlers Incorporated for several months now. "I love this job," you tell Lynn Greenbrier one day. "I've learned so much, yet there's so much more I don't know. Sometimes, I look at a JApplet that I've created and think how far I've come; other times, I realize I barely have a start in Java."

"Go on," Lynn urges, "what do you need to know more about right now?"

"Well, I wish it were easier to place components accurately within applets and frames," you say. "I want to be able to create more complex applets and applications, and one thing I'm really confused about is handling events. You've taught me about registering objects as listeners and about listening and handling, but I want to learn more about the big picture."

"Event handling is a complicated system," Lynn says. "Let's see if I can help you organize it in your mind. After all, we are the Event Handlers!"

LEARNING ABOUT LAYOUT MANAGERS

When you add more than one or two components to a JFrame, JApplet, or any other container, you can spend a lot of time computing exactly where to place each component so that the layout is attractive and no component obscures another one. An alternative is to use a layout manager. A **layout manager** is an object that controls the size and position (that is, the layout) of components inside a Container object. For example, a window is a container that includes components such as buttons and labels. The layout manager that you assign to the window determines how the components are sized and positioned within the window. Layout managers are interface classes that are part of the Java SDK (Software Development Kit); they align your components so they neither crowd each other nor overlap. For example, one layout manager arranges components in equally spaced columns and rows; another layout manager centers components within their container.

Each layout manager defines methods that arrange components within a Container, and each component you place within a Container can also be a Container itself, so you can assign layout managers within layout managers. The Java platform supplies layout managers that range from the very simple (FlowLayout and GridLayout) to the special purpose (BorderLayout and CardLayout) to the very flexible (GridBagLayout and BoxLayout). Table 14-1 shows each layout manager and situations in which each is commonly used.

> **»NOTE** Usually, JPanels and content panes are the only Containers whose layout managers you need to set (when you do not want to use their default layout managers).

USING BorderLayout

The **BorderLayout manager** is the default manager class for all content panes. You can use the BorderLayout class with any container that has five or fewer components. (However, any of the components could be a container that holds even more components.) When you use the BorderLayout manager, the components fill the screen in five regions: north, south, east, west, and center. Figure 14-1 shows an applet containing five JButton objects that fill the five regions in a content pane that uses BorderLayout.

Layout Manager	When to Use
BorderLayout	Use when you add components to a maximum of five sections arranged in north, south, east, west, and center positions.
FlowLayout	Use when you need to add components from left to right; FlowLayout automatically moves to the next row when needed, and each component takes its preferred size.
GridLayout	Use when you need to add components into a grid of rows and columns; each component is the same size.
CardLayout	Use when you need to add components that are displayed one at a time.
BoxLayout	Use when you need to add components into a single row or a single column.
GridBagLayout	Use when you need to set size, placement, and alignment constraints for every component that you add.

Table 14-1 Java layout managers

```java
import javax.swing.*;
import java.awt.*;
public class JDemoBorderLayout extends JApplet
{
    private JButton nb = new JButton("North Button");
    private JButton sb = new JButton("South Button");
    private JButton eb = new JButton("East Button");
    private JButton wb = new JButton("West Button");
    private JButton cb = new JButton("Center Button");
    public void init()
    {
      setLayout(new BorderLayout());
      add(nb, BorderLayout.NORTH);
      add(sb, BorderLayout.SOUTH);
      add(eb, BorderLayout.EAST);
      add(wb, BorderLayout.WEST);
      add(cb, BorderLayout.CENTER);
    }
}
```

Figure 14-1 The JDemoBorderLayout application

»NOTE In the JApplet in Figure 14-1, you could create a Container to hold the value returned by getContentPane() and add each component to the Container. You learned about the ramifications of this technique in Chapter 13. To keep the examples in this chapter as simple as possible, the call to getContentPane() will not be made explicitly unless there is a compelling reason to do so.

When you add a component to a container that uses BorderLayout, the add() method uses two arguments—the component and the region to which the component is added. The

BorderLayout class provides five named constants for the regions—BorderLayout.NORTH, .SOUTH, .EAST, .WEST, and .CENTER—or you can use the Strings those constants represent: "North", "South", "East", "West", or "Center". Figure 14-2 shows an HTML document that hosts the applet, and Figure 14-3 shows the output, in which each button fills one of the five regions.

> **»NOTE** When using BorderLayout, you can use the constants PAGE_START, PAGE_END, LINE_START, LINE_END, and CENTER instead of NORTH, SOUTH, EAST, WEST, and CENTER. Rather than using geographical references, these constants correspond to positions as you might picture them on a printed page.

```
<html>
<object code = "JDemoBorderLayout.class" width = 375
   height = 200>
</object>
</html>
```

Figure 14-2 The TestJDemoBorderLayout HTML document

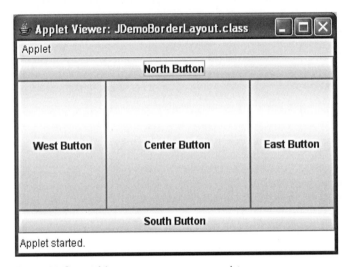

Figure 14-3 Output of the JDemoBorderLayout applet

> **»NOTE** A feature in Java 5.0 and later is the **static import feature**, which allows you to use a static constant without the class name. For example, if you add the following import statement at the top of your file, you can simply refer to CENTER instead of BorderLayout.CENTER.
>
> `import static java.awt.BorderLayout.*;`
>
> In Chapter 12, you learned about the more commonly used import declaration that imports classes from packages, allowing them to be used without package qualification. Similarly, the static import declaration imports static members from classes, allowing them to be used without class qualification. The disadvantage to using multiple static import statements is that someone who reads your code will not know the package from which a constant originated.

> **»NOTE** Swing provides three generally useful top-level container classes: JFrame, JDialog, and JApplet. Each program that uses Swing components has at least one top-level container. To appear onscreen, every GUI component, such as a JButton or JLabel, must be part of a containment hierarchy. A **containment hierarchy** is a tree of components that has a top-level container as its root.

When you place exactly five components in a container and use `BorderLayout`, each component fills one entire region, as illustrated in Figure 14-3. When the application runs, Java determines the exact size of each component based on the component's contents. When you resize a `Container` that uses `BorderLayout`, the regions also change in size. If you drag the `Container`'s border to make it wider, the north, south, and center regions become wider, but the east and west regions do not change. If you increase the `Container`'s height, the east, west, and center regions become taller, but the north and south regions do not change.

When you create a `Container` named con, you can set its layout manager to `BorderLayout` with the following statement:

```
con.setLayout(new BorderLayout());
```

Similarly, within a `JApplet`, you can use either of the following statements to set the layout manager:

```
setLayout(new BorderLayout());
this.setLayout(new BorderLayout());
```

However, it's not necessary to use any of these statements to specify `BorderLayout` because it is the default layout manager for all content panes (and `JApplets`); that's why, in previous chapters, you had to specify `FlowLayout` to acquire the easier-to-use manager.

As Figure 14-1 shows, when you use the `add()` method to add a component to a `JApplet` that uses `BorderLayout`, you use one of the five area names to specify the region of the container in which the component should be placed. For example, when you place a `JButton` named someButton into an applet, the following statement places the object in the south region of the `JApplet`'s `Container`:

```
add(someButton, BorderLayout.SOUTH);
```

When you use `BorderLayout`, you are not required to add components into each of the five regions. If you add fewer components, any empty component regions disappear and the remaining components expand to fill the available space. If any or all of the north, south, east, or west areas are left out, the center area spreads into the missing area or areas. However, if the center area is left out, the north, south, east, or west areas do not change.

> **»NOTE** A common mistake when using `BorderLayout` is to use `add(Component)` without naming the region. This can result in some of the components not being visible.

USING `FlowLayout`

Recall from Chapter 9 that you can use the **FlowLayout manager** class to arrange components in rows across the width of a `Container`—you used `FlowLayout` with the content panes of `JApplets` in that chapter. With `FlowLayout`, each `Component` that you add is placed to the right of previously added components in a row; or, if the current row is filled, the `Component` is placed to start a new row.

When you use `BorderLayout`, the `Components` you add fill their regions—that is, each `Component` expands or contracts based on its region's size. However, when you use `FlowLayout`, each `Component` retains its default size, or **preferred size**. For example, a `JButton`'s preferred size is the size that is large enough to hold the `JButton`'s text. When you use `BorderLayout` and then resize the window, the components change size accordingly because their regions change. When you use FlowLayout and then resize the window, each component retains its size, but it might become partially obscured or change position.

The FlowLayout class contains three constants you can use to align Components with a Container:

» FlowLayout.LEFT

» FlowLayout.CENTER

» FlowLayout.RIGHT

If you do not specify alignment, Components are center-aligned in a FlowLayout Container by default. Figure 14-4 shows a JApplet that uses the FlowLayout.LEFT and

```
import javax.swing.*;
import java.awt.*;
import java.awt.event.*;
public class JDemoFlowLayout extends JApplet implements ActionListener
{
    private JButton lb = new JButton("L Button");
    private JButton rb = new JButton("R Button");
    private Container con = getContentPane();
    private FlowLayout layout = new FlowLayout();
    public void init()
    {
        con.setLayout(layout);
        con.add(lb);
        con.add(rb);
        lb.addActionListener(this);
        rb.addActionListener(this);
    }
    public void actionPerformed(ActionEvent event)
    {
        Object source = event.getSource();
        if(source == lb)
            layout.setAlignment(FlowLayout.LEFT);
        else
            layout.setAlignment(FlowLayout.RIGHT);
        con.invalidate();
        con.validate();
    }
}
```

Figure 14-4 The JDemoFlowLayout applet

»NOTE In Figure 14-4, notice that a Container is created and the getContentPane() method is called explicitly. In Chapter 13, you learned that when you use the add(), remove(), or setLayout() methods with an applet in Java 5 or later, you don't need to get a content pane reference. However, when you use the invalidate() and validate() methods, you need a content pane reference. Instead of creating a Container object, as in the applet in Figure 14-4, you could add the buttons without using a reference, and then use an anonymous reference to the content pane in the validate() and invalidate() calls, as in the following:

```
getContentPane().invalidate();
```

In Chapter 7, you learned to use the term *anonymous* to describe unnamed references.

FlowLayout.RIGHT constants to reposition JButtons. In this example, a FlowLayout object named layout is used to set the layout of the content pane. When the user clicks a button, the highlighted code in the actionPerformed() method changes the alignment to left or right using the FlowLayout class setAlignment() method. The last shaded statements call invalidate() and validate(). The invalidate() call marks the container (and any of its parents) as needing to be laid out. The validate() call causes the components to be rearranged based on the newly assigned layout. Figure 14-5 shows the JApplet when it starts, Figure 14-6 shows how the JButtonComponents are repositioned after the user clicks the "L" button, and Figure 14-7 shows how the Components are repositioned after the user clicks the "R" button.

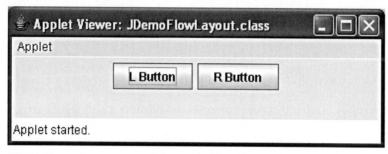

Figure 14-5 The JDemoFlowLayout applet as it first appears on the screen

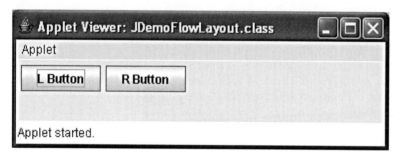

Figure 14-6 The JDemoFlowLayout applet after the user chooses the "L" button

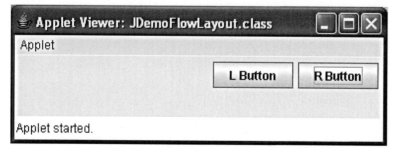

Figure 14-7 The JDemoFlowLayout applet after the user chooses the "R" button

» NOTE FlowLayout is the default layout manager for every JPanel. You first learned about JPanels in Chapter 13 and will learn more about the JPanel class later in this chapter.

USING GridLayout

If you want to arrange components into equal rows and columns, you can use the **GridLayout manager** class. When you create a GridLayout object, you indicate the numbers of rows and columns you want, and then the container surface is divided into a grid, much like the screen you see when using a spreadsheet program. For example, the following statement establishes an anonymous GridLayout with four horizontal rows and five vertical columns in a Container named con:

```
con.setLayout(new GridLayout(4, 5));
```

Similarly, within a JApplet, you can establish the same layout with either of the following:

```
this.setLayout(new GridLayout(4, 5));
setLayout(new GridLayout(4, 5));
```

>> **NOTE** When you use GridLayout, you specify rows first and then columns, which is the same approach you take when specifying two-dimensional arrays, as you learned in Chapter 8.

As you add new Components to a GridLayout, they are positioned from left to right across each row, in sequence. Unfortunately, you can't skip a position or specify an exact position for a component. (However, you can add a blank label to a grid position to give the illusion of skipping a position.) You can also specify a vertical and horizontal gap measured in pixels, using two additional arguments. For example, Figure 14-8 shows a JDemoGridLayout JApplet that uses the following statement (shaded in the figure) to establish a GridLayout with three horizontal rows and two vertical columns, and horizontal and vertical gaps of five pixels each:

```
private GridLayout layout = new GridLayout(3, 2, 5, 5);
```

Five JButton Components are added to the JApplet's automatically retrieved content pane. Figure 14-9 shows the result. The Components are placed into the pane across the rows. Because there are six positions but only five Components, one spot remains available.

```
import javax.swing.*;
import java.awt.*;
public class JDemoGridLayout extends JApplet
{
    private JButton b1 = new JButton("Button 1");
    private JButton b2 = new JButton("Button 2");
    private JButton b3 = new JButton("Button 3");
    private JButton b4 = new JButton("Button 4");
    private JButton b5 = new JButton("Button 5");
    private GridLayout layout = new GridLayout(3, 2, 5, 5);
    public void init()
    {
        setLayout(layout);
        add(b1);
        add(b2);
        add(b3);
        add(b4);
        add(b5);
    }
}
```

Figure 14-8 The JDemoGridLayout applet

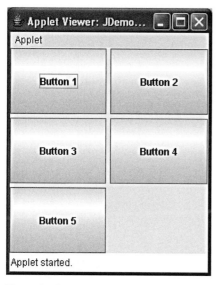

Figure 14-9 Output of the `JDemoGridLayout` applet

> **»NOTE** With `GridLayout`, you can specify the number of rows only, you can use 0 for the number of columns and let the layout manager determine the number of columns, or you can use 0 for the number of rows, specify the number of columns, and let the layout manager calculate the number of rows. Even when you do not specify rows or columns, the components placed in a `GridLayout` are in fixed rows and columns, filling the available space. When you use `FlowLayout`, Java determines the rows and columns, but components are not placed in rigid rows and they retain their "natural" size—that is, the minimum size they need so their contents are fully visible.

USING `CardLayout`

The **CardLayout manager** generates a stack of containers or components, one on top of another, much like a blackjack dealer reveals playing cards one at a time from the top of a deck. Each component in the group is referred to as a card, and each card can be any component type—for example, a `JButton`, `JLabel`, or `JPanel`. You use a `CardLayout` when you want multiple components to share the same display space.

A card layout is created from the `CardLayout` class using one of two constructors:

» `CardLayout()` creates a card layout without a horizontal or vertical gap.

» `CardLayout(int hgap, int vgap)` creates a card layout with the specified horizontal and vertical gaps. The horizontal gaps are placed at the left and right edges. The vertical gaps are placed at the top and bottom edges.

For example, Figure 14-10 shows a `JDemoCardLayout JApplet` that uses a `CardLayout` manager to create a stack of `JButtons` that contain the labels "Ace of Hearts", "Three of Spades", and "Queen of Clubs". In the `init()` method of the applet, you need a slightly different version of the `add()` method to add a component to a content pane whose layout manager is `CardLayout`. The format of the method is:

```
add(aString, aContainer);
```

In this statement, `aString` represents a name you want to use to identify the `Component` card that is added.

```
import javax.swing.*;
import java.awt.*;
import java.awt.event.*;
public class JDemoCardLayout extends JApplet
    implements ActionListener
{
    private CardLayout cards = new CardLayout();
    private JButton b1 = new JButton("Ace of Hearts");
    private JButton b2 = new JButton("Three of Spades");
    private JButton b3 = new JButton("Queen of Clubs");
    public void init()
    {
        setLayout(cards);
        add("ace", b1);
        b1.addActionListener(this);
        add("three", b2);
        b2.addActionListener(this);
        add("queen", b3);
        b3.addActionListener(this);
    }
    public void actionPerformed(ActionEvent e)
    {
        cards.next(getContentPane());
    }
}
```

Figure 14-10 The `JDemoCardLayout` JApplet

> **» NOTE** The example applet in Figure 14-10 does not use the `String`s in the `add()` method calls as anything but placeholders. However, the `String`s are required; the applet compiles but does not execute if you do not include them. `Container`s with a `CardLayout` manager can use these `String`s to identify specific cards; you can use any names you want within your programs. More details are available at *http://java.sun.com*.

> **» NOTE** In the code in Figure 14-10, you might prefer to name a `Container` reference, assign the content pane to it, and use the reference name with the `setLayout()` statement, with each `add()` call, and as the argument to the `next()` call. That way, no matter how many times the `next()` method executes, `getContentPane()` is called only once in the applet.

In a program that has a `CardLayout` manager, a change of cards is usually triggered by a user's action. For example, in the `JDemoCardLayout` applet, each `JButton` can trigger the `actionPerformed()` method. Within this method, the statement `next(getContentPane())` flips to the next card of the container. (The order of the cards depends on the order in which you add them to the container.) You can also use `previous(getContentPane())`, `first(getContentPane());`, and `last(getContentPane());` to flip to the previous, first, and last card, respectively. You can go to a specific card by using the `String` name assigned in the `add()` method call. For example, in the application in Figure 14-10, the following statement would display the "Three of Spades":

```
cards.show(getContentPane()), "three";)
```

Figure 14-11 shows the output of the `JDemoCardLayout` applet when it first appears on the screen, after the user clicks the button once, and after the user clicks the button a second time. Because each `JButton` is a card, each `JButton` consumes the entire viewing area in the container that uses the `CardLayout` manager.

 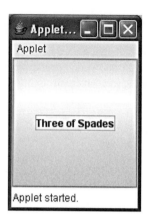 

NOTE
If the user continued to click the card buttons in Figure 14-11, the cards would continue to cycle in order.

Figure 14-11 Output of `JDemoCardLayout` when it first appears on the screen, after the user clicks once, and after the user clicks twice

NOTE Explore the `JTabbedPane` class at the *http://java.sun.com* Web site; the class operates like a container with a `CardLayout`, but folder-type tabs are in place for the user to select the various components.

USING ADVANCED LAYOUT MANAGERS

Just as professional Java programmers are constantly creating new `Component`s, they also create new layout managers. You are certain to encounter new and interesting layout managers during your programming career; you might even create your own.

For example, when `GridLayout` is not sophisticated enough for your purposes, you can use `GridBagLayout`. The **GridBagLayout manager** allows you to add `Component`s to precise locations within the grid, as well as to indicate that specific `Component`s should span multiple rows or columns within the grid. For example, if you want to create a `JPanel` with six `JButtons`, in which two of the `JButtons` are twice as wide as the others, you can use `GridBagLayout`. This class is difficult to use because you must set the position and size for each component. `GridBagLayout` is more complicated to use than `GridLayout`; more than 20 methods are associated with the class. To use a `GridBagLayout` effectively, you must customize one or more of the `GridBagConstraints` objects that are associated with its components. Visit *http://java.sun.com* for details on how to use this class.

Another layout manager option is the **BoxLayout manager**, which allows multiple components to be laid out either vertically or horizontally. The components do not wrap, so a vertical arrangement of components, for example, stays vertically arranged when the frame is resized. The Java Web site can provide you with details.

USING JPanels TO INCREASE LAYOUT OPTIONS

Using the `BorderLayout`, `FlowLayout`, `GridLayout`, and `CardLayout` managers would provide a limited number of screen arrangements if you could place only one `Component` in a section of the layout. Fortunately, you can greatly increase the number of possible component arrangements by using the `JPanel` class. In Chapter 13, you learned that a `JPanel` is similar to a `JWindow` and a `JFrame`, in that a `JPanel` is a surface on which you can place components. But a `JPanel` is *not* a child of the `JWindow` or `JFrame` class; it is a type of `JComponent`, as shown in the class hierarchy in Figure 14-12. A JPanel is a Container, which means that it can contain other components. For example, you can create a JApplet using BorderLayout and place a JPanel in any of the five regions. Then, within the north JPanel, you can place four JButtons using GridLayout, and within the east JPanel, you can place three JLabels using FlowLayout. By using JPanels within JPanels, you can create an infinite variety of screen layouts.

```
java.lang.Object
  !--java.awt.Component
        !--java.awt.Container
              !--javax.swing.JComponent
                    !--javax.swing.JPanel
```

Figure 14-12 The inheritance hierarchy of the JPanel class

When you create a JPanel object, you can use one of four constructors. The different constructors allow you to use default values or to specify a layout manager and whether the JPanel is double buffered. If you indicate **double buffering**, which is the default buffering strategy, you specify that additional memory space be used to draw the JPanel offscreen when it is updated. With double buffering, a redrawn JPanel is displayed only when it is complete; this provides the viewer with updated screens that do not flicker while being redrawn. The four constructors are as follows:

» JPanel() creates a JPanel with double buffering and a flow layout.

» JPanel(LayoutManager layout) creates a JPanel with the specified layout manager and double buffering.

» JPanel(Boolean isDoubleBuffered) creates a JPanel with flow layout and the specified double-buffering strategy.

» JPanel(LayoutManager layout, Boolean isDoubleBuffered) creates a JPanel with the specified layout manager and the specified buffering strategy.

>>**NOTE** When you employ double buffering, the visible screen surface is called the **primary surface**, and the off-screen image is called the **back buffer**. The act of copying the contents from one surface to another is frequently referred to as a **block line transfer**, or blitting, because of the acronym "blt," pronounced "blit." Double buffering prevents "tearing," the visual effect that occurs when you see parts of different images because the redrawing rate is not fast enough. As with most beneficial features, double buffering has a cost—additional memory requirements.

For example, the following statements create a JPanel that uses a named BorderLayout manager.

```
BorderLayout border = new BorderLayout();
JPanel myPanel = new JPanel(border);
```

The following statement accomplishes the same thing as the previous two, combining both statements by using an anonymous layout manager:

```
JPanel myPanel = new JPanel(new BorderLayout());
```

After a JPanel has been created, you can set its layout manager using the setLayout() method. The next two statements have the same result as the last one:

```
JPanel myPanel = new JPanel();
myPanel.setLayout(new BorderLayout());
```

You add components to a JPanel with the add() method—the same method you use to add components to a content pane. Figure 14-13 shows a JDemoManyPanels JApplet containing

> **NOTE** Specifying a layout manager when you create a `JPanel` is preferable for performance reasons; if you create the `JPanel` first and change its layout later, you automatically create an unnecessary `FlowLayout` object.

```java
import javax.swing.*;
import java.awt.*;
public class JDemoManyPanels extends JApplet
{
  // Twelve buttons
    JButton button01 = new JButton("One");
    JButton button02 = new JButton("Two");
    JButton button03 = new JButton("Three");
    JButton button04 = new JButton("Four");
    JButton button05 = new JButton("Five");
    JButton button06 = new JButton("Six");
    JButton button07 = new JButton("Seven");
    JButton button08 = new JButton("Eight");
    JButton button09 = new JButton("Nine");
    JButton button10 = new JButton("Ten");
    JButton button11 = new JButton("Eleven");
    JButton button12 = new JButton("Twelve");
  // Four panels
    JPanel panel01 = new JPanel(new GridLayout(2, 0));
    JPanel panel02 = new JPanel(new FlowLayout());
    JPanel panel03 = new JPanel(new FlowLayout());
    JPanel panel04 = new JPanel(new GridLayout(2, 0));

    public void init()
    {
        setLayout(new BorderLayout());
        add(panel01, BorderLayout.WEST);
        add(panel02, BorderLayout.CENTER);
        add(panel03, BorderLayout.SOUTH);
        add(panel04, BorderLayout.EAST);

        panel01.add(button01);
        panel01.add(button02);
        panel01.add(button03);

        panel02.add(button04);
        panel02.add(button05);
        panel02.add(button06);

        panel03.add(button07);

        panel04.add(button08);
        panel04.add(button09);
        panel04.add(button10);
        panel04.add(button11);
        panel04.add(button12);
    }
}
```

Figure 14-13 The `JDemoManyPanels` `JApplet`

>> **NOTE** If you were creating a program with as many buttons and panels as the one in Figure 14-13, you might prefer to create arrays of the components instead of so many individually named ones. This example does not use an array so you can more easily see how each component is placed.

four JPanels and 12 JButtons that each display a single spelled-out number so you can better understand their positions. The automatically supplied content pane for the JApplet is assigned a BorderLayout, and each JPanel is assigned either a GridLayout or FlowLayout and placed in one of the applet's regions (leaving the north region empty). One or more JButtons are then placed on each JPanel. Figure 14-14 shows the output as the user adjusts the borders of the Applet Viewer window to change its size. Using the code as a guide, be certain you understand why each JButton appears as it does in the JApplet.

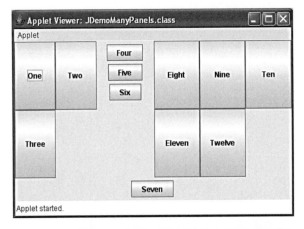

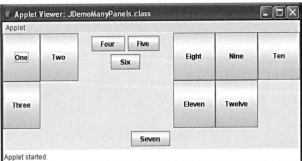

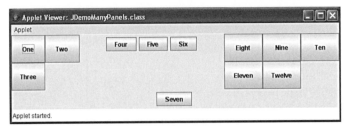

Figure 14-14 Output of the JDemoManyPanels JApplet: three views as the user adjusts the Applet Viewer window borders

NOTE Swing containers other than JPanel and content panes generally provide Application Program Interface (API) methods that you should use instead of the add() method. See the Java Web site at *http://java.sun.com* for details.

GridLayout provides you with rows and columns that are similar to a two-dimensional array. Therefore, it particularly lends itself to displaying arrays of objects. For example, Figure 14-15 contains a Checkerboard class that displays a pattern of eight rows and columns in alternating colors. The JPanel placed in the content pane has a GridLayout of eight by eight.

```
import java.awt.*;
import javax.swing.*;
public class Checkerboard extends JFrame
{
    final int ROWS = 8;
    final int COLS = 8;
    final int GAP = 2;
    final int NUM = ROWS * COLS;
    int x;
    JPanel pane = new JPanel(new GridLayout(ROWS, COLS, GAP, GAP));
    JPanel[] panel = new JPanel[NUM];
    Color color1 = Color.WHITE;
    Color color2 = Color.BLUE;
    Color tempColor;
    public Checkerboard()
    {
        super("Checkerboard");
        setDefaultCloseOperation(JFrame.EXIT_ON_CLOSE);
        add(pane);
        for(x = 0; x < NUM; ++x)
        {
            panel[x] = new JPanel();
            pane.add(panel[x]);
            if(x % COLS == 0)
            {
                tempColor = color1;
                color1 = color2;
                color2 = tempColor;
            }
            if(x % 2 == 0)
                panel[x].setBackground(color1);
            else
                panel[x].setBackground(color2);
        }
    }
    public static void main(String[] arguments)
    {
        Checkerboard frame = new Checkerboard();
        final int SIZE = 300;
        frame.setSize(SIZE, SIZE);
        frame.setVisible(true);
    }
}
```

Figure 14-15 The Checkerboard class

Sixty-four `JPanel`s are declared, and in a loop, one by one, they are instantiated and assigned to a section of the grid (see shaded statements). After each set of eight `JPanel`s is assigned to the grid (when x is evenly divisible by 8), the first and second color values are reversed, so that the first row starts with a blue square, the second row starts with a white square, and so on. Within each row, all the even-positioned squares are filled with one color, and the odd-positioned squares are filled with the other. Figure 14-16 shows the output.

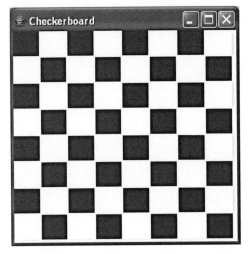

Figure 14-16 Output of the `Checkerboard` application

UNDERSTANDING EVENTS AND EVENT HANDLING

You have already worked with many events in the programs you have written. Beginning in Chapter 9, you learned how to create applets that contain widgets controlled by user-initiated events. Now that you understand inheritance and abstract classes, you can take a deeper look at event handling.

Like all Java classes, events are `Object`s. Specifically, **events** are `Object`s that the user initiates, such as key presses and mouse clicks. Many events that occur have significance only for specific components within a program. For example, you have written programs, as well as used programs written by others, in which pressing Enter or double-clicking a specific component has no effect. Other events have meaning outside your program; for example, clicking the Close button in the Applet Viewer window sends a message to your computer's operating system, which closes the window and stops the program.

The parent class for all event objects is named `EventObject`, which descends from the `Object` class. `EventObject` is the parent of `AWTEvent`, which in turn is the parent of specific event classes such as `ActionEvent` and `ComponentEvent`. Figure 14-17 illustrates the inheritance hierarchy of these relationships.

You can see in Figure 14-17 that `ComponentEvent` is itself a parent to several event classes, including `InputEvent`, which is a parent of `KeyEvent` and `MouseEvent`. The family tree for events has roots that go fairly deep, but the class names are straightforward and they share

```
java.lang.Object
  !--java.util.EventObject
       !--java.awt.AWTEvent
            !--java.awt.event.ActionEvent
            +--java.awt.event.AdjustmentEvent
            +--java.awt.event.ItemEvent
            +--java.awt.event.TextEvent
            +--java.awt.event.ComponentEvent
                 !--java.awt.event.ContainerEvent
                 +--java.awt.event.FocusEvent
                 +--java.awt.event.PaintEvent
                 +--java.awt.event.WindowEvent
                 +--java.awt.event.InputEvent
                      !--java.awt.event.KeyEvent
                      +--java.awt.event.MouseEvent
```

Figure 14-17 The inheritance hierarchy of event classes

>>**NOTE** The abstract class `AWTEvent` is contained in the package `java.awt.event`.

basic roles within your programs. For example, `ActionEvents` are generated by components that users can click, such as `JButtons` and `JCheckBoxes`, and `TextEvents` are generated by components into which the user enters text, such as a `JTextField`. `MouseEvents` include determining the location of the mouse and distinguishing between a single- and double-click. Table 14-2 lists some common user actions and the events that are generated from them.

User Action	Resulting Event Type
Click a button	`ActionEvent`
Click a component	`MouseEvent`
Click an item in a list box	`ItemEvent`
Click an item in a check box	`ItemEvent`
Change text in a text field	`TextEvent`
Open a window	`WindowEvent`
Iconify a window	`WindowEvent`
Press a key	`KeyEvent`

Table 14-2 Examples of user actions and their resulting event types

Because `ActionEvents` involve the mouse, it is easy to confuse `ActionEvents` and `MouseEvents`. If you are interested in `ActionEvents`, you focus on changes in a component (for example, a `JButton` on a `JFrame` being pressed); if you are interested in `MouseEvents`, your focus is on what the user does manually with the mouse (for example, clicking the left mouse button).

When you write programs with GUI interfaces, you are always handling events that originate with the mouse or keys on specific `Components` or `Containers`. Just as your telephone notifies you when you have a call, the computer's operating system notifies the user when an `AWTEvent` occurs; for example, when the mouse is clicked. Just as you can ignore your phone when you're not expecting or interested in a call, you can ignore `AWTEvents`. If you don't care about an event, such as when your program contains a component that produces no effect when clicked, you simply don't look for a message to occur.

>>**NOTE**
There is no prewritten, built-in Java class named `Event`; the general event class is `AWTEvent`.

When you care about events—that is, when you want to listen for an event—you can implement an appropriate interface for your class. Each event class shown in Table 14-2 has a listener interface associated with it, so that for every event class, such as `<name>Event`, there is a similarly named `<name>Listener` interface.

> **NOTE** Remember that an interface contains only abstract methods, so all interface methods are empty. If you implement a listener, you must provide your own methods for all the methods that are part of the interface. Of course, you can leave the methods empty in your implementation, providing a header and curly braces, but no statements.

> **NOTE** Every `<name>Event` class has a `<name>Listener`. The `MouseEvent` class has an additional listener, the `MouseMotionListener`.

Every `<name>Listener` interface method has the return type `void`, and each takes one argument—an object that is an instance of the corresponding `<name>Event` class. Thus, the `ActionListener` interface has a method named `actionPerformed()`, and its header is `void actionPerformed(ActionEvent e)`. When an action takes place, the `actionPerformed()` method executes, and e represents an instance of that event. Interface methods such as `actionPerformed()`, which are called automatically when an appropriate event occurs, are called **event handlers**.

Instead of implementing a listener class, you can extend an adapter class. An **adapter class** implements all the methods in an interface, providing an empty body for each method. For example, the `MouseAdapter` class provides an empty method for all the methods contained in `MouseListener`. When you extend an adapter class, you need to write only those methods you want to use, and you do not have to bother creating empty methods for all the others.

> **NOTE** If a listener has only one method, there is no need for an adapter. For example, the `ActionListener` class has one method, `actionPerformed()`, so there is no `ActionAdapter` class.

Whether you use a listener or an adapter, you create an event handler when you write code for the listener methods; that is, you tell your class how to handle the event. After you create the handler, you must also register an instance of the class with the component that you want the event to affect. For any `<name>Listener`, you must use the form `object.add<name>Listener(Component)` to register an object with the `Component` that will listen for objects emanating from it. The `add<name>Listener()` methods, such as `addActionListener()` and `addItemListener()`, all work the same way. They register a listener with a `Component`, return `void`, and take a `<name>Listener` object as an argument. For example, if a `JApplet` is an `ActionListener` and contains a `JButton` named pushMe, then the following statement registers this applet as a listener for the pushMe `JButton`:

```
pushMe.addActionListener(this);
```

Table 14-3 lists the events with their listeners and handlers.

AN EVENT-HANDLING EXAMPLE: `KeyListener`

You use the **KeyListener interface** when you are interested in actions the user initiates from the keyboard. The `KeyListener` interface contains three methods—keyPressed(), keyTyped(), and keyReleased(). For most keyboard applications in which the user must

Event	Listener	Handlers
ActionEvent	ActionListener	actionPerformed(ActionEvent)
ItemEvent	ItemListener	itemStateChanged(ItemEvent)
TextEvent	TextListener	textValueChanged(TextEvent)
AdjustmentEvent	AdjustmentListener	adjustmentValueChanged(AdjustmentEvent)
ContainerEvent	ContainerListener	componentAdded(ContainerEvent)
		componentRemoved(ContainerEvent)
ComponentEvent	ComponentListener	componentMoved(ComponentEvent)
		componentHidden(ComponentEvent)
		componentResized(ComponentEvent)
		componentShown(ComponentEvent)
FocusEvent	FocusListener	focusGained(FocusEvent)
		focusLost(FocusEvent)
MouseEvent	MouseListener	mousePressed(MouseEvent)
	MouseMotionListener	mouseReleased(MouseEvent)
		mouseEntered(MouseEvent)
		mouseExited(MouseEvent)
		mouseClicked(MouseEvent)
		mouseDragged(MouseEvent)
		mouseMoved(MouseEvent)
KeyEvent	KeyListener	keyPressed(KeyEvent)
		keyTyped(KeyEvent)
		keyReleased(KeyEvent)
WindowEvent	WindowListener	windowActivated(WindowEvent)
		windowClosing(WindowEvent)
		windowClosed(WindowEvent)
		windowDeiconified(WindowEvent)
		windowIconified(WindowEvent)
		windowOpened(WindowEvent)

Table 14-3 Events with their related listeners and handlers

type a keyboard key, it is probably not important whether you take resulting action when a user first presses a key, during the key press, or upon the key's release; most likely these events occur in quick sequence. However, on those occasions when you don't want to take action while the user holds down the key, you can place the actions in the keyReleased() method. It is best to use the keyTyped() method when you want to discover which character was typed. When the user presses a key that does not generate a character, such as a function key (sometimes called an **action key**), keyTyped() does not execute. The methods keyPressed() and keyReleased() provide the only ways to get information about keys that don't generate characters. The KeyEvent class contains constants known as **virtual key codes**, which represent keyboard keys that have been pressed. For example, when you type "A", two virtual key codes

>>**NOTE** Java programmers call `keyTyped()` events "higher-level" events because they do not depend on the platform or keyboard layout. (For example, the key that generates `VK_Q` on a U.S. keyboard layout generates `VK_A` on a French keyboard layout.) In contrast, `keyPressed()` and `keyReleased()` events are "lower-level" events and do depend on the platform and keyboard layout. According to the Java documentation, using `keyTyped()` is the preferred way to find out about character input.

are generated—Shift and "a". The virtual key code constants have names such as VK_SHIFT and VK_ALT. See the Java Web site for a complete list of virtual key codes.

Figure 14-18 shows a JDemoKeyFrame class that uses the keyTyped() method to discover which key the user typed last. A prompt in the north border area asks the user to type in the text field in

```java
import javax.swing.*;
import java.awt.*;
import java.awt.event.*;
public class JDemoKeyFrame extends JFrame
  implements KeyListener
{
    JLabel prompt = new JLabel("Type keys below:");
    JLabel outputLabel = new JLabel("Key Typed:");
    JTextField textField = new JTextField(10);
    public JDemoKeyFrame()
    {
        setTitle("JKey Frame");
        setDefaultCloseOperation(JFrame.EXIT_ON_CLOSE);
        setLayout(new BorderLayout());
        add(prompt, BorderLayout.NORTH);
        add(textField, BorderLayout.CENTER);
        add(outputLabel, BorderLayout.SOUTH);
        addKeyListener(this);
        textField.addKeyListener(this);
    }
    public void keyTyped(KeyEvent e)
    {
        char c = e.getKeyChar();
        outputLabel.setText("Last key typed: " + c);
    }
    public void keyPressed(KeyEvent e)
    {
    }
    public void keyReleased(KeyEvent e)
    {
    }
    public static void main(String[] args)
    {
        JDemoKeyFrame keyFrame = new JDemoKeyFrame();
        final int WIDTH = 250;
        final int HEIGHT = 100;
        keyFrame.setSize(WIDTH, HEIGHT);
        keyFrame.setVisible(true);
    }
}
```

Figure 14-18 The JDemoKeyFrame class

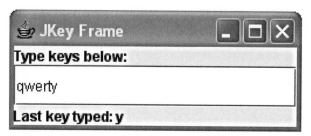

Figure 14-19 Output of the `JDemoKeyFrame` application after the user has typed several characters

the center area. With each key press by the user, the `keyTyped()` method changes the label in the south border area of the frame to display the key that generated the most recent `KeyEvent`. Figure 14-19 shows the output after the user has typed several characters into the text field.

USING `AWTEvent` CLASS METHODS

In addition to the handler methods included with the event listener interfaces, the `AWTEvent` classes themselves contain methods. You use many of these methods to determine the nature of and the facts about an event in question. For example, the `ComponentEvent` class contains a `getComponent()` method that returns the `Component` involved in the event. You use the `getComponent()` method when you create an application with several components; the `getComponent()` method allows you to determine which `Component` is generating the event. The `WindowEvent` class contains a similar method, `getWindow()`, that returns the `Window` that was the source of the event. Table 14-4 lists some useful methods for many of the event classes. All `Component`s have these methods:

» `addComponentListener()`

» `addFocusListener()`

» `addMouseListener()`

» `addMouseMotionListener()`

You can call any of the methods listed in Table 14-4 by using the object-dot-method format that you use with all class methods. For example, if you have an `InputEvent` named `inEvent` and an integer named `modInt`, the following statement is valid:

```
modInt = inEvent.getModifiers();
```

You use the `getModifiers()` method with an `InputEvent` object, and you can assign the return value to an integer variable. Thus, when you use any of the handler methods from Table 14-3, such as `actionPerformed()` or `itemStateChanged()`, they provide you with an appropriate event object. You can use the event object within the handler method to obtain information; you simply add a dot and the appropriate method name from Table 14-4.

When you use an event such as `KeyEvent`, you can use any of the event's methods. Through the power of inheritance, you can also use methods that belong to any class that is a super-class of the event with which you are working. For example, any `KeyEvent` has access to the `InputEvent`, `ComponentEvent`, `AWTEvent`, `EventObject`, and `Object` methods, as well as to the `KeyEvent` methods.

Class	Method	Purpose
EventObject	Object getSource()	Returns the Object involved in the event
ComponentEvent	Component getComponent()	Returns the Component involved in the event
WindowEvent	Window getWindow()	Returns the Window involved in the event
ItemEvent	Object getItem()	Returns the Object that was selected or deselected
ItemEvent	int getStateChange()	Returns an integer named ItemEvent.SELECTED or ItemEvent.DESELECTED
InputEvent	int getModifiers()	Returns an integer to indicate which mouse button was clicked
InputEvent	int getWhen()	Returns a time indicating when the event occurred
InputEvent	boolean isAltDown()	Returns whether the Alt key was pressed when the event occurred
InputEvent	boolean isControlDown()	Returns whether the Ctrl key was pressed when the event occurred
InputEvent	boolean isShiftDown()	Returns whether the Shift key was pressed when the event occurred
KeyEvent	int getKeyChar()	Returns the Unicode character entered from the keyboard
MouseEvent	int getClickCount()	Returns the number of mouse clicks; lets you identify the user's double-clicks
MouseEvent	int getX()	Returns the x-coordinate of the mouse pointer
MouseEvent	int getY()	Returns the y-coordinate of the mouse pointer
MouseEvent	Point getPoint()	Returns the Point Object that contains the x- and y-coordinates of the mouse location

Table 14-4 Useful Event class methods

HANDLING MOUSE EVENTS

Even though Java program users sometimes type characters from a keyboard, when you write GUI programs you probably expect users to spend most of their time operating a mouse. The **MouseMotionListener interface** provides you with methods named mouseDragged() and mouseMoved() that detect the mouse being rolled or dragged across a component surface. The **MouseListener interface** provides you with methods named mousePressed(), mouseClicked(), and mouseReleased() that are analogous to the keyboard event methods keyPressed(), keyTyped(), and keyReleased(). With a mouse, however, you are interested in more than its key presses; you sometimes simply want to know where a mouse is pointing. The additional interface methods mouseEntered() and mouseExited() inform you when the user positions the mouse over a component (entered) or moves the mouse off a component (exited). The **MouseInputListener interface** implements all the methods in both the MouseListener and MouseMotionListener interfaces; although it has no methods of its own, it is a convenience when you want to handle many different types of mouse events. Tables 14-5 and 14-6 show the methods of the MouseListener and MouseMotionListener classes, respectively.

Method	Description
void mouseClicked(MouseEvent e)	Invoked when the mouse button has been clicked (pressed and released) on a component
void mouseEntered(MouseEvent e)	Invoked when the mouse pointer enters a component
void mouseExited(MouseEvent e)	Invoked when the mouse pointer exits a component
void mousePressed(MouseEvent e)	Invoked when a mouse button has been pressed on a component
void mouseReleased(MouseEvent e)	Invoked when a mouse button has been released on a component

Table 14-5 MouseListener methods

>> NOTE Many of the methods in Tables 14-5 and 14-6 also appear in tables earlier in this chapter. They are organized by class here so you can better understand the scope of methods that are available for mouse actions. Don't forget that because MouseListener, MouseMotionListener, and MouseInputListener are interfaces, you must include each method in every program that implements them, even if you choose to place no instructions within some of the methods.

Method	Description
void mouseDragged(MouseEvent e)	Invoked when a mouse button is pressed on a component and then dragged
void mouseMoved(MouseEvent e)	Invoked when the mouse pointer has been moved onto a component but no buttons have been pressed

Table 14-6 MouseMotionListener methods

Each of the methods in Tables 14-5 and 14-6 accepts a MouseEvent argument. A **MouseEvent** is the type of event generated by mouse manipulation. Figure 14-20 shows the inheritance hierarchy of the MouseEvent class. From this diagram, you can see that a MouseEvent is a type of InputEvent, which is a type of ComponentEvent. The MouseEvent class contains many instance methods and fields that are useful in describing mouse-generated events. Table 14-7 lists some of the more useful methods of the MouseEvent class, and Table 14-8 lists some fields.

```
java.lang.Object
  !--java.util.EventObject
        !--java.awt.AWTEvent
              !--java.awt.event.ComponentEvent
                    !--java.awt.event.InputEvent
                          !--java.awt.event.MouseEvent
```

Figure 14-20 The inheritance hierarchy of the MouseEvent class

Method	Description
int getButton()	Returns which, if any, of the mouse buttons has changed state; uses fields NOBUTTON, BUTTON1, BUTTON2, and BUTTON3
int getClickCount()	Returns the number of mouse clicks associated with the current event
int getX()	Returns the horizontal x-position of the event relative to the source component
int getY()	Returns the vertical y-position of the event relative to the source component

Table 14-7 Some useful MouseEvent methods

Field	Description
static int BUTTON1	Indicates mouse button #1; used by getButton()
static int BUTTON2	Indicates mouse button #2; used by getButton()
static int BUTTON3	Indicates mouse button #3; used by getButton()
static int NOBUTTON	Indicates no mouse buttons; used by getButton()
static int MOUSE_CLICKED	The "mouse clicked" event
static int MOUSE_DRAGGED	The "mouse dragged" event
static int MOUSE_ENTERED	The "mouse entered" event
static int MOUSE_EXITED	The "mouse exited" event

Table 14-8 Some useful MouseEvent fields

Figure 14-21 shows a JMouseActionsFrame application that demonstrates several of the mouse listener and event methods. JMouseActionsFrame extends JFrame and, because it implements the MouseListener interface, it must include all five methods—mouseClicked(), mouseEntered(), mouseExited(), mousePressed(), and mouseReleased() —even though no actions are included in the mousePressed() or mouseReleased() methods.

```java
import javax.swing.*;
import java.awt.*;
import java.awt.event.*;
public class JMouseActionsFrame extends JFrame implements MouseListener
{
    final int MAX = 20;
    final int STARTX = 10;
    final int STARTY = 20;
    int x, y;
    String message[] = new String[MAX];
    int msgCount = 0;

    public JMouseActionsFrame()
    {
        setTitle("Mouse Actions");
        setDefaultCloseOperation(JFrame.EXIT_ON_CLOSE);
        addMouseListener(this);
    }

    public void mouseClicked(MouseEvent e)
    {
        int whichButton = e.getButton();
        String msg;
        if(msgCount == MAX)
            clearScreen();
        message[msgCount] = "You pressed the mouse.";
        if(whichButton == MouseEvent.BUTTON1)
            msg = "button 1.";
        else if(whichButton == MouseEvent.BUTTON2)
            msg = "button 2.";
        else msg = "button 3.";
        message[msgCount] = message[msgCount] +
            " You used " + msg;
        message[msgCount] = message[msgCount] +
            " You are at position " +
        e.getX() + ", " + e.getY() + ".";
        if(e.getClickCount() == 2)
            message[msgCount] = message[msgCount] +
                " You double-clicked";
        else
            message[msgCount] = message[msgCount] +
                " You single-clicked";
        ++msgCount;
        repaint();
    }
```

Figure 14-21 The JMouseActionsFrame application (*continued*)

▶

```
   public void mouseEntered(MouseEvent e)
   {
      if(msgCount == MAX)
         clearScreen();
      message[msgCount] = "You entered the frame";
      ++msgCount;
      repaint();
   }
   public void mouseExited(MouseEvent e)
   {
      if(msgCount == MAX)
         clearScreen();
      message[msgCount] = "You exited the frame";
      ++msgCount;
      repaint();
   }

   public void mousePressed(MouseEvent e)
   {
   }

   public void mouseReleased(MouseEvent e)
   {
   }

   public void paint(Graphics g)
   {
      super.paint(g);
      x = STARTX;
      y = STARTY;
      for(int a = 0; a < msgCount; ++a)
         g.drawString(message[a], x, y += 20);
   }

   public void clearScreen()
   {
      msgCount = 0;
      for(int a = 0; a < MAX; ++a)
         message[a] = " ";
      repaint();
   }
   public static void main(String[] args)
   {
      JMouseActionsFrame mFrame = new JMouseActionsFrame();
      final int WIDTH = 750;
      final int HEIGHT = 500;
      mFrame.setSize(WIDTH, HEIGHT);
      mFrame.setVisible(true);
   }
}
```

Figure 14-21 The JMouseActionsFrame application

The JMouseActionsFrame application in Figure 14-21 displays messages as the user takes mouse actions. In the application, a named constant is declared to hold the maximum number of messages that can appear on-screen at any time. Named constants are also declared for the starting x- and y-coordinate position of the messages. In the first unshaded section of the figure, three fields are declared—integers to hold the mouse position x- and y-coordinates, and an array of 20 Strings to hold messages that inform the user of the mouse actions taken. An integer is declared to count the number of messages displayed so that the capacity of the String array is not exceeded.

In the first shaded section of Figure 14-21, the constructor sets a frame title by passing it to the parent of JMouseActionsFrame, sets a close operation, and enables the frame to listen for mouse events.

In Figure 14-21, most of the action occurs in the mouseClicked() method (the second unshaded area in the figure). The method constructs descriptive messages to place in the array of messages that appear on the screen. The same actions could have been placed in the mousePressed() or mouseReleased() method because the statements could be placed in the frame just as well at either of those times. Within the mouseClicked() method, the getButton() method is used to determine which mouse button the user clicked. If 20 messages have been displayed on the screen, a clearScreen() method is called. Then a String is built in the next available spot in the array; it contains information about the action that generated the method call. The msgCount variable is increased so that the next time the method is called, a message will be stored in the next available array location. The last statement in the method calls repaint(), which calls paint().

>> NOTE
You learned about the repaint() method in Chapter 10.

The MouseEvent generated when the mouseClicked() method executes is named e. The e object is used several times within the method. First, e is used with the getButton() instance method in the first line of the mouseClicked() method; it returns an integer that, later in the method, is compared to the MouseEvent fields, BUTTON1 and BUTTON2, to determine which button message to display. Later, e is used with getX() and getY() so the coordinates at which the user clicks can be displayed. Finally, e is used with getClickCount(), returning the number of clicks generated.

In Figure 14-21, messages are also generated in the mouseEntered() and mouseExited() methods, so the user is notified when the mouse pointer has "entered"—that is, passed over the surface area of—the JFrame, the component that is listening for actions.

Using a loop, the paint() method displays as many messages as have been stored in locations indicated by the x- and y-coordinates. The y-coordinate value is increased by 20 on each pass through the loop, so that subsequent messages appear lower on the frame.

The clearScreen() method, which is called after 20 messages have been generated, sets each String in the array of messages to a blank and repaints the screen with 20 blank lines so a new set of 20 messages can begin.

>> NOTE The first statement within the paint() method in the JMouseActionsFrame class is super.paint(g);. This statement is a call to the paint() method that is part of the parent class (JFrame), and it passes the local Graphics object (named g) in this method. In Chapter 10, you took the same action in JApplets. If you remove this statement, the JFrame surface is not repainted and the surface appears to be transparent, revealing the items that were on your screen before the application started.

The main() method at the end of the class creates one instance of the JMouseActionsFrame class and sets its size and visibility.

Figure 14-22 shows one execution of the JMouseActionsFrame application. At this point, the user has generated several mouse actions. Of course, in your own applications you might not want to only notify users of their mouse actions; instead, you might want to perform calculations, create files, or generate any other programming tasks.

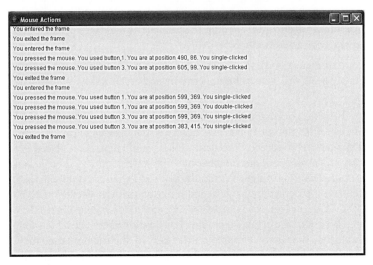

Mouse Actions
You entered the frame
You exited the frame
You entered the frame
You pressed the mouse. You used button,1. You are at position 490, 86. You single-clicked
You pressed the mouse. You used button 3. You are at position 605, 99. You single-clicked
You exited the frame
You entered the frame
You pressed the mouse. You used button 1. You are at position 599, 369. You single-clicked
You pressed the mouse. You used button 1. You are at position 599, 369. You double-clicked
You pressed the mouse. You used button 3. You are at position 599, 369. You single-clicked
You pressed the mouse. You used button 3. You are at position 383, 415. You single-clicked
You exited the frame

Figure 14-22 Typical execution of the JMouseActionsFrame application

YOU DO IT

USING BorderLayout

Using layout managers in your applets and other containers in your applications allows flexibility in arranging the components that users see on the screen. In this section, you will create a JApplet that uses a BorderLayout and place components in each region. In the following sections, you will observe how the same components appear when other layout managers are used.

To create a JApplet that uses BorderLayout with a button in each region:

1. Open a new file in your text editor, and then type the following first few lines of a JApplet that demonstrates BorderLayout with five objects:

```
import javax.swing.*;
import java.awt.*;
public class JBorderLayout extends JApplet
{
```

2. Instantiate five JButton objects, each with a label that is the name of one of the regions used by BorderLayout:

```
private JButton nb = new JButton("North");
private JButton sb = new JButton("South");
private JButton eb = new JButton("East");
private JButton wb = new JButton("West");
private JButton cb = new JButton("Center");
```

3. Write the `init()` method that sets the applet content pane's layout manager and adds each of the five `JButtons` to the appropriate region. Also add the closing curly brace for the class:

```
public void init()
{
    setLayout(new BorderLayout());
    add(nb, BorderLayout.NORTH);
    add(sb, BorderLayout.SOUTH);
    add(eb, BorderLayout.EAST);
    add(wb, BorderLayout.WEST);
    add(cb, BorderLayout.CENTER);
}
}
```

4. Save the file as **JBorderLayout.java** in the Chapter.14 folder on your Student Disk, then compile it using the **javac** command.

5. Open a new file in your text editor, then create the following HTML document to host the `JApplet`:

```
<html>
<object code = "JBorderLayout.class" width = 300
    height = 300>
</object>
</html>
```

6. Save the file as **TestJBorderLayout.html**. Run the applet using **appletviewer TestJBorderLayout.html**. The output looks like Figure 14-23. Each `JButton` entirely

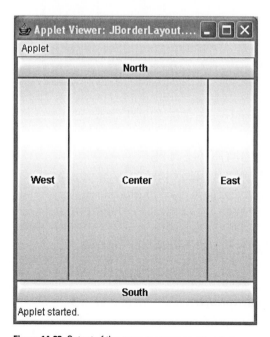

Figure 14-23 Output of the `JBorderLayout` JApplet

fills its region. (If you click the JButtons, they appear to be pressed, but because you have not implemented ActionListener, no other action is taken.)

7. So you can observe the effects of changing the size of the viewing area, use your mouse to drag the right border of the Applet Viewer to increase the width to approximately that shown in Figure 14-24. Notice that the center region expands, while the east and west regions retain their original size.

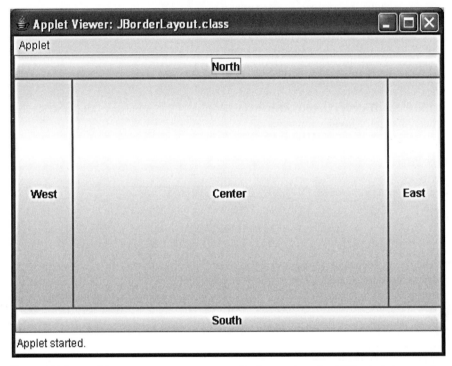

Figure 14-24 Output of the JBorderLayout JApplet after the user drags the right border to increase the width

8. Experiment with resizing both the width and height of the Applet Viewer window. Close the window when you finish.

USING FEWER THAN FIVE COMPONENTS WITH THE BorderLayout MANAGER

When you use JBorderLayout, you are not required to place components in every region. For example, you might use only four components, leaving the north region empty. Next, you will remove one of the objects from the JBorderLayout JApplet to observe the effect.

To create a Container that uses BorderLayout with only four objects:

1. Open the **JBorderLayout.java** file in your text editor. Immediately save it as **JBorderLayoutNoNorth.java**.

2. Change the class name to **JBorderLayoutNoNorth**.

3. Remove the declaration of the "North" button, and within the init() method, remove the statement that adds the "North" button to the content pane.

4. Save the file and compile it.

5. Open the **TestJBorderLayout.html** file in your text editor. Change the class reference to **JBorderLayoutNoNorth.class**, and save the file as **TestJBorderLayoutNoNorth.html**.

6. Run the applet using the **appletviewer** command. The output appears as shown in Figure 14-25. The center region occupies the space formerly held by the north region.

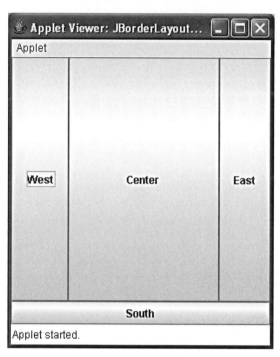

Figure 14-25 Output of the `JBorderLayoutNoNorth` JApplet

7. Experiment with removing some of the other components from the `JBorderLayoutNoNorth` JApplet. Create an HTML host document for your new class and execute it, observing the results.

USING FlowLayout

Next, you will modify the `JBorderLayout` JApplet to demonstrate how the same components appear when using `FlowLayout`.

To demonstrate `FlowLayout`:

1. Open the **JBorderLayout.java** file in your text editor, and immediately save it as **JFlowLayoutRight.java**.

2. Change the class name from `JBorderLayout` to **JFlowLayoutRight**.

3. Within the `init()` method, change the `setLayout()` statement to use `FlowLayout` and right alignment:

```
setLayout(new FlowLayout(FlowLayout.RIGHT));
```

4. Alter each of the five `add()` statements so that just the button name appears within the parentheses and the region is omitted. For example, `add(nb, BorderLayout.NORTH);` becomes the following:

```
add(nb);
```

5. Save the file and compile it using the **javac** command.

6. Open a new text file and create the following HTML document to host the `JApplet`:

```
<html>
<object code = "JFlowLayoutRight.class" width = 300
    height = 300>
</object>
</html>
```

7. Save the HTML document as **TestJFlowLayoutRight.html** in the Chapter.14 folder on your Student Disk, then run the applet using the **appletviewer** command. Your output should look like Figure 14-26. The components have their "natural" size (or preferred size)— the minimum size the buttons need to display their labels. The buttons flow across the applet surface in a row until no more can fit; in Figure 14-26, the last button added cannot fit in the first row, so it appears in the second row, right-aligned.

8. Experiment with widening and narrowing the Applet Viewer window, and observe how the components realign.

9. Close the Applet Viewer window.

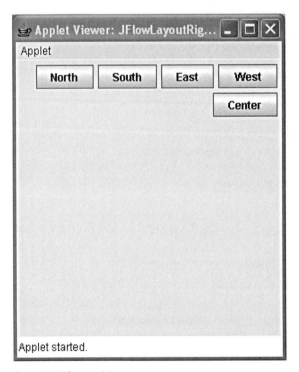

Figure 14-26 Output of the `JFlowLayoutRight` JApplet

USING GridLayout

Next, you will modify a JApplet to demonstrate GridLayout.

To demonstrate GridLayout:

1. Open the **JFlowLayoutRight.java** file in your text editor and save the file as **JGridLayout.java**.

2. Change the class name from JFlowLayoutRight to **JGridLayout**.

   Within the init() method, change the setLayout() statement to establish a GridLayout with two rows, three columns, a horizontal space of two pixels, and a vertical space of four pixels:

   ```
   setLayout(new GridLayout(2, 3, 2, 4));
   ```

3. Save the file and compile it using the **javac** command.

4. Open the **TestJFlowLayoutRight.html** file in your text editor, change the class reference to **JGridLayout.class**, and then save the file as **TestJGridLayout.html** in the Chapter.14 folder on your Student Disk.

5. Use the **appletviewer** command to run the applet, then compare your output to Figure 14-27. The components are arranged in two rows and three columns from left to right across each row, in the order they were added to their container. Because there are only five components, one grid position is still available.

6. Close the Applet Viewer window.

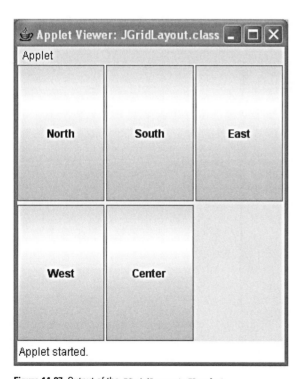

Figure 14-27 Output of the JGridLayout JApplet

USING CardLayout

Next, you will create a CardLayout with five cards, each holding one of the JButtons used in the previous examples.

To demonstrate CardLayout:

1. Open the **JGridLayout.java** file in your text editor and save the file as **JCardLayout.java**.

2. Change the class name from JGridLayout to **JCardLayout**.

3. Within the init() method, change the setLayout() statement to establish a CardLayout:

   setLayout(new CardLayout());

4. Change the five add() statements that add the buttons to the content pane so that each includes a String that names the added component, as follows:

   ```
   add("north", nb);
   add("south", sb);
   add("east", eb);
   add("west", wb);
   add("center", cb);
   ```

5. Save the file, then compile it using the **javac** command.

6. Open the **TestJGridLayout.html** file in your text editor, change the class reference to **JCardLayout.class**, and then save the file as **TestJCardLayout.html** in the Chapter.14 folder on your Student Disk.

7. Use the **appletviewer** command to run the applet; your output should look like Figure 14-28. You see only the "North" JButton because, as the first one added, it is the top card.

Figure 14-28 Output of the JCardLayout JApplet

You can click the button, but no actions take place because you have not implemented `ActionListener`.

8. Close the Applet Viewer window.

VIEWING ALL THE CARDS IN CardLayout

Next, you will modify the `JCardLayout` `JApplet` so that its buttons can initiate events that allow you to view all five `JButtons` you add to the content pane.

To view all the cards in `CardLayout`:

1. Open the **JCardLayout.java** file in your text editor and save the file as **JCardLayout2.java**.

2. Change the class name from `JCardLayout` to **JCardLayout2**.

3. At the top of the file, add the `import` statement that adds the classes and methods that allow the applet to respond to events:

   ```
   import java.awt.event.*;
   ```

4. At the end of the class header, insert the following phrase so the `JApplet` can respond to button clicks:

   ```
   implements ActionListener
   ```

5. Instead of an anonymous layout manager, you need to create a `CardLayout` manager with an identifier that you can use with the `next()` method when the user clicks a button. Immediately after the five `JButton` declaration statements, insert the following statement:

   ```
   CardLayout cardLayout = new CardLayout();
   ```

6. Within the `init()` method, change the `setLayout()` statement so it uses the named layout manager:

   ```
   setLayout(cardLayout);
   ```

7. At the end of the `init()` method, add five statements that allow each of the buttons to initiate an `ActionEvent`:

   ```
   nb.addActionListener(this);
   sb.addActionListener(this);
   eb.addActionListener(this);
   wb.addActionListener(this);
   cb.addActionListener(this);
   ```

8. Just before the closing curly brace for the class, add an `actionPerformed()` method that responds to user clicks. The method uses the `next()` method to display the next card (next button) in the collection.

   ```
   public void actionPerformed(ActionEvent e)
   {
       cardLayout.next(getContentPane());
   }
   ```

9. Save the file and compile it using the **javac** command.

10. Open the **TestJCardLayout.html** file in your text editor, change the class reference to **JCardLayout2.class**, and then save the file as **TestJCardLayout2.html** in the Chapter.14 folder on your Student Disk.

11. Use the **appletviewer** command to run the applet. Your output looks the same as in Figure 14-28—you see only the "North" JButton. However, when you click it, the button changes to "South", "East", "West", and "Center" in succession. Close the Applet Viewer window when you finish.

USING JPanels TO ACHIEVE COMPLEX LAYOUTS

Next, you will create a JApplet for Event Handlers Incorporated that uses a layout manager and contains a JPanel that uses a different layout manager. To begin, you create one JPanel named wp (for "western panel") and place it in the west region of an applet that uses BorderLayout. The wp JPanel holds JButtons indicating the states in which Event Handlers Incorporated does business. Using GridLayout, you will place three JButtons and a JLabel in this JPanel. When the user clicks a JButton representing a state, the applet displays the locations of Event Handlers offices in that state.

To create the JWesternPanel JApplet:

1. Open a new file in your text editor and enter the following first few lines of the JWesternPanel class. The JWesternPanel class extends JApplet and implements ActionListener because the JPanel contains clickable JButtons.

```
import javax.swing.*;
import java.awt.*;
import java.awt.event.*;
public class JWesternPanel extends JApplet
   implements ActionListener
{
```

2. Create three JButtons that, when clicked, display location information about Wyoming, Colorado, and Nevada. Add a label indicating that location information will display.

```
JButton wyButton = new JButton("Wyoming");
JButton coButton = new JButton("Colorado");
JButton nvButton = new JButton("Nevada");
JLabel infoLabel = new JLabel(" Location Info ");
```

3. Next, add a panel that uses a GridLayout of two rows high by two columns wide, with gaps of two pixels.

```
JPanel wp = new JPanel(new GridLayout(2, 2, 2, 2));
```

4. In the init() method for the JApplet, set the applet's container to use BorderLayout. Add the Wyoming, Colorado, and Nevada buttons to the western panel, wp, and apply the addActionListener() message to each one so that the JApplet can respond to click events.

```
public void init()
{
   setLayout(new BorderLayout());
   wp.add(wyButton);
   wyButton.addActionListener(this);
   wp.add(coButton);
```

```
coButton.addActionListener(this);
wp.add(nvButton);
nvButton.addActionListener(this);
wp.add(infoLabel);
```

5. Continue the `init()` method by declaring four buttons to be used as placeholders in the remaining four regions of the `JApplet`. These buttons will not be made "live"—that is, no actions are associated with them. They simply hold the unused regions of the `JApplet` for you. Add each button to a region of the `JApplet` and then type the closing curly brace for the `init()` method.

```
JButton nb = new JButton("North Region");
JButton sb = new JButton("South Region");
JButton eb = new JButton("East Region");
JButton cb = new JButton("Center Region");
add(nb,BorderLayout.NORTH);
add(sb,BorderLayout.SOUTH);
add(eb,BorderLayout.EAST);
add(wp,BorderLayout.WEST);
add(cb,BorderLayout.CENTER);
}
```

6. Create an `actionPerformed()` method that accepts an `ActionEvent` and uses the `getSource()` method with it to determine whether the action was initiated by the user clicking the Wyoming, Colorado, or Nevada button. Depending on the button, display different city names indicating Event Handlers Incorporated office locations. Finally, include the closing brace for the class.

```
public void actionPerformed(ActionEvent e)
{
    Object source = e.getSource();
    if (source == wyButton)
        infoLabel.setText("Cody");
    else
        if (source == coButton)
            infoLabel.setText("Denver    Aspen");
        else
            infoLabel.setText("Las Vegas    Reno");
}
}
```

7. Save the file as **JWesternPanel.java** in the Chapter.14 folder on your Student Disk, and compile the file using the **javac** command.

8. Open a new text file and create the following HTML document to host the `JApplet`:

```
<html>
<object code = "JWesternPanel.class" width = 400
    height = 300>
</object>
</html>
```

9. Save the HTML document as **TestJWesternPanel.html** in the Chapter.14 folder on your Student Disk, then run the `JApplet` using the **appletviewer** command. Your

output should look like Figure 14-29. The applet shows five regions, with the north, south, east, and center regions containing large buttons. The west region is complex; it is a panel with `GridLayout` containing three buttons and a label.

10. Click one of the buttons in the panel in the west region of the `JApplet`. For example, Figure 14-30 shows the `JApplet` after the user clicks the Colorado button; the information label shows Colorado cities.

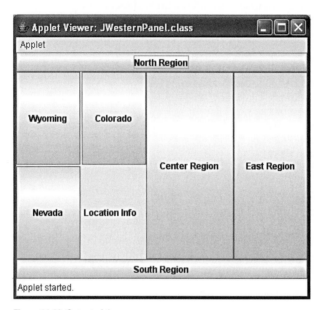

Figure 14-29 Output of the `JWesternPanel JApplet`

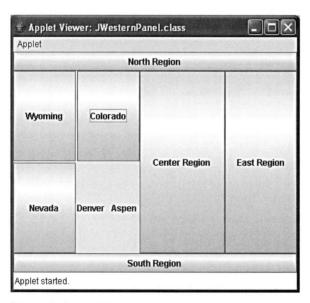

Figure 14-30 Output of the `JWesternPanel JApplet` after the user clicks the Colorado button

11. Click the **North**, **South**, **Center**, and **East** JButtons. Nothing happens because you have not activated these JButtons.

12. Close the Applet Viewer window.

13. Open the JWesternPanel JApplet and resave it as **JRegionalPanels.java**. Change the class name and modify the JApplet so that at least one other region contains a JPanel that contains at least two buttons representing states, and so that when the user clicks a button, you display city information for those states. For example, you might create a JPanel to display in the north region of the JApplet and include buttons for North Dakota and Minnesota in the JPanel that is shown there.

IMPLEMENTING KeyListener

Next, you will create a JPanel for Event Handlers Incorporated that allows the user to select a midwestern state by entering a number from the keyboard. The JPanel implements KeyListener so that it can respond to user-initiated keyboard events. Recall that you use the KeyListener interface when you are interested in actions the user initiates from the keyboard. The KeyListener interface contains three methods—keyPressed(), keyTyped(), and keyReleased().

To create a class that implements KeyListener:

1. Open a new file in your text editor and enter the following first few lines for the JMidwestPanel class that implements KeyListener:

```
import javax.swing.*;
import java.awt.*;
import java.awt.event.*;
public class JMidwestPanel extends JPanel implements
    KeyListener
{
```

2. Create three labels. One provides instruction ("Select a state:"), another provides a list of states from which to choose, and a third is empty. The cities in which Event Handlers maintains an office in the selected state appear in this third label.

```
JLabel label1 = new JLabel("Select a state:");
JLabel label2 = new
        JLabel("(1) Illinois (2) Kansas (3) Iowa");
JLabel offices = new JLabel("");
```

3. In the JMidwestPanel constructor, set the layout to FlowLayout, add the labels to the panel, and prepare the panel to respond to keystrokes with the addKeyListener() method.

```
public JMidwestPanel()
{
    setLayout(new FlowLayout());
    add(label1);
    add(label2);
    add(offices);
    addKeyListener(this);
}
```

4. The following `keyTyped()` method is one of the three abstract methods contained in `KeyListener`. When the user presses a key, this method determines the key pressed and sets the text of the `offices` label to a list of cities in the selected state.

```
public void keyTyped(KeyEvent e)
{
    char c = e.getKeyChar();
    if(c == '1')
        offices.setText("Illinois: Chicago, Rockford, Springfield");
    else
        if(c == '2')
            offices.setText("Kansas: Topeka, Wichita");
        else
            offices.setText("Iowa: Iowa City, Des Moines");
}
```

5. Because `KeyListener` contains `keyPressed()` and `keyReleased()` methods, you are required to implement them, even if you leave their bodies without statements. Add them as follows, and add the closing curly brace for the class.

```
    public void keyPressed(KeyEvent e)
    {
    }
    public void keyReleased(KeyEvent e)
    {
    }
}
```

6. Save the file as **JMidwestPanel.java** in the Chapter.14 folder on your Student Disk. Compile the file using the **javac** command.

7. Next, write the following application, which instantiates a JFrame that can hold the JMidwestPanel. The application allows the frame to listen for key events generated on the JMidwestPanel object, adds the panel to the frame, sets the close operation, and sets the size and visibility of the JFrame.

```
import javax.swing.*;
import java.awt.*;
public class TestPanel
{
    public static void main(String[] args)
    {
        JFrame frame = new JFrame();
        JMidwestPanel midwestPanel =
            new JMidwestPanel();
        final int WIDTH = 250;
        final int HEIGHT = 140;
        frame.addKeyListener(midwestPanel);
        frame.add(midwestPanel);
        frame.setDefaultCloseOperation(JFrame.EXIT_ON_CLOSE);
        frame.setSize(WIDTH, HEIGHT);
        frame.setVisible(true);
    }
}
```

8. Save the application as **TestPanel.java** in the Chapter.14 folder on your Student Disk. Compile and execute the application. The output looks like the left screen in Figure 14-31. Press a number key on the keyboard. For example, when the user presses 2, the output looks like the screen on the right side of the figure—the appropriate label listing cities has been added to the JPanel surface.

9. Make as many keyboard selections as you want and observe how the label containing the city list changes. When you are done, click the **Close** button on the JFrame.

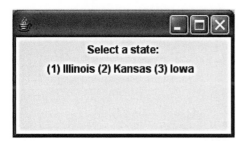
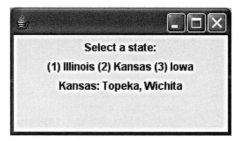

Figure 14-31 Output of the TestPanel application before the user presses any key, and after the user presses 2

USING THE getSource() METHOD TO DETERMINE AN EVENT

Next, you will use an EventObject method with an ActionEvent. You can accomplish this because every ActionEvent is a descendant of EventObject. Therefore, when you create a Component with several JButton objects, you can use EventObject's getSource() method to determine the source of the ActionEvent.

To write a class that uses the EventObject getSource() method with an ActionEvent:

1. Open a new file in your text editor, then type the following first few lines of the JButtonFrame class that implements the ActionListener interface to respond to JButton clicks:

```
import javax.swing.*;
import java.awt.*;
import java.awt.event.*;
public class JButtonFrame extends JFrame
   implements ActionListener
{
```

2. Create the following three JButtons from which the user can choose to change the JFrame's background color. Create a Container to hold the JFrame components.

```
JButton redButton = new JButton("Red");
JButton blueButton = new JButton("Blue");
JButton greenButton = new JButton("Green");
Container con = getContentPane();
```

>> **NOTE** In this application, you need to get the content pane reference explicitly. Although the add() operation would work with an implicitly retrieved JFrame content pane object, the methods that set the background and foreground colors would not.

3. Write the `JButtonFrame` constructor. Set a title for the `JFrame`. Set the default close operation and set the layout manager to `FlowLayout`. Then add the three `JButtons` to the container and set the foreground and background colors for the container. Finally, register the `JButtonFrame` as an `ActionListener` for each of the three `JButton` objects, and then close the constructor method.

>> NOTE
Earlier in this chapter, you learned that the default layout for a `JFrame` is `BorderLayout`.

```
public JButtonFrame()
{
    setTitle("JButtonFrame");
    setDefaultCloseOperation(JFrame.EXIT_ON_CLOSE);
    con.setLayout(new FlowLayout());
    con.add(redButton);
    con.add(blueButton);
    con.add(greenButton);
    con.setBackground(Color.WHITE);
    con.setForeground(Color.BLACK);
    redButton.addActionListener(this);
    blueButton.addActionListener(this);
    greenButton.addActionListener(this);
}
```

4. Add the following `main()` method that creates a new `JButtonFrame` named `bFrame`, declares size constants, sizes the frame using the `setSize()` method, and sets its visible property to `true`.

```
public static void main(String[] args)
{
    JButtonFrame bFrame = new JButtonFrame();
    final int WIDTH = 350;
    final int HEIGHT = 250;
    bFrame.setSize(WIDTH, HEIGHT);
    bFrame.setVisible(true);
}
```

5. Because `JButtonFrame` implements `ActionListener`, you are required to write code for `ActionListener`'s only method, `actionPerformed()`. The `actionPerformed()` method provides you with an `ActionEvent` object with which you can use the `EventObject` method named `getSource()` to return the source of the event as an `Object` class instance. Using the `if...else` structure allows you to compare the source `Object` with possible event sources and take the appropriate action. Remember to add the closing curly braces for the method and class.

```
public void actionPerformed(ActionEvent e)
{
    Object source = e.getSource();
    if(source == redButton)
        con.setBackground(Color.RED);
    else if (source == blueButton)
        con.setBackground(Color.BLUE);
    else if (source == greenButton)
        con.setBackground(Color.GREEN);
}
}
```

6. Save the file as **JButtonFrame.java** in the Chapter.14 folder on your Student Disk. Compile the file using the **javac** command, then run the application using the **java JButtonFrame** command. Click any of the three JButtons and note the change in the JFrame's background color. Note that the JFrame listens for action on each of the JButtons, and the single actionPerformed() method executes no matter which JButton is clicked. You achieve different background colors in the JFrame because you use the ObjectEvent method getSource() with the ActionEvent generated by each button click. The output of the application after the user clicks the Blue button is shown in Figure 14-32.

7. Close the frame.

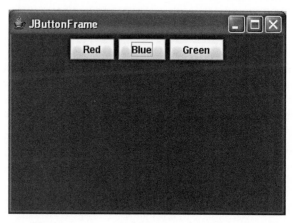

Figure 14-32 The JButtonFrame application after the user clicks the Blue button

USING MouseEvents

The MouseListener class provides you with many interesting, interactive methods. To illustrate, you will create a JMouseFrame class that employs some of these methods. In addition, you will use three MouseEvent methods—getX() and getY(), which return the mouse coordinates, and getButton(), which returns a value that indicates which mouse button was clicked to generate an event. The application will allow you to draw large or small circles on a frame at the point where you click with the left or right mouse button.

To write the JMouseFrame class:

1. Open a new file in your text editor and type the following first few lines of the JMouseFrame class:

```
import javax.swing.*;
import java.awt.*;
import java.awt.event.*;
public class JMouseFrame extends JFrame
    implements MouseListener
{
```

2. Create the following Container and three integer variables. Two hold the x- and y-positions of the mouse; the third holds the size of an oval you draw when the mouse is clicked. Also include constants that hold sizes for large and small circles.

```
Container con = getContentPane();
int x, y;
```

```
int size;
final int LARGE = 10;
final int SMALL = 4;
```

3. Enter the following JMouseFrame constructor, which sets the title, sets the close operation, and adds the MouseListener:

```
public JMouseFrame()
{
    setTitle("Mouse Frame");
    setDefaultCloseOperation(JFrame.EXIT_ON_CLOSE);
    con.addMouseListener(this);
}
```

4. Enter the following mouseClicked() method to get the x- and y-coordinates from the MouseEvent that initiates the method call. The x and y variables hold the exact position of the mouse location at the time of the event. If the user clicks the left mouse button, set the size variable to the larger size (10) to draw a larger oval; if the user clicks the right mouse button, set the size variable to the smaller size (4) to draw a small oval. Then, the mouseClicked() method calls repaint().

```
public void mouseClicked(MouseEvent e)
{
    x = e.getX();
    y = e.getY();
    if(e.getButton() == MouseEvent.BUTTON1)
        size = LARGE;
    else size = SMALL;
    repaint();
}
```

5. Enter the following code to change the JFrame background color to yellow when the user positions the mouse pointer over the JFrame, and then change the background to black when the user places the mouse pointer somewhere else on the screen:

```
public void mouseEntered(MouseEvent e)
{
    con.setBackground(Color.YELLOW);
}
public void mouseExited(MouseEvent e)
{
    con.setBackground(Color.BLACK);
}
```

6. You don't need any special code for the mousePressed() or mouseReleased() methods, but you must provide the methods because the abstract interface MouseListener contains them:

```
public void mousePressed(MouseEvent e)
{
}
public void mouseReleased(MouseEvent e)
{
}
```

7. Recall from Chapter 10 that when you call `paint()`, you should call `JMouseFrame`'s parent's `paint()` method. You will execute this application first with the call to the `super.paint()` method commented out, and then with the statement executing. Recall that the `Graphics` method `drawOval()` requires four arguments. Envision a rectangle surrounding an oval, and provide arguments for the x- and y-coordinates of the upper-left corner and the width and height of the rectangle. The `mouseClicked()` method sets the size to either 4 or 10, depending on the mouse button the user clicks. Then, `mouseClicked()` calls `repaint()`, which calls the following `paint()` method. To draw an oval that appears as a circle with a diameter of either 8 or 20 pixels, use `x - size` and `y - size` for the upper-left corner of the rectangle, and use `size * 2` for the width and the height. For example, when the user clicks at location 10, 20 and the size is 4, the circle is drawn in a square that extends from coordinates 6, 16 to 14, 24.

```
public void paint(Graphics g)
{
    // super.paint(g);
    g.drawOval(x - size, y - size, size * 2, size * 2);
}
```

8. Add the following `main()` method that creates a new `JMouseFrame` named `mFrame`, declares size constants, sizes the frame using the `setSize()` method, and sets its visible property to `true`. Add the closing curly brace for the class.

```
public static void main(String[] args)
{
    JMouseFrame mFrame = new JMouseFrame();
    final int WIDTH = 250;
    final int HEIGHT = 150;
    mFrame.setSize(WIDTH, HEIGHT);
    mFrame.setVisible(true);
}
}
```

9. Save the file as **JMouseFrame.java** in the Chapter.14 folder on your Student Disk. Compile the file, then run the application using the **java JMouseFrame** command. When the `JFrame` appears on your screen, roll the mouse pointer over the `JFrame` surface so it turns yellow. When you roll the mouse pointer off the `JFrame` surface, it turns black. When you roll the mouse pointer over the `JFrame` surface and right-click, the surface turns yellow and a small circle appears above the mouse position. When you click in a new position with the left mouse button, a larger circle appears. Figure 14-33 shows the output after the user has clicked several times with each mouse button, but before the user has rolled the mouse pointer off the frame surface.

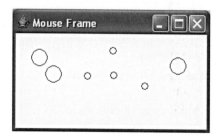

Figure 14-33 Output of the `JMouseFrame` application after the user has clicked several times with each mouse button

10. When you roll the mouse pointer off the JMouseFrame, the surface turns black, appearing to erase the ovals you have created. Roll the mouse pointer back over the JMouseFrame and the surface turns yellow, ready for you to click for more ovals. Close the JFrame when you finish.

11. Remove the two comment slashes (//) from in front of the call to super.paint(). Save the application (as **JMouseFrame.java**) and recompile the program. Execute the program again. When you click the frame's surface, a circle appears, but this time, when you click again, the first circle disappears and only the new circle is visible. Because the frame is repainted with each action, only the most recent drawing appears. Depending on the results you want in your final product, you might choose to keep or remove the superclass paint() method.

KEY TERMS

A **layout manager** is an object that controls the size and position (that is, the layout) of components inside a Container object.

The **BorderLayout manager** is the default manager class for all content panes. You can use the BorderLayout class with any container that has five or fewer components. When you use the BorderLayout manager, the components fill the screen in five regions: north, south, east, west, and center.

Java's **static import feature** allows you to add a statement at the top of a class file so that you can use a static constant without the class name.

A **containment hierarchy** is a tree of components that has a top-level container as its root.

The **FlowLayout manager** arranges components in rows across the width of a Container. FlowLayout is the default layout manager for every JPanel.

A Component's **preferred size** is its default size.

The **GridLayout manager** arranges components into equal rows and columns.

The **CardLayout manager** generates a stack of containers or components, one on top of another. You use a CardLayout when you want multiple components to share the same display space.

The **GridBagLayout manager** allows you to add Components to precise locations within the grid, as well as to indicate that specific Components should span multiple rows or columns within the grid.

The **BoxLayout manager** allows multiple components to be laid out either vertically or horizontally. The components do not wrap, so a vertical arrangement of components, for example, stays vertically arranged when the frame is resized.

Double buffering, which is the default buffering strategy for JPanel objects, is the strategy in which you specify that additional memory space be used to draw a component offscreen when it is updated.

The **primary surface** is the visible screen surface when double buffering.

The **back buffer** is the offscreen image used for double buffering.

Block line transfer, or blitting, is the act of copying the contents from one surface to another when double buffering.

Events are Objects that the user initiates, such as key presses and mouse clicks.

Event handlers are interface methods that are called automatically when an appropriate event occurs.

An **adapter class** implements all the methods in an interface, providing an empty body for each method.

You use the **KeyListener interface** when you are interested in actions the user initiates from the keyboard.

Action keys are keyboard keys that do not generate a character, such as function keys.

Virtual key codes are constants that represent keyboard keys.

The **MouseMotionListener interface** provides you with methods named mouseDragged() and mouseMoved() that detect the mouse pointer being rolled or dragged across a component surface.

The **MouseListener interface** provides you with methods named mousePressed(), mouseClicked(), mouseReleased(), mouseEntered(), and mouseExited().

The **MouseInputListener interface** implements all the methods in both the MouseListener and MouseMotionListener interfaces.

A **MouseEvent** is the type of event generated by mouse manipulation.

CHAPTER SUMMARY

» A layout manager is an object that controls the size and position (that is, the layout) of components inside a Container object. Each layout manager defines methods that arrange components within a Container, and each component you place within a Container can also be a Container itself, so you can assign layout managers within layout managers.

» The BorderLayout manager is the default manager class for all content panes. You can use the BorderLayout class with any container that has five or fewer components. When you use the BorderLayout manager, the components fill the screen in five regions: north, south, east, west, and center.

» You can use the FlowLayout manager class to arrange components in rows across the width of a Container. When you use BorderLayout, the Components you add fill their regions—that is, each Component expands or contracts based on its region's size. However, when you use FlowLayout, each Component retains its default size; for example, a JButton is large enough to hold its text.

» You can use the GridLayout manager class to arrange components into equal rows and columns. As you add new Components to a GridLayout, they are positioned from left to right across each row, in sequence.

» The CardLayout manager generates a stack of containers or components, one on top of another. You use a CardLayout when you want multiple components to share the same display space. In a program that has a CardLayout manager, a change of cards is usually triggered by a user's action.

» The GridBagLayout manager allows you to add Components to precise locations within the grid and to indicate that specific Components should span multiple rows or columns within the grid. Another layout manager option is the BoxLayout manager, which allows multiple components to be laid out either vertically or horizontally. The components do not wrap, so a vertical arrangement of components, for example, stays vertically arranged when the frame is resized.

» A JPanel is a surface on which you can place components. A JPanel is also a container, which means it can contain other components. By using JPanels within other JPanels, you can create an infinite variety of screen layouts.

» Events are Objects that the user initiates, such as key presses and mouse clicks. The parent class for all event objects is named EventObject, which descends from the Object class. EventObject is the parent of AWTEvent, which in turn is the parent of specific event classes such as ActionEvent and ComponentEvent.

» When you want to listen for an event, you can implement an appropriate interface for your class, such as ActionListener or WindowListener. The class becomes an event listener. For every event class named <name>Event, there is a listener that is similarly named <name>Listener. Every <name>Listener interface method has the return type void, and each takes one argument—an object that is an instance of the corresponding <name>Event class.

» Interface methods that are automatically called when an appropriate event occurs are called event handlers.

» The KeyListener interface contains three methods: keyPressed(), keyTyped(), and keyReleased().

» The MouseListener interface provides you with methods named mousePressed(), mouseClicked(), and mouseReleased(). The additional interface methods mouseEntered() and mouseExited() inform you when the user positions the mouse over a component (entered) or moves the mouse off a component (exited). A MouseEvent is the type of event generated by mouse manipulation.

REVIEW QUESTIONS

1. If you add fewer than five components to a BorderLayout, _____ .

   a. any empty component regions disappear

   b. the remaining components expand to fill the available space

   c. both a and b

   d. none of the above

2. When you resize a Container that uses BorderLayout, _____ .

   a. the Container and the regions both change in size

   b. the Container changes in size, but the regions retain their original sizes

   c. the Container retains its size, but the regions change or might disappear

   d. nothing happens

3. When you create a JFrame named myFrame, you can set its layout manager to BorderLayout with the statement _____ .

   a. myFrame.setLayout = new BorderLayout();

   b. myFrame.setLayout(new BorderLayout());

   c. setLayout(myFrame = new BorderLayout());

   d. setLayout(BorderLayout(myFrame));

4. Which is the correct syntax for adding a `JButton` named b1 to a `Container` named con when using `CardLayout`?

a. `con.add(b1);`

b. `con.add("b1");`

c. `con.add("Options", b1);`

d. none of the above

5. You can use the _____ class to arrange components in a single row or column of a container.

a. `FlowLayout`   c. `CardLayout`

b. `BorderLayout`   d. `BoxLayout`

6. When you use _____, the components you add fill their region; they do not retain their default size.

a. `FlowLayout`   c. `FixedLayout`

b. `BorderLayout`   d. `RegionLayout`

7. The statement _____ ensures that components are placed from left to right across a `JApplet` surface until the first row is full, at which point a second row is started at the applet surface's left edge.

a. `setLayout(FlowLayout.LEFT);`

b. `setLayout(new FlowLayout(LEFT));`

c. `setLayout(new FlowLayout(FlowLayout.LEFT));`

d. `setLayout(FlowLayout(FlowLayout.LEFT));`

8. The `GridBagLayout` class allows you to _____ .

a. add components to precise locations within the grid

b. indicate that specific components should span multiple rows or columns within the grid

c. both a and b

d. none of the above

9. The statement `setLayout(new GridLayout(2,7));` establishes a `GridLayout` with _____ horizontal row(s).

a. zero   c. two

b. one   d. seven

10. As you add new components to a `GridLayout`, _____ .

a. they are positioned left-to-right across each row in sequence

b. you can specify exact positions by skipping some positions

c. both of the above

d. none of the above

11. A `JPanel` is a _____ .

    a. `Window`

    b. `Container`

    c. both of the above

    d. none of the above

12. The _____ class allows you to arrange components as if they are stacked like index or playing cards.

    a. `GameLayout`

    b. `CardLayout`

    c. `BoxLayout`

    d. `GridBagLayout`

13. `AWTEvent` is the child class of _____ .

    a. `EventObject`

    b. `Event`

    c. `ComponentEvent`

    d. `ItemEvent`

14. When a user clicks a `JPanel` or `JFrame`, the action generates a(n) _____ .

    a. `ActionEvent`

    b. `MouseEvent`

    c. `PanelEvent`

    d. `KeyboardEvent`

15. Event handlers are _____ .

    a. abstract classes

    b. concrete classes

    c. listeners

    d. methods

16. The return type of `getComponent()` is _____ .

    a. `Object`

    b. `Component`

    c. `int`

    d. `void`

17. The `KeyEvent` method `getKeyChar()` returns a(n) _____ .

    a. `int`

    b. `char`

    c. `KeyEvent`

    d. `AWTEvent`

18. The `MouseEvent` method that allows you to identify double-clicks is _____ .

    a. `getDouble()`

    b. `isClickDouble()`

    c. `getDoubleClick()`

    d. `getClickCount()`

19. You can use the _____ method to determine the `Object` in which an `ActionEvent` originates.

    a. `getObject()`

    b. `getEvent()`

    c. `getOrigin()`

    d. `getSource()`

20. The `mousePressed()` method is originally defined in the _____ .

    a. `MouseListener` interface

    b. `MouseEvent` event

    c. `MouseObject` object

    d. `AWTEvent` class

EXERCISES

1. Create a `JFrame` and set the layout to `BorderLayout`. Place a `JButton` containing the name of a politician in each region (left, center, and right, or west, center, and east). Each politician's physical position should correspond to your opinion of his political stance. Save the file as **JPoliticalFrame.java**.

2. Create 26 `JButtons`, each labeled with a single, different letter of the alphabet. Create a `JApplet` to hold five `JPanels` in a five-by-one grid. Place six `JButtons` within each of the first four `JPanels` and two `JButtons` within the fifth `JPanel` of the applet. Add a `JLabel` to the fifth `JPanel`. When the user clicks a `JButton`, the text of the `JLabel` is set to "Folder X", where X is the letter of the alphabet that is clicked. Save the file as **JFileCabinet.java**. Also, create an HTML document named **TestJFileCabinet.html** to host the applet.

3. Create a `JFrame` that holds four buttons with the names of four different fonts. Draw any `String` using the font that the user selects. Save the file as **JFontFrame.java**.

4. Create a `JFrame` that uses `BorderLayout`. Place a `JButton` in the center region. Each time the user clicks the `JButton`, change the background color in one of the other regions. Save the file as **JColorFrame.java**.

5. Create a `JFrame` with `JPanels`, a `JButton`, and a `JLabel`. When the user clicks the `JButton`, reposition the `JLabel` to a new location in a different `JPanel`. Save the file as **JMovingFrame.java**.

6. Create a class named `JPanelOptions` that extends `JPanel` and whose constructor accepts two colors and a `String`. Use the colors for background and foreground to display the `String`. Create an application named `JTeamColors` with `GridLayout`. Display four `JPanelOptions` `JPanels` to display the names (in their team colors) of four of your favorite sports teams. Save the files as **JPanelOptions.java** and **JTeamColors.java**.

7. Write an application that lets you determine the integer value returned by the `InputEvent` method `getModifiers()` when you click your left, right, or (if you have one) middle mouse button on a `JFrame`. Save the file as **JLeftOrRight.java**.

8. Write a `JApplet` that displays car maintenance services, such as oil changes and tune-ups. Allow the user to select any number of services. If the user clicks the right mouse button, display a message that the user wants service ASAP. Display a list of the user's

choices so that unselected choices appear dim (use a light color) and selected choices appear dark. Save the `JApplet` file as **JMaintenance.java** and save a host HTML file as **TestJMaintenance.html**.

9. Write a `JApplet` that uses a `JPanel` to show the messages "Mouse Entered" and "Mouse Exited" when the mouse enters and exits the applet. Also, when the mouse is clicked on the applet, a message "Mouse Clicked Here" should appear near the clicked location. Save the file as **JMouse.java** and save its host file as **TestJMouse.html**.

DEBUGGING EXERCISES

Each of the following files in the Chapter.14 folder on your Student Disk has syntax and/or logic errors. In each case, determine the problem and fix the program. After you correct the errors, save each file using the same filename preceded with Fix. For example, DebugFourteen1.java will become FixDebugFourteen1.java. DebugFourteen2 is a `JApplet`. You can use the file TestFixDebugFourteen2.html on your Student Disk to test this applet.

    a. DebugFourteen1.java

    b. DebugFourteen2.java

    c. DebugFourteen3.java

    d. DebugFourteen4.java

CASE PROJECT

COMPUTING PROFESSIONALS' ORGANIZATION

The Computing Professionals' Organization wants you to create a `JApplet` that allows a user to select a type of hardware (for example, a mainframe computer), a programming language (for example, Java), and an application (for example, word processing) with which the user is most familiar so the organization can keep track of its members' talents. Provide the user with at least three options in each category and display the user's selections. Save the `JApplet` as **JExperience.java** and save a host document as **TestJExperience.html** in the Chapter.14 folder on your Student Disk.

GAME ZONE

Now that you can position components accurately in a frame and handle mouse-generated events, you can create many interesting games. You or your instructor might prefer to wait until you work through Chapter 15 to create some of the following games.

1. Use the `CardLayout` class to write a `JApplet` that displays a series of cards that make a royal flush in hearts (Ace, King, Queen, Jack, and 10). Save the file as **JRoyalFlush.java** in the Chapter.14 folder on your Student Disk. Also, create an HTML document named **TestJRoyalFlush.html** to host the applet.

2. a. Create a `MineField` game in which the user attempts to click 10 panels of a grid before hitting the "bomb." Set up a four-by-five grid using `GridLayout` and populate the grid with

JPanels. Set the background color for all the JPanels to Color.BLUE. Randomly choose one of the panels to be the bomb; the other 19 panels are "safe." Allow the player to click on grids. If the player chooses a safe panel, turn the panel to Color.WHITE. If the player chooses the bomb panel, turn the panel to Color.RED and turn all the remaining panels WHITE. If the user successfully chooses 10 safe panels before choosing the bomb, display a congratulatory message. Save the game as **MineField.java**.

b. Improve the MineField game by allowing the user to choose a difficulty level before beginning. Using a BorderLayout, place three buttons labeled "Easy", "Intermediate", and "Difficult" in one region and place the game grid in another region. Require the user to select a difficulty level before starting the game, then disable the buttons. If the user chooses "Easy", the user must select only five safe panels to win the game. If the user selects "Intermediate", require 10 safe panels as in the original game. If the user selects "Difficult", require 15 safe panels. Save the game as **MineField2.java**.

3. a. Create a game that helps new mouse users improve their hand-eye coordination. Within a JFrame, display an array of 48 JPanels in a GridLayout using six rows and eight columns. Randomly display an X on one of the panels. When the user clicks the correct panel (the one displaying the X), remove the X and display it on a different panel. After the user has successfully "hit" the correct panel 10 times, display a congratulatory message that includes the user's percentage (hits divided by clicks). Save the file as **JCatchTheMouse.java**.

b. Review how to use the GregorianCalendar class from Chapter 4, then revise the JCatchTheMouse game to conclude by displaying the number of seconds it took the user to click all 10 X's. When the application starts, create a GregorianCalendar object and use the get(Calendar.SECOND) and get(Calendar.MINUTE) methods with it to get the SECOND and MINUTE values at the start of the game. When the user has clicked all 10 X's, create a second GregorianCalendar object and get the SECOND and MINUTE values at the end of the game. If the user starts and ends a game during the same minute, then the playing time is simply the difference between the two SECOND values. Make sure your application times the game correctly even if the start and stop times do not occur during the same MINUTE. Save the file as **JCatchTheMouseTimed.java**.

c. In the JCatchTheMouseTimed game described in Exercise 3b, the timer does not work correctly if the user happens to play when the hour (or day or year) changes. Use the *http://java.sun.com* Web site to find out how to use the GregorianCalendar class method getTimeInMillis(), then modify the game to measure playing time accurately, no matter when the user plays the game. Save the file as **JCatchTheMouseTimed2java**.

> **»NOTE** If you were writing a professional timed game, you would test the timer's accuracy regardless of when the user decided to play. For example, if the user played over the midnight hour on New Year's Eve, you would either have to test the game then (which is impractical), or reset your system's clock to simulate New Year's Eve. If you are writing the programs in this book on a school's computer network, you might be blocked by the administrator from changing the date and time. Even if you are working on your own computer, do not attempt to change the date and time unless you understand the impact on other installed applications. For example, your operating system might assume that an installed virus-protection program is expired, or a financial program might indicate that automatically paid bills are overdue.

4. The game Corner the King is played on a checkerboard. To begin, a checker is randomly placed in the bottom row. The player can move one or two squares to the left or upwards, then the computer can move one or two squares left or up. The first to reach the upper-left corner wins. Design a game in which the computer's moves are chosen randomly.

When the game ends, display a message that indicates the winner. Save the game as **CornerTheKing.java**.

5. Create a target practice game that allows the user to click moving targets and displays the number of hits in a 10-second period. Create a grid of at least 100 `JPanel`s. Randomly display an X on five panels to indicate targets. As the user clicks each X, change the label to indicate a hit. When all five Xs have been hit, randomly display a new set of five targets. Continue with as many sets as the user can hit in 10 seconds. (Use the *http://java.sun.com* Web site to find how to use the `GregorianCalendar` class method `getTimeInMillis()` to calculate the time change.) When the time is up, display a count of the number of targets hit. Save the file as **JTargetPractice.java**.

6. You set up the card game Concentration by placing pairs of cards face down in a grid. The player turns up two cards at a time, exposing their values. If the cards match, they are removed from the grid. If the cards do not match, they are turned back over so their values are hidden again, and the player selects two more cards to expose. Using the knowledge gained by the previously exposed cards, the player attempts to remove all the pairs of cards from play. Create a Java version of this game using a `GridLayout` that is four rows high and five columns wide. Place randomly assigned number pairs in 20 `JPanel`s, and place one of the 20 `JPanel`s in each cell of the grid. Initially, show only "backs" of cards by setting each panel's background to a solid color. When the user clicks a first card, change its color and expose its value. After the user clicks a second card, change its color to the same color as the first exposed card, expose the second card's value, and keep both cards exposed until the user's mouse pointer exits the second card. If the two exposed cards are different, hide the cards again. If the two turned cards match, then "remove" the pair from play by setting their background colors to white. When the user has matched all 20 cards into 10 pairs, display a congratulatory message. Save the game as **JConcentration.java**.

7. Create a Mine Sweeper game by setting up a grid of rows and columns in which "bombs" are randomly hidden. You choose the size and difficulty of the game; for example, you might choose to create a fairly simple game by displaying a four-by-five grid that contains four bombs. If a player clicks a panel in the grid that contains a bomb, then the player loses the game. If the clicked panel is not a bomb, display a number that indicates how many adjacent panels contain a bomb. For example, if a user clicks a panel containing a 0, the user knows it is safe to click any panel above, below, beside, or diagonally adjacent to the cell, because those cells cannot possibly contain a bomb. If the player loses by clicking a bomb, display all the numeric values as well as the bomb positions. If the player succeeds in clicking all the panels except those containing bombs, the player wins and you should display a congratulatory message. Figure 14-34 shows the progression of a typical game. In the first screen, the user has clicked a panel, and the display indicates that three adjacent cells contain bombs. In the second screen, the user has clicked a second panel, and the display indicates that no adjacent cells contain bombs. In the last screen, the user has clicked a bomb panel, and all the bomb positions are displayed. Save the game as **MineSweeper.java**.

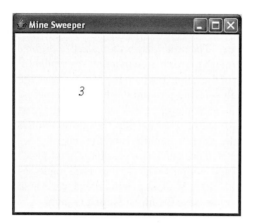

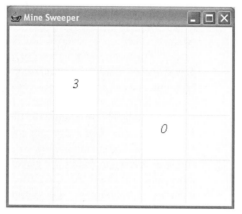

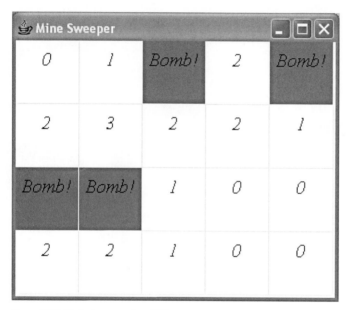

Figure 14-34 Typical progression of Minesweeper game

8. Create the game Lights Out using a five-by-five grid of panels. Randomly set each panel in the grid to a dark color or light color. The object of the game is to force all the panels to be dark, thus turning the "lights out." When the player clicks a panel, turn all the panels in the same row and column (including the clicked panel) to the opposite color. For example, if the user clicks the panel in the second row, third column, then darken all the light-colored panels in the second row and third column, and lighten all the dark-colored panels in that row and column. When all the panels in the grid are dark, all the lights are out, so display a congratulatory message. Save the game as **LightsOut.java**.

9. The game Stop Gate is played on a checkerboard with a set of dominoes; each domino is large enough to cover two checkerboard squares. One player places a domino horizontally on the checkerboard, covering any two squares. The other player then places a domino vertically to cover any other two squares. When a player has no more moves available, that player loses. Create a computerized version of the game in which the player places the horizontal pieces and the computer randomly selects a position for the vertical pieces. (Game construction will be simpler if you allow the player to select only the left square of a two-square area and assume the domino covers that position plus the position immediately to the right.) Use a different color for the player's dominoes and the computer's. Display a message naming the winner when no more moves are possible. Figure 14-35 shows a typical game after the player (blue) and computer (black) have each made one move, and near the end of the game when the player is about to win—the player has several moves remaining but the computer has none. Save the file as **StopGate.java**.

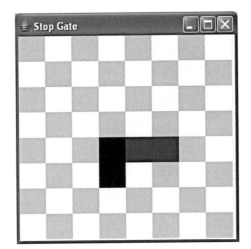 

Figure 14-35 A typical game of StopGate just after play begins and near the end of the game

UP FOR DISCUSSION

1. If you are completing all the programming exercises in this book, you know that working programs require a lot of time to write and test. Professional programs require even more hours of work. In the workplace, programs frequently must be completed by strict deadlines—for example, a tax-calculating program must be completed by year's end or an advertising Web site must be completed by the launch of the product. Programmers often find themselves working into the evenings or on weekends to complete "rush" projects. How do you feel about having to do this? What types of compensation would make the hours worthwhile for you?

2. Suppose your organization asks you to develop a code of ethics for the Information Technology Department. What would you include?

15

EXCEPTION HANDLING

In this chapter, you will:

Learn about exceptions
Understand the limitations of traditional error handling
Try code and catch Exceptions
Throw and catch multiple Exceptions
Use the finally block
Understand the advantages of exception handling
Specify the Exceptions a method can throw
Trace Exceptions through the call stack
Create your own Exceptions
Use an assertion

JAVA ON THE JOB, SCENE 15

You're muttering to yourself at your desk at Event Handlers Incorporated.

"Anything wrong?" Lynn Greenbrier asks as she passes by.

"It's these errors!" you complain.

"Aren't you going overboard?" Lynn asks. "Everyone makes errors when they code programs."

"Oh, I expect typos and compiler errors while I'm developing my programs," you say, "but no matter how well I write my code, the user can still mess everything up by inputting bad data. The Event Planning Department told me that it has events planned for the 32nd day of the month and for negative five attendees. Even if my code is perfect, the user can enter mistakes."

"Then your code isn't perfect yet," Lynn says. "Besides writing programs that can handle ordinary situations, you must enable your programs to handle exceptions."

LEARNING ABOUT EXCEPTIONS

An **exception** is an unexpected or error condition. The programs you write can generate many types of potential exceptions, such as when you do the following:

- » You issue a command to read a file from a disk, but the file does not exist there.
- » You attempt to write data to a disk, but the disk is full or unformatted.
- » Your program asks for user input, but the user enters invalid data.
- » The program attempts to divide a value by 0, access an array with a subscript that is too large, or calculate a value that is too large for the answer's variable type.

> **NOTE**
> Providing for exceptions involves an oxymoron; you must expect the unexpected.

These errors are called exceptions because, presumably, they are not usual occurrences; they are "exceptional." The object-oriented techniques to manage such errors comprise the group of methods known as **exception handling**.

Like all other classes in Java, exceptions are `Objects`. Java has two basic classes of errors: `Error` and `Exception`. Both of these classes descend from the `Throwable` class, as shown in Figure 15-1.

> **NOTE**
> Unplanned exceptions that occur during a program's execution are also called **runtime exceptions**.

> **NOTE** With Java SE 6 (Java Standard Edition version 6.0), Java acknowledges more than 75 categories of `Exceptions` with unusual names such as `ActivationException`, `AlreadyBoundException`, `AWTException`, `CloneNotSupportedException`, `PropertyVetoException`, and `UnsupportedFlavorException`. See the *http://java.sun.com* Web site for more details about these and other `Exceptions`.

The **Error class** represents more serious errors from which your program usually cannot recover. You probably have made these errors in your own programs when you spelled a class name incorrectly or stored a required class in the wrong folder. When a program cannot locate a required class or your system runs out of memory, an `Error` condition occurs. Of course, a person can recover from such errors by respelling a name correctly, moving a file to the correct folder, or by physically installing more memory, but a program cannot recover from these kinds of mistakes on its own.

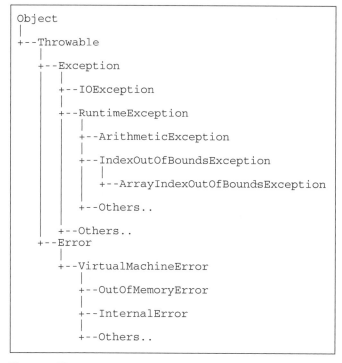

```
Object
|
+--Throwable
    |
    +---Exception
    |   |
    |   +--IOException
    |   |
    |   +--RuntimeException
    |   |   |
    |   |   +--ArithmeticException
    |   |   |
    |   |   +--IndexOutOfBoundsException
    |   |   |   |
    |   |   |   +--ArrayIndexOutOfBoundsException
    |   |   |
    |   |   +--Others..
    |   |
    |   +--Others..
    +--Error
        |
        +--VirtualMachineError
            |
            +--OutOfMemoryError
            |
            +--InternalError
            |
            +--Others..
```

Figure 15-1 The Exception and Error class inheritance hierarchy

The **Exception class** comprises less serious errors that represent unusual conditions that arise while a program is running and from which the program *can* recover. Some examples of Exception class errors include using an invalid array subscript or performing certain illegal arithmetic operations.

When your code causes a program error, whether inadvertently or purposely, you can determine whether the type of Throwable object generated is an Error or an Exception by examining the message you receive from Java after the error occurs.

For example, in Figure 15-2, the user is trying to compile a Java file named xyz.java that does not exist in the current folder. The "cannot read" Error in Figure 15-2 must be remedied by typing a different class name or by storing a file with the name xyz.java in the Chapter.15 folder. In other words, a person must take action before the command can successfully execute; there is no program code you could write that would prevent the Error message.

Figure 15-2 Error message generated when a user compiles a class that does not exist

> **NOTE** In this chapter, when you see the word "error" with a lowercase "e," think of a general mistake-generating condition. When you see "Error" with an uppercase "E," think of the Error class. For example, even though in Figure 15-2 the user generated an Error (that is, an instance of the Error class), the error message displays with a lowercase "e."

However, when you generate a recoverable Exception, which is less severe than an Error, you see a different type of message. An Exception message indicates that you could have prevented the message by using specific code within your program.

A different type of message is generated when the programmer could have prevented the error. For example, Figure 15-3 shows a class named MathMistake that contains a single, small main() method. The method declares three integers, assigns values to two of them, and calculates the value of the third integer by dividing the first two values. However, the variable used as the divisor, denom, is 0, and division by 0 is a mathematically undefined operation. Figure 15-4 shows the output when the MathMistake application executes.

```java
public class MathMistake
{
    public static void main(String[] args)
    {
        int num = 13, denom = 0, result;
        result = num / denom;
    }
}
```

Figure 15-3 The MathMistake class

```
C:\Java>java MathMistake
Exception in thread "main" java.lang.ArithmeticException: / by zero
        at MathMistake.main(MathMistake.java:6)

C:\Java>
```

Figure 15-4 Output of the attempted execution of the MathMistake application

> **NOTE** You should never write a program that purposely divides a value by 0. However, this situation certainly could occur by accident—for example, if a variable used as a divisor gets its value as the result of user input.

> **NOTE**
> You learned about subclasses and inheritance in Chapters 11 and 12.

In Figure 15-4, the Exception is a java.lang.ArithmeticException. ArithmeticException is one of many subclasses of Exception. You also get some information about the error ("/ by zero"), the method that generated the error (MathMistake.main), and the file and line number for the error (MathMistake.java, line 6).

Just because an Exception occurs, you don't necessarily have to deal with it. In the MathMistake class, you can simply let the offending program terminate. However, the program termination is abrupt and unforgiving. When a program divides two numbers (or performs a less trivial task such as balancing a checkbook), the user might be annoyed if the program ends abruptly. However, if the program is used for a more critical task such as air-traffic control or to monitor a patient's vital statistics during surgery, an abrupt conclusion could be disastrous. Object-oriented error-handling techniques provide more elegant (and safer) solutions.

UNDERSTANDING THE LIMITATIONS OF TRADITIONAL ERROR HANDLING

Programmers had to deal with error conditions long before object-oriented methods were conceived. Probably the most often used error-handling solution has been to terminate the offending program. For example, you can change the `main()` method of the `MathMistake` class to halt the program before dividing by 0, as shown in Figure 15-5.

```
public class MathMistake
{
    public static void main(String[] args)
    {
        int num = 13, denom = 0, result;
        if(denom == 0)
            System.exit(1);
        result = num / denom;
    }
}
```

Figure 15-5 A `MathMistake` application using a traditional error-handling technique

» NOTE You first used the `System.exit()` method in Chapter 1 when you wrote code to close a dialog box, and you have used it in every application that uses `Swing` components. On those occasions, you used 0 as the argument to `System.exit()` to indicate that the program was ending normally. Here, you use 1, which conventionally indicates a problem or error situation.

When you use the `System.exit()` method, the current application ends and control returns to the operating system. The convention is to return 1 if an error is causing program termination, or 0 if the program is ending normally. Using this `exit()` method circumvents displaying the error message shown in Figure 15-4 because the program ends before the division error occurs.

Exception handling provides a more elegant solution for handling error conditions. In object-oriented terminology, you "try" a procedure that might cause an error. A method that detects an error condition or `Exception` "throws an exception," and the block of code that processes the error "catches the exception."

» NOTE Programs that can handle exceptions appropriately are said to be more fault-tolerant and robust. **Fault-tolerant** applications are designed so that they continue to operate, possibly at a reduced level, when some part of the system fails. **Robustness** represents the degree to which a system is resilient to stress, maintaining correct functioning.

TRYING CODE AND CATCHING Exceptions

When you create a segment of code in which something might go wrong, you place the code in a **try block**, which is a block of code you attempt to execute while acknowledging that an exception might occur. A `try` block consists of the following elements:

» The keyword `try`
» An opening curly brace
» Executable statements, including some that might cause exceptions
» A closing curly brace

You usually code at least one `catch` block immediately following a `try` block. A **catch block** is a segment of code that can handle an exception that might be thrown by the `try` block that precedes it. A **throw statement** is one that sends an `Exception` out of a method so it can be handled elsewhere. Each `catch` block can "catch" one type of exception—that is, one object that is an object of type `Exception` or one of its child classes. You create a `catch` block by typing the following elements:

> **» NOTE** If you do not include a `catch` block immediately after a `try` block, then you must code a `finally` block. You will learn about `finally` blocks later in this chapter.

» The keyword `catch`
» An opening parenthesis
» An `Exception` type
» A name for an instance of the `Exception` type
» A closing parenthesis
» An opening curly brace
» The statements that take the action you want to use to handle the error condition
» A closing curly brace

Figure 15-6 shows the general format of a method that includes a shaded `try...catch` pair.

```
returnType methodName(optional arguments)
{
    optional statements prior to code that is tried
    try
    {
        // statement or statements that might generate an exception
    }
    catch(Exception someException)
    {
        // actions to take if exception occurs
    }
    // optional statements that occur after try,
    // whether catch block executes or not
}
```

Figure 15-6 Format of `try...catch` pair

>> NOTE A catch block looks a lot like a method named catch() that takes an argument that is some type of Exception. However, it is not a method; it has no return type, and you can't call it directly.

>> NOTE Some programmers refer to a catch block as a catch clause.

In Figure 15-6, someException represents an object of the Exception class or any of its subclasses. If an Exception occurs during the execution of the try block, the statements in the catch block execute. If no Exception occurs within the try block, the catch block does not execute. Either way, the statements following the catch block execute normally.

Figure 15-7 shows an application named MathMistakeCaught that improves on the MathMistake class. The main() method in the class contains a try block with code that attempts division. When the illegal division by 0 takes place, an ArithmeticException is automatically created and the catch block executes, displaying the output shown in Figure 15-8.

```
public class MathMistakeCaught
{
    public static void main(String[] args)
    {
        int num = 13, denom = 0, result;
        try
        {
            result = num / denom;
        }
        catch(ArithmeticException mistake)
        {
            System.out.println("Attempt to divide by zero!");
        }
    }
}
```

Figure 15-7 The MathMistakeCaught application

>> NOTE In the application in Figure 15-7, the throw and catch operations reside in the same method. Later in this chapter, you will learn that throws and their corresponding catches frequently reside in separate methods.

Figure 15-8 Output of the MathMistakeCaught application

>> NOTE If you want to send error messages to a different location from "normal" output, you can use System.err instead of System.out. For example, if an application writes a report to a specific disk file, you might want errors to write to a different location—perhaps to a different disk file or to the screen.

When the `MathMistakeCaught` application displays the error message ("Attempt to divide by zero!"), you cannot confirm that division by 0 was the source of the error. In reality, *any* `ArithmeticException` generated within the `try` block in the program would be caught by the `catch` block in the method. Instead of writing your own message, you can use the `getMessage()` method that `ArithmeticException` inherits from the `Throwable` class. To retrieve Java's message about any `ThrowableException` named `someException`, you code `someException.getMessage()`.

> **» NOTE** As an example of another condition that could generate an `ArithmeticException`, if you create an object using Java's `BigDecimal` class and then perform a division that results in a nonterminating decimal division such as 1/3, but specify that an exact result is needed, an `ArithmeticException` is thrown. As another example, you could create your own class containing a method that creates a new instance of the `ArithmeticException` class and throws it under any conditions you specify.

For example, Figure 15-9 shows a `MathMistakeCaught2` class that uses the `getMessage()` method (see shading) to generate the message that "comes with" the caught `ArithmeticException` argument to the `catch` block. Figure 15-10 shows the output; the message is "/ by zero".

```
public class MathMistakeCaught2
{
    public static void main(String[] args)
    {
        int num = 13, denom = 0, result;
        try
        {
            result = num / denom;
        }
        catch(ArithmeticException mistake)
        {
            System.out.println(mistake.getMessage());
        }
    }
}
```

Figure 15-9 The `MathMistakeCaught2` application

Figure 15-10 Output of the `MathMistakeCaught2` application

> **NOTE** It should be no surprise that the automatically generated error message when dividing by 0 is "/ by zero"; you saw the same message in Figure 15-4 when the programmer provided no exception handling and the message was automatically supplied.

Of course, you might want to do more in a `catch` block than print an error message; after all, Java did that for you without requiring you to write the code to catch any `Exceptions`. You also might want to add code to correct the error; for example, such code could force the arithmetic to divide by 1 rather than by 0. Figure 15-11 shows `try...catch` code in which the `catch` block computes the result by dividing by 1 instead of by the `denom` value. After the `catch` block, the application could continue with a guarantee that `result` holds a valid value—either the division worked in the `try` block and the `catch` block did not execute, or the `catch` block remedied the error.

```
try
{
    result = num / denom;
}
catch(ArithmeticException mistake)
{
    result = num / 1;
}
// program continues here; result is guaranteed to have a valid value
```

Figure 15-11 A `try...catch` block in which the `catch` block corrects the error

> **NOTE** In the code in Figure 15-11, you can achieve the same result in the `catch` block by coding `result = num;` instead of `result = num / 1;`. Explicitly dividing by 1 simply makes the code's intention clearer, but it does require an additional operation. As an alternative, you could make the program more efficient by omitting the division by 1 and adding clarity with a comment.

THROWING AND CATCHING MULTIPLE Exceptions

You can place as many statements as you need within a `try` block, and you can `catch` as many `Exceptions` as you want. If you `try` more than one statement, only the first error-generating statement `throws` an `Exception`. As soon as the `Exception` occurs, the logic transfers to the `catch` block, which leaves the rest of the statements in the `try` block unexecuted.

When a program contains multiple `catch` blocks, they are examined in sequence until a match is found for the type of `Exception` that occurred. Then, the matching `catch` block executes and each remaining `catch` block is bypassed.

For example, consider the application in Figure 15-12. The `main()` method in the `TwoMistakes` class `throws` two types of `Exceptions`: an `ArithmeticException` and an `IndexOutOfBoundsException`. (An `IndexOutOfBoundsException` occurs when an array subscript is not within the allowed range.)

```
public class TwoMistakes
{
    public static void main(String[] args)
    {
        int num[] = { 4, 0, 0};
        try
        {
            num[2] = num[0] / num[1];
            num[2] = num[3] / num[0];
        }
        catch(ArithmeticException e)
        {
            System.out.println("Arithmetic error");
        }
        catch(IndexOutOfBoundsException e)
        {
            System.out.println("Out of bounds error");
        }
        System.out.println("End of program");
    }
}
```

Figure 15-12 The TwoMistakes class

The TwoMistakes class declares an integer array with three elements. In the main() method, the try block executes; at the first statement within the try block (shaded), an Exception occurs because the divisor in the division problem, num[1] , is 0. The try block is abandoned, and the logic transfers to the first catch block (shaded). Division by 0 causes an ArithmeticException; because the first catch block receives an ArithmeticException, the message "Arithmetic error" displays. In this example, the second statement in the try block is never attempted, and the second catch block is skipped. Figure 15-13 shows the output.

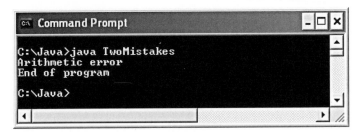

Figure 15-13 Output of the TwoMistakes application

If you make any one of several minor changes to the class in Figure 15-12, you can force the second catch block, the one with the IndexOutOfBoundsException argument, to execute. For example, you can force the division in the try block to succeed by substituting a nonzero value for the divisor in the first arithmetic statement of the first shaded statement in the try block, as shown in Figure 15-14. Alternatively, you could reverse the positions of the two arithmetic statements or comment out the first statement. With any of these changes, division by 0 does not take place. In the code in Figure 15-14, the first statement in the try block succeeds,

```
public class TwoMistakes2
{
    public static void main(String[] args)
    {
        int num[] = { 4, 0, 0};
        try
        {
            num[2] = num[0] / 10;
            num[2] = num[3] / num[0];
        }
        catch(ArithmeticException e)
        {
            System.out.println("Arithmetic error");
        }
        catch(IndexOutOfBoundsException e)
        {
            System.out.println("Out of bounds error");
        }
        System.out.println("End of program");
    }
}
```

Figure 15-14 The TwoMistakes2 class

and the logic proceeds to the second statement in the try block. This shaded statement attempts to access element 3 of a three-element array (whose subscripts should only be 0, 1, or 2), so it throws an IndexOutOfBoundsException. The try block is abandoned, and the first catch block is examined and found unsuitable because it does not catch an IndexOutOfBoundsException. The program logic proceeds to the second catch block (shaded), whose Exception argument type is a match for the thrown Exception, so the message "Out of bounds error" displays. Figure 15-15 shows the output.

```
C:\Java>java TwoMistakes2
Out of bounds error
End of program

C:\Java>
```

Figure 15-15 Output of the TwoMistakes2 application

Sometimes, you want to execute the same code no matter which Exception type occurs. For example, within the TwoMistakes2 application in Figure 15-14, each of the two catch blocks prints a unique message. Instead, you might want both the ArithmeticException's catch block and the IndexOutOfBoundsException's catch block to use their parent's getMessage() method. Because ArithmeticExceptions and IndexOutOfBoundsExceptions are both subclasses of Exception, you can rewrite the TwoMistakes class as shown in Figure 15-16, using a single generic catch block (shaded) that can catch any type of Exception.

```
public class TwoMistakes3
{
    public static void main(String[] args)
    {
        int num[] = { 4, 0, 0};
        try
        {
            num[2] = num[0] / num[1];
            num[2] = num[3] / num[0];
        }
        catch( Exception e)
        {
            System.out.println(e.getMessage());
        }
    }
}
```

Figure 15-16 The `TwoMistakes3` application

The `catch` block in Figure 15-16 accepts a more generic `Exception` argument type than that thrown by either of the potentially error-causing `try` statements, so the generic `catch` block can act as a "catch-all" block. When either an arithmetic error or array error occurs, the thrown exception is "promoted" to an `Exception` error in the `catch` block. Through inheritance, `ArithmeticExceptions` and `IndexOutOfBoundsExceptions` are `Exceptions`, and because an `Exception` is `Throwable`, you can use the `Throwable` class `getMessage()` method.

» NOTE
Programmers also call unreachable code **dead code**.

When you list multiple `catch` blocks following a `try` block, you must be careful that some `catch` blocks don't become unreachable. **Unreachable code** statements are program statements that can never execute under any circumstances. For example, if two successive `catch` blocks catch an `IndexOutOfBoundsException` and an ordinary `Exception`, the `IndexOutOfBoundsException` errors cause the first `catch` to execute and other `Exceptions` "fall through" to the more general `Exception` `catch` block. However, if you reverse the sequence of the `catch` blocks so that the one that catches general `Exception` objects is first, even `IndexOutOfBoundsExceptions` are caught by the `Exception` `catch`. The `IndexOutOfBoundsException` `catch` block is unreachable because the `Exception` `catch` block is in its way and the class does not compile.

» NOTE
Creating an unreachable `catch` block causes a compiler error. The message generated indicates that the unreachable exception "has already been caught."

Although a method can throw any number of `Exception` types, many developers believe that it is poor style for a method to throw more than three or four types. If it does, one of the following conditions might be true:

» Perhaps the method is trying to accomplish too many diverse tasks and should be broken up into smaller methods.

» Perhaps the `Exception` types thrown are too specific and should be generalized, as they are in the `TwoMistakes3` application in Figure 15-16. As another example, both `EOFExceptions` (which occur when the end of a file is reached) and `FileNotFoundExceptions` (which occur when a method attempts to open a file that it cannot find) are children of the `IOException` class (which, in turn, is a child of the `Exception` class). If a method throws both subclass `Exception` types, using the one superclass type might be sufficient.

» NOTE Chapter 16 describes `EOFExceptions` and `FileNotFoundExceptions` and uses both types in sample programs.

USING THE finally BLOCK

When you have actions you must perform at the end of a `try...catch` sequence, you can use a **finally block**. The code within a `finally` block executes regardless of whether the preceding `try` block identifies an `Exception`. Usually, you use a `finally` block to perform cleanup tasks that must happen whether or not any `Exceptions` occurred, and whether or not any `Exceptions` that occurred were caught. Figure 15-17 shows the format of a `try...catch` sequence that uses a `finally` block.

```
try
{
    // statements to try
}
catch(Exception e)
{
    // actions that occur if exception was thrown
}
finally
{
    // actions that occur whether catch block executed or not
}
```

Figure 15-17 Format of `try...catch...finally` sequence

Compare Figure 15-17 to Figure 15-7 shown earlier in this chapter. When the `try` code works without error in Figure 15-7, control passes to the statements at the end of the method. Also, when the `try` code fails and `throws` an `Exception`, and the `Exception` is caught, the `catch` block executes and control again passes to the statements at the end of the method. At first glance, it seems as though the statements at the end of the method always execute. However, the final set of statements might never execute for at least two reasons:

» An unplanned `Exception` might occur.

» The `try` or `catch` block might contain a `System.exit();` statement.

Any `try` block might throw an `Exception` for which you did not provide a `catch` block. After all, `Exceptions` occur all the time without your handling them, as one did in the first `MathMistake` application in this chapter. In the case of an unhandled `Exception`, program execution stops immediately, the `Exception` is sent to the operating system for handling, and the current method is abandoned. Likewise, if the `try` block contains an `exit()` statement, execution stops immediately.

When you include a `finally` block, you are assured that the `finally` statements will execute before the method is abandoned, even if the method concludes prematurely. For example, programmers often use a `finally` block when the program uses data files that must be closed. You will learn more about writing to and reading from data files in Chapter 16. For now, however, consider the format shown in Figure 15-18, which represents part of the logic for a typical file-handling program.

```
try
{
    // Open the file
    // Read the file
    // Place the file data in an array
    // Calculate an average from the data
    // Display the average
}
catch(IOException e)
{
    // Issue an error message
    // System exit
}
finally
{
    // If the file is open, close it
}
```

Figure 15-18 Pseudocode that tries reading a file and handles an `IOException`

>> **NOTE** If an application might throw several types of exceptions, you can try some code, catch the possible exception, try some more code, catch the possible exception, and so on. Usually, however, the superior approach is to try all the statements that might throw exceptions, then include all the needed `catch` blocks and an optional `finally` block. This is the approach shown in Figure 15-18, and it usually results in logic that is easier to follow.

>> **NOTE** You can avoid using a `finally` block, but you would need repetitious code. For example, instead of using the `finally` block in the pseudocode in Figure 15-18, you could insert the statement "If the file is open, close it" as both the last statement in the `try` block and the second-to-last statement in the `catch` block, just before `System exit`. However, writing code just once in a `finally` block is clearer and less prone to error.

The pseudocode in Figure 15-18 represents an application that opens a file; in Java, if a file does not exist when you open it, an input/output exception, or `IOException`, is thrown and the `catch` block handles the error. However, because the application uses an array (see the statement "Place the file data in an array"), it is possible that, even though the file opened successfully, an uncaught `IndexOutOfBoundsException` might occur. In such an event, close the file before proceeding. By using the `finally` block, you ensure that the file is closed because the code in the `finally` block executes before control returns to the operating system. The code in the `finally` block executes no matter which of the following outcomes of the `try` block occurs:

>> The `try` ends normally.

>> The `catch` executes.

>> An `Exception` causes the method to abandon prematurely—perhaps the array is not large enough to hold the data, or calculating the average results in division by 0. These `Exceptions` do not allow the `try` block to finish, nor do they cause the `catch` block to execute.

>> **NOTE**
C++ programmers are familiar with `try` and `catch` blocks, but C++ does not provide a `finally` block.

>> **NOTE** If a `try` block calls the `System.exit()` method and the `finally` block calls the same method, the `exit()` method in the `finally` block executes. The `try` block's `exit()` method call is abandoned.

UNDERSTANDING THE ADVANTAGES OF EXCEPTION HANDLING

Before the inception of object-oriented programming languages, potential program errors were handled using somewhat confusing, error-prone methods. For example, a traditional, non-object-oriented, procedural program might perform three methods that depend on each other using code that provides error checking similar to the pseudocode in Figure 15-19.

The pseudocode represents an application in which the logic must pass three tests before a final result can be displayed. It performs methodA(); it then performs methodB() only if methodA() is successful. Similarly, methodC() executes only when methodA() and methodB() are both successful. When any method fails, the program sets an appropriate errorCode to 'A', 'B', or 'C'. (Presumably, the errorCode is used later in the application.) The logic in Figure 15-19 is difficult to follow, and the application's purpose and intended outcome—to print the finalResult—is lost in the maze of if statements. Also, you can easily make coding mistakes within such a program because of the complicated nesting, indenting, and opening and closing of curly braces.

```
call methodA()
if methodA() worked
{
    call methodB()
    if methodB() worked
    {
        call methodC()
        if methodC() worked
            everything's okay so print finalResult
        else
            set errorCode to 'C'
    }
    else
        set errorCode to 'B'
}
else
    set errorCode to 'A'
```

Figure 15-19 Pseudocode representing traditional error checking

Compare the same program logic using Java's object-oriented, error-handling technique shown in Figure 15-20. Using the try...catch object-oriented technique provides the same results as the traditional method, but the statements of the program that do the "real" work (calling methods A, B, and C and printing finalResult) are placed together, where their logic is easy to follow. The try steps should usually work without generating errors; after all, the errors are "exceptions." It is convenient to see these business-as-usual steps in one location. The unusual, exceptional events are grouped and moved out of the way of the primary action.

Besides clarity, an advantage to object-oriented exception handling is the flexibility it allows in the handling of error situations. When a method you write throws an Exception, the same method can catch the Exception, although it is not required to do so, and in most object-oriented programs it does not. Often, you don't want a method to handle its own Exception. In many cases, you want the method to check for errors, but you do not want to require a method to

```
try
{
    call methodA() and maybe throw an exception
    call methodB() and maybe throw an exception
    call methodC() and maybe throw an exception
    everything's okay, so display finalResult
}
catch(methodA()'s error)
{
    set errorCode to 'A'
}
catch(methodB()'s error)
{
    set errorCode to 'B'
}
catch(methodC()'s error)
{
    set errorCode to 'C'
}
```

Figure 15-20 Pseudocode representing object-oriented exception handling

handle an error if it finds one. Another advantage to object-oriented exception handling is that you gain the ability to appropriately deal with Exceptions as you decide how to handle them. When you write a method, it can call another, catch a thrown Exception, and you can decide what you want to do. Just as a police officer can deal with a speeding driver differently depending on circumstances, you can react to Exceptions specifically for your current purposes.

Methods are flexible partly because they are reusable—that is, a well-written method might be used by any number of applications. Each calling application might need to handle the error differently, depending on its purpose. For example, an application that uses a method that divides values might need to terminate if division by 0 occurs. A different program simply might want the user to reenter the data to be used, and a third program might want to force division by 1. The method that contains the division statement can throw the error, but each calling program can assume responsibility for handling the error detected by the method in an appropriate way.

If a method throws an Exception that it will not catch but that will be caught by a different method, you must also use the keyword throws followed by an Exception type in the method header. For example, Figure 15-21 shows a PriceList class used by a company to hold a list of prices for items it sells. For simplicity, there are only four prices and a single method that displays the price of a single item. The displayPrice() method accepts an argument to use as the array subscript, but because the subscript could be out of bounds, the method contains a shaded throws clause, acknowledging it could throw an exception.

```
public class PriceList
{
    private static final double[] price = {15.99, 27.88, 34.56, 45.89};
    public static void displayPrice(int item)
        throws IndexOutOfBoundsException
    {
        System.out.println("The price is $" + price[item]);
    }
}
```

Figure 15-21 The PriceList class

Figures 15-22 and 15-23 show two applications in which programmers have chosen to handle the exception differently. In the first class, PriceListApplication1, the programmer has chosen to handle the exception in the shaded catch block by displaying a price of $0. In the

```
public class PriceListApplication1
{
    public static void main(String[] args)
    {
        int item = 4;
        try
        {
            PriceList.displayPrice(item);
        }
        catch(IndexOutOfBoundsException e)
        {
            System.out.println("Price is $0");
        }
    }
}
```

Figure 15-22 The PriceListApplication1 class

```
import javax.swing.*;
public class PriceListApplication2
{
    public static void main(String[] args)
    {
        int item = 4;
        try
        {
            PriceList.displayPrice(item);
        }
        catch(IndexOutOfBoundsException e)
        {
            while(item < 0 || item > 3)
            {
                String answer = JOptionPane.showInputDialog(null,
                    "Please reenter a value 0, 1, 2 or 3");
                item = Integer.parseInt(answer);
            }
            PriceList.displayPrice(item);
        }
        System.exit(0);
    }
}
```

Figure 15-23 The PriceListApplication2 class

>> **NOTE** In Figures 15-22 and 15-23, the item variable is set to 4 to demonstrate how the catch blocks work when an Exception is generated. In an actual application, it would be more likely that the item number is input by a user or retrieved from a data file.

second class, `PriceListApplication2`, the programmer has chosen to continue using an input dialog box in the shaded `catch` block to prompt the user for a new item number until it is within the correct range. Other programmers could choose still different actions, but they all can use the flexible `displayPrice()` method because it throws the error but doesn't limit the calling method's choice of recourse.

> **» NOTE** With exception handling, a program can continue after dealing with a problem. This is especially important in mission-critical applications. The term **mission critical** refers to any process that is crucial to an organization.

SPECIFYING THE Exceptions A METHOD CAN THROW

When you write a method that might throw an `Exception`, such as the `displayPrice()` method in Figure 15-21, you can type the clause `throws <name>Exception` after the method header to indicate the type of `Exception` that might be thrown. Every Java method you write has the potential to throw an `Exception`. Some `Exceptions`, such as an `InternalErrorException`, can occur anywhere at any time. However, for most Java methods that you write, you do not use a `throws` clause. For example, you have not needed to use a `throws` clause in any of the many programs you have written while working through this book; however, in those methods, if you divided by 0 or went beyond an array's bounds, an `Exception` was thrown nevertheless. Most of the time, you let Java handle any `Exception` by shutting down the program. Imagine how unwieldy your programs would become if you were required to provide instructions for handling every possible error, including equipment failures and memory problems. Most exceptions never have to be explicitly thrown or caught, nor do you have to include a `throws` clause in the headers of methods that automatically throw these `Exceptions`.

Java's exceptions can be categorized into two types:

> » Checked exceptions
> » Unchecked exceptions

Unchecked exceptions come in two types:

> » Errors
> » Runtime exceptions

Checked exceptions are the type that programmers should anticipate and from which programs should be able to recover. For example, suppose a program prompts a user for the name of a data file to open. If the file can't be found, you might want to provide the user with additional opportunities to provide the correct filename. In contrast, programmers usually cannot anticipate errors or runtime exceptions. Errors are mistakes that are external to the program—for example, hardware failures. Runtime exceptions are internal to the program—for example, logic errors. Although an application could catch either type of error, it usually makes sense for a technician to fix external problems or for a programmer to fix internal problems. On the other hand, a program can fix checked exceptions while it is executing.

All exceptions that you explicitly throw are checked exceptions, which descend from the `Exception` class. Checked exceptions are exceptions that are not runtime exceptions; the compiler checks that these exceptions are either caught or specified to be thrown in the method header. If you throw a checked exception, you must do one of the following:

» Catch it.

» Declare the exception in your method header's `throws` clause.

If you write a method with a `throws` clause in the header, then any programmer who uses your method must do one of the following:

» Catch and handle the exception.

» Declare the exception in the `throws` clause of their method. Their method can then throw the exception to yet another method.

In other words, when an exception is a checked exception, client programmers are forced to deal with the possibility that an exception will be thrown.

`Errors` and `RuntimeExceptions` are unchecked exceptions. You never have to throw these exceptions explicitly. Most of the errors you received earlier in this book when you made mistakes in your Java programs are runtime exceptions—members of the `RuntimeException` class that represent unplanned exceptions that occur during a program's execution. Runtime exceptions can occur anywhere in a program and can be numerous in a typical program. Most Java programmers feel that the cost of checking for many runtime exceptions exceeds the benefit of catching or specifying them. Those that represent logical errors should be fixed in the code.

If you write a method that explicitly throws a checked `Exception` that is not caught within the method, Java requires that you use the `throws` clause in the header of the method. Using the `throws` clause does not mean that the method *will* throw an `Exception`—everything might go smoothly. Instead, it means the method *might* throw an `Exception`. You include the `throws` clause in the method header so applications that use your methods are notified of the potential for an `Exception`.

To be able to use a method to its full potential, you must know the method's name and three additional pieces of information:

» The method's return type
» The type and number of arguments the method requires
» The type and number of Exceptions the method throws

To use a method, you must first know what types of arguments are required. You can call a method without knowing its return type, but if you do, you can't benefit from any value that the method returns. (Also, if you use a method without knowing its return type, you probably don't understand the purpose of the method.) Likewise, you can't make sound decisions about what to do in case of an error if you don't know what types of Exceptions a method might throw.

When a method might throw more than one Exception type, you can specify a list of potential Exceptions in the method header by separating them with commas. As an alternative, you could specify that the methods might throw an object of a more general Exception parent class to cover all specific instances. For example, if your method might throw either an ArithmeticException or an ArrayIndexOutOfBoundsException, you can just specify that your method throws a RuntimeException. One advantage to this technique is that when your method is modified to include more specific RuntimeExceptions in the future, the method signature will not change. This saves time and money for users of your methods, who will not have to modify their own methods to accommodate new RuntimeException types.

An extreme alternative is to simply specify that your method throws a general Exception, so that all exceptions are included in one clause. However, using this latter technique disguises information about the specific types of exceptions that might occur, and such information usually is of great value to the users of your methods.

>>**NOTE** Usually, you declare only checked exceptions. Runtime exceptions can occur anywhere in a program, and can be numerous. Programs would be less clear if you had to account for runtime exceptions in every method declaration. Therefore, the compiler does not require that you catch or specify runtime exceptions.

TRACING Exceptions THROUGH THE CALL STACK

When one method calls another, the computer's operating system must keep track of where the method call came from, and program control must return to the calling method when the called method is completed. For example, if methodA() calls methodB(), the operating system has to "remember" to return to methodA() when methodB() ends. Likewise, if methodB() calls methodC(), the computer must "remember" while methodC() executes to return to methodB() and eventually to methodA(). The memory location known as the **call stack** is where the computer stores the list of method locations to which the system must return.

When a method throws an Exception and the method does not catch it, the Exception is thrown to the next method up the call stack, or in other words, to the method that called the offending method. Figure 15-24 shows how the call stack works. If methodA() calls methodB(), and methodB() calls methodC(), and methodC() throws an Exception, Java first looks for a catch block in methodC(). If none exists, Java looks for the same thing in methodB(). If methodB() does not have a catch block, Java looks to methodA().

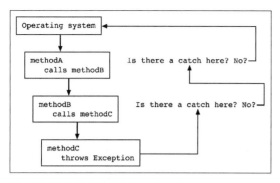

Figure 15-24 Cycling through the call stack

If methodA() cannot catch the Exception, it is thrown to the Java virtual machine, which displays a message at the command prompt.

For example, examine the application in Figure 15-25. The main() method of the application calls methodA(), which displays a message and calls methodB(). Within methodB(), another message displays and methodC() is called. In methodC(), yet another message displays. Then, a JFrame object is defined, but instead of calling the JFrame constructor using the new

```java
import javax.swing.*;
public class DemoStackTrace
{
    public static void main(String[] args)
    {
        methodA();   // line 6
    }
    public static void methodA()
    {
        System.out.println("In methodA()");
        methodB();   // line 11
    }
    public static void methodB()
    {
        System.out.println("In methodB()");
        methodC();   // line 16
    }
    public static void methodC()
    {
        System.out.println("In methodC()");
        JFrame frame = null;
        frame.setVisible(true);   // line 22
    }
}
```

Figure 15-25 The DemoStackTrace class

>> NOTE In Figure 15-25, the comments indicating line numbers were added so you could more easily follow the sequence of generated error messages. You probably would not add such comments to a working application.

operator, the reference is set to null. This statement compiles correctly—it is always acceptable to set a reference to null and use the new operator to call its constructor later. However, methodC() never calls the JFrame constructor. Instead, an attempt is made to set the JFrame object's visible property. Figure 15-26 shows the output when the application executes.

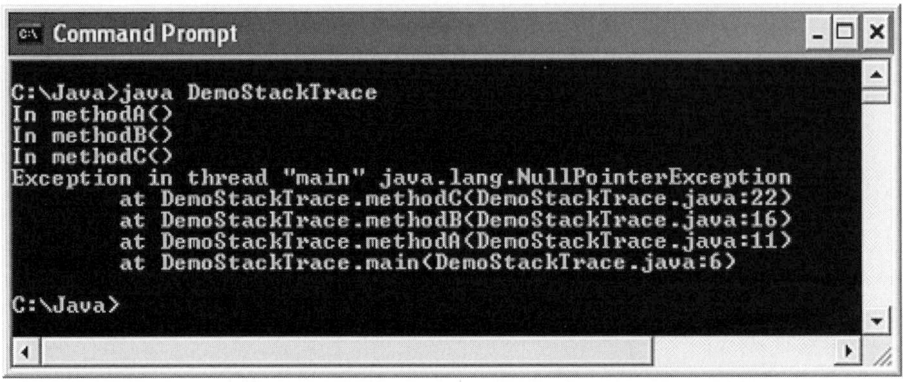

```
C:\Java>java DemoStackTrace
In methodA()
In methodB()
In methodC()
Exception in thread "main" java.lang.NullPointerException
        at DemoStackTrace.methodC(DemoStackTrace.java:22)
        at DemoStackTrace.methodB(DemoStackTrace.java:16)
        at DemoStackTrace.methodA(DemoStackTrace.java:11)
        at DemoStackTrace.main(DemoStackTrace.java:6)

C:\Java>
```

Figure 15-26 Error messages generated by the DemoStackTrace application

>> **NOTE**
Within a class, you have used the this reference to refer to the current object. C++ programmers call the this reference the "this pointer".

As you can see in Figure 15-26, three messages display, indicating that methodA(), methodB(), and methodC() were called in order. However, when methodC() attempts to use the uninitialized JFrame object, a NullPointerException is automatically thrown. The error message generated, as shown in Figure 15-26, shows that the exception occurred in methodC() at line 22 of the file, which was called by methodB() in line 16 of the file, which was called by methodA() in line 11 of the file, which was called by the main() method in line 6 of the file. Using this list of error messages, you could track down the location where the error was generated. Of course, in a larger application containing thousands of lines of code, the stack trace history list would be even more useful.

>> **NOTE** A **pointer** is a reference variable—that is, a variable that holds a memory address. C++ programmers use the term "pointer" frequently; Java programmers do not. However, the error generated by using an unassigned reference in Java is called a NullPointerException.

The technique of cycling through the methods in the stack has great advantages because it allows methods to handle Exceptions wherever the programmer has decided it is most appropriate—including allowing the operating system to handle the error. However, when a program uses several classes, the disadvantage is that the programmer finds it difficult to locate the original source of an Exception.

You have already used the Throwable method getMessage() to obtain information about an Exception. Another useful Exception method is the printStackTrace() method. When you catch an Exception, you can call printStackTrace() to display a list of methods in the call stack so you can determine the location of the Exception.

For example, Figure 15-27 shows a `DemoStackTrace2` application in which the `printStackTrace()` method produces a trace of the trail taken by a thrown exception. The differences from the `DemoStackTrace` application are shaded. The call to `methodB()` has been placed in a `try` block so that the exception can be caught. Instead of throwing the exception to the operating system, this application catches the exception, displays a stack trace, and continues to execute. The output of the list of methods in Figure 15-28 is similar to the one shown in Figure 15-26, but the application does not end abruptly.

```java
import javax.swing.*;
public class DemoStackTrace2
{
    public static void main(String[] args)
    {
        methodA();   // line 6
    }
    public static void methodA()
    {
        System.out.println("In methodA()");
        try
        {
            methodB();   // line 13
        }
        catch(RuntimeException e)
        {
            System.out.println("In methodA() - The stack trace:");
            e.printStackTrace();
        }
        System.out.println("Method ends normally.");
        System.out.println("Application could continue here.");
    }
    public static void methodB()
    {
        System.out.println("In methodB()");
        methodC();   // line 26
    }
    public static void methodC()
    {
        System.out.println("In methodC()");
        JFrame frame = null;
        frame.setVisible(true);   // line 32
    }
}
```

Figure 15-27 The `DemoStackTrace2` class

Often, you do not want to place a `printStackTrace()` method call in a finished program. The typical application user has no interest in the cryptic messages that display. However, while you are developing an application, `printStackTrace()` can be a useful tool for diagnosing your class's problems.

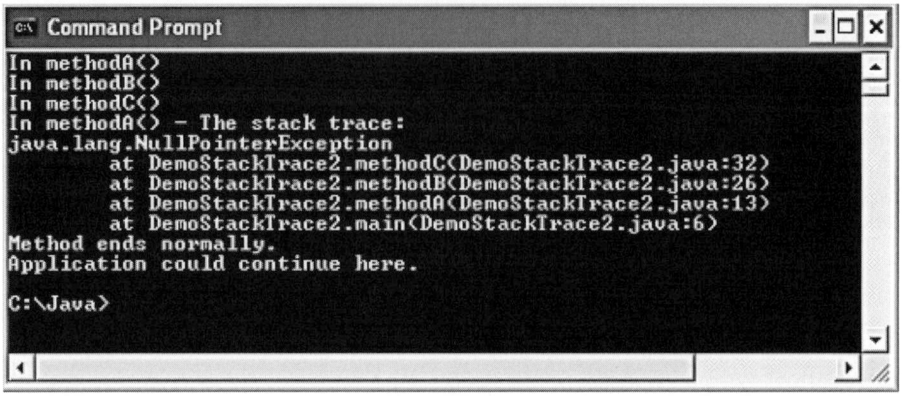

Figure 15-28 Output of the `DemoStackTrace2` application

CREATING YOUR OWN `Exceptions`

Java provides over 40 categories of `Exceptions` that you can use in your programs. However, Java's creators could not predict every condition that might be an `Exception` in your applications. For example, you might want to declare an `Exception` when your bank balance is negative or when an outside party attempts to access your e-mail account. Most organizations have specific rules for exceptional data; for example, an employee number must not exceed three digits, or an hourly salary must not be less than the legal minimum wage. Of course, you can handle these potential error situations with `if` statements, but Java also allows you to create your own `Exceptions`.

» NOTE When you create an `Exception`, it's conventional to end its name with `Exception`.

To create your own throwable `Exception`, you must extend a subclass of `Throwable`. Recall from Figure 15-1 that `Throwable` has two subclasses, `Exception` and `Error`, which are used to distinguish between recoverable and nonrecoverable errors. Because you always want to create your own `Exceptions` for recoverable errors, you should extend your `Exceptions` from the `Exception` class. You can extend any existing `Exception` subclass, such as `ArithmeticException` or `NullPointerException`, but usually you want to inherit directly from `Exception`.

The `Exception` class contains four constructors. You can provide no arguments, include a `String` containing the message that can be returned by the `getMessage()` method, include a `Throwable` object that is the cause of the exception, or include both. The constructors are:

- `Exception()`—Constructs a new exception with `null` as its detail message
- `Exception(String message)`—Constructs a new exception with the specified detail message
- `Exception(String message, Throwable cause)`—Constructs a new exception with the specified detail message and cause
- `Exception(Throwable cause)`—Constructs a new exception with the specified cause and a detail message of `cause.toString()`, which typically contains the class and the detail message of `cause`, or `null` if the cause argument is `null`

For example, Figure 15-29 shows a `HighBalanceException` class. Its constructor contains a single statement that passes a description of an error to the parent `Exception` constructor. This `String` would be retrieved if you called the `getMessage()` method with a `HighBalanceException` object.

```
public class HighBalanceException extends Exception
{
    public HighBalanceException()
    {
        super("Customer balance is high");
    }
}
```

Figure 15-29 The `HighBalanceException` class

Figure 15-30 shows a `CustomerAccount` class that uses a `HighBalanceException`. The `CustomerAccount` constructor header indicates that it might throw a `HighBalanceException` (see the first shaded statement); if the balance used as an argument to the constructor exceeds a set limit, a new, unnamed instance of the `HighBalanceException` class is thrown (see the second shaded statement).

```
public class CustomerAccount
{
    private int acctNum;
    private double balance;
    public static double HIGH_CREDIT_LIMIT = 20000.00;
    public CustomerAccount(int num, double bal)
        throws HighBalanceException
    {
        acctNum = num;
        balance = bal;
        if(balance > HIGH_CREDIT_LIMIT)
            throw(new HighBalanceException());
    }
}
```

Figure 15-30 The `CustomerAccount` class

> **NOTE**
> When a constructor throws an exception, no object is constructed; its intended reference variable value will be `null`.

> **NOTE** In the `CustomerAccount` class in Figure 15-30, you could choose to instantiate a named `HighBalanceException` and throw it when the balance exceeds the credit limit. By waiting and instantiating an unnamed object only when it is needed, you improve program performance.

Figure 15-31 shows an application that instantiates a `CustomerAccount`. In this application, a user is prompted for an account number and balance. After the values are entered, an attempt is made to construct a `CustomerAccount` in a `try` block (as shown in the first shaded section). If the attempt is successful—that is, if the `CustomerAccount` constructor does not throw an `Exception`—the `CustomerAccount` information is displayed in a dialog box. However, if the `CustomerAccount` constructor does throw a `HighBalanceException`, the `catch` block receives it (as shown in the second shaded section) and displays a message.

```
import javax.swing.*;
public class UseCustomerAccount
{
    public static void main(String[] args)
    {
        int num;
        double balance;
        String input;
        input = JOptionPane.showInputDialog(null,
            "Enter account number");
        num = Integer.parseInt(input);
        input = JOptionPane.showInputDialog(null, "Enter balance due");
        balance = Double.parseDouble(input);
        try
        {
            CustomerAccount ca = new CustomerAccount(num, balance);
            JOptionPane.showMessageDialog(null, "Customer #" +
                num + " has a balance of $" + balance);
        }
        catch( HighBalanceException hbe)
        {
            JOptionPane.showMessageDialog(null, "Customer #" +
                num + " has a balance higher than the credit limit");
        }
        System.exit(0);
    }
}
```

Figure 15-31 The UseCustomerAccount class

A different application could take any number of different actions; for example, it could display the return value of the getMessage() method, construct a CustomerAccount object with a lower balance, or construct a different type of object—perhaps a child of CustomerAccount called PreferredCustomerAccount that allows a higher balance. Figure 15-32 shows a typical execution of the application in which a customer's balance is too high.

Instead of hard coding error messages into your exception classes, as shown in Figure 15-32, you might consider creating a catalog of possible messages to use. This approach provides several advantages:

» NOTE
In Exercises 11 and 12 at the end of this chapter, you will create catalogs of error messages for applications to use.

» All the messages are stored in one location instead of being distributed throughout the program, making them easier to see and modify.

» The list of possible errors serves as a source of documentation, listing potential problems when running the application.

» Other applications might want to use the same catalog of messages.

» If your application will be used internationally, you can provide messages in multiple languages and other programmers can use the version that is appropriate for their country.

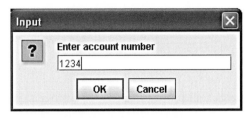

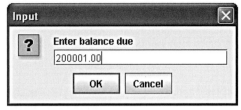

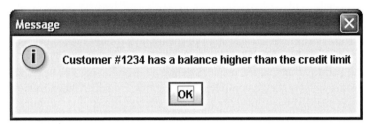

Figure 15-32 Typical execution of `UseCustomerAccount` application

> **» NOTE** You can throw any type of `Exception` at any time, not just `Exception`s of your own creation. For example, within any program you can code `throw(new RuntimeException());`. Of course, you would want to do so only with good reason because Java handles `RuntimeException`s for you by stopping the program. Because you cannot anticipate every possible error, Java's automatic response is often the best course of action.

You should not create an excessive number of special `Exception` types for your classes, especially if the Java development environment already contains an `Exception` that will `catch` the error. Extra `Exception` types add complexity for other programmers who use your classes. However, when appropriate, specialized `Exception` classes provide an elegant way for you to handle error situations. They enable you to separate your error code from the usual, nonexceptional sequence of events; they allow errors to be passed up the stack and traced; and they allow clients of your classes to handle exceptional situations in the manner most suitable for their application.

USING ASSERTIONS

In Chapter 1, you learned that you might inadvertently create syntax or logical errors when you write a program. Syntax errors are mistakes using the Java language; they are compile-time errors that prevent a program from compiling and creating an executable file with a .class extension.

In Chapter 1, you also learned that a program might contain logical errors even though it is free of syntax errors. Some logical errors cause runtime errors, or errors that cause a program to terminate. In this chapter, you learned how to use `Exception`s to handle many of these kinds of errors.

Some logical errors do not cause a program to terminate, but nevertheless produce incorrect results. For example, if a payroll program should determine gross pay by multiplying hours worked by hourly pay rate, but you inadvertently divide the numbers, no runtime error occurs and no `Exception` is thrown, but the output is wrong. An **assertion** is a Java language feature that can help you detect such logic errors and debug a program. You use an

assert statement to create an assertion; when you use an `assert` statement, you state
a condition that should be true, and Java throws an `AssertionError` when it is not.

The syntax of an `assert` statement is:

```
assert booleanExpression : optionalErrorMessage
```

The Boolean expression in the `assert` statement should always be `true` if the program is
working correctly. The `optionalErrorMessage` is displayed if the `booleanExpression` is
`false`.

Figure 15-33 contains an application that prompts a user for an hourly pay rate and is
intended to calculate the user's new weekly pay after all the following steps have occurred: a
raise has been applied to the hourly rate, the weekly gross pay has been calculated assuming a
40-hour work week, and withholding tax and insurance have been deducted. The application
in Figure 15-33 is free from syntax errors; it compiles and executes. However, when the user
enters a current pay rate of 12.00, the output (which should be a positive amount of more
than $355) is negative $140. The result does not make sense—a user's weekly pay after a raise
should not be less than the hourly pay before the raise, and certainly should not be negative.
(See Figure 15-34.)

```
import javax.swing.*;
class PayRaise
{
    public static void main(String[] args)
    {
        double oldPay = 0;
        double newPay = 0;
        final double INCREASE = 0.04;
        final double TAXRATE = 0.28;
        final double HRSPERWEEK = 40;
        final double INSURANCE = 140.00;
        String entry;
        entry = JOptionPane.showInputDialog(null,
            "Enter old pay per hour");
        oldPay = Double.parseDouble(entry);
        oldPay = oldPay + oldPay * INCREASE;
        newPay = (newPay * HRSPERWEEK) -
            (newPay * TAXRATE) - INSURANCE;
        JOptionPane.showMessageDialog(null,
            "New net pay is $" + newPay + " per week");
        System.exit(0);
    }
}
```

Figure 15-33 The flawed `PayRaise` application without any assertion

If you carefully examine the code in Figure 15-33, you might be able to find the logical error
that is the source of the incorrect output. However, in a more complicated program, you
might prefer to use an assertion to help you debug the application. Figure 15-35 contains the
same `PayRaise` application to which the shaded `assert` statement has been added. The
statement asserts that `oldPay` is less than `newPay`—a condition that should always be true

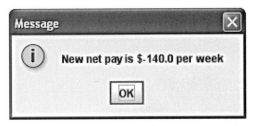

Figure 15-34 Incorrect output produced by `PayRaise` application in Figure 15-33

after a pay raise has been applied. If the expression is not true, a message is created using the values of both `oldPay` and `newPay`.

```java
import javax.swing.*;
class PayRaise
{
    public static void main(String[] args)
    {
        double oldPay = 0;
        double newPay = 0;
        final double INCREASE = 0.04;
        final double TAXRATE = 0.28;
        final double HRSPERWEEK = 40;
        final double INSURANCE = 140.00;
        String entry;
        entry = JOptionPane.showInputDialog(null,
            "Enter old pay per hour");
        oldPay = Double.parseDouble(entry);
        oldPay = oldPay + oldPay * INCREASE;
        newPay = (newPay * HRSPERWEEK) -
            (newPay * TAXRATE) - INSURANCE;
        assert oldPay < newPay:
            "Old Pay is " + oldPay +
            "\nNew pay is $" + newPay +
            "\nNew pay should be more than old pay";
        JOptionPane.showMessageDialog(null,
            "New net pay is $" + newPay + " per week");
        System.exit(0);
    }
}
```

Figure 15-35 The flawed `PayRaise` application containing an assertion

If you compile and execute the application in Figure 15-35 in the usual way, you get the same incorrect output as in Figure 15-34. To enable the assertion, you must compile the program using the `-source 1.6` option. (Notice the hyphen at the start of the option.) Then, when you execute the program, you must use the `-ea` option; *ea* stands for *enable assertion*. Figure 15-36 shows the command-line instructions needed to compile and execute the application and enable the assertion.

> **»NOTE** If you are not using Java version 6 (version 6 is the product version; 1.6 is used by developers), you should use the appropriate number with the `-source` compiler option. The assertion option was not available in its present form in versions earlier than 1.4.

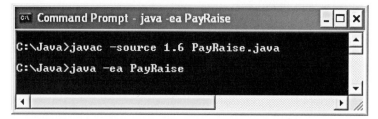

Figure 15-36 Compiling and executing an application using the enable assertion option

When the `PayRaise` program executes and the user enters 12.00, as shown in Figure 15-37, the program displays the message in Figure 15-38 instead of displaying incorrect output. You can see from the message that an `AssertionError` was thrown and that both the `oldPay` value (which is 12.48 but should be only 12.00) and the `newPay` value are incorrect.

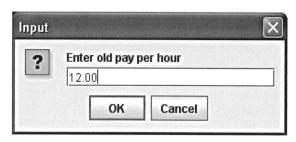

Figure 15-37 Input dialog box in `PayRaise` application

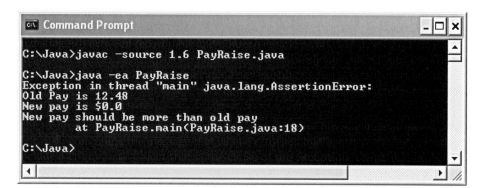

Figure 15-38 Message displayed by assertion in `PayRaise` application

When the programmer sees that the `oldPay` value is not what was entered, the reasonable course of action is to return to the source code and examine all the changes that are applied to the oldPay variable. The programmer can see that oldPay is correctly declared as a double in the first statement in the main() method. The next two statements that alter oldPay are:

```
oldPay = Double.parseDouble(entry);
oldPay = oldPay + oldPay * INCREASE;
```

In the first of these statements, the user's entry is correctly converted to a double and stored in oldPay. In the second statement, oldPay is increased by a percentage of itself. This is an incorrect statement; newPay should be a factor of oldPay. The programmer should make the shaded change shown in Figure 15-39. When this new version is compiled and executed using a $12.00 starting pay, the output appears as in Figure 15-40.

```
import javax.swing.*;
class PayRaise
{
    public static void main(String[] args)
    {
        double oldPay = 0;
        double newPay = 0;
        final double INCREASE = 0.04;
        final double TAXRATE = 0.28;
        final double HRSPERWEEK = 40;
        final double INSURANCE = 140.00;
        String entry;
        entry = JOptionPane.showInputDialog(null,
            "Enter old pay per hour");
        oldPay = Double.parseDouble(entry);
        newPay = oldPay + oldPay * INCREASE;
        newPay = (newPay * HRSPERWEEK) -
            (newPay * TAXRATE) - INSURANCE;
        assert oldPay < newPay:
            "Old Pay is " + oldPay +
            "\nNew pay is $" + newPay +
            "\nNew pay should be more than old pay";
        JOptionPane.showMessageDialog(null,
            "New net pay is $" + newPay + " per week");
        System.exit(0);
    }
}
```

Figure 15-39 The correct PayRaise application

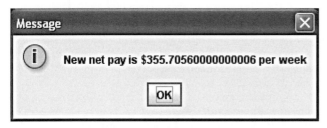

Figure 15-40 Output of PayRaise application when user enters 12.00

An experienced programmer could have found the error in the original `PayRaise` application without using an assertion. For example, the programmer might have found the error simply by examining the code carefully. Alternatively, the programmer could have inserted print statements to display variable values at strategic points in the program. However, after the mistake is found and fixed, the extra print statements should be removed when the final product is ready for distribution to users. In contrast, any `assert` statements can be left in place, and if the user does not use the `-ea` option when running the program, the user will see no evidence that the `assert` statements exist. Placing `assert` statements in key program locations can reduce development and debugging time.

>> **NOTE** When you run the `PayRaise` program that contains an assertion, you do not need to use the `-ea` option; you can use it only if you modify the program in the future and want to test the `oldPay` and `newPay` values again.

>> **NOTE** You do not want to use assertions to check for every type of error that could occur in a program. For example, if you want to ensure that a user enters numeric data, you should use exception-handling techniques that provide the means for your program to recover from the mistake. If you want to ensure that the data falls within a specific range, you should use a decision or a loop. Assertions are meant to be helpful in the development stage of a program, not when it is in production and in the hands of users.

YOU DO IT

CATCHING AN `Exception` AND USING `getMessage()`

In this section, you will create an application that catches an `ArithmeticException` if you attempt to divide by 0, and you will use the `getMessage()` method to display the automatically generated message for the exception.

To write an application that catches an `ArithmeticException`:

1. Open a new file in your text editor and type the first few lines of an interactive application named `PerformDivision`.

```
import javax.swing.*;
public class PerformDivision
{
    public static void main(String[] args)
    {
```

2. Declare three integers—two to be input by the user and a third to hold the result after dividing the first two. Also declare an input `String` to hold the return value of the `JOptionPane showInputDialog()` method.

```
int num1, num2, result;
String inputString;
```

3. Add code to prompt the user for two values, and convert each entered `String` to an integer.

```
inputString = JOptionPane.showInputDialog(null,
    "Enter a number to be divided");
num1 = Integer.parseInt(inputString);
    inputString = JOptionPane.showInputDialog(null,
        "Enter a number to divide into the first number");
num2 = Integer.parseInt(inputString);
```

4. Place the division operation in a `try` block. Follow the block with a `catch` clause that catches an `ArithmeticException` if an attempt is made to divide by 0. If the `try` is successful, it holds the result of the division. If the `try` fails, the `catch` block displays the `String` returned by the `getMessage()` method message and sets the result to 0.

```
try
{
    result = num1 / num2;
}
catch(ArithmeticException exception)
{
    JOptionPane.showMessageDialog(null,
        exception.getMessage());
    result = 0;
}
```

5. Whether the `try` block succeeds or not, display the result (which might have been set to 0) and exit the application. Include closing curly braces for the `main()` method and for the class.

```
        JOptionPane.showMessageDialog(null, num1 +
            " / " + num2 + "\nResult is " + result);
        System.exit(0);
    }
}
```

6. Save the file as **PerformDivision.java** in the Chapter.15 folder on your Student Disk. Compile and then execute the application. Enter two nonzero values. For example, Figure 15-41 shows the output when the user enters 12 and 4 as the two input values.

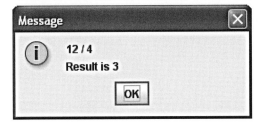

Figure 15-41 Output of the `PerformDivision` application when the user enters 12 and 4

7. Close the application. Execute it again using 0 as the second input value. For example, when the user enters 12 and 0, the first output looks like the dialog box on the left in Figure 15-42.

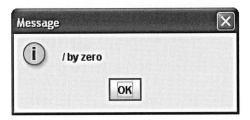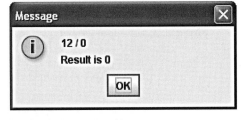

Figure 15-42 Output of the `PerformDivision` application when the user enters 12 and 0

8. Click **OK**. The next dialog box looks like the one on the right in Figure 15-42. The output shows that the Exception was caught successfully, setting the result to 0.

9. Close the application.

GENERATING A NumberFormatException

The PerformDivision application works, dividing numbers it can and handling any attempt to divide by 0. However, the application is not forgiving if you do not enter numeric values when prompted. Next, you will test the PerformDivision application using non-numeric input, and then you will remedy the error caused by the unhandled exception.

To test the PerformDivision application with non-numeric input:

1. Run the PerformDivision application again. When prompted for the first value, enter some text instead of a number. For example, when the user enters "a", the screen looks like Figure 15-43. The automatically generated error messages indicate that a NumberFormatException has been thrown for the input string "a".

```
Command Prompt                                              _ □ ×

C:\Java>java PerformDivision
Exception in thread "main" java.lang.NumberFormatException: For input string: "a
"
        at java.lang.NumberFormatException.forInputString(NumberFormatException.
java:48)
        at java.lang.Integer.parseInt(Integer.java:447)
        at java.lang.Integer.parseInt(Integer.java:497)
        at PerformDivision.main(PerformDivision.java:10)

C:\Java>
```

Figure 15-43 Messages generated when the user types a letter as input for the PerformDivision application

ADDING NumberFormatException HANDLING CAPABILITIES TO AN APPLICATION

Next, you will modify the PerformDivision application so that the statements that convert the input strings to integers are within try blocks; in this way, any thrown Exception can be handled.

To handle the NumberFormatException in the PerformDivision application:

1. If it is not still open, open the **PerformDivision.java** file in your text editor. Change the class name to **PerformDivision2** and save the file as **PerformDivision2.java**.

2. Provide initial values for the num1 and num2 variables, changing the integer declaration statement to the following:

```
int num1 = 0, num2 = 0, result;
```

This step is necessary because you will place the statements that provide values for num1 and num2 in a try block. The compiler understands that a try block might not complete; that is, it might throw an Exception before it is through. Therefore, when the application reaches the point where num1 and num2 are displayed following the try and catch blocks, it might attempt to display invalid, or "garbage," values. In other words, the compiler does not allow you to display num1 and num2 at the end of the application if it is not certain that these variables were provided with legitimate values beforehand.

3. Cut the two lines containing `try` and its opening curly brace from their current position just before the division operation, and insert them immediately after the statement that declares the `inputString`. In other words, now all the input statements and their conversion to integers are within the `try` block, along with the division operation.

4. After the closing curly brace of the `catch` block that catches the `ArithmeticException`, add a second `catch` block to handle potential `NumberFormatExceptions` by displaying a message, setting num1 and num2 to 999, and forcing the `result` to 1.

```
catch(NumberFormatException exception)
{
    JOptionPane.showMessageDialog(null,
        "This application accepts digits only!");
    num1 = 999;
    num2 = 999;
    result = 1;
}
```

5. Save the application, then compile and execute it. This time, if you type some letters instead of a number, the program does not end abruptly—instead, the dialog boxes in Figure 15-44 appear. Click **OK** to dismiss each dialog box.

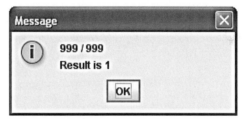

Figure 15-44 Output of the `PerformDivision2` application when the user types letters for an input value

CREATING A CLASS THAT AUTOMATICALLY THROWS Exceptions

Next, you will create a class that contains two methods that throw `Exceptions` but don't catch them. The `PickMenu` class allows Event Handlers Incorporated customers to choose a dinner menu selection as part of their event planning. Before you create `PickMenu`, you will create the `Menu` class, which lists dinner choices for customers and allows them to make a selection.

To create the Menu class:

1. Open a new file in your text editor, then enter the following import statement, class header, and opening curly brace for the `Menu` class:

```
import javax.swing.*;
public class Menu
{
```

2. Type the following `String` array for three entree choices. Also include a `String` to build the menu that you will display and an integer to hold the numeric equivalent of the selection.

```
private String[] entreeChoice = {"Rosemary Chicken",
    "Beef Wellington", "Maine Lobster"};
private String menu = "";
private int choice;
```

3. Add the `displayMenu()` method, which lists each entree option with a corresponding number the customer can type to make a selection. Even though the allowable `entreeChoice` array subscripts are 0, 1, and 2, most users would expect to type 1, 2, or 3. So, you code `x + 1` rather than `x` as the number in the prompt. After the user enters a selection, convert it to an integer. Return the `String` that corresponds to the user's menu selection—the one with the subscript that is 1 less than the entered value. After the closing curly brace for the `displayMenu()` method, add the closing curly brace for the class.

```
public String displayMenu()
{
    for(int x = 0; x < entreeChoice.length; ++x)
    {
        menu = menu + "\n" + (x + 1) + " for " +
            entreeChoice[x];
    }
    String input = JOptionPane.showInputDialog(null,
        "Type your selection, then press Enter." + menu);
    choice = Integer.parseInt(input);
    return(entreeChoice[choice - 1]);
}
}
```

> **NOTE** The curly braces are not necessary in the `for` loop of the `displayMenu()` method because the loop contains only one statement. However, in a later exercise, you will add another statement within this block.

4. Examine the code within the `displayMenu()` method. Consider the exceptions that might occur. The user might not type an integer, so the `parseInt()` method can fail, and even if the user does type an integer, it might not be in the range allowed to access the `entreeChoice` array. Therefore, the `displayMenu()` method, like most methods in which you rely on the user to enter data, might throw exceptions that you can anticipate. (Of course, any method might throw an unanticipated exception.)

5. Save the file as **Menu.java** in the Chapter.15 folder on your Student Disk, and compile the class using the **javac** command.

CREATING A CLASS THAT PASSES ON AN Exception

Next, you will create the `PickMenu` class, which lets the customer choose from the available dinner entree options. The `PickMenu` class declares a `Menu` and a `String` named `guestChoice` that holds the name of the entree the customer selects.

To enable the `PickMenu` class to operate with different kinds of `Menu`s in the future, you will pass a `Menu` to `PickMenu`'s constructor. This technique provides two advantages: First, when the menu options change, you can alter the contents of the Menu.java file without changing any of the code in programs that use Menu. Second, you can extend Menu, perhaps to VegetarianMenu, LowSaltMenu, or KosherMenu, and still use the existing PickMenu class. When you pass any Menu or Menu subclass into the PickMenu constructor, the correct customer options appear.

The PickMenu class is unlikely to directly generate any exceptions because it does not request user input. (Keep in mind that any class might generate an exception for such uncontrollable events as the system not having enough memory available.) However, PickMenu declares a Menu object; the Menu class, because it relies on user input, is likely to generate an Exception.

To create the PickMenu class:

1. Open a new file in your text editor, then add the following first few lines of the PickMenu class with its data fields (a Menu and a String that reflect the customer's choice):

```
import javax.swing.*;
public class PickMenu
{
    private Menu briefMenu;
    private String guestChoice = new String();
```

2. Enter the following PickMenu constructor, which receives an argument representing a Menu. The constructor assigns the Menu that is the argument to the local Menu, then calls the setGuestChoice() method, which prompts the user to select from the available menu. The PickMenu() constructor method might throw an Exception because it calls setGuestChoice(), which calls displayMenu(), a method that uses keyboard input and might throw an Exception.

```
public PickMenu(Menu theMenu)
{
    briefMenu = theMenu;
    setGuestChoice();
}
```

3. The following setGuestChoice() method displays the menu and reads keyboard data entry (so the method throws an Exception). It also displays instructions and then retrieves the user's selection.

```
public void setGuestChoice()
{
    JOptionPane.showMessageDialog(null,
        "Choose from the following menu:");
    guestChoice = briefMenu.displayMenu();
}
```

4. Add the following getGuestChoice() method that returns a guest's String selection from the PickMenu class. Also, add a closing curly brace for the class.

```
    public String getGuestChoice()
    {
        return(guestChoice);
    }
}
```

5. Save the file as **PickMenu.java** in the Chapter.15 folder on your Student Disk, and compile it using the **javac** command.

CREATING AN APPLICATION
THAT CAN CATCH Exceptions

You have created a Menu class that simply holds a list of food items, displays itself, and allows the user to make a selection. You also created a PickMenu class with fields that hold a user's specific selection from a given menu and methods to get and set values for those fields. The PickMenu class might throw Exceptions, but it contains no methods that catch those Exceptions. Next, you will write an application that uses the PickMenu class. This application can catch Exceptions that PickMenu throws.

To write the PlanMenu class:

1. Open a new file in your text editor, and start entering the following PlanMenu class, which has just one method—a main() method:

```
import javax.swing.*;
public class PlanMenu
{
    public static void main(String[] args)
    {
```

2. Construct the following Menu named briefMenu, and declare a PickMenu object that you name entree. You do not want to construct a PickMenu object yet because you want to be able to catch the Exception that the PickMenu constructor might throw. Therefore, you want to wait and construct the PickMenu object within a try block. For now, you just declare entree and assign it null. Also, you declare a String that holds the customer's menu selection.

```
Menu briefMenu = new Menu();
PickMenu entree = null;
String guestChoice = new String();
```

3. Write the following try block that constructs a PickMenu item. If the construction is successful, the next statement assigns a selection to the entree object. Because entree is a PickMenu object, it has access to the getGuestChoice() method in the PickMenu class, and you can assign the method's returned value to the guestChoiceString.

```
try
{
    PickMenu selection = new PickMenu(briefMenu);
    entree = selection;
    guestChoice = entree.getGuestChoice();
}
```

4. The catch block must immediately follow the try block. When the try block fails, guestChoice will not have a valid value, so recover from the Exception by assigning a value to guestChoice within the following catch block:

```
catch(Exception error)
{
    guestChoice = "an invalid selection";
}
```

5. After the `catch` block, the application continues. Use the following code to display the customer's choice at the end of the `PlanMenu` application, and then add closing curly braces for the `main()` method and the class:

```
JOptionPane.showMessageDialog(null,
    "You chose " + guestChoice);
System.exit(0);
    }
}
```

6. Save the file as **PlanMenu.java** in the Chapter.15 folder on your Student Disk, then compile and execute it. Read the instructions, click **OK**, choose an entree by typing its number from the menu, and click **OK** again. Confirm that the menu selection displayed is the one you chose, and click **OK** to dismiss the last dialog box. Figure 15-45 shows the first dialog box of instructions, the menu that displays, and the output when the user selects option 2.

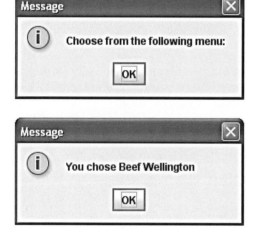
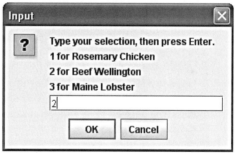

Figure 15-45 Typical execution of the `PlanMenu` application

7. The `PlanMenu` application works well when you enter a valid menu selection. One way that you can force an `Exception` is to enter an invalid menu selection at the prompt. Run the `PlanMenu` application again, and type **4**, **A**, or any invalid value at the prompt. Entering "4" produces an `ArrayIndexOutOfBoundsException`, and entering "A" produces a `NumberFormatException`. If the program lacked the `try...catch` pair, either entry would halt the program. However, because the `setGuestChoice()` method in the `PickMenu` class `throws` the `Exception` and the `PlanMenu` application catches it, `guestChoice` takes on the value "an invalid selection" and the application ends smoothly, as shown in Figure 15-46.

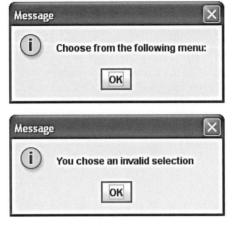
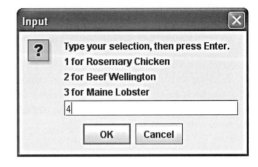

Figure 15-46 Exceptional execution of the `PlanMenu` application

EXTENDING A CLASS THAT THROWS Exceptions

An advantage to using object-oriented `Exception` handling techniques is that you gain the ability to handle error conditions differently within each program you write. Next, you will extend the `Menu` class to create a class named `VegetarianMenu`. Subsequently, when you write an application that uses `PickMenu` with a `VegetarianMenu` object, you can deal with any thrown `Exception` differently than when you wrote the `PlanMenu` application.

To create the `VegetarianMenu` class:

1. Open the **Menu.java** file in your text editor and change the access specifier for the `entreeChoice` array from `private` to `protected`. That way, when you extend the class, the derived class will have access to the array. Save the file and recompile it using the **javac** command.

2. Open a new file in your text editor, then type the following class header for the `VegetarianMenu` class that extends `Menu`:

```
public class VegetarianMenu extends Menu
{
```

3. Provide new menu choices for the `VegetarianMenu` as follows:

```
String[] vegEntreeChoice = {"Spinach Lasagna",
   "Cheese Enchiladas", "Fruit Plate"};
```

4. Add the following constructor that calls the superclass constructor and assigns each vegetarian selection to the `Menu` superclass `entreeChoice` array, and then add the closing curly brace for the class:

```
public VegetarianMenu()
{
    super();
    for(int x = 0; x < vegEntreeChoice.length; ++x)
        entreeChoice[x] = vegEntreeChoice[x];
}
}
```

5. Save the class as **VegetarianMenu.java** in the Chapter.15 folder on your Student Disk, then compile it.

6. Now write an application that uses `VegetarianMenu`. You could write any program, but for demonstration purposes, you can simply modify PlanMenu.java. Open the **PlanMenu.java** file in your text editor, then immediately save it as **PlanVegetarianMenu.java**.

7. Change the class name in the header to **PlanVegetarianMenu**.

8. Change the first statement within the `main()` method as follows so it declares a `VegetarianMenu` instead of a `Menu`:

```
VegetarianMenu briefMenu = new VegetarianMenu();
```

9. Change the `guestChoice` assignment statement in the `catch` block as follows so it is specific to the program that uses the `VegetarianMenu`:

```
guestChoice = "an invalid vegetarian selection";
```

10. Save the file in the Chapter.15 folder on your Student Disk, compile it, and run the application. When you see the vegetarian menu, enter a valid selection and confirm that the program works correctly. Run the application again and enter an invalid selection. The error message shown in Figure 15-47 identifies your invalid entry as "an invalid vegetarian selection". Remember that you did not change the `PickMenu` class. Your new `PlanVegetarianMenu` application uses the `PickMenu` class that you wrote and compiled before a `VegetarianMenu` ever existed. However, because `PickMenu` throws uncaught `Exceptions`, you can handle those `Exceptions` as you see fit in any new applications in which you `catch` them. Click **OK** to end the application.

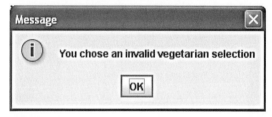

Figure 15-47 Output of the `PlanVegetarianMenu` application when the user makes an invalid selection

USING THE `printStackTrace()` METHOD

The `printStackTrace()` method can help you locate the origin of a thrown `Exception`. In this section, you will add a call to `printStackTrace()` in the `catch` block in the `PlanMenu` class.

To use the `printStackTrace()` method:

1. Open the **PlanMenu.java** file in your text editor and save it as **PlanMenuWithStackTrace.java**.

2. Change the class header to **PlanMenuWithStackTrace**.

3. Position your insertion point within the `catch` block after the statement `guestChoice = "an invalid selection";`, then press **Enter** to start a new line. Type the following

two new statements to identify and print the stack trace using the object named `error` that is the `Exception` passed into the `catch` block:

```
System.out.println("StackTrace");
error.printStackTrace();
```

4. Save the file in the Chapter.15 folder on your Student Disk, then compile and execute it. After the menu appears, enter an invalid selection. If you enter "4", your command screen looks like Figure 15-48. If you read the list that follows the Stack Trace heading, you see that an `ArrayIndexOutOfBoundsException` occurred in the method `Menu.displayMenu()`, and that the value that caused the `Exception` was 3 (the 4 you entered, minus 1). That method was called by the `PickMenu.setGuestChoice()` method, which in turn was initiated by the `PickMenu` constructor. The `PickMenu` constructor was called from the `PlanMenuWithStackTrace.main()` method. You see the line number as additional information within each method in which the `Exception` occurred. (Your line numbers might be different if you added comments to your classes or changed the layout of your lines from that shown in this book.) If you did not understand why entering 4 caused an error, you would use the stack trace information to first examine the `Menu.displayMenu()` method as the original source of the error. Using `printStackTrace()` can be a helpful debugging tool.

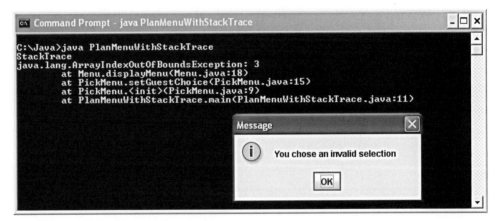

Figure 15-48 Messages generated by `printStackTrace()` after the user enters 4

5. Close the application by clicking **OK** in the dialog box or by pressing **Ctrl+C**.

Run the **PlanMenuWithStackTrace** application again, and enter **A** for the user selection. You can see from the stack trace that this time the `Exception` does not originate directly in the `Menu.displayMenu()` method. This execution of the application generates a `NumberFormatException` at the `parseInt()` method within the `displayMenu()` method before the application attempts to access the array. See Figure 15-49.

6. Close the application by clicking **OK** in the dialog box or by pressing **Ctrl+C** when the command prompt window is the active window.

Figure 15-49 Messages generated by `printStackTrace()` after the user enters A

CREATING AN Exception CLASS

Besides using the built-in `Exceptions` such as `NumberFormatException` and `IndexOutOfBoundsException`, you can create your own `Exception` classes. For example, suppose that although you have asked a user to type a number representing a menu selection, you realize that some users might mistakenly type the initial letter of an option, such as "R" for "Rosemary Chicken". Although the user has made an error, you want to treat this type of error more leniently than other errors, such as typing a letter that has no discernable connection to the presented menu. In the next section, you will create a `MenuException` class that you can use with the `Menu` class you created earlier to represent a specific type of error.

To create the `MenuException` class:

1. Open a new file in your text editor and enter the `MenuException` class. The class extends `Exception`. Its constructor requires a `String` argument, which is passed to the parent class to be used as a return value for the `getMessage()` method.

```
public class MenuException extends Exception
{
    public MenuException(String choice)
    {
        super(choice);
    }
}
```

2. Save the file as **MenuException.java** in the Chapter.15 folder on your Student Disk. Compile the class.

USING AN Exception YOU CREATED

Next, you will modify the `Menu`, `PickMenu`, and `PlanMenu` classes to demonstrate how to use a `MenuException` object.

To modify the `Menu` class to throw a `MenuException` object:

1. Open the **Menu** class in your text editor, and immediately save the file as **Menu2.java**.

2. Change the class name to **Menu2**.

3. At the end of the list of class data fields, add an array of characters that can hold the first letter of each of the entrees in the menu.

```
protected char initial[] = new char[entreeChoice.length];
```

4. At the end of the method header for the `displayMenu()` class, add the following clause:

```
throws MenuException
```

You add this clause because you are going to add code that throws such an exception.

5. Within the `displayMenu()` method, just before the closing curly brace of the `for` loop that builds the menu `String`, add a statement that takes the first character of each `entreeChoice` and stores it in a corresponding element of the `initial` array. At the end of the `for` loop, the `initial` array holds the first character of each available entree.

```
initial[x] = entreeChoice[x].charAt(0);
```

6. After displaying the `JOptionPane` dialog box that displays the menu and receives the user's input, add a loop that compares the first letter of the user's choice to each of the initials of valid menu options. If a match is found, throw a new instance of the `MenuException` class that uses the corresponding entree as its `String` argument. In other words, when this thrown `Exception` is caught by another method, the assumed entree is the `String` returned by the `getMessage()` method. By placing this test before the call to `parseInt()`, you cause entries of "R", "B", or "M" to throw a `MenuException` before they can cause a `NumberFormatException`.

```
for(int y = 0; y < entreeChoice.length; ++ y)
   if(input.charAt(0) == initial[y])
      throw (new MenuException(entreeChoice[y]));
```

7. Take a moment to compare your new class with Figure 15-50, in which all of the changes to the `Menu` class are shaded.

8. Save the class and compile it.

To modify the `PickMenu` class to throw a `MenuException` object:

1. Open the **PickMenu** file in your text editor and immediately save it as **PickMenu2.java**.

2. Change the class name to **PickMenu2** and change the declaration of the `Menu` object to a **Menu2** object. Change the constructor name to **PickMenu2** and its argument to type **Menu2**. Also add a `throws` clause to the `PickMenu2` constructor header so that it **throws MenuException**. This constructor does not throw an `Exception` directly, but it calls the `setGuestChoice()` method, which calls the `displayMenu()` method, which throws a `MenuException`.

3. Add the following `throws` clause to the `setGuestChoice()` method header:

```
throws MenuException
```

4. Compare your modifications to the `PickMenu2` class in Figure 15-51, in which the changes from the `PickMenu` class are shaded. Save your file and compile it.

```
import javax.swing.*;
public class Menu2
{
    protected String[] entreeChoice = {"Rosemary Chicken",
        "Beef Wellington", "Maine Lobster"};
    private String menu = "";
    private int choice;
    protected char initial[] = new char[ entreeChoice.length];
    public String displayMenu() throws MenuException
    {
        for(int x = 0; x < entreeChoice.length; ++x)
        {
            menu = menu + "\n" + (x + 1) + " for " +
                entreeChoice[ x];
            initial[ x] = entreeChoice[ x].charAt(0);
        }
        String input = JOptionPane.showInputDialog(null,
            "Type your selection, then press Enter." + menu);
        for(int y = 0; y < entreeChoice.length; ++ y)
            if(input.charAt(0) == initial[ y])
                throw (new MenuException(entreeChoice[ y]));
        choice = Integer.parseInt(input);
        return(entreeChoice[ choice - 1]);
    }
}
```

Figure 15-50 The Menu2 class

```
import javax.swing.*;
public class PickMenu2
{
    private Menu2 briefMenu;
    private String guestChoice = new String();
    public PickMenu2(Menu2 theMenu) throws MenuException
    {
        briefMenu = theMenu;
        setGuestChoice();
    }
    public void setGuestChoice() throws MenuException
    {
        String inputString = new String();
        JOptionPane.showMessageDialog(null,
            "Choose from the following menu:");
        guestChoice = briefMenu.displayMenu();
    }
    public String getGuestChoice()
    {
        return(guestChoice);
    }
}
```

Figure 15-51 The PickMenu2 class

To modify the `PlanMenu` class to handle a `MenuException` object:

1. Open the **PlanMenu.java** file in your text editor and immediately save it as **PlanMenu2.java**.

2. Change the class name to **PlanMenu2**. Within the `main()` method, declare a **Menu2** object and a **PickMenu2** reference instead of the current `Menu` object and `PickMenu` reference.

3. Within the `try` block, change both references of `PickMenu` to **PickMenu2**.

   Using Figure 15-52 as a reference, add a `catch` block after the `try` block and before the existing `catch` block. This `catch` block will catch any thrown `MenuExceptions` and display their messages. The message will be the name of a menu item, based on the initial the user entered. All other `Exceptions`, including `NumberFormatExceptions` and `IndexOutOfBoundsExceptions`, will fall through to the second `catch` block and be handled as before.

```
import javax.swing.*;
public class PlanMenu2
{
    public static void main(String[] args)
    {
        Menu2 briefMenu = new Menu2();
        PickMenu2 entree = null;
        String guestChoice = new String();
        try
        {
            PickMenu2 selection = new PickMenu2(briefMenu);
            entree = selection;
            guestChoice = entree.getGuestChoice();
        }
        catch( MenuException error)
        {
            guestChoice = error.getMessage();
        }
        catch(Exception error)
        {
            guestChoice = "an invalid selection";
        }
        JOptionPane.showMessageDialog(null,
            "You chose " + guestChoice);
        System.exit(0);
    }
}
```

Figure 15-52 The `PlanMenu2` class

4. Save the file, then compile and execute it several times. When you are asked to make a selection, try entering a valid number, an invalid number, an initial letter that is part of the menu, and a letter that is not one of the initial menu letters, and observe the results each time. Whether you enter a valid number or not, the application works as expected. Entering an invalid number still results in an error message. When you enter a letter or a string of letters, the application assumes your selection is valid if you enter the same initial letter, using the same case, as one of the menu options.

KEY TERMS

An **exception** is an unexpected or error condition.

Exception handling is an object-oriented technique for managing errors.

Runtime exceptions are unplanned exceptions that occur during a program's execution. The term is also used more specifically to describe members of the `RuntimeException` class.

The **`Error` class** represents more serious errors than the `Exception` class—those from which your program usually cannot recover.

The **`Exception` class** comprises less serious errors than those from the `Error` class; the `Exception` class represents unusual conditions that arise while a program is running, and from which the program can recover.

Fault-tolerant applications are designed so that they continue to operate, possibly at a reduced level, when some part of the system fails.

Robustness represents the degree to which a system is resilient to stress, maintaining correct functioning.

When you create a segment of code in which something might go wrong, you place the code in a **`try` block**, which is a block of code you attempt to execute while acknowledging that an exception might occur.

A **`catch` block** is a segment of code that can handle an exception that might be thrown by the `try` block that precedes it.

A **throw statement** is one that sends an `Exception` out of a method so it can be handled elsewhere.

Unreachable code statements are program statements that can never execute under any circumstances.

Programmers also call unreachable code **dead code**.

When you have actions you must perform at the end of a `try...catch` sequence, you can use a **`finally` block**.

The term **mission critical** refers to any process that is crucial to an organization.

Checked exceptions are those that a programmer should plan for and from which a program should be able to recover. They are not runtime exceptions; the compiler checks that these exceptions are caught or specified.

The **catch or specify requirement** is the Java rule that checked exceptions require catching or declaration.

Syntactic sugar is a term to describe aspects of a computer language that make it "sweeter," or easier, for programmers to use.

Syntactic salt describes a language feature designed to make it harder to write bad code.

A **thread** is the flow of execution of one set of program statements.

The memory location known as the **call stack** is where the computer stores the list of method locations to which the system must return.

A **pointer** is a reference variable. The term is used in C++ programming more frequently than in Java programming.

An **assertion** is a Java language feature that can help you detect logic errors and debug a program.

You use an **assert statement** to create an assertion.

CHAPTER SUMMARY

» An exception is an unexpected or error condition. The object-oriented techniques to manage such errors comprise the group of methods known as exception handling. In Java, the two basic classes of errors are `Error` and `Exception`; both descend from the `Throwable` class.

» Exception handling provides an elegant solution for handling error conditions. In object-oriented terminology, you "try" a procedure that might cause an error. A method that detects an error condition or `Exception` "throws an exception," and the block of code that processes the error "catches the exception."

» When you create a segment of code in which something might go wrong, you place the code in a `try` block, which is a block of code you attempt to execute while acknowledging that an exception might occur. You must code at least one `catch` block immediately following a `try` block (or else you must code a `finally` block). A `catch` block is a segment of code that can handle an exception that might be thrown by the `try` block that precedes it.

» You can place as many statements as you need within a `try` block, and you can `catch` as many `Exceptions` as you want. If you `try` more than one statement, only the first error-generating statement `throws` an `Exception`. As soon as the `Exception` occurs, the logic transfers to the `catch` block, which leaves the rest of the statements in the `try` block unexecuted. When a program contains multiple `catch` blocks, they are examined in sequence until a match is found for the type of `Exception` that occurred. Then, the matching `catch` block executes and each remaining `catch` block is bypassed.

» When you have actions you must perform at the end of a `try...catch` sequence, you can use a `finally` block. The code within a `finally` block executes regardless of whether the preceding `try` block identifies an `Exception`. Usually, you use a `finally` block to perform cleanup tasks that must happen whether or not any `Exceptions` occurred, and whether or not any `Exceptions` that occurred were caught.

» Besides clarity, an advantage to object-oriented exception handling is the flexibility it allows in the handling of error situations. Each calling application might need to handle the same error differently, depending on its purpose.

» When you write a method that might throw a checked `Exception` that is not caught within the method, you must type the clause `throws <name>Exception` after the method header to indicate the type of `Exception` that might be thrown. Methods in which you explicitly throw a checked exception require a catch or a declaration. Every Java method you write has the potential to throw an `Exception`. Some `Exceptions` can occur anywhere at any time. However, for most Java methods that you write, you do not use a `throws` clause.

» When one method calls another, the computer's operating system must keep track of where the method call came from, and program control must return to the calling method when the called method is completed. The memory location known as the call stack is where the computer stores the list of method locations to which the system must return. A useful `Exception` method is the `printStackTrace()` method. When you catch an `Exception`, you can call `printStackTrace()` to display a list of methods in the call stack so you can determine the location of the `Exception`.

» Java provides over 40 categories of `Exceptions` that you can use in your programs. However, Java's creators could not predict every condition that might be an `Exception` in your applications, so Java also allows you to create your own `Exceptions`. To create your own throwable `Exception`, you must extend a subclass of `Throwable`.

» An assertion is a Java language feature that can help you detect logic errors and debug a program. When you use an assertion, you state a condition that should be true, and Java throws an `AssertionError` when it is not.

REVIEW QUESTIONS

1. In object-oriented programming terminology, an unexpected or error condition is a(n) _____ .

   a. anomaly   c. deviation

   b. aberration   d. exception

2. All Java `Exceptions` are _____ .

   a. `Errors`

   b. `RuntimeExceptions`

   c. `Throwables`

   d. `Omissions`

3. Which of the following statements is true?

   a. `Exceptions` are more serious than `Errors`.

   b. `Errors` are more serious than `Exceptions`.

   c. `Errors` and `Exceptions` are equally serious.

   d. `Exceptions` and `Errors` are the same thing.

4. The method that ends the current application and returns control to the operating system is _____ .

   a. `System.end()`   c. `System.exit()`

   b. `System.done()`   d. `System.abort()`

5. In object-oriented terminology, you _____ a procedure that might not complete correctly.

   a. `try`   c. `handle`

   b. `catch`   d. `encapsulate`

6. A method that detects an error condition or Exception _____ an Exception.

   a. throws   c. handles

   b. catches   d. encapsulates

7. A try block includes all of the following elements except _____ .

   a. the keyword try

   b. the keyword catch

   c. curly braces

   d. statements that might cause Exceptions

8. The segment of code that handles or takes appropriate action following an exception is a _____ block.

   a. try   c. throws

   b. catch   d. handles

9. You _____ within a try block.

   a. must place only a single statement

   b. can place any number of statements

   c. must place at least two statements

   d. must place a catch block

10. If you try three statements and include three catch blocks, and the second try statement throws an Exception, _____ .

    a. the first catch block executes

    b. the first two catch blocks execute

    c. only the second catch block executes

    d. the first matching catch block executes

11. When a try block does not generate an Exception and you have included multiple catch blocks, _____ .

    a. they all execute

    b. only the first one executes

    c. only the first matching one executes

    d. no catch blocks execute

12. The catch block that begins catch (Exception e) can catch Exceptions of type _____ .

    a. IOException

    b. ArithmeticException

    c. both of the above

    d. none of the above

13. The code within a `finally` block executes when the `try` block _____.

    a. identifies one or more `Exceptions`

    b. does not identify any `Exceptions`

    c. either a or b

    d. neither a nor b

14. An advantage to using a `try...catch` block is that exceptional events are _____.

    a. eliminated

    b. reduced

    c. integrated with regular events

    d. isolated from regular events

15. Which methods can `throw` an `Exception`?

    a. methods with a `throws` clause

    b. methods with a `catch` block

    c. methods with both a `throws` clause and a `catch` block

    d. any method

16. A method can _____.

    a. check for errors but not handle them

    b. handle errors but not check for them

    c. either of the above

    d. neither of the above

17. Which of the following is least important to know if you want to be able to use a method to its full potential?

    a. the method's return type

    b. the type of arguments the method requires

    c. the number of statements within the method

    d. the type of `Exceptions` the method `throws`

18. The memory location where the computer stores the list of method locations to which the system must return is known as the _____.

    a. registry   c. chronicle

    b. call stack   d. archive

19. You can get a list of the methods through which an `Exception` has traveled by using the _____ method.

    a. `getMessage()`   c. `getPath()`

    b. `callStack()`   d. `printStackTrace()`

20. A(n) _____ is a statement used in testing programs that should be true; if it is not true, an Exception is thrown.

 a. verification

 b. throwable

 c. assertion

 d. declaration

EXERCISES

1. Write an application named GoTooFar in which you declare an array of five integers and store five values in the array. Write a try block in which you loop to display each successive element of the array, increasing a subscript by 1 on each pass through the loop. Create a catch block that catches the eventual ArrayIndexOutOfBoundsException and displays the message, "Now you've gone too far." Save the file as **GoTooFar.java**.

2. The Integer.parseInt() method requires a String argument, but fails if the String cannot be converted to an integer. Write an application in which you try to parse a String that does not represent an integer value. Catch the NumberFormatExceptionError that is thrown, and then display an appropriate error message. Save the file as **TryToParseString.java**.

3. Write an application that prompts the user to enter a number to use as an array size, and then attempt to declare an array using the entered size. If the array is created successfully, display an appropriate message. Java generates a NegativeArraySizeException if you attempt to create an array with a negative size, and a NumberFormatException if you attempt to create an array using a non-numeric value for the size. Use a catch block that executes if the array size is non-numeric or negative, displaying a message that indicates the array was not created. Save the file as **NegativeArray.java**.

4. Write an application that throws and catches an ArithmeticException when you attempt to take the square root of a negative value. Prompt the user for an input value and try the Math.sqrt() method on it. The application either displays the square root or catches the thrown Exception and displays an appropriate message. Save the file as **SqrtException.java**.

5. Create an EmployeeException class whose constructor receives a String that consists of an employee's ID and pay rate. Save the file as **EmployeeException.java**. Create an Employee class with two fields, idNum and hourlyWage. The Employee constructor requires values for both fields. Upon construction, throw an EmployeeException if the hourlyWage is less than $6.00 or over $50.00. Save the class as **Employee.java**. Write an application that establishes at least three Employees with hourlyWages that are above, below, and within the allowed range. Display an appropriate message when an Employee is successfully created and when one is not. Save the file as **ThrowEmployee.java**.

6. a. Create an `IceCreamConeException` class whose constructor receives a `String` that consists of an ice cream cone's flavor and an integer representing the number of scoops in the `IceCreamCone`. Pass this `String` to the `IceCreamConeException`'s parent so it can be used in a `getMessage()` call. Save the class as **IceCreamConeException.java**. Create an `IceCreamCone` class with two fields—`flavor` and `scoops`. The `IceCreamCone` constructor calls two data-entry methods—`setFlavor()` and `setScoops()`. The `setScoops()` method throws an `IceCreamConeException` when the scoop quantity exceeds three. Save the class as **IceCreamCone.java**. Write an application that establishes several `IceCreamCone` objects and handles the `Exceptions`. Save the file as **ThrowIceCream.java**.

    b. Create an `IceCreamCone2` class in which you modify the `IceCreamCone setFlavor()` method to ensure that the user enters a valid flavor. Allow at least four flavors of your choice. If the user's entry does not match a valid flavor, throw an `IceCreamConeException`. Write an application that establishes several `IceCreamCone` objects and demonstrates the handling of the new `Exception`. Save the new class file as **IceCreamCone2.java** and save the new application file as **ThrowIceCream2.java**.

7. Write an application that displays a series of at least five student ID numbers (that you have stored in an array) and asks the user to enter a numeric test score for the student. Create a `ScoreException` class, and throw a `ScoreException` for the class if the user does not enter a valid score (less than or equal to 100). `Catch` the `ScoreException` and then display an appropriate message. In addition, store a 0 for the student's score. At the end of the application, display all the student IDs and scores. Save the files as **ScoreException.java** and **TestScore.java**.

8. Write an application that displays a series of at least 10 student ID numbers (that you have stored in an array) and asks the user to enter a test letter grade for the student. Create an `Exception` class named `GradeException` that contains a `static public` array of valid grade letters ('A', 'B', 'C', 'D', 'F', and 'I'), which you can use to determine whether a grade entered from the application is valid. In your application, throw a `GradeException` if the user does not enter a valid letter grade. `Catch` the `GradeException` and then display an appropriate message. In addition, store an 'I' (for Incomplete) for any student for whom an exception is caught. At the end of the application, display all the student IDs and grades. Save the files as **GradeException.java** and **TestGrade.java**.

9. Write an applet that prompts the user for a color name. If it is not red, white, or blue, throw an `Exception`. Otherwise, change the applet's background color appropriately. Create an HTML document to host the `JApplet`. Save the applet file as **RWBApplet.java**, and save the host document as **TestRWB.html**.

10. Write an applet that prompts the user for an ID number and an age. Create an `Exception` class and throw an `Exception` of that class if the ID is not in the range of valid ID numbers (0 through 999), or if the age is not in the range of valid ages (0 through 119). Catch the `Exception` and then display an appropriate message. Create an HTML document to host the `JApplet`. Save the files as **DataEntryException.java**, **BadIDAndAge.java**, and **TestBadIDAndAge.html**.

11. A company accepts user orders by part numbers interactively. Users might make the following errors as they enter data:

   » The part number is not numeric.

   » The quantity is not numeric.

   » The part number is too low (less than 0).

   » The part number is too high (more than 999).

   » The quantity ordered is too low (less than 1).

   » The quantity ordered is too high (more than 5000).

   Create a class that stores an array of usable error messages; save the file as **DataMessages.java**. Create a `DataException` class that displays one of the messages; save the file as **DataException.java**. Create a `JApplet` that prompts the user for a part number and quantity. Allow for the possibility of non-numeric entries as well as out-of-range entries, and display the appropriate message when an error occurs. If no error occurs, display the message "All data is OK". Save the applet as **DataEntryExceptions.java**. Create an HTML document to host the `JApplet`; save it as **TestDataEntryExceptions.html**.

12. A company accepts user orders for its products interactively. Users might make the following errors as they enter data:

   » The item number ordered is not numeric.

   » The quantity is not numeric.

   » The item number is too low (less than 0).

   » The item number is too high (more than 9999).

   » The quantity ordered is too low (less than 1).

   » The quantity ordered is too high (more than 12).

   » The item number is not a currently valid item.

   Although the company might expand in the future, its current inventory consists of the following items:

Item Number	Price ($)
111	0.89
222	1.47
333	2.43
444	5.99

   Create a class that stores an array of usable error messages; save the file as **OrderMessages.java**. Create an `OrderException` class that displays one of the messages; save the file as **OrderException.java**. Create a `JFrame` that contains prompts for an item number and quantity. Allow for the possibility of non-numeric entries as well as out-of-range entries and entries that do not match any of the currently available item numbers. The user should click a button when all the data for an order is ready to submit; the program should then display an appropriate message if an error has occurred. If no errors exist in the entered data, compute the user's total amount due (quantity times price each) and display it. Save the applet as **PlaceAnOrder.java**.

DEBUGGING EXERCISES

Each of the following files in the Chapter.15 folder on your Student Disk has syntax and/ or logic errors. In each case, determine the problem and fix the program. After you correct the errors, save each file using the same filename preceded with Fix. For example, DebugFifteen1.java will become FixDebugFifteen1.java. You will also use a file named DebugEmployeeIDException.java with the DebugFifteen4.java file.

a. DebugFifteen1.java   c. DebugFifteen3.java

b. DebugFifteen2.java   d. DebugFifteen4.java

CASE PROJECT
GADGETS BY MAIL

1. a. Gadgets by Mail sells many interesting items through its catalogs. Write an application that prompts the user for order details, including item numbers and quantity of each item ordered, based on the available items shown in Table 15-1.

Item #	Description	Price ($)
101	Electric hand warmer	12.99
124	Battery-operated plant waterer	7.55
256	Gerbil trimmer	9.99
512	Talking bookmark	6.89

Table 15-1 Items offered by Gadgets by Mail

The shipping and handling fee for an order is based on the total order price, as shown in Table 15-2.

Price of Order ($)	Shipping and Handling ($)
0–24.99	5.55
25.00–49.99	8.55
50.00 or more	11.55

Table 15-2 Shipping and handling fees charged by Gadgets by Mail

Create the following classes:

» Gadget, which contains an item number, description, and price for a gadget; a constructor that sets all the fields; and get methods to retrieve the field values.

» Order, which contains an order number, customer name, and address (assume you need just a street address, not city, state, and zip code); a list of item numbers ordered (up to four); the total price of all items ordered; and a shipping and handling fee for the order. Include a constructor to set the field values and get methods to retrieve the field values.

» GadgetOrderTaker, which is an interactive application that takes four customer orders. The class contains an array of the four Gadget objects offered (from Table 15-1). The application prompts each user for a name and street address and assigns a unique order number to each customer, starting with 101. The application asks each user to enter an item number and quantity wanted. When the user enters 999 for the item number, the order is complete, and the next customer can enter data. Each customer can order up to four item numbers. When a customer's order is complete (the customer has entered 999 for an item number, or has ordered four different items), calculate the shipping and handling charges. After all four customers have placed Orders, display each Order's data, including the order number, the name and address of the customer, and the list of items ordered, including the item number, description, and price of each Order, the total price for the order, and the shipping and handling charge. The GadgetOrderTaker class handles all thrown Exceptions by displaying an explanatory message and ending the application.

» OrderException, which is an Exception that is created and thrown under any of the following conditions:

  » A customer attempts to order more than four different items.

  » A customer orders more than 100 of any item.

  » A customer enters an invalid item number.

» Also, catch the Exception generated by either of these conditions:

  » A customer enters a non-numeric character as the item number.

  » A customer enters a non-numeric character as the quantity.

Save the files as **Gadget.java**, **Order.java**, **GadgetOrderTaker.java**, and **OrderException.java**.

b. The GadgetOrderTaker class handles all thrown Exceptions by displaying an explanatory message and ending the application. Create a new application that handles all Exceptions by requiring the user to reenter the offending data. Save the file as **GadgetOrderTaker2.java**.

GAME ZONE

Chapter 14 provided you with many opportunities to create games. If you did not complete all the Game Zone assignments in Chapter 14, you might want to complete more of them now.

1. In Chapter 1, you created a class called RandomGuess. In this game, the application generates a random number for a player to guess. In Chapter 5, you improved the application to display a message indicating whether the player's guess was correct, too high, or too low. In Chapter 6, you further improved the game by adding a loop that continually prompts the user to enter the correct value, if necessary. As written, the game should work as long as the player enters numeric guesses. However, if the player enters a letter or other non-numeric character, the game throws an exception. Discover the type of Exception thrown, then improve the game by handling the exception so that the user is

informed of the error and allowed to attempt correct data entry again. Save the file as **RandomGuess4.java**.

2. In Chapter 8, you created a `Quiz` class containing an array of 10 multiple-choice quiz questions to which the user was required to respond with an A, B, or C. At the time, you knew how to handle the user's response if an invalid character was entered. Rerun the program now to determine whether an exception is thrown if the user enters nothing—that is, the user just presses the Enter key without making an entry. If so, improve the program now by catching the exception, displaying an appropriate error message, and presenting the same question to the user again. Save the file as **QuizWithExceptionsCaught.java**.

UP FOR DISCUSSION

1. The terms *syntactic sugar* and *syntactic salt* were described in this chapter. There are no hard and fast rules to assigning these terms to language features; it is somewhat a matter of opinion. From your knowledge of the Java programming language, list as many syntactic sugar and salt features as you can.

2. Have you ever been victimized by a computer error? For example, were you ever incorrectly denied credit, billed for something you did not purchase, or assigned an incorrect grade in a course? How did you resolve the problem? On the Web, find the most outrageous story you can involving a computer error.

3. Search the Web for information about educational video games in which historical simulations are presented in an effort to teach students about history. For example, Civilization III is a game in which players control a society as it progresses through time. Do you believe such games are useful to history students? Does the knowledge gained warrant the hours it takes to master the games? Do the makers of the games have any obligations to present history factually? Do they have a right to penalize players who choose options of which the game-writers disapprove (such as using nuclear weapons or allowing slavery)? Do game creators have the right to create characters who possess negative stereotypical traits—for example, a person of a specific nationality portrayed as being stupid, weak, or evil? Would you like to take a history course that uses similar games?

16

FILE INPUT AND OUTPUT

In this chapter, you will:

Understand computer files
Use the `File` class
Understand data file organization and streams
Use streams
Write to and read from a file
Write formatted file data
Read formatted file data
Use a variable filename
Create and use random access files
Write records to a random access file
Read records from a random access file
Read and write objects to and from files

JAVA ON THE JOB, SCENE 16

"Haven't I seen you spending a lot of time at the keyboard lately?" asks Lynn Greenbrier one day at Event Handlers Incorporated.

"I'm afraid so," you answer. "I'm trying to write a program that displays a month's scheduled events, one at a time. Every time I run it to test it, I have to enter the data for every event—the host's name, the number of guests, and so on."

"You're typing all the data over and over again?" Lynn asks in disbelief. "It's time for me to show you how to save data to a file."

"What would I do without you?" you ask.

"Well, now that you mention it, there is always more to learn about Java and I won't always be here to help you. Fortunately, there are many advanced books you can graduate to, and the Java Web site at *http/java.sun.com* holds a wealth of information. You will always need to download newer versions of Java."

"Why?" you ask. "My Java compiler works fine."

"Yes," Lynn says, "but there are always new developments. For example, in 2007, the United States started using new rules for calculating daylight saving time. If you don't have the latest Java version, some of your time-dependent applications could be inaccurate."

"There certainly is a lot to keep up with," you say.

"Yes, but you have a good foundation and you've come very far," Lynn says. "I'm proud of you!"

UNDERSTANDING COMPUTER FILES

When data items are stored in a computer system, they can be stored for varying periods of time—temporarily or permanently.

» Temporary storage is usually called computer memory or **random access memory** (RAM). When you write a Java program that stores a value in a variable, you are using temporary storage; the value you store is lost when the program ends or the computer loses power. This type of storage is **volatile**.

» Permanent storage, on the other hand, is not lost when a computer loses power; it is **nonvolatile**. When you write a Java program and save it to a disk, you are using permanent storage.

> **» NOTE** When discussing computer storage, "temporary" and "permanent" refer to volatility, not length of time. For example, a "temporary" variable might exist for several hours in a large program or one that the user forgets to close, but a "permanent" piece of data might be saved and then deleted within a few seconds.

A **computer file** is a collection of information stored on a nonvolatile device in a computer system. Files exist on **permanent storage devices**, such as hard disks, floppy disks, Zip disks, USB drives, reels or cassettes of magnetic tape, and compact discs. Some files are **data files** that contain facts and figures, such as a payroll file that contains employee numbers, names, and salaries; some files are **program files** or **application files** that store software instructions. (You have created many such files throughout this book.) Other files can store graphics, text, or operating system instructions (such as the compiled files with a .class extension that your compiler has created for every .java class that you compile). Although their contents vary, files have many common characteristics—each file occupies space on a section of disk (or other storage device) and has a name and a specific time of creation.

Computer files are the electronic equivalent of paper files often stored in file cabinets in offices. When you store a permanent file, you can place it in the main or **root directory** of your storage device. If you picture computer storage as similar to a file cabinet drawer, this is equivalent to tossing a loose document into the drawer. However, for better organization, most office clerks place documents in folders, and most computer users also organize their files into **folders** or **directories**. Users can also place folders within folders to form a hierarchy. A complete list of the disk drive plus the hierarchy of directories in which a file resides is its **path**. For example, in the Windows operating system, the complete path for a file named Data.txt on the C drive in a folder named Chapter.16 in a folder named Java is:

```
C:\\Java\Chapter.16\Data.txt
```

When you work with stored files in an application, you typically perform all or some of the following tasks:

» Determining whether and where the file exists

» Opening the file

» Reading data from the file

» Writing information to the file

» Closing the file

Java provides built-in classes that contain methods to help you with all these tasks.

USING THE File CLASS

You can use Java's **File class** to gather file information such as its size, whether it is open, its most recent modification date, and whether the file even exists. You must include the statement `import java.io.*` in any program that uses the File class. The `java.io` package contains all the classes you use in file processing. The File class is a direct descendant of the `Object` class. You can create a File object using a constructor that includes a filename as its argument; for example, you make the following statement when Data.txt is a file on the default disk drive:

```
File someData = new File("Data.txt");
```

You can also specify a path for the file; for example, the following argument to the constructor contains a disk drive and path:

```
File someData = new File("C:\\Java\\Chapter.16\Data.txt");
```

> **NOTE**
> The *io* in `java.io` stands for input/output. The io package contains 50 classes, a dozen interfaces, and 15 specific Exceptions.

> **NOTE** In the file path, the backslash character (\) separates folders and files. On a Windows computer, the backslash is the separator character, but on a UNIX computer the forward slash (/) is the separator character. Java processes both characters identically when they are used in a path. However, if you use the backslash, you must recall that it is also used as part of an escape sequence in Java. (For example, '\n' represents a newline character.) You must type two backslashes to indicate a single backslash to the operating system. You learned about escape sequences in Chapter 2. Instead of explicitly using "\\" or "/" as part of a string representing a path, you can also use the File class String field File.separator. This field holds the correct separator for the current operating system.

> **NOTE** For Microsoft Windows platforms, the prefix of an absolute pathname that contains a disk-drive specifier consists of the drive letter followed by ":". For UNIX platforms, the prefix of an absolute pathname is always "/".

Table 16-1 lists some useful `File` class methods.

» NOTE
The `File` class contains over 40 methods. See the documentation at *http://java.sun.com* for a complete list.

Method Signature	Purpose
`boolean canRead()`	Returns `true` if a file is readable
`boolean canWrite()`	Returns `true` if a file is writable
`boolean exists()`	Returns `true` if a file exists
`String getName()`	Returns the file's name
`String getPath()`	Returns the file's path
`String getParent()`	Returns the name of the folder in which the file can be found
`long length()`	Returns the file's size
`long lastModified()`	Returns the time the file was last modified; this time is system dependent and should be used only for comparison with other files' times, not as an absolute time

Table 16-1 Selected `File` class methods

Figure 16-1 contains an application that demonstrates some of the `File` class methods. In the `main()` method, a `File` object named `myFile` is declared. The `String` passed to the constructor is "SomeData.txt", which is the stored file's system name. In other words, although SomeData.txt might be the name of a stored file when the operating system refers to it, the file is known as

```
import java.io.*;
public class FileDemo
{
    public static void main(String[] args)
    {
        File myFile = new File("SomeData.txt");
        if(myFile.exists())
        {
            System.out.println(myFile.getName() + " exists");
            System.out.println("The file is " +
                myFile.length () + " bytes long");
            if(myFile.canRead())
                System.out.println(" ok to read");
            else
                System.out.println(" not ok to read");
            if(myFile.canWrite())
                System.out.println(" ok to write");
            else
                System.out.println(" not ok to write");
        }
        else
            System.out.println("File does not exist");
    }
}
```

Figure 16-1 The `FileDemo` class

myFile within the application. The idea of a file having one name when referenced by the operating system and a different name within an application is similar to the concept of how a method can contain a variable with one name, but a method that uses the value can refer to the same value using a different name. In both cases, a specific item has an "outside" name and an "inside" name, just as a student known as "Arthur" in school might be "Junior" at home. To use this application with a different file, you would change only the String passed to the File constructor.

In the main() method of the FileDemo class, an if statement tests for the existence of the file. If the file exists, its name, length, and reading and writing capabilities display; otherwise, a message indicates "File does not exist". Figure 16-2 shows the output when the application executes and no such file is stored in the same folder as the application, and then again after such a file has been created.

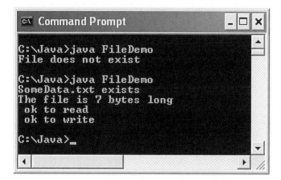

Figure 16-2 Output of the FileDemo application when run before and after creation of the SomeData.txt file

In the second execution of the FileDemo application shown in Figure 16-2, the application found the file named SomeData.txt because the file was physically located in the current directory—that is, the directory in which the application was stored and from which it was executed. You can check the status of files in other directories by using a File constructor with two String arguments. The first String represents a path to the filename, and the second String represents the filename. For example, the following statement refers to the SomeData.txt file located in the EventHandlers folder within the com folder in the current drive:

```
File someFile = new File("\\com\\EventHandlers", "SomeData.txt");
```

You can also refer to files on other storage devices. For example, the following statement refers to the SomeOtherData.txt file in the Temp folder on the A drive:

```
File someOtherFile = new File("A:\\Temp", "SomeOtherData.txt");
```

UNDERSTANDING DATA FILE ORGANIZATION AND STREAMS

Most businesses generate and use large quantities of data every day. You can store data in variables within a program, but this type of storage is temporary. When the application ends, the variables no longer exist and the data is lost. Variables are stored in the computer's main or primary memory (RAM). When you need to retain data for any significant amount of time, you must save the data on a permanent, secondary storage device, such as a floppy disk, hard drive, or compact disc (CD).

> **NOTE** Because you can erase data from files, some programmers prefer the term "*persistent* storage" to permanent storage. In other words, you can remove data from a file stored on a device such as a disk drive, so it is not technically permanent. However, the data remains in the file even when the computer loses power, so, unlike RAM, the data persists, or perseveres.

> **NOTE**
> Java uses Unicode to represent its characters. You first learned about Unicode in Chapter 1, and more information is contained in Appendix B.

Businesses store data in a hierarchy, as shown in Figure 16-3. The smallest useful piece of data to most people is the character. A character can be any one of the letters, numbers, or other special symbols, such as punctuation marks, that comprise data. Characters are made up of bits (the zeros and ones that represent computer circuitry), but people who use data are not concerned with whether the internal representation for an 'A' is 01000001 or 10111110; rather, they are concerned with the meaning of 'A'—for example, it might represent a grade in a course, a person's initial, or a company code.

> **NOTE** In computer terminology, a character can be any group of bits, and it does not necessarily represent a letter or number. Some of these do not correspond to characters in natural language; for example, some "characters" produce a sound or control display. You have also used the '\n' character to start a newline.

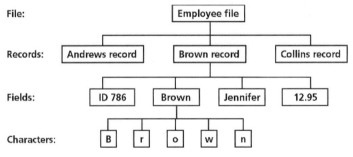

Figure 16-3 Data hierarchy

> **NOTE** Sometimes, you can think of a character as a unit of information instead of data with a particular appearance. For example, the mathematical character pi (π) and the Greek letter pi look the same, but have two different Unicode values.

When businesses use data, they group characters into fields. A **field** is a group of characters that has some meaning. For example, the characters *T*, *o*, and *m* might represent your first name. Other data fields might represent items such as last name, Social Security number, zip code, and salary.

Fields are grouped together to form records. A **record** is a collection of fields that contain data about an entity. For example, a person's first and last names, Social Security number, zip code, and salary represent that person's record. When programming in Java, you have created many classes, such as an `Employee` class or a `Student` class. You can think of the data typically stored in each of these classes as a record. These classes contain individual variables that represent data fields. A business's data records usually represent a person, item, sales transaction, or some other concrete object or event.

Records are grouped to create files. Data files consist of related records, such as a company's personnel file that contains one record for each company employee. Some files have only a few records; perhaps your professor maintains a file for your class with 25 records—one record for each student. Other files contain thousands or even millions of records. For example, a large insurance company maintains a file of policyholders, and a mail-order catalog company maintains a file of available items. A data file is used as a **sequential access file** when each record is stored in order based on the value in some field; for example, employees might be stored in Social Security number order, or inventory items might be stored in item number order.

Before an application can use a data file, it must open the file. A Java application **opens a file** by creating an object and associating a stream of bytes with that object. Similarly, when you finish using a file, the program should **close the file**—that is, make it no longer available to your application. If you fail to close an input file—that is, a file from which you are reading data—there usually are no serious consequences; the data still exists in the file. However, if you fail to close an output file—a file to which you are writing data—the data might become inaccessible. You should always close every file you open, and you should close the file as soon as you no longer need it. When you leave a file open for no reason, you use computer resources and your computer's performance suffers. Also, particularly within a network, another program might be waiting to use the file.

Whereas people view files as a series of records, with each record containing data fields, Java views files as a series of bytes. When you perform an input operation in an application, you can picture bytes flowing into your program from an input device through a **stream**, which functions as a pipeline or channel. When you perform output, some bytes flow out of your application through another stream to an output device, as shown in Figure 16-4. A stream is an object, and like all objects, streams have data and methods. The methods allow you to perform actions such as opening, closing, and flushing (clearing) the stream.

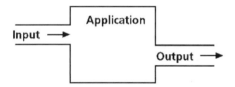

Figure 16-4 File streams

Most streams flow in only one direction; each stream is either an input or output stream. You might open several streams at once within an application. For example, an application that reads a data disk and separates valid records from invalid ones might require three streams. The data arrives via an input stream, and as the program checks the data for invalid values, one output stream writes some records to a file of valid records, and another output stream writes other records to a file of invalid records.

USING STREAMS

Figure 16-5 shows a partial hierarchical relationship of Java's Stream classes; it shows that InputStream and OutputStream are subclasses of the Object class. **InputStream** and **OutputStream** are abstract classes that contain methods for performing input and output, respectively. As abstract classes, these classes contain methods that must be overridden in their child classes. The capabilities of the most commonly used classes that provide input and output are summarized in Table 16-2.

» NOTE
When records are not used in sequence, the file is used as a random access file. You will learn more about random access files later in this chapter.

» NOTE
Random access files use streams that flow in two directions. You will use a random access file later in this chapter.

```
Object
|
+--InputStream
|   |
|   +--FileInputStream
|   |
|   +--FilterInputStream
|      |
|      +--DataInputStream
|      |
|      +--BufferedInputStream
|
+--OutputStream
|   |
|   +--FileOutputStream
|   |
|   +--FilterOutputStream
|      |
|      +--DataOutputStream
|      |
|      +--BufferedOutputStream
|      |
|      +--PrintStream
|
+--RandomAccessFile
```

Figure 16-5 Partial Stream class hierarchy

Class	Description
InputStream	Abstract class containing methods for performing input
OutputStream	Abstract class containing methods for performing output
FileInputStream	Child of InputStream that provides the capability to read from disk files
FileOutputStream	Child of OutputStream that provides the capability to write to disk files
PrintStream	Child of FilterOutputStream, which is a child of OutputStream; PrintStream handles output to a system's standard (or default) output device, usually the monitor
BufferedInputStream	Child of FilterInputStream, which is a child of InputStream; BufferedInputStream handles input from a system's standard (or default) input device, usually the keyboard

Table 16-2 Description of selected classes used for input and output

Java's `System` class instantiates a `PrintStream` object. This object is `System.out`, which you have used extensively in this book with its `print()` and `println()` methods. Besides `System.out`, the `System` class defines an additional `PrintStream` object named `System.err`. The output from `System.err` and `System.out` can go to the same device; in fact, `System.err` and `System.out` by default are both directed to the command line on the monitor. The difference is that `System.err` is usually reserved for error messages, and `System.out` is reserved for valid output. You can direct either `System.err` or `System.out` to a new location, such as a disk file or printer. For example, you might want to keep a hard-copy (printed) log of the error messages generated by a program, but direct the standard output to a disk file.

Java also contains a `FileWriter` class, which is a convenience class for writing character files. A **convenience class** is one that has been designed to make the programmer's job easier.

Figure 16-5 shows that the `InputStream` class is the parent to `FilterInputStream`, which is the parent to `BufferedInputStream`. The object `System.in` is a `BufferedInputStream` object. The `System.in` object captures keyboard input. A **buffer** is a memory location that you use to hold data temporarily. The `BufferedInputStream` class allows keyboard data to be entered at the command line and held until the user presses Enter. That way, the user can backspace over typed characters to change the data before the application stores it. This allows the operating system—instead of your program—to handle the complicated tasks of deleting characters as the user backspaces, and then replacing the deleted characters with new ones.

> **» NOTE** Using a buffer to hold input or output before the actual IO command is issued improves program performance. Input and output operations are relatively slow compared to computer processor speeds. Holding input or output until there is a "batch" makes programs run faster.

> **» NOTE** You can create your own `InputStream` and `OutputStream` objects and assign `System.in` and `System.out` to them, respectively. Then, you can use the `InputStream`'s `read()` method to read one character at a time from the location you choose. The `read()` method returns an integer that represents the Unicode value of the typed character; it returns a value of –1 when it encounters an end-of-file condition, known as **EOF**. Whenever you use the `read()` or `close()` methods, there is a possibility that they might throw an `IOException`. Therefore, any method that contains these statements might throw `Exception`s and must either catch the `Exception`s or pass them through to another method that catches them. You learned about `Exception` objects in Chapter 15. You can also identify EOF by throwing an `EOFException`; you will use this technique later in this chapter.

Figure 16-6 contains a demonstration application named `ReadAndWrite`. In the application's `main()` method, `InputStream` and `OutputStream` objects are declared and `System.in` and `System.out` are assigned to them. After the prompt "Type some characters", a `try` block holds the shaded `while` statement. The `while` statement continues to read while it does not return –1, the EOF value. In the case of keyboard input, –1 is returned when you press Ctrl+Z. Until you enter EOF, the `while` statement displays the input character and retrieves another. Figure 16-7 shows a sample run of the application. To create this output, the user types "abcdefg". After each input character, a character is written to the `OutputStream` but held until the user presses Enter. Next, the user types "the quick brown fox" followed by Enter, and the output displays again. Finally, the user presses Ctrl+Z and Enter at the beginning of a line, indicating EOF, so the logic continues with the `finally` block, where the files are closed in their own `try` block. Notice that the keystroke combination Ctrl+Z appears on the screen as ^Z.

> **» NOTE** Pressing Ctrl+Z to end a program is an operating system command, not a Java command.

> **» NOTE** Ctrl+Z represents EOF in Windows. You can create an EOF character on a UNIX keyboard by using Ctrl+D.

```java
import java.io.*;
public class ReadAndWrite
{
    public static void main(String[] args)
    {
        InputStream istream;
        OutputStream ostream;
        int c;
        istream = System.in;
        ostream = System.out;
        System.out.println("Type some characters ");
        try
        {
            while((c = istream.read()) != -1)
                ostream.write(c);
        }
        catch(IOException e)
        {
            System.out.println("Error: " + e.getMessage());
        }
        finally
        {
            try
            {
                istream.close();
                ostream.close();
            }
            catch (IOException e)
            {
                System.out.println("File did not close");
            }
        }
    }
}
```

Figure 16-6 The `ReadAndWrite` class

>> **NOTE** Throughout this book, you have learned that defining named constants for numeric values makes programs easier to read and understand. In the application in Figure 16-6, instead of testing for the end of data input while comparing the `read()` method value to –1, you might prefer to define and use a named constant such as:

```java
final int END = -1;
```

>> **NOTE** Before you knew about input and output streams, you wrote applications that read data from the keyboard and displayed it on the screen, so the application in Figure 16-6 initially might seem to contain a lot of unnecessary work. However, soon you will see that the `InputStream` and `OutputStream` objects can be assigned other input and output devices, allowing your applications to save and retrieve data using storage devices.

```
C:\Java>java ReadAndWrite
Type some characters
abcdefg
abcdefg
the quick brown fox
the quick brown fox
^Z

C:\Java>
```

Figure 16-7 Sample execution of the `ReadAndWrite` application

> **NOTE** The `while` loop in the `ReadAndWrite` application continues until the `read()` method returns –1. However, you cannot end the program by typing –1. Typing a minus sign (–) and a one (1) causes two additional characters to be sent to the buffer, and neither character represents –1. Instead, you must press Ctrl+Z, which forces the `read()` method to return –1, and which the operating system recognizes as the end of the file.

WRITING TO AND READING FROM A FILE

Instead of assigning files to the standard input and output devices, you can also assign a file to the `InputStream` or `OutputStream`. For example, you can read data items from the keyboard and store them permanently on a disk. To accomplish this, you can construct a `FileOutputStream` object and assign it to the `OutputStream`. If you want to change an application's output device, you don't have to make any other changes to the application other than assigning a new object to the `OutputStream`; the rest of the logic remains the same. Java lets you assign a file to a `Stream` object so that screen output and file output work in exactly the same manner.

You can associate a `File` object with the output stream in one of two ways:

» You can pass the filename to the constructor of the `FileOutputStream` class.

» You can create a `File` object by passing the filename to the `File` constructor. Then, you can pass the `File` object to the constructor of the `FileOutputStream` class.

The second method has some benefits: if you create a `File` object, you can use the `File` class methods, such as `exists()` and `lastModified()`, to retrieve file information. Figure 16-8 shows a `ReadAndWriteToAFile` application that is similar to the `ReadAndWrite` application, but it writes output to a file rather than to the screen. In Figure 16-8, the first shaded statement declares a `File` object named `outputFile` that creates a file named MyData.dat in the current folder. (The filename and the extension are the programmer's choice; in this case, .dat is used to stand for "data," but any extension that is acceptable to the current operating system could be used.)

When you call the `FileOutputStream` constructor, it might throw a `FileNotFoundException`, so the creation of the assignment to the `ostream` object is placed in a `try` block (shaded). Near the end of the code in Figure 16-8, a shaded `catch` block catches any thrown

```java
import java.io.*;
public class ReadAndWriteToAFile
{
    public static void main(String[] args)
    {
        InputStream istream;
        OutputStream ostream;
        File outputFile = new File("MyData.dat");
        int c;
        istream = System.in;
        try
        {
            ostream = new FileOutputStream(outputFile);
            System.out.println("Type some characters ");
            try
            {
                while((c = istream.read()) != -1)
                    ostream.write(c);
            }
            catch(IOException e)
            {
                System.out.println("Error: " + e.getMessage());
            }
            finally
            {
                try
                {
                    istream.close();
                    ostream.close();
                }
                catch(IOException e)
                {
                    System.out.println("File did not close");
                }
            }
        }
        catch(FileNotFoundException e)
        {
            System.exit(1);
        }
    }
}
```

Figure 16-8 The ReadAndWriteToAFile class

FileNotFoundException. In this case, the application ends with a System.exit() call, but the programmer could choose to display a message or take any other action. As an alternative, the programmer could add the clause throws Exception to the end of the main() method header and remove all the try and catch clauses from the application. Then, any thrown Exceptions would simply be thrown to the operating system, and error messages would display at the command line.

Other than the shaded changes, the ReadAndWriteToAFile class in Figure 16-8 is the same as the ReadAndWrite class in Figure 16-6. However, the outcome when you execute the application is different; although the user still types input at the keyboard and presses Ctrl+Z when done, the output is sent to a file instead of to the screen. Figure 16-9 shows the execution of the application along with the file output displayed in a text editor.

Figure 16-9 Execution of the ReadAndWriteToAFile application and the file output

> **NOTE** You can write to a file in an application, but not in a standard applet. Applets are designed for distribution over the Internet, and because applets that write to a client's file could destroy a client's existing data, writing files is usually prohibited. It is possible to create a **signed applet**, which is one that contains a digital signature, to prove that it came from a trusted source and so has more privileges than an ordinary applet. See *http://java.sun.com* for details.

READING FROM A FILE

The process you use to read data from a file is similar to the one you use to write data to a file. You can create a File object and assign it to the input stream, as shown in the shaded statements in the ReadFromAFileAndWrite application in Figure 16-10. The only other differences between this application and the ReadAndWriteToAFile class in Figure 16-8 are that the OutputStream has been reassigned to the screen (the screen object is System.out), and the prompt to enter characters has been removed because a storage device does not need a prompt the way a human user does. If the MyFile.dat file exists and opens successfully, its contents display on the screen. For example, Figure 16-11 shows the output produced from the MyData.dat file created in Figure 16-9.

```
import java.io.*;
public class ReadFromAFileAndWrite
{
    public static void main(String[] args)
    {
        InputStream istream;
        OutputStream ostream;
        File inputFile = new File("MyData.dat");
        int c;
```

Figure 16-10 The ReadFromAFileAndWrite class (*continued*)

```
            ostream = System.out;
            try
            {
                istream = new FileInputStream(inputFile);
                try
                {
                    while((c = istream.read()) != -1)
                        ostream.write(c);
                }
                catch(IOException e)
                {
                    System.out.println("Error: " + e.getMessage());
                }
                finally
                {
                    try
                    {
                        istream.close();
                        ostream.close();
                    }
                    catch(IOException e)
                    {
                        System.out.println("File did not close");
                    }
                }
            }
            catch(FileNotFoundException e)
            {
                System.exit(1);
            }
        }
    }
```

Figure 16-10 The `ReadFromAFileAndWrite` class

Figure 16-11 Output of the `ReadFromAFileAndWrite` class, using the data file created in the execution of `ReadAndWriteToAFile` in Figure 16-9

WRITING FORMATTED FILE DATA

Frequently, it is inconvenient to read a data file as a series of characters. For example, you might have a data file that contains personnel records that include an `int` employee ID number, a `String` name, and `double` salary for each employee in your organization. Rather than reading a series of bytes, it is more useful to be able to read such a file in groups of bytes that constitute a record containing an `int`, a `String`, and a `double`. You can use the `DataInputStream` and `DataOutputStream` classes to accomplish formatted input and output.

`DataOutputStream` objects enable you to write binary data to an `OutputStream`. Much of the data that you write with `DataOutputStream` objects is not readable in a text editor because it is not stored as characters. Instead, the data is formatted correctly for its type. For example, a `double` with the value 123.45 is not stored as six separate readable characters that can correctly display in a text editor. Instead, numeric values are stored in a more compact form that you can read later with a `DataInputStream` object.

The `DataOutput` interface is implemented by `DataOutputStream`. The `DataOutput` interface includes methods such as `writeBoolean()`, `writeChar()`, `writeDouble()`, `writeFloat()`, and `writeInt()`. Each method writes data in the correct format for the data type indicated by its name. You can use the method `writeUTF()` to write Unicode format strings.

> **»NOTE**
> **Binary data** is data stored in machine-readable code that must be read by an application before you can understand it. Text data can be read by people.

> **»NOTE** The meaning of the acronym UTF is disputed by various sources. The most popular interpretations include Unicode Transformation Format, Unicode Transfer Format, and Unicode Text Format.

When you create a `DataOutputStream`, you can assign a `FileOutputStream` object to it so that your data is stored in a file. Using `DataOutputStream` with a `FileOutputStream` allows you to use the correct write method that is appropriate for your data. When you use a `DataOutputStream` connected to `FileOutputStream`, the approach is known as **chaining the stream objects**. That is, if you define a `DataOutputStream` object with a statement such as `DataOutputStream out;`, and then call the `DataOutputStream` constructor, you pass a `FileOutputStream` object to it. For example:

```
out = new DataOutputStream(new FileOutputStream ("someFile"));
```

Figure 16-12 contains a class named `CreateEmployeeFileFrame`, which demonstrates an application that writes formatted data to a file. The class creates a `JFrame` containing text fields and a button. The user can type employee data into the text fields, and when finished, click a button that causes the data to be written to a file for storage. Then, the fields are cleared so data for the next employee can be entered and stored. Because `CreateEmployeeFileFrame` has so many components, its code is lengthy. However, you can think about all the statements coded in the class in six broad sections.

In the first unshaded section of the class in Figure 16-12, all the necessary declarations are made. The `JFrame` contains fields in which the user enters an employee last name and hourly salary and contains labels to provide a title and descriptions of each text field. The `JFrame` also contains a button that the user clicks when the entered data is ready to be submitted. Objects are created for a content pane and a `DataOutputStream`—the file where the entered data is stored.

In the first shaded area in Figure 16-12, the constructor for the `CreateEmployeeFileFrame` class passes a title ("Employee Data") to the `JFrame` constructor. (You can use the `super()`

» NOTE In the `CreateEmployeeFileFrame` class, no call is made to `getContentPane()` because only the `setLayout()` and `add()` methods are used. Recall from Chapter 13 that if you used other methods or were using a version of Java older than version 5, you would have to explicitly call `getContentPane()`.

```java
import java.io.*;
import java.awt.*;
import java.awt.event.*;
import javax.swing.*;
public class CreateEmployeeFileFrame extends JFrame
   implements ActionListener
{
   private JLabel title = new JLabel("Employee Data Entry");
   private Font bigFont = new Font("Arial", Font.BOLD, 24);
   private JTextField lastNameField = new JTextField(10);
   private JTextField hourlyPayField = new JTextField(4);
   private JLabel lastNameLabel = new JLabel("Last name");
   private JLabel hourlyPayLabel = new JLabel("Hourly pay rate");
   private JButton enterDataButton = new JButton("Enter data");
   DataOutputStream ostream;
   final int WIDTH = 260;
   final int HEIGHT = 200;

   public CreateEmployeeFileFrame()
   {
      super("Employee Data");
      try
      {
         ostream = new DataOutputStream
            (new FileOutputStream("EmpData.dat"));
      }
      catch(IOException e)
      {
         System.err.println("File not opened");
         System.exit(1);
      }

      setLayout(new FlowLayout());
      title.setFont(bigFont);
      add(title);
      add(lastNameLabel);
      add(lastNameField);
      add(hourlyPayLabel);
      add(hourlyPayField);
      add(enterDataButton);
      enterDataButton.addActionListener(this);
      setSize(WIDTH, HEIGHT);
      setVisible(true);
      setDefaultCloseOperation(JFrame.EXIT_ON_CLOSE);
   }
```

Figure 16-12 The `CreateEmployeeFileFrame` class (*continued*) ▶

```
public void actionPerformed(ActionEvent e)
{
    double pay;
    try
    {
        pay = Double.parseDouble(hourlyPayField.getText());
        ostream.writeUTF(lastNameField.getText());
        ostream.writeDouble(pay);
        lastNameField.setText("");
        hourlyPayField.setText("");
    }
    catch(NumberFormatException e2)
    {
        System.err.println("Invalid hourly pay data");
    }
    catch(IOException e3)
    {
        System.err.println("Error writing file");
        System.exit(1);
    }
}

public static void main(String[] args)
{
    CreateEmployeeFileFrame frame = new
        CreateEmployeeFileFrame();
}
}
```

Figure 16-12 The `CreateEmployeeFileFrame` class

method because the `CreateEmployeeFileFrame` class descends from `JFrame`.) Then, a
`try...catch` pair attempts to create a new output file. The file creation code is written
within a `try` block because creating a `File` object might throw an `Exception`. For example,
if the default storage device is full or write-protected, no file can be created. If that happens,
the application displays a message and ends.

The second unshaded area in Figure 16-12 shows the setup tasks for the `JFrame`—setting its
layout manager, adding all the components to its surface, activating the button, setting the
frame's size and visibility, and setting its close operation.

The beginning of the `actionPerformed()` method is contained in the second shaded area
in the figure. A local variable named `pay` is declared to hold the pay rate the user enters.
The `getText()` method is used with the `hourlyPayField` object to retrieve the `String` the
user enters; as part of the same statement, the `String` is converted to a `double` using the
`Double` class `parseDouble()` method. This conversion appears in a `try` block because it
might fail (for example, if the user enters character data in the hourly pay rate field). When
the conversion is successful and no exception is thrown, the `writeUTF()` method writes a
`String` representing the employee's last name to the output file and the `writeDouble()`
method writes the employee's pay rate. Then, the text fields are cleared so the user can enter
new data for another employee.

The catch blocks in the third unshaded section of Figure 16-12 handle the exceptions thrown in the try block. If the user enters invalid pay data, a message displays, but the application continues and the user can reenter data for that employee. However, if there is an error writing to the output file, the catch block handling that exception exits the application.

The final shaded portion of Figure 16-12 is the main() method that creates a JFrame instance. When you execute the application, the screen looks like Figure 16-13, awaiting data entry. When users see the JFrame, they can enter data in each of the available JTextFields. When a user completes a record for a single employee, he or she clicks the JButton, which causes the actionPerformed() method to execute, retrieving the text from each of the JTextFields and writing it to a data file in the correct format. The user can quit the application by clicking the Close button in the upper-right corner of the frame.

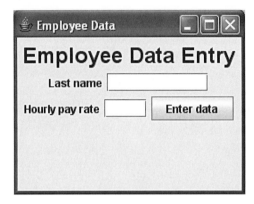

Figure 16-13 Input screen displayed by the CreateEmployeeFileFrame application

After you execute the CreateEmployeeFileFrame application, you can examine its contents in a text editor. For example, Figure 16-14 shows the output file after a user has entered data for four employees. Some of the data, the String names, is readable. However, the numbers that represent the pay rates of each employee are not understandable. Data written with writeDouble() is stored in a condensed format that you cannot easily interpret; the same would be true for data written with writeInteger() or any of the other DataOutput interface write methods. Although it is interesting to view the file data in an editor, data written to a file is never intended for human consumption; file data is simply stored for later use. For example, you might want to write an application that reads stored file data and sends it to a printer or to a monitor.

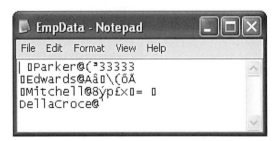

Figure 16-14 The EmpData.dat file in a text editor after the user enters data for four employees

READING FORMATTED FILE DATA

`DataInputStream` objects enable you to read binary data from an `InputStream`. The `DataInput` interface is implemented by `DataInputStream`. The `DataInput` interface includes methods such as `readByte()`, `readChar()`, `readDouble()`, `readFloat()`, `readInt()`, and `readUTF()`. In the same way that the different write methods of `DataOutput` correctly format data you write to a file, each `DataInput` read method correctly reads the type of data indicated by its name.

When you want to create a `DataInputStream` object that reads from a file, you use the same chaining technique you used for output files. In other words, if you define a `DataInputStream` object as `DataInputStream in;`, you can associate it with a file when you call its constructor, as in the following:

```
in = new DataInputStream(FileInputStream("someFile"));
```

When you read data from a file, you need to determine when the end of the file has been reached. Earlier in this chapter, you learned that you can determine EOF by checking for a return value of –1 from the `read()` method. Alternatively, if you attempt each file `read()` from within a `try` block, you can catch an `EOFException`. When you catch an `EOFException`, it means you have reached the end of the file and you should take appropriate action, such as closing the file.

> **» NOTE** Most `Exception`s represent error conditions. An `EOFException` is more truly an "exception" in that most `read()` method calls do not result in EOF. For example, when a file contains 999 records, only the 1000th, or last, `read()` for a file causes an `EOFException`.

Figure 16-15 contains a `ReadEmployeeFileFrame` application that reads an EmpData.dat file created by the `CreateEmployeeFileFrame` application. The `ReadEmployeeFileFrame` class is very similar to the class that created the file; however, instead of requiring a user to type data that is written to a file, this application reads data from the file and displays each record, one at a time, in a `JFrame`.

In the first shaded section in Figure 16-15, the input file object is created and the file is opened. The code is in a `try` block because an exception might be thrown if the system is unable to open the file (for example, if it does not exist in the default folder).

The second shaded block in Figure 16-15 shows the beginning of the `actionPerformed()` method—the method that executes when a user clicks the button on the frame. Within this method, local variables are declared for the employee's name and pay, and then values for these variables are retrieved from the input stream using the `readUTF()` and `readDouble()` methods. This code is in a `try` block because it might encounter an error reading the file. Also, at some point, the code encounters the end-of-file exception. When the user clicks the button, the name and pay rate from the first record are retrieved from the file and placed in text fields. The user can view this data and then click the button to retrieve the next set of data. If the user continues to click, eventually the end of file is encountered and an `EOFException` is thrown, causing the first `catch` block to execute. The `catch` block calls a `closeFile()` method. In this example, the file-closing statements were placed in their own method for convenience. The more separate final actions you want to take, the more it makes sense to encapsulate them into their own method.

```java
import java.io.*;
import java.awt.*;
import java.awt.event.*;
import javax.swing.*;
public class ReadEmployeeFileFrame extends JFrame
    implements ActionListener
{
   private JLabel title =
       new JLabel("Employee Data");
   private Font bigFont = new Font("Arial", Font.BOLD, 24);
   private JLabel prompt =  new
       JLabel("View the employees");
   private JTextField lastNameField = new JTextField(10);
   private JTextField hourlyPayField = new JTextField(4);
   private JButton viewRecordsButton = new
       JButton("View Records");
   private JLabel lastNameLabel = new JLabel("Name");
   private JLabel hourlyPayLabel = new JLabel("Rate");
   DataInputStream istream;
   final int WIDTH = 325;
   final int HEIGHT = 200;
   public ReadEmployeeFileFrame()
   {
       super("Read File");
       try
       {
           istream = new DataInputStream
               (new FileInputStream ("EmpData.dat"));
       }
       catch(IOException e)
       {
           System.err.println("File not opened");
           System.exit(1);
       }
       setLayout(new FlowLayout());
       title.setFont(bigFont);
       add(title);
       add(prompt);
       add(lastNameLabel);
       add(lastNameField);
       add(hourlyPayLabel);
       add(hourlyPayField);
       add(viewRecordsButton);
       viewRecordsButton.addActionListener(this);
       setSize(WIDTH, HEIGHT);
       setVisible(true);
       setDefaultCloseOperation(JFrame.EXIT_ON_CLOSE);
   }
```

Figure 16-15 The ReadEmployeeFileFrame class (*continued*)

```
public void actionPerformed(ActionEvent e1)
{
    String last;
    double pay;
    try
    {
        last = istream.readUTF();
        pay = istream.readDouble();
        lastNameField.setText(last);
        hourlyPayField.setText(String.valueOf(pay));
    }
    catch(EOFException e)
    {
        closeFile();
    }
    catch(IOException e2)
    {
        System.err.println("Error reading file");
        System.exit(1);
    }
}
public void closeFile()
{
    try
    {
        istream.close();
        System.exit(0);
    }
    catch(IOException e)
    {
        System.err.println("Error closing file");
        System.exit(1);
    }
}
public static void main(String[] args)
{
    ReadEmployeeFileFrame frame = new
        ReadEmployeeFileFrame();
}
}
```

Figure 16-15 The `ReadEmployeeFileFrame` class

The third shaded code block in Figure 16-15 contains the `closeFile()` method. This method contains its own `try...catch` pair, because closing a file could result in an exception. If the `try` is successful (that is, if the input file closes correctly), the application ends with a `System.exit(0)` call.

Figure 16-16 shows the output of the `ReadEmployeeFileFrame` application, using the data file displayed in Figure 16-14, after the user has clicked the View Records button one time to retrieve the first data record. Notice that although Parker's pay rate is not decipherable when

Figure 16-16 Output of the `ReadEmployeeFileFrame` application, using the EmpData.dat data file, after the user clicks the button once

the data file is displayed in the text editor in Figure 16-14, the `readDouble()` method has read it correctly in the application, so it can be displayed legibly in the `JFrame` in Figure 16-16.

> **》NOTE** In Java 5 and later, you can also use the `Scanner` class to read from files. This class provides the ability to read formatted data; you can search the Java Web site for more details. The `Scanner` class is used in a programming example later in this chapter.

USING A VARIABLE FILENAME

A program that reads a data file and displays its contents for you is useful. A program that can read any data file, regardless of what you name it, is even more useful. For example, suppose data files for employees exist for several branches of an organization, or suppose inventory files exist for each month of the year. Instead of hard-coding a filename to be written or read, it is more flexible to use a variable filename; then, the same application can process different data sets.

One approach to using a variable filename is to pass the name to the method that opens the file. For example, in the `ReadEmployeeFileFrame` application in Figure 16-15, you could alter the constructor header to include a `String` argument that you use as the filename. Figure 16-17 shows the first portion of the altered constructor; the shaded sections show how the filename is used.

```
public ReadEmployeeFileFrame(String nameOfFile)
{
    super("Read File");
    try
    {
        istream = new DataInputStream(new
            FileInputStream(nameOfFile));
    }
```

Figure 16-17 First part of the `ReadEmployeeFileFrame` constructor using a `String` argument

When `ReadEmployeeFileFrame` executes, you pass a filename into it. You could obtain the desired filename in several ways. For example, Figure 16-18 shows a `main()` method that declares a `String` variable named `name` (shaded), prompts the user using a dialog box, and passes the entered name to the `ReadEmployeeFileFrame` constructor.

```
public static void main(String[] args)
{
    String name;
    name = JOptionPane.showInputDialog(null,
       "Enter filename for processing");
    ReadEmployeeFileFrame frame = new
       ReadEmployeeFileFrame(name);
}
```

Figure 16-18 A `main()` method that prompts a user for a filename and passes it to a constructor that opens the file

Figure 16-19 presents an alternative. In this `main()` method, the first element of the `args` array that is passed to the `main()` method becomes the filename. When you execute the application with this approach, instead of the command `java ReadEmployeeFileFrame`, you provide a list of arguments with the command by typing a statement similar to the following:

```
java ReadEmployeeFileFrame EmpData.dat
```

This command not only executes the application, but the `String` following the application name becomes the zero-element argument in the `args` array. When a user wants to run the `ReadEmployeeFileFrame` application, the user simply types the correct current data filename at the end of the command to execute it.

» NOTE You can use `args[1]`, `args[2]`, and so on as `String`s passed to the `main()` method of any application by listing as many `String`s as you need, separated by spaces, after the application name when you use the `java` command.

```
public static void main(String[] args)
{
    ReadEmployeeFileFrame frame = new
       ReadEmployeeFileFrame(args[0]);
}
```

Figure 16-19 A `main()` method that uses the first element of the `args` array as the filename

CREATING AND USING RANDOM ACCESS FILES

The examples of files that have been written to and read from in this chapter are sequential access files, which means that you access the records in sequential order from beginning to end. For example, if you wrote an employee record with a last name of Parker, and then you created a second record with a last name of Brown, you would see when you retrieved the records that they remain in the original data-entry order. Businesses store data in sequential order when they use the records for **batch processing**, or processing that involves performing the same tasks with many records, one after the other. For example, when a company produces paychecks, the records for the pay period are gathered in a batch and the checks are calculated and printed in sequence. It really doesn't matter whose check is produced first because none are distributed to employees until all have been printed.

> **»»NOTE** Besides indicating a system that works with many records, the term "batch processing" can also be used to mean a system in which you issue many operating-system commands as a group.

For many applications, sequential access is inefficient. These applications, known as **real-time** applications, require that a record be accessed immediately while a client is waiting. For example, if a customer telephones a department store with a question about a monthly bill, the customer service representative does not need or want to access every customer account in sequence. With tens of thousands of account records to read, it would take too long to access the customer's record. Instead, customer service representatives require **random access files**, files in which records can be located in any order. Files in which records must be accessed immediately are also called **instant access files**. Because they enable you to locate a particular record directly (without reading all of the preceding records), random access files are also called **direct access files**. You can use Java's RandomAccessFile class to create your own random access files.

The RandomAccessFile class contains the same read(), write(), and close() method names as InputStream and OutputStream, but it also contains a seek() method that lets you select a beginning position within a file before you read or write data, and places a file pointer at the selected location. A **file pointer**, or **file position pointer**, is an automatically created variable that holds the byte number of the next file position to be used. For example, if you declare a RandomAccessFile object named myFile, the following statement selects the 200th position within the file:

```
myFile.seek(200);
```

The 200th position represents the 201st byte because, as with Java arrays, the numbering of file positions begins at zero. The next read() or write() method operates from the newly selected starting point.

When you declare a RandomAccessFile object, you include a filename as you do with other file objects. You also include "r" or "rw" as a String within double quotation marks as a second argument, which indicates that the file is open for reading only ("r") or for both reading and writing ("rw"). For example, the following statement opens the SomeData.dat file so that either the read() or write() method can be used on the file:

```
RandomAccessFile myFile = new
    RandomAccessFile("C:\\Temp\\SomeData.dat","rw");
```

This feature is particularly useful in random access processing. Consider a business with 20,000 customer accounts. When the customer who has the 14,607th record in the file acquires a new telephone number, it is convenient to directly access the 14,607th record. The read() method confirms that it represents the correct customer, and then the write() method writes the new telephone number to the file in the location in which the old number was previously stored.

Figure 16-20 shows an application named `AccessACharacter` that creates a `RandomAccessFile` object using a file named AQuote.txt, the contents of which are shown in Figure 16-21. An integer named `pos` is declared and assigned the value 34. In the first shaded statement, the `seek()` method is used with the input file object to access position 34 in the file; in the second shaded statement, the file is read. Position 34 holds a "W", which is the character that is displayed as output in Figure 16-22.

```java
import java.io.*;
public class AccessACharacter
{
    public static void main(String[] args) throws IOException
    {
        OutputStream ostream;
        int c;
        RandomAccessFile inFile = new RandomAccessFile("AQuote.txt","r");
        ostream = System.out;
        int pos = 34;
        try
        {
            inFile.seek(pos);
            c = inFile.read();
            System.out.print("The character in position " + pos + " is ");
            ostream.write(c);
        }
        catch(IOException e)
        {
            System.out.println("Error: " + e.getMessage());
        }
        finally
        {
            System.out.println();
            inFile.close();
            ostream.close();
        }
    }
}
```

Figure 16-20 The `AccessACharacter` class

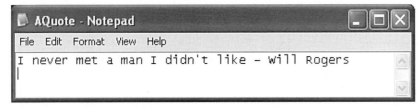

Figure 16-21 The AQuote.txt file used as input to the `AccessACharacter` application

Figure 16-22 Output of the `AccessACharacter` application

In the `AccessACharacter` application, only one `read()` command was issued, yet the application accessed a byte 34 positions into the file. When you access a file randomly, you do not read all the data that precedes the data you are seeking. Accessing data randomly is one of the major features that makes large data systems maintainable.

WRITING RECORDS TO A RANDOM ACCESS FILE

Accessing one character in a text file is of limited value. When you store records in a file, it is often more useful to be able to access the 34th record, rather than the 34th byte. In this case, you multiply each record's size by the position you want to access. For example, if you store records that are 50 bytes long, you can access the *n*th record using the following statement:

```
myFile.seek((n-1) * 50);
```

One approach to writing a random file is to place records into the file based on a key field. A **key field** is the field in a record that makes the record unique from all others. For example, in a file of students, many records might have the same last name, first name, or grade point average, but each record has a key field, such as a student ID number or Social Security number.

> **» NOTE** Although the Social Security Administration (SSA) intended that Social Security numbers be unique, occasionally the same number has been given to multiple people. If you completed the Up for Discussion questions at the end of Chapter 11, you have researched this topic.

Figure 16-23 contains an example that asks a user to enter student data and writes a random data file using the student's ID number as a key field. So that the example can be brief and concentrate on the random access file writing, this application makes several assumptions:

- » A student record contains only an ID number and a grade point average. In a real application, each student would require many more data fields, such as name, address, phone number, and so on.
- » Each student ID number is three digits or fewer. In a real application, ID numbers would be longer to ensure unique values. (Three-digit numbers provide only 1000 unique combinations.)
- » The user will enter a valid ID number. In a real application, this would be a foolhardy assumption. However, to streamline the code and concentrate on the writing of a random access file, error checking for valid ID numbers is eliminated from this example.

» The user will not duplicate student ID numbers. In a real application, a key field should be checked against all existing key fields to ensure that a record is unique before adding it to a file.

» Each student's record will be placed in the random access file position that is one less than the student's ID number. In many real applications, the mathematical computations performed on a key field to determine file placement are more complicated.

» The user will enter a valid grade point average. Again, this assumption is seldom reasonable in a professional application, but it is made here to streamline the code.

```java
import javax.swing.*;
import java.io.*;
public class WriteRandomStudentFile
{
    public static void main(String[] args) throws IOException
    {
        int pos;
        RandomAccessFile stuFile =
            new RandomAccessFile("StudentData.dat", "rw");
        String inputString;
        int id;
        double gpa;
        final int RECORDSIZE = 12;
        final int NUMRECORDS = 1000;
        final int STOP = 999;
        try
        {
            for(int x = 0; x < NUMRECORDS; ++x)
            {
                stuFile.writeInt(0);
                stuFile.writeDouble(0.0);
            }
        }

        catch(IOException e)
        {
            System.out.println("Error: " + e.getMessage());
        }
        finally
        {
            stuFile.close();
        }
        stuFile =
            new RandomAccessFile("StudentData.dat","rw");
        inputString = JOptionPane.showInputDialog(null,
            "Enter student ID number or 999 to quit");
        id = Integer.parseInt(inputString);
```

Figure 16-23 The `WriteRandomStudentFile` class (*continued*) ▶

```
        try
        {
            while(id != STOP)
            {
                inputString = JOptionPane.showInputDialog(null,
                    "Enter grade point average");
                gpa = Double.parseDouble(inputString);
                pos = id - 1;
                stuFile.seek(pos * RECORDSIZE);
                stuFile.writeInt(id);
                stuFile.writeDouble(gpa);
                inputString = JOptionPane.showInputDialog(null,
                    "Enter student ID number or " + STOP + " to quit");
                id = Integer.parseInt(inputString);
            }
        }
        catch(IOException e)
        {
            System.out.println("Error: " + e.getMessage());
        }
        finally
        {
            stuFile.close();
        }
        System.exit(0);
    }
}
```

Figure 16-23 The `WriteRandomStudentFile` class

At the start of the `WriteRandomStudentFile` application in Figure 16-23, an integer is declared to hold a calculated file position. A `RandomAccessFile` named StudentData.dat is opened, and variables are declared to hold the input `String` that is returned from interactive dialog boxes and the `int` ID number and `double` grade point average to which the input `Strings` will be converted. Two constants are declared; one of them, `RECORDSIZE`, is set to 12 because each student record consists of a four-byte `int` ID number plus an eight-byte `double` grade point average. Table 16-3 shows the byte sizes of the standard data types in Java.

» NOTE
You first learned about the sizes of data types, as well as the minimum and maximum values they can hold, in Chapter 2.

Type	Size in Bytes
byte	1
short	2
int	4
float	4
long	8
double	8

Table 16-3 Sizes of data types

The application in Figure 16-23 also declares a constant for the number of records the file can hold. For this application, assume there can be no more than 1000 students stored. For convenience, also assume that each student's ID number is at least 1 but no more than 998. Because you begin numbering the disk storage locations with 0, each student's record is stored on the data disk at the location that corresponds to the student's ID number minus 1.

The first shaded section of the `WriteRandomStudentFile` application is a `try` block that executes preparation statements before the data-entry portion of the application begins. Within the `try` block, the application writes 1000 "empty" student records to the output file—that is, it writes 1000 records with an ID number of 0 and a grade point average of 0.0. When the user enters actual data later in the application, some of these records are replaced with "real" data. Writing the 1000 zero-filled records provides a blank slate that is 12,000 bytes long, into which actual records can later be inserted in the appropriate locations.

When the `try` block finishes writing 1000 records, the `finally` block executes, as shown in the second shaded section in Figure 16-23. In the `finally` block, the open file is closed. Then, it is immediately reopened so the true work of the application can begin.

After the second shaded section of code in Figure 16-23, a dialog box prompts the user to enter an ID number or 999 to quit. The user enters a number, it is converted from a `String` to an integer, and while it is not 999, the user is prompted for a grade point average, which is converted from a `String` to a `double`. Next, the file position for the record is calculated by subtracting one from the student's ID number.

In the final shaded statement in the application, the `seek()` method is used to locate a position on the disk. For example, if the student's ID number is 123, the position that is 122 times 12 bytes (or 1464 bytes) from the beginning of the disk file is accessed. At that location, the student's ID number and grade point average are written as an integer and `double`, respectively. Then, the user is prompted for the next student ID number.

Suppose that student data exists as shown in Figure 16-24.

Student ID	Grade Point Average
123	3.2
004	4.0
003	2.7
087	3.5
086	2.9

Figure 16-24 Sample student data

When a user executes the `WriteRandomStudentFile` application, a dialog box appears, as shown in Figure 16-25. Assuming that the user enters the data from the sample student data table in Figure 16-24, the output file looks like Figure 16-26 when opened in a text editor. The data file appears mostly "blank," but if you examine the characters closely, you can see that some characters have been placed near the beginning of the file—these represent the data for student IDs 003 and 004. Several lines down, there is another "chunk" of data—these characters represent student records 086 and 087. The characters near the bottom of the viewing area for the file represent the data for student 123. As with the data you viewed in Figure 16-14 earlier in the chapter, this numeric data is not humanly readable; instead, it can be read by another Java application in which it can be interpreted for human consumption.

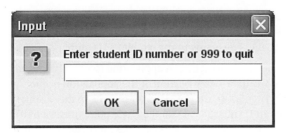

Figure 16-25 Dialog box created by the `WriteRandomStudentFile` application

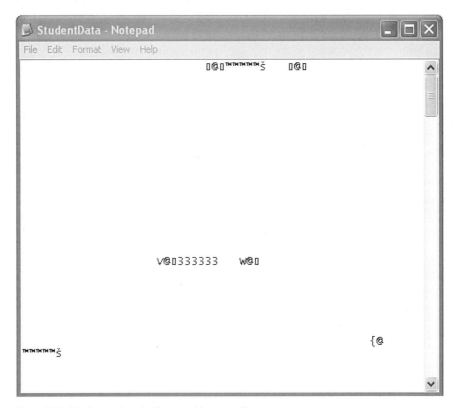

Figure 16-26 The StudentData.dat file viewed in a text editor

READING RECORDS FROM A RANDOM ACCESS FILE

Just because a file is created as a random access file does not mean it has to be used as a random access file. You can process a random access file either sequentially or randomly.

ACCESSING A RANDOM ACCESS FILE SEQUENTIALLY

The StudentData.dat random access file created by the `WriteRandomStudentFile` application in Figure 16-23 contains 1000 records. However, only five of them contain valuable data; displaying every record would result in many irrelevant lines of data. It makes more sense to display only those records for which an ID number has been inserted. The `ReadRandomStudentFile` application in Figure 16-27 reads through the 1000-record StudentData.dat file sequentially in a `for` loop (shaded), reading `int-double` pairs. When an ID number value is 0, it means no user-entered record was stored at that point, so the application does not bother to print it. Figure 16-28 shows the application's output—a list of the entered records, conveniently in student ID number order, which reflects their relative positions within the file.

```java
import javax.swing.*;
import java.io.*;
public class ReadRandomStudentFile
{
    public static void main(String[] args) throws IOException
    {
        RandomAccessFile stuFile =
            new RandomAccessFile("StudentData.dat","rw");
        int id;
        double gpa;
        final int NUMRECORDS = 1000;
        try
        {
            for(int x = 0; x < NUMRECORDS; ++x)
            {
                id = stuFile.readInt();
                gpa = stuFile.readDouble();
                if(id != 0)
                    System.out.println("ID# " + id + "   GPA: " + gpa);
            }
        }
        catch(IOException e)
        {
            System.out.println("Error: " + e.getMessage());
        }
        finally
        {
            stuFile.close();
        }
        System.exit(0);
    }
}
```

Figure 16-27 The `ReadRandomStudentFile` class

» NOTE In Figure 16-28, notice that the student ID numbers do not align because they display as integers—that is, without leading zeros even though they are assumed to be three-digit numbers. If you wanted the lower numbers to print with leading zeros, you could take several approaches, including using an `if` statement to decide to display extra zeros, storing the ID numbers as `Strings` instead of integers, and using formatted output as discussed in Appendix C.

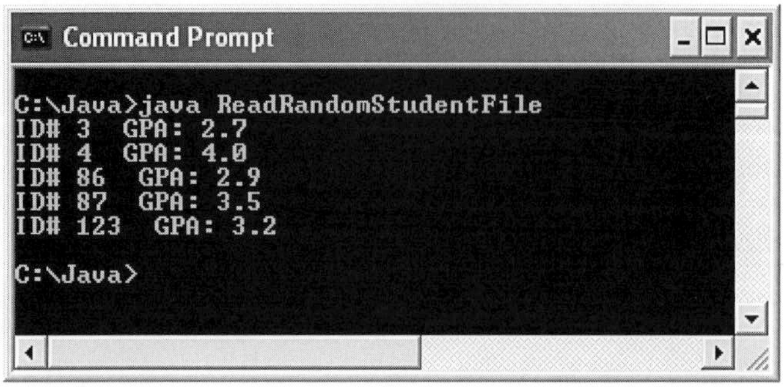

Figure 16-28 Output of the `ReadRandomStudentFile` application

ACCESSING A RANDOM ACCESS FILE RANDOMLY

If you simply want to display records in order based on their key field, you do not need to create a random access file and waste so much unneeded storage. Instead, you could sort the records using one of the sorting techniques you learned about in Chapter 8. The true benefit of using a random access file is the ability to retrieve a specific record from a file directly, without reading through other records to locate the desired one.

The `ReadRandomStudentFile2` application in Figure 16-29 allows the user to enter a student's ID number. The application then calculates the student record's position in the data file (one less than the ID number) and positions the file pointer at the correct location to begin reading. In the application, a dialog box prompts the user for an ID number, which is converted to an integer with the `parseInt()` method. (To keep this example brief, the application does not check for a valid ID number, so the `parseInt()` method might throw an exception to the operating system, ending the execution of the application.) Then, in the shaded portion of the application in Figure 16-29, while the user does not enter 999 to quit, the position of the sought-after record is calculated by subtracting one from the ID number, multiplying it by the record size, and positioning the file pointer at the desired location with the `seek()` method. (Again, to keep the example short, the ID number is not checked to ensure it is 999 or less.) The student record `int-double` pair is retrieved from the data file and displayed in a dialog box. Then, the user is prompted for the next desired student ID number. Figure 16-30 shows the output when the user requests student number 086.

```
import javax.swing.*;
import java.io.*;
public class ReadRandomStudentFile2
{
    public static void main(String[] args) throws IOException
    {
        int pos;
        RandomAccessFile stuFile =
            new RandomAccessFile("StudentData.dat","rw");
        String inputString;
        int id;
```

Figure 16-29 The `ReadRandomStudentFile2` class (*continued*) ▶

```
        double gpa;
        final int RECORDSIZE = 12;
        final int STOP = 999;
        inputString = JOptionPane.showInputDialog(null,
            "Enter student ID number or 999 to quit");
        id = Integer.parseInt(inputString);
        try
        {
            while(id != STOP)
            {
                pos = id - 1;
                stuFile.seek(pos * RECORDSIZE);
                id = stuFile.readInt();
                gpa = stuFile.readDouble();
                JOptionPane.showMessageDialog(null, "For ID # " + id +
                    "  GPA is " + gpa);
                inputString = JOptionPane.showInputDialog(null,
                    "Enter student ID number or 999 to quit");
                id = Integer.parseInt(inputString);
            }
        }
        catch(IOException e)
        {
            System.out.println("Error: " + e.getMessage());
        }
        finally
        {
            stuFile.close();
        }
        System.exit(0);
    }
}
```

Figure 16-29 The `ReadRandomStudentFile2` class

»NOTE In the application in Figure 16-29, you could eliminate the `readInt()` statement that retrieves the student's ID number; after all, the user has already entered the desired ID number. In this case, the `seek` statement would become:

```
stuFile.seek(pos * RECORDSIZE + 4);
```

You would add four bytes to the beginning of the desired record to access only the `double` grade point average of the appropriate student.

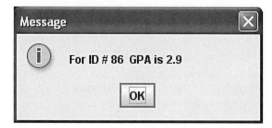

Figure 16-30 Output of the `ReadRandomStudentFile2` application when the user enters 086

READING AND WRITING OBJECTS TO AND FROM FILES

Creating objects is a fundamental feature of Java and all other object-oriented languages. Throughout this book, you have created classes from which you can instantiate objects. Therefore, it makes sense that Java allows you to write entire objects to files, instead of separately writing individual fields.

Consider the Employee class in Figure 16-31. It is similar to many you have created throughout this book. It contains three data fields, a constructor, and a display() method. The only feature of this class that is new to you is the shaded clause in the class header: implements Serializable. **Serialization** is Java's built-in mechanism for manipulating objects as streams of bytes; the Serializable interface endows your class with the ability to be serialized.

> **NOTE** A full-blown Employee class might contain many more data fields and get and set methods for each field, but this class is purposely brief so you can more easily follow the program examples that use it.

> **NOTE** Serializable is an unusual class in that it has no methods or fields. Its purpose is only to identify the class as being serializable.

```java
import java.io.*;
public class Employee implements Serializable
{
    private int idNum;
    String name;
    private double payRate;
    public Employee(int num, String name, double rate)
    {
        idNum = num;
        this.name = name;
        payRate = rate;
    }
    public void display()
    {
        System.out.println("ID# " + idNum + " " +
            name + " Pay rate: $" + payRate);
    }
}
```

Figure 16-31 The Employee class

When you create an Employee object from the class in Figure 16-31, it will be a **serialized object**—one that is represented as a sequence of bytes and includes the object's data as well as information about the types of data stored in the object. After a serialized object has been written into a file, it can be read from the file and deserialized. **Deserialization** is the process of recreating an object in computer memory after it is retrieved from a file.

Figure 16-32 contains an application that creates Employee objects and saves them in a file. The main() method throws an IOException because opening and closing files might cause

```
import java.io.*;
import java.util.*;
public class CreateEmployeeFile
{
    public static void main(String[] args) throws IOException
    {
        ObjectOutputStream output =
            new ObjectOutputStream
            (new FileOutputStream("Employees.txt"));
        Employee emp;
        int num = 0;
        String name;
        double rate;
        Scanner in = new Scanner(System.in);
        System.out.println
            ("Enter employee number, name, and pay rate: ");
        while(in.hasNext())
        {
            try
            {
                num = in.nextInt();
                name = in.next();
                rate = in.nextDouble();
                emp = new Employee(num, name, rate);
                output.writeObject(emp);
            }
            finally
            {
                System.out.println
                    ("Enter employee number, name, and " +
                    "pay rate, or Ctrl+Z to quit" );
            }
        }
        output.close();
    }
}
```

Figure 16-32 The `CreateEmployeeFile` class

such an exception. Also, the statements that read data from the keyboard might encounter the wrong data type. Again, in a full-blown application, you might choose to handle these exceptions within the application.

In the `CreateEmployeeFile` class, an `ObjectOutputStream` object is created using a `FileOutputStream` argument. In the first shaded statement, a `Scanner` class object is created using `System.in`. A **Scanner object** is a text reader that can pull primitive types and strings from input data streams. The scanner works by dividing input into pieces called **tokens**, which are single, small elements of text. Table 16-4 describes the `Scanner` class methods used in the `CreateEmployeeFile` class.

Method	Description
`boolean hasNext()`	Remains `true` if scanner has more input
`double nextDouble()`	Scans the next input token as a `double`
`int nextInt()`	Scans the next input token as an `int`
`String next()`	Scans the next complete token

Table 16-4 Selected `Scanner` class methods

In the loop that starts with the shaded `while` statement in Figure 16-32, while there is more input data available—for example, while the user has not typed Ctrl+Z when using Windows—the scanner retrieves an `int`, `String`, and `double` and passes them to the `Employee` class constructor. The scanning statements are placed in a `try` block because an exception might be thrown if the scanner encounters invalid data. In this example, the `main()` method would simply throw such exceptions to the operating system, but you could alter the program to catch and handle the exceptions. After a set of data has been entered, a new prompt is displayed before a new record is entered.

Figure 16-33 shows a typical execution of the `CreateEmployeeFile` class. The user is repeatedly prompted to enter employee data, and presses Ctrl+Z when finished.

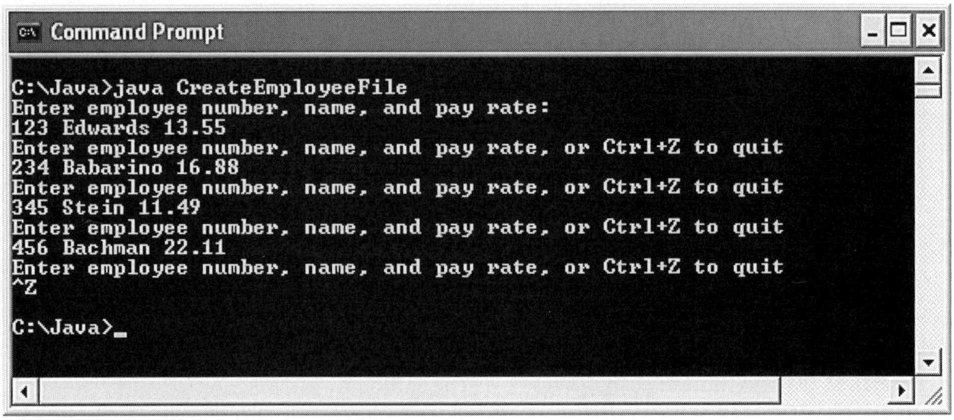

```
C:\Java>java CreateEmployeeFile
Enter employee number, name, and pay rate:
123 Edwards 13.55
Enter employee number, name, and pay rate, or Ctrl+Z to quit
234 Babarino 16.88
Enter employee number, name, and pay rate, or Ctrl+Z to quit
345 Stein 11.49
Enter employee number, name, and pay rate, or Ctrl+Z to quit
456 Bachman 22.11
Enter employee number, name, and pay rate, or Ctrl+Z to quit
^Z

C:\Java>
```

Figure 16-33 Typical execution of `CreateEmployeeFile`

The `ReadEmployeeFile` class in Figure 16-34 creates an `ObjectInputStream` object using the same filename as in the `CreateEmployeeFile` application. The shaded `readObject()` method returns an `Object` that is cast to an `Employee` before being stored in an `Employee` object. Then the `Employee` class `display()` method can be used. Figure 16-35 shows the output.

```
import java.io.*;
public class ReadEmployeeFile
{
    public static void main(String[] args)
        throws IOException, ClassNotFoundException
    {
        ObjectInputStream in = new
          ObjectInputStream
          (new FileInputStream("Employees.txt"));
        Employee emp;
        try
        {
          while(true)
          {
              emp = (Employee)in.readObject();
              emp.display();
          }
        }
        catch(EOFException e)
        {
            in.close();
        }
    }
}
```

Figure 16-34 The ReadEmployeeFile application

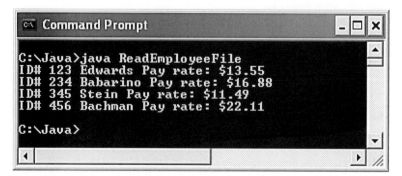

Figure 16-35 Execution of ReadEmployeeFile application

>> NOTE Many sophisticated file-handling techniques exist that are beyond the scope of this chapter. In particular, the package java.nio contains features for handling buffers, channels, and file locks that make input and output more efficient.

YOU DO IT

USING THE `File` CLASS TO EXAMINE FILE STATUS

In this section, you will write a class that examines a file and prints appropriate messages concerning its status.

To create a class that examines a `File` object:

1. Open a new file in your text editor and type the following first few lines of a class that checks a file's status:

```
import java.io.*;
public class CheckFile
{
    public static void main(String[] args)
    {
```

2. Enter the following line to create a `File` object that represents a disk file named Data.txt. Although the filename on the disk is Data.txt, within the program the filename is `myFile`.

```
File myFile = new File("Data.txt");
```

3. Enter the following `if...else` statements to test for the file's existence. If the `File` object `myFile` exists, display its name and size, and then test whether the file can be read or written. Also display the date the file was last modified. The result is a long integer. If the file does not exist, simply print an appropriate message.

```
if(myFile.exists())
{
    System.out.println(myFile.getName() + " exists");
    System.out.println("It is " +
        myFile.length() + " bytes long");
    if(myFile.canRead())
        System.out.println("It can be read");
    if(myFile.canWrite())
        System.out.println("It can be written to");
    System.out.println("It was last modified " +
        myFile.lastModified());
}
else
    System.out.println("File does not exist");
```

4. Add a closing curly brace for the `main()` method and a closing curly brace for the class.

5. Save the file as **CheckFile.java** and compile the class.

6. Compile the application and execute it. Unless you have stored a file named Data.txt in the default folder, you see the message "File does not exist".

7. Open a new file in your text editor and type the company name:

```
Event Handlers Incorporated!
```

Save this file as **Data.txt** in the current directory (also called the current folder).

8. Run the `CheckFile` application again. Your output is similar to the output in Figure 16-36. The file exists and is 28 bytes long because each character you typed, including spaces and

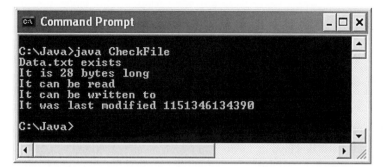

Figure 16-36 Output of the CheckFile application

NOTE
If you added comments to the beginning of your Data.txt file or mistyped the company name, the total number of characters in your file might differ from 28.

punctuation, consumes one byte of storage. The file has read and write capabilities. The date your file was last modified is represented by a different long integer.

COMPARING TWO FILE DATES

Next, you will create a second data file so that you can compare its size and time stamp with those of the Data.txt file.

To create a Data2.txt file and an application to compare two files' dates:

1. Open a new file in your text editor and type a shorter version of the company name:

```
Event Handlers
```

Save the file as **Data2.txt** in the current folder.

2. Open a new file in your text editor and type the following first few lines of the CheckTwoFiles application:

```
import java.io.*;
public class CheckTwoFiles
{
    public static void main(String[] args)
    {
```

3. Enter the following code to declare two file objects:

```
File f1 = new File("Data.txt");
File f2 = new File("Data2.txt");
```

4. Enter the following code to determine whether both files exist. If they do, comparing their creation times determines which file has the more recent time stamp, and comparing their lengths determines which file is longer.

```
if(f1.exists() && f2.exists())
{
    System.out.print("The more recent file is ");
    if(f1.lastModified() > f2.lastModified())
        System.out.println(f1.getName());
    else
        System.out.println(f2.getName());
```

```
        System.out.print("The longer file is ");
        if(f1.length() > f2.length())
            System.out.println(f1.getName());
        else if(f1.length() < f2.length())
            System.out.println(f2.getName());
        else System.out.println("neither one");
    }
```

5. Add two more closing curly braces—one for the `main()` method and one for the class.

6. Save the file as **CheckTwoFiles.java** in the current folder, then compile and run the application. The output appears in Figure 16-37. Note that the Data2.txt file was created after the Data.txt file, so it is more recent, but it contains fewer characters.

Figure 16-37 Output of the `CheckTwoFiles` application

USING InputStream AND OutputStream OBJECTS

Next, you will create `InputStream` and `OutputStream` objects so you can read from the keyboard and write to the screen. Of course, you have already written many programs that read from the keyboard and write to the screen without using these objects. By using them here with the default input/output devices, you can easily modify the `InputStream` and `OutputStream` objects later, and use whatever input and output devices you choose.

To create an application that reads from the keyboard and writes to the screen:

1. Open a new file in your text editor and type the following first few lines of a program that allows a user to enter data from the keyboard and then echo that data to the screen. The class name is `ReadKBWriteScreen`:

```
import java.io.*;
public class ReadKBWriteScreen
{
```

2. Add the following header and opening curly brace for the `main()` method. The `main()` method `throws` an `IOException` because you will perform input and output operations.

```
public static void main(String[] args) throws IOException
{
```

3. Enter the following code to declare `InputStream` and `OutputStream` objects, as well as an integer to hold each character the user types:

```
InputStream istream;
OutputStream ostream;
int c;
```

4. Enter the following code to assign the `System.in` object to `istream` and the `System.out` object to `ostream`. Then add a multiline prompt telling the user to enter some characters, and to press Ctrl+Z when the user is finished.

```
istream = System.in;
ostream = System.out;
System.out.println("Please enter some characters.");
System.out.println
        ("Press Enter after each group of characters");
System.out.println
        ("to see your input echoed to the screen.");
System.out.println("Press Ctrl+Z when you are done.");
```

5. Use the following `try` block to read from the file. If an `IOException` occurs, you can print an appropriate message. Within the `try` block, execute a loop that reads from the keyboard until the end-of-file condition occurs (when the `read()` method returns –1). While there is not an end-of-file condition, send the character to the `ostream` object.

```
try
{
    while((c = istream.read()) != -1)
        ostream.write(c);
}
```

6. Use the following `catch` block to handle any `IOException`:

```
catch(IOException e)
{
    System.out.println("Error: " + e.getMessage());
}
```

7. Regardless of whether an `IOException` occurs, you want to close the streams. Use the following `finally` block to ensure that the streams are closed:

```
finally
{
    istream.close();
    ostream.close();
}
```

8. Add a closing curly brace for the `main()` method and another for the class.

9. Save the file as **ReadKBWriteScreen.java**, then compile and run the application. At the command line, type any series of characters and press **Enter**. As you type characters, the buffer holds them until you press Enter, at which time the stored characters echo to the screen. When you have entered a few lines of characters, press **Ctrl+Z**, then press **Enter** to end the application. Figure 16-38 shows a typical application execution. Notice that the keystroke combination Ctrl+Z appears on the screen as ^Z.

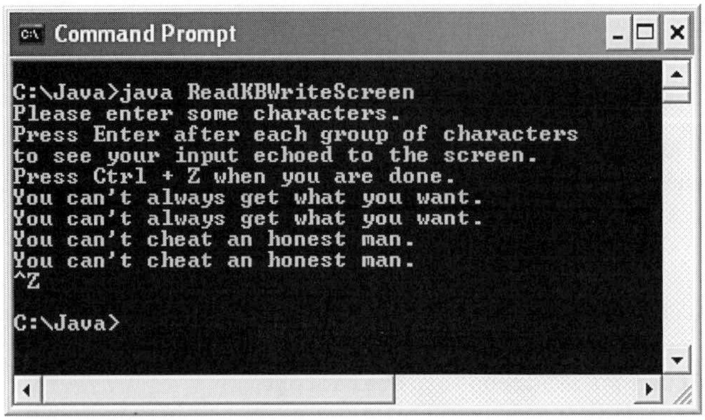

Figure 16-38 Typical execution of the `ReadKBWriteScreen` application

> **NOTE** Do not press Ctrl+C to end the `ReadKBWriteScreen` application. Doing so breaks out of the program before its completion and does not properly close the files.

WRITING TO AN OUTPUT FILE

In the next set of steps, you will use a `FileOutputStream` to write keyboard-entered data to a file you create.

To create an application that writes keyboard data to a file:

1. Open the **ReadKBWriteScreen.java** file in your text editor and immediately save the file as **ReadKBWriteFile.java**.

2. Change the class header to **public class ReadKBWriteFile**.

3. Position your insertion point at the end of the line that defines the `ostream` object (`OutputStream ostream;`), then press **Enter** to start a new line. On the new line, define a `File` object as follows:

   ```
   File outFile = new File("Datafile.dat");
   ```

4. Replace the statement that assigns `System.out` to the `ostream` object with the following statement:

   ```
   ostream = new FileOutputStream(outFile);
   ```

5. Save the file, then compile and execute the application. At the command line, type **Event Handlers handles events of all sizes**, then press **Enter**. After you press Enter, the characters do not appear on the screen; instead, they are output to a file named Datafile.dat that is written in the default directory, the current directory from which you are working.

6. Press **Ctrl+Z**, then press **Enter** to stop the program.

7. In your text editor, open the **Datafile.dat** file. The characters are an exact copy of the ones you entered at the keyboard.

> **NOTE** You could enter any number of characters to the output stream before ending the program, and they would be saved in the output file. If you run the `ReadKBWriteFile` program again, the program overwrites the existing Datafile.dat file with your new data.

READING DATA FROM A FILE

Next, you will read data from a file and write it to the screen.

To read data from a file:

1. In your text editor, open the **ReadKBWriteFile.java** file and immediately save it as **ReadFileWriteScreen.java**.

2. Change the class header to **public class ReadFileWriteScreen**.

3. In the `File` object declaration, change the object name to `inFile`; the object refers to the Datafile.dat file you created. Of course, the name `outFile` would also work, but it would not be as descriptive because the file will be read into this application, not written from it. The statement becomes the following:

```
File inFile = new File("Datafile.dat");
```

4. Change the statement that assigns the `System.in` object to `istream` (`istream = System.in`) so that you can use the `File` object for input instead of the keyboard. Replace the statement with the following:

```
istream = new FileInputStream(inFile);
```

5. Change the `ostream` assignment to `System.out` so that output will display on the monitor:

```
ostream = System.out;
```

6. Remove the four statements that prompt the user for input; a disk file does not need a prompt.

7. Save the file, then compile and run the application. The data you stored in the Datafile.dat file ("Event Handlers handles events of all sizes") appears on the screen, and the application ends.

CREATING A FILE OF SEQUENTIAL DATA RECORDS

In the next series of steps, you will create a full-blown project for Event Handlers Incorporated. The application uses a GUI interface to capture data about an event from a user, and writes that data to an output file using the `DataOutput` interface. The data required includes the host's name, the date, and the number of guests. For simplicity, this application accepts event dates for the current month only, so the date field is an integer. Figure 16-39 shows a preliminary sketch of the user's interface.

Figure 16-39 Sketch of the user's interface

To create a `JFrame` for data entry:

1. Open a new file in your text editor and type the following first few lines of the `CreateEventFile` class. `CreateEventFile` is a `JFrame` that reacts to a mouse click when you click an object within the `JFrame`. Therefore, you must extend `JFrame` and implement `ActionListener`.

```java
import java.io.*;
import java.awt.*;
import java.awt.event.*;
import javax.swing.*;
public class CreateEventFile extends JFrame
    implements ActionListener
{
```

2. Enter the following code to create constants for the frame size, a `JLabel` for the company name, and a `Font` object to use with the company name:

```java
final int WIDTH = 320;
final int HEIGHT = 200;
private JLabel companyName =
    new JLabel("Event Handlers Incorporated");
private Font bigFont =
    new Font("Helvetica", Font.ITALIC, 24);
```

3. Enter the following code to create a prompt that tells the user to enter data, and enter `JTextField`s for the host, date, and guests. Because a host's name is usually several characters long, the field for the host's name should be wider than the fields for the date and number of guests.

```java
private JLabel prompt =
    new JLabel("Enter this month's events");
private JTextField host = new JTextField(10);
private JTextField date = new JTextField(4);
private JTextField guests = new JTextField(4);
```

4. Enter the following code to create a `JLabel` for each of the `JTextField`s. Include a `JButton` object that the user can click when a data record is completed and ready to be written to the data file.

```java
private JLabel hLabel = new JLabel("Host");
private JLabel dLabel = new JLabel("Date");
private JLabel gLabel = new JLabel("Guests");
private JButton enterDataButton =
    new JButton("Enter data");
```

5. When you write the user's data to an output file, you will use the `DataOutputStream` class, so create a `DataOutputStream` object as follows:

```java
DataOutputStream ostream;
```

6. Save the work you have done so far as **CreateEventFile.java**.

ADDING A CONSTRUCTOR THAT OPENS A FILE

Next, you will add CreateEventFile's constructor to the class. The constructor calls its parent's constructor, which is the JFrame class constructor, and passes it a title to use for the JFrame. The constructor also attempts to open an Events.dat file for output. If the attempt fails, the constructor's catch block handles the Exception; otherwise, you add all the JTextField, JLabel, and JButtonComponents to the JFrame.

To write the CreateEventFile class constructor:

1. In the **CreateEventFile.java** file, press **Enter** to start a new line below the statement that declares the DataOutputStream object, type the following constructor header and opening curly brace, and then call the superclass constructor:

```
public CreateEventFile()
{
    super("Create Event File");
```

2. Add the following try...catch block to handle the file creation:

```
try
{
    ostream = new DataOutputStream
        (new FileOutputStream("Events.dat"));
}
catch(IOException e)
{
    System.err.println("File not opened");
    System.exit(1);
}
```

> **》NOTE** Notice the use of the System.err object to display an error message. Alternatively, you can display the message on System.out.

3. After the file is open, use the following code to set the JFrame's size, choose a layout manager, and add all the necessary Components to the JFrame:

```
setSize(WIDTH, HEIGHT);
setLayout(new FlowLayout());
companyName.setFont(bigFont);
add(companyName);
add(prompt);
add(hLabel);
add(host);
add(dLabel);
add(date);
add(gLabel);
add(guests);
add(enterDataButton);
```

4. To finish the JFrame constructor, enter the following code to register the JFrame as a listener for the JButton, make the JFrame visible, and set the default close operation for the JFrame. Finally, add a closing curly brace for the constructor.

```
        enterDataButton.addActionListener(this);
        setVisible(true);
        setDefaultCloseOperation(JFrame.EXIT_ON_CLOSE);
    }
```

5. Save the file. Don't compile the file yet; you will add more code in the next set of steps.

ADDING AN actionPerformed() METHOD

When users see the JFrame, they can enter data in each of the available JTextFields. When users complete a record for a single event, they click the JButton, which causes the actionPerformed() method to execute. This method must retrieve the text from each of the JTextFields and write it to a data file in the correct format. You will write a usable actionPerformed() method now.

To add the actionPerformed() method to the CreateEventFile program:

1. At the end of the existing code within the **CreateEventFile.java** file, press **Enter** to start a new line below the constructor method, and then type the following header for the actionPerformed() method. Within the method, create an integer variable to hold the number of guests at an event.

```
public void actionPerformed(ActionEvent e1)
{
    int numGuests;
```

2. Use a try block to hold the data retrieval and the subsequent file-writing actions so that you can handle any I/O errors that occur. You will use the parseInt() method to convert the JTextField guest number to a usable integer, but you will accept the host and date fields as simple text. You can use the appropriate DataOutputStream methods to write formatted data to the output file.

```
try
{
    numGuests = Integer.parseInt(guests.getText());
    ostream.writeUTF(host.getText());
    ostream.writeUTF(date.getText());
    ostream.writeInt(numGuests);
```

3. Continue the try block by removing the data from each JTextField after it is written to the file. That way, each JTextField will be clear and ready to receive data for the next record. Notice that to clear the fields, you use a pair of quotes with no space between them. Then, end the try block.

```
    host.setText("");
    date.setText("");
    guests.setText("");
}
```

4. There are two types of Exceptions that you might want to deal with in this application. Because the host name and date fields are text, the user can enter any type of data. However, the guest field must be an integer. When you use the parseInt() method with data that cannot be converted to an integer (such as alphabetic letters), a NumberFormatException error occurs. In this case, you can write an error message to the standard error device and explain the problem as follows:

```
catch(NumberFormatException e2)
{
    System.err.println("Invalid number of guests");
}
```

5. A second and more serious `Exception` occurs when the application cannot write the output file, so you should `catch` the potential `IOException`, display an error message, and exit using the following code:

```
catch(IOException e3)
{
    System.err.println("Error writing file");
    System.exit(1);
}
```

6. Add a closing curly brace for the `actionPerformed()` method.

ADDING A `main()` METHOD

Next, you will create a `main()` method that creates an instance of the `CreateEventFile` `JFrame`.

To write a `main()` method that instantiates a `CreateEventFile` `JFrame`:

1. Type the following method:

```
public static void main(String[] args)
{
    CreateEventFile cef = new CreateEventFile();
}
```

2. Add a closing curly brace for the class. Then save the file and compile it.

3. When the class compiles successfully, execute the application and enter some data. Figure 16-40 shows the input screen into which the user has typed the first record: **Sagami** as the event host, on the **3**(rd), with **150** guests. After entering the data into the three fields, click the **Enter data** button. Your data is sent to the file, and the fields are cleared. Enter a second record by making up your own record information, then click the **Enter data** button again. Repeat this process until you have entered five data records.

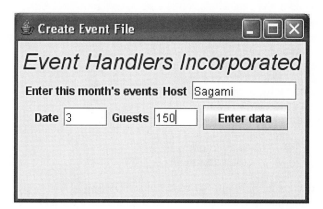

Figure 16-40 Data entry screen for the `CreateEventFile` application

While entering at least one record, type non-numeric data in the guests field. Notice the error message that displays on the standard error device at the command line.

4. Click the **Close** button in the `CreateEventFile JFrame` to close it.

5. Examine your Student Disk using any file-management program or the DOS command-line directory command, `dir`. Confirm that your program created the Events.dat data file. You will write an application to read the file in the next series of steps.

READING FROM A SEQUENTIAL ACCESS FILE

Next, you will create a `JFrame` in which employees of Event Handlers Incorporated can view each individual record stored in the Events.dat file. The user interface will look like the interface used in the `CreateEventFile JFrame`, but the user will not enter data within this `JFrame`. Instead, the user will click a `JButton` to see each succeeding record in the Events.dat file.

To create a `JFrame` for viewing file data:

1. Open a new file in your text editor and type the following first few lines of the `ReadEventFile` class:

```
import java.io.*;
import java.awt.*;
import java.awt.event.*;
import javax.swing.*;
public class ReadEventFile extends JFrame
    implements ActionListener
{
```

2. Enter the following code to declare constants for the frame size and to declare all of the `JLabel`s, `JTextField`s, and associated values that will appear in the `JFrame`. The text of the prompt and `JButton` have changed, but these statements basically echo those in the CreateEventFile.java file. (To save typing, you might want to copy the corresponding statements from the `CreateEventFile` class and make minor adjustments.)

```
final int WIDTH = 325;
final int HEIGHT = 200;
private JLabel companyName =
    new JLabel("Event Handlers Incorporated");
private Font bigFont =
    new Font("Helvetica", Font.ITALIC, 24);
private JLabel prompt = new
    JLabel("View this month's events");
private JTextField host = new JTextField(10);
private JTextField date = new JTextField(4);
private JTextField guests = new JTextField(4);
private JButton viewEventButton = new
    JButton("View Event");
private JLabel hLabel = new JLabel("Host");
private JLabel dLabel = new JLabel("Date");
private JLabel gLabel = new JLabel("Guests");
```

3. Enter the following code to declare a `DataInputStream` object. Then write the `ReadEventFile` constructor method that uses a `try...catch` block to open a file. Notice that you can chain the `DataInputStream` object and a `FileInputStream` object

using the same technique you used for output. (*Note:* If you have stored your Events.dat file in a location other than the default folder, change the location in the `FileInputStream` constructor in your own version of the class.)

```
DataInputStream istream;
public ReadEventFile()
{
    super("Read Event File");
    try
    {
        istream = new
            DataInputStream(new FileInputStream
            ("Events.dat"));
    }
    catch(IOException e)
    {
            System.err.println("File not opened");
            System.exit(1);
    }
}
```

4. After successfully opening the file, set the `JFrame` size, layout manager, and `Font` for the `JFrame` as follows:

```
setSize(WIDTH, HEIGHT);
setLayout(new FlowLayout());
companyName.setFont(bigFont);
```

5. Add the `JFrame`'s `Components` as follows:

```
add(companyName);
add(prompt);
add(hLabel);
add(host);
add(dLabel);
add(date);
add(gLabel);
add(guests);
add(viewEventButton);
```

6. Enter the following code to ensure that the `JFrame` listens for `JButton` messages, to make the `JFrame` visible, and to set the default close operation:

```
viewEventButton.addActionListener(this);
setVisible(true);
setDefaultCloseOperation(JFrame.EXIT_ON_CLOSE);
```

7. Add the closing curly brace for the `ReadEventFile` constructor.

8. Type the beginning of the following `actionPerformed()` method. This method declares variables for the file field data, and then uses a `try` block to call the appropriate `read()` method for each field. Each data field then appears in the correct `JTextField`.

```
public void actionPerformed(ActionEvent e1)
{
    String theHost, theDate;
```

```
        int numGuests;
        try
        {
            theHost = istream.readUTF();
            theDate = istream.readUTF();
            numGuests = istream.readInt();
            host.setText(theHost);
            date.setText(theDate);
            guests.setText(String.valueOf(numGuests));
        }
```

9. Code the following two `catch` blocks for the `try` block that reads the data fields. The first `catch` block catches the `EOFException` and calls a `closeFile()` method. The second `catch` block catches `IOExceptions` and exits the application if there is a problem with the file. Notice that the `Exceptions` have unique names (e2 and e3) because you cannot declare two data items with the same name within the same method.

```
catch(EOFException e2)
{
    closeFile();
}
catch(IOException e3)
{
    System.err.println("Error reading file");
    System.exit(1);
}
```

10. Add the closing curly brace for the `actionPerformed()` method.

Write the following `closeFile()` method that closes the `DataInputStream` object and exits the application:

```
public void closeFile()
{
    try
    {
        istream.close();
        System.exit(0);
    }
    catch(IOException e)
    {
        System.err.println("Error closing file");
        System.exit(1);
    }
}
```

11. Add a `main()` method that instantiates a `ReadEventFile` object, and add a final closing curly brace for the class:

```
    public static void main(String[] args)
    {
        ReadEventFile ref = new ReadEventFile();
    }
}
```

12. Save the file as **ReadEventFile.java** and then compile the class using the **javac** command. Execute the application using the **java** command, then click the **View Event** JButton to view the first record. Your output should look like Figure 16-41. Click the **View Event** button again to see the second record. Continue clicking the **View Event** button until you reach the end of the file; when you do, the JFrame closes and the program ends.

Figure 16-41 Output of the ReadEventFile application after clicking the View Event button one time

CREATING A RANDOM ACCESS FILE

When you create a random access file, you provide some basis for the placement of records on the file so that later you can use the seek() method to access the records directly. Frequently, you use an account number or ID number as a key field that you can manipulate to determine a file position. In the next sets of steps, you will create and use a random access file for Event Handlers Incorporated in which you use the event's data as the key fields. In these examples, you assume that only one event is scheduled per day. If that were not the case, you would have to differentiate events on some other basis, perhaps by assigning an event number to each.

To create a random access file for Event Handlers Incorporated:

1. Open the **CreateEventFile.java** class in your text editor. Immediately save the file as **CreateRandomEventFile.java**.

2. Change the class name to **CreateRandomEventFile**.

3. You need to declare a RandomAccessFile object for this application, then declare two constants. The first constant holds a record size. Each record contains 18 bytes—10 for the host's name, and four each for the integer data and number of guests. The second constant holds a number of records—one for each day in a month. Also declare a blank name that is 10 characters long. To accomplish these tasks, add four new statements at the end of the list of declared Components as follows:

```
RandomAccessFile eventsFile;
final int RECORD_SIZE = 18;
final int NUM_RECORDS = 31;
StringBuffer blankName = new StringBuffer(10);
```

4. Change the constructor name to match the class: **CreateRandomEventFile**.

5. Within the constructor, replace the existing `try` block with the following code. A new file named RandomEventsData.dat is opened, and a `for` loop writes 31 "empty" records in which each name is null, each date is 0, and each guest count is 0.

```
try
{
    eventsFile =
        new RandomAccessFile("RandomEventsData.dat","rw");
    for(int x = 0; x < NUM_RECORDS; ++x)
    {
        eventsFile.writeUTF(blankName.toString());
        eventsFile.writeInt(0);
        eventsFile.writeInt(0);
    }
}
```

6. The `actionPerformed()` method executes when the user clicks the `JButton`. However, instead of just writing the data from the text fields to a storage device, this method first calculates the correct position for the data, so you replace the first part of the `actionPerformed()` method (up to the first `catch` block) with this new version. Add an integer to hold a numeric date; this number will be used to determine each event's file position. Within the `try` block, retrieve the number of guests and the date from the text fields. Use the `seek()` method to set the file pointer to a position that is one less than the date (because the first file position is 0) times the size of a record. Then write the data to the output file and clear the text fields.

```
public void actionPerformed(ActionEvent e1)
{
    int numGuests;
    int numDate;
    try
    {
        numGuests = Integer.parseInt(guests.getText());
        numDate = Integer.parseInt(date.getText());
        eventsFile.seek((numDate-1) * RECORD_SIZE);
        eventsFile.writeUTF(host.getText());
        eventsFile.writeInt(numDate);
        eventsFile.writeInt(numGuests);
        host.setText("");
        date.setText("");
        guests.setText("");
    }
```

7. In the `main()` method, replace both occurrences of `CreateEventFile` with **CreateRandomEventFile**.

8. Save the file and compile it. Execute the application. The interface looks the same as the interface you used in the `CreateEventFile` application earlier. However, when you enter data this time, each record is stored in a file based on the date. Enter records for at least four or five events, clicking the **Enter data** button after you type each entry. Be careful that you do not enter any host names longer than 10 characters; you have not coded this application to handle errors that will occur when you read from the file in the next section if a host's name is too long. Close the frame when you are finished.

9. Open the RandomEventsData.dat file in your text editor. For example, Figure 16-42 shows a file for which events have been stored for the 1st, 3rd, 19th, 20th, and 21st days of the month. The text names are readable, but the date and guest values are not.

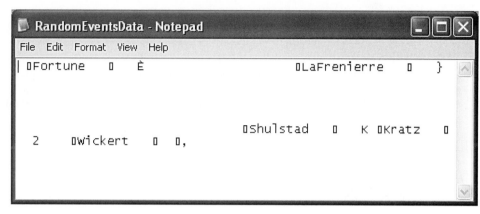

Figure 16-42 The RandomEventsData.dat file

ACCESSING RECORDS RANDOMLY

Next, you will create an application that reads the RandomEventsData.dat file you just created, and then allows you to enter a date and view the host and number of guests scheduled for that date.

1. Open the **CreateRandomEventFile.java** file in your text editor and immediately save it as **ReadRandomEventFile.java**.

2. Change the class name to **ReadRandomEventFile**.

3. Change the text on the JButton from "Enter data" to "Enter **date**".

4. Change the constructor name to **ReadRandomEventFile**.

5. Remove the for loop that writes 31 empty records to the output file.

6. The actionPerformed() method executes when the user clicks the JButton after entering a date in the date field. The new actionPerformed() method retrieves the date, converts it to an integer, and calculates a file position where the requested record can be found. Then, the host, date, and number of guests are retrieved from the file, and their values are placed in the text fields. To accomplish these tasks, change the first part of the actionPerformed() method (up to the first catch block) as follows:

```
public void actionPerformed(ActionEvent e1)
{
    String eventHost;
    int numGuests;
    int numDate;
    try
    {
        numDate = Integer.parseInt(date.getText());
        eventsFile.seek((numDate-1) * RECORD_SIZE);
        eventHost = eventsFile.readUTF();
        numDate = eventsFile.readInt();
```

```
            numGuests = eventsFile.readInt();
            host.setText(eventHost);
            date.setText("" + numDate);
            guests.setText("" + numGuests);
    }
```

7. In the `main()` method, change both instances of `CreateRandomEventFile` to **ReadRandomEventFile**.

8. Save the file, then compile and execute it. When the frame appears, type a date and press the button. The host and number of guests for the event scheduled for the date appear. If you choose a date for which you have not scheduled an event, the host field appears blank and the guest field contains a 0.

9. View records for as many dates as you want, then close the application.

KEY TERMS

Random access memory (RAM) is temporary, volatile storage.

Volatile memory requires power to retain information.

Nonvolatile storage does not require power to retain information.

A **computer file** is a collection of stored information in a computer system.

Permanent storage devices retain data even when power is lost. Examples include hard disks, floppy disks, Zip disks, USB drives, reels or cassettes of magnetic tape, and compact discs.

Data files consist of related records that contain facts and figures, such as employee numbers, names, and salaries.

Program files or **application files** store software instructions.

The **root directory** of a storage device is its main directory, outside any folders.

Folders or **directories** provide a storage organization hierarchy.

A **path** is the complete list of the disk drive plus the hierarchy of directories in which a file resides.

Java's **File class** provides methods to gather file information.

A **field** is a group of characters that has some meaning.

A **record** is a collection of fields that contain data about an entity.

A data file is used as a **sequential access file** when each record is stored in order, based on the value in some field.

A Java application **opens a file** by creating an object and associating a stream of bytes with that object.

When an application **closes a file**, it is no longer available to an application.

A **stream** functions as a pipeline or channel through which bytes flow into and out of an application.

InputStream is an abstract class that contains methods for performing input.

OutputStream is an abstract class that contains methods for performing output.

A **convenience class** is one that has been designed to make the programmer's job easier.

A **buffer** is a memory location that you use to hold data temporarily.

EOF is the end-of-file condition.

A **signed applet** is one that contains a digital signature to prove that it came from a trusted source and so has more privileges than an ordinary applet.

Binary data is data stored in machine-readable code that must be read by an application before you can understand it.

When you use a `DataOutputStream` connected to `FileOutputStream`, the approach is known as **chaining the stream objects**.

Batch processing is processing that involves performing the same tasks with many records, one after the other.

Real-time applications require that a record be accessed immediately while a client is waiting.

Random access files are files in which records can be located in any order.

Files in which records must be accessed immediately are also called **instant access files**.

Random access files are also called **direct access files**.

A **file pointer**, or **file position pointer**, is an automatically created variable that holds the byte number of the next file position to be used.

A **key field** is the field in a record that makes the record unique from all others.

Serialization is Java's built-in mechanism for manipulating objects as streams of bytes.

A **serialized object** is represented as a sequence of bytes and includes the object's data as well as information about the types of data stored in the object.

Deserialization is the process of recreating an object in computer memory after it is retrieved from a file.

A **Scanner object** is a text reader that can pull primitive types and strings from input data streams.

Tokens are single, small elements of text used by a `Scanner`.

CHAPTER SUMMARY

» Files are objects that you store on nonvolatile, permanent storage devices, such as floppy disks, CDs, or external drives.

» You can use the `File` class to gather file information, such as its size, whether it is open, its most recent modification date, and whether the file even exists.

» Data used by businesses is generally stored in a data hierarchy that includes files, records, fields, and characters.

» Java views a file as a series of bytes, and views a stream as an object through which input and output data (in the form of bytes) flow. `InputStream` and `OutputStream` are abstract subclasses of `Object` that contain methods for performing input and output. `FileInputStream` and `FileOutputStream` provide the capability to read from and write to files. You can use the `InputStream read()` method to read in one character at a time.

» You can use the `DataOutputStream` class to accomplish formatted output. The `DataOutput` interface includes methods such as `writeBoolean()`, `writeChar()`, `writeDouble()`, `writeFloat()`, and `writeInt()`. Each method writes data in the correct format for the data type indicated by its name. You can use the method `writeUTF()` to write Unicode format strings.

» `DataInputStream` objects enable you to read binary data from an `InputStream`. The `DataInput` interface includes methods such as `readByte()`, `readChar()`, `readDouble()`, `readFloat()`, `readInt()`, and `readUTF()`. Each `DataInput read()` method correctly reads the type of data indicated by its name.

» You can provide a variable filename to a program with techniques such as prompting the user or including the filename in the command-line instruction to execute an application.

» In random access files, or direct access files, records can be located in any order. The `RandomAccessFile` class contains the same `read()`, `write()`, and `close()` methods as `InputStream` and `OutputStream`, but it also contains a `seek()` method that lets you select a beginning position within a file before you read or write.

» You can write objects to files if they implement the `Serializable` interface. Serialization is Java's built-in mechanism for manipulating objects as streams of bytes.

REVIEW QUESTIONS

1. Files always _____ .

   a. hold software instructions

   b. occupy a section of storage space

   c. remain open until the end of an application that uses them

   d. all of the above

2. The `File` class enables you to _____ .

   a. open a file

   b. close a file

   c. determine a file's size

   d. all of the above

3. The _____ package contains all the classes you use in file processing.

   a. `java.file`   c. `java.lang`

   b. `java.io`   d. `java.process`

4. The statement `File aFile = new File("myFile");` creates a file _____ .

   a. on the disk in drive A

   b. on the hard drive (drive C)

   c. in the Temp folder on the hard drive (drive C)

   d. on the default disk drive in the default directory

5. The `File` method `canWrite()` returns a(n) _____ value.

   a. `int`

   b. `Boolean`

   c. `Object`

   d. `void`

6. Data used by businesses is stored in a data hierarchy that includes the following items, from largest to smallest:

   a. file, field, record, character

   b. record, file, field, character

   c. file, record, field, character

   d. record, field, file, character

7. A group of characters that has meaning is a _____ .

   a. file

   b. record

   c. field

   d. byte

8. Files consist of related _____ .

   a. records

   b. fields

   c. data segments

   d. archives

9. Before an application can read data from any file, the program must _____ the file.

   a. create

   b. open

   c. store

   d. close

10. When you perform an input operation in a Java application, you use a _____ .

   a. pipeline

   b. channel

   c. moderator

   d. stream

11. Most streams flow _____ .

   a. in

   b. out

   c. either in or out, but only in one direction

   d. both in and out concurrently

12. The output from `System.err` and `System.out` _____ go to the same device.

   a. must

   b. cannot

   c. might

   d. The answer depends on whether a mainframe or PC system is used.

13. A memory location that is used to temporarily hold data is a _____ .

    a. stream   c. bulwark

    b. buffer   d. channel

14. The `read()` method returns a value of –1 when it encounters a(n) _____ .

    a. input error   c. end-of-file condition

    b. integer   d. negative value

15. Much of the data that you write with `DataOutputStream` objects is not readable in a text editor because _____ .

    a. it does not exist in any physical sense

    b. it is stored in a noncharacter format

    c. you can read it only with a special piece of hardware called a Data Reader

    d. Java's security features prohibit it

16. You use a `DataOutputStream` connected to `FileOutputStream` by using a method known as _____ .

    a. sequencing   c. piggybacking

    b. iteration   d. chaining

17. When you `catch` an `EOFException`, it means you have _____ .

    a. failed to find the end of the file

    b. forgotten to open a file

    c. forgotten to close a file

    d. reached the end of a file

18. Which of the following applications is most likely to use random file processing?

    a. an application that schedules airline reservations

    b. a credit card company's end-of-month billing application

    c. a college's application that lists honor students at the end of each semester

    d. a manufacturing company's quarterly inventory reporting system

19. The method contained in the `RandomAccessFile` class, but which does not exist in the `InputStream` class, is _____ .

    a. `read()`   c. `seek()`

    b. `close()`   d. `delete()`

20. You can open a `RandomAccessFile` object for _____ .

    a. reading   c. both of the above

    b. writing   d. none of the above

EXERCISES

1. Create a file using any word-processing program or text editor. Write an application that displays the file's name, parent, size, and time of last modification. Save the file as **FileStatistics.java**.

2. Create two files using any word-processing program or text editor. Write an application that determines whether the two files are located in the same folder. Save the file as **SameFolder.java**.

3. Create a file that contains your favorite movie quote. Use a text editor such as Notepad and save the file as **quote.txt**. Copy the file contents and paste them into a word-processing program such as Word. Save the file as **quote.doc**. Write an application that displays the sizes of the two files as well as the ratio of their sizes to each other. Save the file as **FileStatistics2.java**.

4. Write an application that determines which, if any, of the following files are stored in the folder where you have been saving the exercises created in this chapter: autoexec.bat, SameFolder.java, FileStatistics.class, and Hello.java. Save the file as **FindSelectedFiles.java**.

5. a. Create a JFrame that allows the user to enter a series of friends' names and phone numbers and creates a file from the entered data. The main() method in the class creates an instance of the JFrame. Save the file as **CreatePhoneList.java**.

   b. Write an application that reads the file created by the CreatePhoneList application and displays one record at a time in a JFrame. Save the file as **ReadPhoneList.java**.

6. a. Create a data-entry JFrame for a mail-order company. Allow a user to type an item number and a quantity into text fields, and when the user clicks a button, write the record to a file. Continue until the user closes the frame. Save the file as **MailOrderFrame.java**. Write an application that creates an instance of the frame and save the file as **MailOrderWrite.java**.

   b. Write an application that reads the data file created by the MailOrderWrite application and displays one record at a time on the screen. Save the file as **MailOrderRead.java**.

7. a. Create a data-entry JFrame for a mail-order company. Allow a user to type an item number and a quantity into text fields. The valid item numbers and prices are as follows:

Item Number	Price ($)
101	4.59
103	29.95
107	36.50
125	49.99

When the user enters an item number, check the number to ensure that it is valid. If it is valid, write a record that includes the item number, quantity, price per item, and total price.

Continue until the user closes the frame. Save the file as **MailOrderFrame2.java**. Write an application that creates an instance of the frame, and save the file as **MailOrderWrite2.java**.

   b. Write an application that reads the data file created by the `MailOrderWrite2` application and displays one record at a time on the screen. Save the file as **MailOrderRead2.java**.

8. a. Write an application that allows a user to enter a filename and an integer representing a file position. Access the requested position within the file and display the character there. Save the file as **SeekPosition.java**.

   b. Modify the `SeekPosition` application so that you display the next five characters after the requested position. Save the file as **SeekPosition2.java**.

   c. Modify the `SeekPosition2` application so that instead of displaying five characters, the user enters the number of characters to display, beginning with the requested position. Save the file as **SeekPosition3.java**.

9. a. Write an application that creates a `JFrame` with text fields for order processing for a tee-shirt manufacturer. Include `JTextFields` for size, color, and slogan. Write each complete record to a file. Save the file as **TeeShirtWrite.java**.

   b. Write an application that reads the data file created by the `TeeShirtWrite` program and displays one record at a time in a `JFrame` on the screen. Save the file as **TeeShirtRead.java**.

10. Write an application that allows the user to type any number of characters and save them to a file. Then display the file contents backward. Save the file as **ReadBackwards.java**.

11. a. Create a `JFrame` that allows you to enter student data—ID number, last name, and first name. Include two buttons and instruct the user to click "Grad" or "Undergrad" after entering the data for each student. Depending on the user's choice, write the data to either a graduate student file or an undergraduate student file. Save the file as **GradAndUndergrad.java**.

   b. Create a `JFrame` that, in turn, accesses each record in the graduate file and then in the undergraduate file created in the `GradAndUndergrad` application. When the end of the first file is reached, change a label in the frame to notify the user which file is currently accessed. Save the file as **StudentRead.java**.

12. a. The Rochester Bank maintains customer records in a random access file. Write an application that creates 10,000 blank records, and then allows the user to enter a balance and customer account information using an account number that is 9999 or less. Insert each new record into a data file at a location that is equal to the account number. Assume that the user will not enter invalid account numbers. Save the file as **CreateBankFile.java**.

   b. Create an application that uses the file created by the user in Exercise 11a and displays all existing accounts in account-number order. Save the file as **DisplayBankFileSequentially.java**.

   c. Create an application that uses the file created by the user in Exercise 11a and allows the user to enter an account number to view the account balance. Allow the user to view additional account balances until entering an application-terminating value. Save the file as **DisplayBankFileRandomly.java**.

d. Create an Exception class for which you instantiate an object when a user attempts to create a bank account with an account number that has already been used. Save the file as **DuplicateAccountException.java**. Modify the CreateBankFile application created in Exercise 12a so that duplicate account numbers are not allowed and an appropriate error message is displayed. Save the file as **CreateBankFile2.java**. Make sure that the completed data file created by the new application still displays correctly with both DisplayBankFileSequentially.java and DisplayBankFileRandomly.java.

13. You first learned about the GregorianCalendar class in Chapter 4. GregorianCalendar implements Serializable. Write an application that prompts the user for a month, day, and year and creates GregorianCalendar objects that are saved to a file. Save the application as **CreateDateFile.java**. Create another application that reads the dates from the file and displays them formatted with slashes separating the month, day, and year. Save the second application as **ReadDateFile.java**.

14. You first learned about the JLabel class in Chapter 9 when you used Swing components. JLabel implements Serializable. Write an application that prompts the user for a series of words to display on JLabels. Also, give the user the choice of making each JLabel's foreground red or blue. Save the JLabels to a file, and save the application as **CreateLabelFile.java**. Create another application that retrieves the JLabels from the file and displays them in a JFrame. Save the second application as **ReadLabelFile.java**.

DEBUGGING EXERCISES

Each of the following files in the Chapter.16 folder on your Student Disk has syntax and/or logic errors. In each case, determine the problem and fix the program. After you correct the errors, save each file using the same filename preceded with Fix. For example, DebugSixteen1.java will become FixDebugSixteen1.java.

  a. DebugSixteen1.java

  b. DebugSixteen2.java

  c. DebugSixteen3.java

  d. DebugSixteen4.java

CASE PROJECT

MOWERS INC.

Create a data-entry and retrieval system for Mowers Inc., a lawn-mowing service.

Use a JFrame to enter data for the customer's account number, name, and lawn size in square feet. Allowed account numbers are 1 through 9999; do not allow duplicate account numbers. If the user enters invalid data while creating a record, throw an Exception, display an error message, and allow the user to continue. Create a random access output file named **Mowers.dat** to hold the customer account number, name, lawn size, and fee per mowing—$50 for lawns under 1000 square feet and $75 for lawns of 1000 square feet or more. Save the application file as **MowersInc.java** in the Chapter.16 folder on your Student Disk.

Create an application that uses the Mowers.dat file and displays all existing accounts in account-number order. Save the file as **DisplayMowersSequentially.java** in the Chapter.16 folder on your Student Disk.

Create an application that uses the Mowers.dat file and allows the user to enter an account number to view the account details. (If the user enters a non-numeric value for the account number, display the first account.) Allow the user to view additional accounts until closing the frame. Save the file as **DisplayMowersRandomly.java** in the Chapter.16 folder on your Student Disk.

GAME ZONE

1. In several Game Zone assignments earlier in this book, you have created games similar to Hangman in which the user guesses a secret phrase by selecting a series of letters. These versions had limited appeal because each contained only a few possible phrases to guess; after playing the games a few times, the user would have memorized all the possible phrases. Now create a version in which possible secret phrases can be saved to a file before the game is played. First create an application in which a user can enter any number of phrases to store. Save the application as **WritePhrases.java**. Then, create a guessing game that randomly selects a phrase from the file and allows the user to guess the phrase letter by letter. Save the game as **SecretPhraseUsingFile.java**.

>> **NOTE** In the SecretPhraseUsingFile game, the creator of the secret phrases and the player would most likely be different people. For example, a teacher might use the WritePhrases application to store famous quotes from history or scientific terms that correspond to the current lesson so that students could learn while playing the game.

2. a. In Chapter 13, you created a game named HedgeYourBet in which the user could respond to multiple-choice questions by selecting one answer (for more points) or multiple answers (for fewer points). Modify the game so that it stores the player's score from the last game in a file and displays the previous score at the start of each new game. (The first time you play the game, the previous score should be 0.) Save the game as **HedgeYourBetUsingFile.java**.

   b. Modify the HedgeYourBetUsingFile game so that it records and displays the best previous score rather than the most immediate previous score. Save the game as **HedgeYourBetUsingFile2.java**.

3. In Chapter 14, you created a game called JCatchTheMouseTimed2 in which a user attempts to click randomly placed Xs in the shortest possible time. Modify the game so the user's best time is saved in a file. When the user completes the game, display a message indicating whether the current attempt is the user's best time ever, or if not, what the best time was. Save the file as **JCatchTheMouseTimed3.java**.

4. In Chapter 14, you created a game named StopGate in which a player competed against the computer to place dominoes across checkerboard squares. Modify the game so that it creates a file containing the number of games played to date, as well as the number of times the player has won. After each game, display the player's cumulative winning percentage. Save the game as **StopGate2.java**.

UP FOR DISCUSSION

1. In Exercise 3 earlier in this chapter, what did you discover about the size difference of files that held the same contents but were created using different software (such as Word and Notepad)? Why do you think the file sizes are so different, even though the files contain the same data?

2. Locate several .class files that resulted from compiling any Java programs you have written. (If you have deleted all your .class files, simply compile a few of your Java programs to recreate them.) Using a text editor, such as Notepad, open these files. Confirm that the first four characters (Êþ°¾) are the same in each of the compiled files. Find an online program that translates characters to their hexadecimal values and discover the translated value of this character set. What is the significance of the value? Why do all .class files start with the same set of characters?

3. Suppose your employer asks you to write a program that lists all the company's employees, their salaries, and their ages. You are provided with the personnel file to use as input. You decide to take the file home so you can create the report over the weekend. Is this acceptable? What if the file contained only employees' names and departments, but not more sensitive data such as salaries and ages?

APPENDIX A

WORKING WITH THE JAVA PLATFORM

In this appendix, you will:

Configure Windows to work with the Java SE
Development Kit
Use Notepad to save and edit source code
Use TextPad to work with Java

CONFIGURING WINDOWS TO WORK WITH THE JAVA SE DEVELOPMENT KIT

»NOTE
For downloading help, visit *http://java.sun.com/downloads/faq.html#113.*

Several versions of Java are available for free at the Java Web site (*http://java.sun.com*). The official name of the most recent version is Java Platform, Standard Edition 6, often called **Java SE 6** for short. Two version numbers (1.6.0 and 6) are used to identify this release of the Java Platform. Version 6 is the product version and 1.6.0 is the developer version. The number 6 is used to reflect Java's evolving level of maturity. As new versions containing advanced features emerge, you can download them. Alternatively, you can use the version that comes with this book.

»NOTE Each new version of Java has a code name. The code name for version 6 is Mustang. The name for version 5 was Tiger and the scheduled name for version 7 is Dolphin.

»NOTE   Over the years, Java has been inconsistent in numbering new versions. Before version 6, the standard editions were called JDK 1.0.3, JDK 1.1.2 through 1.1.8, J2SE 1.2.0 through 1.4.2, and J2SE 5.0. With version 6, Java is attempting to simplify the name and number changes.

The different names for Java versions are somewhat confusing, and frequently misused. If you download Java to use with this book, you want to acquire the Java Standard Edition (SE) Development Kit, also known as the **JDK**. Java also supports the **Java Enterprise Edition** (EE), which includes all of the classes in the Java SE, plus a number of classes that are more useful to programs running on servers than on workstations. The Java EE Development Kit is known as **SDK**. The names of the development kits have changed frequently; originally, JDK meant "Java Development Kit," but that interpretation was used with the earliest Java versions and no longer is used officially.

»NOTE
The **Java Micro Edition** (ME) is another Java platform, which is used for small devices such as PDAs (personal digital assistants), cell phones, and other consumer appliances.

To configure your Windows operating system with the JDK, you must add the Java bin directory to the command path of your operating system (OS). That way, your OS will know where to look for the Java commands that you use.

One way to update the OS path for Windows XP or Windows 2000 is to edit or set the OS path in the autoexec.bat file. This file is automatically executed every time you start your computer. A simpler and less error-prone alternative is to type two commands at the OS prompt when you want to begin a session of working on Java programs. (These two commands are described later in this appendix.)

You do not need to be an operating system expert to issue operating system commands. Learning just a few commands allows you to create and run all the examples in this book.

FINDING THE COMMAND PROMPT

Locating the command prompt on your computer depends on which operating system it uses.

»NOTE
In Microsoft Windows/95/98/ME, the console window was called the MS-DOS (Microsoft Disk Operating System) prompt. In other versions of Windows, it is the command prompt.

» In Windows XP, click Start, point to All Programs, point to Accessories, then click Command Prompt.

» In Windows 2000, click Start, point to Programs, point to Accessories, then click Command Prompt.

COMMAND PROMPT ANATOMY

The command prompt contains at least a disk drive name followed by a colon, a backslash, and a greater-than sign (for example, C:\>). You might also see folder or directory names within the command prompt just before the greater-than sign, as shown in the following examples:

C:\Documents and Settings>

C:\Documents and Settings\Administrator>

Each directory in the path is separated by a backslash.

CHANGING DIRECTORIES

You can back up one directory level by typing cd for "change directory," followed by two periods:

```
cd..
```

For example, if your OS prompt contains C:\Documents and Settings\Primary> and you type cd.., the command prompt changes to C:\Documents and Settings>. If you type cd.. again, the prompt changes to C:\>, indicating the root directory. Figure A-1 shows this progression.

Figure A-1 Results following two cd.. commands

When you have multiple directories to back through, it is easier to use the following command:

```
cd\
```

This takes you immediately to the root directory instead of backing up one level at a time.

At the command prompt, you can change to another disk drive by typing its name and a colon, then pressing Enter. For example, the following command changes the command prompt to refer to the A drive:

```
A:
```

You can change the directory by typing cd followed by the name of the directory. For example, if you have a folder named Java and it contains a folder named Chapter.01, you can change the command prompt to the Chapter.01 folder by backing up to the root directory and typing the following:

```
cd Java
cd Chapter.01
```

As shown in Figure A-2, the command prompt now reads C:\Java\Chapter.01>. When you compile and execute your Java programs, you should start from the command prompt where the files are stored.

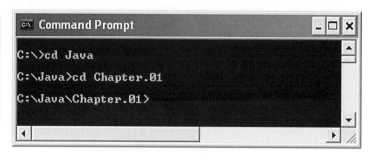

Figure A-2 Changing to the Java\Chapter.01 directory

> **NOTE**
> When your command prompt display is filled with commands, it can look confusing. If you want, you can type cls (for Clear Screen) to remove old commands.

SETTING THE class AND classpath VARIABLES

When you start a Java session, you might need to set the class and classpath options. These settings tell the operating system where to find the Java compiler and your classes. If you or someone else has altered your autoexec.bat file to contain these commands, you do not need to type them. Otherwise, every time you want to compile and execute Java programs, you need to type statements similar to the following:

```
path = c:\program files\java\jdk1.6.0\bin
set classpath=.
```

After you have typed these statements, you can compile and run as many Java programs as you want without typing these commands again. You must type them again if you close the Command Prompt window or restart your computer.

The first statement sets the path and allows the OS to recognize the javac command you use when compiling programs. Consider the following example:

```
path = c:\program files\java\jdk1.6.0\bin
```

This example assumes that you are using JDK 1.6.0 and that it is stored in the java folder in the program files folder. These are the defaults when you download Java from the Java Web site; if you installed Java in a different location, you need to alter the command accordingly.

The command set classpath=. tells Java to find your compiled classes in the current directory when you execute your applications and applets. There must be no space between classpath and the equal sign, or between the equal sign and the period.

After you set the path correctly, you should be able to use the javac command. If you attempt to compile a Java class and see an error message that javac is not a recognized command, either Java was not properly installed or the path command was incorrect. On the other hand, if classes compile successfully but do not execute, you might have entered the classpath command incorrectly.

CHANGING A FILE'S NAME

When working through the examples in this book, you will often find it convenient to change the name of an existing file—for example, when you want to experiment with altering code without losing the original version, or if you find that when you previously saved a file, you mistyped a filename so that it did not match the class name within the .java file you created. You can take at least three approaches:

» Open the existing file using the appropriate software application (for example, Notepad), click File on the menu bar, and then click Save As. Select the folder you want, then type a new filename for the file. Now you have two versions—one with the old name and one with the new.

» In Windows, open My Computer and locate the misnamed file. Select the file and then click the filename. (Do not double-click the filename unless you want to open the file.) Now, you can edit the filename by using a combination of the Backspace, Delete, and new character keys. Press Enter when the filename is correct.

» At the command prompt, use the `rename` command. You type `rename`, a space, the old filename, another space, and the new filename. For example, to change a file named xyz.java to abc.java, type the following at the command prompt for the directory containing the existing file:

```
rename xyz.java abc.java
```

COMPILING AND EXECUTING A JAVA PROGRAM

At the command prompt, change from the default drive prompt to the drive where your application is stored. Then change the directory (or folder) to the directory that holds your application.

To compile an application or applet, you type the `javac` command to start the Java compiler, then type a space and the complete name of the .java file—for example, First.java. If the application doesn't compile successfully, the path might not be set correctly to the Java JDK bin directory where the javac.exe file is located. Also, you might have failed to use the same spelling as the Java filename.

When you compile a .java file correctly, the Java compiler creates a .class file that has the same filename as the .java file. Thus, a successful compilation of the First.java file creates a file named First.class. To run a Java application, you use the `java` command and the class name without the .class extension. For example, after an application named First.java is compiled, producing First.class, you execute the program using the command `java First`.

When the program ends, control is returned to the command prompt. If a program does not end on its own, or you want to end it prematurely, you can press Ctrl+C to return to the command prompt.

After you compile a Java program, you can execute it as many times as you want without recompiling. If you change the source code, you must save and compile again before you can see the changed results in an executed application.

>>**NOTE** When you are testing a Java program, you often issue the commands to compile and execute it many times before you are satisfied with the results. If you press the Up Arrow key at the command line, the previous commands repeat in reverse succession. When you find the command you want to repeat, just press Enter.

USING NOTEPAD TO SAVE AND EDIT SOURCE CODE

You can use the Windows Notepad text editor to save and edit the source code for Java programs. To start Notepad using Windows 2000, click the Start menu, point to Programs, point to Accessories, and click Notepad. To start Notepad using Windows XP, click the Start menu, point to All Programs, point to Accessories, and click Notepad. After you start Notepad, you can enter and edit the code just as you would with any text editor.

Saving source code in Notepad requires that the Java source file be saved with a .java extension. Because Java is case sensitive, you must save a file with the proper capitalization. If the class name of the file and the filename do not match in both spelling and case, you receive an error when you attempt to execute compiled source code. The default extension for Notepad documents is .txt. To create a file with a .java extension, you can use one of the following approaches:

» Use Save As, locate the folder you want, and type the filename with double quotation marks around it, as in "First.java". This ensures that the file is not saved as "First.java.txt". Then click Save.

» Use Save As, locate the folder you want, and type the filename. Click the Save as type list box below the File name list box, select All Files, and then click Save. With this approach, you do not need double quotes around the filename, but you do need to use the Save as type list box.

» Save the file as a .txt file, and then change it to a .java file using one of the techniques outlined in the previous section.

USING TEXTPAD TO WORK WITH JAVA

As an alternative to Notepad, you can use TextPad—a text editor that includes many features helpful to Java programmers. You can download a trial version from *www.textpad.com*. Unlike Notepad, TextPad is not included with Windows; to install TextPad, run the setup file after downloading it from the TextPad Web site, and then respond to the dialog box options. Because you download a trial version, you should purchase TextPad if you decide to use it beyond the trial period. Note that TextPad runs only under the Windows operating system. If you are not using Windows, you can use the text editor that comes with your operating system, or you can search the Web to find a text editor that better suits your needs.

To enter and edit source code in TextPad, you can use the same techniques that you use with any other Windows text editor. In short, you can use the standard Windows shortcut keystrokes and menus to enter, edit, and save your code. You can use the File menu to open and close files. You can use the Edit menu to cut, copy, and paste text, and you can use the Search menu to find and replace text. In addition, TextPad color-codes the source files so it is easier to recognize the Java syntax. TextPad also makes it easier to save Java files with the proper capitalization and extension. To compile the current source code, you can select the Compile Java command from the Tools menu. If the source code does not compile cleanly, TextPad displays a Command Results window, including line numbers that identify the source of problems. With TextPad, you can choose to display line numbers in your code.

KEY TERMS

Java SE 6 is the most recent version of Java. The full, official name is Java Platform, Standard Edition 6.

The **JDK** is the Java Standard Edition Development Kit.

The **Java Enterprise Edition** (EE) includes all of the classes in the Java SE, plus a number of classes that are more useful to programs running on servers.

The **SDK** is the Java EE Development Kit.

The **Java Micro Edition** (ME) is another Java platform, which is used for small devices such as PDAs, cell phones, and other consumer appliances.

APPENDIX B

LEARNING ABOUT ASCII AND UNICODE

The characters used in Java are represented in Unicode, which is a 16-bit coding scheme for characters. For example, the letter A actually is stored in computer memory as a set of 16 zeros and ones as 0000 0000 0100 0001 (a space is inserted after each set of four digits for readability). Because 16-digit numbers are difficult to read, programmers often use a shorthand notation called hexadecimal, or base 16. In hexadecimal shorthand, 0000 becomes 0, 0100 becomes 4, and 0001 becomes 1, so the letter A is represented in hexadecimal as 0041. You tell the compiler to treat the four-digit hexadecimal 0041 as a single character by preceding it with the \u escape sequence. Therefore, there are two ways to store the character A:

```
char letter = 'A';
char letter = '\u0041';
```

The second option, using hexadecimal, is obviously more difficult and confusing than the first method, so it is not recommended that you store letters of the alphabet using the hexadecimal method. However, you can produce some interesting values using the Unicode format. For example, the sequence '\u0007' is a bell that produces a noise if you send it to output. Letters from foreign alphabets that use characters instead of letters (Greek, Hebrew, Chinese, and so on) and other special symbols (foreign currency symbols, mathematical symbols, geometric shapes, and so on) are available using Unicode, but not on a standard keyboard, so it is important that you know how to use Unicode characters.

>> **NOTE** Two-digit, base-16 numbers can be converted to base-10 numbers by multiplying the left digit by 16 and adding the right digit. For example, hexadecimal 41 is 4 times 16 plus 1, or 65.

>> **NOTE**
For more information about Unicode, go to *www.unicode.org*.

>> **NOTE**
The ASCII character set is more limited than Unicode because it contains only letters and symbols used in the English language.

In the United States, the most widely used character set traditionally has been ASCII (American Standard Code for Information Interchange). The ASCII character set contains 128 characters, some of which are shown in Table B-1 with their decimal or numerical code and equivalent character representation. The first 32 characters and the last character are control characters and are nonprintable. You can enter these characters by holding down Ctrl and pressing a letter on the keyboard. For example, the Tab key or ^I (Ctrl+I) produces a character 9, which produces a hard tab when pressed.

You can create any Unicode character by adding eight zeros to the beginning of the ASCII character value. This means that the decimal value of any ASCII character is the same as that of the corresponding Unicode character. For example, 'B' has the value 66 in both character sets. The decimal values are important because they allow you to show nonprintable characters, such as a carriage return, in decimal codes. Also, the numeric values of the coding schemes are used when a computer sorts numbers and strings. When you sort characters in ascending order, for example, numbers are sorted first (because their Unicode values begin with decimal code 48), followed by capital letters (starting with decimal 65), and then lowercase letters (starting with decimal 97).

Table B-1 contains a list of Unicode values for some commonly used characters. For a complete list, see *www.unicode.org/charts*. There you will find Greek, Armenian, Hebrew, Tagalog, Cherokee, and a host of other character sets. Unicode also contains characters for mathematical symbols, geometric shapes, and other unusual characters.

Decimal Value	Explanation	Character
48	Digit zero	0
49	Digit one	1
50	Digit two	2
51	Digit three	3
52	Digit four	4
53	Digit five	5
54	Digit six	6
55	Digit seven	7
56	Digit eight	8
57	Digit nine	9
58	Colon	:
59	Semicolon	;
60	Less-than sign	<
61	Equal sign	=
62	Greater-than sign	>
63	Question mark	?
64	At sign	@
65	Letter A	A
66	Letter B	B
67	Letter C	C
68	Letter D	D

Table B-1 Decimal values, descriptions, and characters for commonly used Unicode values (*continued*) ▶

Decimal Value	Explanation	Character
69	Letter E	E
70	Letter F	F
71	Letter G	G
72	Letter H	H
73	Letter I	I
74	Letter J	J
75	Letter K	K
76	Letter L	L
77	Letter M	M
78	Letter N	N
79	Letter O	O
80	Letter P	P
81	Letter Q	Q
82	Letter R	R
83	Letter S	S
84	Letter T	T
85	Letter U	U
86	Letter V	V
87	Letter W	W
88	Letter X	X
89	Letter Y	Y
90	Letter Z	Z
91	Left square bracket	[
92	Backslash	\
93	Right square bracket	]
94	Circumflex accent	^
95	Underscore	_
96	Grave accent	`
97	Letter a	a
98	Letter b	b
99	Letter c	c
100	Letter d	d
101	Letter e	e
102	Letter f	f
103	Letter g	g

Table B-1 Decimal values, descriptions, and characters for commonly used Unicode values (*continued*)

Decimal Value	Explanation	Character
104	Letter h	h
105	Letter i	i
106	Letter j	j
107	Letter k	k
108	Letter l	l
109	Letter m	m
110	Letter n	n
111	Letter o	o
112	Letter p	p
113	Letter q	q
114	Letter r	r
115	Letter s	s
116	Letter t	t
117	Letter u	u
118	Letter v	v
119	Letter w	w
120	Letter x	x
121	Letter y	y
122	Letter z	z
123	Left curly brace	{
124	Pipe		
125	Right curly brace	}
126	Tilde	~

Table B-1 Decimal values, descriptions, and characters for commonly used Unicode values

APPENDIX C

FORMATTING OUTPUT

In this appendix, you will:

Understand the limitations of the `println()` method
Use multiplication and division to supply formatting
Use the `printf()` method
Use the `DecimalFormat` class

UNDERSTANDING THE LIMITATIONS OF THE `println()` METHOD

When you display numbers using the `println()` method in Java applications, it is sometimes difficult to make numeric values appear as you want. For example, suppose you have declared variables named `price`, `taxRate`, and `totalPrice`, as shown in the `ComputePriceWithTax` application in Figure C-1. As the output shows in Figure C-2, the application correctly calculates a final price of $21.3893. Although this answer is mathematically correct, you might prefer to express the final sale price with tax in dollars and cents—that is, to show the output value rounded to two decimal places.

```
public class ComputePriceWithTax
{
    public static void main(String[] args)
    {
        double price = 19.99;
        double taxRate = .07;
        double totalPrice = price + (price * taxRate);
        System.out.println("Total price is $" + totalPrice);
    }
}
```

Figure C-1 The `ComputePriceWithTax` application

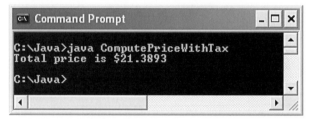

Figure C-2 Output of the `ComputePriceWithTax` application

You encounter another formatting problem when you want to align a column of numeric values. For example, Figure C-3 shows a `NumberList` application that contains an array of integer values. The application displays the values using a `for` loop, but, as the output in

```
public class NumberList
{
    public static void main(String[] args)
    {
        int[] list = {1, 23, 456, 7890, 987, 65};
        int x;
        for(x = 0; x < list.length; ++x)
            System.out.println(list[ x ]);
    }
}
```

Figure C-3 The `NumberList` application

> **NOTE** If you are interested in mathematically correct output, the programs in Figures C-1 and C-3 are adequate. However, to improve the appearance of your output, a number of techniques are available to help you. If you are just starting to learn Java and are not yet comfortable with classes and methods, you might prefer to use multiplication and division to achieve better-looking output, as described in the next section. If you are comfortable using new methods and classes, then you can explore using the `printf()` method or the `DecimalFormat` class, as described in later sections of this appendix.

Figure C-4 shows, the numbers are not aligned by the (implied) decimal point as you usually would want numbers to be aligned. Because the `println()` method displays values as `Strings`, the displayed values are left-aligned, just as series of words would be. The numeric values are accurate; they just are not attractively arranged.

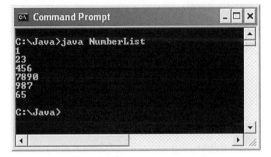

Figure C-4 Output of the `NumberList` application

FORMATTING USING MULTIPLICATION AND DIVISION

A simple way to convert a longer number to a fixed number of decimal places involves multiplying, then dividing the number by a fixed value. For example, to convert a value with more than two decimal places to one that contains only two decimal places, you can perform the following steps:

» Multiply the number by 100.
» Remove the decimal portion.
» Divide by 100.

Figure C-5 shows a sample application in which the value 123.45678 is multiplied by 100, giving 12345.678, and truncated to a temporary `int` with the value 12345. When this value is

```
public class TwoPlacesNoRounding
{
   public static void main(String[] args)
   {
      double money = 123.45678;
      System.out.println("Before conversion: " + money);
      int temp;
      temp = (int)(money * 100);
      money = temp / 100.0;
      System.out.println("After conversion: " + money);
   }
}
```

> **NOTE** The eighth line in Figure C-5 performs a cast, forcing a `double` to become an `int`. Chapter 2 describes casting.

Figure C-5 The `TwoPlacesNoRounding` class

divided by 100.0 and stored in a `double`, the result is 123.45, which is the original value reduced to two decimal places. Figure C-6 shows the application's execution.

Figure C-6 Output of the `TwoPlacesNoRounding` program

》NOTE If you decide to use the formatting technique used in the `TwoPlacesNoRounding` class, you might want to provide a named constant to use for the 100.0 value. You should also provide program comments to explain your intention.

In the output in Figure C-6, you can see that the original value is reduced to two decimal places, without rounding. Rounding requires a simple trick, as shown in the class in Figure C-7. The only changes in this class from the one in Figure C-5 are in the class name and the shaded addition of 0.5 to the `money * 100` calculation. Using this trick causes any value not to be rounded when the third position to the right of the decimal point is 4 or less, but to be rounded up when the digit in that position is 5 or more. Figure C-8 shows the program execution.

```java
public class TwoPlacesWithRounding
{
   public static void main(String[] args)
   {
      double money = 123.45678;
      System.out.println("Before conversion: " + money);
      int temp;
      temp = (int)(money * 100 + 0.5);
      money = temp / 100.0;
      System.out.println("After conversion: " + money);
   }
}
```

Figure C-7 The `TwoPlacesWithRounding` class

》NOTE Another option for rounding is to use the `Math` class `round()` method. For example, in the program in Figure C-7, the value of `Math.round(money * 100)` would be 12346. The `Math` class is covered in Chapter 4.

Using this multiply-and-divide technique to display values has its limitations. For example, the applications in Figures C-5 and C-7 display values to no more than two decimal places, but not to exactly two decimal places. If you change the value of `money` in the `TwoPlacesWithRounding` class to 123.40, it displays as 123.4 both before and after the

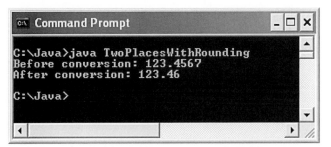

Figure C-8 Output of the `TwoPlacesWithRounding` program

arithmetic. Although you could determine whether the last digits of values were zeros and then display extra zeros accordingly, this approach is cumbersome. To conveniently achieve output that displays values to a fixed number of decimal places, you should explore the `System.out.printf()` method and the `DecimalFormat` class presented in the next sections.

> **NOTE** You can determine whether a number ends with 0 by using the modulus operator (%). In the decimal system, if there is no remainder when a value is divided by 10, then the value ends with 0. Similarly, if there is no remainder when a value is divided by 100, the value ends with two 0s.

USING THE `printf()` METHOD

The **`System.out.printf()` method** is used to format numeric values. It is a newer Java feature that was first included in the `Formatter` class in Java 1.5.0. (This is the internal version number of the Java Development Kit; the external version number is 5.0.) Because this class is contained in the `java.util` package, you do not need to include any import statements to use it. The `printf()` method allows you to format numeric values in two useful ways:

» By specifying the number of decimal places to display
» By specifying the field size in which to display values

> **NOTE** The `Formatter` class contains many formats that are not covered here. To view the details of formatting data types such as `BigDecimal` and `Calendar`, visit the Java Web site at *http://java.sun.com*.

> **NOTE** C programmers use a `printf()` function that is very similar to Java's `printf()` method. Although the `printf()` method is used in these examples, in Java, you can substitute `System.out.format()` for `System.out.printf()`. There is no difference in the way you use these two methods.

When creating numeric output, you can specify a number of decimal places to display by using the `printf()` method with two types of arguments that represent the following:

» A format string
» A list of arguments

A **format string** is a string of characters; it includes optional text (that is displayed literally) and one or more format specifiers. A **format specifier** is a placeholder for a numeric value.

Within a call to `printf()`, you include one argument (either a variable or a constant) for each format specifier.

The format specifiers for general, character, and numeric types contain the following elements, in order:

» **NOTE**
Other conversion characters include those used to display hexadecimal numbers and scientific notation. If you need these display formats, you can find more details at *http://java.sun.com*.

» A percent sign (%), which indicates the start of every format specifier.

» An optional argument index, which is an integer indicating the position of the argument in the argument list. The integer is followed by a dollar sign. You will learn more about this option later in this appendix.

» Optional flags that modify the output format. The set of valid flags depends on the data type you are formatting. You can find more details about this feature at the Java Web site.

» An optional field width, which is an integer indicating the minimum number of characters to be written to the output. You will learn more about this option later in this appendix.

» An optional precision, which is a decimal point followed by a number and typically used to control decimal places displayed. You will learn more about this option in the next section.

» The required conversion character, which indicates how its corresponding argument should be formatted. Java supports a variety of conversion characters, but the three you want to use most frequently are d, f, and s, the characters that represent decimal (base-10 integer), floating-point (`float` and `double`), and string values, respectively.

For example, you can use the `ConversionCharacterExamples` class in Figure C-9 to display a declared integer and `double`. The `main()` method of the class contains three `printf()` statements. The three calls to `printf()` in this class each contain a format string; the first two calls contain a single additional argument, and the last `printf()` statement contains two arguments after the string. None of the format specifiers in this class use any of the optional parameters—only the required percent sign and conversion character. The first `printf()` statement uses `%d` in its format string as a placeholder for the integer argument at the end. The second `printf()` statement uses `%f` as a placeholder for the floating-point argument at the end. The last `printf()` statement uses both a `%d` and `%f` to indicate the positions of the integer and floating-point values at the end, respectively. Figure C-10 shows the output, in which the strings display with the values inserted in the appropriate places. As Figure C-10 shows, floating-point values are displayed with six decimal positions by default.

» **NOTE**
If you attempt to use a conversion character that is invalid for the data type, the program will compile but not execute.

```
public class ConversionCharacterExamples
{
    public static void main(String[] args)
    {
        int age = 23;
        double money = 123.45;
        System.out.printf("Age is %d\n", age);
        System.out.printf("Money is $%f\n", money);
        System.out.printf
            ("Age is %d and money is $%f\n", age, money);
    }
}
```

Figure C-9 The `ConversionCharacterExamples` application

Figure C-10 Output of the `ConversionCharacterExamples` application

Notice that in the `ConversionCharacterExamples` class, the output appears on three separate lines only because the newline character ('\n') has been included at the end of each `printf()` format string. Unlike the `println()` statement, `printf()` does not include an automatic new line.

SPECIFYING A NUMBER OF DECIMAL PLACES TO DISPLAY WITH `printf()`

You can control the number of decimal places displayed when you use a floating-point value in a `printf()` statement by adding the optional precision factor to the format specifier. Between the percent sign and the conversion character, you can add a decimal point and the number of decimal positions to display. For example, the following statements produce the output "Money is $123.45", displaying the `money` value with just two decimal places instead of six, which would occur without the precision factor:

```
double money = 123.45;
System.out.printf("Money is $%.2f\n", money);
```

Similarly, the following statements display 8.10. If you use the `println()` equivalent with `amount`, only 8.1 is displayed; if you use a `printf()` statement without inserting the `.2` precision factor, 8.100000 is displayed.

```
double amount = 8.1;
System.out.printf("%.2f", amount);
```

When you use a precision factor on a value that contains more decimal positions than you want to display, the result is rounded. For example, the following statements produce 100.457 (not 100.456), displaying three decimals because of the precision factor.

```
double value = 100.45678;
System.out.printf("%.3f", value);
```

You cannot use the precision factor with an integer value; if you do, your program will throw an `IllegalFormatConversionException`.

SPECIFYING A FIELD SIZE WITH `printf()`

You can indicate a field size in which to display output by using an optional integer as the field width. For example, the `NumberList2` class in Figure C-11 displays each element in an array of integers in a field with a size of 6. Each value is displayed right-aligned in its field; for

> **NOTE**
> If a numeric value contains more positions than you indicate for its `printf()` field size, the field size is ignored, and the entire value displays.

example, a single digit is preceded by five blank spaces, and a two-digit number is preceded by four blank spaces. Figure C-12 shows the output of the application.

```
public class NumberList2
{
  public static void main(String[] args)
  {
      int[] list = {1, 23, 456, 7890, 987, 65};
      int x;
      for(x = 0; x < list.length; ++x)
         System.out.printf("%6d\n", list[x]);
  }
}
```

Figure C-11 The NumberList2 class

Figure C-12 Output of the NumberList2 class

Throughout this book, you have been encouraged to use named constants for numeric values instead of literal constants, so that your programs are clearer. In the program in Figure C-11, you could define a constant such as:

```
final int DISPLAY_WIDTH = 6;
```

Then the printf() statement would be:

```
System.out.printf("%" + SIZE + "d\n", list[x]);
```

Another, perhaps clearer alternative is to define a format string such as the following:

```
final String FORMAT = "%6d\n";
```

Then the printf() statement would be:

```
System.out.printf(FORMAT, list[x]);
```

With floating-point values, you can combine a field size with a decimal position indicator if you want. For example, to produce four spaces followed by 98.6, you could write the following:

```
double temperature = 98.602;
System.out.printf("%8.1", temperature);
```

In this example, the entire field size displayed is 8; this includes four blanks, the number 98, the decimal point, and the single decimal place digit, 6. (In this case, no rounding occurs because the digit following the 6 is not 5 or greater.)

You can specify that a value be left-aligned in a field instead of right-aligned by inserting a negative sign in front of the width. Although you can do this with numbers, most often you choose to left-align strings. For example, the following code displays five spaces followed by "hello" and then five spaces followed by "there". Each string is left-aligned in a field with a size of 10.

```
String string1 = "hello";
String string2 = "there";
System.out.printf("%-10s%-10s", string1, string2);
```

USING THE OPTIONAL ARGUMENT INDEX WITH printf()

The **argument index** is an integer that indicates the position of an argument in the argument list of a printf() statement. To separate it from other formatting options, the argument index is followed by a dollar sign ($). The first argument is referenced by "1$", the second by "2$", and so on.

For example, the printf() statement in the following code contains four format specifiers but only two variables in the argument list:

```
int x = 56;
double y = 78.9;
System.out.printf("%1$6d%2$6.2f%1$6d%2$6.2f",x,y);
```

The printf() statement displays the value of the first argument, x, in a field with a size of 6, and then it displays the second argument, y, in a field with a size of 6 with two decimal places. Then, the value of x displays again, followed by the value of y. The output appears as follows:

```
    56 78.90     56 78.90
```

USING THE DecimalFormat CLASS

The **DecimalFormat class** provides ways to easily convert numbers into strings, allowing you to control the display of leading and trailing zeros, prefixes and suffixes, grouping (thousands) separators, and the decimal separator. You specify the formatting properties of DecimalFormat with a pattern String. The **pattern String** is composed of symbols that determine what the formatted number looks like; it is passed to the DecimalFormat class constructor.

The symbols you can use in a pattern String include:

» A pound sign (#), which represents a digit

» A period (.), which represents a decimal point

» A comma (,), which represents a thousands separator

» A zero (0), which represents leading and trailing zeros when it replaces the pound sign

> **» NOTE** The pound sign is typed using Shift+ 3 on standard computer keyboards. It is also called an **octothorpe**, a number sign, a hash sign, square, tic-tac-toe, gate, and crunch.

For example, the following lines of code result in `value` being displayed as 12,345,678.90.

```
double value = 12345678.9;
DecimalFormat aFormat = new DecimalFormat("#,###,###,###.00");
System.out.printf("%s\n", aFormat.format(value));
```

A `DecimalFormat` object is created using the pattern #,###,###,###.00. When the object's `format()` method is used in the `printf()` statement, the first two pound signs and the comma between them are not used because `value` is not large enough to require those positions. The value displays with commas inserted where needed, and the decimal portion is displayed with a trailing 0 because the 0s at the end of the pattern indicate that they should be used to fill out the number to two places.

When you use the `DecimalFormat` class, you must use the import statement `import java.text.*;`. Figure C-13 shows a class that creates a `String` pattern that it passes to the `DecimalFormat` constructor to create a `moneyFormat` object. The class displays an array of values, each in a field that is 10 characters wide. Some of the values require commas and some do not. Figure C-14 shows the output.

```
import java.text.*;
public class DecimalFormatTest
{
   public static void main(String[] args)
   {
      String pattern = "###,###.00";
      DecimalFormat moneyFormat = new DecimalFormat(pattern);
      double[] list = { 1.1, 23.23, 456.249, 7890.1, 987.5678, 65.0};
      int x;
      for(x = 0; x < list.length; ++x)
         System.out.printf("%10s\n", moneyFormat.format(list[x]));
   }
}
```

Figure C-13 The `DecimalFormatTest` class

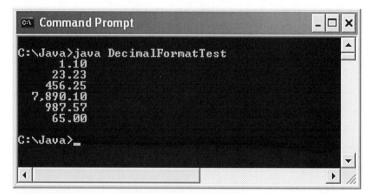

Figure C-14 Output of the `DecimalFormatTest` program

KEY TERMS

The **System.out.printf() method** is used to format numeric values.

A **format string** in a printf() statement is a string of characters; it includes optional text (that is displayed literally) and one or more format specifiers.

A **format specifier** in a printf() statement is a placeholder for a numeric value.

The **argument index** in a printf() statement is an integer that indicates the position of an argument in the argument list.

The **DecimalFormat class** provides ways to easily convert numbers into strings, allowing you to control the display of leading and trailing zeros, prefixes and suffixes, grouping (thousands) separators, and the decimal separator.

A **pattern String** is composed of symbols that determine what a formatted number looks like; it is passed to the DecimalFormat class constructor.

An **octothorpe** is a pound sign.

APPENDIX D

GENERATING RANDOM NUMBERS

In this appendix, you will:

Understand random numbers generated by computers

Use the `Math.random()` method to generate random numbers

Use the `Random` class to generate random numbers

UNDERSTANDING RANDOM NUMBERS GENERATED BY COMPUTERS

A **random number** is one whose value cannot be predicted. Many types of programs use random numbers. For example, simulations that predict phenomena such as urban traffic patterns, crop production, and weather systems typically use random numbers. You might want to use random numbers to change your screen's appearance; for example, screen savers often use random numbers so that a changing pattern remains interesting.

Random numbers are also used in many computer game applications. When you play games with human opponents, their choices are often unpredictable (and sometimes even irrational). Computers usually are predictable and rational, so when you play a game against a computer opponent, you frequently need to generate random numbers. For example, a guessing game would not be very interesting if you were asked to guess the same number every time you played.

> **»NOTE**
> Computers are said to be **deterministic**; that is, their output is determined by their input—they are consistent.

Most computer programming languages, including Java, come with built-in methods that generate random numbers. The random numbers are calculated based on a starting value, called a **seed**. The random numbers generated using these methods are not truly random; they are **pseudorandom** in that they produce the same set of numbers whenever the seed is the same. Therefore, if you seed a random-number generator with a constant, you always receive the same sequence of values. Many computer programs use the time of day as a random number-generating seed. For game applications, this method works well, as a player is unlikely to reset his computer's clock and attempt to replay a game beginning at exactly the same moment in time.

> **»NOTE** For applications in which randomness is more crucial than in game-playing, you can use other methods (such as using the points in time at which a radioactive source decays) to generate truly random starting numbers.

There are two approaches to generating random numbers in Java. Both techniques are explained in this appendix and summarized in Table D-1.

Method/Class	Advantages
`Math.random()` method	You do not need to create an object.
	You do not need to understand constructors and multiple methods.
`Random` class and its methods	You can generate numbers in the format you need without arithmetic manipulation.
	You can create reproducible results if necessary.

Table D-1 Generating random numbers in Java

USING THE `Math.random()` METHOD

> **»NOTE**
> Chapter 4 provides details about Java's `Math` class.

Java's `Math` class provides a `random()` method that returns a `double` value in the range of 0.0 up to, but not including, 1.0. For example, the application in Figure D-1 generates three random numbers and displays them. Figure D-2 shows three successive executions of the program.

```
public class SomeRandomNumbers
{
    public static void main (String[] args)
    {
        double ran;
        ran = Math.random();
        System.out.println(ran);
        ran = Math.random();
        System.out.println(ran);
        ran = Math.random();
        System.out.println(ran);
    }
}
```

Figure D-1 The SomeRandomNumbers class

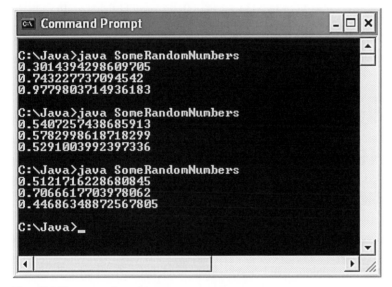

Figure D-2 Three executions of the SomeRandomNumbers program

The values displayed in Figure D-2 appear to be random, but are not typical of the values you need in a game-playing program. Usually, you need a relatively small number of whole values. For example, a game that involves a coin flip might only need two values to represent heads or tails, and a dice game might need only six values to represent rolls of a single die. Even in a complicated game in which 40 types of space aliens might attack the player, you need only 40 whole numbers generated to satisfy the program requirements.

For example, suppose you need a random number from 1 to 10. To change any value generated by the Math.random() method to fall between 0 and 10, you can multiply the generated number by 10. For example, the last three numbers in Figure D-2 would become approximately 5.12, 7.07, and 4.47. Then, you can eliminate the fractional part of each number by casting it to an int; after this step, every generated number will be a value from 0 to 9 inclusive. Finally, you can add 1 to a value so it falls in the range from 1 to 10 instead of 0 to 9. In short,

» NOTE
Chapter 2 describes casting.

the following statement generates a random number from 1 through 10 inclusive, and assigns it to `ran`:

```
int ran = 1 + (int)(Math.random() * 10);
```

Suppose that, instead of 1 through 10, you need random numbers from 1 through 13. (For example, standard decks of playing cards have 13 values from which you might want to select.) When you use the modulus operator (%) to find a remainder, the remainder is always a value from 0 to one less than the number. For example, if you divide any number by 4, the remainder is always a value from 0 through 3. Therefore, to find a number from 1 through 13, you can use a statement like the following:

```
int ranCardValue = ((int)(Math.random() * 100) % 13 + 1);
```

» NOTE
Chapter 2 describes using the modulus operator.

In this statement, a randomly generated value (for example, 0.447) is multiplied by 100 (producing 44.7). The result is converted to an `int` (44). The remainder after dividing by 13 is 5. Finally, 1 is added so the result is 1 through 13 instead of 0 through 12 (giving 6). In short, the general format for assigning a random number to a variable is:

```
int result = ((int)(Math.random() * 100) %
    HIGHEST_VALUE_WANTED + LOWEST_VALUE_WANTED);
```

> **» NOTE** Instead of 100 as the multiplier, you might prefer to use a higher value such as 1000 or 10,000. For most games, the randomness generated using 100 is sufficient.

USING THE Random CLASS

The `Random` class provides a generator that creates a list of random numbers. To use this class, you must use one of the following import statements:

```
import java.util.*;
import java.util.Random;
```

You must also instantiate a random-number generator object using one of the following constructors:

» `Random()`, in which the seed comes from the operating system. This constructor sets the seed of the random-number generator to a value that is probably distinct from any other invocation of this constructor.

» `Random(long seed)`, in which you provide a starting seed so that your results are reproducible.

After you create a random-number generator object, you can use any of the methods in Table D-2 to get the next random number from the generator.

For example, Figure D-3 contains an application that declares a `Random` generator named `ran`, using the version of the constructor that takes no arguments. This ensures that the results will be different each time the application runs. The program then defines `LIMIT` as 10, and calls `ran.nextInt(LIMIT)` three times, displaying the results (see Figure D-4).

Method	Explanation
nextInt(int n)	Returns a pseudorandom int value between 0 (inclusive) and the specified value *n* (exclusive), drawn from the random-number generator's sequence
nextInt()	Returns a pseudorandom int value between 0 (inclusive) and 1.0 (exclusive), drawn from the random-number generator's sequence
nextLong()	Returns the next pseudorandom long value from the generator's sequence
nextFloat()	Returns the next pseudorandom float value between 0.0 and 1.0 from the generator's sequence
nextDouble()	Returns the next pseudorandom double value between 0.0 and 1.0 from the generator's sequence
nextBoolean()	Returns the next pseudorandom boolean value from the generator's sequence

Table D-2 Selected Random class methods

```
import java.util.*;
public class SomeRandomNumbers2
{
public static void main(String[] args)
    {
        Random ran = new Random();
        final int LIMIT = 10;
        System.out.println(ran.nextInt(LIMIT));
        System.out.println(ran.nextInt(LIMIT));
        System.out.println(ran.nextInt(LIMIT));
    }
}
```

Figure D-3 The SomeRandomNumbers2 class

In Figure D-4, each displayed value falls between 0 and LIMIT. Of course, to select values between 1 and LIMIT inclusive, you could add 1 to each result. Even though the three method calls to ran.nextInt(LIMIT) are written identically, you can see that each call results in the retrieval of a new value.

Figure D-5 shows a class using the version of the Random constructor that takes an argument (shaded). In this example, a value between 0 and 7 is generated 15 times. Figure D-6 shows the output when the program is run three times. Although the 15 numbers displayed for each execution constitute a random list, the list is identical in each program execution. You use a seed when you want random but reproducible results. For games, you usually want to use the no-argument version of the Random constructor.

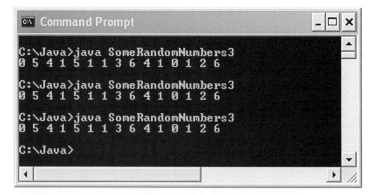

Figure D-4 Three executions of the SomeRandomNumbers2 program

```java
import java.util.*;
public class SomeRandomNumbers3
{
    public static void main(String[] args)
    {
        Random ran = new Random(129867L);
        final int TIMES = 15;
        final int LIMIT = 7;
        for(int x = 0; x < TIMES; ++x)
            System.out.print(ran.nextInt(LIMIT) + " ");
        System.out.println();
    }
}
```

Figure D-5 The SomeRandomNumbers3 class

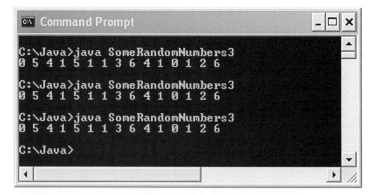

Figure D-6 Three executions of the SomeRandomNumbers3 program

KEY TERMS

A **random number** is one whose value cannot be predicted.

Deterministic is an adjective that describes the predictability and consistency of computer output.

A **seed** is a starting value.

Pseudorandom numbers appear to be random, but are the same set of numbers whenever the seed is the same.

INDEX

& (ampersand), 176–178

<> (angle brackets), 321–322

* (asterisk), 13, 141

@ (at sign), 490

\ (backslash), 47, 695, 758

: (colon), 758

, (comma), 17, 775

{} (curly braces), 11, 19, 78, 171–173, 270, 289, 640

$ (dollar sign), 9, 775

" (double quotes), 327

= (equal sign), 37, 92, 168, 169

! (exclamation point), 185

/ (forward slash), 13, 624

> (greater-than sign), 758

– (minus sign), 151

( ) (parentheses), 269, 640

% (percent sign), 772

. (period), 9, 78, 512, 775

+ (plus sign), 39, 246, 441, 446

(pound sign), 775

; (semicolon), 8, 169, 178, 270

' (single quotes), 45

_ (underscore), 9

| (vertical bar), 177

A

abs method, 139

abstract classes

  creating, 282–285

  described, **282**, **397**

  extending, 504–506

  interfaces and, 499

  naming, 503–504

abstract keyword, 10, 483

abstract methods, **483**

abstraction, **77**, 107

access modifiers, **10**, 77

AccessACharacter application, 717–718

accessor methods, **108**, 257

accumulating, **213**

aChar variable, 240

AChildClass application, 458

acos method, 139

action keys, **597**

ActionEvent class, 594–595, 597

ActionEvent interface, 338, 594–595, 597

ActionListener interface, 336, 350, 536, 537, 500, 535, 536, 596, 619–620, 736

actionPerformed method, 336, 338–341, 343, 345, 350, 353, 354, 372, 374, 378, 400, 407–409, 423–424, 538, 554–556, 585, 588, 596, 599, 613, 615, 619, 621, 709, 738–742, 744–745

actual parameters, **84**

acyclic gradients, **392**

adapter classes, **596**

add method, 326, 338–339, 534, 546, 548, 550, 581, 583, 590–591, 593, 610, 612, 619